"RECREATION LAKES OF CALIFORNIA"

By D. J. DIRKSEN & R. A. REEVES

Sail Sales Publishing
P.O. Box 1028
Aptos, California 95001
Phone: 408-662-2456

Seventh Edition

ISBN 0-943798-08-6

CREDITS

MAPS by RENEE REEVES

CARTOONS by GREG DIRKSEN

PRINTING by DELTA LITHOGRAPH COMPANY

ALL FEES AND INFORMATION ARE SUBJECT TO CHANGE

MAPS ARE NOT TO SCALE

ORDER FORM

"RECREATION LAKES OF CALIFORNIA"

SEVENTH EDITION

TO: Sail Sales Publishing
P.O. Box 1028
Aptos, CA 95001

$ 10.95	BOOK
.71	TAX
1.84	POSTAGE & HANDLING
$ 13.50	CHECK ENCLOSED

NAME: ______________________________

ADDRESS: ______________________________

____

ACKNOWLEDGMENTS

We are ever grateful to the many people who have contributed to "Recreation Lakes of California" with their timely suggestions and support. The U. S. Forest Service, the California State Park System, the California Department of Fish and Game, along with other Federal, State and Local Agencies were indispensable in helping compile the many details required for this publication. The people operating the facilities and the various Chambers of Commerce were of tremendous help. The patience and expertise of Greg Sirakides of Digital Consultants and Carm Delano of Aptos Word Processing are greatly appreciated. Most of all we want to thank you, our readers, for your continued support through our many editions.

INTRODUCTION

We are pleased to present this seventh edition of "Recreation Lakes of California." As in our previous editions, this guide presents in a clear concise manner the location and recreational opportunities at California's Lakes.

California is blessed with an abundance and variety of Lakes. From a quiet alpine setting at 10,000 feet, an urban Lake at sea level, to a large inland sea 228 feet below sea level, each Lake is unique in its own way. No matter where you are in the State, there is a Lake nearby awaiting you.

Each Lake is described according to environment, elevation, size and facilities. The locations of campgrounds, picnic areas, launch ramps and marinas are noted on each map. Bicycle, hiking and equestrian trails are presented. The maps also show important recreation areas near or at each Lake, such as State and National Parks, Wilderness Areas, the Pacific Crest Trail and the California Aqueduct Bikeway.

While boating, fishing and camping are basic to most Lakes, we have also included swimming, hiking, backpacking, hunting, and equestrian information. Water slides, boat tours, golf courses and other specific attractions are noted. Nature and campfire programs are included. Name your interest from a ferry ride to a John Muir Wilderness Area trailhead to drag boat racing at Lake Havasu. There is a Lake somewhere in California you should visit.

TABLE OF CONTENTS

GENERAL INFORMATION

SECTION MAP

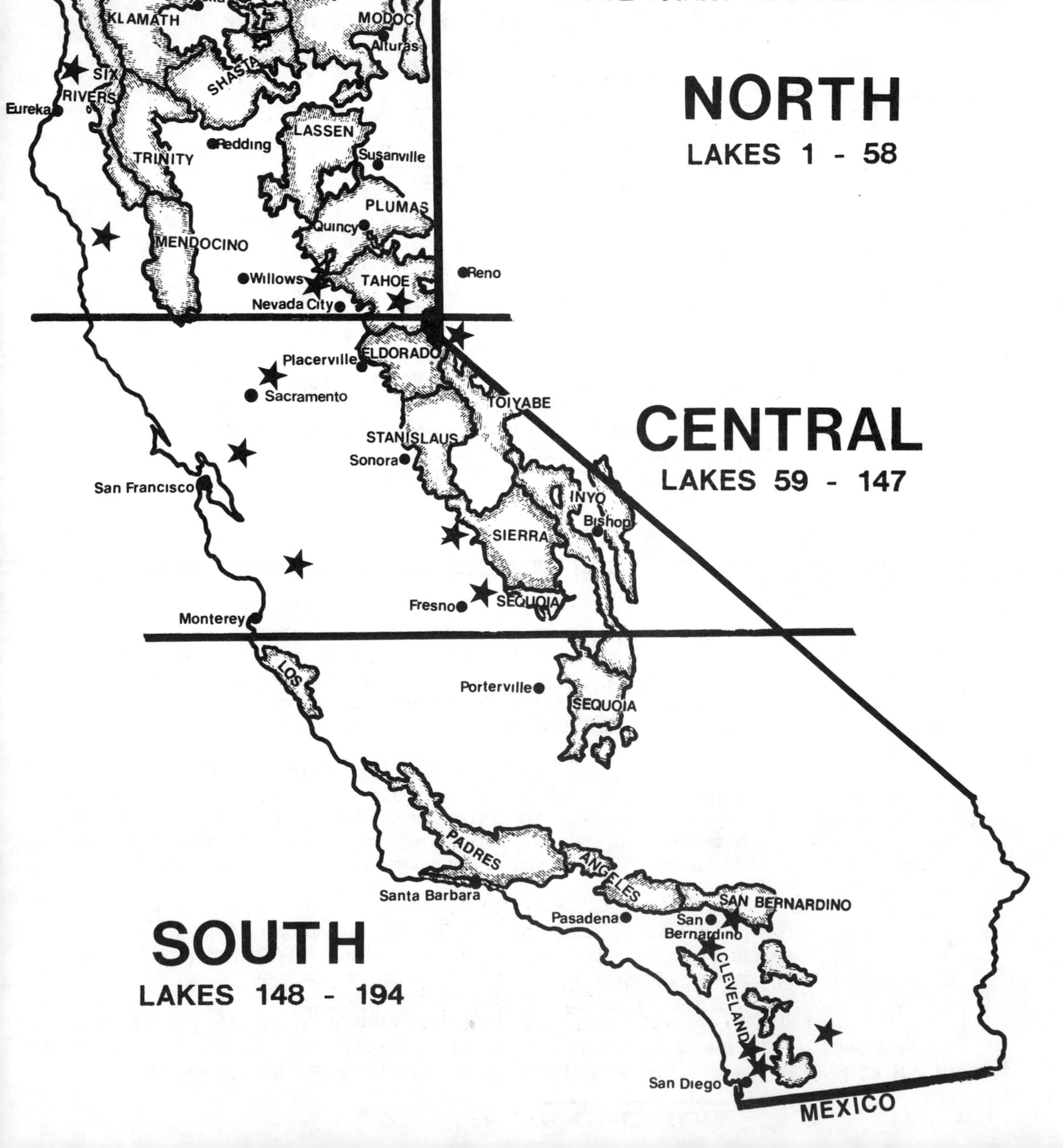
NATIONAL FORESTS OF CALIFORNIA
STATE PARKS LOCATED AT LAKES
NORTH
LAKES 1 - 58
CENTRAL
LAKES 59 - 147
SOUTH
LAKES 148 - 194
OREGON
MEXICO
KLAMATH
Yreka
MODOC
Alturas
SIX RIVERS
SHASTA
Eureka
LASSEN
Redding
TRINITY
Susanville
PLUMAS
Quincy
MENDOCINO
Willows
TAHOE
Reno
Nevada City
Placerville
ELDORADO
Sacramento
TOIYABE
STANISLAUS
Sonora
San Francisco
INYO
Bishop
SIERRA
Fresno
SEQUOIA
Monterey
LOS
Porterville
PADRES
ANGELES
Santa Barbara
SAN BERNARDINO
Pasadena
San Bernardino
CLEVELAND
San Diego

NORTH SECTION

LAKES 1 - 58

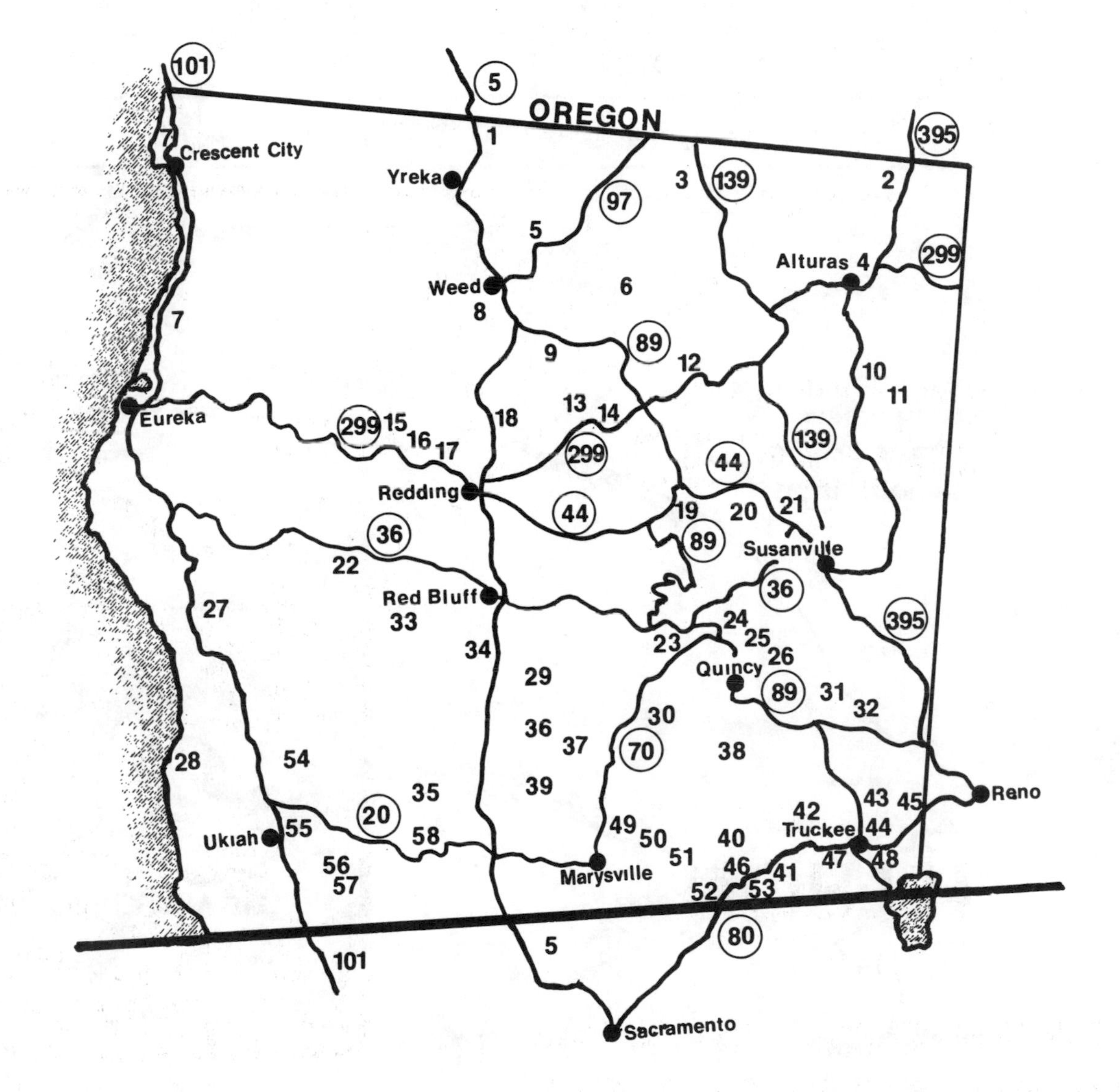

NUMBERS REPRESENT LAKES IN NUMERICAL ORDER IN BOOK

IRON GATE RESERVOIR AND COPCO LAKE

Iron Gate Reservoir and Copco Lake are east of Interstate 5 at a relatively low elevation of 2,607 feet near the Oregon border. The Lakes are administered by the Pacific Power and Light Company which operates the campsites. Fed by the Klamath River, the Lakes offer a variety of fish from warm water species to trout. In the River, there are trout, steelhead and salmon, and Riverboat Guides are available from September through March. This is a hunter's paradise with California's largest deer herd per acre along with an abundance of waterfowl, quail, dove, and even stocked with wild turkey.

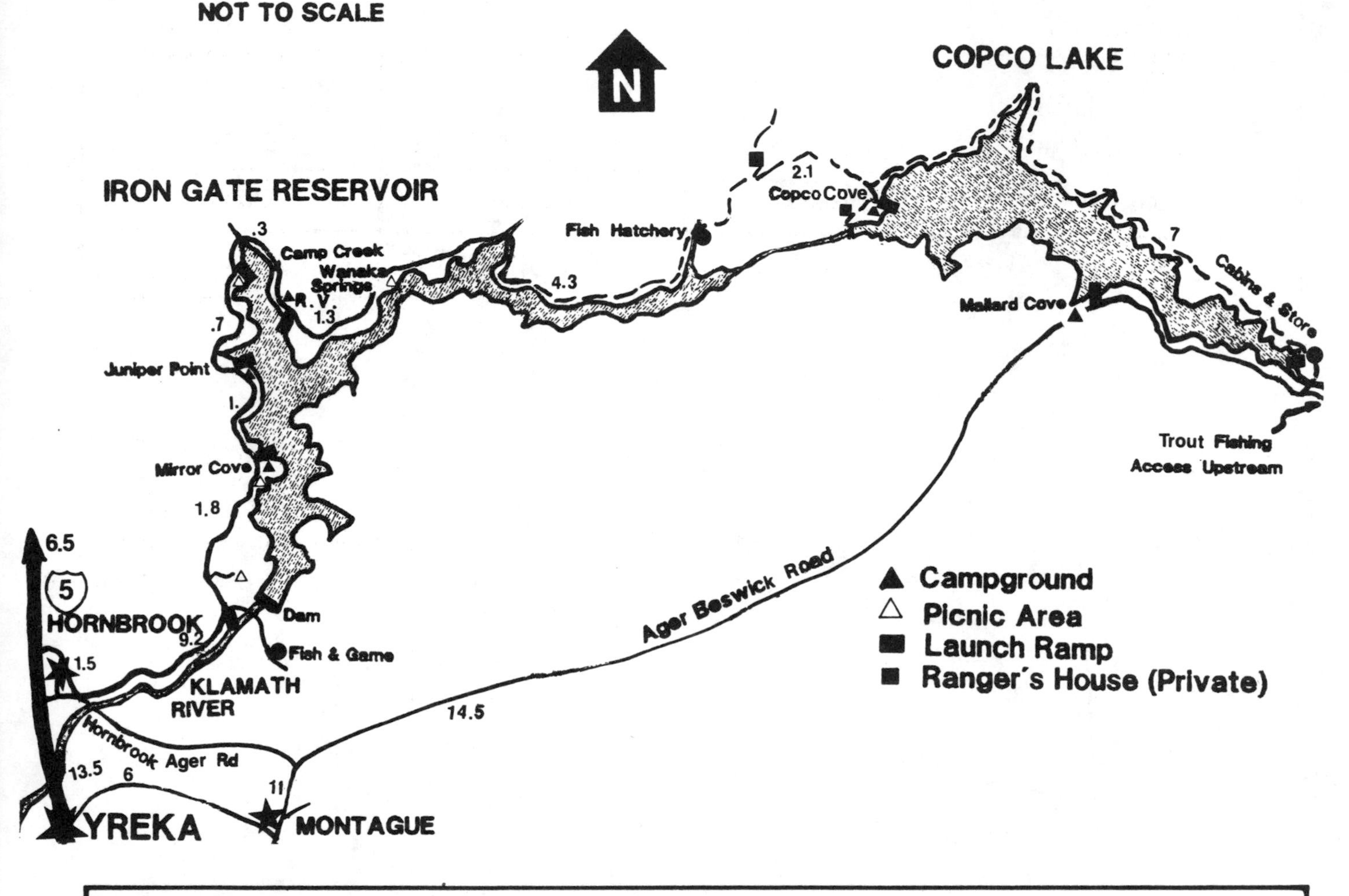

INFORMATION: Pacific Power Light, 300 S. Main, Yreka 96097, Ph: 916-842-3521

CAMPING	BOATING	RECREATION	OTHER
Iron Gate Reservoir: Camp Creek - 12 Sites with Water Juniper Point - 9 Sites, No Water Mirror Cove - 10 Sites, No Water Copco Lake: Copco Cove - 1 Site Mallard Cove - 1 Site	Power, Row, Canoe, Sail & Inflatable 10 MPH Speed Limit in Designated Areas Copco Lake - Upper 1/3 Set Aside for Fishing (No Wake) Launch Ramps Rentals: Fishing Boats with Motors - Copco Lake Only Docks	Fishing: Trout, Catfish, Crappie, Perch, Salmon & Steelhead-Klamath River Swimming Picnicking Hiking & Riding Trail Rafting Hunting: Deer, Quail, Dove, Waterfowl, Wild Turkey	Copco Only: Cabins - Reserve: Copco Lake Store Star Route 1, Box 188 Montague 96064 Ph: 916-459-3655 Full Facilities at Hornbrook

GOOSE, CAVE AND LILY LAKES, FEE RESERVOIR

Goose Lake rests on the California-Oregon border at an elevation of 4,800 feet. This huge 108,800 surface acre Lake is used primarily for waterfowl hunting and boating. Trout fishing is considered poor. In contrast, nearby Cave and Lily Lakes offer excellent fishing for Brook and Rainbow Trout, but boating is limited. These two small mountain Lakes are neighbors at 6,000 feet in the Modoc National Forest. Poor access roads limit the use of trailers. Fee Reservoir, at 4,000 feet, is under the jurisdiction of Modoc County, and it is known for its large Rainbow Trout.

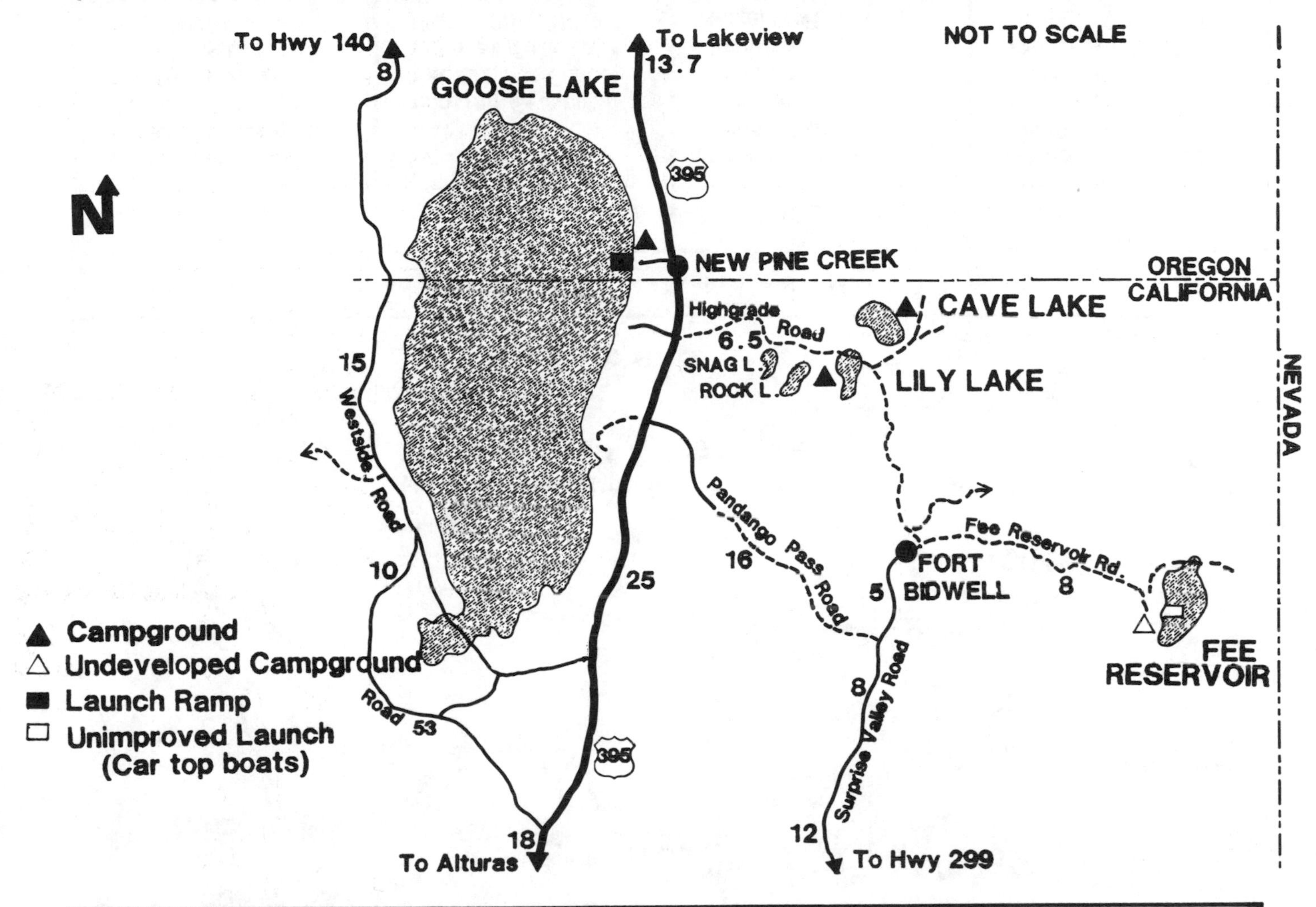

INFORMATION: Warner Mountain Ranger Dist., P.O. Box 220, Cedarville 96104, Ph: 916-279-6116

CAMPING	BOATING	RECREATION	OTHER
Lily & Cave Lakes: 6 Tent & R.V. Sites to 30 People-Drinking Water at Cave Lake Goose Lake: Oregon State Parks 48 Tent & R.V. Sites Water & Electric Hookups Disposal Station Fee: Undev. Sites	Lily & Cave Lakes No Motors Hand Launch Goose Lake: Open to All Boating Paved Launch Ramp Fee Reservoir: Unimproved Launch Ramp Shallow Draft Boats Advised	Fishing: Brook & Rainbow Trout Picnicking Hiking & Riding Trails Backpacking & Nature Study Swimming Hunting: Upland Game Waterfowl, Deer Birdwatching	Oregon State Parks Region 4 P.O. Box 5309 Bend, Oregon 97708 Ph: 503-388-6211 Facilities Limited to Nearby Towns

LOWER KLAMATH, TULE AND CLEAR LAKES

KLAMATH BASIN NATIONAL WILDLIFE REFUGE

This is waterfowl country! These Lakes are within the Klamath Basin National Wildlife Refuge which has one of the greatest concentrations of migratory waterfowl in the world. Photography and wildlife observation (over 270 species of birds have been identified) are popular activities. This is a hunter's paradise. Since rules and boundaries are strictly enforced, it is essential you contact the Fish and Wildlife Service for detailed information. Except for canoeing at Tule Lake, boating is auxiliary to hunting. There is no fishing. Accommodations can be a problem, especially during hunting season, so plan ahead by contacting the facilities listed below or the Tule Lake Chamber of Commerce, P.O. Box 592, Tule Lake 96134, Ph: 916-667-5178.

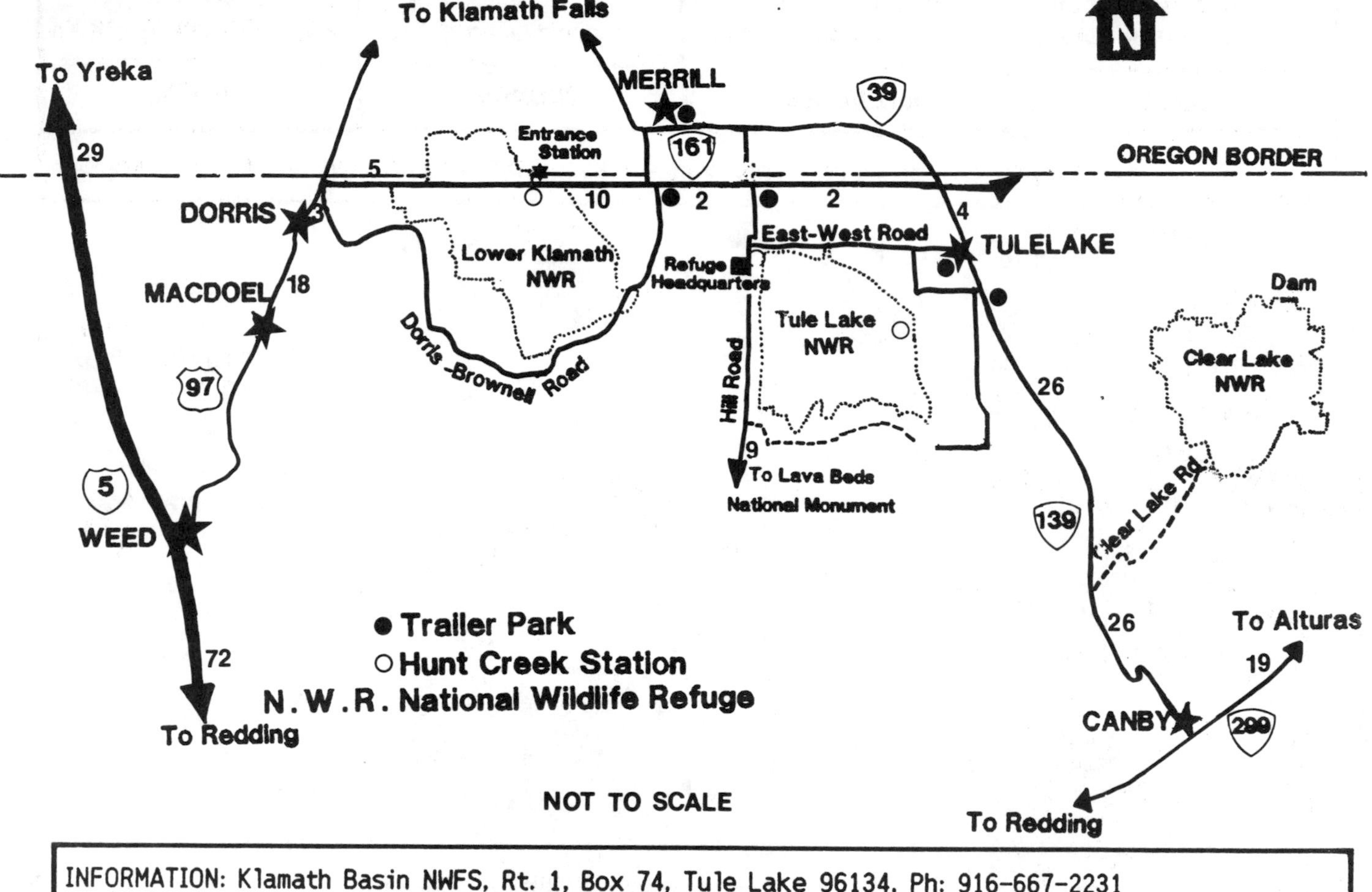

INFORMATION: Klamath Basin NWFS, Rt. 1, Box 74, Tule Lake 96134, Ph: 916-667-2231

CAMPING	BOATING	RECREATION	OTHER
Shady Lanes Trailer Park: P.O. Box 297 Tule Lake 96134 Ph: 916-667-2617 58 R.V. Sites Full Hookups Sheepy Ridge Camp Rt. 1, Box 45-A Tule Lake 96134 Ph: 916-667-5370 60 Tent/R.V. Sites Full Hookups: $10.50	Boats are Allowed Only During Hunting Season Except for Canoe Area at Tule Lake NWR - Open July Through September Air Thrust & Water Thrust Boats are Prohibited	Hunting: Geese, Ducks, Coots, Snipe & Pheasants *Steel Shot is Required for Waterfowl Hunting Birdwatching Nature Study Photography	Westside Grocery & Trailer Park Rt. 1, Box 46F Tule Lake 96134 Ph: 916-667-5225 14 Tent/R.V. Sites Full Hookups Fee: $9 Lava Beds National Monument 40 Tent/R.V. Sites

BIG SAGE, "C", "F", DUNCAN, GRAVEN, BAILEY AND DORRIS RESERVOIRS, DELTA LAKES

Although facilities are limited, Mother Nature has provided an abundance of recreational opportunities at these Lakes in the Modoc National Forest and Modoc County. Big Sage Reservoir rests at an elevation of 4,400 feet on a sage and juniper covered plateau. This 5,400 acre Reservoir is open to all boating and provides a warm water fishery. Nearby Reservoirs "C", and "F" and Duncan provide a good opportunity to catch the large Eagle Lake Trout. Dorris Lake is in the Modoc National Wildlife Refuge. It is closed during waterfowl hunting season. The angler will find trout and a warm water fishery. Graven, Bailey and Delta are under the jurisdiction of Modoc County and are primarily known for their good catfishing.

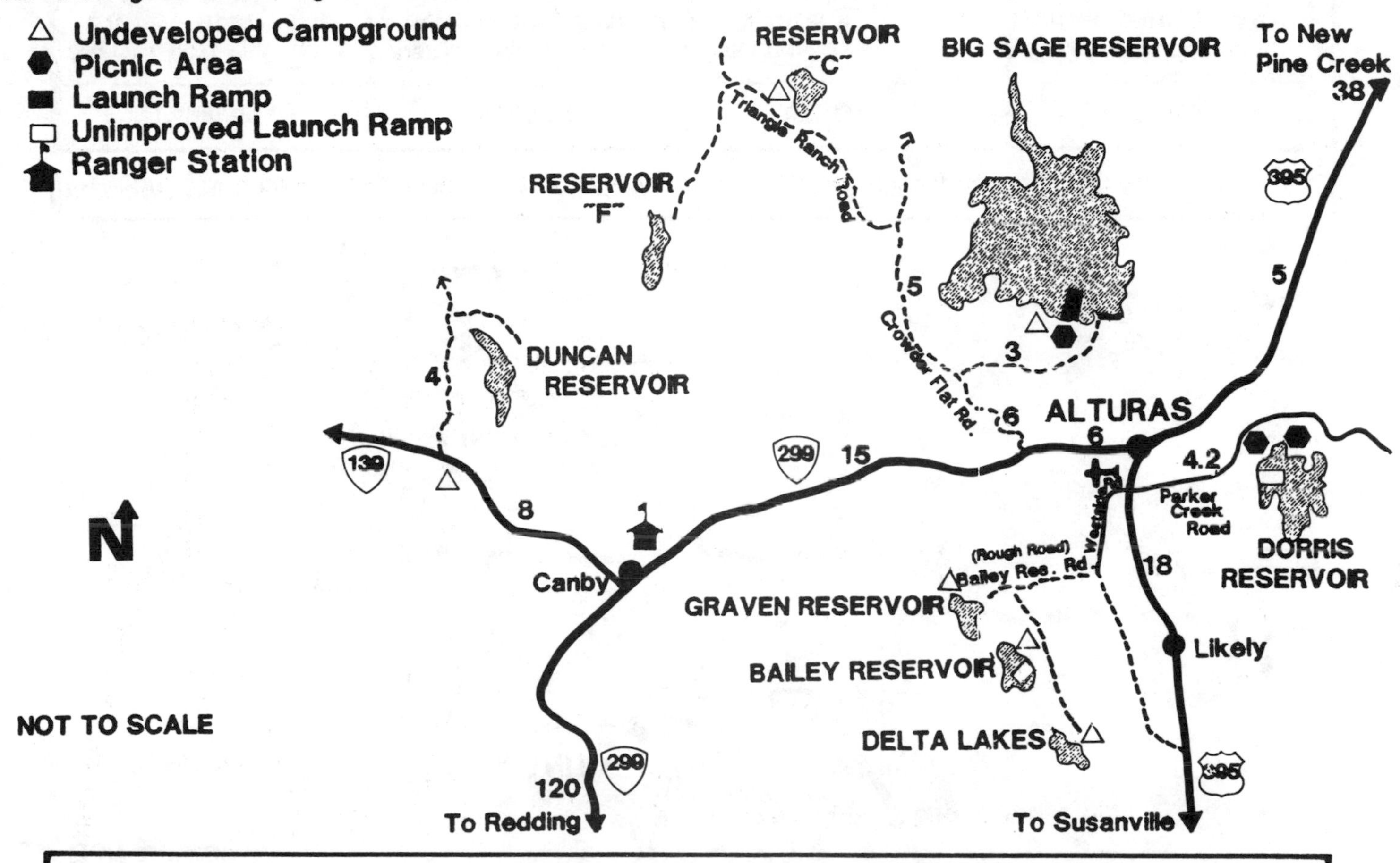

INFORMATION: Devils Garden Ranger Dist., P.O. Box 5, Canby 96015, Ph: 916-233-4611

CAMPING	BOATING	RECREATION	OTHER
Undeveloped Campsites as Shown on Map No Drinking Water Limited Trailer Access	Big Sage: Open to All Boating Paved Launch Ramp Dorris: Open to All Boating Unimproved Ramp Underwater Hazards Other Lakes Open to Small Hand Launched Boats	Fishing: Trout, Bass, Catfish & Panfish, Eagle Lake Trout at Res. "C", Res. "F", & Duncan Hiking & Riding Trails Nature & Bird Study Hunting: Waterfowl, Upland Game, Deer & Antelope No Hunting at Dorris	Dorris Reservoir: Modoc National Wildlife Refuge Alturas 96101 Ph: 916-233-3572 Graven, Bailey & Delta Modoc County 202 W. 4th St. Alturas 96101 Ph: 916-233-2582

INDIAN TOM, MEISS, JUANITA, ORR AND SHASTINA LAKES

These Lakes along Highway 97 from Weed to the Oregon Border provide a variety of recreational experiences. The alkaline waters in Indian Tom support a unique Cutthroat fishery. Meiss Lake is within the Butte Valley State Wildlife Refuge. Waterfowl hunting and observation are the primary activities. Juanita is a pretty mountain Lake resting at an elevation of 5,100 feet. There is a nice campground and good trout fishing. Orr is a small private Lake open to the public for boating and fishing. Lake Shastina is a popular private facility providing good fishing and all boating. Contact the Chamber of Commerce at P.O. Box 366, Weed 96094 or phone 916-938-4624 for information.

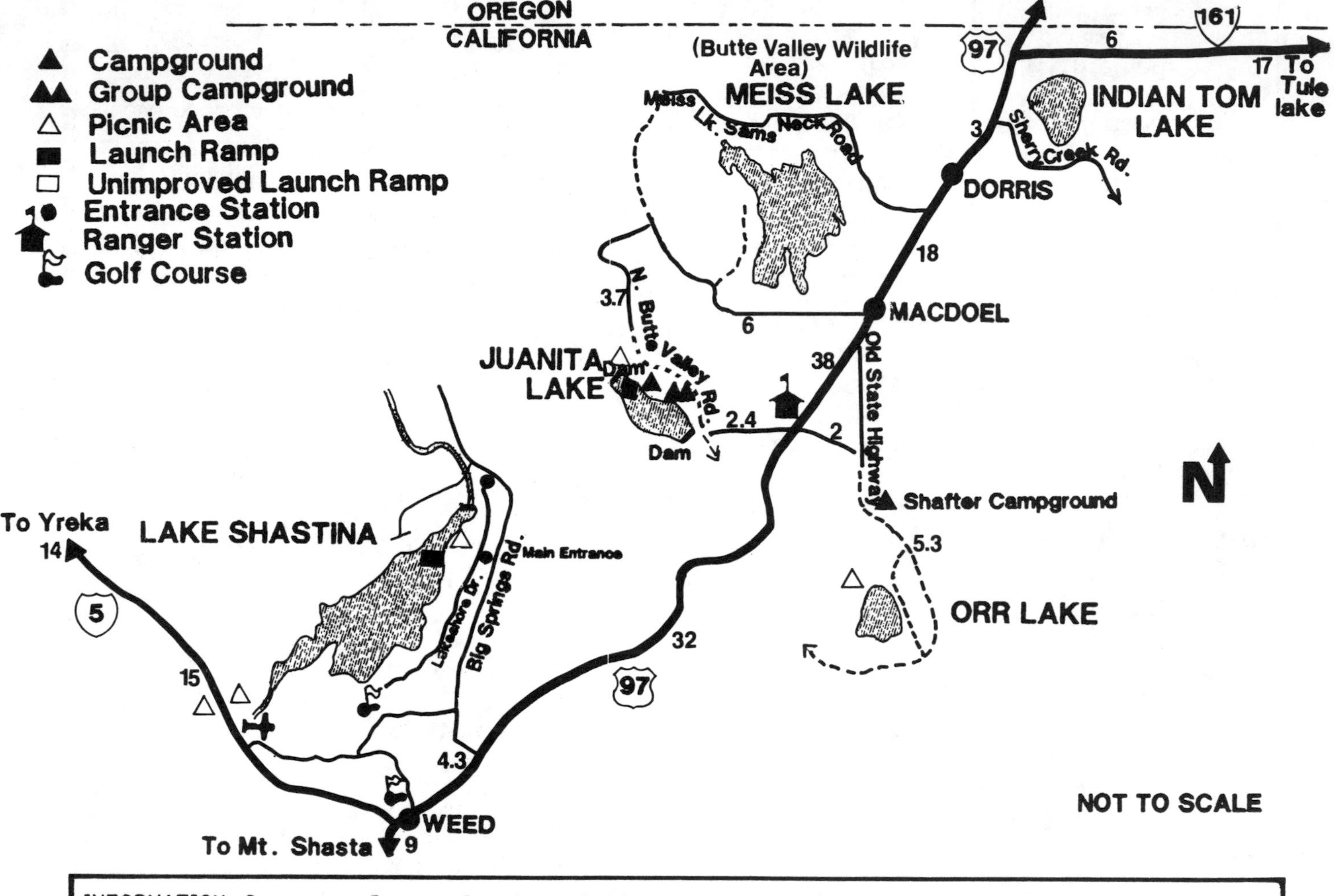

INFORMATION: Goosenest Ranger Station, 37805 Hwy. 97, Macdoel 96058, Ph: 916-398-4391

CAMPING	BOATING	RECREATION	OTHER
Juanita Lake: 23 Dev. Sites Fee: $4 1 Group Site Fee: $6 No Firearms Dis-charged in Campground Shafter: 10 Sites - Fee: $4	Juanita: Open to All Non-powered Boating Launch Ramp Shastina: Open to All Boating Orr & Indian Tom: Small Hand Launch Craft - Max. 10 HP Meiss: Shallow Draft Non-powered Boating	Fishing: Juanita: Brown & Rainbow Trout Shastina: Trout, Silver Salmon, Bass, Catfish & Crappie Indian Tom: Cutthroat Hunting: Waterfowl, Deer & Quail Swimming & Picnicking Hiking & Backpacking	Full Facilities in Weed & Tule Lake Gas & Grocery Store at Macdoel & Mt. Hebron Butte Valley Wildlife Area P.O. Box 249 Macdoel 96058 Ph: 916-398-4627

MEDICINE LAKE

Medicine Lake is in the Modoc National Forest at an elevation of 6,700 feet. Once the center of a volcano, this 640-acre Lake has no known outlets and is said to be 150 feet deep in places. The pine-covered campgrounds are maintained by The U. S. Forest Service. Points of interest include the Lava Beds National Monument, Glass Mountain, Burnt Lava Flow, Medicine Lake Glass Flow and Undertakers Crater. Although remote, this is a popular Lake for boating, waterskiing and sailing. The fishing is good from shore or boat, and Little Medicine Lake offers an opportunity unique to Californians with a population of Arctic Greyling.

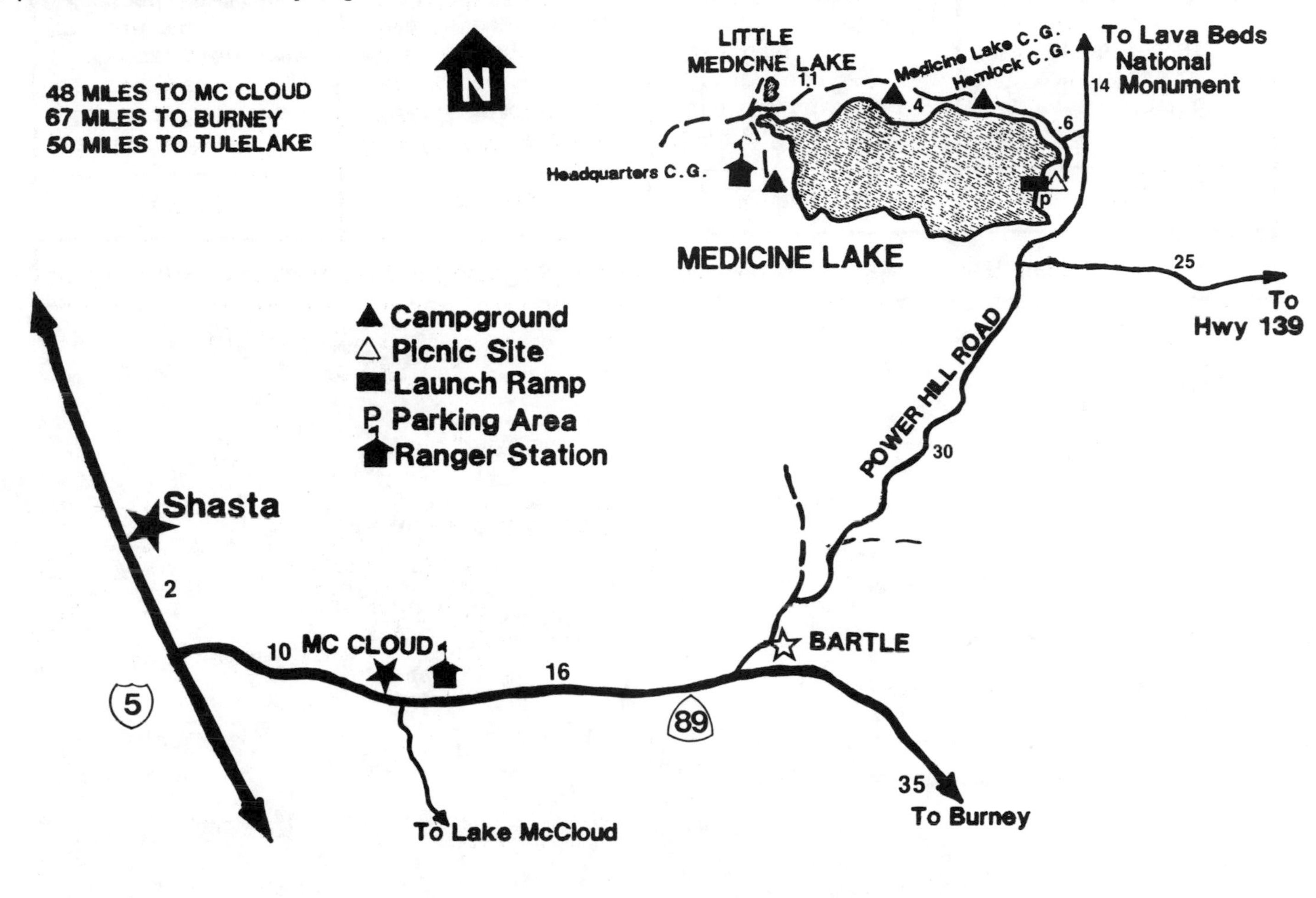

INFORMATION: Doublehead Ranger Dist., Box 818, Tulelake 96134, Ph: 916-667-2246

CAMPING	BOATING	RECREATION	OTHER
76 Dev. Sites for Tents & R.V.s Fee: $3 & $4 No Hook-ups No Reservations	Power, Row, Canoe, Sail, Inflatable, Waterski, Jet Ski Launch Ramp - Paved	Fishing: Rainbow & Brook Trout, Arctic Greyling Swimming Picnicking Hiking Horseback Riding Hunting: Deer, Bear, Grouse	Full Facilities: 14 Miles at Lava Beds Nat. Mon. Full Facilities: 33 Miles at Bartle

LAKE EARL, FISH LAKE, FRESHWATER LAGOON, STONE LAGOON AND BIG LAGOON

Big Lagoon and the smaller Stone and Freshwater Lagoons are three of California's most unusual Lakes. These clear, brackish water Lakes are separated from the Pacific Ocean by a thin strip of sand. The angler may fish for trout, and then cross the sand and surf-cast for perch. Earl is a large shallow Lake just north of Crescent City used primarily by fishermen. Fish is a small Lake, 28 acres, at an elevation of 1,800 feet. Motors are not allowed on this popular fishing Lake. The Forest Service maintains a nice campground amid fir and huckleberries. There is also a self-guided nature trail and other trails leading to Red Mountain Lake and on to Blue Lake.

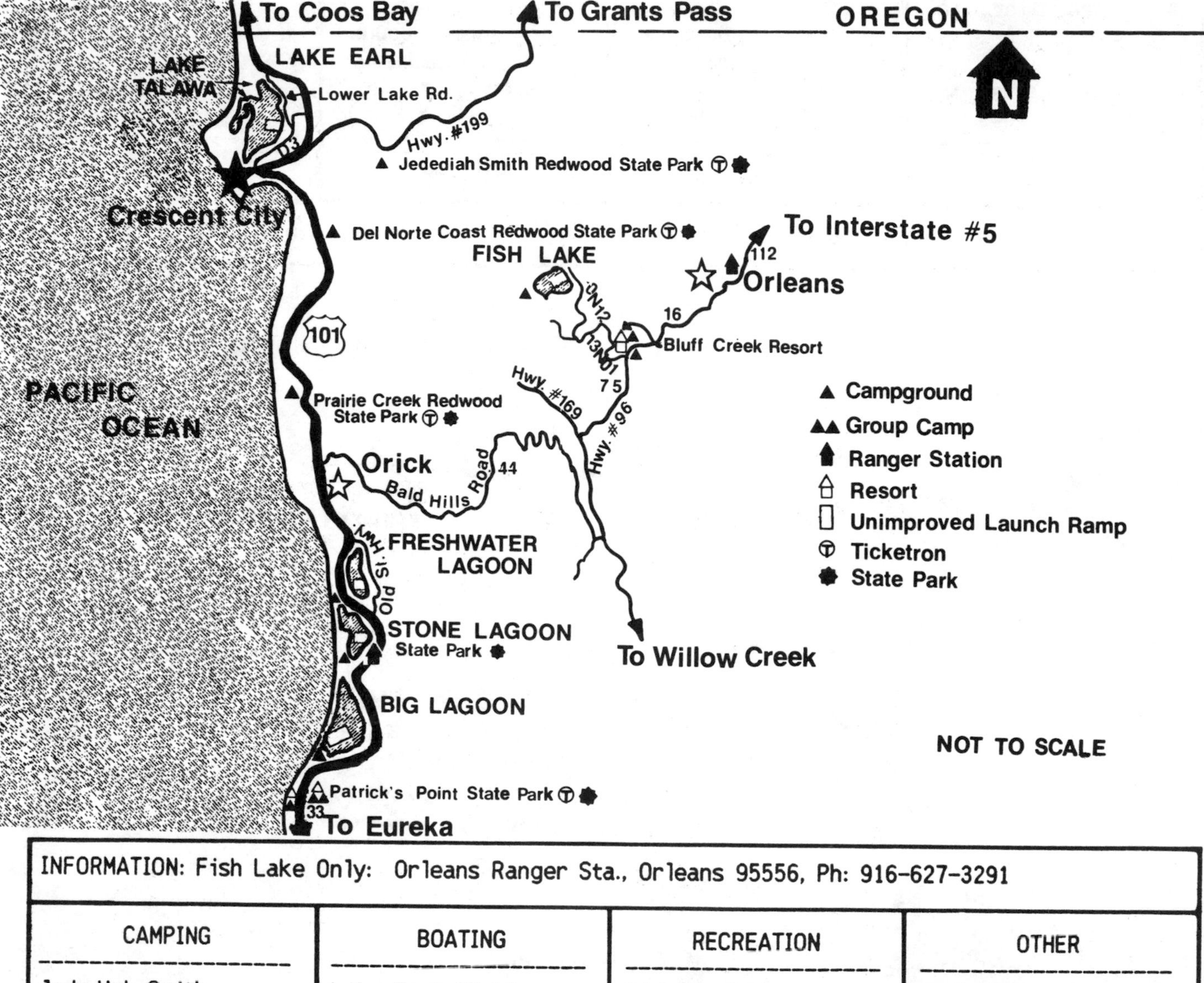

INFORMATION: Fish Lake Only: Orleans Ranger Sta., Orleans 95556, Ph: 916-627-3291

CAMPING	BOATING	RECREATION	OTHER
Jedediah Smith Redwoods State Park Del Norte Coast Redwoods State Park Prairie Creek Redwoods State Park Humboldt Lagoons State Park Stone Lagoon: 30 Primitive Sites First Come Basis Others: Ticketron	Lake Earl: Fishing Boats—Beach Launch Freshwater Lagoon: Waterskiing Stone Lagoon: Canoes & Fishing Boats Big Lagoon: Fishing & Small Sailboats Fish Lake: Non-Power Boats Only Unimproved Ramp	Fishing: Rainbow, Brown & Cutthroat Trout Picnicking Swimming at Lagoons Hiking & Nature Trails Beach Combing Tidal Pools Redwood Groves	Fish Lake: Orleans Ranger Sta. Orleans 95556 Ph: 916-627-3291 Store, Gas, Trailer Park at Bluff Creek Resort

LAKE SISKIYOU AND CASTLE LAKE

Lake Siskiyou is a man-made Reservoir, at an elevation of 3,181 feet, located in the morning shadows of awesome Mount Shasta. On the headwaters of the Sacramento River, the Lake has 437 surface acres with 5-1/4 shoreline miles surrounded by pine trees. The campground offers complete facilities for the varied recreational activities such as its 1,000 feet of sandy swimming beach, complete marina and store. The Pacific Crest Trail is located nearby and the fishing is good. Castle Lake is a small Lake located just south of Lake Siskiyou. It is very pretty with crystal clear water. This is primarily a fishing Lake but swimming is allowed. There is a small picnic area near the Lake and 5 campsites for tents.

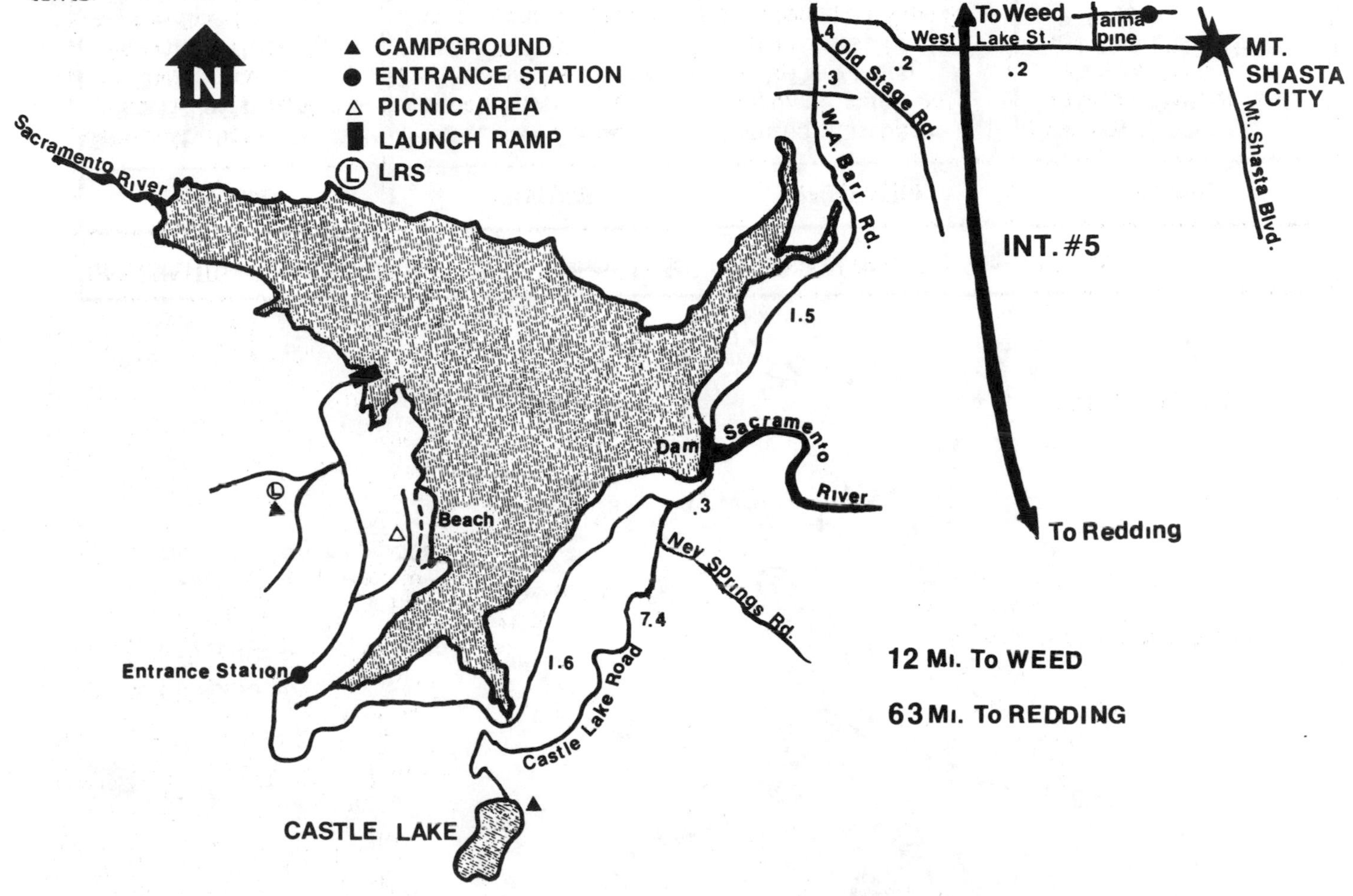

INFORMATION: Lake Siskiyou, P.O. Box 276, Mt. Shasta 96067, Ph: 916-926-2618

CAMPING	BOATING	RECREATION	OTHER
299 Dev. Sites for Tents & R.V.s Full Hook-ups Fee: $8 - $10 Group Camps Reservations: LRS or Above Castle Lake: Mount Shasta Ranger District 5 Tent Sites	Power, Row, Canoe, Windsurfing, Sail, & Inflatables 10 MPH Speed Limit Full Service Marina Launch Ramp Rentals: Fishing, Canoe, Paddleboat, Pontoon Berths, Docks, Gas, Moorings, Dry Storage	Fishing: Rainbow, Kamloop, Brown, & Brook Trout, Largemouth Bass Swimming Picnicking Hiking Backpacking-Parking 2 Children's Playgrounds	Snack Bar Grocery Store Bait & Tackle Laundromat Disposal Station Propane Community-Sized Barbecue Handicap Fishing Patio Full Facilities - 3.5 Miles at Mt. Shasta

LAKE MC CLOUD

The Dam on the McCloud River was constructed by P.G.&E. in 1965. At an elevation of 3,000 feet, the surface area of this 520-acre Lake belongs to P.G.&E., and the surrounding land belongs to the Hearst Corporation. The U. S. Forest Service was deeded a narrow strip of land between the road and high water mark from Tarantula Gulch to Star City Creek. The steep shoreline provides a beautiful setting for the Lake with pine trees towering above the rocky terrain. This is a popular Lake for fishing. There are no developed campsites, but there is a small unimproved campground and picnic area at Star City Creek. A Forest Service campground is located on the McCloud River at Ah-Di-Na.

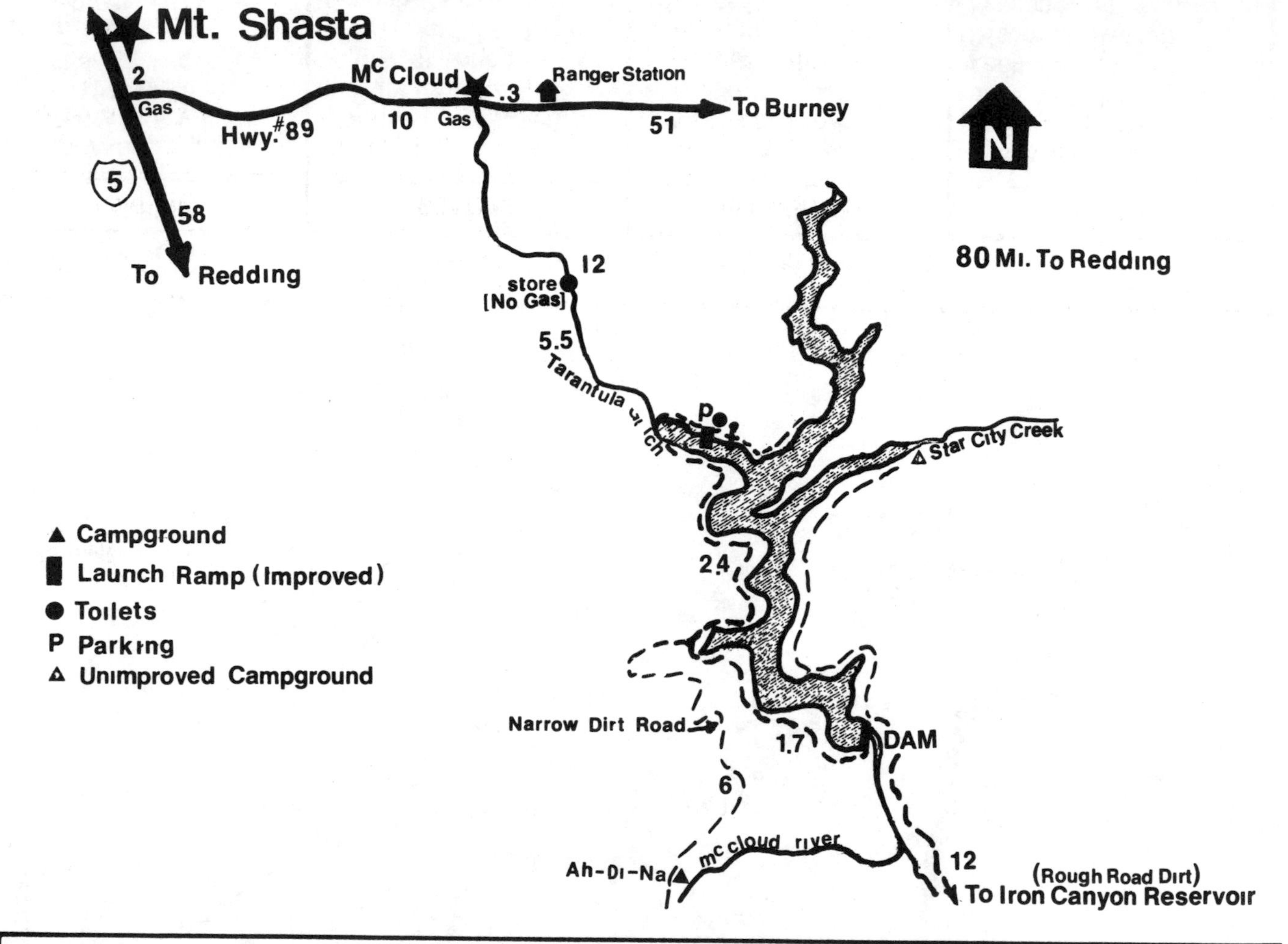

INFORMATION: McCloud Ranger Dist., Drawer I, McCloud 96057, Ph: 916-964-2184

CAMPING	BOATING	RECREATION	OTHER
Star City Creek: Small Unimproved Campground with Toilets Ah-Di-Na: 16 Camper Sites Narrow Dirt Road Not Advised for Large Trailers	Power, Row, Canoe Launch Ramp	Fishing: Rainbow & Brown Trout *Dolly Varden Trout must be Released Picnicking Hiking Nature Study	Grocery Store - 5-1/2 Miles Full Facilities in McCloud

WEST VALLEY RESERVOIR

West Valley Reservoir is in the northeastern corner of California at an elevation of 4,770 feet, east of Highway 395. This 970-acre Reservoir has a shoreline of 7 miles which is usually frozen over from December to early March. West Valley is owned and administered by Modoc County. This is a good Lake for boating, and waterskiing is popular. The angler will find good warm water fishing, but Eagle Lake Trout are the main attraction. Although somewhat remote and limited in facilities, West Valley Reservoir offers the dedicated fisherman an opportunity to land the big one.

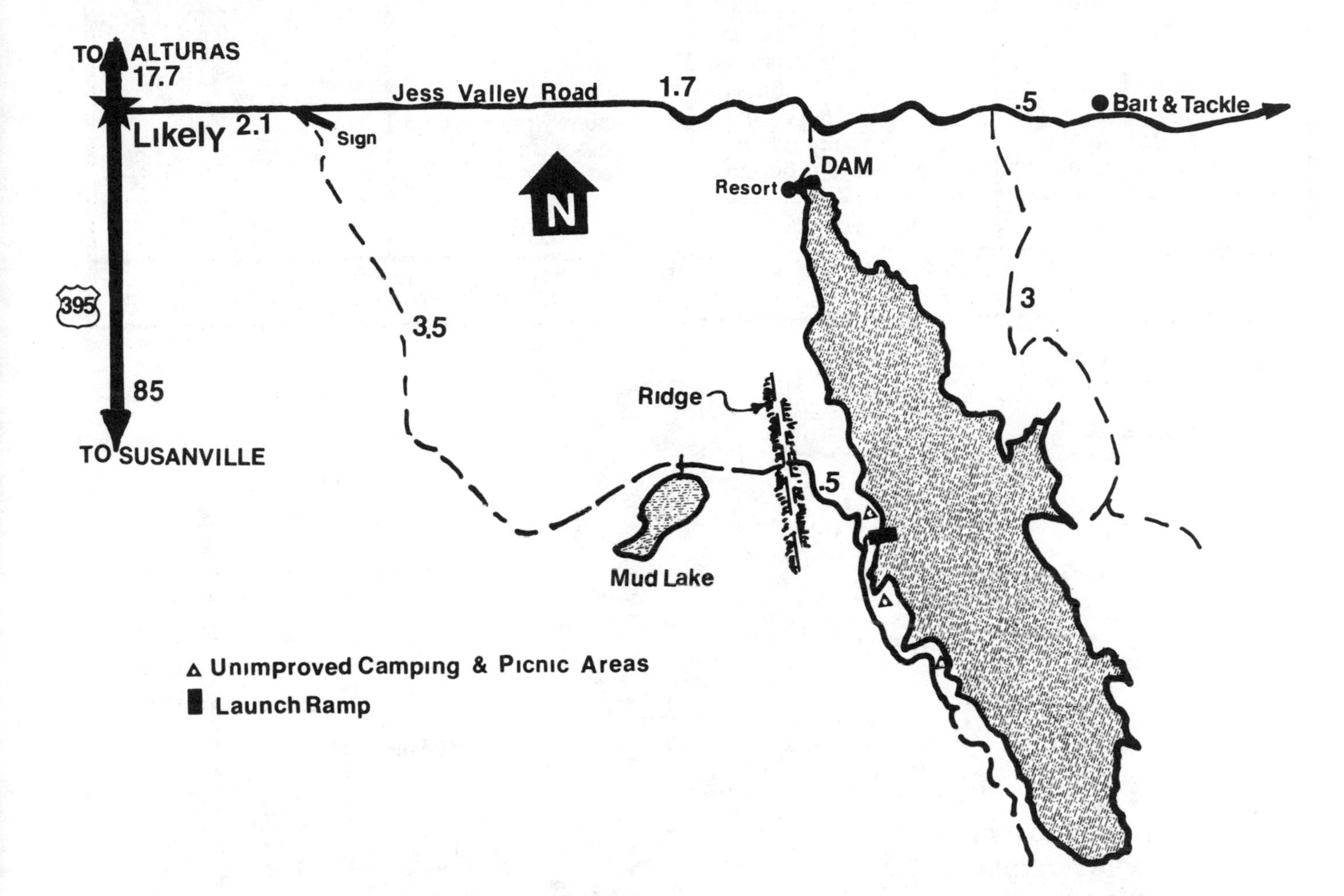

INFORMATION: Modoc County, 202 W. 4th St., Alturas 96101, Ph: 916-233-2582			
CAMPING	BOATING	RECREATION	OTHER
Primitive Camping Water & Toilets	Power, Row, Canoe, Sail, Waterski, Jet Ski, Windsurfing & Inflatable Overnight Camping In Boat Permitted Anywhere High Winds Can Be Hazardous	Fishing: Eagle Lake Trout, Catfish, Perch Swimming Picnicking Hiking Backpacking-Parking Hunting: Deer & Rabbit	Full Facilities - 6 Miles at Likely

BLUE LAKE

Blue Lake, 28 miles southeast of Alturas, is in the Modoc National Forest. This pretty mountain Lake of 160 surface acres is surrounded by Ponderosa Pine, White Fir and meadows at an elevation of 6,000 feet. This is a popular, well-used facility near the South Warner Wilderness area. The Lake fishing is good for Rainbow and Brown Trout. There are no boating facilities other than an unimproved launch ramp, but all boating is permitted. For the hiker, backpacker, horseback rider or energetic fisherman, the South Warner Wilderness offers good trails. A Wilderness Permit is not required for the South Warner Wilderness.

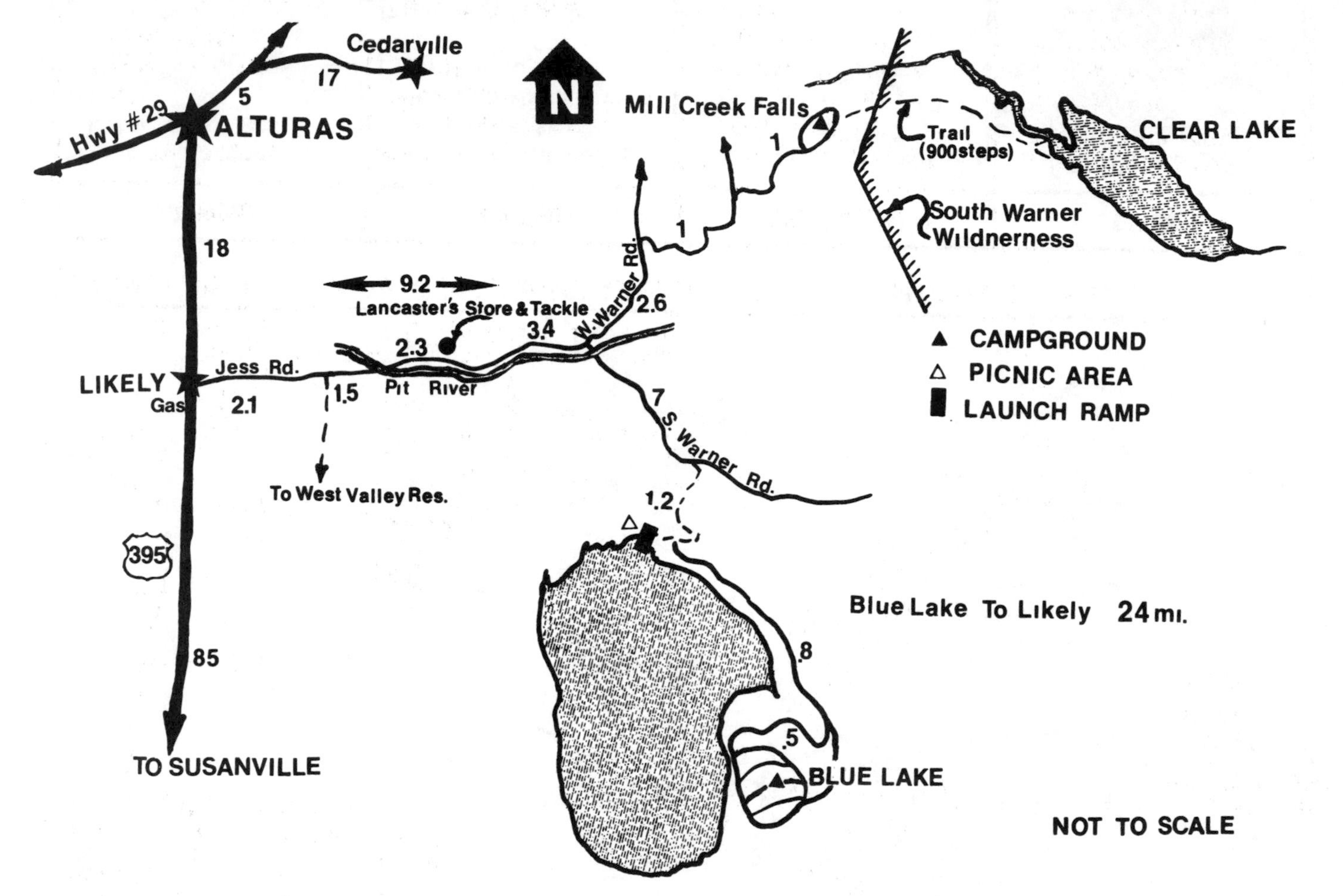

INFORMATION: Warner Mountain R.D., Box 220, Cedarville 96104, Ph: 916-279-6116

CAMPING	BOATING	RECREATION	OTHER
Blue Lake Camp: 48 Dev. Sites for Tents & R.V.s under 22 feet Fee: $4 Mill Creek Falls: 19 Dev. Sites for Tents & R.V.s under 22 feet	Power, Row, Canoe, Sail, & Inflatable Unimproved Launch Ramp	Fishing: Rainbow & Brown Trout Picnicking Hiking Swimming Hunting: Deer in Vicinity	Lancaster's Store: Groceries, Bait & Tackle, Licenses Likely: Grocery Store, Restaurant, Gas Station Full Facilities - 28 Miles at Alturas

EASTMAN, TULE, BIG, FALL RIVER, CRYSTAL AND BAUM LAKES

At an elevation of 2,980 feet, these Lakes in the Fall River Valley are fed by the famous Hat Creek, Pit River and Fall River. Baum Lake, 89 acres, and Crystal Lake, 60 acres, are contiguous. Non-powered boating is allowed, and trophy sized brown trout along with Eastern brook and rainbow await the fisherman. Big, Tule, Eastman and Fall River Lakes rest an elevation of 3,300 feet and are connected together as shown. There is a good warm water fishery. Rainbows of 1-1/2 to 4 pounds are fairly common. The creeks and rivers in this area are also inviting to the serious angler.

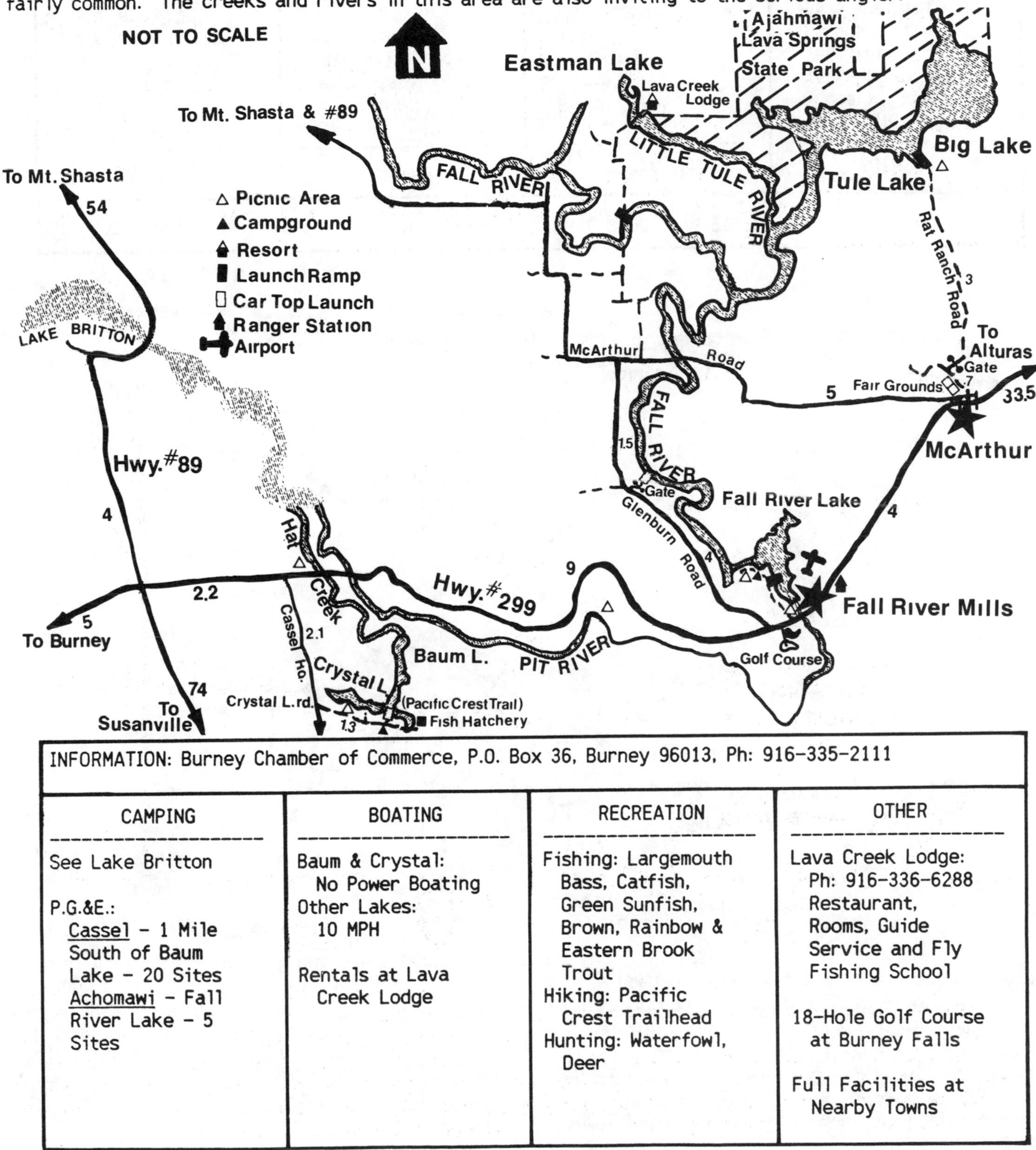

INFORMATION: Burney Chamber of Commerce, P.O. Box 36, Burney 96013, Ph: 916-335-2111

CAMPING	BOATING	RECREATION	OTHER
See Lake Britton P.G.&E.: Cassel - 1 Mile South of Baum Lake - 20 Sites Achomawi - Fall River Lake - 5 Sites	Baum & Crystal: No Power Boating Other Lakes: 10 MPH Rentals at Lava Creek Lodge	Fishing: Largemouth Bass, Catfish, Green Sunfish, Brown, Rainbow & Eastern Brook Trout Hiking: Pacific Crest Trailhead Hunting: Waterfowl, Deer	Lava Creek Lodge: Ph: 916-336-6288 Restaurant, Rooms, Guide Service and Fly Fishing School 18-Hole Golf Course at Burney Falls Full Facilities at Nearby Towns

IRON CANYON RESERVOIR

Iron Canyon Reservoir is at an elevation of 2,700 feet in the Shasta-Trinity National Forest. This beautiful 500-surface acre Lake rests in a gentle mountainous area with 15 miles of forested shoreline. Larger boats with deep draft are not recommended due to shallow Lake levels, but owners of smaller, low-speed boats find Iron Canyon ideal. The Lake level varies greatly during the year depending on weather and P.G.&E. power needs. There are some big trout in the Lake, and the fishing can be good. The U. S. Forest Service has a Self-Service Campground providing a quiet atmosphere amid pine and fir trees. P.G.&E., in co-operation with U.S.F.S., has opened a new campground and paved launch ramp at Hawkins Landing. This Lake is perfect for those seeking solitude.

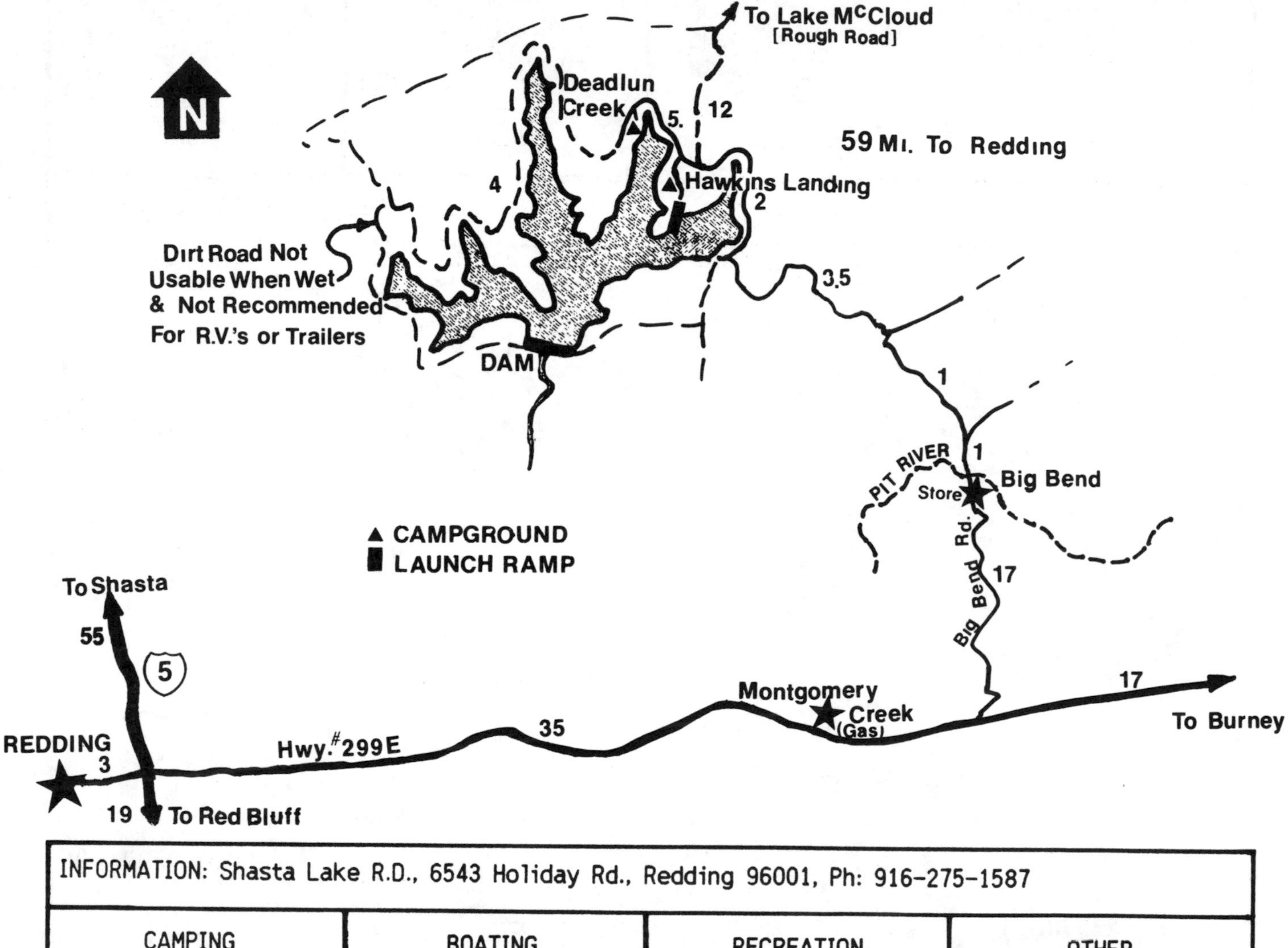

INFORMATION: Shasta Lake R.D., 6543 Holiday Rd., Redding 96001, Ph: 916-275-1587			
CAMPING	**BOATING**	**RECREATION**	**OTHER**
U.S.F.S. - Deadlun Creek: 30 Dev. Sites for Tents & R.V.s to 15 feet - No Fee U.S.F.S. and P.G.E. Hawkins Landing: 10 Dev. Sites for Tents & R.V.s Fee: $5	Power, Row, Canoe, & Inflatables Speedboats & Waterskiing Not Permitted Launch Ramp at Hawkins Landing Campground	Fishing: Rainbow & Brown Trout Swimming Picnicking Hiking Bird Watching Hunting: Deer	At Big Bend: Grocery Store Bait & Tackle Gas Station (Hours of Operation are Limited) U.S.F.S. Guard Station and Fire Station Caution: Heavy Logging Truck Traffic at Times

LAKE BRITTON

Lake Britton, located in the Shasta-Trinity National Forest, is at an elevation of 2,760 feet. This 1,600 surface acre Lake has 18 shoreline miles and is nestled amid the evergreen forests near the Pit River. The McArthur-Burney Falls Memorial State Park has 853 acres stretching from Burney Falls along Burney Creek to the shoreline of Lake Britton. Burney Creek is planted with trout weekly in season. This Park, established in 1920, is not only one of the oldest in the State Park System, but one of the best facilities in Northern California. There are also U. S. Forest Service and P.G.&E. campgrounds around the Lake. Burney Falls, called by Teddy Roosevelt, "the eighth wonder of the world," is the popular attraction of the area. This is a good boating Lake although caution should be used as there can be floating debris. Fishing can be excellent in both the Lake and streams.

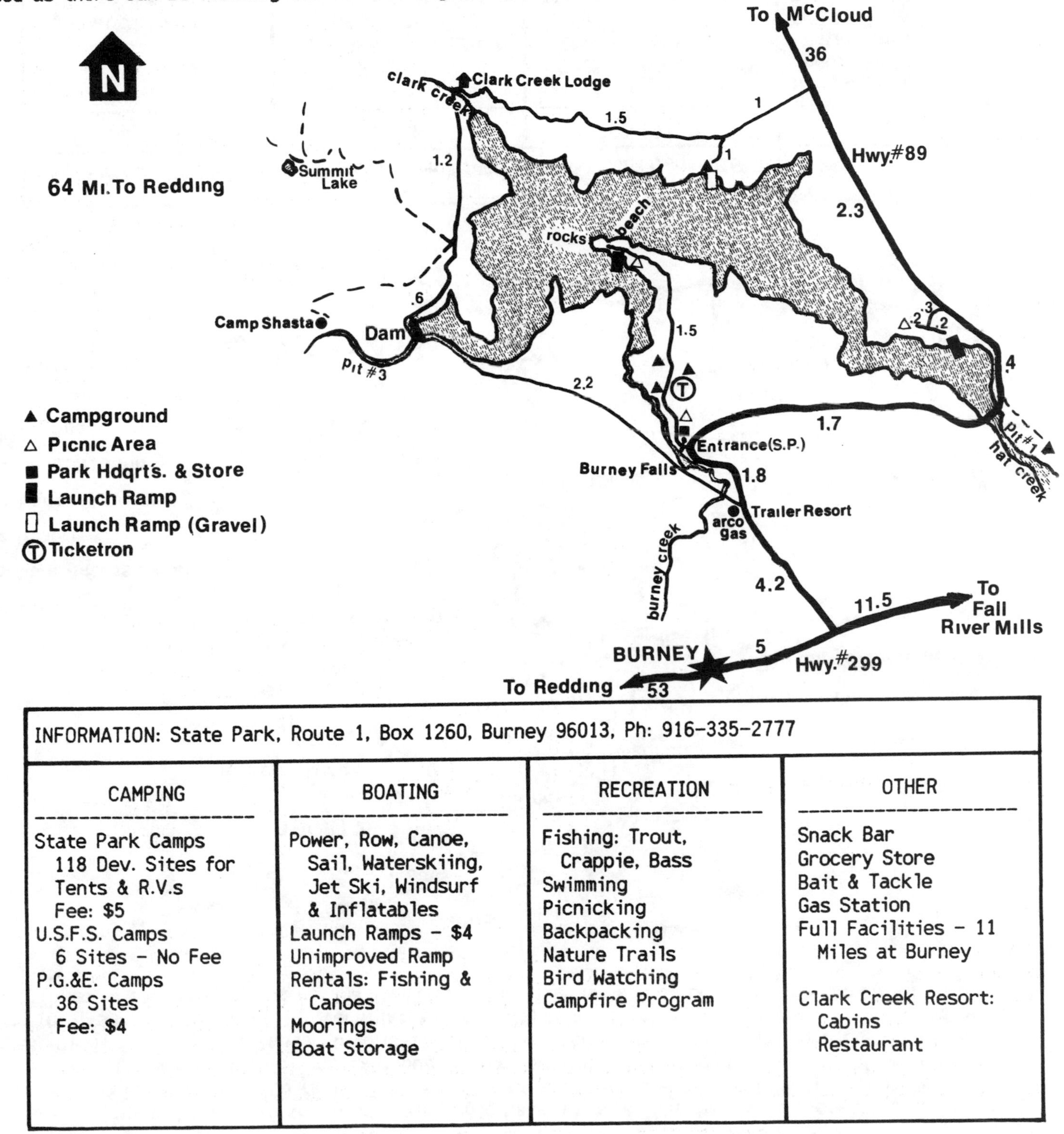

INFORMATION: State Park, Route 1, Box 1260, Burney 96013, Ph: 916-335-2777

CAMPING	BOATING	RECREATION	OTHER
State Park Camps 118 Dev. Sites for Tents & R.V.s Fee: $5 U.S.F.S. Camps 6 Sites - No Fee P.G.&E. Camps 36 Sites Fee: $4	Power, Row, Canoe, Sail, Waterskiing, Jet Ski, Windsurf & Inflatables Launch Ramps - $4 Unimproved Ramp Rentals: Fishing & Canoes Moorings Boat Storage	Fishing: Trout, Crappie, Bass Swimming Picnicking Backpacking Nature Trails Bird Watching Campfire Program	Snack Bar Grocery Store Bait & Tackle Gas Station Full Facilities - 11 Miles at Burney Clark Creek Resort: Cabins Restaurant

TRINITY LAKE

Trinity Lake, also known as Clair Engle Lake, rests at the foot of the spectacular Trinity Alps at an elevation of 2,400 feet. The 145 miles of shoreline are covered by pine, cedar and oak trees creating a camper's delight. Although water level fluctuation can cause considerable hazards, the boater will find plenty of water in this 17,000 surface acre Lake. There are hundreds of quiet coves for the fisherman to tie up in overnight and catch fish for dinner. Campgrounds, marinas and other facilities are extensive, and recreational opportunities range from boating to mountain climbing in the Trinity Alps.

. . . Continued . . .

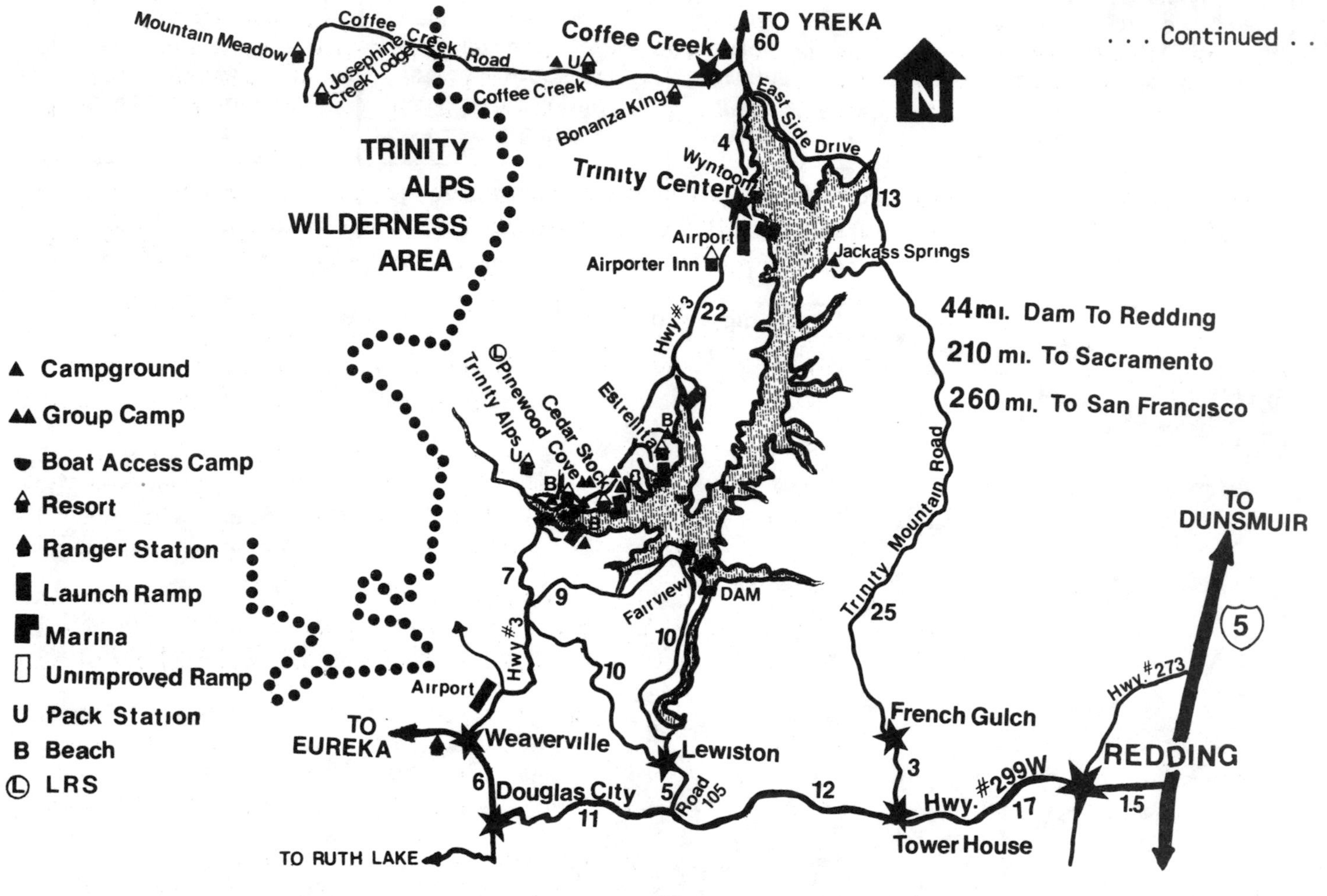

INFORMATION: U.S. Forest Service, Drawer T., Weaverville 96093, Ph: 916-623-2121			
CAMPING	BOATING	RECREATION	OTHER
424 Dev. Sites for Tents & R.V.s Fees: $4 - $6 35 Boat Access Sites - No Fee Group Camps - 150 People Maximum Reservations at Weaverville R.S. Only Additional Campsites at Private Resorts	Power, Row, Canoe, Sail, Waterski, Jet Skis, Windsurf & Inflatables Full Service Marinas Launch Ramps Rentals: Fishing, Ski, Houseboats & Pontoons Docks, Berths, Moorings, Storage, Gas	Fishing: Trout, Catfish, Bluegill, Bass, Kokanee Swimming Picnicking Hiking Backpacking Horseback Riding - Trails & Rentals Campfire Programs Hunting: Deer, Fowl	Motels & Cabins Snack Bars Restaurants Grocery Stores Bait & Tackle Laundromat Disposal Stations Gas Stations Airports - Trinity Center & Weaverville

TRINITY LAKE

LAUNCH RAMPS: *Fairview Public Launch Ramp* - Adjacent to Fairview Marina - Bait and Tackle, Boat Gas, Snack Bar, Rentals: Houseboats, Fishing, Waterski & Patio Boats; *Tannery Gulch* - 84 Campsites - Amphitheater; *Stuart Fork Ramp*: *Cedar Stock Resort & Marina* - Grocery Store, Gas, Cabins, Restaurant, Slips, Boat Rentals: Houseboats, Fishing, Waterski & Patio Boats; *Minersville* - Low Water Ramp Adjacent to Minersville Campground; *Estrellita Marina* - Grocery Store, Gas, Snack Bar, LP Gas at Dock, Rentals: Houseboats, Fishing & Waterski Boats & Ski Equipment, Slips; *Bowerman Ramp* - *Recreation Plus* - Store, Bait & Tackle, Slips, Boat Rentals: Houseboats, Fishing, Waterski & Patio Boats.

FOR A COMPLETE LIST OF FACILITIES, WRITE: **TRINITY COUNTY CHAMBER OF COMMERCE**, P.O. Box 517, Weaverville 96093, Ph: 916-623-6101.

TRINITY ALPS RESORT, Star Route, Box 490, Lewiston 96052, Ph: 916-286-2205, Weaverville Exch.
15 Miles North on Highway 3, 1 Mile Left on Trinity Alps Road. The oldest Resort in Trinity - Completely equipped, rustic housekeeping cabins situated along Stuart Fork River, restaurant, full vacation facilities, gas, store, phone, Family Resort.

PINEWOOD COVE RESORT, P.O. Box 388, Weaverville 96093, Ph: 916-623-6919
14 Miles North of Weaverville on Highway 3 - 95 Campsites for tents & R.V.s, full hookups, disposal station, showers, grocery store, ramp, dock, slips, fishing boat rentals for patrons only, private beach, group area, game room, recreation hall, laundromat, movies.

CEDAR STOCK RESORT, Star Route, Box 510, Lewiston 96052, Ph: 916-286-2225, Weaverville Exchange
About 15 Miles North on Highway 3 - Housekeeping cabins, restaurant, lounge, grocery store, full service marina, house boat rentals for up to 10 people, boat, gas, phone.

AIRPORTER INN RESORT, P.O. Box 59, Trinity Center 96091, Ph: 916-266-3223
Fly-In, boat-in motel, housekeeping units, restaurant, cocktail lounge. Bicycle rentals, boat rentals and free launch ramp in co-operation with Recreation Plus Marina. Scott Museum Tours and an annual Labor Day Fly-In barbecue.

WYNTOON PARK RESORT, P.O. Box 70, Trinity Center 96091, Ph: 916-266-3337
1/2 Mile North of Trinity Center on Highway 3 - Complete 90-acre recreation village, cabins, 136 R.V. sites with full hookups, 80 tent sites, grocery store, gas station and propane, snack bar, private dock, rental boats for patrons, laundromat, showers.

RIPPLE CREEK CABINS, Box 3899, St. Rt. 2, Trinity Center 96091, Ph: 916-266-3505
4 miles north of Coffee Creek Road off Highway 3 - Fully equipped housekeeping cabins each with wood stoves, kitchens, porches, barbecues, recreation and game area. Two trailheads nearby, stream fishing.

BONANZA KING, Coffee Creek Route, Trinity Center 96091, Ph: 916-266-3305
3 Miles from Upper End of Trinity Lake on Coffee Creek - Fully equipped housekeeping cabins, some with fireplaces, each with porch, barbecue and picnic table, swimming pond, stream fishing, lawn games, pack station nearby.

COFFEE CREEK RANCH, Star Route 2, Box 4940, Dept. RL, Trinity Center 96091, Ph: 916-266-3343
13 Miles Northwest of Trinity Center on Coffee Creek Road - Full American Plan cabins, some with fireplaces, restaurant, swimming pool, weekly steak fry, square dancing, horseback riding, stream fishing on Coffee Creek which runs through the Ranch, pack trips and deer hunting in season. Added Amenities: trout pond, European Plan--spring, fall, winter, satellite TV, R.V. sites, self-contained only, "Kiddie Korral"--babysitting for 2-9 year olds.

LEWISTON LAKE

Lewiston Lake is at an elevation of 1,902 feet in the Shasta Trinity National Forest. This beautiful Lake is nine miles long and has a surface area of 750 acres. It is open to all boating but subject to a 10 MPH speed limit. The cold, constantly moving water flows into Lewiston Lake from the bottom waters of Trinity Lake providing an ideal habitat for large trout. Just below Lewiston Dam, the Trinity River, Rush Creek and other streams offer prize salmon and steelhead as well as trout. The Lewiston Fish Hatchery is the world's most automated salmon and steelhead hatchery.

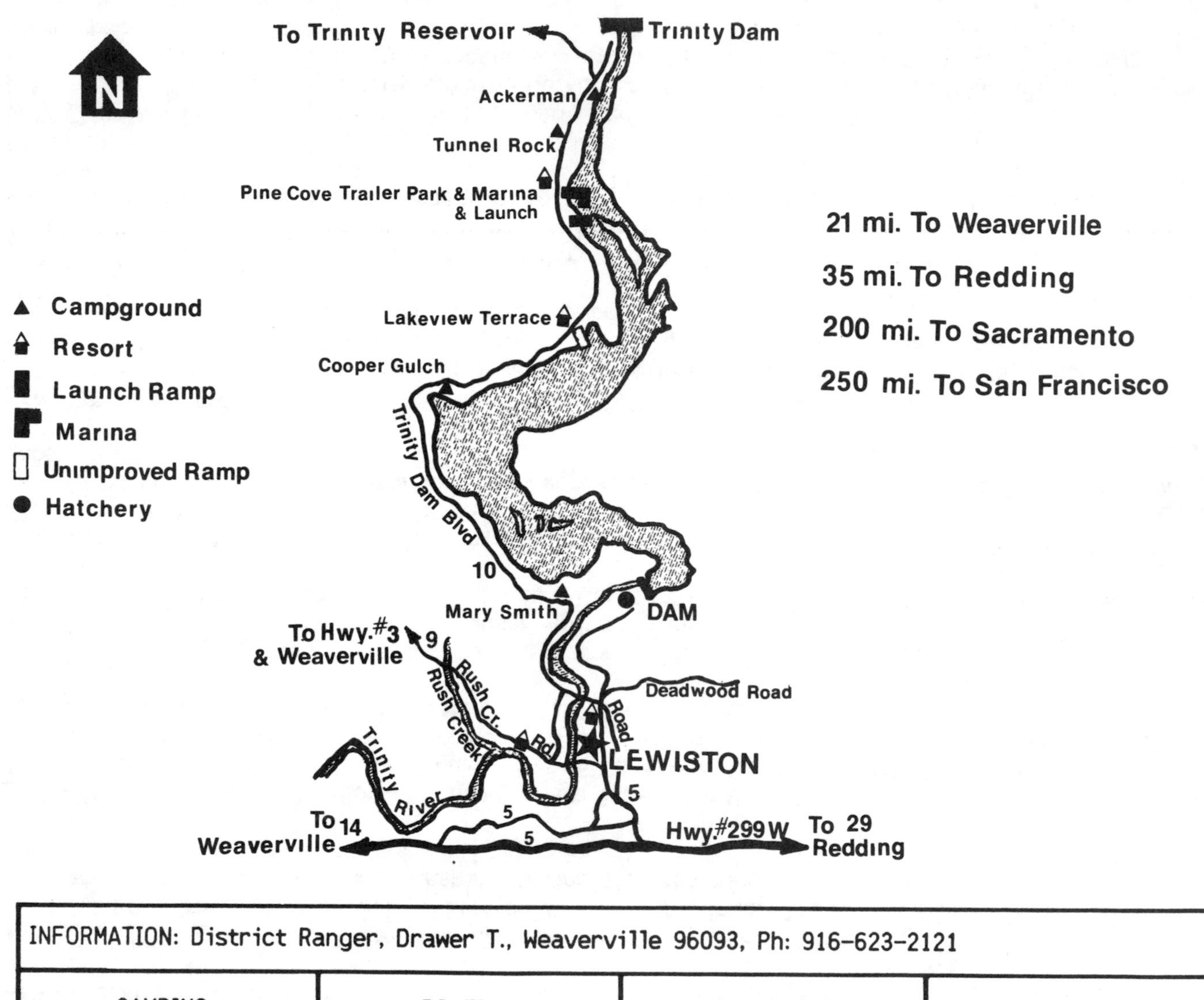

INFORMATION: District Ranger, Drawer T., Weaverville 96093, Ph: 916-623-2121

CAMPING	BOATING	RECREATION	OTHER
24 Dev. Sites for Tents Only 77 Dev. Sites for Tents & R.V.s Fee: $0 - $5 Disposal Station at Ackerman Camp Additional Campsites At Private Resorts	Power, Row, Canoe, Sail & Inflatable Speed Limit - 10 MPH Launch Ramps Rentals: Fishing Boats Docks, Gas, Dry Storage	Fishing: Rainbow & Brown Trout, Kokanee Salmon Picnicking Hunting: Deer, Bear Fowl & Squirrel	Resorts: Contact - Trinity County Chamber of Commerce Box 517 Weaverville 96093 Snack Bars Restaurants Grocery Stores Bait & Tackle

WHISKEYTOWN LAKE AND KESWICK RESERVOIR

Whiskeytown, at an elevation of 1,209 feet, has 36 miles of coniferous shoreline. Tree shaded islands, numerous coves, and 3,220 surface acres of clear blue water invite the watersport enthusiast. The boater will find complete marine facilities and over 5 square miles of open water. Waterskiing and sailing are excellent. Fishing is good from bank or shore for trout, Kokanee salmon, bass and pan fish. The National Park Service maintains the facilities which include picnic areas and campgrounds. Keswick Reservoir is at an elevation of 587 feet and has a surface area of 630 acres. Fed by cold water released from Shasta Dam, Keswick provides the angler with lunker rainbows. Keswick is open to all boating and the launch ramp and picnic area are operated by Shasta County.

INFORMATION: Superintendent, P.O. Box 188, Whiskeytown 96095, Ph: 916-241-6584			
CAMPING	**BOATING**	**RECREATION**	**OTHER**
Brandy Creek: 37 Self-Contained R.V. Sites Disposal Station Oak Bottom: 105 Dev. Tent Sites & 50 R.V. Sites Disposal Station Dry Creek: Group Camp to 200 People-Reserve	Whiskeytown: Open to All Boats Full Service Marina Rentals: Fishing, Ski, Sail, Canoe & Pontoon Boats Sailing Regattas Keswick: Open to All Boats Paved Launch Ramp	Fishing: Kokanee Salmon, Brown, & Rainbow Trout, Spotted, Large & Smallmouth Bass, Bluegill, Crappie & Catfish Swimming Picnicking - Groups Hiking & Riding Trails	Campground Programs Scuba Diving Hunting: Deer & Waterfowl Grocery Store Snack Bar Bait & Tackle Keswick Reservoir: Info: Shasta CDPW 1855 Placer St. Redding 96001 Ph: 916-246-5661

SHASTA LAKE

Shasta Lake is at an elevation of 1,067 feet at the northern tip of the Sacramento Valley on Interstate 5. This huge Lake has over 370 shoreline miles, one-third more than the San Francisco Bay. The four main arms, Sacramento River, McCloud River, Squaw Creek and Pit River, encompass a total surface area of 29,500 acres, making this the largest man-made Lake in California. The steep shoreline is covered with tall pine trees. Called by many, "California's Water Wonderland," Shasta is truly a boater's paradise. There are over 16 varieties of fish including the Alabama spotted bass. Complete vacation facilities await the visitor. Tours of the Caverns and Shasta Dam are available.

. . . Continued . . .

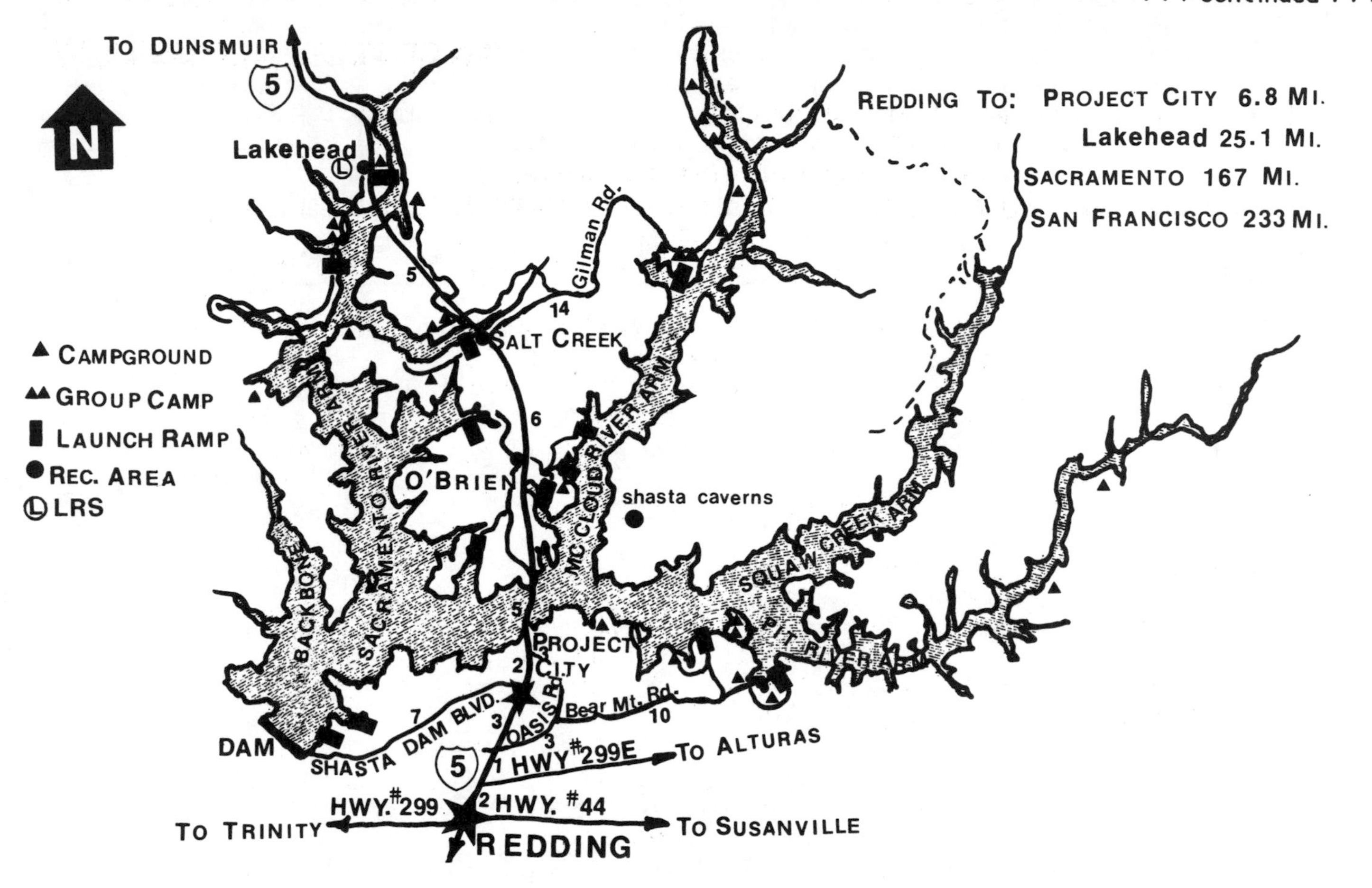

INFORMATION: Chamber of Commerce, Box 1368, Central Valley 96019, Ph: 916-275-8862

CAMPING	BOATING	RECREATION	OTHER
U.S.F.S. 84 Walk-In Sites Fee: $2 - $3 346 Dev. Sites for Tents & R.V.s Fee: $3- $4 108 Boat-In Sites No Fee 2 Group Camps See Following Pages	Power, Row, Canoe, Sail, Waterski, Jet Ski, Windsurf & Inflatable Full Service Marinas Launch Ramps Rentals: Houseboats, Fishing & Ski Boats Docks, Berths, Gas, Moorings, Storage Overnight in Boat Permitted Anywhere	Fishing: Trout, Bass, Catfish, Bluegill, Perch, Crappie & Kokanee Salmon Swimming-Lake & Pools Picnicking Hiking Backpacking Campfire Programs Sightseeing Tours Hunting: Deer, Elk, Waterfowl	Motels & Cabins Snack Bars Restaurants Grocery Stores Bait & Tackle Laundromats Gas Stations Trailer Parks Disposal Stations Floating Toilets on Lake

. . . Continued . . .

U. S. F. S. CAMPING FACILITIES WITH WATER AND TOILETS - FOR INFORMATION CONTACT: DISTRICT RANGER, 6543 HOLIDAY ROAD, REDDING 96003, PH: 916-275-1587

PIT RIVER ARM

From Interstate 5

At Oasis Rd:

11 Miles NE	Rocky Ridge - 10 Tent Sites, Boat Access. Fee: $3
11 Miles NE	Jones Valley - 27 Tent & R.V. Sites, Boat Access. Fee: $3
13 Miles NE	Mariner's Point - 8 Tent Sites, Boat & Vehicle Access. Fee: None

MC CLOUD RIVER ARM

At O'Brien:

1 Mile E	Bailey Cove-10 Tent Sites, 6 Tents & R.V.s Launch Ramp. Fee: $4
2 Miles E	Wintoon - 11 Tent Sites

At Gilman Rd:

9 Miles E	Hirz Bay - 48 Tent & R.V. Sites. Fee: $4. Launch Ramp, Amphitheater.
10 Miles E	Dekkas Rock - 9 Tent Sites. Fee: $3
11 Miles E	Moore Creek - 13 Tent & R.V. Sites. Fee: $3
13 Miles E	Jennings Creek - 8 Tent Sites, Boat-In & Walk-In Access. Fee: $2
15 Miles E	Ellery Creek - 9 Tent sites, 10 Tent & R.V. Sites. Fee: $3
16 Miles E	Pine Point - 6 Tent Sites, 7 Tent & R.V. Sites. Fee: $3
17 Miles E	McCloud Bridge - 9 Tent Sites, 9 Tent & R.V. Sites. Fee: $3
9 Miles E	Hirz Bay Group Camp - Camp #1: Minimum Capacity - 25 People, Maximum Capacity - 150 People. Fee: $30. Camp #2: Minimum Capacity - 15 People, Max. Capacity - 50 People. Fee: $10

SACRAMENTO RIVER ARM

At Salt Creek:

0 Miles	Upper Salt Creek - 30 Tent Sites. Fee: $2
1 Mile S	Lower Salt Creek - 12 Tent Sites. Launch Ramp. Fee: $3
.5 Mile W	Nelson Point - 8 Multiple Family Sites - Tents & R.V.s. Fee: $3
1 Mile W	Oak Grove - 43 Tent & R.V. Sites. Fee: $4
3 Miles NE	Gregory Creek - 5 Tent Sites, 13 R.V. Sites. Fee: $4

At Lakehead:

1.7 Miles S	Antlers - 59 Tent & R.V. Sites. Launch Ramp. Adjacent to Resort with Full Facilities. Fee: $4.
2.5 Miles S	Lakeshore East - 8 Tent Sites, 15 Tent & R.V. Sites. Adjacent to Resort with Full Facilities. Fee: $4
	Lakeshore West - 13 Tent & R.V. Sites. Fee: $3
7.6 Miles S	Old Man - 10 Tent Sites, Boat Access. Fee: None

BOAT ACCESS CAMPING WITH TOILETS:

Pit River Arm: Rend Island - 18 Sites, Stein Creek - 5 Sites, Arbuckle Flat - 11 Sites

Sacramento River Arm: Slaughterhouse Island - 13 Sites, Gooseneck Cove - 10 Sites, Salt Creek Point - 7 Sites.

Between McCloud River and Squaw Creek: Allie Cove - 5 Sites, Ski Island - 29 Sites with water, amphitheater.

McCloud River Arm: Green Creek - 11 Sites.

. . . Continued . . .

SHASTA LAKE

. . . Continued . . .

PUBLIC LAUNCH RAMPS: No Fee

Pit River Arm: Jones Valley Ramp - 11 Miles NE on Oasis Road.
Packers Bay Launch Ramp - 2 Miles SW of O'Brien.

McCloud River Arm: Bailey Cove - 1.5 Miles E. of O'Brien.
Hirz Bay Ramp - 9 Miles E of Gilman Road.

Sacramento River Arm: Centimudi Launch Ramp - 1 Mile E of Dam.
Antlers Ramp - 1.4 Miles S of Lakehead at Sugarloaf.

PRIVATE RESORTS AND FACILITIES:

Bridge Bay - At South Interstate 5 Crossing
Bridge Bay Resort and Marina: Lodging, Houseboat Rentals, Restaurant, Grocery Store, Supplies. For Brochure & Reservations: 10300 Bridge Bay Road, Redding 96001, Ph: 916-275-3021 or 213-691-2235 or 714-871-1476

Jones Valley Resort & Marina, Silverthorn Resort, Bear Mountain R.V. Park

Lakehead Recreation Area - Antler Resorts - Campground & R.V. Park (LRS for Reservations), Lakehead Campground (LRS for Reservations), Sierra Outdoor Resort (Membership Park Only)

Lakeshore Recreation Area - Lakeshore Resort, Margus Houseboat Rentals, Shasta Lake Trailer Resort & Campground

O'Brien Recreation Area - At McCloud River - Lakeview Marina Resort, Westair Flotels, Holiday Flotels, Shasta Marina, Lake Shasta Caverns Tour, Holiday Harbor, Kamloops Campground (Membership Park Only)

Project City - Central Valley - Digger Bay Marina, Shasta Dam Visitors Center

Salt Creek Recreation Area - Cascade Cove Resort, Salt Creek Lodge & Marina, American Trails Campground (Membership Park Only)

Sugarloaf Recreation Area - Sugarloaf Marina & Resort, Sugarloaf Cottages, Tsasdi Resort.

Wonderland - Mountain Gate - Fawndale Lodge, Fawndale Oaks R.V. Park & Waterslides

FOR FURTHER INFORMATION ON PRIVATE RESORTS CONTACT:

Shasta Dam Area Chamber of Commerce
P.O. Box 1368 R
Central Valley 96019
Ph: 916-275-8862

Shasta Lake Fishing Reports can be obtained by contacting the Chamber of Commerce.

MANZANITA LAKE, BUTTE LAKE, SUMMIT LAKE AND JUNIPER LAKE

These Lakes are in the Lassen Volcanic National Park at elevations ranging from 5,890 feet to 6,745 feet. The 106,000-acre expanse of volcanic coniferous forest has over 150 miles of trails, including a part of the Pacific Crest Trail, rich in natural beauty. The Park Service provides well-maintained campgrounds at the Lakes. There are no motors allowed for boating, so the fisherman and boater can enjoy the serene pleasure of quiet Lakes. Pets and vehicles are not allowed on trails. Pack and saddle stock may not overnight anywhere except in corrals, and all feed must be brought in by the horseman as grazing is not permitted. Reservations are required for use of horse corrals.

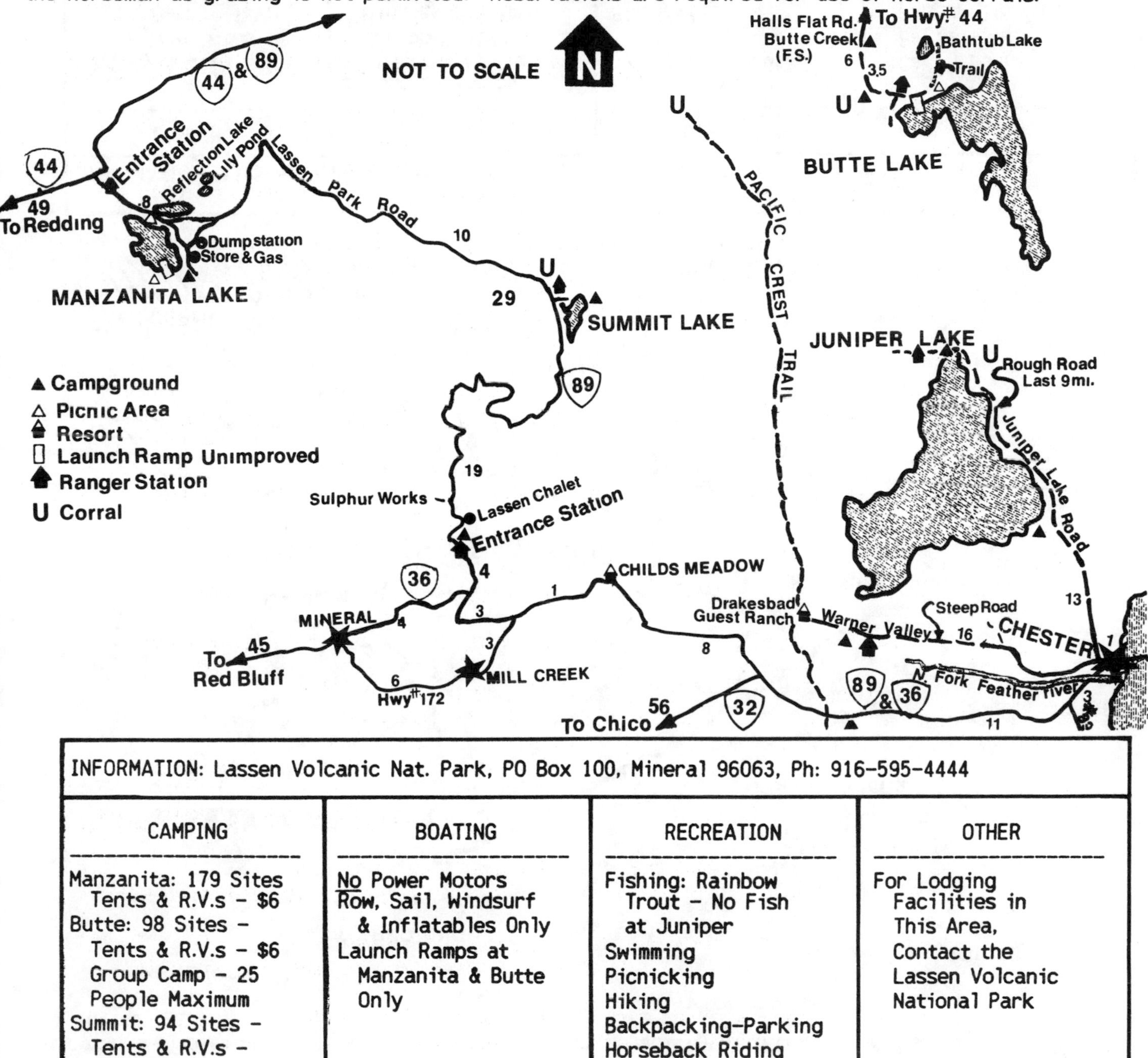

INFORMATION: Lassen Volcanic Nat. Park, PO Box 100, Mineral 96063, Ph: 916-595-4444

CAMPING	BOATING	RECREATION	OTHER
Manzanita: 179 Sites Tents & R.V.s - $6 Butte: 98 Sites - Tents & R.V.s - $6 Group Camp - 25 People Maximum Summit: 94 Sites - Tents & R.V.s - $4 - $6 Juniper: 18 Sites - Tents Only-No Fee No Water - Groups	No Power Motors Row, Sail, Windsurf & Inflatables Only Launch Ramps at Manzanita & Butte Only	Fishing: Rainbow Trout - No Fish at Juniper Swimming Picnicking Hiking Backpacking-Parking Horseback Riding Trails & Corrals Campfire Programs No ORV's	For Lodging Facilities in This Area, Contact the Lassen Volcanic National Park

CRATER, CARIBOU AND SILVER LAKES

In the Lassen National Forest, these Lakes provide a bounty of natural recreational opportunities. Crater Lake, at 6,800 feet elevation, has a surface area of 27 acres. This volcanic crater offers excellent fishing for Eastern Brook trout. The Lakes near Silver Lake border the Caribou Wilderness, a gentle, rolling, forested plateau which can easily be explored by the hiker, backpacker or horseman. Silver Lake and its neighbor, Caribou Lake, provide a quiet remote area for the small boater, camper and fisherman. The roads are dirt and rough, especially into Crater Lake so large trailers are not advised.

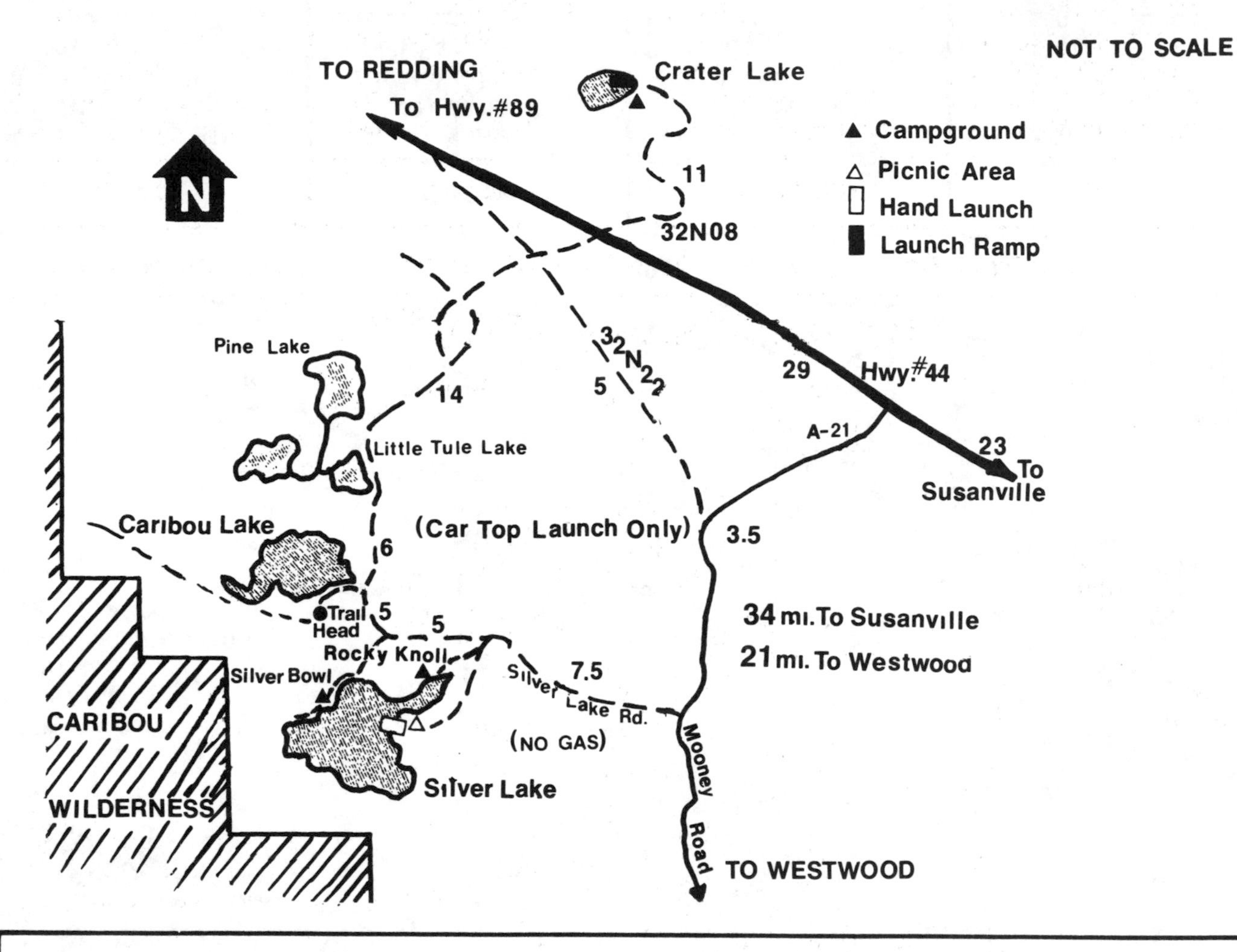

INFORMATION: Almanor Ranger District, Box 767, Chester 96020, Ph: 916-258-2141

CAMPING	BOATING	RECREATION	OTHER
Silver Lake: Rocky Knoll: 7 Tent Sites 11 Tent or R.V. Sites Silver Bowl: 18 Tent Sites Fee: $4	Silver & Caribou Lakes: Cartop Boats Hand Launch Only Crater Lake: No Motors Allowed Launch Ramp	Fishing: Rainbow & Eastern Brook Trout Picnicking Swimming Hiking & Riding Trails Backpacking Hunting: Antelope, Deer, Rabbit, Quail & Grouse	Crater Lake Campground: Eagle Lake Ranger District 472-013 Johnston-ville Road Susanville 96130 Ph: 916-257-2595 or 2161 17 Dev. Sites Trailers Not Recommended

EAGLE LAKE

Eagle Lake is at an elevation of 5,100 feet in the Lassen National Forest. With a surface area of 27,000 acres and over 100 miles of timbered shoreline, it is the second largest natural Lake in California. The slightly alkaline water is the natural habitat for the famous Eagle Lake Trout, a favorite for the fisherman for its size of 3 pounds or better. Eagle Lake is ideal for water sports because there are no snags or underwater obstructions. The water is warm and clear, and the size of the Lake offers plenty of room. There are 4 Forest Service Campgrounds amid tall pines, and full hook-ups for R.V.s are located at Eagle Lake Park.

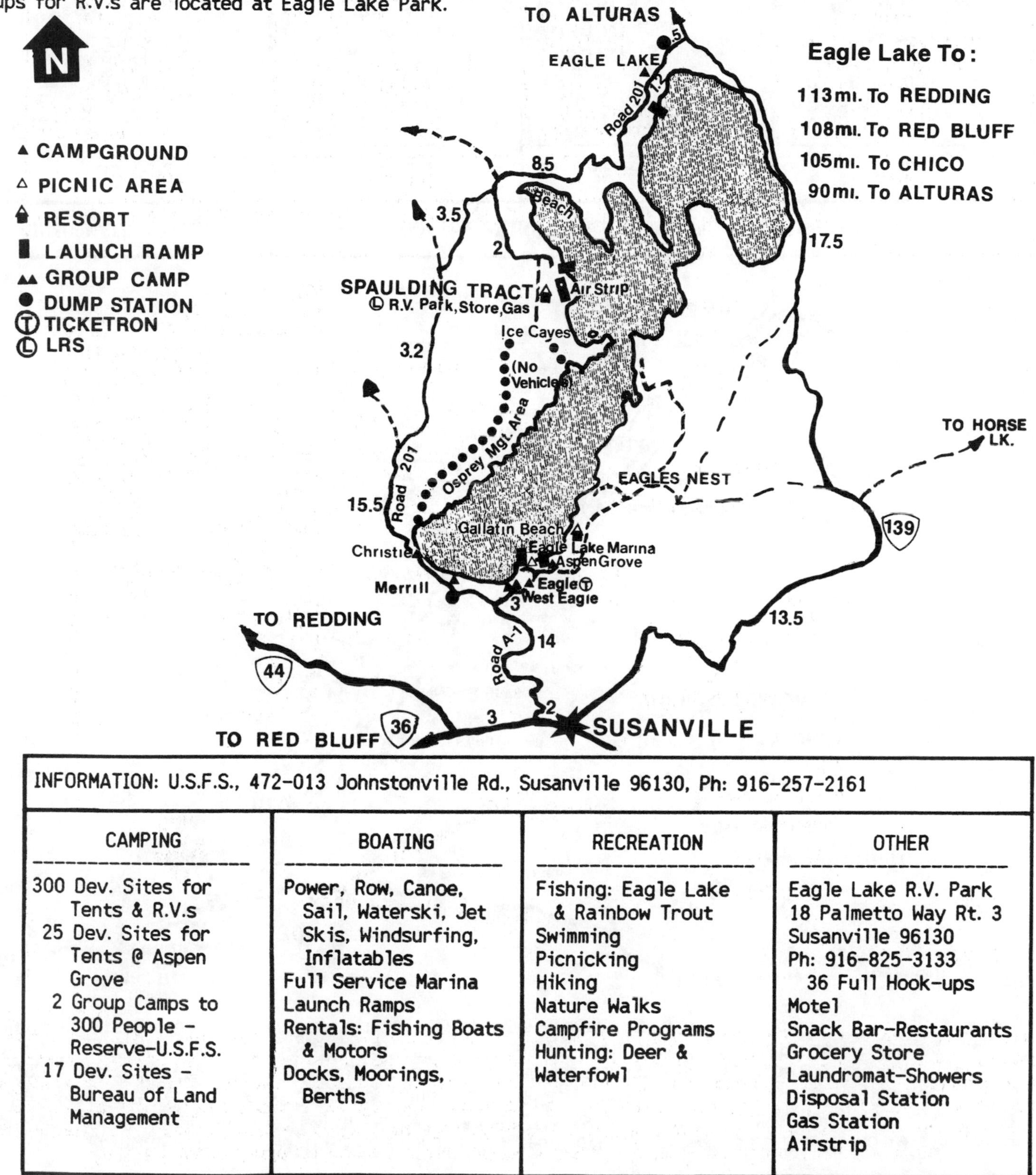

INFORMATION: U.S.F.S., 472-013 Johnstonville Rd., Susanville 96130, Ph: 916-257-2161

CAMPING	BOATING	RECREATION	OTHER
300 Dev. Sites for Tents & R.V.s 25 Dev. Sites for Tents @ Aspen Grove 2 Group Camps to 300 People - Reserve-U.S.F.S. 17 Dev. Sites - Bureau of Land Management	Power, Row, Canoe, Sail, Waterski, Jet Skis, Windsurfing, Inflatables Full Service Marina Launch Ramps Rentals: Fishing Boats & Motors Docks, Moorings, Berths	Fishing: Eagle Lake & Rainbow Trout Swimming Picnicking Hiking Nature Walks Campfire Programs Hunting: Deer & Waterfowl	Eagle Lake R.V. Park 18 Palmetto Way Rt. 3 Susanville 96130 Ph: 916-825-3133 36 Full Hook-ups Motel Snack Bar-Restaurants Grocery Store Laundromat-Showers Disposal Station Gas Station Airstrip

RUTH LAKE

Ruth Lake is half way between Eureka and Red Bluff on Highway 36. This is quite a drive on a narrow road at times, but well worth the trip if you plan to stay awhile in this beautiful country. The Lake rests at an elevation of 2,800 feet and has a surface area of 1,200 acres. It was formed by damming the Mad River in 1962, and it is now a popular recreation facility offering boating of all kinds, fishing and camping. The Flying "AA" Ranch has its own airport, motel, horses, swimming pool, tennis courts and an excellent restaurant featuring a weekend open-pit barbecue.

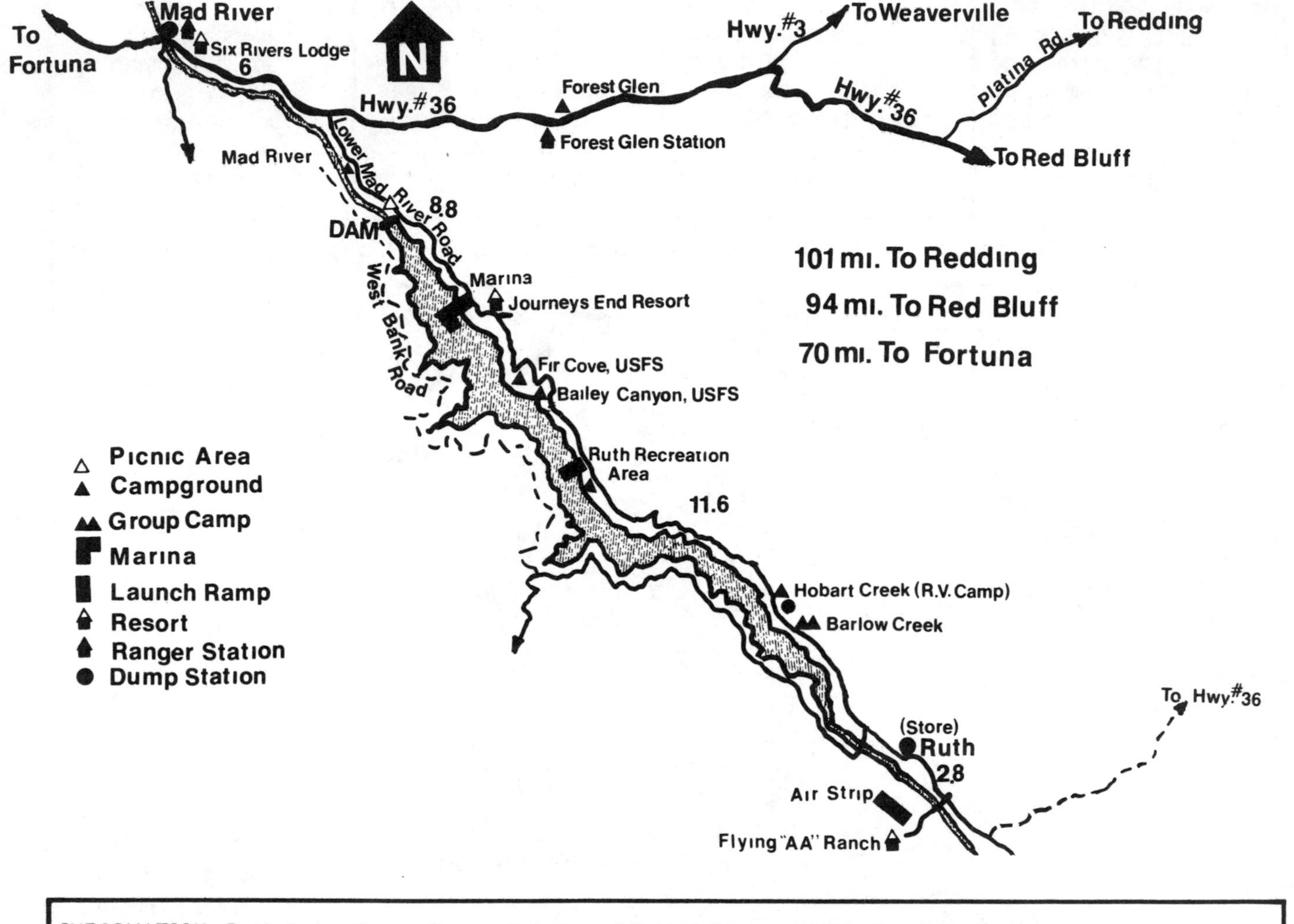

INFORMATION: Ruth Lake Comm. Serv., P.O. Box 31, Mad River 95552, Ph: 707-574-6332

CAMPING	BOATING	RECREATION	OTHER
U.S.F.S. 81 Dev. Sites for Tents & R.V.s Fee: $3 - $4 1 Group Site Reserve Ph: 707-574-6233 Ruth Lake Comm. Service District 100 Dev. Sites for Tents & R.V.s Fee: $3	Power, Row, Canoe, Sail, Waterski, Jet Ski, Windsurf & Inflatables Full Service Marina Launch Ramps Rentals: Fishing Boats & Motors, Waterski, Pontoon Docks	Fishing: Rainbow Trout, Kokanee Salmon, Bass, Catfish Waterplay Picnicking Hiking Horseback Riding - Trails & Rentals Hunting: Deer, Boar, Quail, Grouse, Wild Turkey	Flying "AA" Ranch Ruth Star Rt. P.O. Box 700 Bridgeville 95526 Ph: 707-574-6227 Cabins, Restaurant Tennis, Swimming Pool, Airport, Car Rentals, Full Vacation Facilities Snack Bar-Restaurant Disposal Station

ROUND VALLEY RESERVOIR

Round Valley Reservoir is at an elevation of 4,600 feet in the Plumas National Forest. Located 2 miles south of Greenville, this small secluded Lake is the water supply for Greenville so water sports are limited to fishing and boating. Swimming or body contact with the water is not permitted. Famous for Black Bass, Round Valley is an excellent warm-water Lake. The area offers nice hiking and nature study trails. Campsites are available at the Resort and also at the Greenville County Campground.

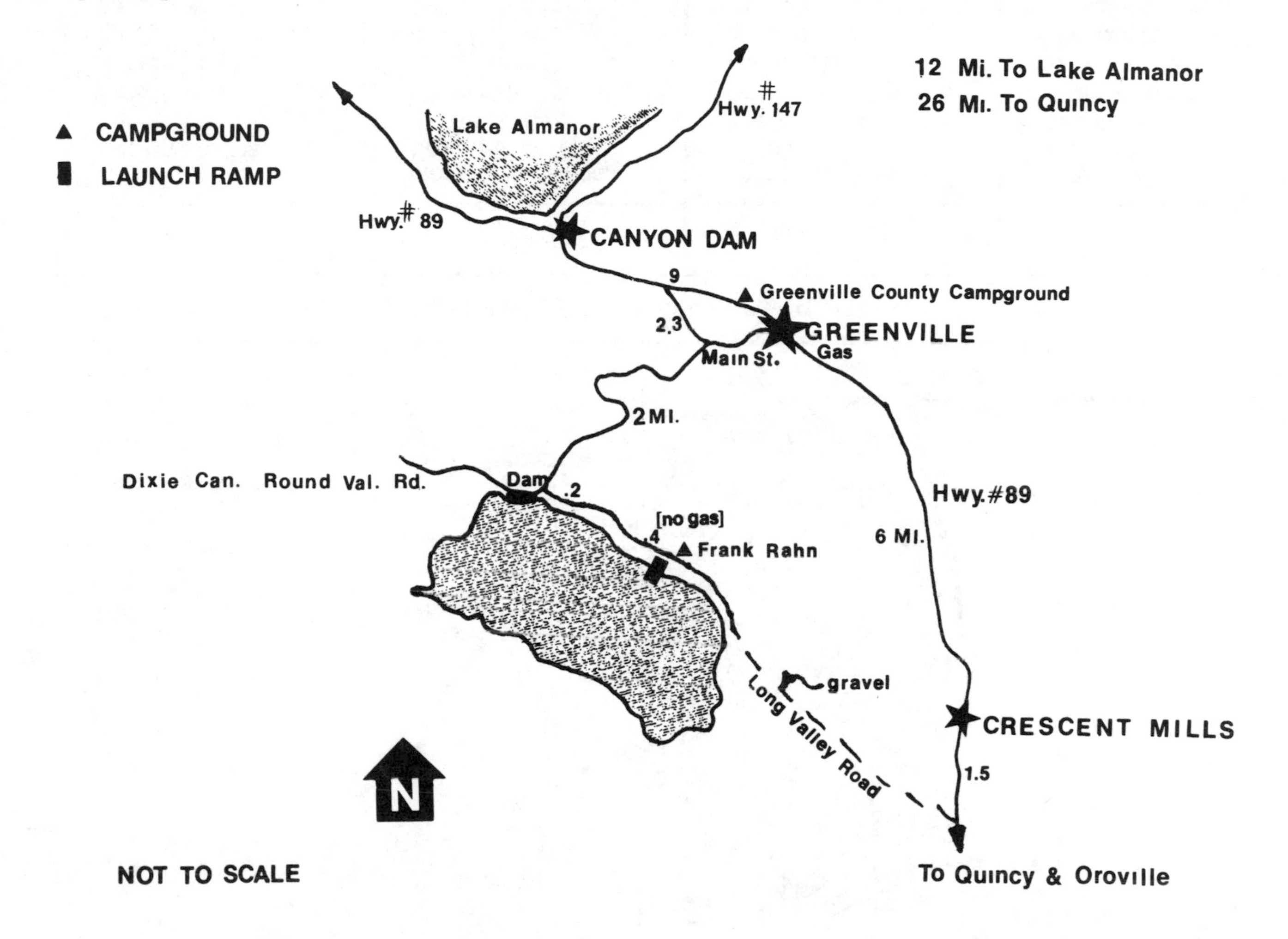

INFORMATION: Round Valley Resort, P.O. Box 65, Greenville 95947, Ph: 916-284-7530

CAMPING	BOATING	RECREATION	OTHER
50 Dev. sites for Tents & R.V.s Fee: $6 Per Vehicle & 2 People - 50 cents Per Each Additional Person Plumas County: Greenville Campground 23 Dev. Sites	Fishing Boats Only 7-1/2 HP Motors Maximum Rocked Launch Ramp Rentals: Rowboats & Motorboats	Fishing: Black Bass, Catfish & Bluegill No Swimming Picnicking Hiking	Hot Showers Included in Camping Fee

LAKE ALMANOR

Lake Almanor rests at an elevation of 4,500 feet in the Lassen National Forest. There is an abundance of pine-sheltered campgrounds operated by P.G.&E., the Forest Service and private resorts. The Lake is 13 miles long and 6 miles wide with a surface area of 28,000 acres. It one of the largest man-made Lakes in California. Almanor's clear, blue waters offer complete boating facilities. Caution is advised for at times small islands are exposed and gusty winds can come up. Fishing can be excellent for a variety of species in the Lake, and the many nearby streams are often productive.

. . . Continued . . .

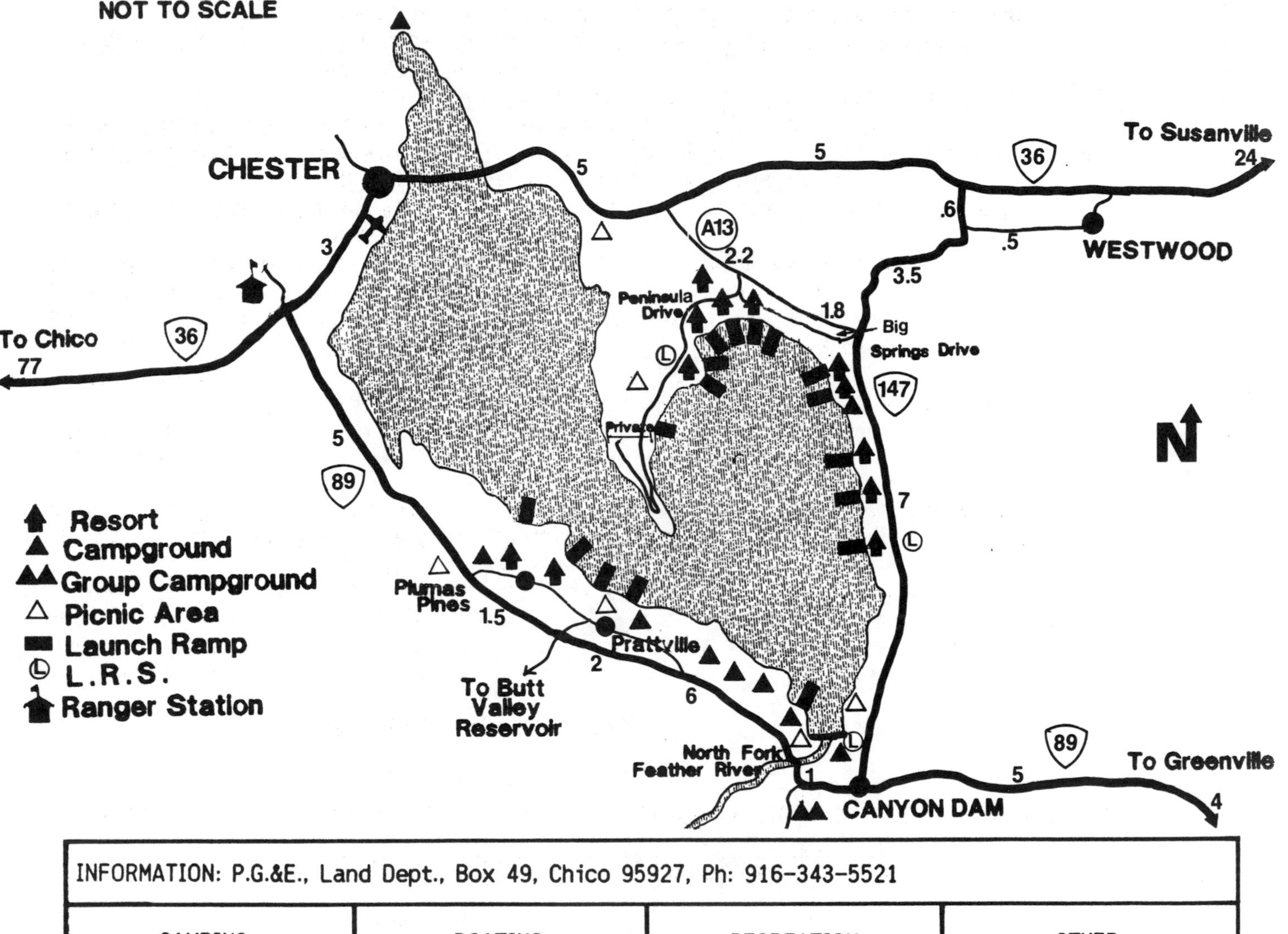

INFORMATION: P.G.&E., Land Dept., Box 49, Chico 95927, Ph: 916-343-5521			
CAMPING	BOATING	RECREATION	OTHER
P.G.&E.: 80 Dev. Sites for Tents & R.V.s - Fee: $4-$5 Group Camp to 40 People Maximum U.S.F.S.: 101 Dev. Sites for Tents & R.V.s - Fee: $4	Power, Row, Canoe, Sail, Waterski, Inflatables Full Service Marinas Launch Ramps Rentals: Fishing, Canoe, Patio & Ski Waterski School at Plumas Pines Resort Docks, Berths, Gas	Fishing: Rainbow & Brown Trout, Large & Smallmouth Bass, Catfish, Kokanee & Coho Salmon Swimming Picnicking Hiking Hunting: Deer, Waterfowl Horseback Riding	Cabins & Motels Snack Bars Restaurant Grocery Stores Bait & Tackle Laundromats Disposal Stations Gas Stations

Approx. Miles From Dam on Hwy. 89	P. G. & E. CAMPING FACILITIES
0.1 E	Skinner Flat Group Camp - 40 People Maximum - Multi-purpose utility building with cook area, grill, refrigeration, showers and 5 bunk houses, swimming beach and picnic area. Reservations Only.
1.5 NW	Fox Farm - 43 Campsites
1.5 NW	Mountain View - 20 Campsites, handicap facilities.
1.5 NW	Rocky Point - 17 Campsites
	Last Chance Creek - 25 Campsites (4 Miles from Chester Via Feather River Rd.)

U. S. FOREST SERVICE - ALMANOR RANGER DISTRICT

7 NW	Almanor Campground - 101 Campsites (15 Tents only, 86 Tents & R.V.s), Handicap Facilities. Fee.

SOME PRIVATELY OWNED RESORTS

NORTHSHORE CAMPGROUND - At Chester Causeway
HARBOR LITES RESORT - 300 Peninsula Drive - R.V. Sites, Cabins, Marina, Dockage.
KNOTTY PINE RESORT - 430 Peninsula Drive - Cabins, Marina, Boat Rentals, Snacks, Store.
LITTLE NORWAY RESORT - 432 Peninsula Drive - Campsites, Cabins, Marina, Store, Snack Bar, Boat Rentals, Docks, Fuel.
THE BOAT DOCK - 440 Peninsula Drive - Cabins, Dockage.
BIG COVE RESORT - 442 Peninsula Drive - Campsites, Chalets, Launch Ramp, Boat Rentals, Store.
MOONSPINNERS COVE RESORT - 508 Peninsula Drive - Campsites, Cabins.
KOKANEE RESORT - End of Peninsula Drive Before Gate to Private Homes - Campsites, Chalets, Cabins, Marina, Boat Rentals, Store - LRS Reservations.
LASSEN VIEW RESORT - On Highway 147 - Campsites, R.V. Sites, Cabins, Marina, Boat Rentals, Store.
LAKE HAVEN RESORT - On Highway 147 - R.V. Sites, Cabins, Marina.
DORADO INN - On Highway 147 - Campsites, Cabins, Marina, Boat Rentals.
CRAWFORDS LAKESIDE RESORT - On Highway 147 - Motel, Housekeeping Cabins, Marina, Boat Rentals.
CANYON DAM MOBILE HOME ESTATES - At Canyon Dam - R.V. Sites, Full Hookups, Snack Bar, Restaurant, Store, Gas - LRS Reservations.
CAMP PRATTVILLE - On Highway 89 in Prattville - Campsites, R.V. Sites, Restaurant, Marina.
PLUMAS PINES RESORT - On Highway 89 Near Prattville - R.V. Sites, Motel, Cabins, Restaurant, Cocktail Lounge, Marina, Store, Boat Rentals, Water Ski School.
CASHMAN'S RESORT - 443 Peninsula Drive - R.V. Hookups, Campsites, Hot Showers, Restaurant, Laundromat, Gift Shop, Video Games, Boat Launching and Dockage, Group Rates Available.
BIG SPRINGS TRAILER PARK - On Big Springs Road.
VAGABOND TRAILER PARK - On Highway 147 - R.V.s only.
LAKE COVE TRAILER LODGE AND MARINA - On Highway 147 - 43 R.V. Sites with Full Hookups, 12 Sites with Water & Electricity, Store, Gas, Marina, Ramp, LRS Reservations.

FOR ADDITIONAL INFORMATION CONTACT: Chamber of Commerce, P.O. Box 1198, Chester 96020, Ph: 916-258-2426

BUTT VALLEY RESERVOIR

Butt Valley Reservoir rests at an elevation of 4,150 feet in the Lassen National Forest. This picturesque mountain Lake is five miles long and three-quarters of a mile at its widest point. It is connected to Lake Almanor by a tunnel, and it is the second level of P.G.&E.'s "stairway of power" which flows down the Feather River into Lake Oroville. This is a nice boating Lake although marina facilities are limited to a launch ramp. There is a good fishery for both planted rainbows and native brown and rainbow trout. The well-kept campground and picnic areas are under the jurisdiction of P.G.&E.

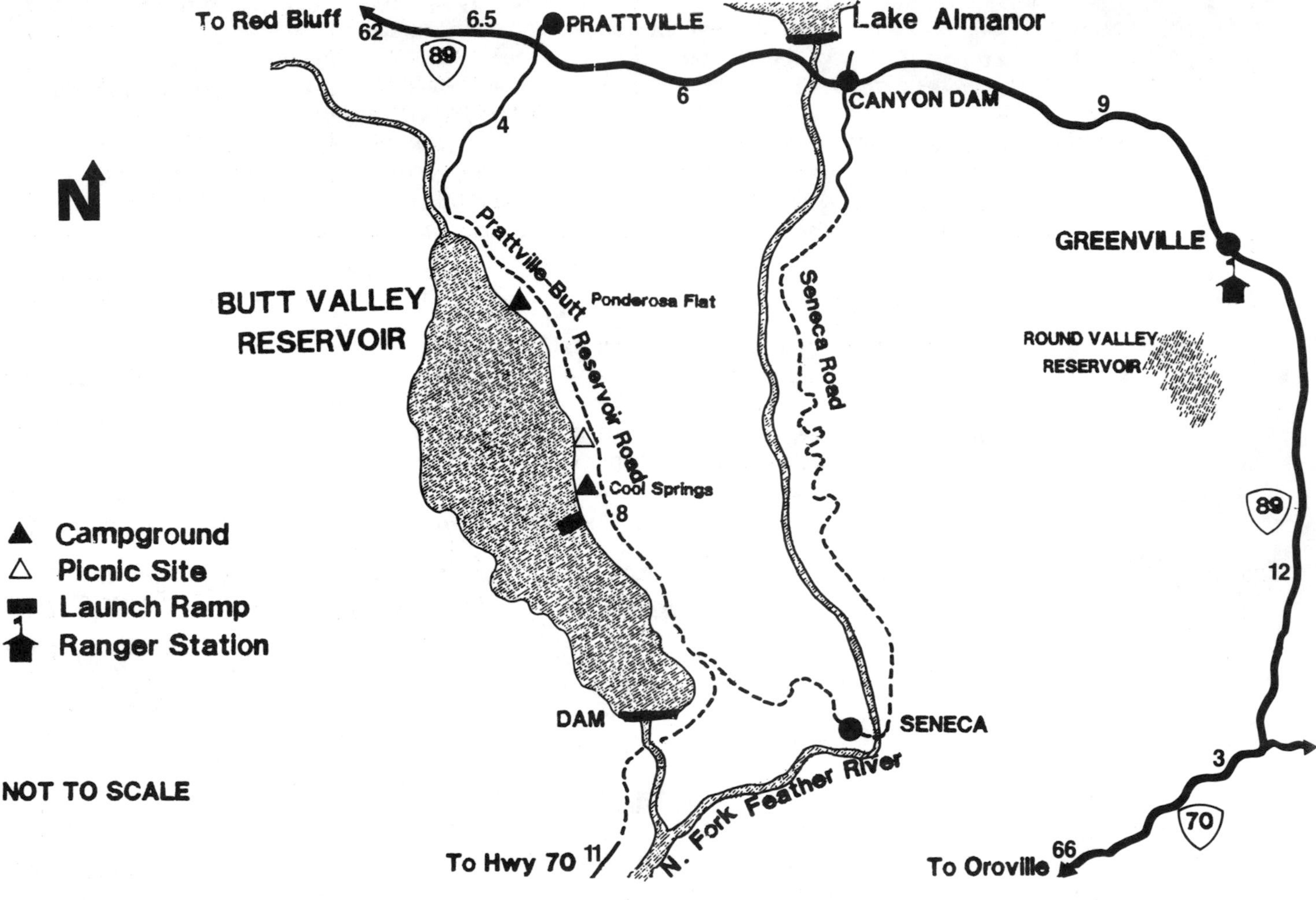

INFORMATION: P.G.&E. Land Dept., Box 49, Chico 95927, Ph: 916-343-5521			
CAMPING	BOATING	RECREATION	OTHER
Cool Springs: 22 Sites for Tents & R.V.s Fee: $4 - $5 Ponderosa Flat: 45 Sites for Tents & R.V.s Fee: $4 - $5	Open to All Boating Launch Ramp No Waterskiing	Fishing: Rainbow, Brown Trout, Catfish Picnicking Swimming Hiking Nature Study Hunting: Waterfowl & Deer Horseback Riding	Full Facilities in Chester

ANTELOPE LAKE

The Antelope Lake Recreation Area rests at an elevation of 5,000 feet in the Plumas National Forest. The Lake has 15 miles of timbered shoreline and a surface area of 930 acres. The sheltered coves and islands make this beautiful Lake a pleasant boating haven. The well maintained Forest Service campgrounds provide the camper with nice sites amid pine and fir trees. Good sized Rainbow and Eagle Lake Trout await the fisherman. Indian Creek, below the Dam, has some large German Brown Trout as well as Rainbow for the stream fisherman.

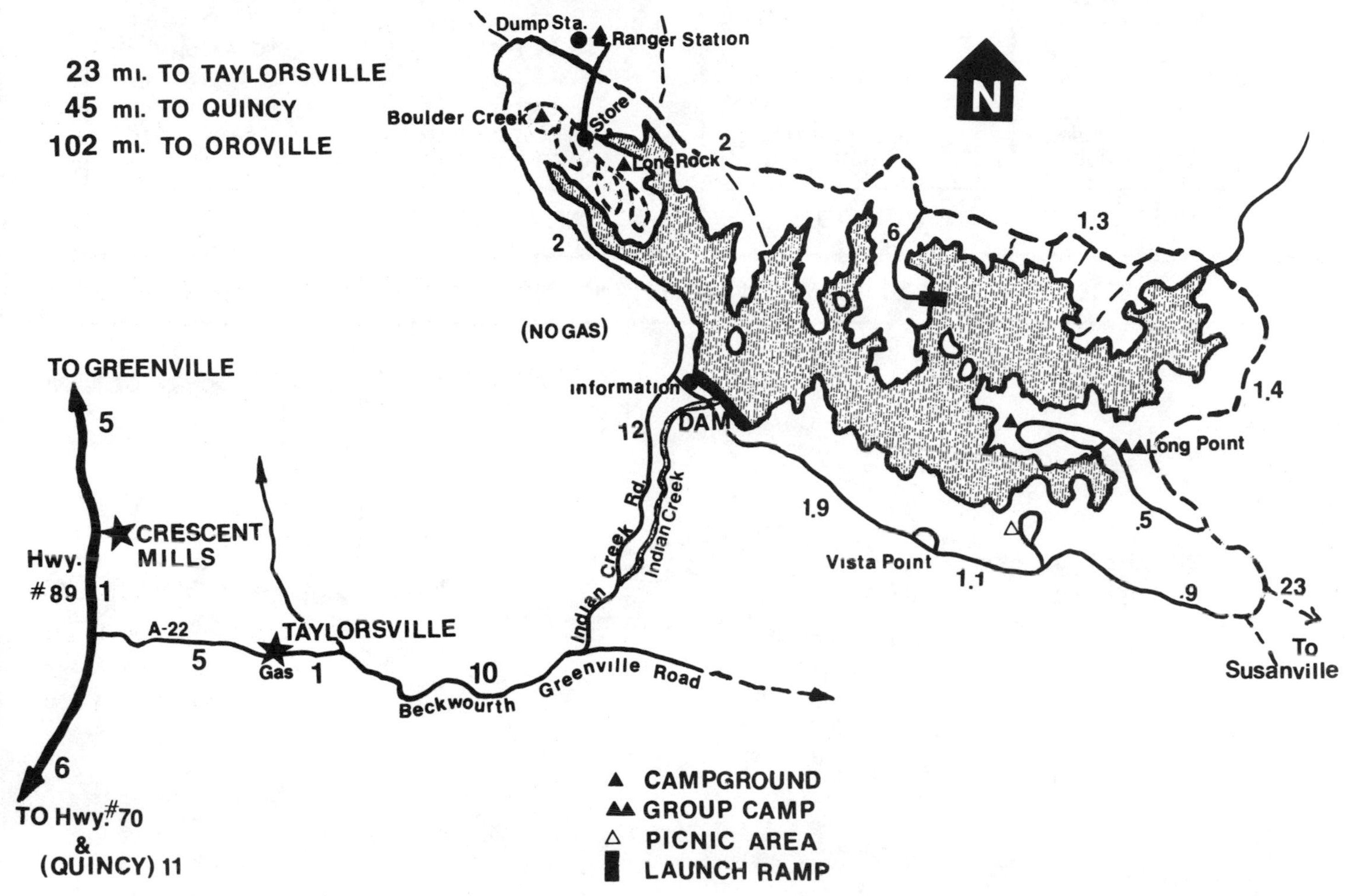

INFORMATION: Greenville, R.D., P.O. Box 329, Greenville 95947, Ph: 916-284-7126

CAMPING	BOATING	RECREATION	OTHER
193 Dev. Sites for Tents & R.V.s Fee: $4 15 Dev. Sites - Can be used for Groups at Long Point Campground	Power, Row, Canoe, Sail, Waterski, Windsurfing & Inflatables Launch Ramp	Fishing: Eagle Lake, Rainbow & German Brown Trout & Catfish Swimming Hiking (No Trails) Nature Trail Campfire Programs Hunting: Deer	Grocery Store Bait & Tackle Disposal Station Full Facilities - 26 Miles at Taylorsville

BENBOW LAKE

Benbow Lake State Recreation Area is at an elevation of 364 feet off Highway 101 in the Redwood Empire. This 230 acre Lake is created every summer by damming the Eel River. Boating is limited to small non-powered craft, yet this is a nice Lake for sailing and rowing. The State of California maintains a park with picnic areas, campground and a swimming beach. The Benbow Inn, adjacent to the Lake, is a lovely old hotel and restaurant. The Benbow Valley R.V. Resort offers 100 pull-through campsites with full hook-ups, cable T.V., swimming pool, jacuzzi and playgrounds.

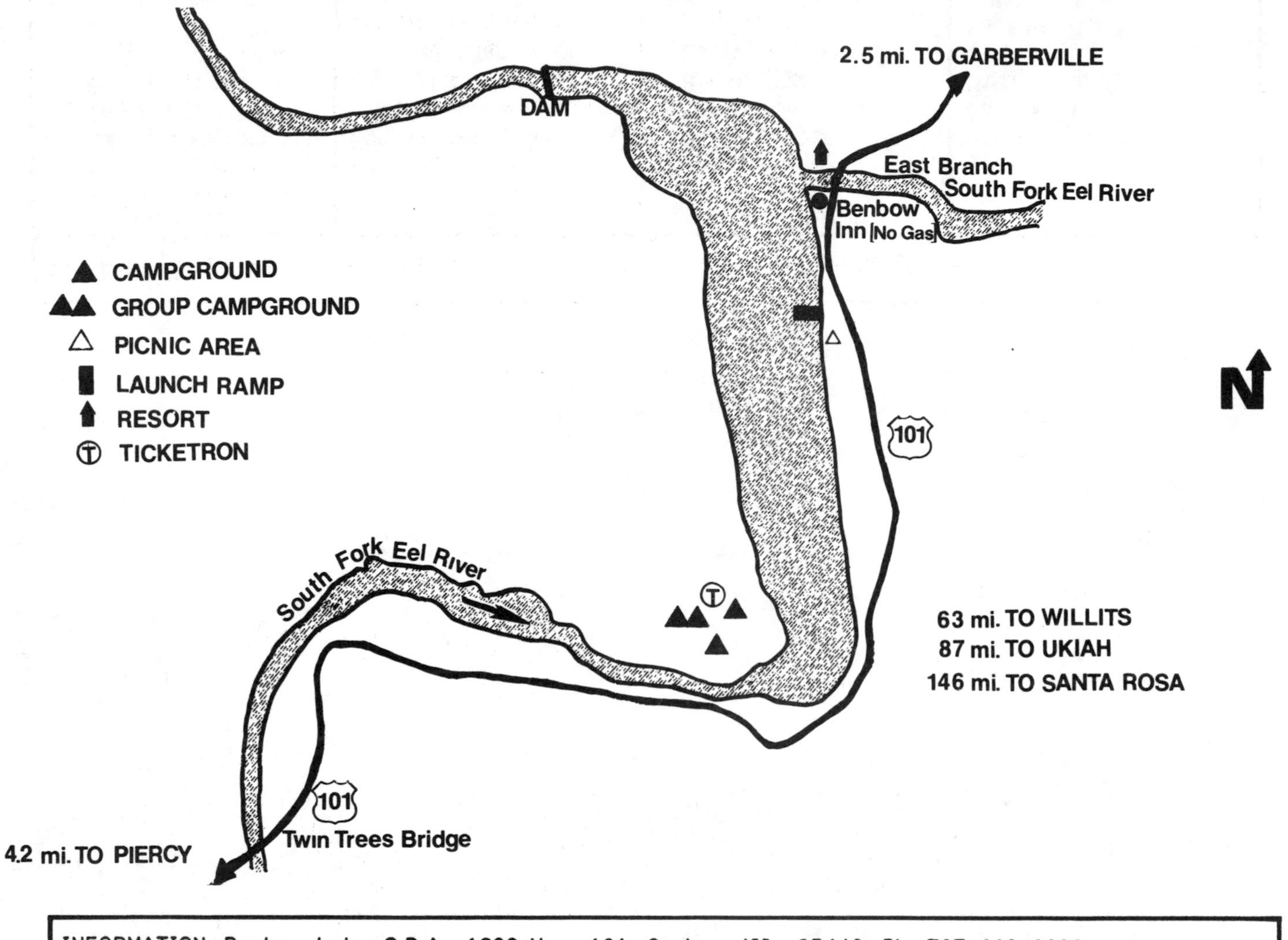

INFORMATION: Benbow Lake S.R.A., 1600 Hwy. 101, Garberville 95440, Ph: 707-923-3238

CAMPING	BOATING	RECREATION	OTHER
State Park 75 Dev. Sites for Tents & Self-Contained Units No Hook-ups Fee: $6 Ph: 707-247-3318	Row, Sail, Canoe, Windsurfing & Inflatables No Motors Rentals: Canoes, Waterbikes & Yak Boards Launch Ramp - Summer Only	Fishing: Not Recommended in Summer due to Young Steelhead & Salmon Swimming Picnicking Hiking Nature Study Campfire Programs	Benbow Valley R.V. Resort 2575 Benbow Dr. Garberville 95440 Ph: 707-923-2777 100 R.V. Sites Full Hook-ups Fee: $13.50 Benbow Inn and Restaurant Full Facilities in Garberville

LAKE CLEONE

Lake Cleone is at elevation of 20 feet within the MacKerricher State Park. This nice Park along the scenic Mendocino Coast provides a variety of natural habitats from forest and wetlands to sand dunes and a six-mile beach. Although swimming is not advised due to cold, turbulent seas, the 500-yard black sandy beach is a popular attraction. Lake Cleone, 300 surface acres, is open to shallow draft non-powered boating. The angler may fish for trout and an occasional bass at the Lake, steelhead and salmon in nearby rivers, and surffish, rock fish and link cod in the ocean. Skin divers find abalone in several of the nearby coves. Hikers, riders and naturalists will find trails around the Lake and along the beach inviting.

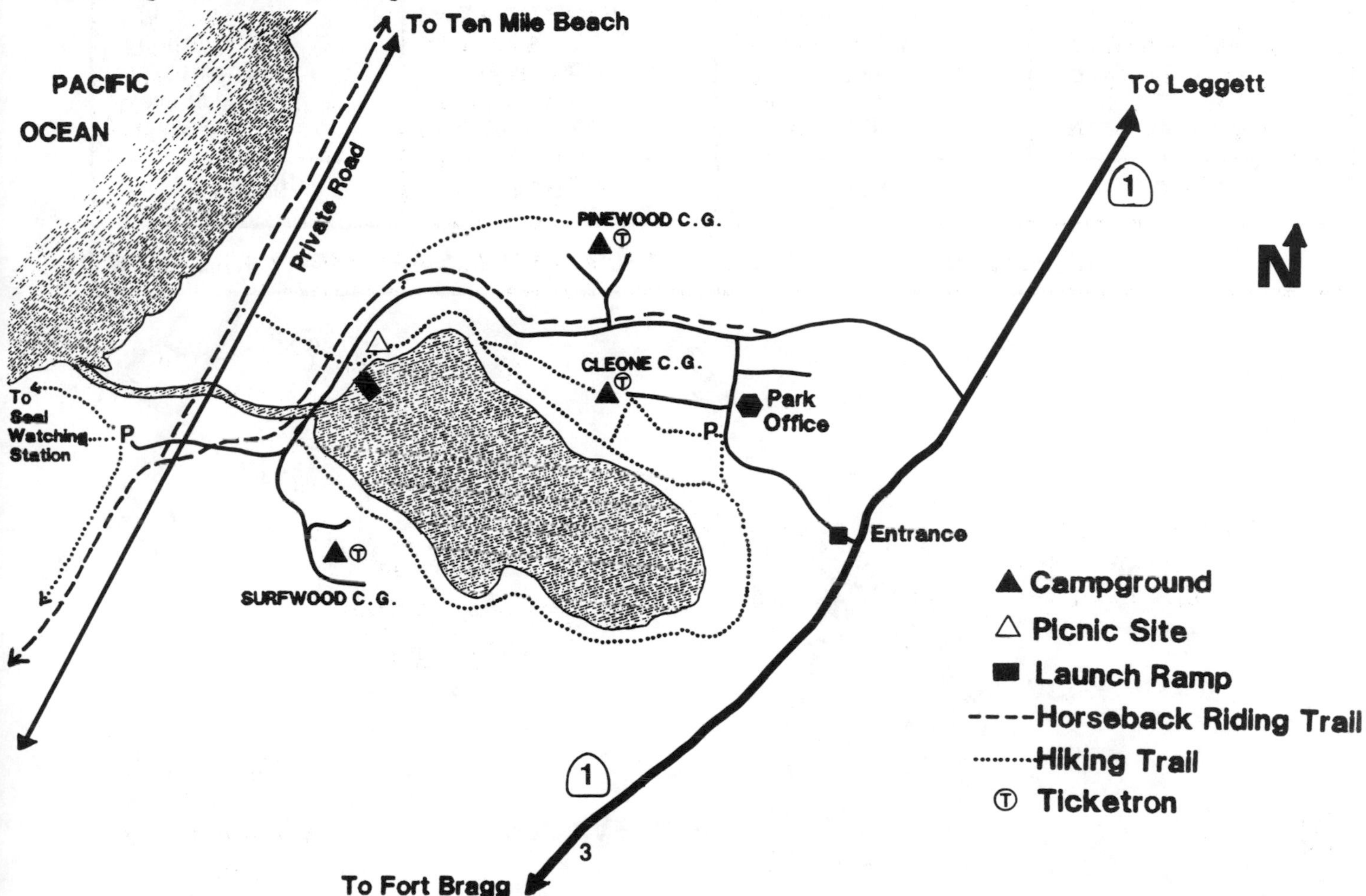

INFORMATION: MacKerricher State Park, Star Rt., Mendocino 95460, Ph: 707-937-5804			
CAMPING	BOATING	RECREATION	OTHER
143 Dev. Sites for Tents & R.V.s Hot Showers Flush Toilets Disposal Station Reservations by Ticketron	Open to Small, Shallow Draft Non-Powered Boats Paved Launch Ramp Rentals: Fishing Boats, Kayaks & Paddle Boats	Fishing: Trout Picnicking Hiking & Nature Study Trails Horseback Riding Trails Campfire Programs Birding Beach Combing Skin Diving Seal Watching Station	Grocery Store Near Park Entrance Full Facilities at Fort Bragg

SNAG, PHILBROOK, DE SABLA AND PARADISE LAKES

These Lakes range in elevation from 3,000 feet at Paradise Lake to 5,500 feet at Philbrook Lake. Snag Lake is barren of game fish. Philbrook is a good fishing Lake, but trailers are not advised on the road. These two Lakes are part of the Lassen National Forest. P.G.&E. maintains a resort for its employees at De Sabla Reservoir, but the public may fish for rainbow and some browns on the south and east sides of the Lake nearest Skyway Blvd. Paradise is a popular day use fishing Lake where the angler will find planted rainbows, some brown trout, largemouth bass and channel catfish.

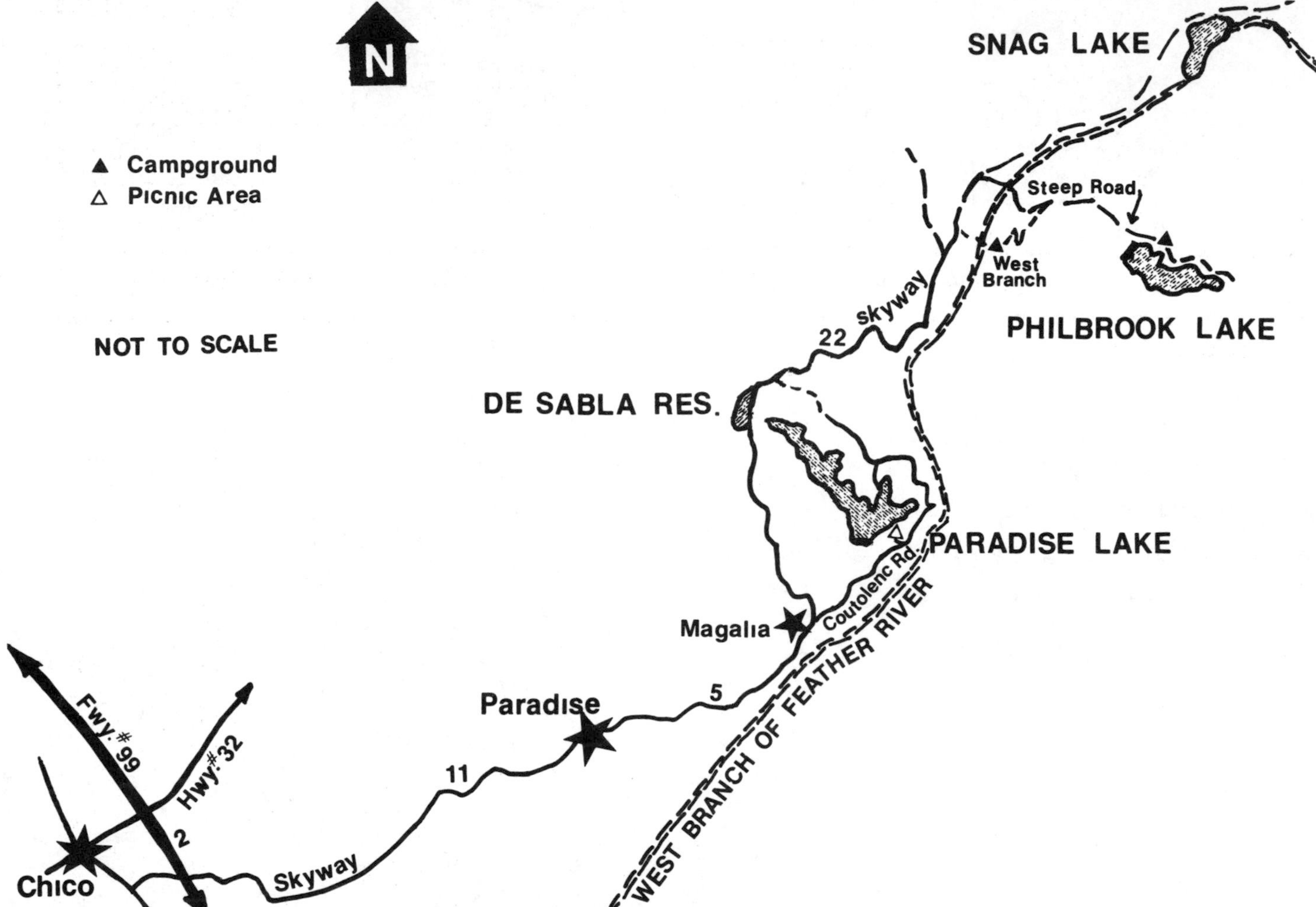

INFORMATION: Almanor Ranger District, P.O. Box 767, Chester 96020, Ph: 916-258-2141			
CAMPING	**BOATING**	**RECREATION**	**OTHER**
U.S.F.S. West Branch: 15 Campsites Fee: $4 P.G.&E.: Philbrook Lake 10 Campsites Fee: $5	Philbrook - Open to All Boating Minimal Facilities Paradise Lake - Rowboats and Canoes Only Minimal Facilities	Fishing: Rainbow, Brown & Eastern Brook Trout, Black Bass & Channel Catfish Picnicking Hiking Backpacking Swimming - Philbrook Lake Only	Recreation Permits and Fees are Required at Paradise Lake

BUCKS, SILVER AND SNAKE LAKES

The Bucks Lake Recreation Area in the Plumas National Forest is rich in wildlife and offers an abundance of outdoor recreation. Bucks Lake, at 5,153 feet elevation, has a surface area of 1,827 acres. There are facilities for all types of boating. Bucks and Silver Lake, at 5,800 feet, offer excellent trout fishing. There is also good stream fishing. Snake Lake, at 4,000 feet, provides a warm water fishery for bass, bluegill and crappie. The newly created Bucks Lake Wilderness Area of 24,000 acres and the Pacific Crest Trail invite the hiker, rider and backpacker to this area of gently rolling terrain, glaciated granite, forested meadows and perennial streams.

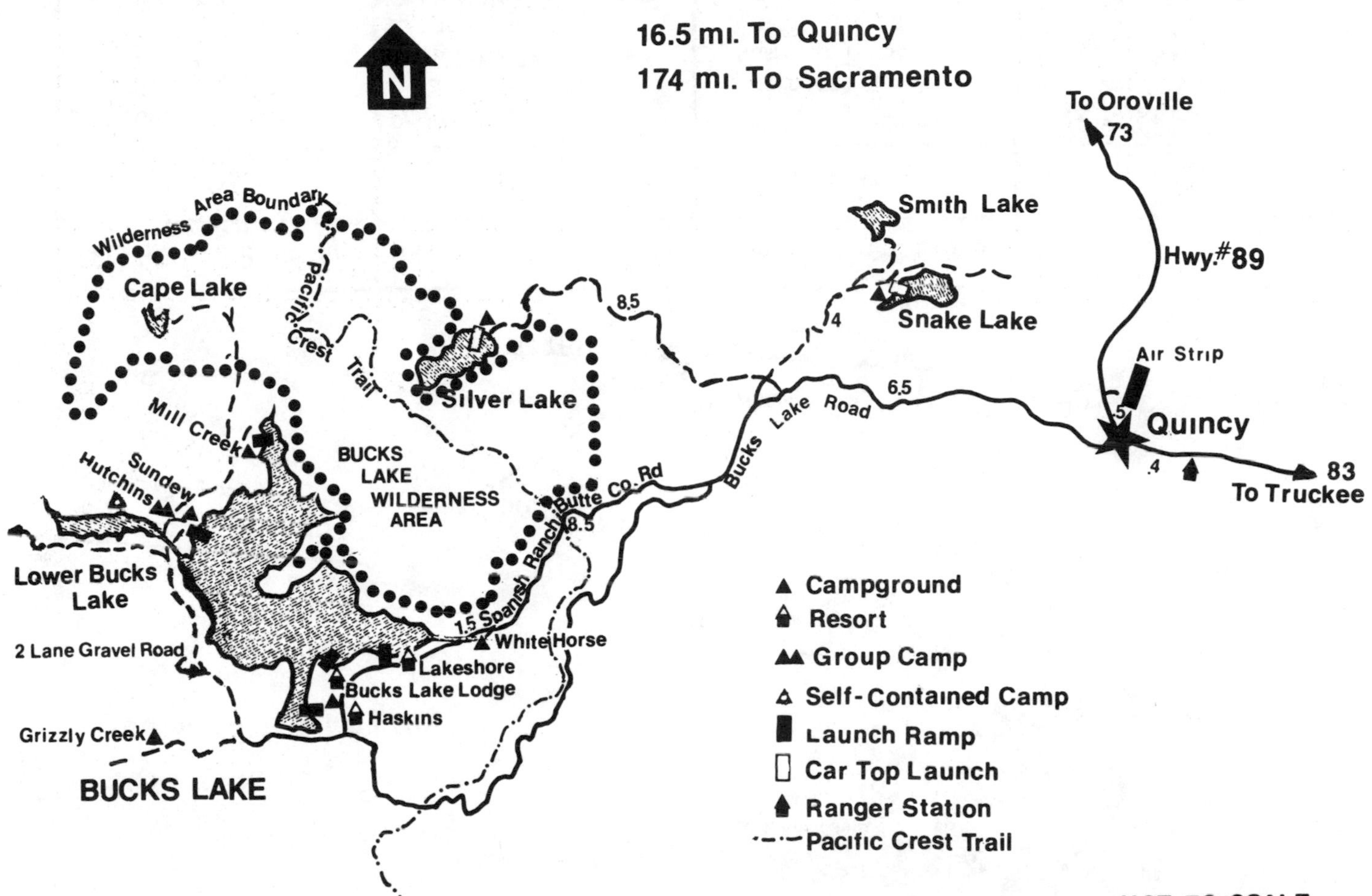

INFORMATION: Plumas Nat. Forest, 875 Mitchell, Oroville 95965, Ph: 916-534-6500

CAMPING	BOATING	RECREATION	OTHER
U.S.F.S. 62 Dev. Sites for Tents & R.V.s to 22 feet - Fee: $5 P.G.&E. 65 Dev. Sites for Tents & R.V.s Group Camp to 25 People Maximum Reservations: Ph: 916-534-6500	Bucks Lake: Open to All Boats Full Service Marina Rental Fishing Boats Snake & Silver Lakes: Rowboats & Canoes Only No Motors Hand Launch	Fishing: Rainbow, German Brown & Brook Trout, Kokanee Salmon Swimming & Ski Beaches Hiking & Picnicking Backpacking-Parking Horseback Riding Trails & Rentals Hunting: Deer, Bear, Rabbits, Waterfowl	Lakeshore Resort Bucks Lake Lodge Valley Resort Cabins & Motel Snack Bars Restaurant Grocery Stores Bait & Tackle Gas Station

LAKE DAVIS

Lake Davis is at an elevation of 5,775 feet with a surface area of 4,026 acres and 32 miles of timbered shoreline. Located in the Plumas National Forest, three campgrounds and launch ramps around the Lake are maintained by the Forest Service. Steady winds make this an ideal sailing Lake, and all types of boating are allowed. Both native and planted trout await the angler. Visitors are welcome at the Smith Peak Lookout to view the area as a fire lookout sees it. Relics of Basque Sheepherders remain on the west and northeast side of the Lake.

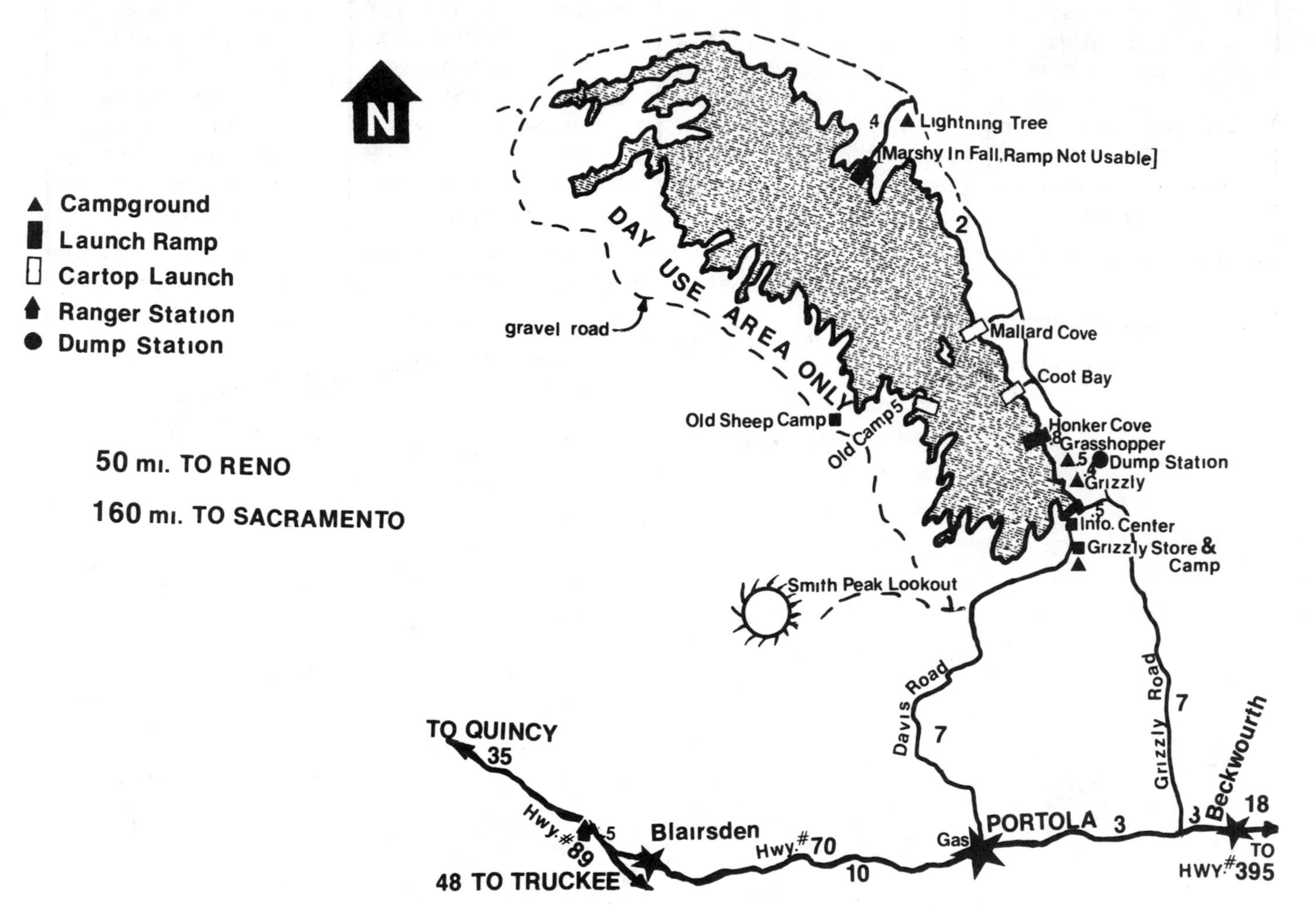

INFORMATION: Beckwourth Ranger Dist., Box 7, Blairsden 96103, Ph: 916-836-2575			
CAMPING	BOATING	RECREATION	OTHER
125 Dev. Sites for Tents & R.V.s Fee: $3 56 Sites for Self-Contained R.V.s Only No Fee Disposal Station	Power, Row, Canoe, Sail, Windsurf & Inflatable Launch Ramps Cartop Boat Launch Areas Rentals: Fishing Boats	Fishing: Rainbow, Cutthroat & Kamloop Trout, Catfish Swimming Picnicking Hiking Backpacking-Parking Hunting: Deer & Waterfowl	Grizzly Store & Camp P.O. Box 203 Portola 96122 Ph: 916-832-4150 26 Dev. Sites for Tents & R.V.s Grocery Store Bait & Tackle Boat Rentals Airport & Full Facilities at Portola

FRENCHMAN LAKE

Frenchman Lake is at an elevation of 5,588 feet in the Plumas National Forest off Highway 70 just north of Chilcoot. The Lake has a surface area of 1,580 acres with 21 miles of shoreline of open sage and pine. The Forest Service maintains numerous campsites including 2 sites modified for the handicapped at Big Cove Campground. This Lake has been stocked with a variety of trout and the fishing is good. Although open to all boating, the Lake level drops in summer and fall, and the launch ramp may be out of the water during extremely dry years. This is a prime hunting area for the Rocky Mountain Mule Deer outside the boundaries of the Recreation Area.

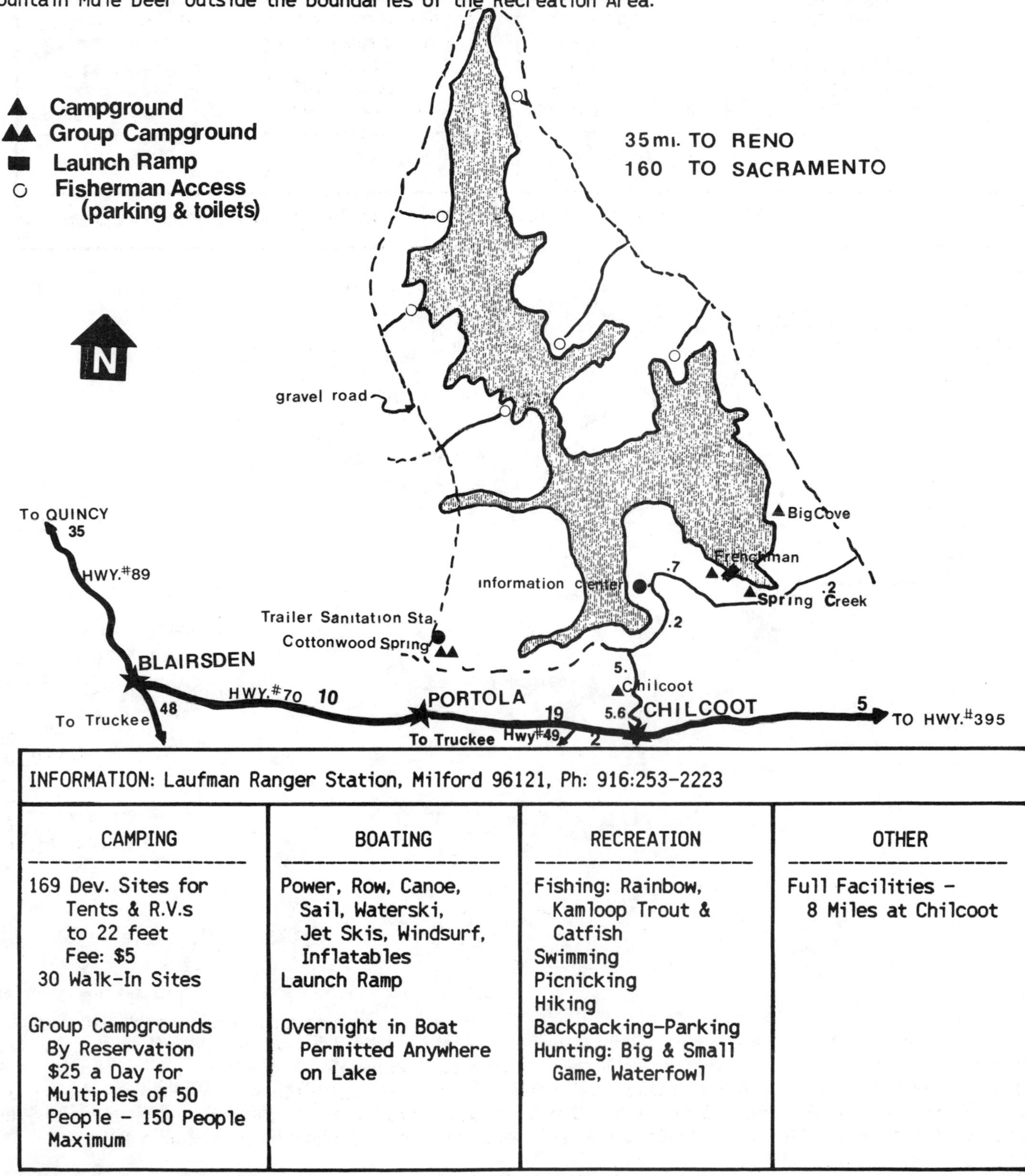

INFORMATION: Laufman Ranger Station, Milford 96121, Ph: 916:253-2223			
CAMPING	BOATING	RECREATION	OTHER
169 Dev. Sites for Tents & R.V.s to 22 feet Fee: $5 30 Walk-In Sites Group Campgrounds By Reservation $25 a Day for Multiples of 50 People - 150 People Maximum	Power, Row, Canoe, Sail, Waterski, Jet Skis, Windsurf, Inflatables Launch Ramp Overnight in Boat Permitted Anywhere on Lake	Fishing: Rainbow, Kamloop Trout & Catfish Swimming Picnicking Hiking Backpacking-Parking Hunting: Big & Small Game, Waterfowl	Full Facilities - 8 Miles at Chilcoot

PLASKETT LAKE, LETTS LAKE AND EAST PARK RESERVOIR

Plaskett Lake at an elevation of 6,000 feet, and Letts Lake at 4,500 feet, are in contrast to the more primitive East Park Reservoir. East Park is a low, warm water fishery known for good bass fishing. It is open to all types of boating with limited facilities. Plaskett and Letts are remote trout Lakes with boating restricted to no motors. The Forest Service maintains good facilities in a mixed coniferous environment. Hikers and backpackers have found Letts Lake a popular attraction with Snow Mountain Wilderness and Summit Springs Trailhead nearby. Trailers over 16 feet are not advised at Plaskett and Letts Lakes due to poor access roads.

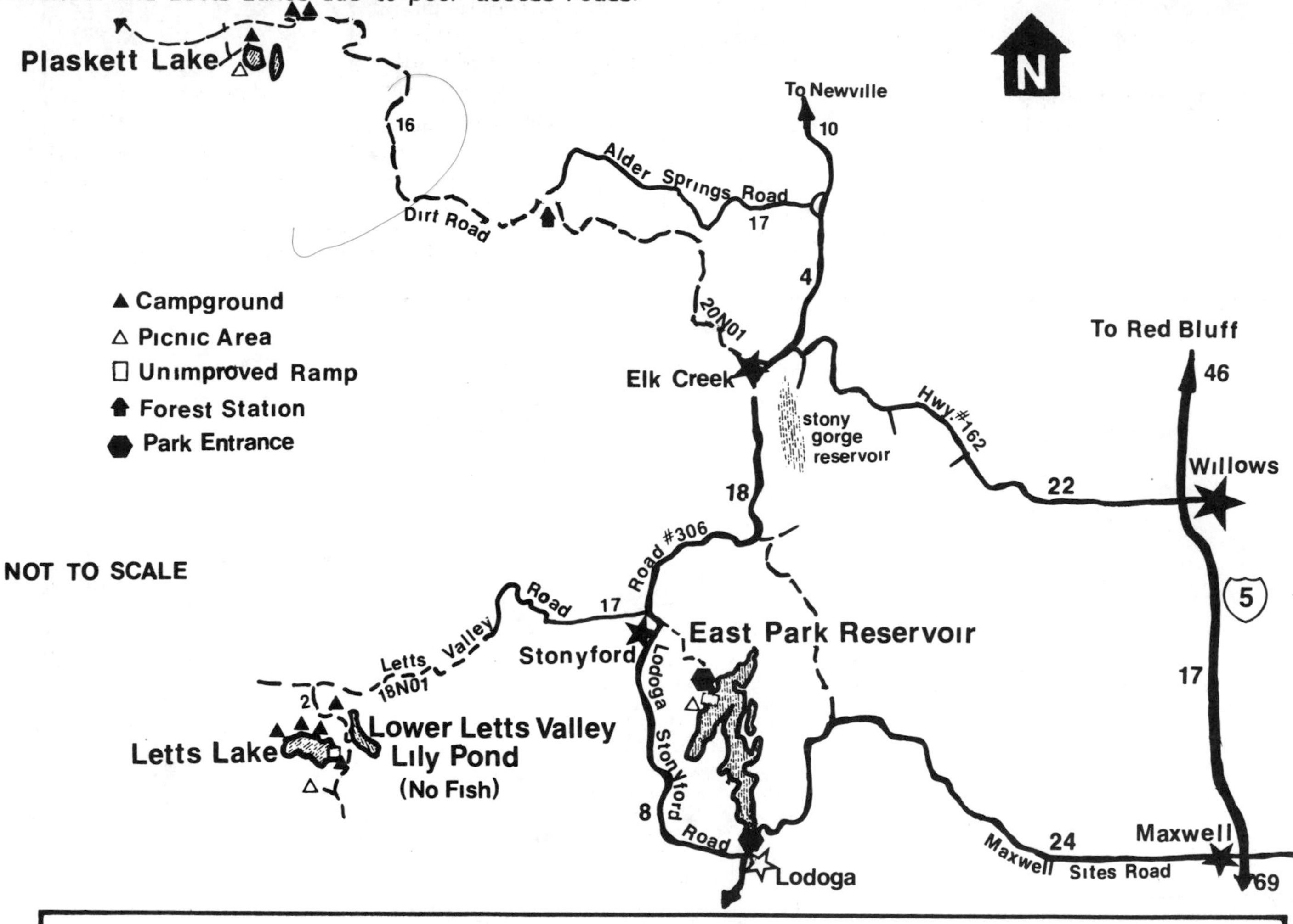

INFORMATION: Stonyford Ranger Dist., Lodoga Rd., Stonyford 95979, Ph: 916-963-3128			
CAMPING	BOATING	RECREATION	OTHER
U.S.F.S. Letts Lake - 42 Sites - Fee: $5 Plaskett Lake Camp - 32 Sites & Masterson Camp 20 Sites Group Site by Reservation: Fee: $15 Per Day	Letts & Plaskett: No Motors - Gas or Electric East Park Reservoir: Open to All Boats Subject to Seasonal Closure - Check with U.S. Bureau of Reclamation Facilities Limited No Houseboats Permitted	Letts & Plaskett: *Fishing: Trout Nature Trails Hiking Backpacking Hunting: Deer, Bear & Squirrel *Bass & Catfish Also in Letts	East Park Reservoir: U.S. Bureau of Reclamation P.O. Box 988 Willows Ph: 916-968-5235 Recreation: Fishing for Black & Spotted Bass, Bluegill, Crappie & Channel Catfish Swimming & Hiking

BLACK BUTTE LAKE

Black Butte is surrounded by rolling hills with basalt buttes and open grassland spotted with oak trees. It rests at an elevation of 470 feet. This 4,500 surface-acre Lake has a shoreline of 40 miles. The U. S. Army Corps of Engineers administers the well-maintained campgrounds and facilities at the Lake. Water level can change rapidly, and boaters are cautioned of possible hazards such as sand bars exposed during low water. This is a good warm water fishery especially in the the spring when the crappie are hungry. There is abundant wildlife, and the bird watcher will find a wide variety of avian life.

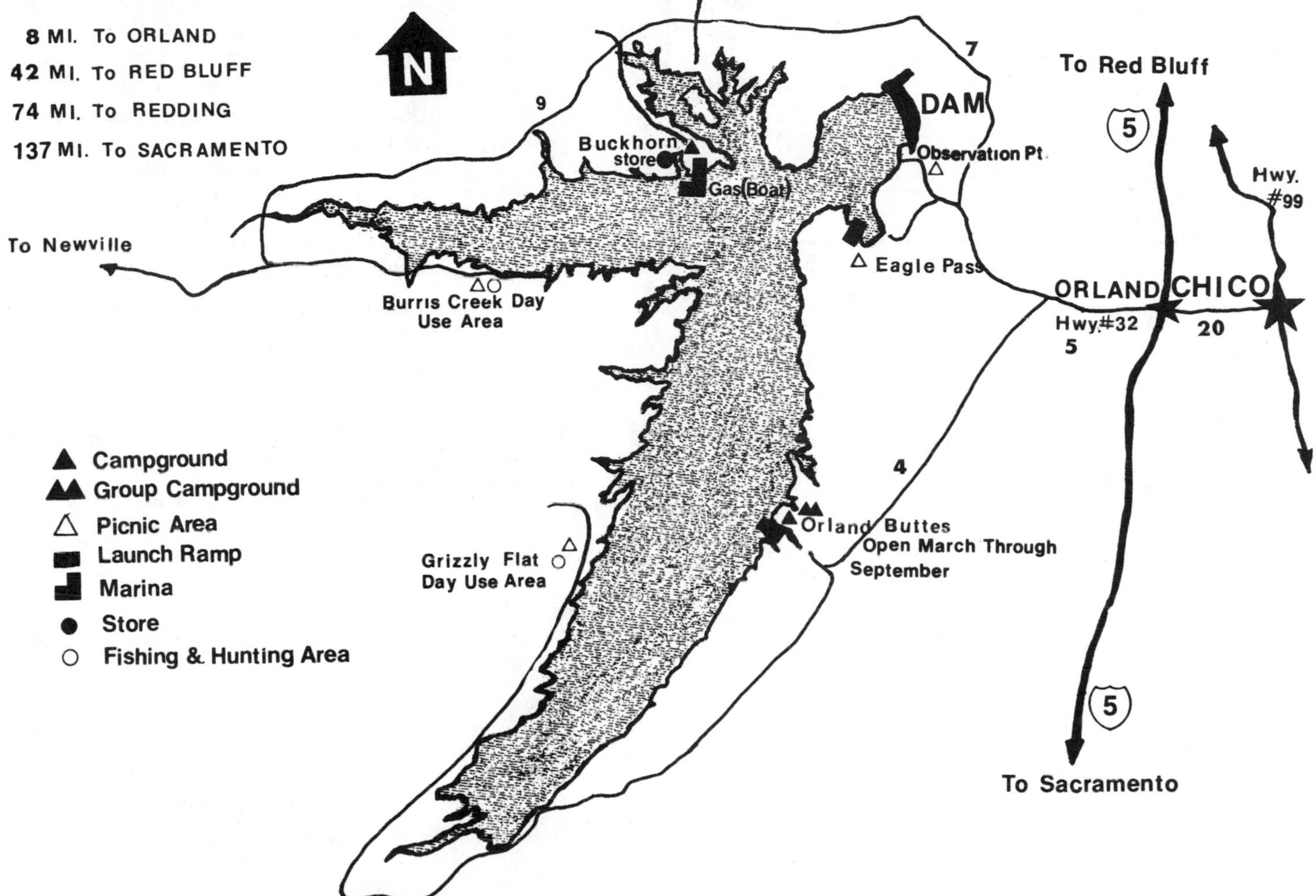

INFORMATION: Park Manager, Star Route, Box 30, Orland 95963, Ph: 916-865-4781			
CAMPING	**BOATING**	**RECREATION**	**OTHER**
Buckhorn: 65 Dev. Sites for Tents & R.V.s - Fee: $6 Orland Buttes: 35 Dev. Sites for Tents & R.V.s - Fee: $6 Group Camp to 150 People - Fee: $25 Reserve for Groups Only. Open March through September. 14 Day Camping Limit.	Power, Row, Canoe, Sail, Waterski, Jet Skis, Windsurf, Inflatables (Maximum Size Boats: 30 x 10) Full Service Marina Launch Ramps Rentals: Fishing Boats & Paddle Boats Docks, Berths, Storage, Gas	Fishing: Catfish, Bluegill, Crappie, Bass Swimming Picnicking Hiking Playgrounds Campfire Programs Hunting: Deer, Dove, Quail, Pheasant, Waterfowl	Snack Bar Grocery Store Bait & Tackle Hot Showers Disposal Station 100-Acre Motorcycle Park - Open June to February Full Facilities - 8 Miles at Orland

STONY GORGE RESERVOIR

Stony Gorge Reservoir is at an elevation of 800 feet in the foothills west of Willows in the upper Sacramento Valley. This Bureau of Reclamation Lake has a surface area of 1,275 acres. The rolling hills surrounding the 25 miles of shoreline are dotted with oak, digger pine and brush. Although there are a number of campsites, they are relatively primitive. Boating facilities are limited to a paved launch ramp which is unusable during late summer and fall. The fishing is good for warm water species in this pretty Lake, and for those who enjoy a natural setting, Stony Gorge will prove a pleasant retreat.

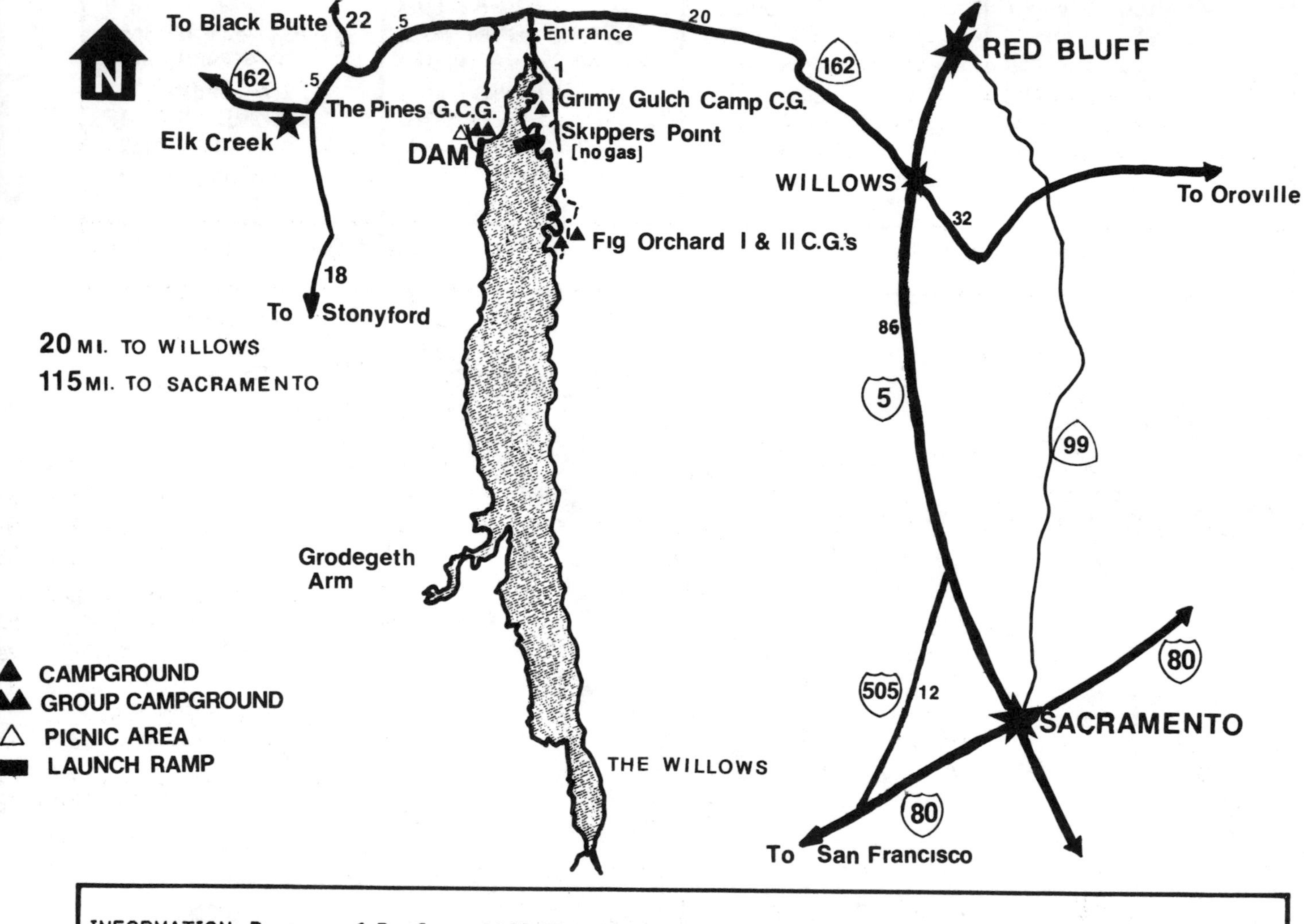

INFORMATION: Bureau of Reclam., 1140 West Wood St., Willows 95988, Ph: 916-968-5235

CAMPING	BOATING	RECREATION	OTHER
150 Sites for Tents & R.V.s Group Camp or Day Use - 200 People Maximum Reservations Only Ph: 916-934-7066 No Fees No Drinking Water	Power, Row, Canoe, Sail, Waterski, Windsurf & Inflatables No Houseboats Permitted Launch Ramp Underwater Hazards Due to Fluctuation in Lake Level	Fishing: Catfish, Bluegill, Crappie, Bass & Perch Swimming Picnicking - 200 People Group site No ORV's and No Hunting	Country Store Gas Station Full Facilities in Elk Creek or Willows

LAKE OROVILLE

Oroville Dam is the highest dam in the United States towering 770 feet above the City of Oroville. Lake Oroville, at 900 feet elevation, has 15,500 surface acres with a shoreline of 167 miles. Although water levels drop late in the summer, the Lake offers unlimited recreation the year around. This is an excellent boating Lake with good marine facilities. There are numerous boat-in campsites, floating campsites and houseboat moorings for those who wish to spend the night on the Lake. The angler will find an extensive variety of game fish from smallmouth bass to king salmon. Thermalito Forebay has 300 surface acres for boating, fishing and swimming.

. . . Continued . . .

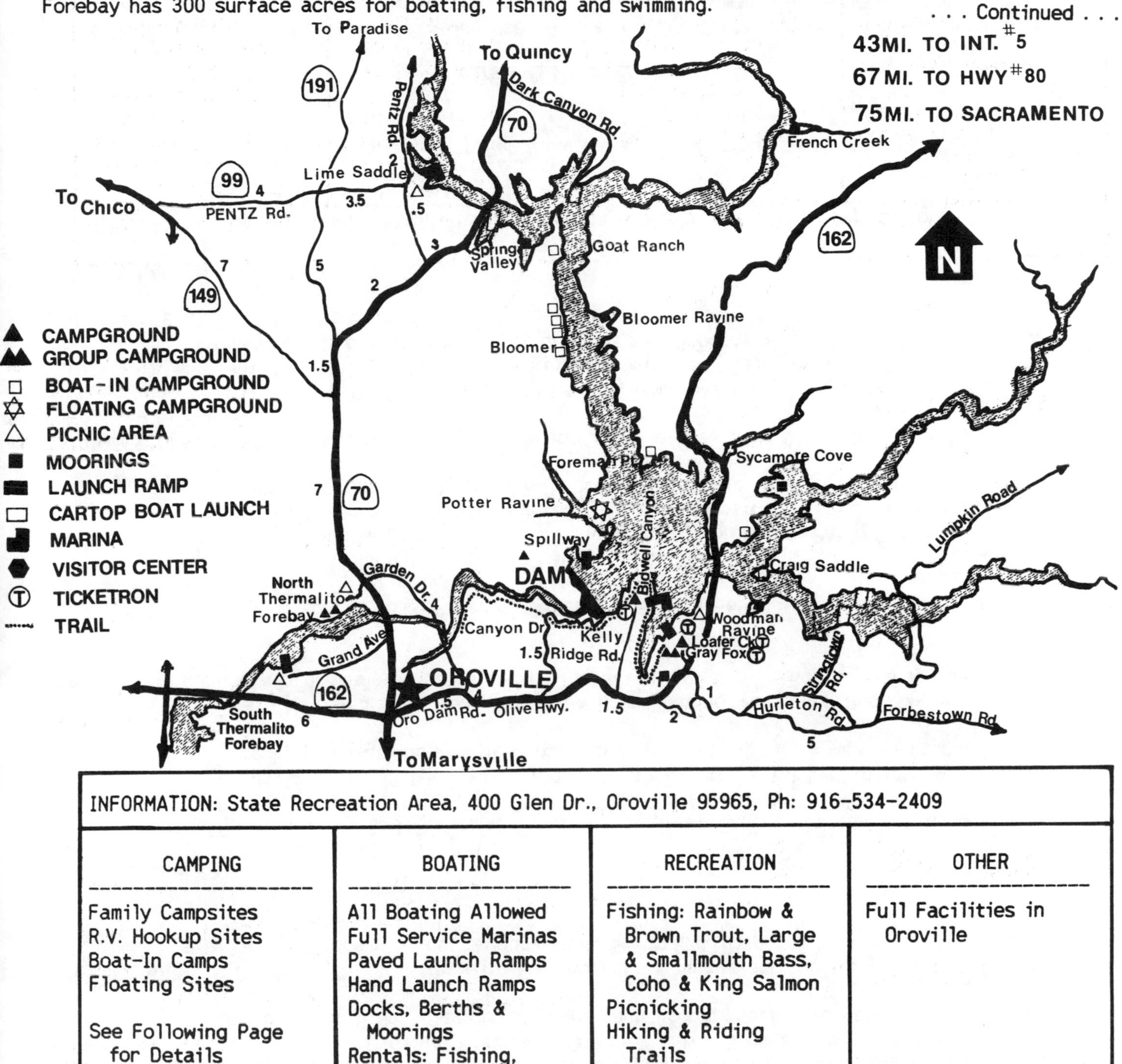

INFORMATION: State Recreation Area, 400 Glen Dr., Oroville 95965, Ph: 916-534-2409			
CAMPING	**BOATING**	**RECREATION**	**OTHER**
Family Campsites R.V. Hookup Sites Boat-In Camps Floating Sites See Following Page for Details	All Boating Allowed Full Service Marinas Paved Launch Ramps Hand Launch Ramps Docks, Berths & Moorings Rentals: Fishing, Waterskiing & Houseboats	Fishing: Rainbow & Brown Trout, Large & Smallmouth Bass, Coho & King Salmon Picnicking Hiking & Riding Trails Hunting: Deer, Upland Game Swimming Visitor Center Fish Hatchery	Full Facilities in Oroville

LAKE OROVILLE

. . . Continued . . .

CAMPING FACILITIES: Reservations Through Ticketron

LOAFER CREEK: 137 Sites for Tents & R.V.s to 31 feet. Water, Flush Toilets, Showers, Laundry Tubs, Disposal Station, 100 Picnic Sites, Swim Beach, Launch Ramp. Group Camps: 6 Well-Developed Camps Each Accommodating 25 People.

BIDWELL CANYON: 75 R.V. Sites with Full Hookups, Launch Ramp, Full Service Marina, Boat Rentals, Grocery Store, Laundry Tubs, Snack Bar, Disposal Station. Ph: 916-589-3165

BOAT-IN CAMPS:

109 SITES AT: Craig Saddle (drinking water), Sycamore Creek, Foreman Point, Goat Ranch, Primitive Area - North Point, Knoll, South Cove, Bloomer.
Group Camp for 75 People Located at South Bloomer - Tables, Toilets, No Drinking Water. Reservations Accepted for Group Site Through Park Headquarters.

4 FLOATING CAMPSITES: Overnight Boating & Houseboating, Moorings, Must be Self-Contained, Outlets Sealed and Be Inspected by Ranger. Contact Park Headquarters for Reservations.

LIME SADDLE MARINA, P.O. Box 1088, Paradise 95969, Ph: 916-534-6950

Full Service Marina, Five-Lane Launch Ramp, Gas
Rentals: Houseboats, Aqua Larks, Fishing & Pontoon Boats, Patio Boats
Overnight Moorings, Docks, Covered & Open Slips, Water Ski Sales and Rentals, Marine Supplies, Grocery Store, Delicatessen, Bait & Tackle, Propane.

BIDWELL CANYON MARINA, 801 Bidwell Canyon Road, Oroville 95965, Ph: 916-589-3165

Full Service Marina, Seven-Lane Launch Ramp, Gas
Rentals: Fishing & Patio & Speed Boats, Water Ski Sales & Rentals
Overnight Moorings, Anchorage, Dry Storage, Grocery Store, Bait & Tackle, Snack Bar, Pumpout Station

PAVED LAUNCH RAMPS ALSO LOCATED AT:

SPILLWAY: 13-Lane Launch Ramp, Parking, Chemical Toilets, Overnight Camping for Self-Contained R.V.s

ENTERPRISE: Free Paved 2-Lane Launch Ramp, Cartop Launch During Low Water.

THERMALITO FOREBAY

The North End of the Forebay is for Day Use. There are 300 Surface Acres. Facilities include a 2-lane launch ramp, sandy swim beach, picnic tables, shade ramadas, potable water and many lovely trees. This area is for sailboats and other non-power boats only. Overnight camping and a group area are by reservations at Park Headquarters.

The South End of the Forebay has a 4-lane launch ramp and is for power boats and fishing boats only. There is no shade or potable water.

LITTLE GRASS VALLEY LAKE, SLY CREEK AND LOST CREEK RESERVOIRS

Little Grass Valley, at 5,040 feet elevation, and Sly Creek, at 3,560 feet elevation, are pretty Lakes in the Plumas National Forest. Little Grass Valley which has a surface area of 1,615 acres is a good boating Lake. There is an abundance of developed campsites in this forested area. Sly Creek Reservoir has 562 surface acres with limited facilities for boating and camping. Its neighbor, Lost Creek Reservoir, is surrounded by private land except for a small portion of Forest Service land on the north side which is relatively unusable due to the steep slopes. These are good fishing Lakes for trout.

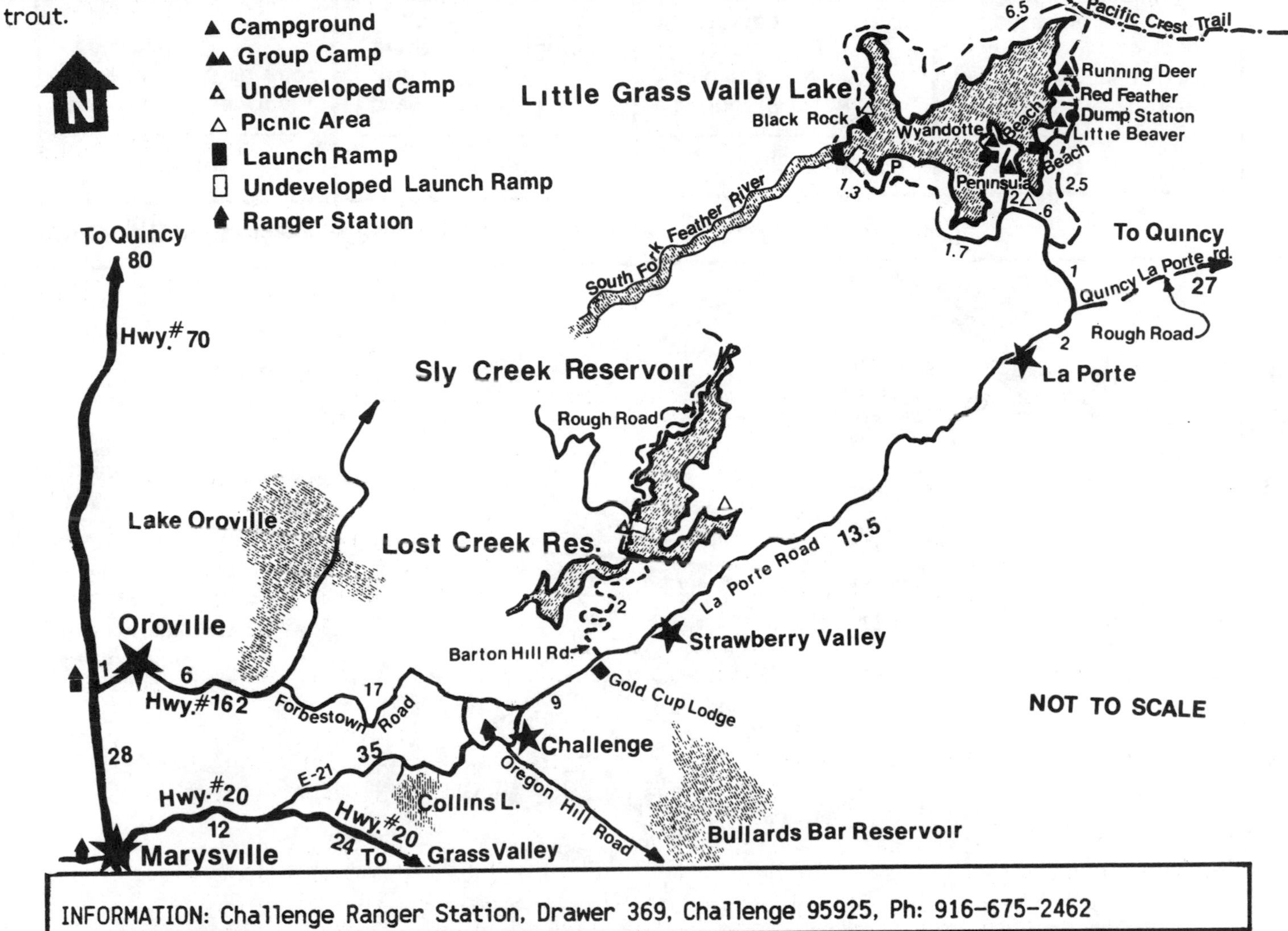

INFORMATION: Challenge Ranger Station, Drawer 369, Challenge 95925, Ph: 916-675-2462

CAMPING	BOATING	RECREATION	OTHER
Little Grass Valley: 280 Dev. Sites for Tents & R.V.s 25 ft. Max. Length Group Campsites Reservations for Any Group of 5 Sites - 58 People Maximum Disposal Station Sly Creek: Primitive Camping	Little Grass Valley: Open to All Boats 3 Paved Launch Ramps Sly Creek: Open to All Boats Cartops Advised - Unimproved Launch Ramp	Fishing: Rainbow, Brook & Brown Trout Swimming Picnicking Hiking Backpacking Nature Study Hunting: Waterfowl Upland Game & Deer	Facilities - 5 Miles at La Porte Abandoned Mining Towns Feather Falls - One of the Highest in the United States

GOLD LAKE AND THE LAKES BASIN RECREATION AREA

More than thirty natural Lakes bless this area of scenic abundance. Gold Lake is the largest of these Lakes which range in elevation from 5,000 top 6,000 feet. While several of the Lakes can be reached by car, many can only be reached by trail. The angler will find good trout fishing in both Lake and stream. This is a popular fly fishing area especially along the Middle Fork of the Feather River which has been designated a natural Wild and Scenic River. The Lakes Basin is in both the Plumas and Tahoe National Fores. The hiker and packer will find numerous trails leading to the Pacific Crest Trail. Although this area remains relatively unspoiled, there are a number of resorts and facilities that complement the natural setting of this beautiful country. (Cover Photograph: Lower Sardine Lake.)

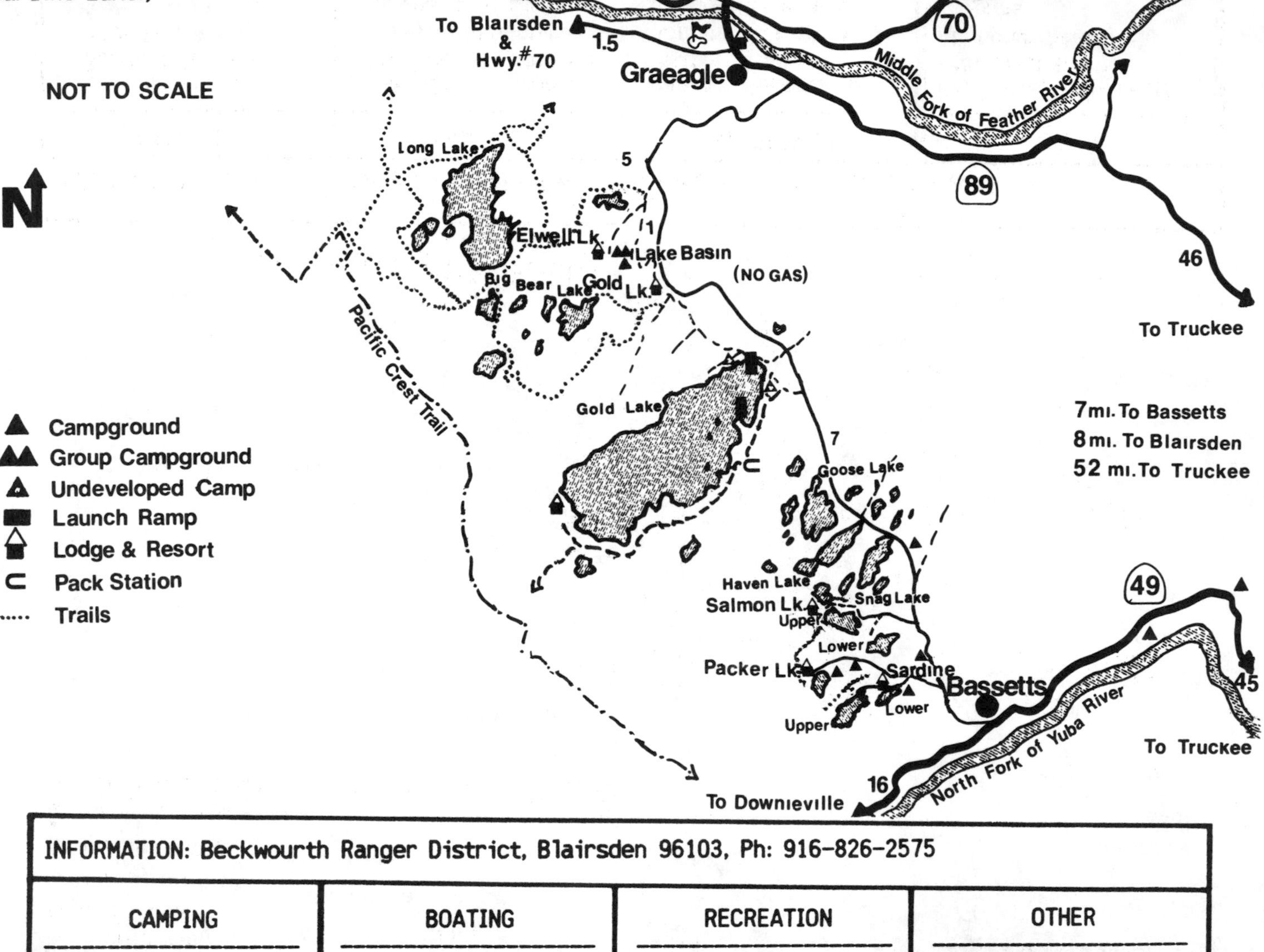

INFORMATION: Beckwourth Ranger District, Blairsden 96103, Ph: 916-826-2575

CAMPING	BOATING	RECREATION	OTHER
Many Forest Service Campgrounds in Area Fee: $5 Group Camp to 25 People by Reservation Fee: $20	Power, Row, Sail, Windsurfing & Waterskiing (Gold Lake) Launch Ramp at Gold Lake	Fishing: Rainbow, Brown & Brook Trout Picnicking Hiking & Riding Trails Backpacking Horse Rentals & Pack Station Swimming Hunting: Deer Golf Courses	Numerous Facilities and Resorts in this Area Contact: Plumas County Chamber of Commerce P.O. Box 1018 Quincy 95971 Ph: 916-283-2045

BULLARDS BAR RESERVOIR

Bullards Bar Reservoir is at an elevation of 2,300 feet in the Tahoe National Forest surrounded by rugged countryside. This large Lake of 4,600 surface acres has 55 shoreline miles of tall hills on three sides with the dam on the southwest end. The area is heavily wooded, so all campsites are shaded by trees. All boating is allowed, but small rowboats and canoes are not advised. During the spring, run-off logs and debris can be a hazard to the waterskier. Water level variation can affect the launch ramps by late summer when water level drops. Swimming is not recommended because of the sharp drop off in the Lake. Fishing is open year around for both warm and cold water fish. There is good swimming at the Oregon Creek Day Use area at the junction of Oregon Creek and the Middle Fork of the Yuba River.

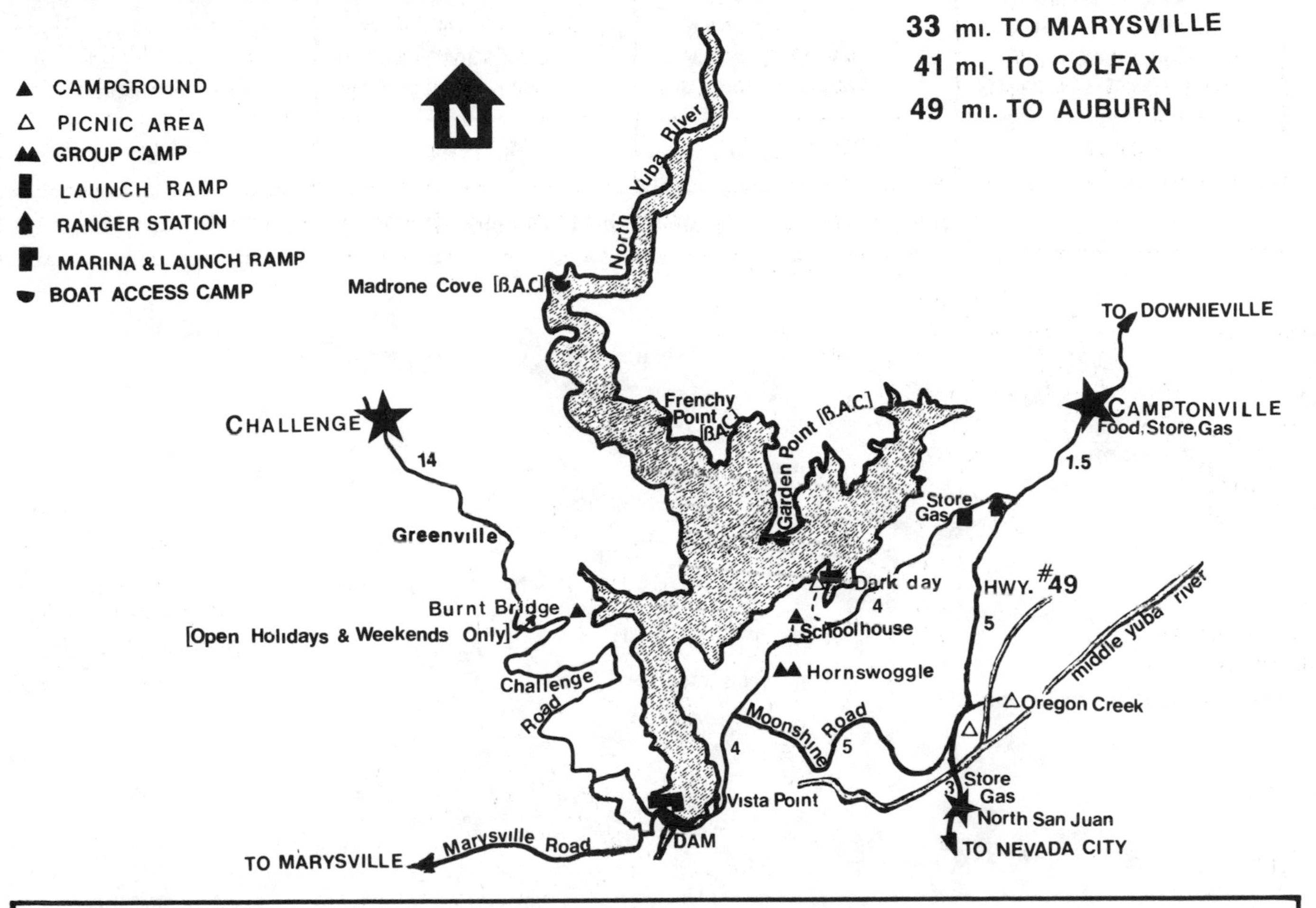

INFORMATION: U.S.F.S., No. Yuba Ranger Station, Camptonville 95922, Ph: 916-288-3231

CAMPING	BOATING	RECREATION	OTHER
67 Dev. Sites for Tents & R.V.s Fee: $4 Group Camps - 150 People Maximum Reservations Req. Water shut off in Campgrounds from September to May. No Fees at that time.	Power, Sail, Waterski, Jet Ski & Inflatable Not Recommended for Rowboats or Canoes Waterskiing Not Advised in Early Summer Launch Ramps, Berths Boat Access Camps: Sports Haven,Box 981 Grass Valley 95945 916-272-1365	Fishing: Rainbow & Brown Trout, Catfish, Bluegill, Crappie, Large & Smallmouth Bass Kokanee Salmon Swimming at Oregon Creek Picnicking Hiking	Full Facilities - 25 Miles at Nevada City or Grass Valley Camptonville & Challenge - 5 Miles Grocery Store Bait & Tackle Restaurant Gas Station

BOWMAN LAKE

Bowman Lake is the largest of several small Lakes in the scenic Bowman Road Area of the Tahoe National Forest. Bowman is 6 miles south of Jackson Meadows Reservoir and 16 miles above Highway 20. The Lakes in the area range in altitude from 5,600 feet to 7,000 feet in this beautiful high Sierra country. The Forest Service maintains a number of campsites as indicated on the map, but be sure to bring your own drinking water as only Grouse Ridge has piped water. Stream and Lake fishing can be good, and the natural setting can make for a pleasant experience.

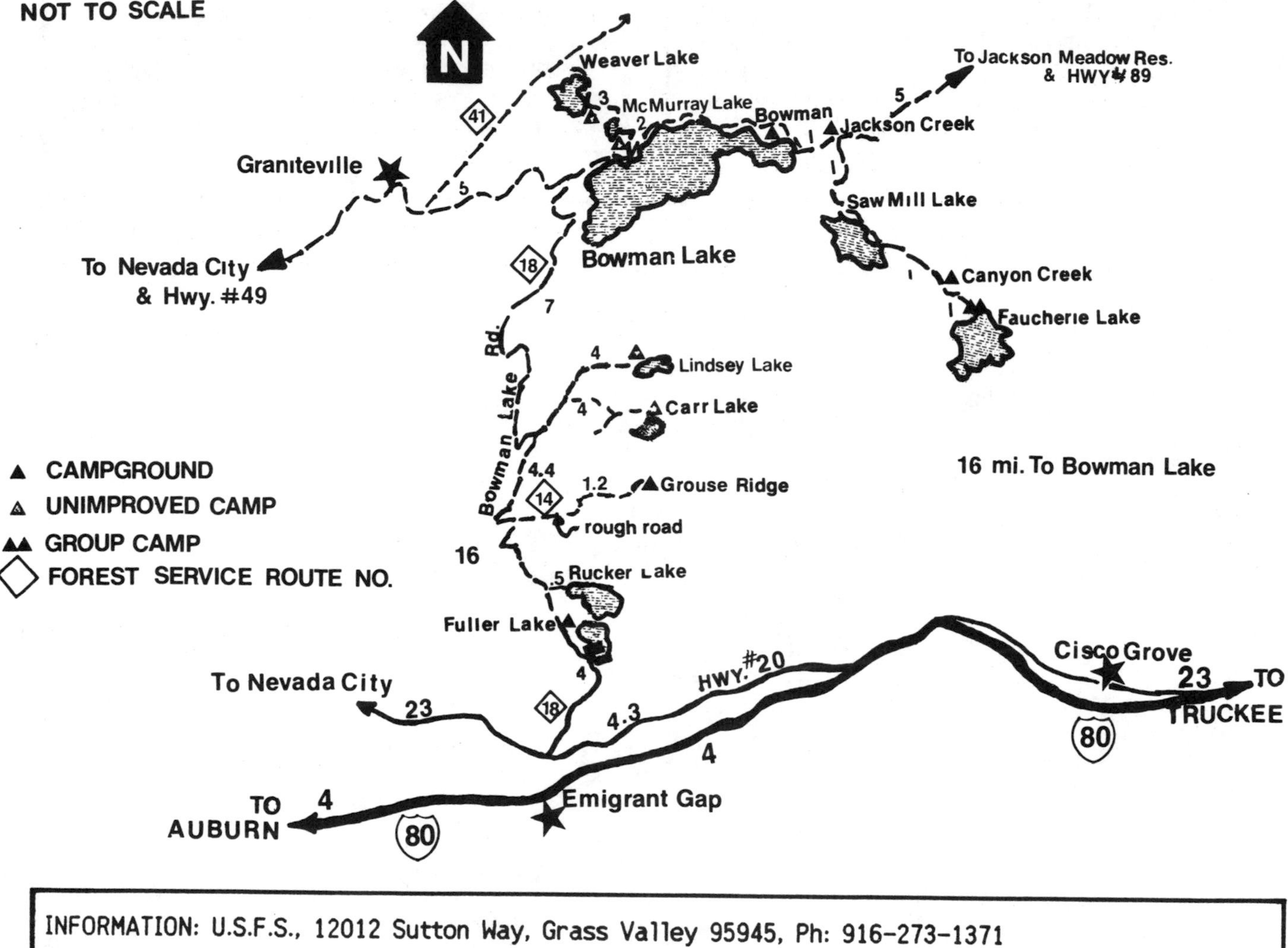

INFORMATION: U.S.F.S., 12012 Sutton Way, Grass Valley 95945, Ph: 916-273-1371			
CAMPING	BOATING	RECREATION	OTHER
Primitive Camping No Fee Group Camp - 25 People Maximum Fee: $20 Reservations Required	Small Boats Only Cartop Launching	Fishing: Rainbow, Brook & Brown Trout Swimming Picnicking Hiking Backpacking Nature Study Hunting: Deer	Full Facilities in Truckee or Along Highway 80 Rough Roads <u>Not</u> Recommended for Cars, Trailers, R.V.s

EAGLE, FORDYCE, STERLING, KIDD, CASCADE, LONG AND SERENE LAKES

These Lakes, off Interstate Highway 80 near Soda Springs, rest at elevations of about 7,000 feet in the Tahoe National Forest. The beautiful high Sierra country offers a variety of recreational opportunities. Boating is limited to non-powered craft and limited facilities, but you will find rentals at Serene Lakes. The serious angler will find trout and catfish. The numerous trails invite the hiker, backpacker and equestrian to get away from it all in this natural paradise.

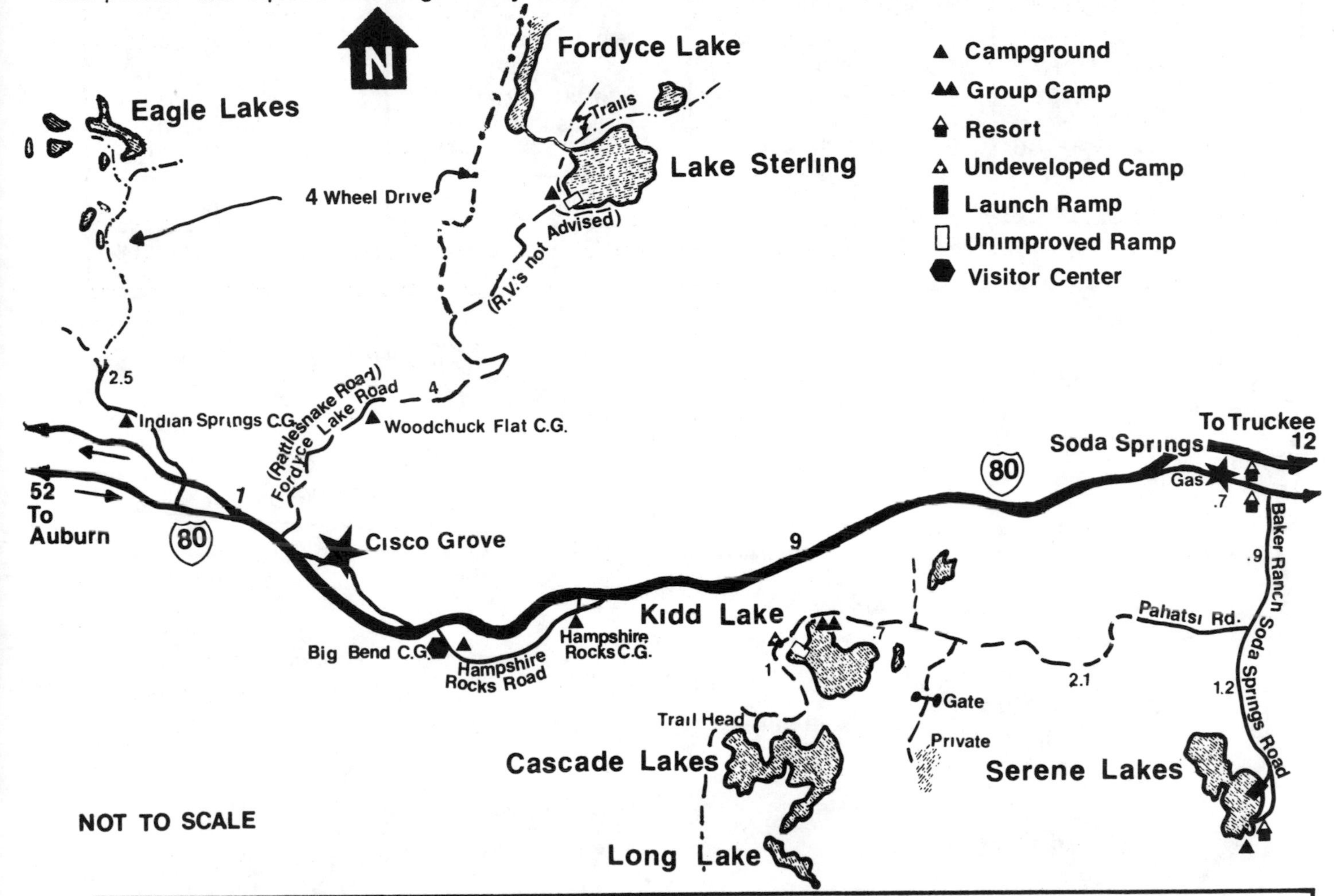

INFORMATION: Chamber of Commerce, P.O. Box 2757, Truckee 95734, Ph: 916-587-2757

CAMPING	BOATING	RECREATION	OTHER
USFS - Nevada City Ranger District Ph: 916-273-1371 Sites for Tents & R.V.s - Fee: $5 Kidd Lake: Groups to 100 - Reserve: P.G.&E. 333 Sacramento St. Auburn 95603 Ph: 916-885-2431	Motors Allowed at Sterling Lake No Motors at Other Lakes Rentals at Serene Lakes	Fishing: Trout & Catfish Swimming Picnicking Numerous Hiking & Riding Trails Horse Rentals Backpacking Nature Study Photography	Serene Lakes Campground: R.V. Hookups Fee: $7.50 Ph: 916-426-3397 Monthly Rentals Motel/Lodge Restaurant & Cocktail Lounge Bait & Tackle Gas Station

JACKSON MEADOW RECREATION AREA

The Jackson Meadow Recreation Area is at an elevation of 6,200 feet in the Tahoe National Forest. This area of forested slopes, alpine meadows, Lakes and streams provides and abundance of recreational opportunities. Jackson Meadows Reservoir is the hub of this area with well maintained camping and recreational facilities dotting its 11 miles shoreline. Nearby Milton and Independence Lakes and their tributaries are subject to specific artificial lure, species and size limitations. Contact the California Sport Fishing Regulations for details. The hiker, backpacker and equestrian will find a trailhead to the Pacific Crest Trail at Pass Creek Bridge. Campsites are also available at Webber and Independence Lakes.

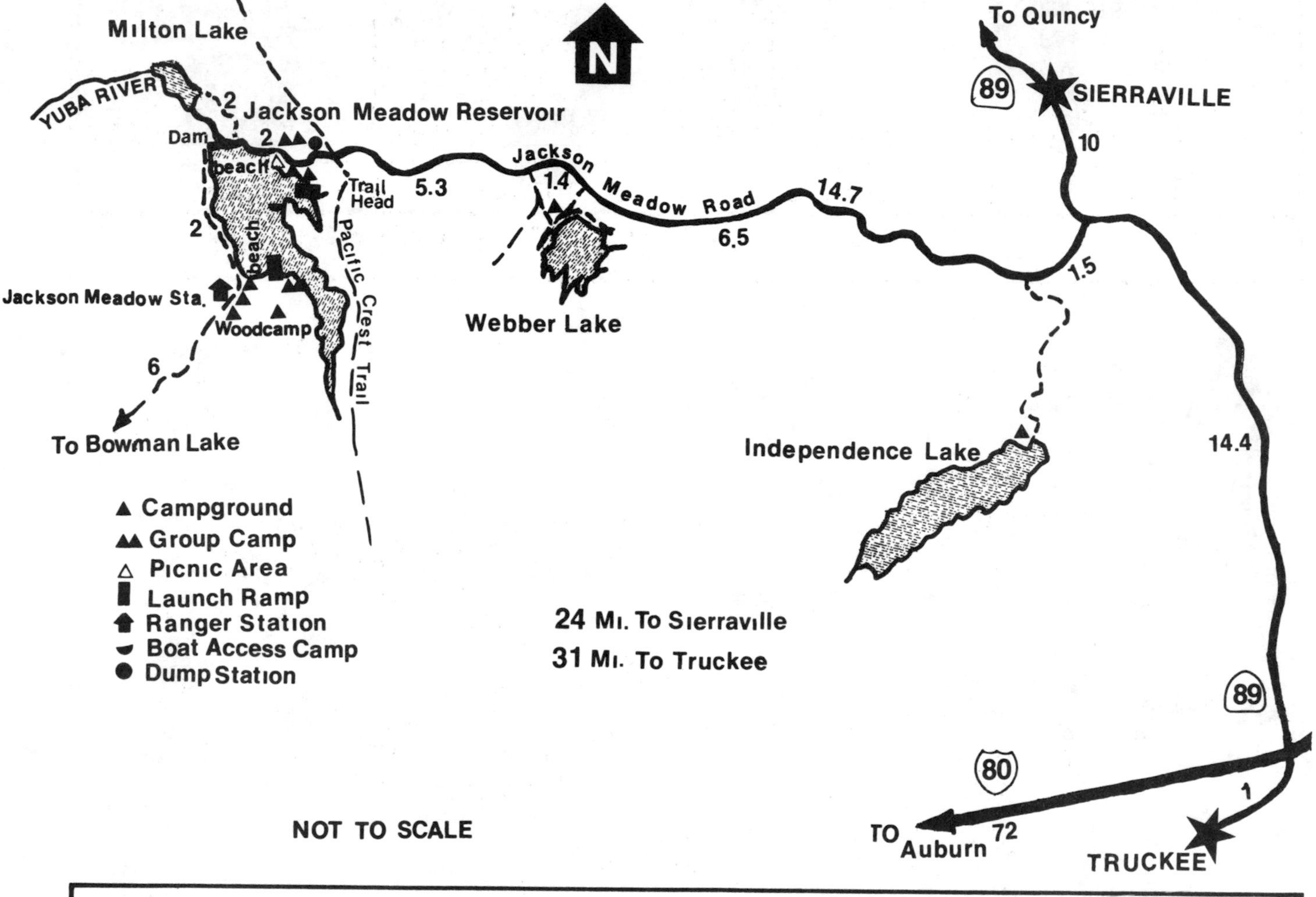

INFORMATION: Sierraville R.S., P.O. Box 95, Sierraville 96216, Ph: 916-994-3401

CAMPING	BOATING	RECREATION	OTHER
139 Dev. Sites for Tents & R.V.s Fee: $5 - $7 10 Boat Access Only Sites Group Camp - 150 People Maximum	Power, Row, Canoe, Sail, Waterski, Jet Ski, Windsurf & Inflatables Noise Level Laws Enforced Launch Ramps	Fishing: Rainbow & Brown Trout Swimming Beaches With Dressing Rooms Picnicking Backpacking-Parking Hiking, Horseback Riding & Nature Trails Hunting: Deer - Outside Recreation Area	Disposal Station Fee: $5 Full Facilities - 24 Miles at Sierraville or 31 Miles at Truckee

STAMPEDE RESERVOIR

Stampede Reservoir is at an elevation of 5,949 feet in the Tahoe National Forest. This large Lake has a surface area of 3,440 acres and 25 miles of sage and coniferous shoreline. The Forest Service maintains numerous campsites at the Lake. This is a good boating Lake with westerly winds for the sailor. Unfortunately, the Lake is very low at the end of the season for water is drained into Pyramid Lake in Nevada via the Truckee River to support two rare species of fish which are near extinction.

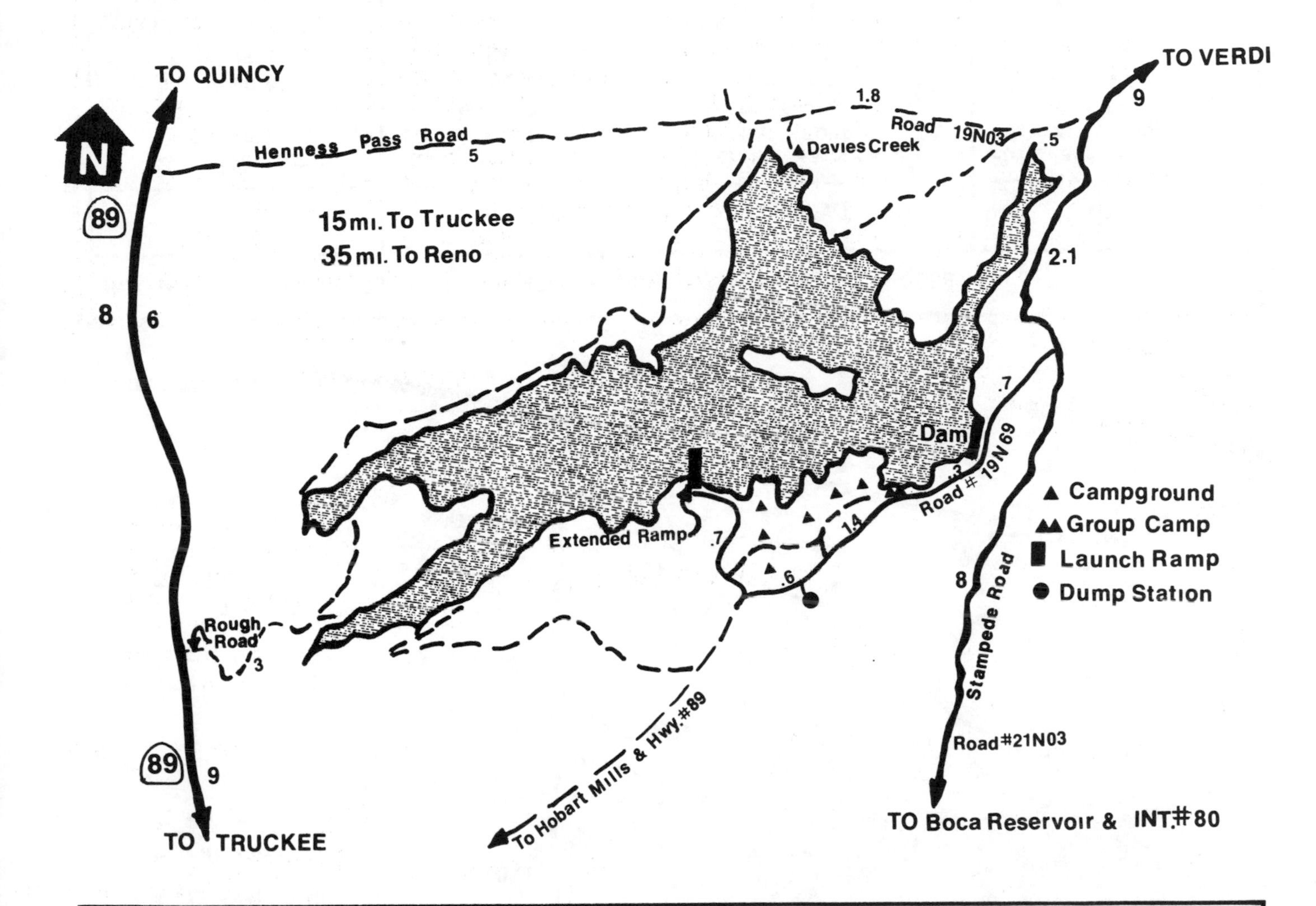

INFORMATION: Truckee R.D., P.O. Box 399, Truckee 95734, Ph: 916-587-3558

CAMPING	BOATING	RECREATION	OTHER
252 Dev. Sites for Tents & R.V.s Fee: $4 10 Sites on Davies Creek - No Fee Group Camp - 150 People Maximum For Reservations Call 415-322-1183	Power, Row, Canoe, Sail, Waterski, Jet Ski, Windsurf & Inflatables Water Very Low In Fall Launch Ramp Extended for Low Water Launching	Fishing: Rainbow & Brown Trout Swimming Picnicking Hiking Hunting: Deer	Full Facilities - 14 Miles at Truckee

PROSSER CREEK RESERVOIR

Prosser Creek Reservoir is at an elevation of 5,711 feet located in the scenic Tahoe National Forest. This 740 surface acre Lake rests in an open canyon surrounded by 11 miles of sage and coniferous-covered hills. The Donner Camp picnic area was the site of the Donner Party tragedy of the winter of 1846-47. Boating is limited to 10 MPH, so waterskiing, power boating and jet skiing are eliminated from this facility. Launching is hampered in the fall by low water conditions. There are trout for the fisherman who will be able to enjoy the serenity of this peaceful facility.

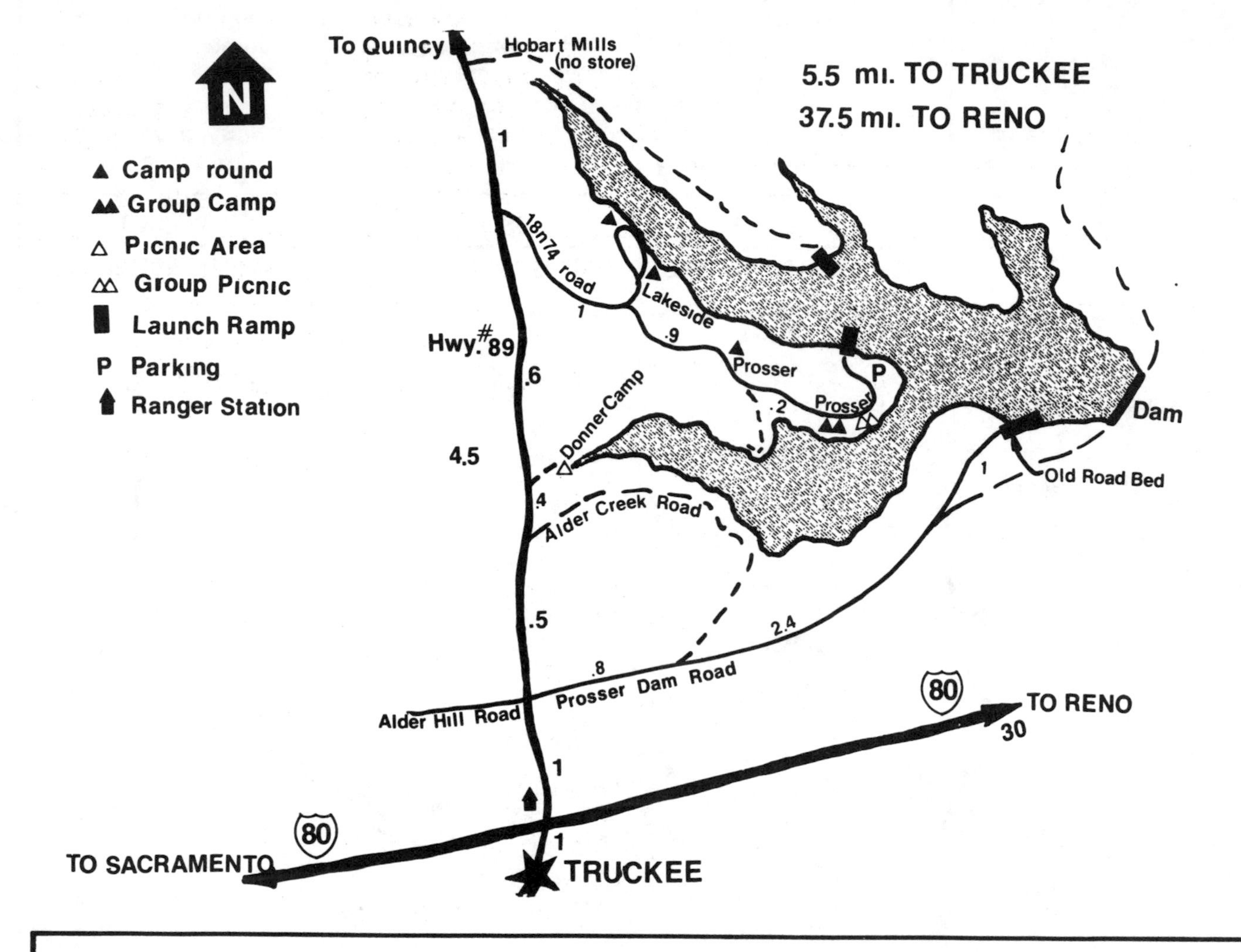

INFORMATION: Truckee R.D., P.O. Box 399, Truckee 95734, Ph: 916-587-3558			
CAMPING	BOATING	RECREATION	OTHER
29 Dev. Sites for Tents & R.V.s Fee: $4 100 Primitive Sites for Tents & R.V.s - No Fee Group Camp - 50 People Maximum Call 916-587-3558 for Reservations	Power, Row, Canoe, Sail, Windsurf, & Inflatables Speed Limit - 10 MPH Launch Ramps	Fishing: Rainbow & Brown Trout Swimming Picnicking Hiking Hunting: Deer	Full Facilities - 5 Miles at Truckee

BOCA RESERVOIR

Boca Reservoir is in the Tahoe National Forest at an elevation of 5,700 feet. The Lake has a surface area of 980 acres and 14 miles of shoreline which is a lovely combination of steep bluffs and low grassy areas amid tall pine trees. The many inlets and prevailing winds create an excellent atmosphere for sailing and boating. The water level is relatively constant as it is fed by Stampede Reservoir, 5 miles above, but there is a drop in late fall.

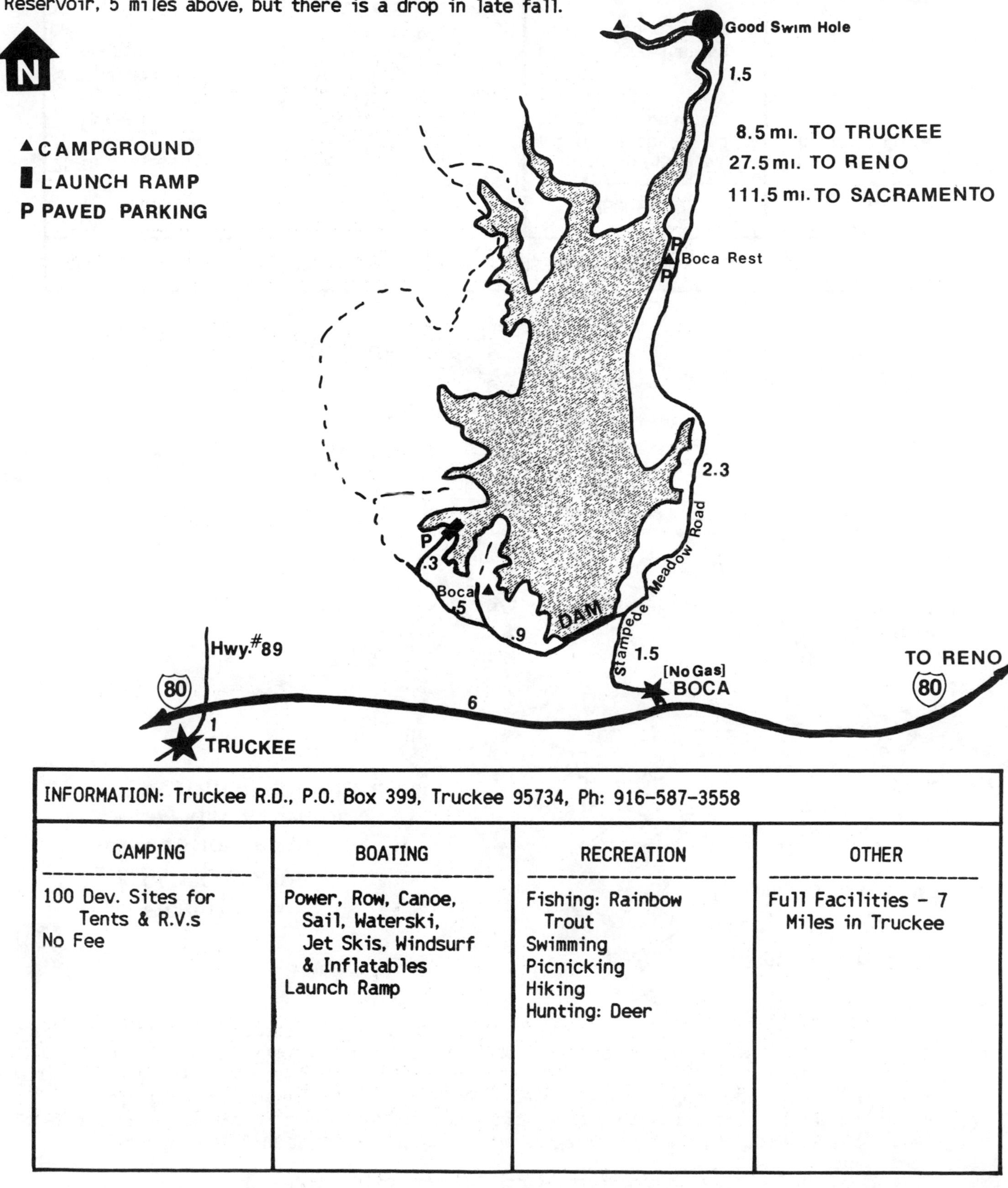

INFORMATION: Truckee R.D., P.O. Box 399, Truckee 95734, Ph: 916-587-3558

CAMPING	BOATING	RECREATION	OTHER
100 Dev. Sites for Tents & R.V.s No Fee	Power, Row, Canoe, Sail, Waterski, Jet Skis, Windsurf & Inflatables Launch Ramp	Fishing: Rainbow Trout Swimming Picnicking Hiking Hunting: Deer	Full Facilities - 7 Miles in Truckee

LAKE SPAULDING

Lake Spaulding is at 5,014 feet in the Sierra Nevadas. The Lake has a surface area of 698 acres and is surrounded by granite rocks intermingled with conifer forest. The Dam was originally built in 1912 for hydraulic mining, and it is now a part of P.G.&E.'s Drum-Spaulding Hydroelectric Project. P.G.&E. operates the campground and launch ramp. Although launching large boats can be difficult, this is a good Lake for boating with huge granite boulders reaching the water, creating a spectacular setting. Fishing from bank or boat is often rewarding.

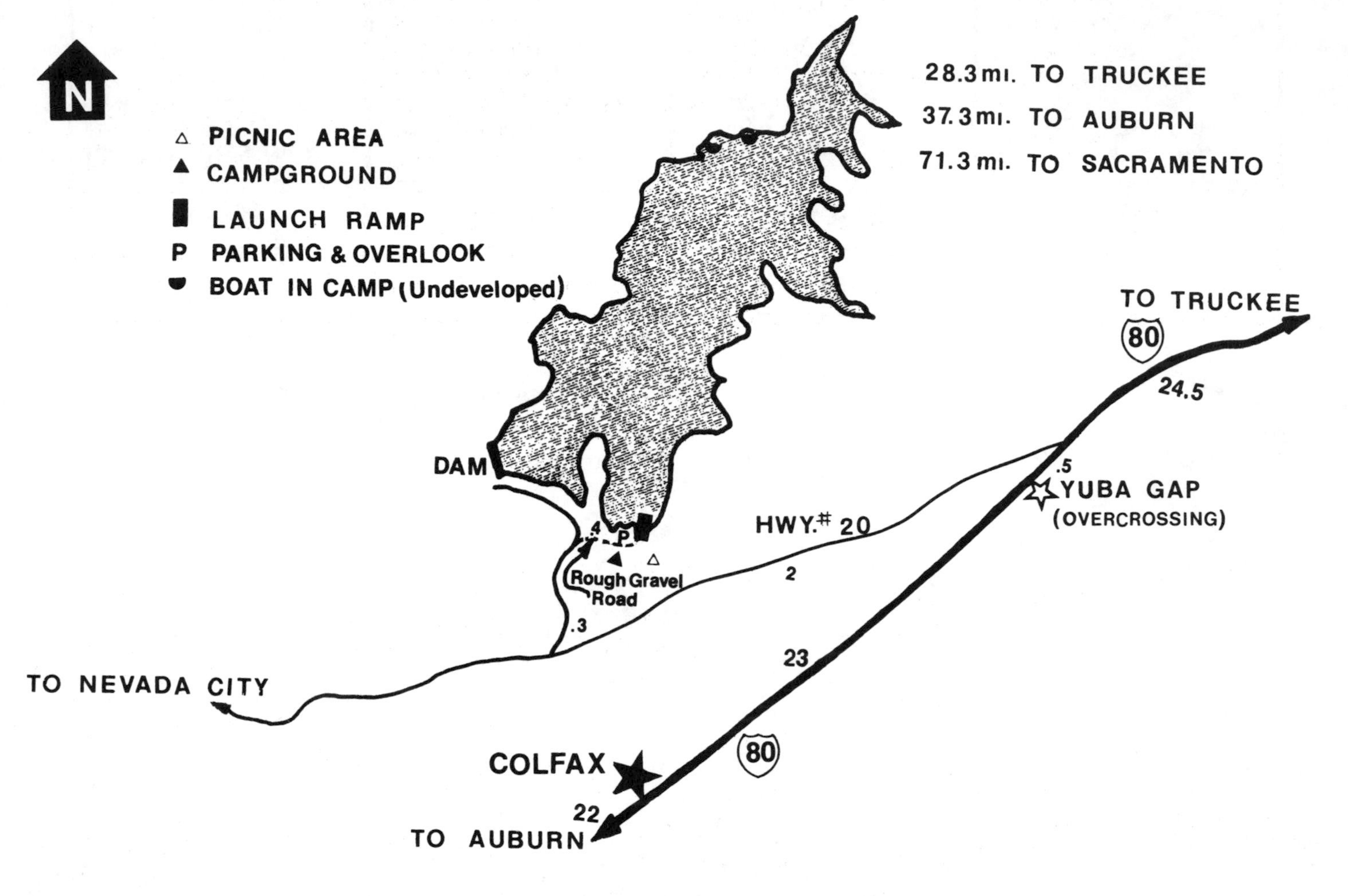

INFORMATION: P.G.&E., 333 Sacramento St., Auburn 95603, Ph: 916-885-2431 X224

CAMPING	BOATING	RECREATION	OTHER
25 Dev. Sites for Tents & R.V.s Fee: $5 Some Undeveloped Boat-In Sites	Power, Row, Canoe, Sail, Waterski, Jet Ski, Windsurf & Inflatables Launch Ramp - Summer Use Only Hazardous Rocks In Late Summer As Water Level Drops	Fishing: Rainbow & Brown Trout Swimming - Beaches Picnicking Hiking Backpacking-Parking Hunting: Deer	Full Facilities - 25 Miles at Colfax

DONNER LAKE

Donner Lake is at an elevation of 5,963 feet in the Tahoe National Forest next to Interstate 80 west of Truckee. The Lake is 3 miles long and 3/4 mile wide with a shoreline of 7-1/2 miles of high alpine woods. The Donner State Memorial Park was named after the tragic Donner Party whose fate in the winter of 1846 attests to the hardships encountered by California's early settlers. This well-maintained Park has 154 developed campsites with campfire programs and nature trails. The Emigrant Trail Museum is open daily from 10:00 a.m. to Noon and from 1:00 p.m. to 4:00 p.m. The water in the Lake is clear and cold, yet refreshing. A popular sailing Lake, Donner has its own local Sailing Club, but beware of periodic afternoon winds that can be hazardous.

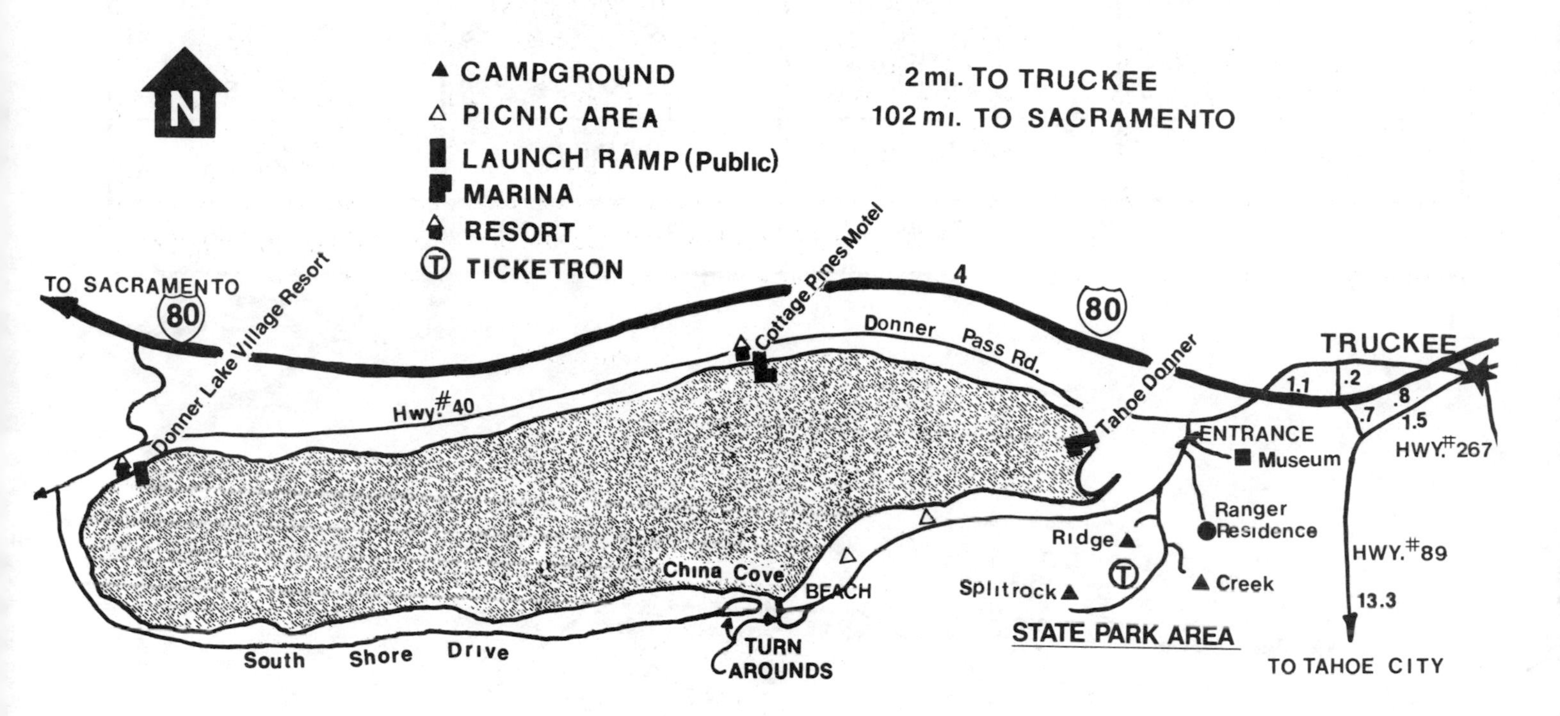

INFORMATION: Chamber of Commerce, P.O. Box 2757, Truckee 95734, Ph: 916-587-2757

CAMPING	BOATING	RECREATION	OTHER
Donner Memorial State Park 154 Dev. Sites for Tents & R.V.s Fee: $5 Ph: 916-587-3841	Power, Row, Canoe, Sail, Waterski, Jet Skis, Windsurf & Inflatables No Launching From State Park Public Launch Ramp At West End Rentals: Fishing, Sail, Pontoon & Paddleboats	Fishing: Rainbow & Brown Trout, Kokanee Salmon Swimming - Beaches Picnicking Hiking Horseback Riding Trails & Rentals Campfire Programs Nature Study Playgrounds	Motels, Cabins Snack Bar Restaurant Cocktail Lounge Grocery Store Bait & Tackle Laundromat Gas Station Airport With Auto Rentals - 2 Miles Tennis, Golf, Movies

MARTIS CREEK LAKE

Martis Creek Lake is located two miles above the confluence of the Truckee River and Martis Creek at an elevation of 5,700 feet. The U. S. Army Corps of Engineers completed the Dam in 1972 as flood protection for Reno. The Lake has a surface area of 700 acres and 4 miles of pine-covered shoreline. Martis Creek Lake is the first to be designated as a "Wild Trout Lake" by the California Department of Fish and Game. Lahonton Cutthroat Trout were introduced in the spring of 1978 and now provide catches up to 24 inches in this catch and release program. Only artificial lures and flies with barbless hooks may be used. The Corps administers a 1,000 acre wildlife area in addition to the camping facilities. The campground is closed in the winter.

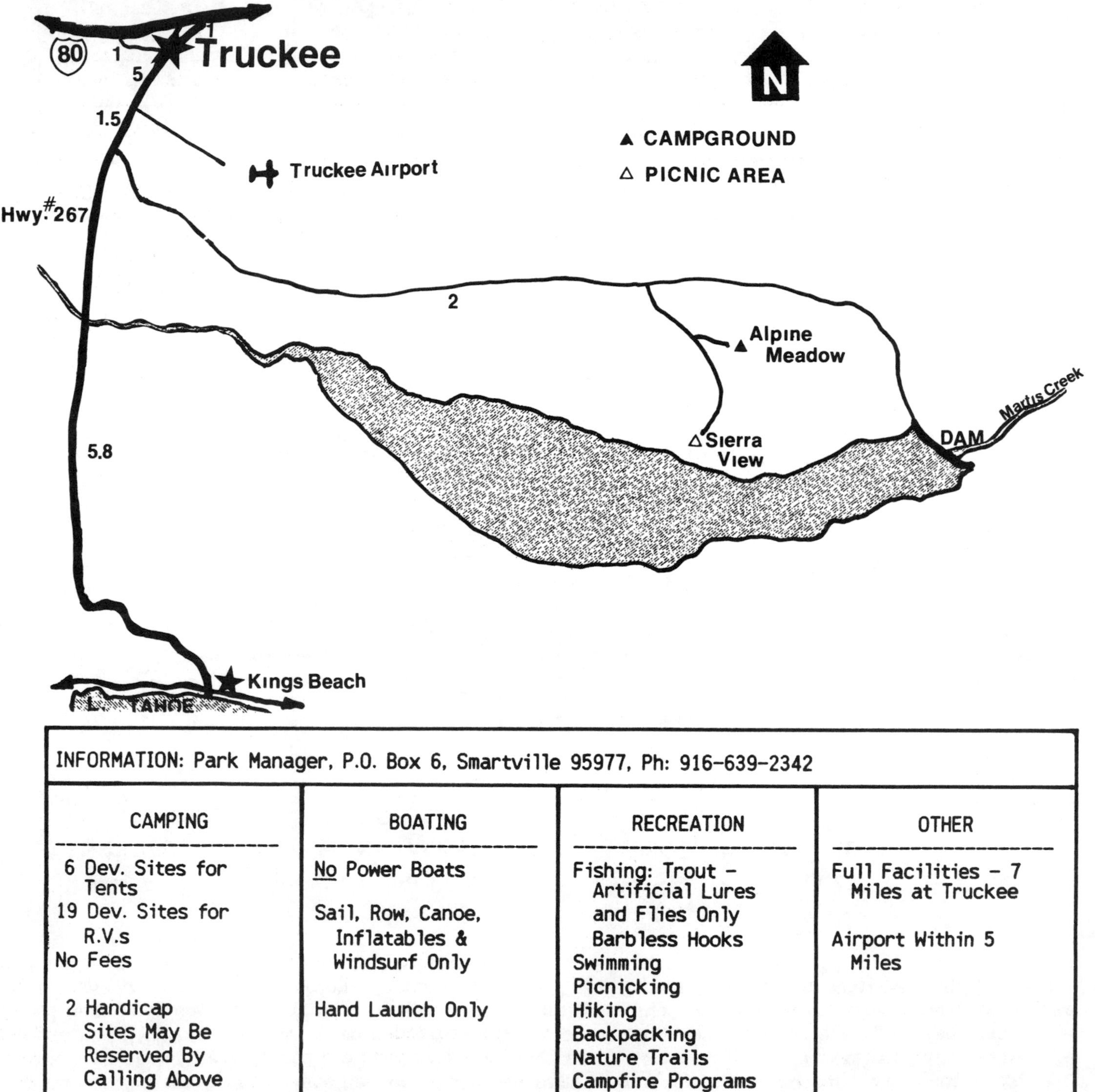

INFORMATION: Park Manager, P.O. Box 6, Smartville 95977, Ph: 916-639-2342

CAMPING	BOATING	RECREATION	OTHER
6 Dev. Sites for Tents 19 Dev. Sites for R.V.s No Fees 2 Handicap Sites May Be Reserved By Calling Above	No Power Boats Sail, Row, Canoe, Inflatables & Windsurf Only Hand Launch Only	Fishing: Trout - Artificial Lures and Flies Only Barbless Hooks Swimming Picnicking Hiking Backpacking Nature Trails Campfire Programs	Full Facilities - 7 Miles at Truckee Airport Within 5 Miles

COLLINS LAKE

The Collins Lake Recreation Area is at an elevation of 1,200 feet in the delightful Mother Lode Country. The Lake has a surface area of over 1,000 acres with 12-1/2 miles of shoreline. The modern campground and R.V. Park provide well-separated sites under oak and pine trees. There is a broad, sandy beach and many family and group picnic sites. All boating is allowed, but waterskiing is permitted only from May 15 through September 15 each year. One of the finest fishing Lakes in California, it is famous for trophy trout along with warm water species. There are zones for the exclusive use of fishermen throughout the year.

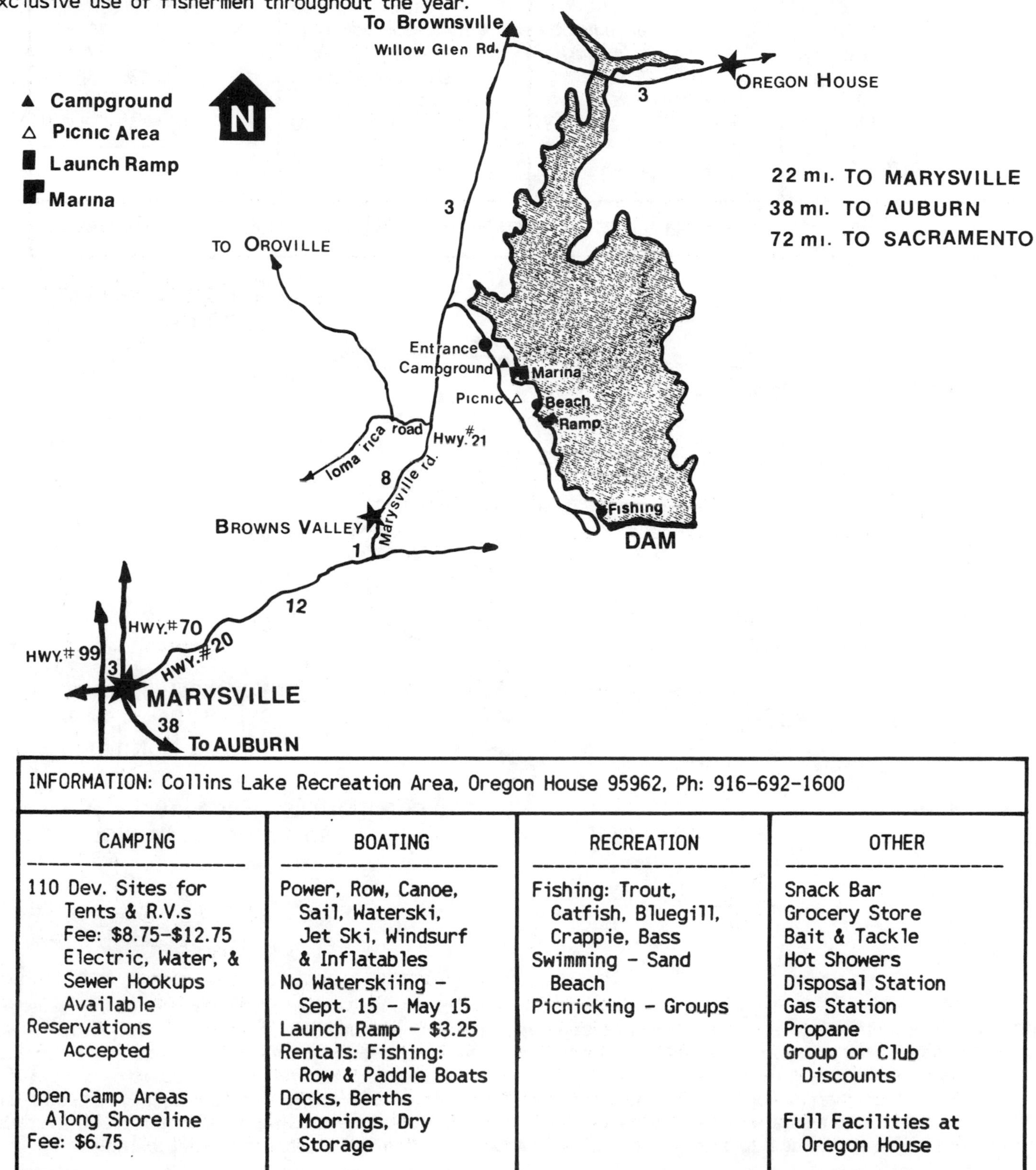

INFORMATION: Collins Lake Recreation Area, Oregon House 95962, Ph: 916-692-1600

CAMPING	BOATING	RECREATION	OTHER
110 Dev. Sites for Tents & R.V.s Fee: $8.75-$12.75 Electric, Water, & Sewer Hookups Available Reservations Accepted Open Camp Areas Along Shoreline Fee: $6.75	Power, Row, Canoe, Sail, Waterski, Jet Ski, Windsurf & Inflatables No Waterskiing - Sept. 15 - May 15 Launch Ramp - $3.25 Rentals: Fishing: Row & Paddle Boats Docks, Berths Moorings, Dry Storage	Fishing: Trout, Catfish, Bluegill, Crappie, Bass Swimming - Sand Beach Picnicking - Groups	Snack Bar Grocery Store Bait & Tackle Hot Showers Disposal Station Gas Station Propane Group or Club Discounts Full Facilities at Oregon House

ENGLEBRIGHT RESERVOIR

Englebright Reservoir is at an elevation of 527 feet northeast of Marysville. The Lake has a surface area of 815 acres with a shoreline of 24 miles that reaches 9 miles above the dam. Englebright is a boat camper's bonanza. Boats can be launched at Headquarters or at Joe Miller, or they can be rented at Skippers Cove. You can then proceed up the Lake to a campsite. The shoreline is steep and rocky except at the campgrounds where there are some sandy beaches with pine and oak trees above the high water line. This Reservoir remains full all year. Fishing is good in the quiet, narrow coves, and waterskiing is not allowed above Upper Boston.

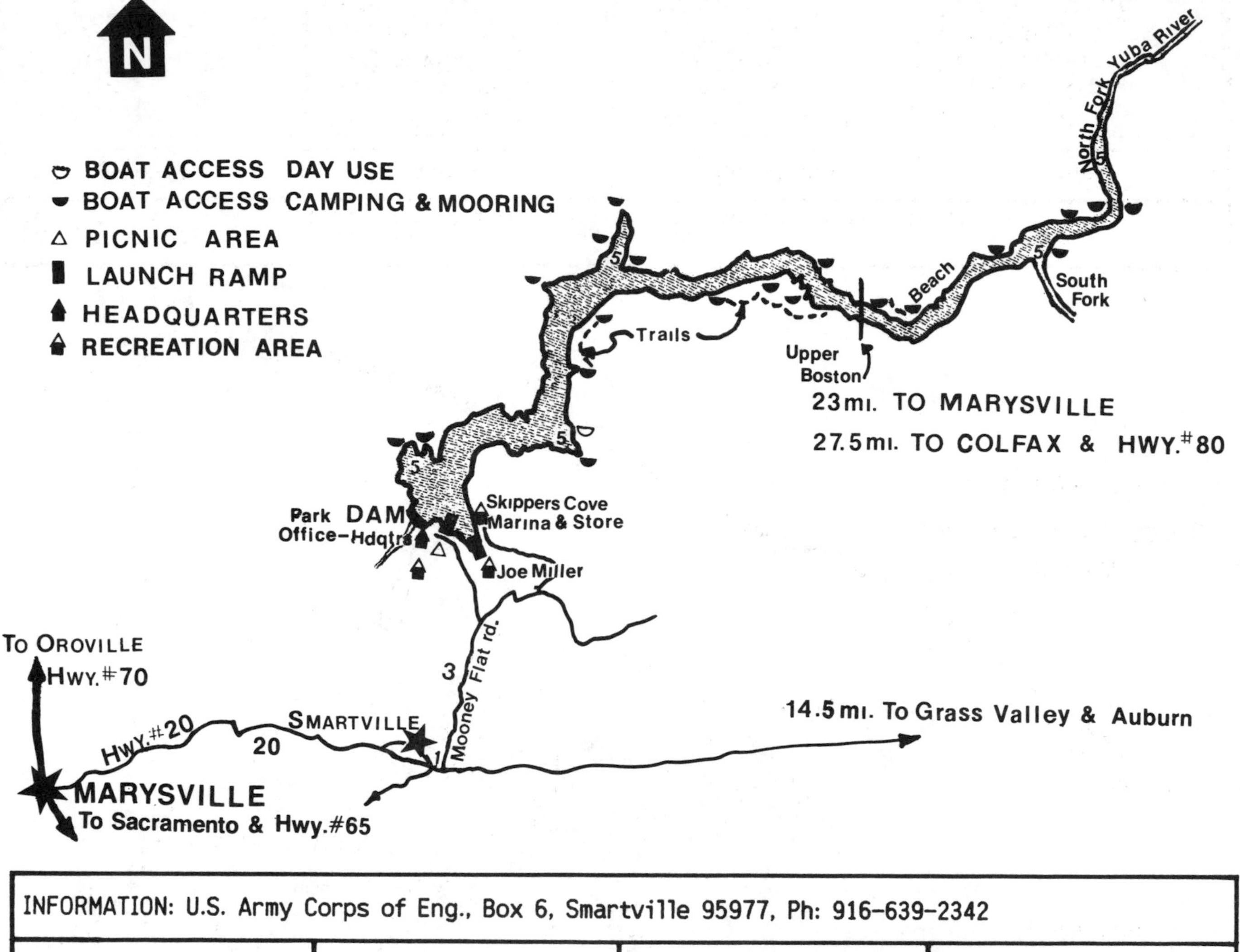

INFORMATION: U.S. Army Corps of Eng., Box 6, Smartville 95977, Ph: 916-639-2342

CAMPING	BOATING	RECREATION	OTHER
100 Plus Dev. Boat-In Sites No Fees	Power, Row, Canoe, Sail, Waterski, Jet Ski, Windsurf & Inflatables Full Service Marina Launch Ramps Rentals: Fishing, Canoe & Waterski Boats, Houseboats & Patio Boats Docks, Berths, Moorings, Gas	Fishing: Trout, Catfish, Bluegill & Bass Swimming Picnicking Hiking Campfire Programs Hunting: Deer & Turkey	Skippers Cove Marina P.O. Box 5 Smartville 95977 Ph: 916-639-2272 Grocery Store Hot Sandwiches Beer & Wine Gas - Propane Bait & Tackle

SCOTTS FLAT LAKE

Scotts Flat Lake is at an elevation of 3,100 feet at the gateway to the Tahoe National Forest. The Lake has a surface area of 850 acres with 7-1/2 miles of coniferous shoreline. This is a good boating Lake with two launch ramps and marina facilities. Fishing is good for trout and warm water fish. The Scotts Flat Campground is family oriented with modern campsites, a picnic area, sandy beaches and a store. This is a quiet, relaxing facility where nature provides a beautiful forested environment. Don't forget a camera.

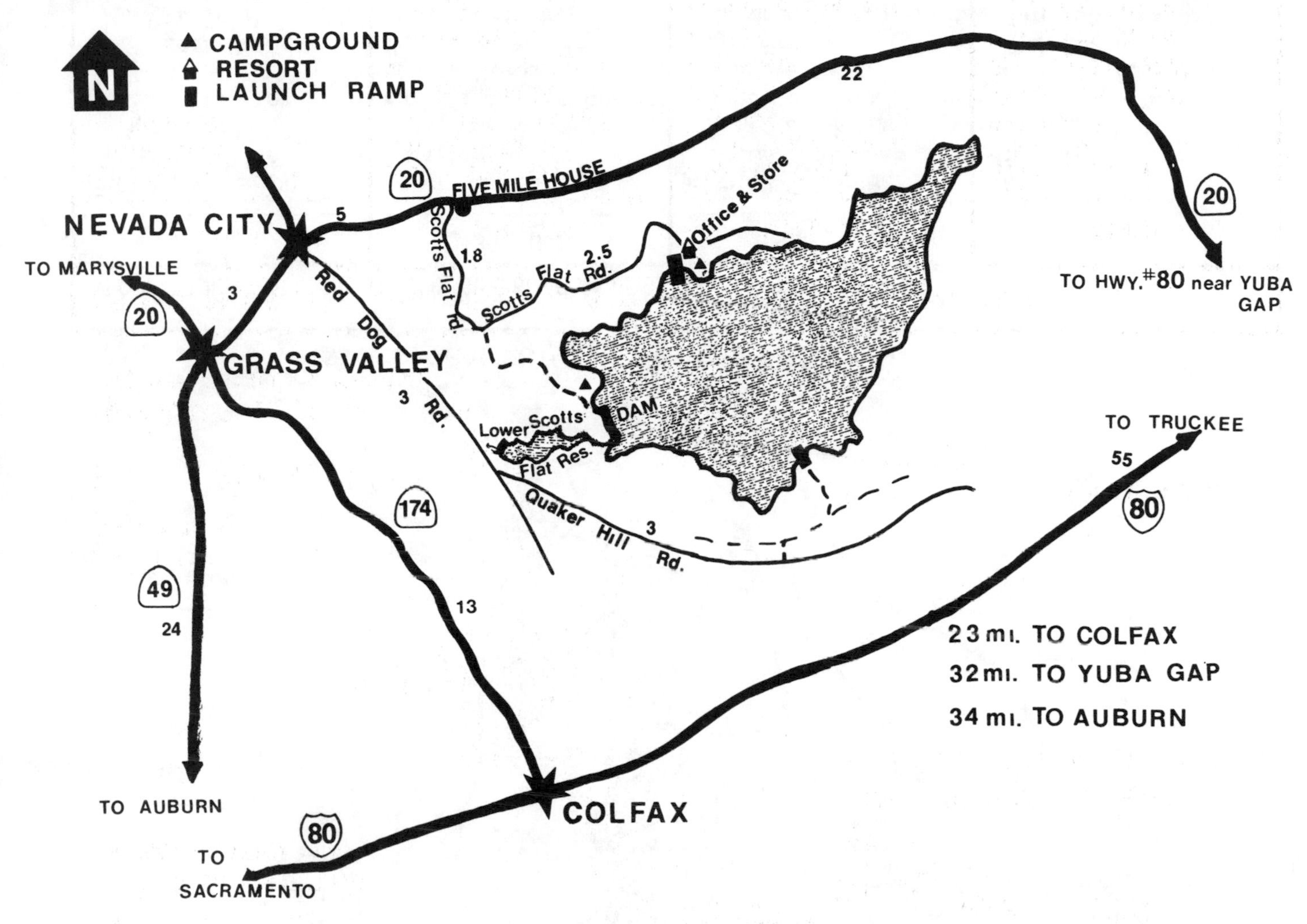

INFORMATION: Scotts Flat, 23333 Scotts Flat Rd., Nevada City 95959, Ph: 916-265-5302

CAMPING	BOATING	RECREATION	OTHER
20 Dev. Sites for Tents 165 Dev. Sites for R.V.s Fee: $7.50 Reservations Accepted	Power, Row, Canoe, Sail, Waterski & Inflatables Full Service Marina Launch Ramps Rentals: Fishing Boats & Pontoons Moorings & Dry Storage	Fishing: Rainbow & German Brown Trout, Large & Smallmouth Bass, Kokanee Swimming Picnicking Hiking Goldpanning No Motorbikes, Motorcycles or Horses	Coffee Shop Grocery Store Bait & Tackle Hot Showers Disposal Station Propane

ROLLINS LAKE

Rollins Lake is at an elevation of 2,100 feet in the Gold Country of the Western Sierras near Colfax. The Lake has a surface area of 900 acres with 26 miles of shoreline. The Rollins Lake Corporation maintains four nicely kept campgrounds around the oak and pine covered shoreline. Each campground has its own personality. Orchard Springs is for group camping. Greenhorn is popular for day use and offers campsites for individuals and large groups. Peninsula is the most remote, and Long Ravine is the most accessible. This is a good Lake for sailing and waterskiing with many coves and long stretches of open water. Fishing is good from both boat and shore for a wide variety of trout and warm water species.

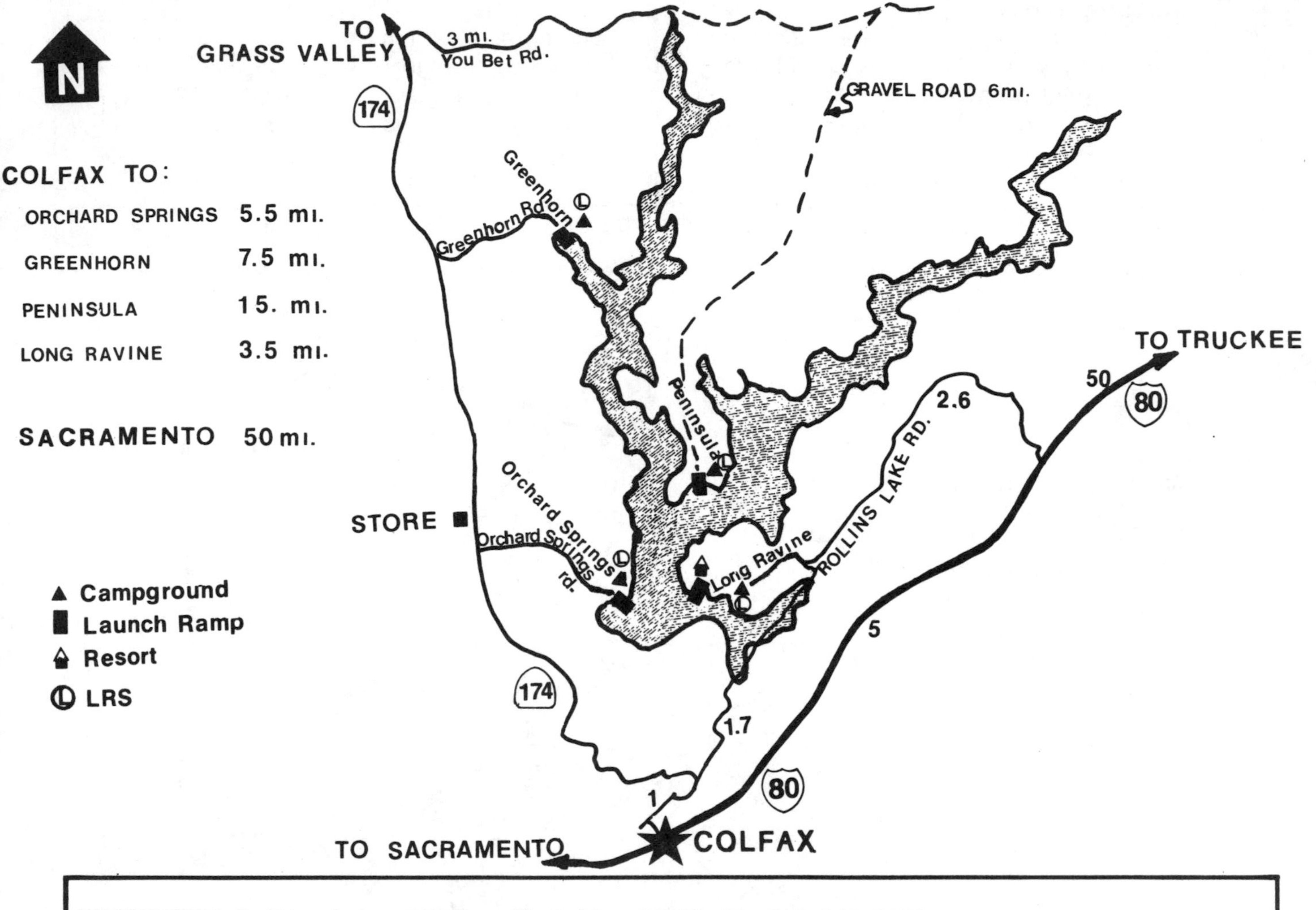

INFORMATION: Rollins Lake, P.O. Box 60, Colfax 95713, Ph: 916-346-6166			
CAMPING	**BOATING**	**RECREATION**	**OTHER**
250 Dev. Sites for Tents & R.V.s Fee: $8.50 Plus $1.50 for Pets 30 Boat In Sites R.V. & Trailer Storage Disposal Station	Power, Row, Canoe, Sail, Waterski, Jet Ski, Windsurf Full Service Marina Launch Ramps Houseboat Mooring Rentals: Fishing Boats with Motors, Canoes & Paddle Boats	Fishing: Rainbow, Brown, Cutthroat & Eagle Lake Trout, Sunfish, Crappie, Bass, Pan Fish & Kokanee Salmon Picnicking Swimming Hiking & Riding Trails	Snack Bar Mini-Mart Bait & Tackle Greenhorn Campground P.O. Box 364 Chicago Park 95712 Ph: 916-272-6100 or 916-272-3500

LAKE VALLEY RESERVOIR

KELLY LAKE

Lake Valley Reservoir is at 5,800 feet elevation. The shoreline is surrounded by tall trees and granite boulders with clear, cold water. The campsites are very pretty, situated under the trees near the Lake. Waterskiing is not allowed. The steep shoreline and steady west wind allows for good sailing. Coming out from Lake Valley to Highway 80, the second right turn goes into Kelly Lake. This is a small, lovely Lake well worth a day's outing, with 5 picnic sites, tables, firepits and toilets. Trout fishing can be excellent at both these High Sierra Lakes.

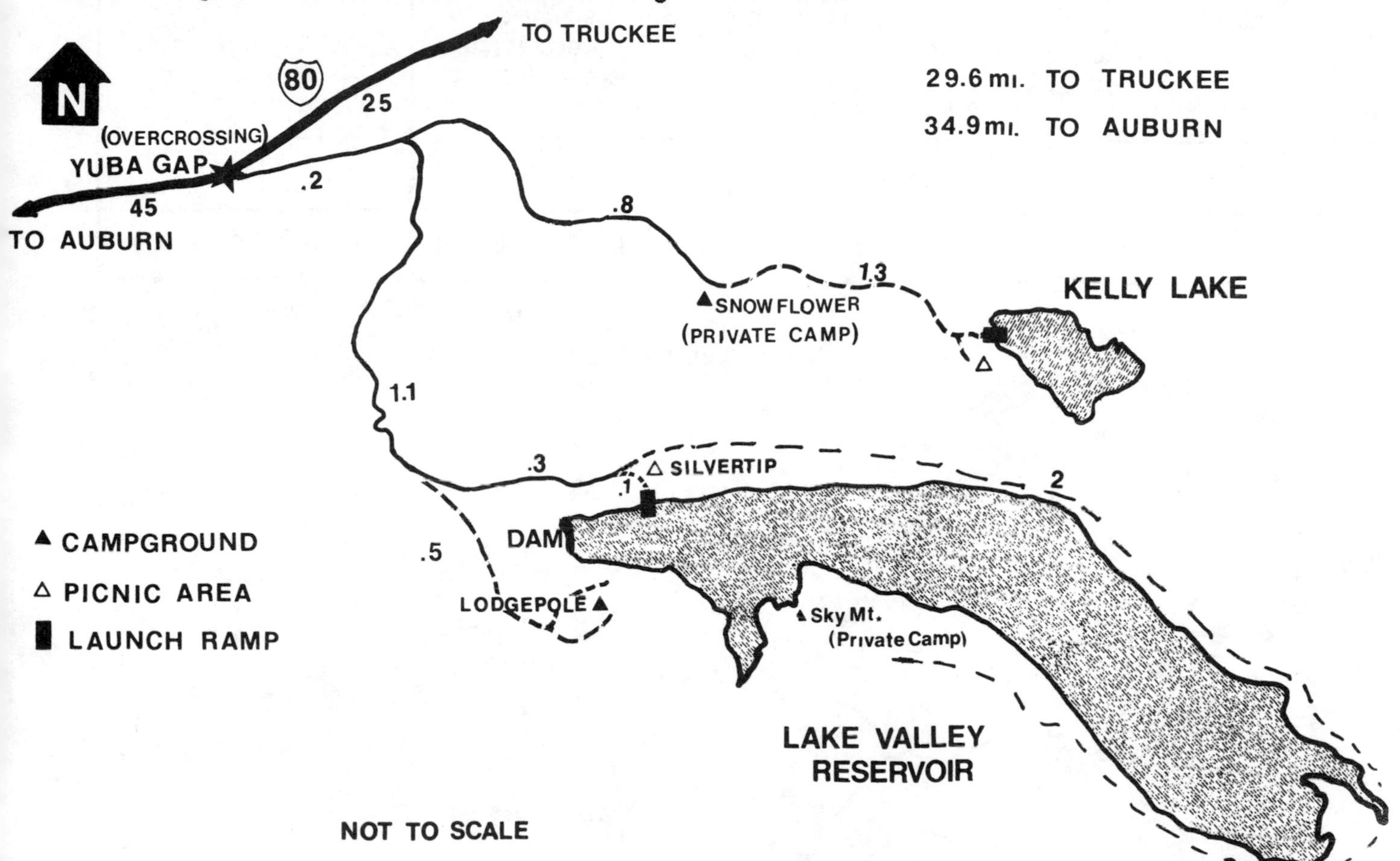

INFORMATION: P.G.&E, 333 Sacramento St., Auburn 95603, Ph: 916-885-2431 X230			
CAMPING	BOATING	RECREATION	OTHER
Lake Valley: 18 Dev. Sites for Tents & R.V.s to 20 feet Fee: $4 Kelly Lake: Day Use Only	Lake Valley: Fishing, Row, Canoe, Sail & Inflatables No Waterskiing Launch Ramp Kelly Lake: No Motors	Fishing: Rainbow & Brown Trout Swimming Picnicking Hiking	Full Facilities at Truckee

LAKE PILLSBURY

Lake Pillsbury is at an elevation of 1,818 feet in the Mendocino National Forest. The surface area of the Lake is 2,000 acres at high water, but the level lowers after Labor Day. All types of boating are allowed. The Lake Pillsbury Recreation Area offers a variety of recreation opportunities from hang gliding at Hull Mountain to horseback riding in the Bloody Rock Area. Fishing in the Lake for trout can be rewarding, and Pogie Point is popular for its "Pogie" or sunfish. The Eel River and its tributaries provide trout and salmon.

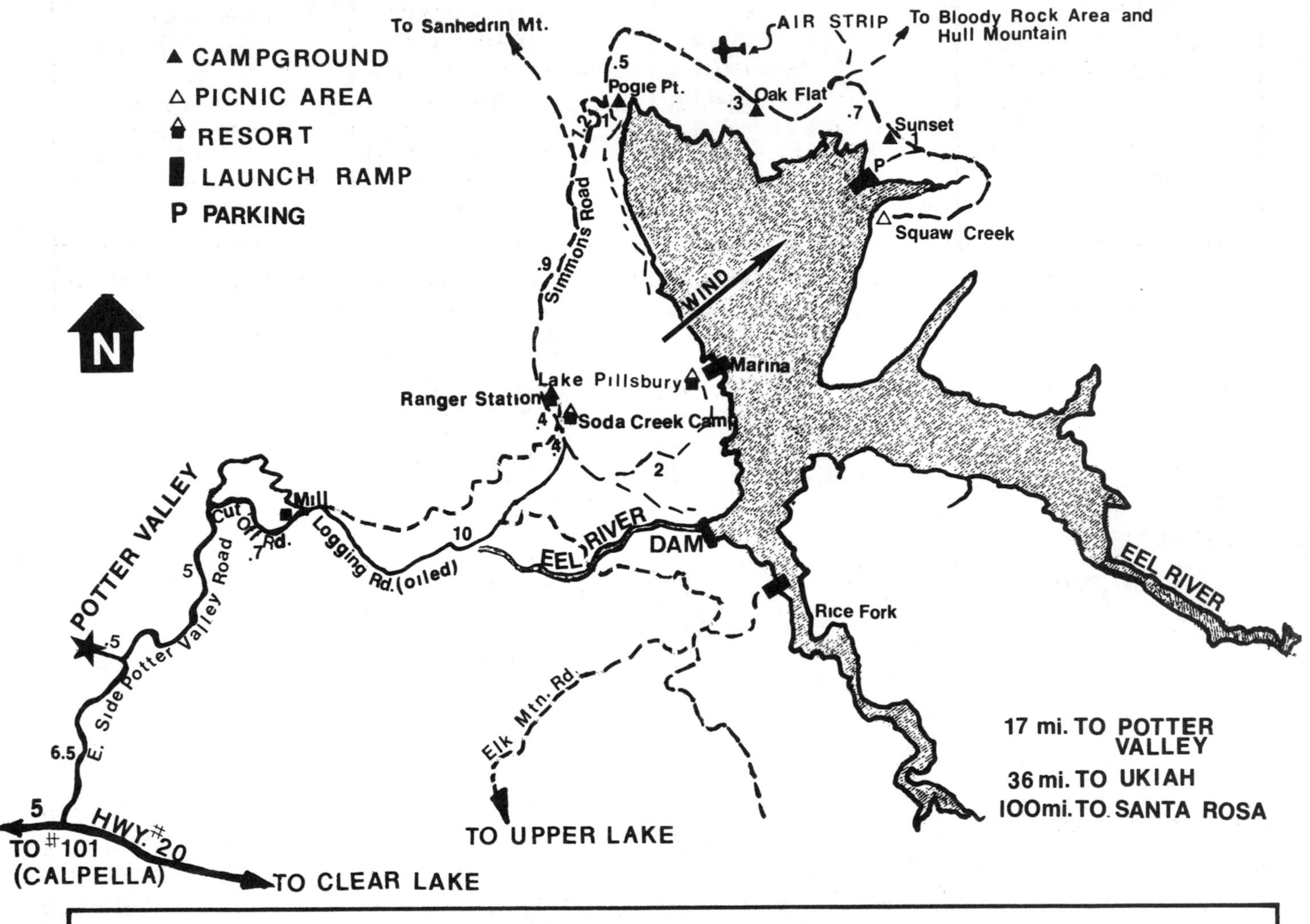

INFORMATION: U.S.F.S., P.O. Box 96, Upper Lake 95485, Ph: 707-275-2361

CAMPING	BOATING	RECREATION	OTHER
115 Dev. Sites for Tents & R.V.s Fee: $5 Additional Sites at 2 Private Resorts Overnight on Boat in Designated Areas	Power, Row, Canoe, Sail, Waterski & Inflatable Launch Ramps Rentals: Fishing, Canoes & Pontoon Boats Marina Supplies	Fishing: Rainbow & Brown Trout, Sunfish, Salmon Swimming Picnicking Hiking Backpacking Horseback Riding Trails ORV's Designated Trails Only	Lake Pillsbury Resort Ph: 707-743-1581 Soda Creek Camp Ph: 707-743-1593 Snack Bars Restaurant Grocery Store Bait & Tackle Gas Station

LAKE MENDOCINO

Lake Mendocino is at an elevation of 748 feet above Coyote Dam on the East Fork of the Russian River. This is wine country with many small valleys of vineyards and pear trees. The Lake has a surface area of 1,740 acres with 15 miles of oak-wooded shoreline. The U.S. Army Corps of Engineers maintain the quality facilities which include numerous campsites, picnic sites and 7 group picnic shelters each with a massive stone barbecue pit. The boater will find two large launch ramps, a marina concession and a large protected swim beach. There is a 5-kilometer hiking trail and several smaller interpretive trails and an Interpretive Cultural Center. The fishing is good with Channel Catfish going to 30 pounds and Stripers to 40 pounds.

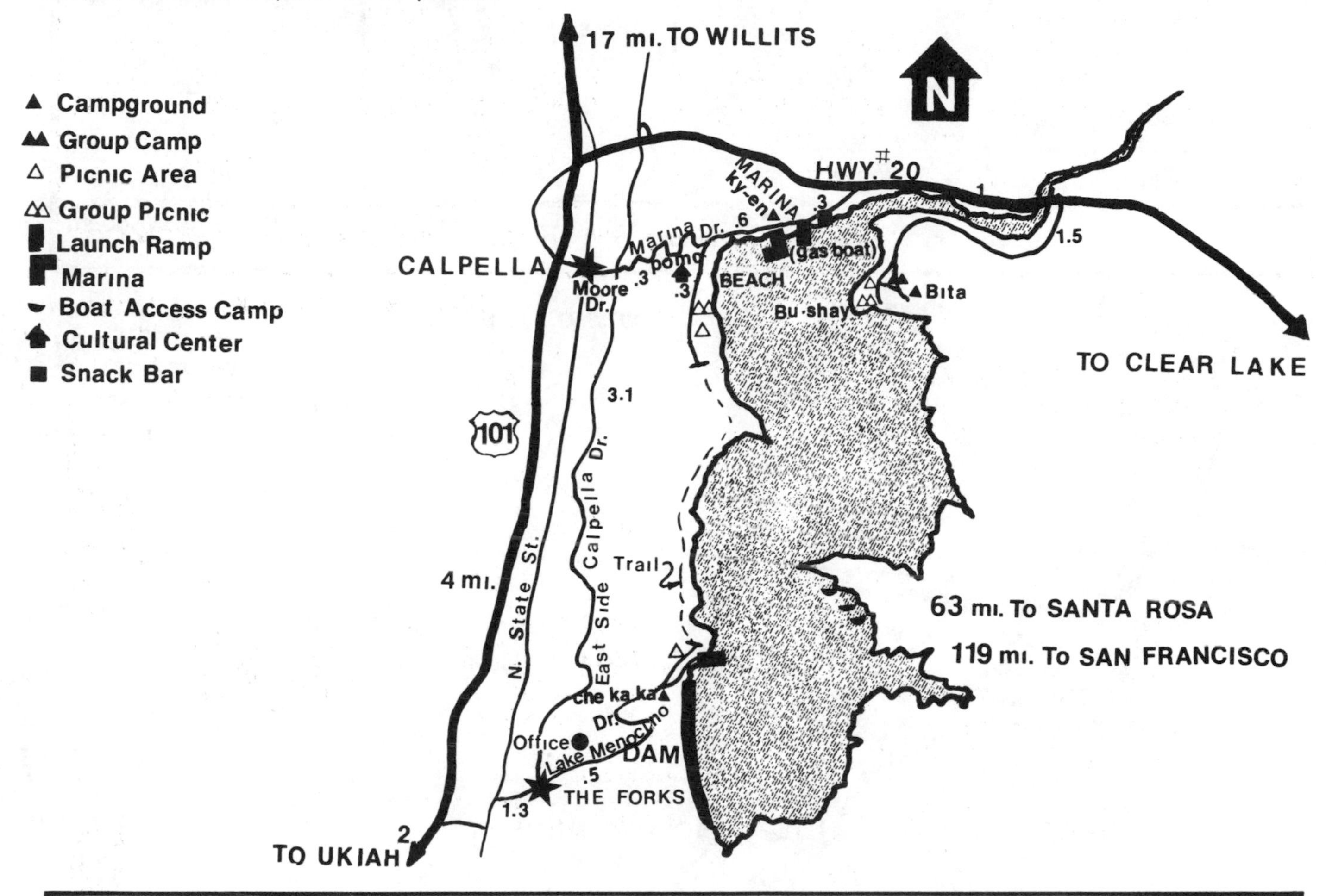

INFORMATION: Park Manager, 1160 Lake Mendocino Dr., Ukiah 95482, Ph: 707-462-7581			
CAMPING	BOATING	RECREATION	OTHER
320 Dev. Sites for Tents & R.V.s Fee: $4 3 Group Camps By Reservation 165 People Maximum 16 Boat Access Only Sites	Power, Row, Canoe, Sail, Waterski & Inflatables Full Service Marina Launch Ramps Rentals: Fishing, Power, Canoe, Waterski & Pontoon Docks, Berths Dry Storage, Gas	Fishing: Catfish, Bluegill, Crappie Large, Smallmouth & Striped Bass Swimming Picnicking Hiking Junior Ranger & Interpretive Programs Hunting: Waterfowl	Lake Mendocino Marina P.O. Box 13 Calpella 95418 Ph: 707-485-8644 (Off Highway 20 at North End) Snack Bar Mini-Market Beer, Wine, Ice

BLUE LAKES – LAKE COUNTY

The Blue Lakes are at an elevation of 1,400 feet located between Clear Lake and Lake Mendocino. These small spring-fed Lakes, which have been in existence for 10,000 years, rest in a beautiful setting of wooded hills and open fields. The clear, blue waters make this a delightful retreat for fishing, swimming, sailing or just plain relaxing. The private Resorts surrounding the Lakes offer complete vacation facilities, including restaurants and lounges, rental boats, swim beaches, picnic areas and shaded campsites.

. . . Continued . . .

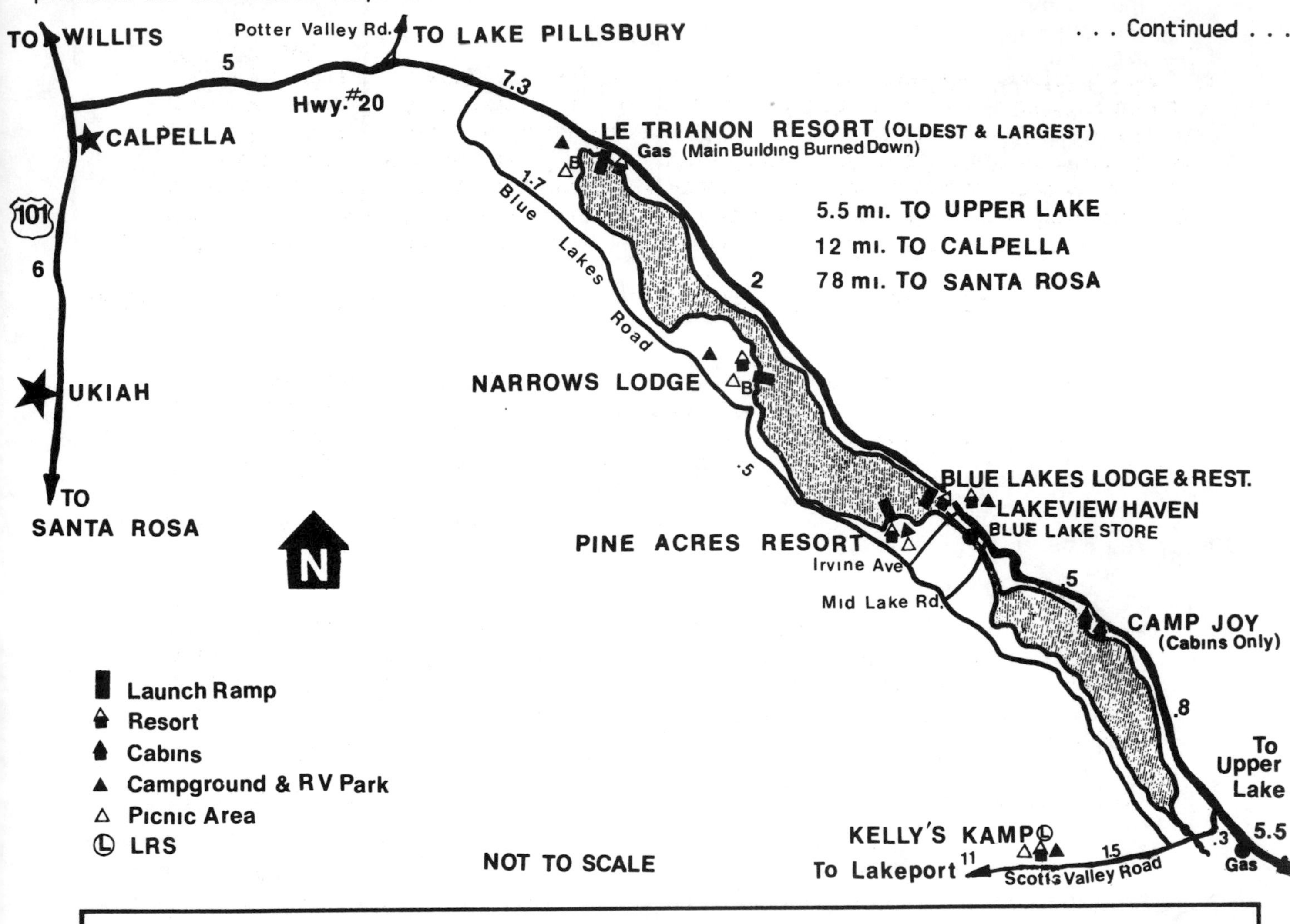

INFORMATION: Contact Individual Resorts - See Following Page

CAMPING	BOATING	RECREATION	OTHER
At Private Resorts: Sites for Tents & R.V.s See Following Page	Power, Row, Canoe, Sail, Windsurf & Inflatables 12 MPH Speed Limit Launch Ramps Rentals: Fishing & Row Boats, Paddle- boats Docks	Fishing: Trout, Catfish, Bluegill & Largemouth Bass Swimming - Beaches Picnicking Hiking	See Following Page

LE TRIANON RESORT: W. Upper Lake Hwy, Upper Lake 95485, Ph: 707-275-2262

Le Trianon Resort offers housekeeping cabins as well as nice areas for tent camping, R.V.s or trailers with 400 picnic tables, electricity, water, toilets and showers. There is a launch ramp, dock swim area and boat rentals along with R.V. storage.

NARROWS LODGE: 5690 Blue Lakes Road, Upper Lake 95485, Ph: 707-275-2718

The Narrows Lodge Resort provides all the comforts of modern conveniences in a lovely tree-studded setting. There are fully equipped housekeeping cabins and motel units. The R.V. Park has 20 sites with complete hookups. Tent sites are also available. The Resort has a launch ramp, fishing dock and swim area. Rowboats and paddleboats can be rented. The Dinner House serves excellent meals and cocktails with piano bar entertainment on Saturday nights. By the way, gnats and mosquitos stay away from this lovely area.

PINE ACRES RESORT: 5328 Blue Lakes Road (off Irvine Ave.), Upper Lake 95485, Ph: 707-275-2811

Pine Acres Resort offers a motel and fully equipped cabins with daily maid service. Complete hookups in R.V. and trailer spaces, including cable T.V. throughout are available. There are shaded lawns, BBQs, picnic tables, horseshoe court, campfire area, swimming beach with float, fishing pier, launch ramp, boat rentals and a bait and tackle shop. A gazebo has been built for pot lucks, square dancing, conferences and other uses.

BLUE LAKES LODGE: 5315 W. Highway 20, Upper Lake 95485, Ph: 707-275-2178

This Resort has a motel with housekeeping units with T.V.s and air conditioning as well as a restaurant and cocktail bar open year round. Live entertainment and dancing is available on weekends. There is a launch ramp, fishing dock, swim area and boat rentals also. A swimming pool and jacuzzi complete this full facility Resort.

KELLY'S KAMP: 8220 Scotts Valley Road, Upper Lake 95485, Ph: 707-263-5754

Kelly's Kamp offers quiet family camping on spacious sites with frontage on Scotts Creek. There are 30 tent sites and 48 R.V. sites with water and electric hookups. Also offered are Kamp Store, modern restrooms, laundromat, disposal station, hot showers, firewood, picnic tables and BBQ grills. Recreational facilities include swimming, 2-acre Lake with floats, fishing, volleyball, badminton, croquet, horseshoes, hiking and planned group activities. R.V. storage is available, and a pavilion area with a built-in barbecue for large groups. Reservations may be made through Leisuretime Reservation Systems, Ph: 800-822-CAMP.

CLEAR LAKE

Clear Lake, at an elevation of 1,326 feet, is the largest natural Lake in California. It has a surface area of 43,000 acres. The Lake's shoreline of 100 miles has been the same for thousands of years. The water level remains constant. This was once the home of the Pomo and Lile'ek tribes who were drawn here by the abundant fish and game. Often called "The Bass Capital of the West", Clear Lake provides the angler with a productive warm water fishery. Miles of open water, many coves and inlets entice the boater, waterskiier and sailor. Numerous launch ramps, marinas, beaches, campgrounds and resorts dot the shoreline. Clear Lake State Park has a nice campground, swim beach, hiking trails and a naturalist program.

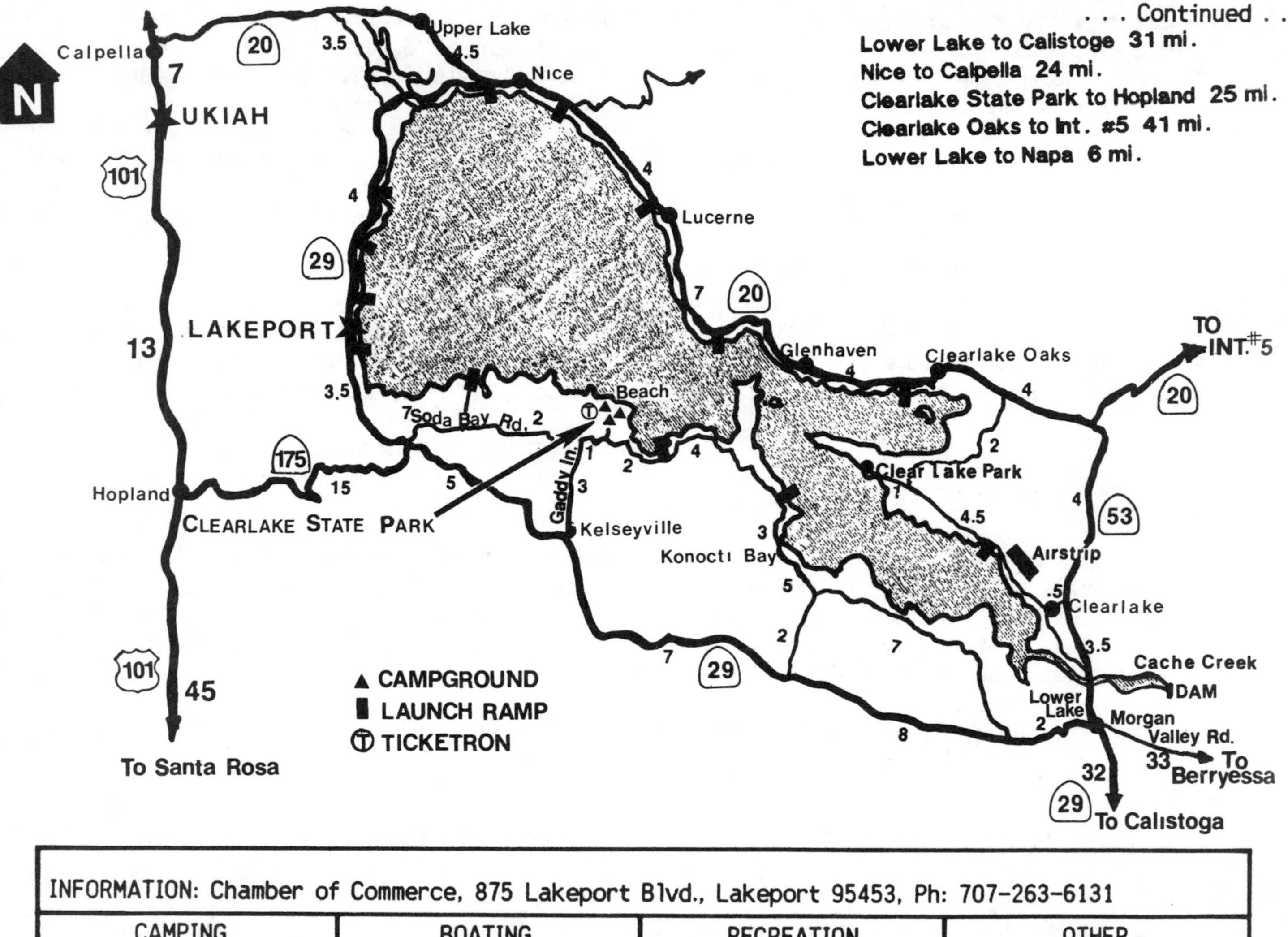

INFORMATION: Chamber of Commerce, 875 Lakeport Blvd., Lakeport 95453, Ph: 707-263-6131

CAMPING	BOATING	RECREATION	OTHER
58 Private Campgrounds Contact: Chamber of Commerce for Information Clear Lake State Park 5300 Soda Bay Rd. Kelseyville 95451 Ph: 707-279-4293 147 Dev. Sites for Tents & R.V.s Fee: $6	Open to All Boating Launch Ramps Full Service Marinas Boat Rentals	Fishing: Black Bass, Bluegill, Crappie & Catfish Picnicking & Swimming Hiking Nature Study Golf Hunting in Nearby National Forest: Deer, Dove, Quail & Waterfowl	Complete Resort Facilities Around Lake

The following is a partial list of Resorts around Clear Lake in counter-clockwise order. Contact the Chamber of Commerce for full details and other Resorts.

SHAW'S SHADY ACRES, 7805 Highway 53, Lower Lake, Ph: 707-994-2236: Camping, R.V.s & Trailers, Store, Launch Ramp.

GARNER'S RESORT, 6235 Old Highway 53, Clearlake, Ph: 707-994-6267: Camping, R.V.s, Full Hookups, Berths, Storage, Marina, Boat Rentals.

LAMPLIGHTER MOTEL, 14165 Lakeshore Dr., Clearlake, Ph: 707-994-2129: Kitchens available, Pool, Restaurant & Lounge, Boat Dock.

SHIP N SHORE RESORT, 13885 Lakeshore Dr., Clearlake, Ph: 707-994-6672: Housekeeping Cottages, Pool, Game Room, Full Service Marina, Launch Ramp, Gas, Beach.

TAMARACK LODGE, 13825 Lakeshore Dr., Clearlake, Ph: 707-994-6660: Cottages, Launch Ramp, Berths, Beach.

LAKE HAVEN MOTEL, 100 Short St., Clearlake Oaks, Ph: 707-998-3908: Housekeeping Cottages, Motel, Pool, Docks, Fishing Pier, Rental Boats.

SUNSET POINT RESORT, 12037 E. Highway 20, Clearlake Oaks, Ph: 707-998-9933: R.V. Park, Restaurant, Docks, Propane.

LAKE MARINA MOTEL, 10215 E. Highway 20, Clearlake Oaks, Ph: 707-998-3787: Units with Kitchenettes, Launch Ramp, Berths, Fishing Pier and Dock.

TIKI TIKI R.V. PARK, 3967 E. Highway 20, Nice, Ph: 707-274-2576: Full Hookups, Laundromat, Disposal Station, Launch Ramp, Dock.

HOLIDAY HARBOR R.V. PARK, 3605 Lakeshore Blvd., Nice, Ph: 707-274-1136: Full Hookups, Laundromat, Disposal Station, Launch Ramp, Dock.

SKYLARK MOTEL, 1120 Main, Lakeport, Ph: 707-263-6151: Units on Water, Launch Ramp.

CLEARLAKE INN, 1010 N. Main, Lakeport, Ph: 707-263-3551: Motel, Pool, Pier, Dock.

ANCHORAGE INN, 950 N. Main, Lakeport, Ph: 707-263-5417: Units, Kitchens, Pool, Dock.

WILL-O-POINT RESORT, One 1st, Lakeport, Ph: 707-263-5407: Camping, R.V. Hookups, Housekeeping Cabins, Restaurant, Store, Launch Ramp, Boat Rentals.

FERNDALE RESORT, 6190 Soda Bay Rd., Kelseyville, Ph: 707-279-4866: Motel, Marina, Gas.

BELL HAVEN RESORT, 3415 White Oak Way, Kelseyville, Ph: 707-279-4329: Cabins, Pier, Beach.

KONOCTI HARBOR INN, 8727 Soda Bay Rd., Kelseyville, Ph: 707-279-4281: Deluxe Rooms, Kitchens, Convention Facilities, Pools, Resort Facilities.

INDIAN VALLEY RESERVOIR

Indian Valley Reservoir is under the jurisdiction of the Yolo County Flood Control District. Resting at an elevation of 1,476 feet, this remote 3,800 acre Lake has 39 shoreline miles. The Lake is an excellent rainbow trout fishery and a developing warm water fishery. Since there is a 10 MPH speed limit, this is a delightfully quiet place for sailing, canoeing and fishing. The crystal clear warm water makes for pleasant swimming. The concession at Indian Valley Store operates a newly developed campground. The area surrounding the Reservoir is an important wintering area for both bald and golden eagles and waterfowl. There is a public launch ramp and an unimproved camping on the North Shore.

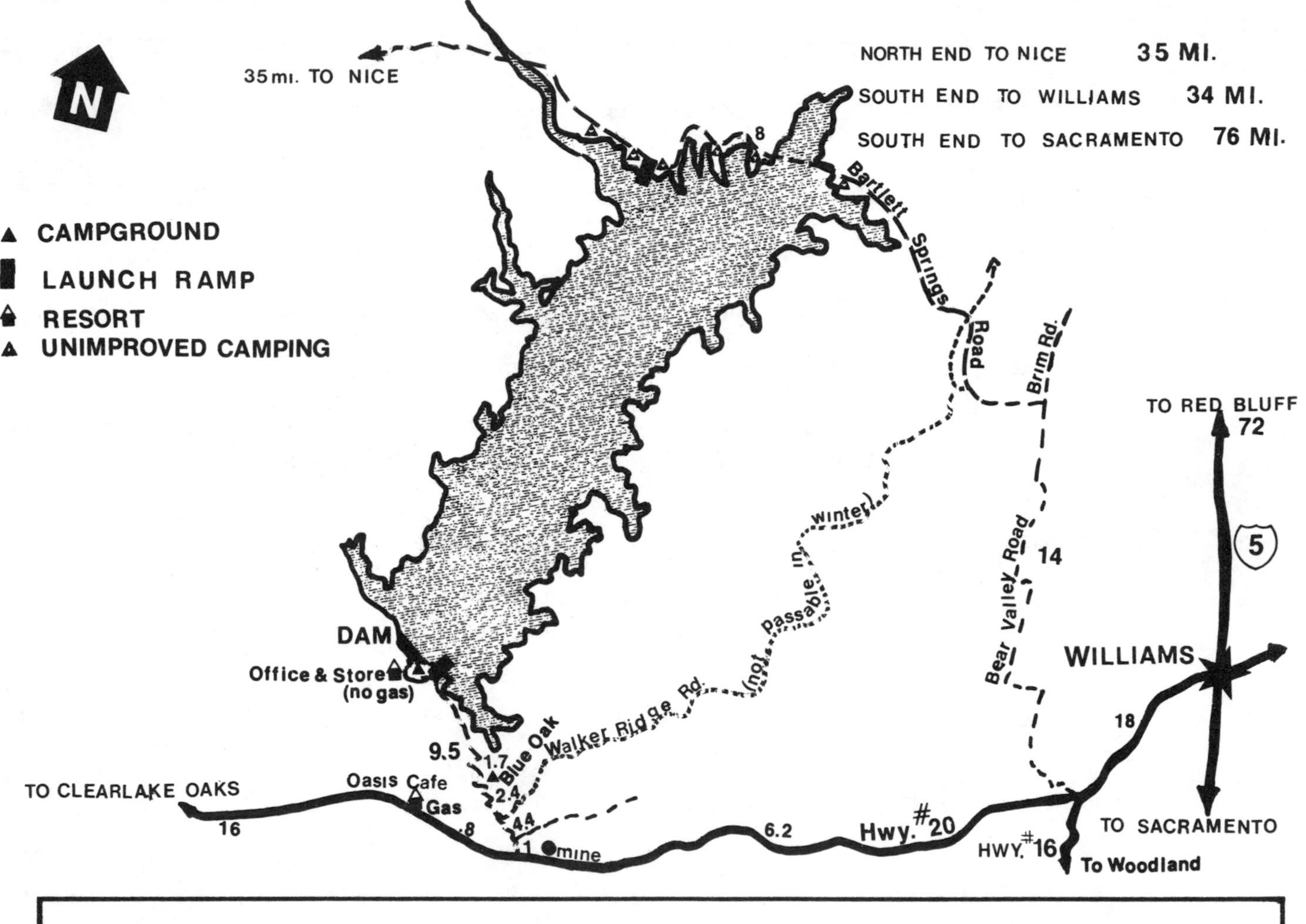

INFORMATION: Indian Valley Store, P.O. Box 4939, Clear Lake 95422, Ph: 916-662-0607

CAMPING	BOATING	RECREATION	OTHER
20 Dev. Sites for Tents 50 Dev. Sites for R.V.s Fee: $5 Disposal Station Hot Showers Day Use Fee: $2	Open to All Boating 10 MPH Speed Limit Paved Launch Ramp Rentals: Fishing Boats and Motors	Fishing: Rainbow Trout, Large & Smallmouth Bass, Catfish & Redear Perch Picnicking & Swimming Hiking Birding Nature Study Hunting: Waterfowl, Quail, Dove, Turkey, Pigs & Bear	Grocery Store Bait & Tackle Propane Gas Oasis Cafe: Restaurant Gas Station

CENTRAL SECTION

LAKES 59 - 147

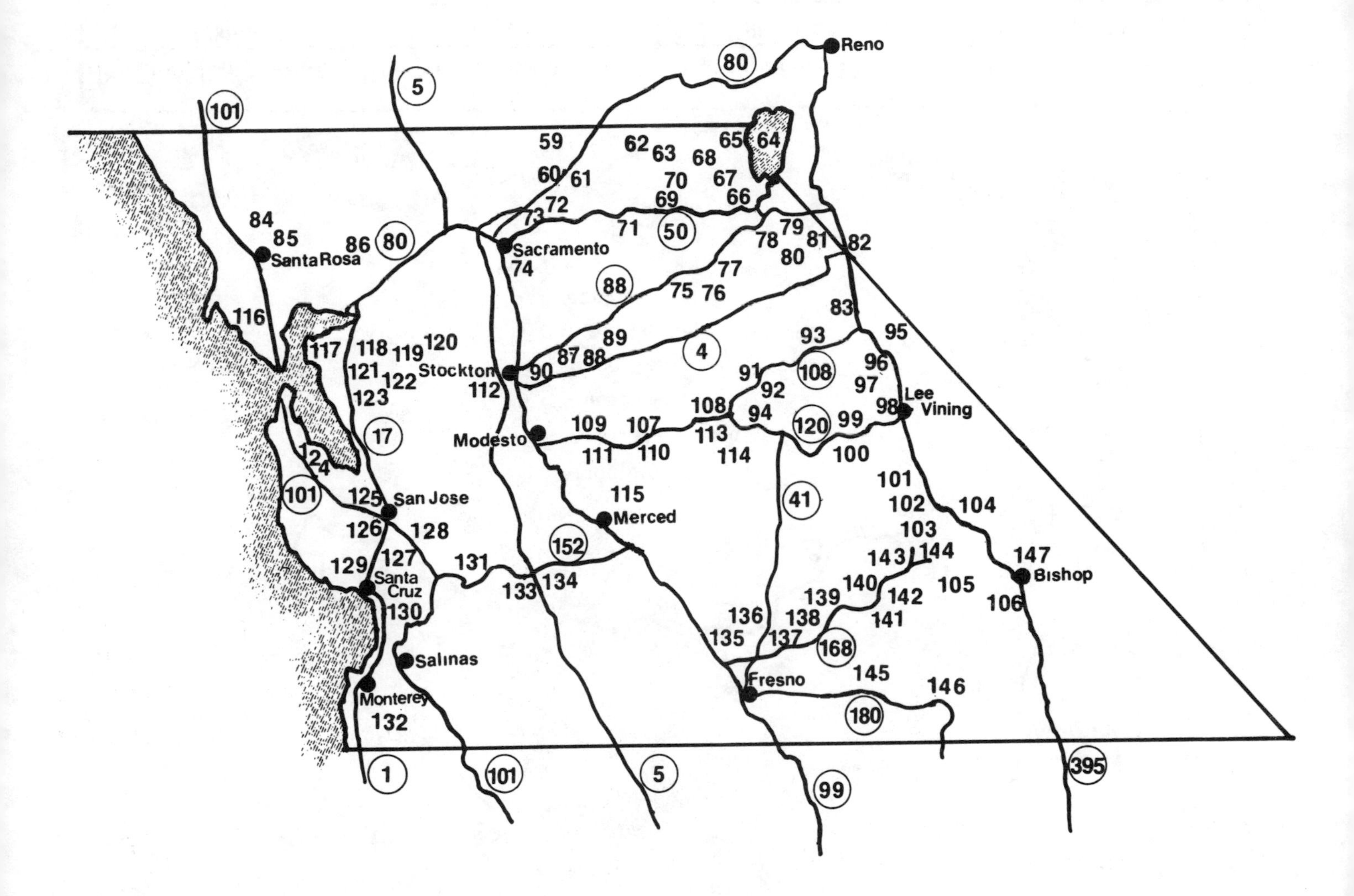

NUMBERS REPRESENT LAKES IN NUMERICAL ORDER IN BOOK

SUGAR PINE AND BIG RESERVOIRS

Sugar Pine Reservoir is at an elevation of 3,500 feet in the Tahoe National Forest. This 160 surface acre Lake is administered by the U. S. Forest Service. The recently completed recreation complex has been designed to accommodate wheelchairs. The campsites will allow for trailers to 30 feet. Big Reservoir, also called Morning Star Lake, rests at an elevation of 4,042 feet in a heavily wooded forest. The facilities of this 70 acre Lake are under the concession of Morning Star Lake Resort. These Lakes are open to boating, subject to the restrictions listed below. The angler will find a good trout and warm water fishery. There are nice swimming beaches and numerous trails for the hiker.

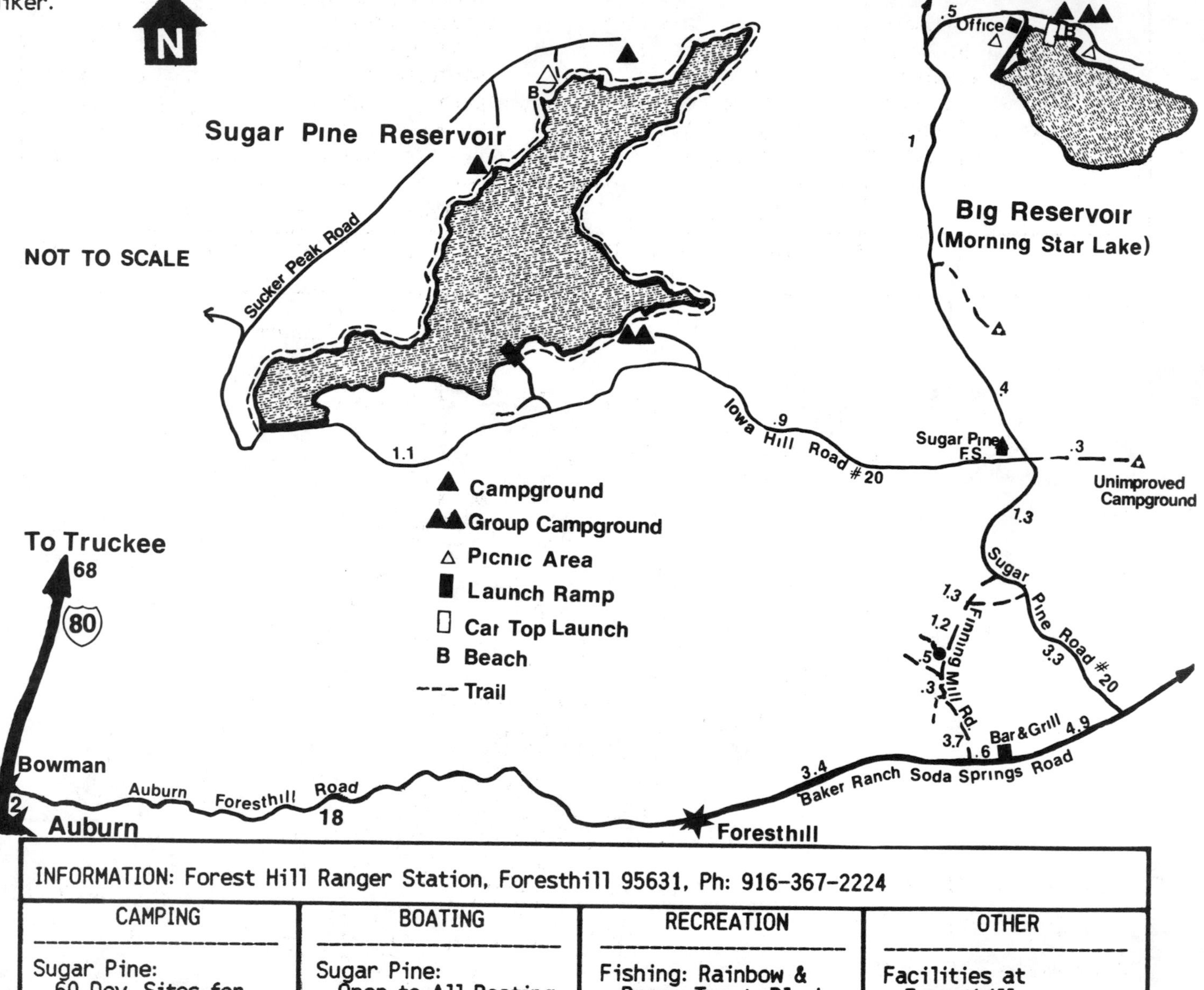

INFORMATION: Forest Hill Ranger Station, Foresthill 95631, Ph: 916-367-2224

CAMPING	BOATING	RECREATION	OTHER
Sugar Pine: 60 Dev. Sites for Tents & R.V.s Fee: $6 2 Group Sites by Reservation Disposal Station Big (Morning Star) 135 Dev. Sites for Tents & R.V.s Fee: $8 2 Group Sites	Sugar Pine: Open to All Boating 10 MPH Speed Limit Launch Ramp No Motor Size Limit Big: Open to Non-Powered Electric Motors Permitted Car Top Launch	Fishing: Rainbow & Brown Trout, Black Bass, Bluegill & Perch Picnicking Paved & Unpaved Trails Swimming Hiking & Backpacking ORV Trails Hunting: Deer & Bear	Facilities at Foresthill Morning Star Lake Resort P.O. Box 119 Foresthill 95631 Ph: 916-367-2129

CAMP FAR WEST LAKE

Camp Far West Lake is at an elevation of 320 feet in the Sierra foothills northeast of Roseville. The Lake has a surface area of 2,000 acres with a shoreline of 29 miles. The water temperature rises up to 85 degrees in the summer when the climate can be quite hot although there are many oak trees providing ample shade. The Lake is open year around, but the north entrance is closed at the end of summer. This is a good Lake for all types of boating and waterskiing, but the boater should be aware of the rocky area as noted on the map. The water level normally is low in late summer. This is a warm water fishery especially for Landlocked Stripers, Smallmouth and Black Bass at Bear River and Rock Creek areas.

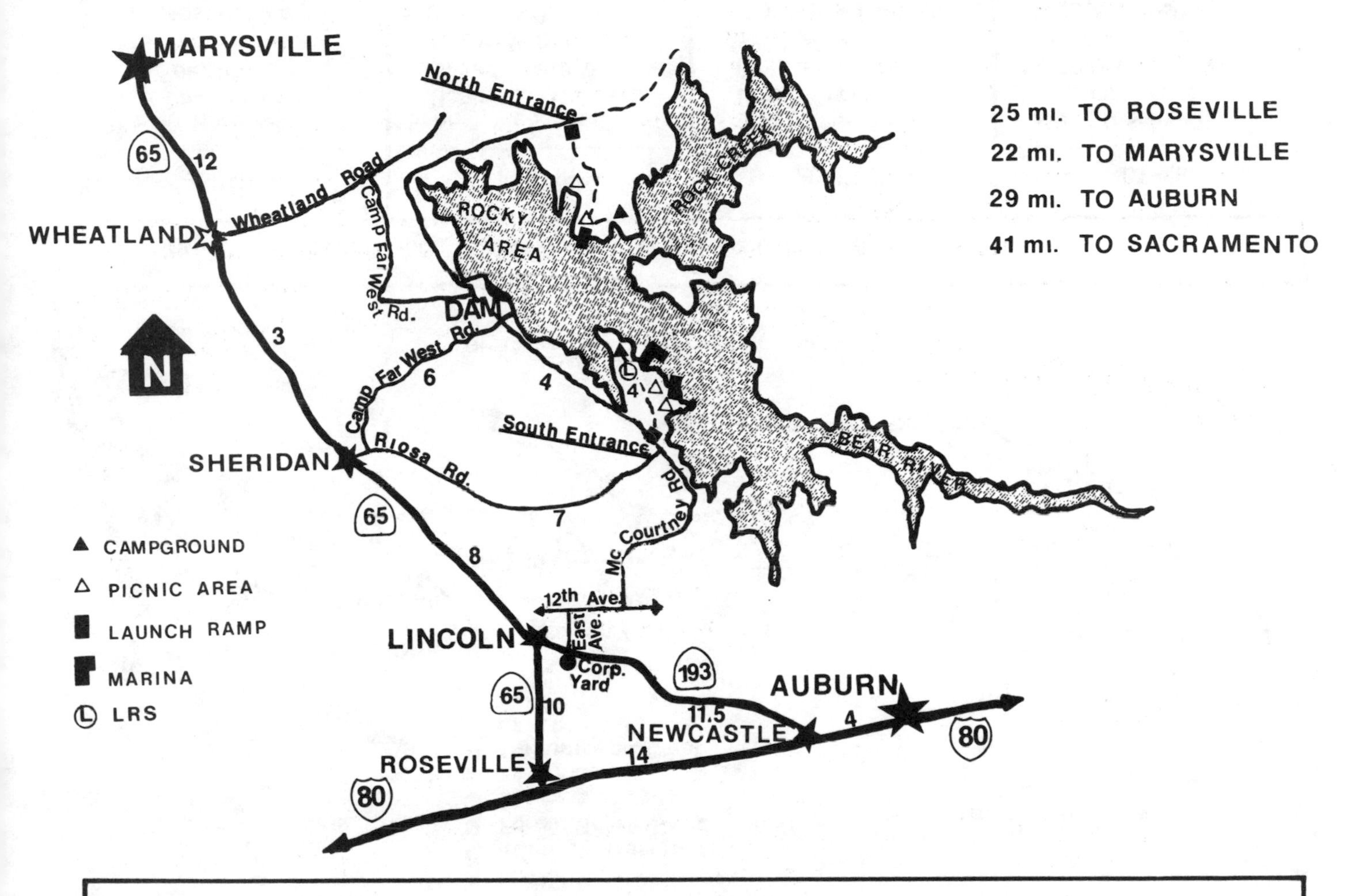

INFORMATION: Camp Far West, P.O. Box 128, Lincoln 95648, Ph: 916-645-8069

CAMPING	BOATING	RECREATION	OTHER
135 Dev. Sites for Tents & R.V.s Fees: $7.50 $10.50 Full Hook-up Overflow Area Group Camp - 50 to 200 People Reservations Accepted	Power, Row, Canoe, Sail, Waterski, Jet Ski, Windsurf & Inflatables Launch Ramps Rentals: Fishing Boats & Canoes Docks, Moorings Gas, Dry Storage	Fishing: Trout, Catfish, Sunfish, Crappie, Black, Smallmouth & Striped Bass Swimming Picnicking Hiking Waterskiing	Snack Bar Grocery Store Bait & Tackle Disposal Stations Propane Game Room

FRENCH MEADOWS RESERVOIR AND LAKE CLEMENTINE

French Meadows Reservoir, administered by the U.S. Forest Service, rests at an elevation of 5,200 feet on the Western slope of the Sierra Nevadas. This man-made Reservoir of 1,920 surface acres is subject to very low water levels in September and October. Although open to all types of boating, there are underwater hazards such as stumps and rocks which prohibit safe speed boating and waterskiing. There is an excellent trout fishery. Lake Clementine is a unit of the California State Park System. This 3-1/2 mile long Lake is open to all boating, and the angler will find a fair warm water fishery in addition to rainbow trout. Swimming areas and beaches are at both Lakes.

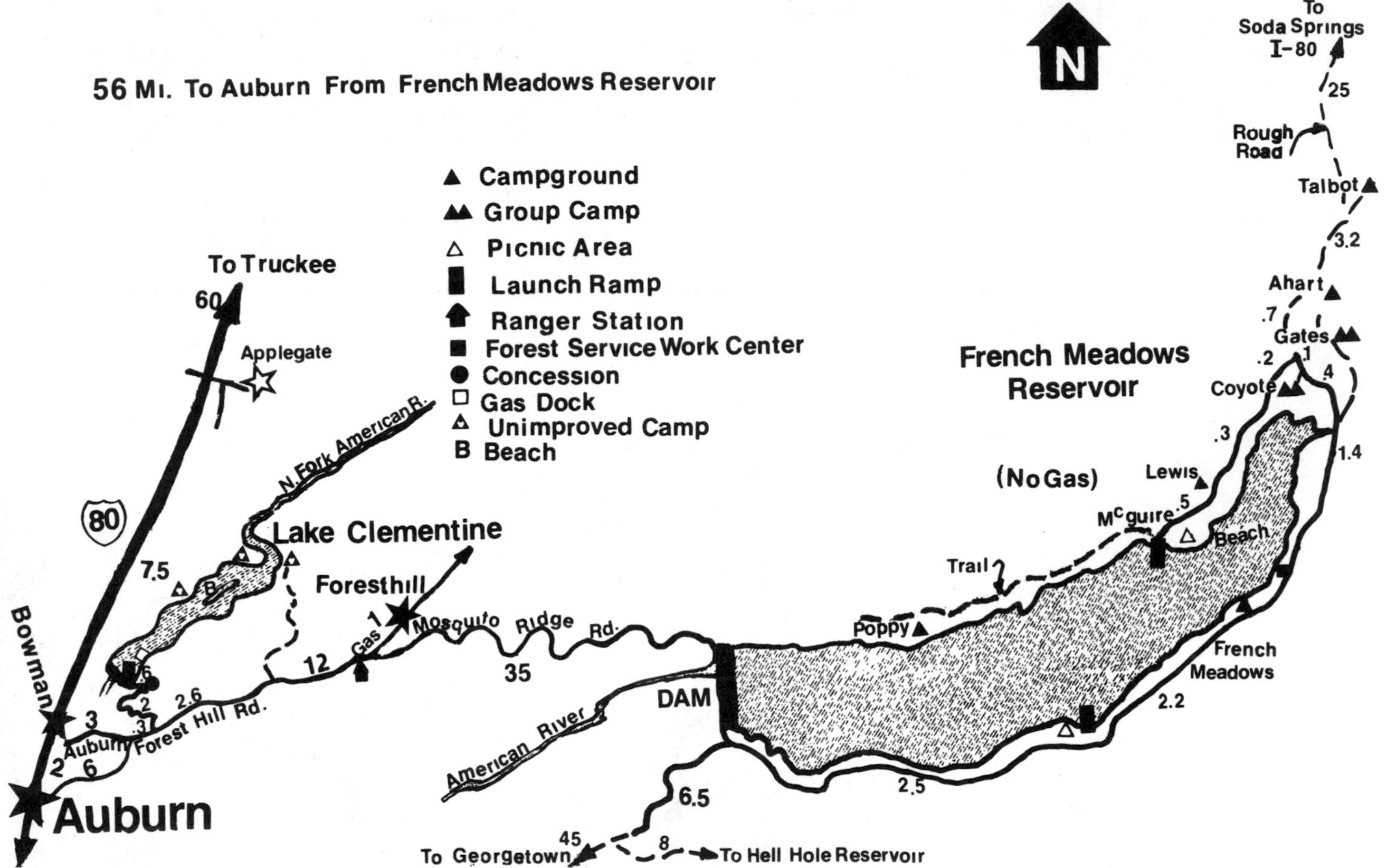

INFORMATION: Foresthill R.D., 22830 Foresthill Rd., Foresthill 95631			
CAMPING	BOATING	RECREATION	OTHER
French Meadows: 115 Dev. Sites Fee: $5 18 Undev. Sites 12 Boat or Walk-In Sites 7 Group Sites - Reservations Ph: 916-367-2224	French Meadows: Open to All Boats Speed Boats & Waterskiing Not Advised Due to Submerged Hazards Lake Clementine: Open to All Boats Speed Limit - 40 MPH	Fishing: Rainbow & Brown Trout Lake Clementine: Smallmouth Bass, Catfish & Panfish Picnicking Swimming Hiking Backpacking-Parking	Lake Clementine: Auburn State Recreation Area P.O. Box 3266 Auburn 95604 Ph: 916-885-4527

HELL HOLE RESERVOIR AND RALSTON AFTERBAY

Hell Hole Reservoir is in the El Dorado National Forest at an elevation of 4,700 feet. The facilities are operated and maintained by the U.S. Forest Service. Hell Hole is 15 miles south of French Meadows Reservoir in a rugged, rocky area on the Rubicon River. The Lake of 1,300 surface acres is in a deep gorge surrounded by granite boulders with cold, clear water, creating an awesome setting. It is especially scenic where the water leaves the power house and drops into the Lake so be sure to bring a camera. There are no facilities other than the launch ramp and campgrounds so come well supplied. Ralston Afterbay is on the Middle Fork of the American River with a nice picnic area and gravel launch ramps.

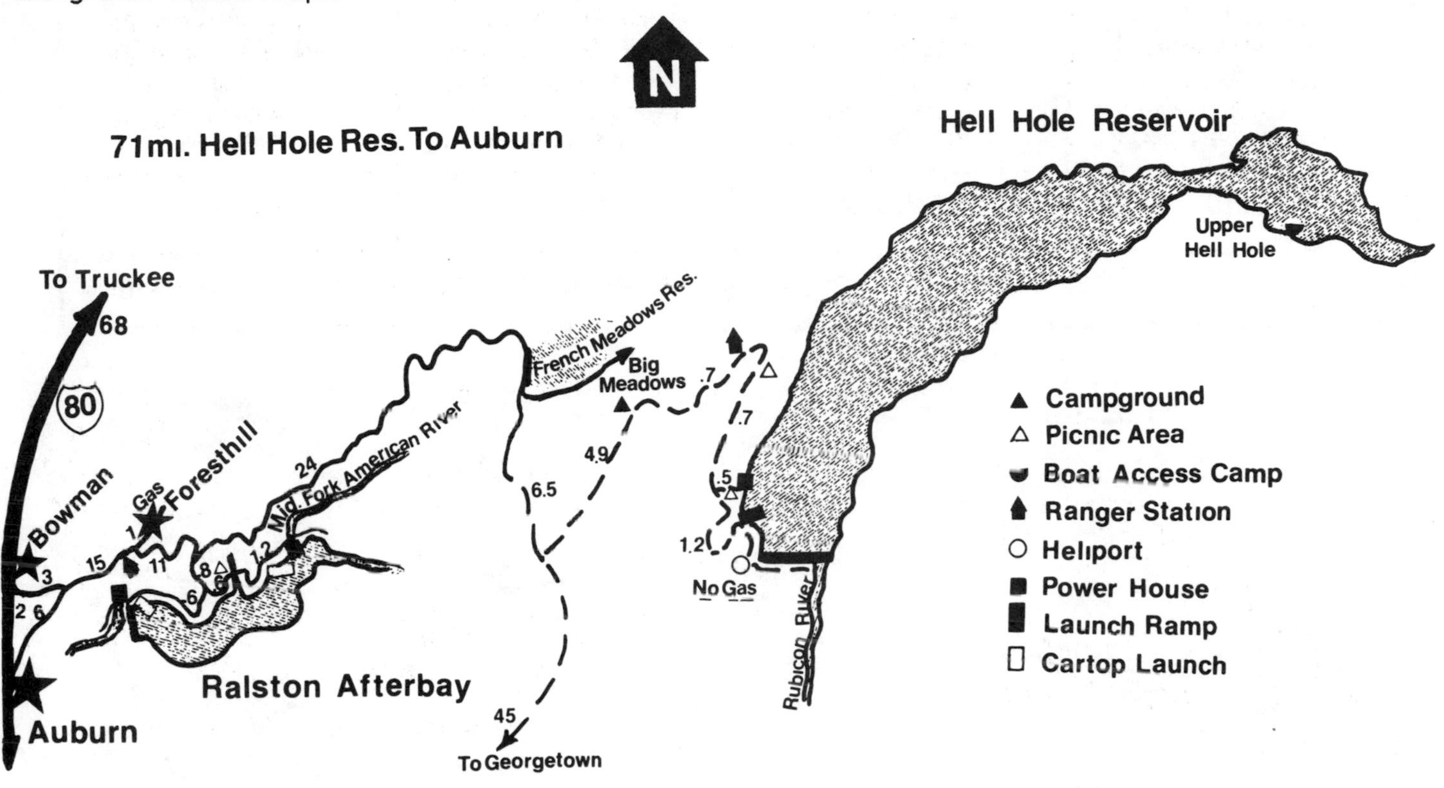

NOT TO SCALE

INFORMATION: Georgetown Ranger District, Georgetown 95634, Ph: 916-333-4312

CAMPING	BOATING	RECREATION	OTHER
Hell Hole: 10 Sites for Tents Only Big Meadows: 55 Sites for Tents & R.V.s 15 Boat Access Sites No Water - No Fee Ralston Afterbay: No Campgrounds	Hell Hole: Power, Row, Canoe, Sail, Waterski & Inflatable Launch Ramp Ralston Afterbay: Small Craft Only Hand Launch	Fishing: Rainbow, Brown, Cutthroat & Kamloop Trout Picnicking Hiking Backpacking Horseback Riding Trails Hunting: Deer, Bear	Nearest Facilities From Hell Hole Reservoir - 55 Miles at Georgetown

STUMPY MEADOWS RESERVOIR AND FINNON LAKE

Stumpy Meadows is at an elevation of 4,260 feet in the Eldorado National Forest. This pretty Lake of 320 acres is surrounded by conifers and the water is clear and cold. Boating is restricted to 5 MPH so waterskiing is not allowed. The angler will find German Brown and Rainbow Trout. Finnon Lake, at 2,420 feet, is a small Lake administered by Eldorado County. Boating is limited to rowboats. Fishing, swimming, hiking and horseback riding are the primary activities. Small trailers only are advised at both of these Lakes.

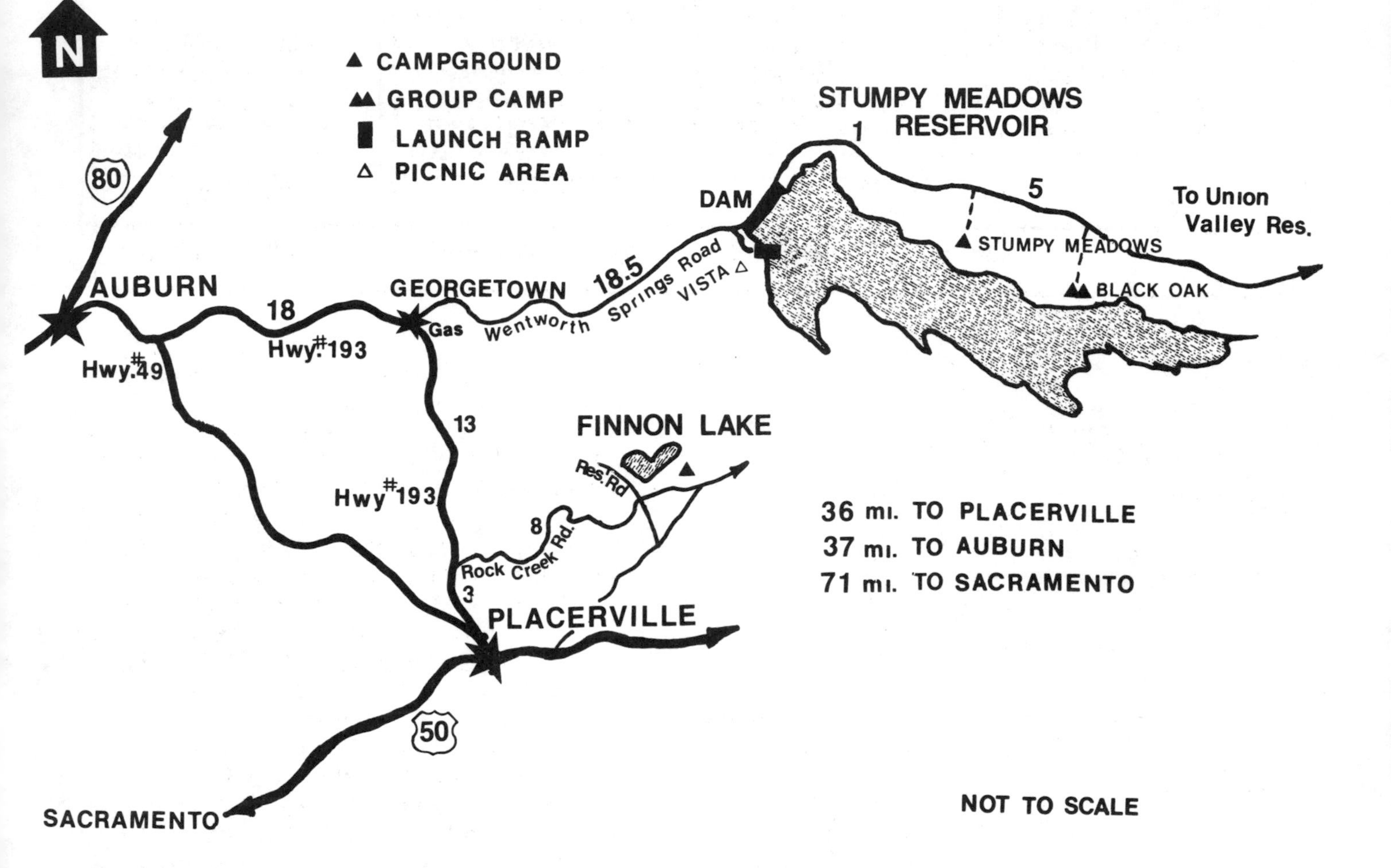

INFORMATION: Georgetown Ranger District, Georgetown 95634, Ph: 916-333-4312

CAMPING	BOATING	RECREATION	OTHER
Stumpy Meadows: 40 Dev. Sites for Tents & R.V.s 4 Group Sites to 225 People by Reservation Max. Trailer Length 22 feet Finnon Lake: 28 Dev. Sites Small Trailers	Stumpy Meadows: Open to All Boats 5 MPH Speed Limit 10 HP Motors Max. Improved Launch Ramp Finnon Lake: Rowboats Only	Fishing: Rainbow & Brown Trout Picnicking Swimming at Finnon Lake Only Hiking & Riding Trails	Finnon Lake Info: Eldorado County Rt. 1, Box 1500 Placerville 95667 Ph: 916-823-4721 Finnon Lake: Store Snack Bar Restaurant

LAKE TAHOE

Mark Twain called Lake Tahoe "The Lake of the Sky". Named Tahoe or "Big Water" by the Washoe Indians, it is 22 miles long, 12 miles wide and at an elevation of 6,229 feet. Although famous for the Casinos at North and South Shores, outdoor recreation facilities are abundant. Campgrounds are described on the following page along with detailed information.

. . . Continued . . .

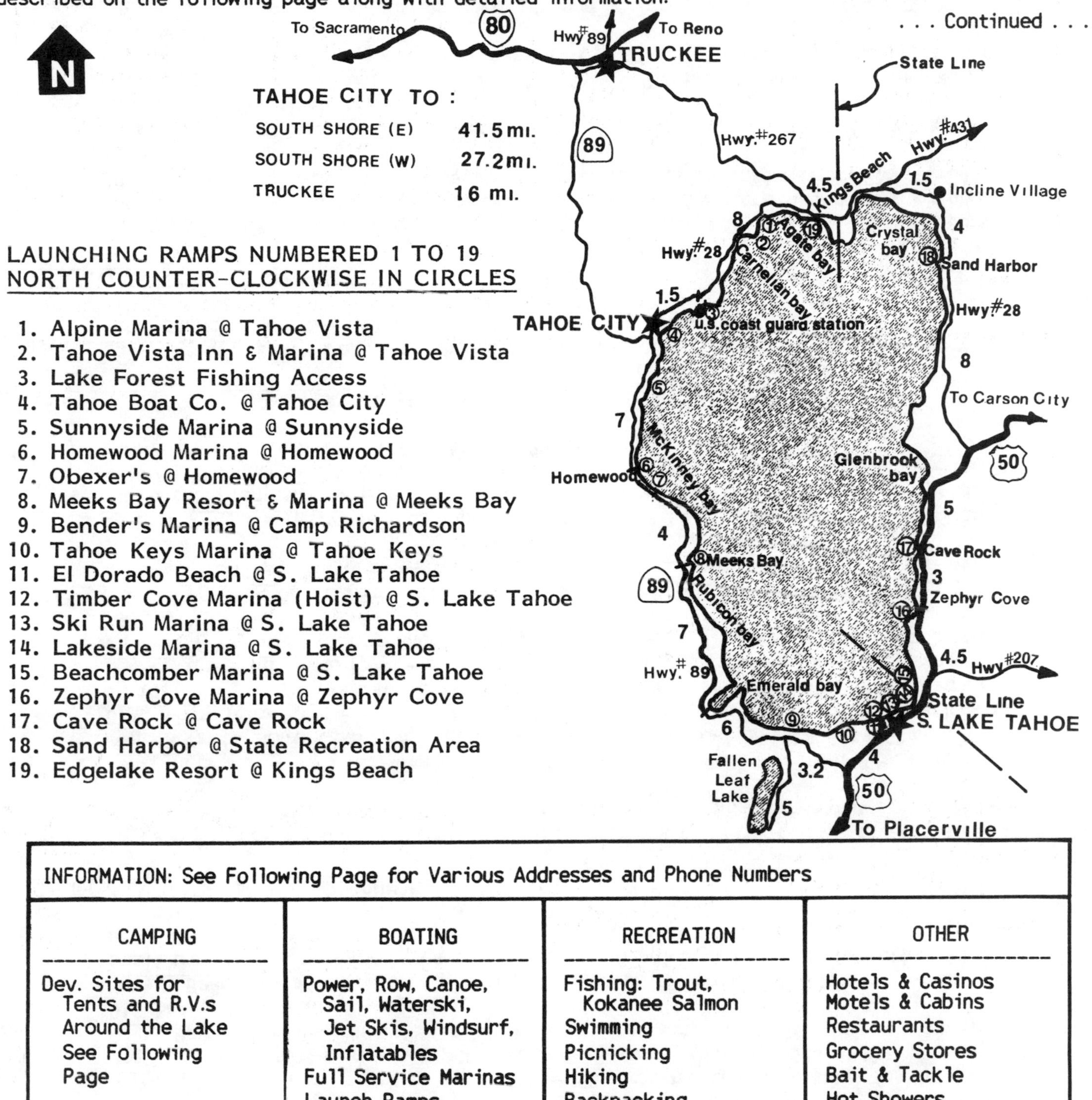

LAUNCHING RAMPS NUMBERED 1 TO 19
NORTH COUNTER-CLOCKWISE IN CIRCLES

1. Alpine Marina @ Tahoe Vista
2. Tahoe Vista Inn & Marina @ Tahoe Vista
3. Lake Forest Fishing Access
4. Tahoe Boat Co. @ Tahoe City
5. Sunnyside Marina @ Sunnyside
6. Homewood Marina @ Homewood
7. Obexer's @ Homewood
8. Meeks Bay Resort & Marina @ Meeks Bay
9. Bender's Marina @ Camp Richardson
10. Tahoe Keys Marina @ Tahoe Keys
11. El Dorado Beach @ S. Lake Tahoe
12. Timber Cove Marina (Hoist) @ S. Lake Tahoe
13. Ski Run Marina @ S. Lake Tahoe
14. Lakeside Marina @ S. Lake Tahoe
15. Beachcomber Marina @ S. Lake Tahoe
16. Zephyr Cove Marina @ Zephyr Cove
17. Cave Rock @ Cave Rock
18. Sand Harbor @ State Recreation Area
19. Edgelake Resort @ Kings Beach

INFORMATION: See Following Page for Various Addresses and Phone Numbers

CAMPING	BOATING	RECREATION	OTHER
Dev. Sites for Tents and R.V.s Around the Lake See Following Page Boat Access Camps at Emerald Bay	Power, Row, Canoe, Sail, Waterski, Jet Skis, Windsurf, Inflatables Full Service Marinas Launch Ramps Boat Rentals Docks, Slips, Mooring, Gas	Fishing: Trout, Kokanee Salmon Swimming Picnicking Hiking Backpacking Horseback Riding Trails & Rentals	Hotels & Casinos Motels & Cabins Restaurants Grocery Stores Bait & Tackle Hot Showers Laundromats Disposal Stations Gas Stations Airport

LAKE TAHOE

. . . Continued . . .

Lake Tahoe has a boat camp at Emerald Bay, and there are numerous campgrounds around the shore of the Lake. Fees vary. The following is a partial list of facilities.

U.S.F.S. CAMPGROUNDS - First-Come, First-Serve

William Kent - 4 miles south of Tahoe City - 55 sites for tents, 40 sites for R.V.s and trailers to 24 feet, swim beach. Information: Summers - Ph: 916-583-3642.
Meeks Bay - 10 miles south of Tahoe City - 40 sites for tents only. Information: Ph: 916-544-6420
Nevada Beach - 1 mile north of Stateline - 23 sites for tents, 21 sites for R.V.s and small trailers, 6 sites for large trailers plus 1 handicapped site. Information: Ph: 916-544-6420.

CALIFORNIA STATE PARKS CAMPGROUNDS

Emerald Bay State Park - 100 sites for tents, trailers to 21 feet, R.V.s to 24 feet, showers plus 20 Boat-Access-Only sites. Reserve: Ticketron, Information: Ph: 916-541-3030.
Tahoe Recreation Area - 1/4 mile east of Tahoe City- 38 sites for tents, trailers to 15 feet, R.V.s to 21 feet, showers. Reserve: Ticketron, Information: 916-583-3074.
D. L. Bliss State Park - 3 miles north of Emerald Bay - 168 sites for tents, trailers to 15 feet, R.V.s to 24 feet, showers. Group Camp. Reserve all Sites through Ticketron.
Sugar Pine Point State Park - 1 mile south of Tahoma - 175 sites for tents, trailers to 24 feet, R.V.s to 30 feet, showers. Group Camp. Reserve all Sites through Ticketron.

CITY OF SOUTH LAKE TAHOE, P.O. Box 1210, South Lake Tahoe 95705, Ph: 916-573-2059
Site fee - $12 per night per site.

El Dorado Recreation Area - on Highway 50 & Rufus Allen Blvd., 1 mile south of Stateline - 170 sites for tents, trailers to 22 feet, motor homes to 28 feet, showers, disposal station, launch ramp. Reserve: Mid-May to Mid-September - 3 weeks in advance - pay 2 nights plus $1, Information: Ph: 916-573-2059.

TAHOE CITY PARKS AND RECREATION, 380 North Lake Blvd., Tahoe City 95730

Lake Forest - 2 miles east of Tahoe City - 20 sites for tents, trailers and R.V.s to 18 feet, showers. No reservations accepted. Information: Ph: 916-583-5544.

PRIVATELY OPERATED CAMPGROUNDS

Tahoe Valley Recreation Area - 1/4 mile west of the "Y" at South Lake Tahoe - 288 sites for tents & R.V.s, 200 full hookups, swimming pool, grocery store, laundromat, propane, recreation room. Reserve: Leisuretime Reservations System, Information: Ph: 916-541-2222.
Camp Richardson Resort - 3 miles west of the "Y" - 180 sites for tents & R.V.s, showers. Information: Ph: 916-541-1801.
Meek's Bay Resort - 10 miles south of Tahoe City - R.V. Park, full hookups, disposal station, showers, motel, launch ramp, marina with 120 slips, boat rentals, snack bar, gas. Information: Ph: 916-525-7242.
Zephyr Cove Resort - 1-1/2 miles north of town of Zephyr Cove - 50 sites for tents, 106 sites for R.V.s and trailers to 35 feet, hookups, showers, cabins & lodge, marina, buoys, market, restaurant. Information: Ph: 702-588-6644.
K O A Campground - on Highway 50 west of Meyers - 50 sites for tents & R.V.s to 38 feet, hookups, showers. Open All Year. Reserve: P.O. Box 11552, Tahoe Paradise 95708, Ph: 916-577-3693.

FALLEN LEAF LAKE

Fallen Leaf Lake is at an elevation of 6,400 feet just south of Lake Tahoe in the Lake Tahoe Basin Management Unit. The lovely property around this Lake is partially private and partially National Forest land. The shoreline is heavily forested with pine trees to the water's edge. This is a nice family recreation Lake with boating facilities and fishing. It is within easy access to the Desolation Wilderness and near the numerous attractions at South Lake Tahoe and the casinos at Stateline.

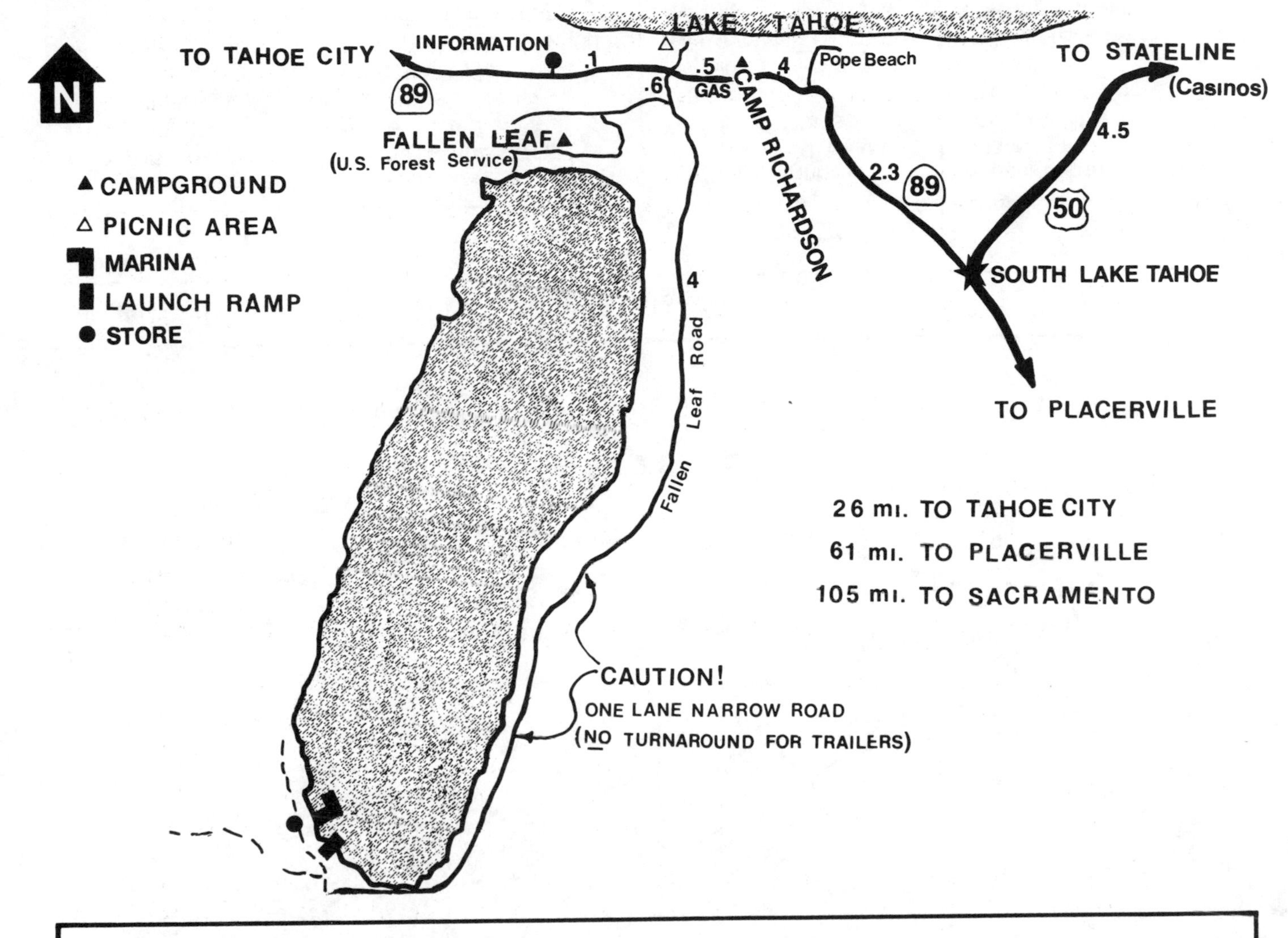

INFORMATION: Lake Tahoe Basin, Box 8465, S. Lake Tahoe 95731, Ph: 916-544-6420

CAMPING	BOATING	RECREATION	OTHER
U.S.F.S. 206 Dev. Sites for Tents & R.V.s	Power, Row, Canoe, Sail Launch Ramp Rentals: Row, Sail, Fishing Boats with Motors, Canoes, Kayaks & Ski Boats	Fishing: Rainbow, German Brown & Mackinaw Trout Swimming Picnicking Hiking Backpacking Horseback Riding Trails Nature Study	Fallen Leaf Lodge Fallen Leaf 95716 Marina 916-544-0787 Store 916-541-4671 Memorial Day to Labor Day Grocery Store Bait & Tackle

ECHO LAKE

Echo Lake is nestled at 7,414 feet in between high mountains near Echo Summit off Highway 50. This is one of the most beautiful natural Lakes to be found in the High Sierras. All types of boating are allowed, but waterskiing is not permitted on Upper Echo Lake. The bordering Desolation Wilderness has 63,475 acres of trails, Lakes, and streams easily accessible for the backpacker or horseman. Echo Chalet, the only facility on the Lake, provides a taxi service to the Upper Lake which shortens the hike into the Wilderness Area by 3-1/2 miles. The Rubicon and American Rivers along with over 50 Lakes and streams welcome expectant anglers to the uncrowded waters of this area.

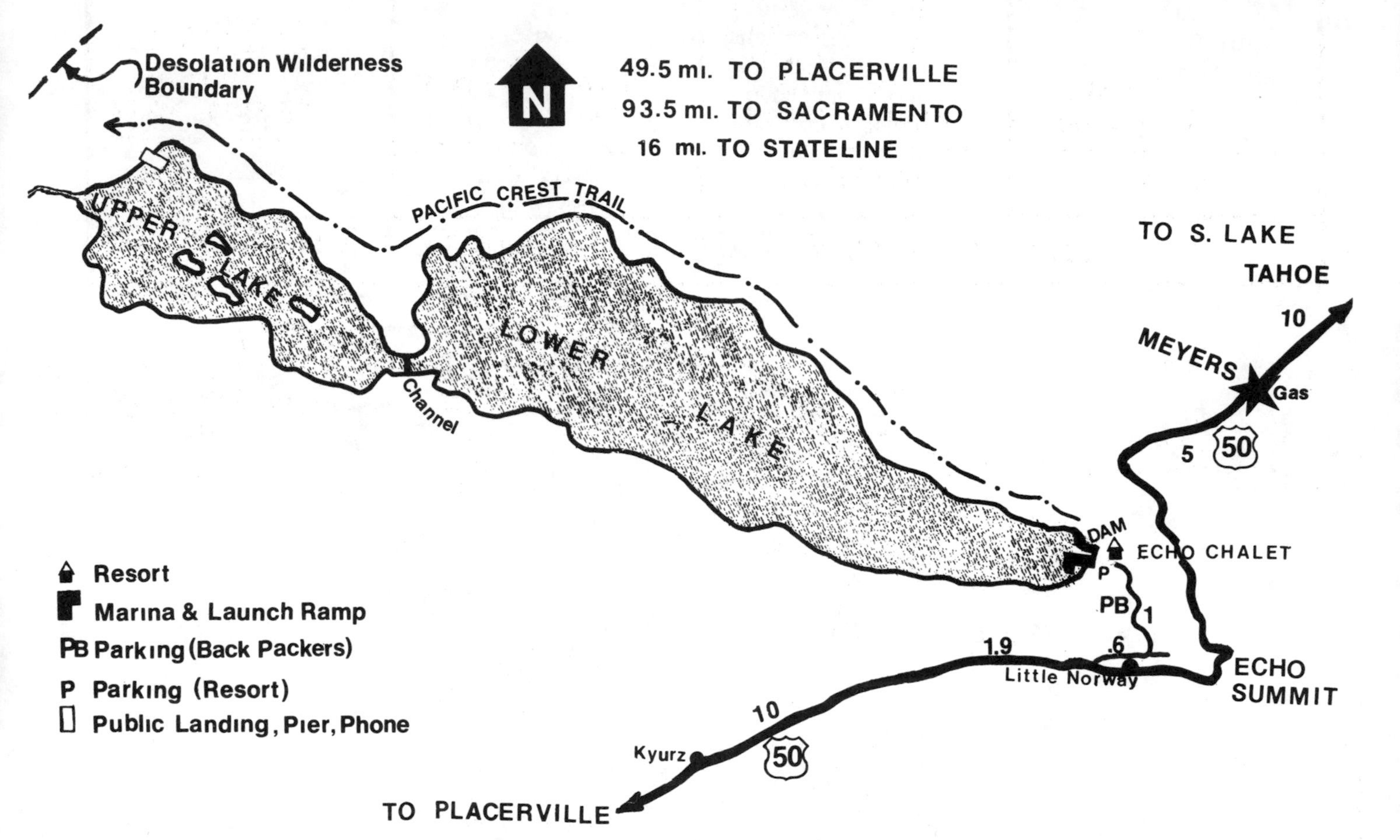

INFORMATION: Echo Chalet, Echo Lake 95721, Ph: 916-659-7207			
CAMPING	BOATING	RECREATION	OTHER
U.S. Forest Service Camping Allowed Only in Desolation Wilderness Area	Power, Row, Canoe, Sail, Waterski, Windsurf & Inflatable Full Service Marina Launch Ramp - $6.00 Rentals: Fishing Boats & Canoes Docks, Berths, Gas, Storage Boat Taxi Service & Tours	Fishing: Rainbow, Brook & Cutthroat Trout; Kokanee Salmon Swimming Picnicking Hiking Backpacking-Parking Horseback Riding Trails Hunting: Deer, Quail	Housekeeping Cabins Snack Bar Grocery Store Hardware & Sporting Goods Bait & Tackle Fishing Licenses Gas Station Day Hike Permits to Wilderness Area

WRIGHTS LAKE

Wrights Lake has a surface area of 65 acres. It is at an elevation of 7,000 feet in the Eldorado National Forest, one of many Lakes in this area. The High Sierra setting provides a unique retreat for the outdoorsman. The Trailheads for Rockbound Pass and Desolation Wilderness Areas border the Lake, making it popular for the equestrian, hiker and backpacker. Wrights Lake offers good fishing, and the other Lakes and streams in this vicinity are equally inviting to the angler. Boating is restricted to hand launching, and no motors are allowed.

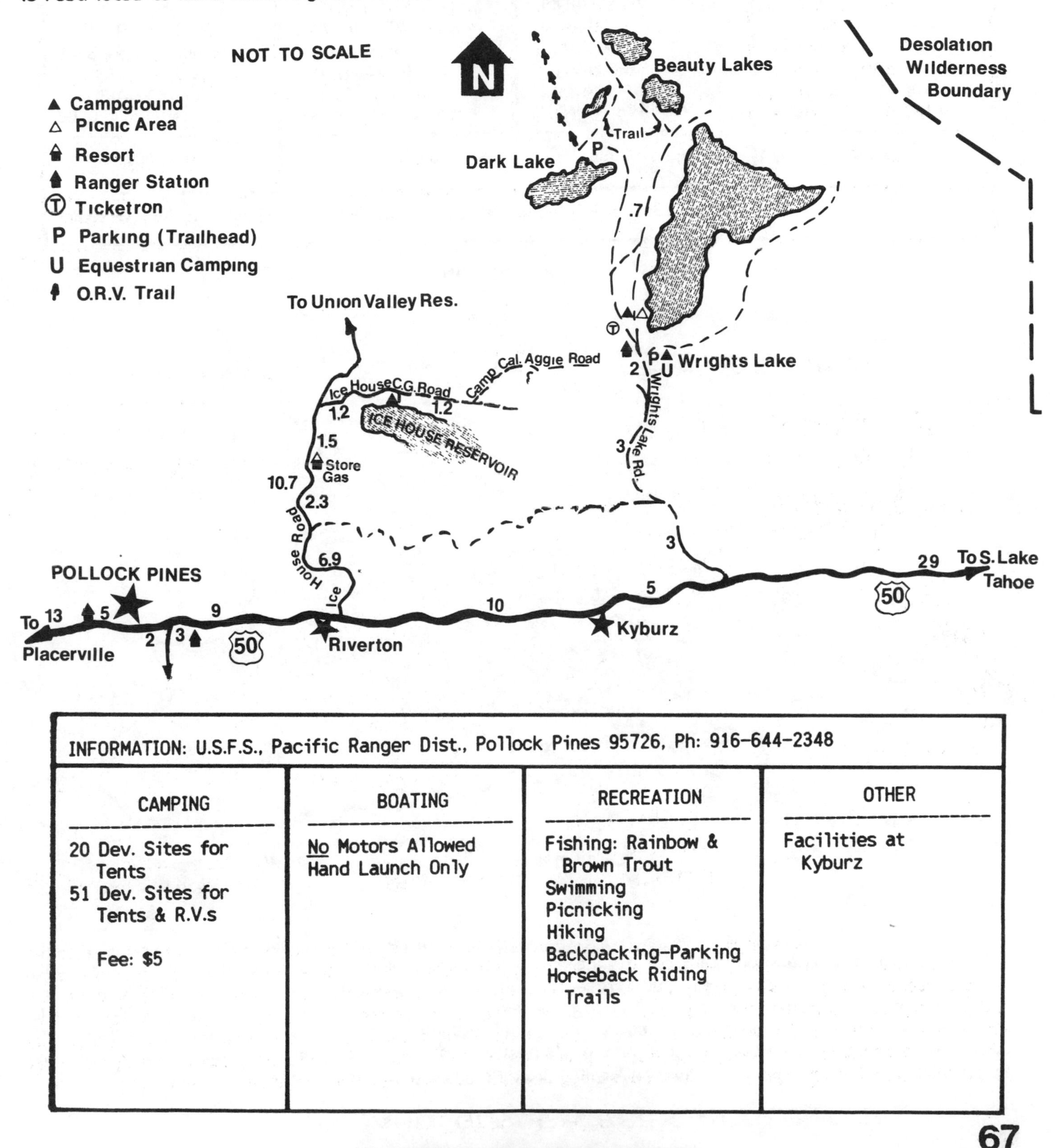

INFORMATION: U.S.F.S., Pacific Ranger Dist., Pollock Pines 95726, Ph: 916-644-2348			
CAMPING	BOATING	RECREATION	OTHER
20 Dev. Sites for Tents 51 Dev. Sites for Tents & R.V.s Fee: $5	No Motors Allowed Hand Launch Only	Fishing: Rainbow & Brown Trout Swimming Picnicking Hiking Backpacking-Parking Horseback Riding Trails	Facilities at Kyburz

LOON LAKE AND GERLE CREEK RESERVOIR

Loon Lake is at an elevation of 6,500 feet in the Crystal Basin Recreation Area of the Eldorado National Forest. The Forest Service maintains the campground, picnic area, paved launch ramp, and a walk-in or boat-in campground. This is a good Lake for sailing and boating in general, but waterskiing is not advised due to extremely cold water. Fishing can be excellent for Rainbow and German Brown Trout. There is trailhead parking for the Desolation Wilderness, and trail conditions are good for hikers and horses. Gerle Creek Reservoir has a 50-site campground and picnic area with limited boating. Motors are not allowed at this nice facility.

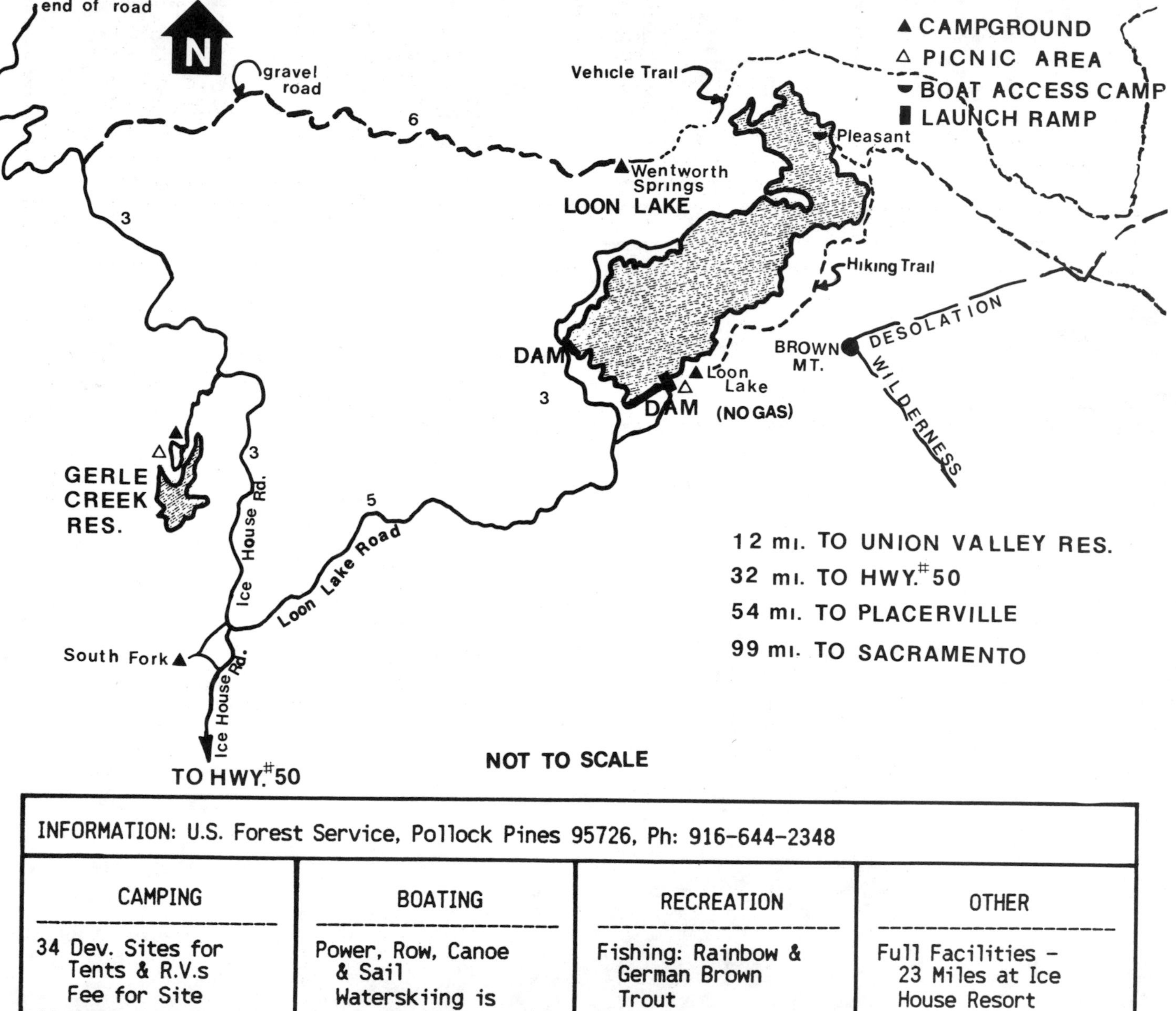

INFORMATION: U.S. Forest Service, Pollock Pines 95726, Ph: 916-644-2348

CAMPING	BOATING	RECREATION	OTHER
34 Dev. Sites for Tents & R.V.s Fee for Site 11 Sites at Wentworth Springs Gerle Creek Reservoir 50 Dev. Sites for Tents & R.V.s Fee for Site	Power, Row, Canoe & Sail Waterskiing is Not Recommended Launch Ramp Gerle Creek Reservoir: No Motors	Fishing: Rainbow & German Brown Trout Picnicking Hiking Backpacking-Parking Entrance to Desolation Wilderness Horseback Riding Trails ORV Trails	Full Facilities - 23 Miles at Ice House Resort

ICE HOUSE RESERVOIR

Ice House Reservoir is at an elevation of 5,500 feet in the Crystal Basin Recreation Area of the Eldorado National Forest. The surface area of the Lake is 678 acres of clear, cold water. The surrounding shoreline is covered with conifers at this high Sierra Lake. In addition to the popular campground, the Forest Service maintains a launch ramp and picnic facilities on the Lake. All types of boating are allowed, and this is a particularly good Lake for sailing. The fisherman will find Trout and Kokanee Salmon.

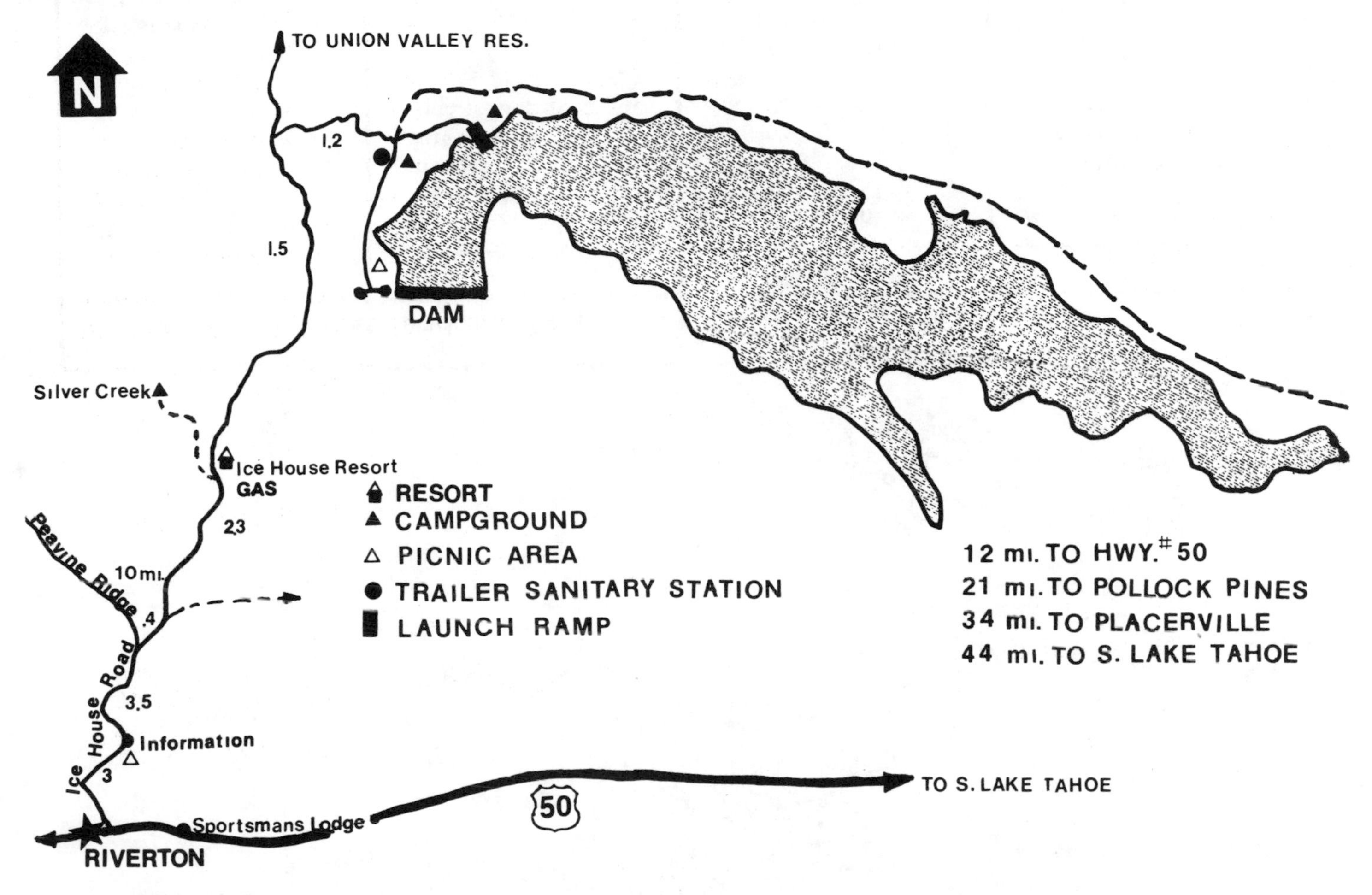

TO PLACERVILLE

INFORMATION: U.S. Forest Service, 100 Forni Rd., Placerville 95667, Ph: 916-622-5061

CAMPING	BOATING	RECREATION	OTHER
Ice House: 83 Dev. Sites for Tents & R.V.s Fees Charged 3 Camp Units Designed for the Handicapped Silver Creek: 11 Primitive Sites for Tents Only No Fees	Power, Row, Canoe, Sail, Waterski, Windsurf & Inflatables Launch Ramp	Fishing: Rainbow & Brown Trout, Kokanee Salmon Swimming Picnicking Hiking	Ice House Resort: Motel Restaurant Grocery Store Gas Station

UNION VALLEY RESERVOIR

Union Valley Reservoir is located at an elevation of 4,900 feet in the Crystal Basin Recreation Area of the Eldorado National Forest. This area is in the pine and fir forests of the Western Sierras and is dominated by the high granite peaks of the Crystal Range. The Reservoir has a surface area of 2,860 acres. The Forest Service maintains two launch ramps on the Lake, one picnic area, three campgrounds and one group campground. Union Valley is an excellent Lake for sailing, and many sailing clubs use this facility during the summer. Fishing is popular by boat or along the shoreline of this lovely Lake.

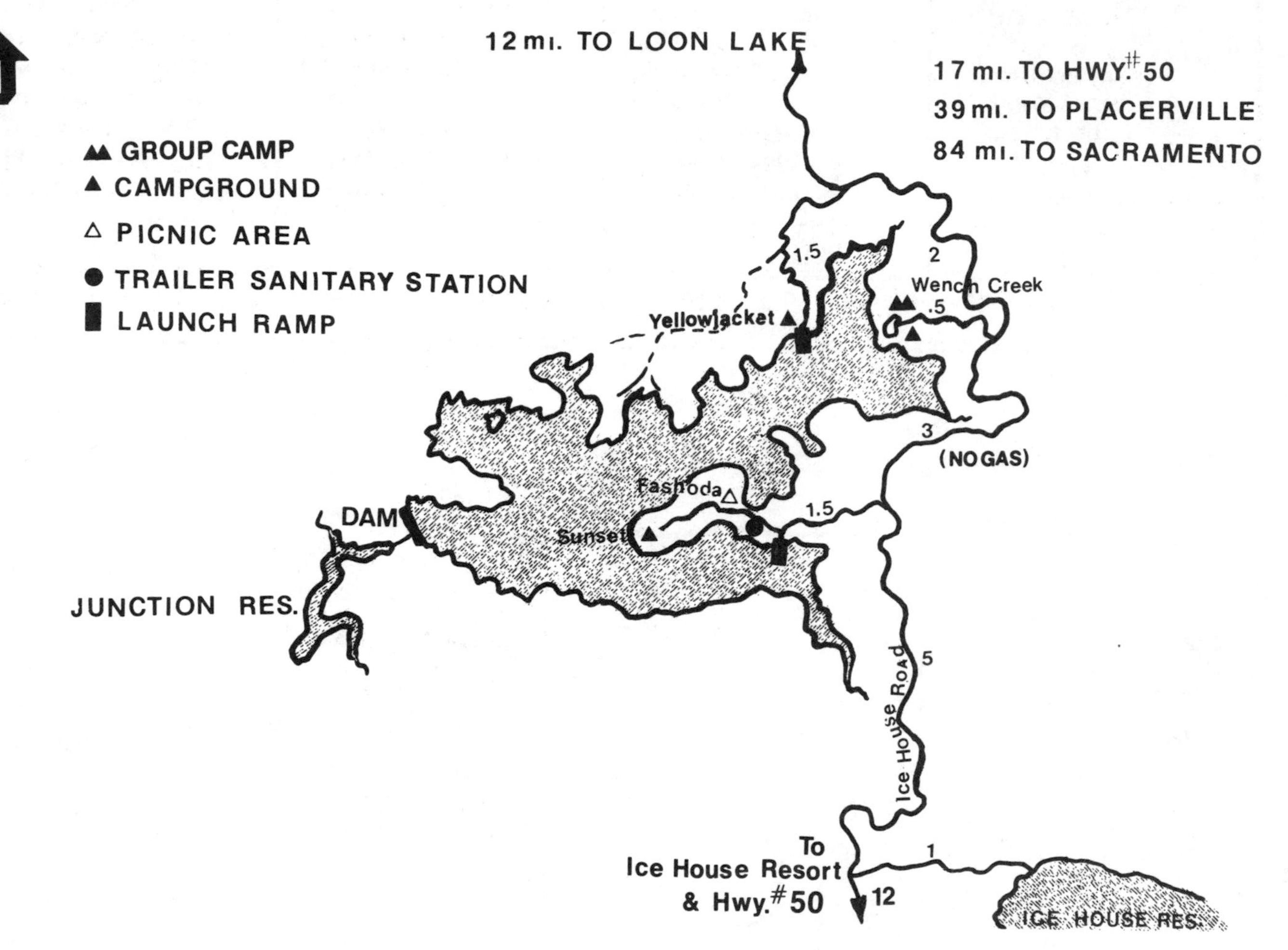

INFORMATION: U.S. Forest Service, 100 Forni Rd., Placerville 95667, Ph: 916-622-5061

CAMPING	BOATING	RECREATION	OTHER
271 Dev. Sites for Tents & R.V.s Fees Charged 2 Group Campgrounds 50 People Maximum Each Reservations	Power, Row, Canoe, Sail, Waterski, Windsurf & Inflatable Launch Ramps	Fishing: Rainbow & Brown Trout Swimming Picnicking Hiking	Disposal Station Facilities - 7 Miles at Ice House Resort

JENKINSON LAKE

SLY PARK RECREATION AREA

Jenkinson Lake is at an elevation of 3,478 feet in the Sly Park Recreation Area south of Pollock Pines. The Lake has a surface area of 640 acres with 8 miles of coniferous-covered shoreline. The Eldorado Irrigation District has jurisdiction over the modern facilities at this pretty Lake. Facilities include a paved 3-lane launch ramp with floats, a nice small marina and a boat storage area. The water is clear, and fishing can be good along the coves. Winds are usually favorable for sailing. Waterskiing is in a counter-clockwise direction in the central section of the Lake. A 5 MPH speed limit is enforced in the northeast area.

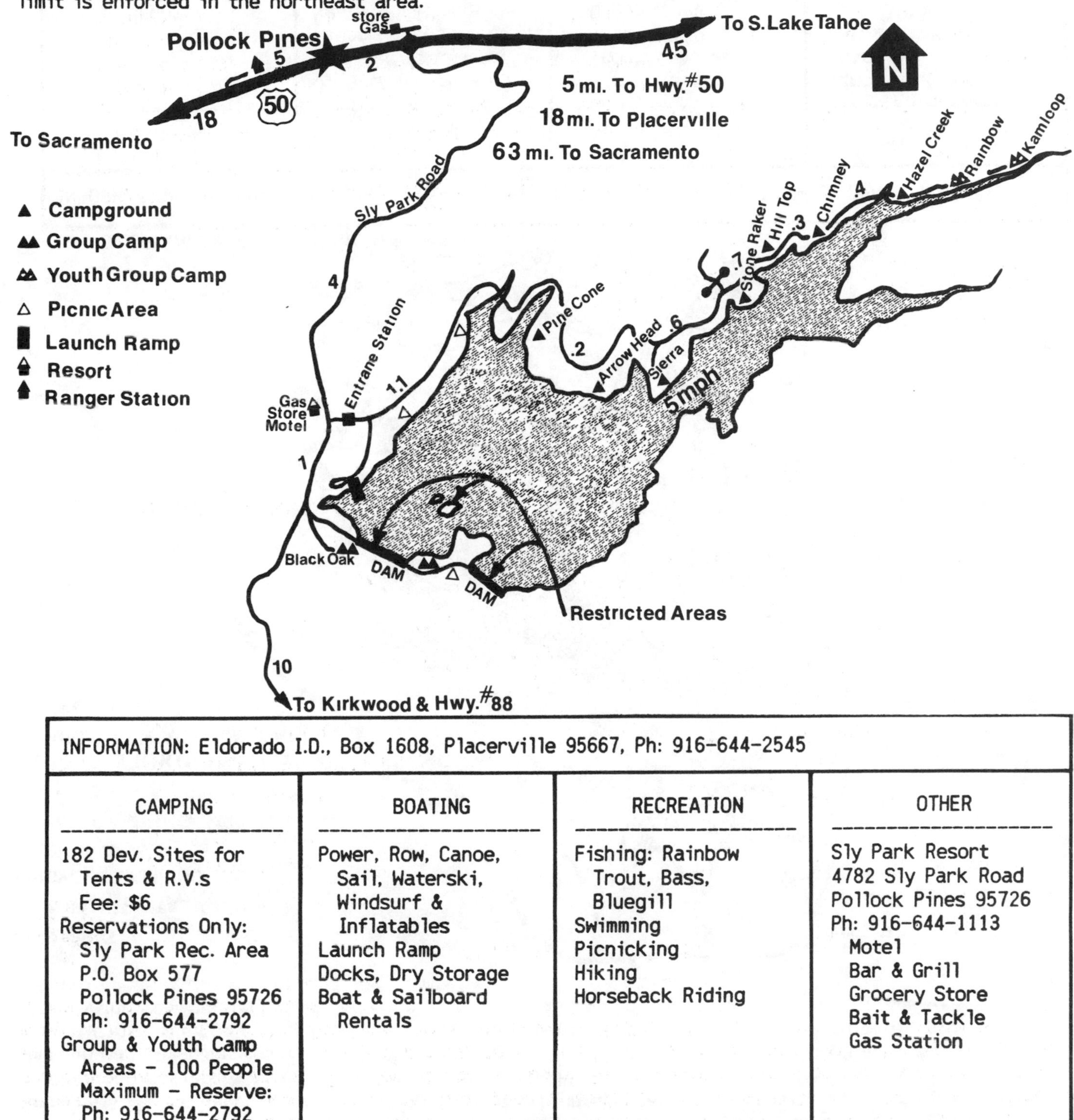

INFORMATION: Eldorado I.D., Box 1608, Placerville 95667, Ph: 916-644-2545

CAMPING	BOATING	RECREATION	OTHER
182 Dev. Sites for Tents & R.V.s Fee: $6 Reservations Only: Sly Park Rec. Area P.O. Box 577 Pollock Pines 95726 Ph: 916-644-2792 Group & Youth Camp Areas - 100 People Maximum - Reserve: Ph: 916-644-2792	Power, Row, Canoe, Sail, Waterski, Windsurf & Inflatables Launch Ramp Docks, Dry Storage Boat & Sailboard Rentals	Fishing: Rainbow Trout, Bass, Bluegill Swimming Picnicking Hiking Horseback Riding	Sly Park Resort 4782 Sly Park Road Pollock Pines 95726 Ph: 916-644-1113 Motel Bar & Grill Grocery Store Bait & Tackle Gas Station

FOLSOM LAKE

The Folsom Lake State Recreation Area is one of the most complete recreation Parks in California. This 18,000 acre Recreation Area offers an abundance of campsites, picnic areas, swimming beaches and marine facilities. Folsom Lake has 11,930 surface acres with 75 shoreline miles. Surrounding the Lake are 75 miles of hiking and riding trails. Fishing is a popular and productive activity with a large variety of game fish. The Lake offers a mixture of boating experiences from waterskiing to windsurfing or canoeing into Rattlesnake Bar's quiet coves. Equestrians will find staging areas and a campground for themselves and their horses.

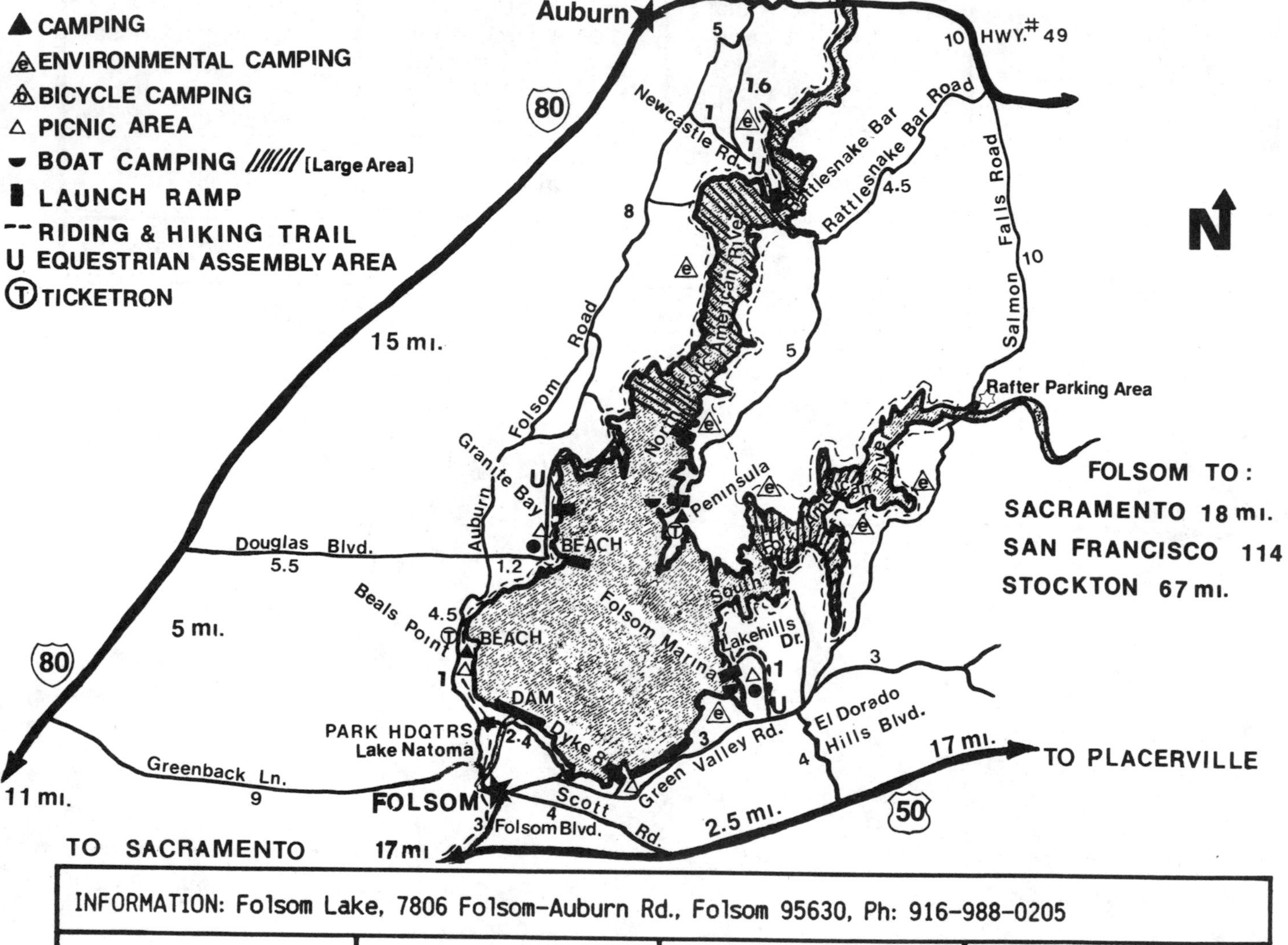

INFORMATION: Folsom Lake, 7806 Folsom-Auburn Rd., Folsom 95630, Ph: 916-988-0205			
CAMPING	**BOATING**	**RECREATION**	**OTHER**
168 Dev. Sites for Tents & R.V.s Fee: $6 12 Environmental Camps Reached by Foot, Boat or Bicycle Equestrian Camp Accommodates up to 50 Riders & Horses Contact Park Hdqtr. Boating Camping	Open to All Boating Full Service Marina Launch Ramps - $2 Rentals: Fishing, Canoe, Sail & Windsurfing Docks, Berths, Dry Storage & Gas Windsurfing Lessons Low Water Hazards	Fishing: Rainbow Trout, Coho Salmon, Catfish, Bluegill, Crappie, Bass, Perch & Sturgeon Picnicking Swimming Beaches Bicycle, Hiking & Riding Trails Horse Rentals	Campfire Programs Snack Bar Bait & Tackle Day Use Fee: $2 Full Facilities in Folsom

LAKE NATOMA

Lake Natoma rests at an elevation of 126 feet just below the Folsom Dam. Natoma is the regulating Reservoir for Folsom Lake. This small body of water has a surface area of 500 acres, and the water is very cold as it comes from under the Dam. There are paved launch ramps at Nimbus Flat and Negro Bar. Boating is limited to 5 MPH so waterskiing is not allowed. The winds are usually good in the afternoon for sailing. There are shade structures with picnic tables, swimming beaches and a campground above Negro Bar. Good trails are available for the equestrian, bicyclist and hiker.

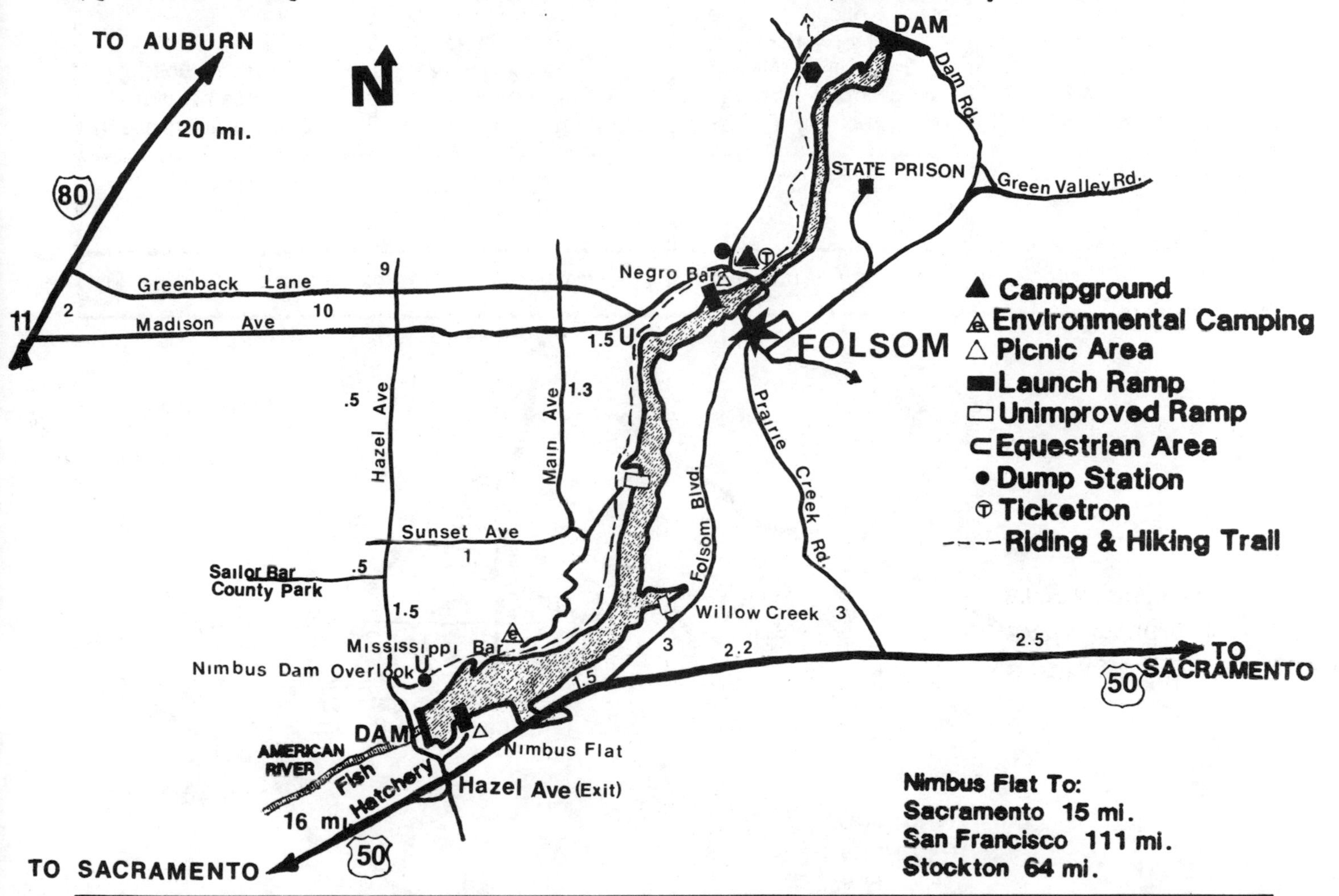

INFORMATION: Folsom Lake, 7806 Folsom-Auburn Rd., Folsom 95630, Ph: 916-988-0205

CAMPING	BOATING	RECREATION	OTHER
20 Dev. Sites for Tents & R.V.s Fee: $6 Can Also Be Reserved As A Group Camp - 100 People Maximum	Power, Row, Canoe, Sail, Windsurf & Inflatables Speed Limit-5 MPH Launch Ramps - $2 CSUS Aquatic Center Rowing, Waterski, Sail & Windsurfing Lessons Students & Members Only	Fishing: Rainbow Trout, Bluegill, Catfish, Crappie, Large & Smallmouth Bass Swimming - Beaches Picnicking Hiking Horseback Riding Trails Bicycle Trails	Day Use Fee: $2 Full Facilities - 1 Mile at Folsom City

RANCHO SECO, GIBSON RANCH, ELK GROVE PARK

All of these Sacramento County Parks provide the angler with a warm water fishery. Rainbow Trout are planted during the Fall and Winter months. Rancho Seco Park is the most water oriented facility with its 165 surface acre Lake which is open to sail and non-powered boating. There are launch ramps, docks, fishing piers, and a sandy swimming beach. Elk Grove Park has a small 3 acre Lake, and within this 125 acre Park are numerous picnic areas, a children's playground, 12 ball fields, a swimming pool, and a multi-purpose lighted equestrian arena. Gibson Ranch has a true ranch character with farm animals, an 8 acre fishing pond, swimming hole and extensive equestrian facilities.

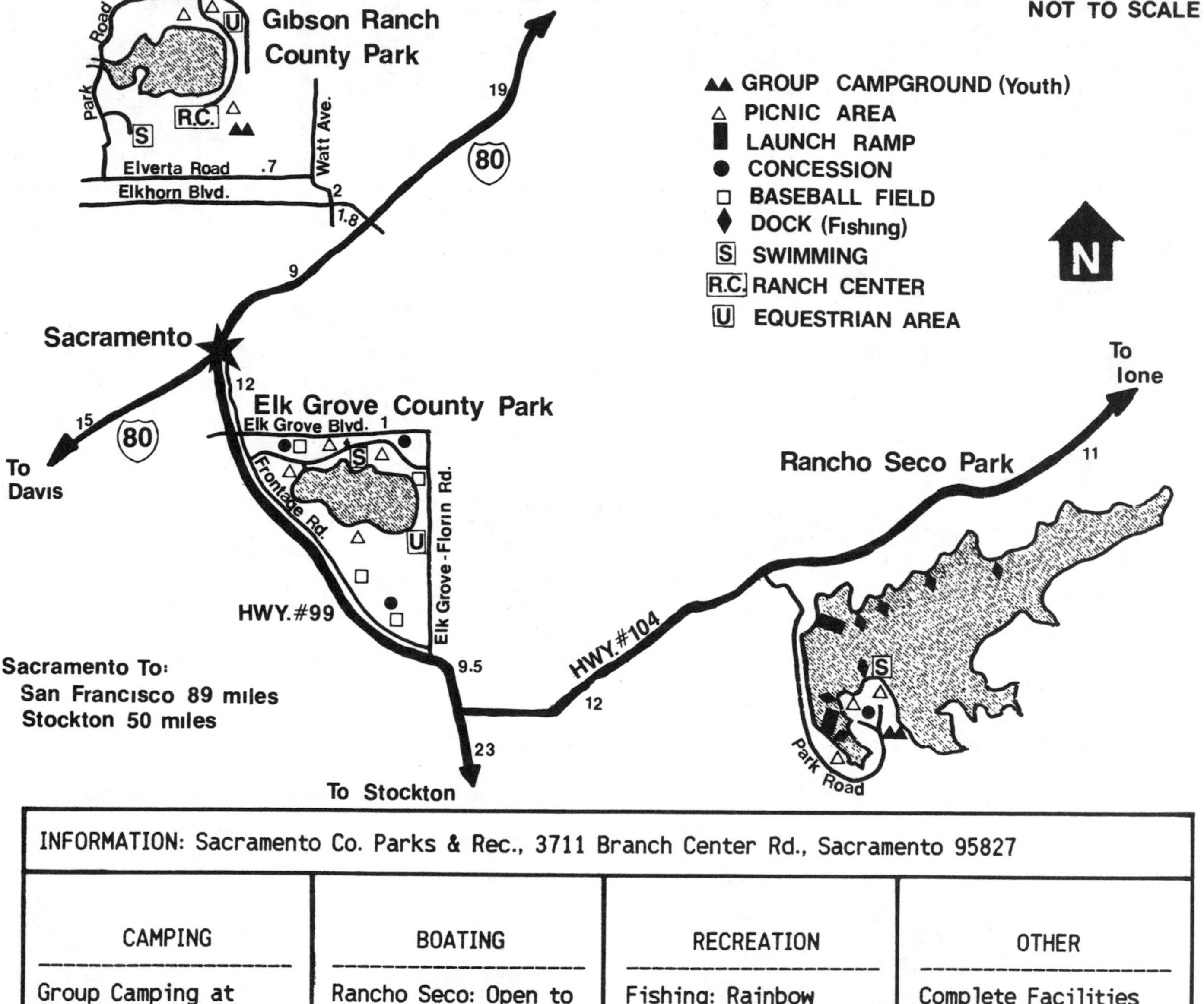

INFORMATION: Sacramento Co. Parks & Rec., 3711 Branch Center Rd., Sacramento 95827

CAMPING	BOATING	RECREATION	OTHER
Group Camping at Rancho Seco & Gibson Ranch Sacramento Co. Parks & Rec. Phone: 916-366-2061	Rancho Seco: Open to Sail & Row Boats Launch Ramps Docks Gibson Ranch & Elk Grove Park: No Boating	Fishing: Rainbow Trout, Florida Bass Bluegill, Red Ear Sunfish & Catfish Family & Group Picnic Areas Swimming Areas & Pool Hiking, Riding & Cycling Equestrian Center Nature Study	Complete Facilities Nearby

SALT SPRINGS RESERVOIR

Salt Springs Reservoir rests at an elevation of 3,900 feet in the spectacular Mokelumne River Canyon of the El Dorado National Forest. This P.G.&E. Reservoir has a surface area of 961 acres. The Forest Service has three campgrounds just below the Lake on the Mokelumne River. This is a good boating Lake, but launching can be a problem especially during periods of low water in the summer and fall. Afternoon winds can be hazardous. Fishing is often excellent in both the Lake and the River. A Trailhead to the beautiful 102,000-acre Mokelumne Wilderness is just above the Dam.

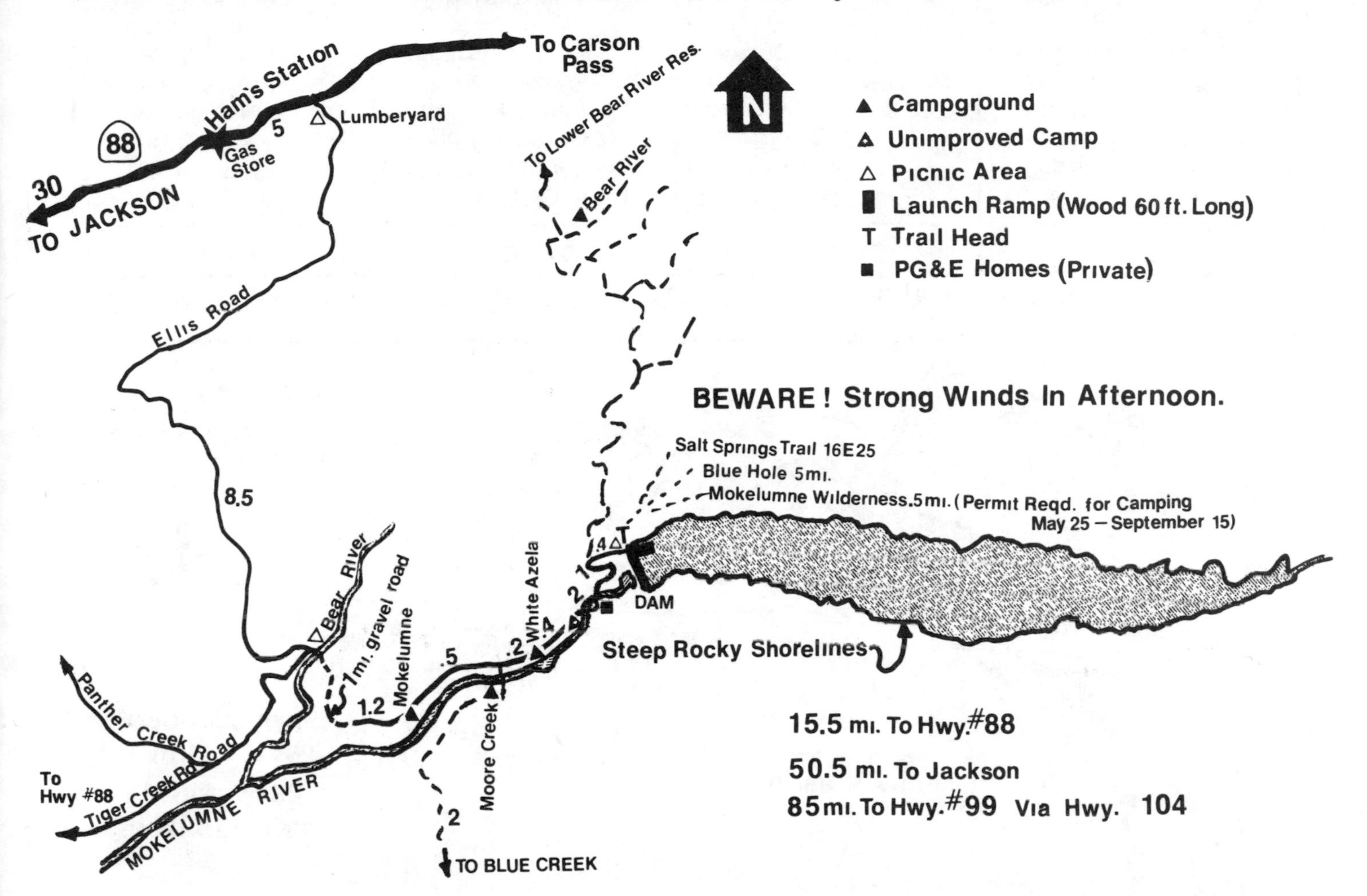

INFORMATION: Amador Ranger Dist., Star Rt. 1, Pioneer 95666, Ph: 209-295-4251

CAMPING	BOATING	RECREATION	OTHER
22 Sites for Tents & R.V.s No Drinking Water No Fee	Power, Row, Canoe & Sail Launch Ramp - 60' Wooden, Steep & Narrow - Usable Only During High Lake Levels - Otherwise Hand Launch Only Hazardous Winds Possible After 10 a.m.	Fishing: Rainbow, Brown & Brook Trout Swimming Picnicking Hiking Backpacking-Parking Horseback Riding Trails Hunting: Deer, Upland Game	Nearest Facilities at Ham's Station Grocery Store Gas Hunting is Allowed Only Above Reservoir - State Game Refuge Below Reservoir

LOWER BEAR RIVER RESERVOIR

Lower Bear River Reservoir rests at an elevation of 5,800 feet in the El Dorado National Forest. This pretty Lake of 727 acres is surrounded by a coniferous forest reaching to water's edge. There are good boating facilities at the Resort. Afternoon breezes make sailing a delight. The Lake is regularly stocked, and fishing is usually productive. The Forest Service campground at South Shore and Bear River is operated by Sierra Recreation Managers, P.O. Box 278, Pioneer 95666. The Bear River Resort has complete camping and marine facilities with hot showers, flush toilets, groceries, bait and tackle, snack bar, trailer rentals and storage. The hiker and backpacker will find parking and trails leading into the Mokelumne Wilderness.

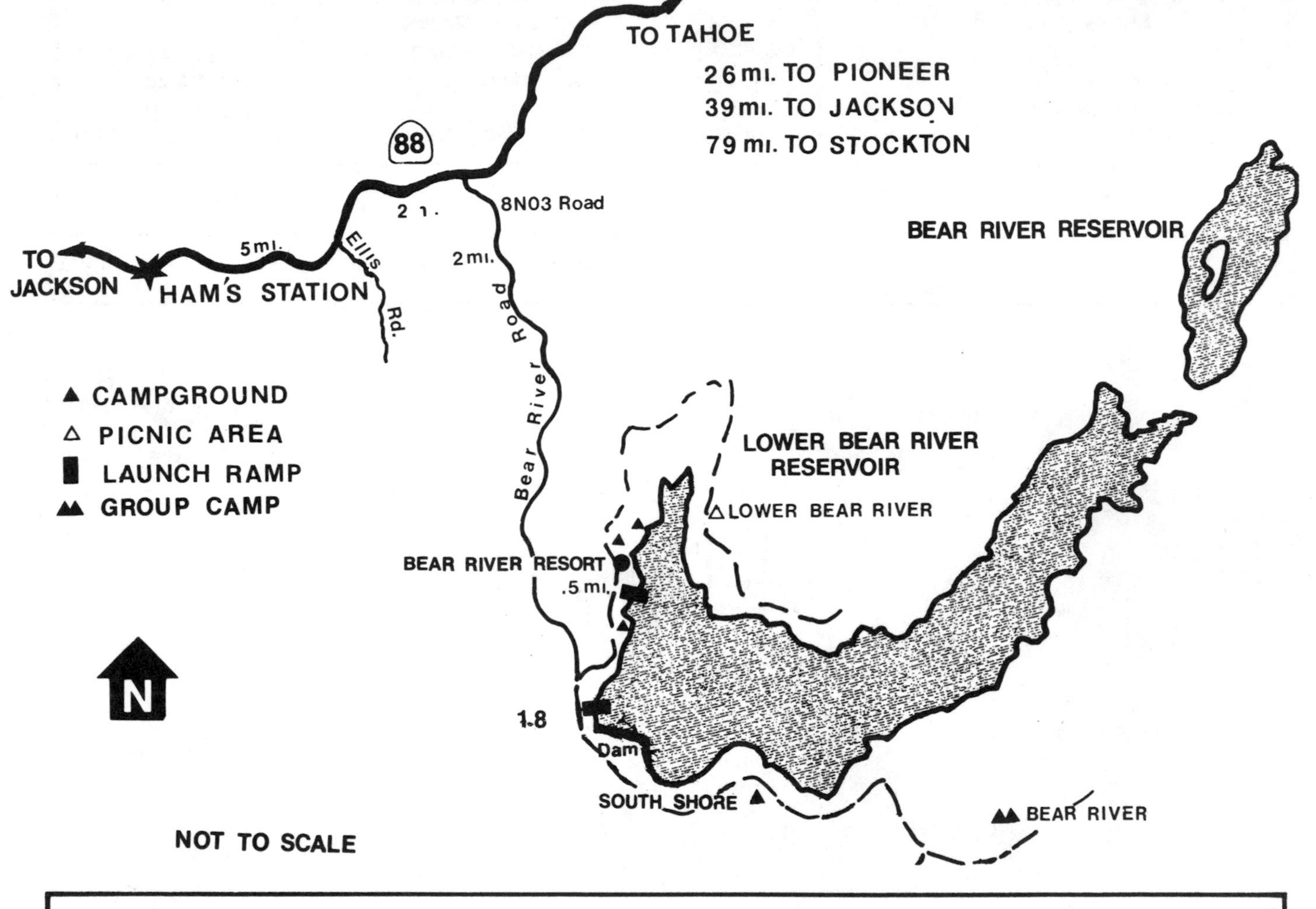

INFORMATION: Amador Ranger Station, Pioneer 95666, Ph: 209-295-4251

CAMPING	BOATING	RECREATION	OTHER
17 Dev. Sites for Tents & R.V.s Fee: $6 5 Double Sites - $12 2 Group Sites - 25 People - $25 1 Group Site - 50 People - $50 Reservations: Ph: 209-295-4521 Campfire Permit Required	Open to All Boating Full Service Marina Paved Launch Ramp Rentals: Fishing, Canoe & Paddle-boats Low Water Hazards Late in Season	Fishing: Rainbow & Brown Trout Picnicking Swimming Hiking - Backpacking Hunting: Deer	Lower Bear River Resort 40800 Hwy. 88 Pioneer 95666 Ph: 209-295-4868 125 Dev. Sites with Hookups--Fee: $9.50 Group Camp to 60 People Disposal Station Storage

SILVER LAKE

Silver Lake rests at an elevation of 7,200 feet in a big granite basin just west of the Sierra summit in the Eldorado National Forest. This exceptionally beautiful Lake was once a resting place on the Emigrant Trail cut by Kit Carson. You can still see the trail markers carved in trees. The descendants of Raymond Peter Plasse, who established a trading post in 1853, operate a Resort at the Lake. A popular recreation area for over a century, Silver Lake offers a variety of natural resources and facilities for the camper, angler, boater, hiker and equestrian.

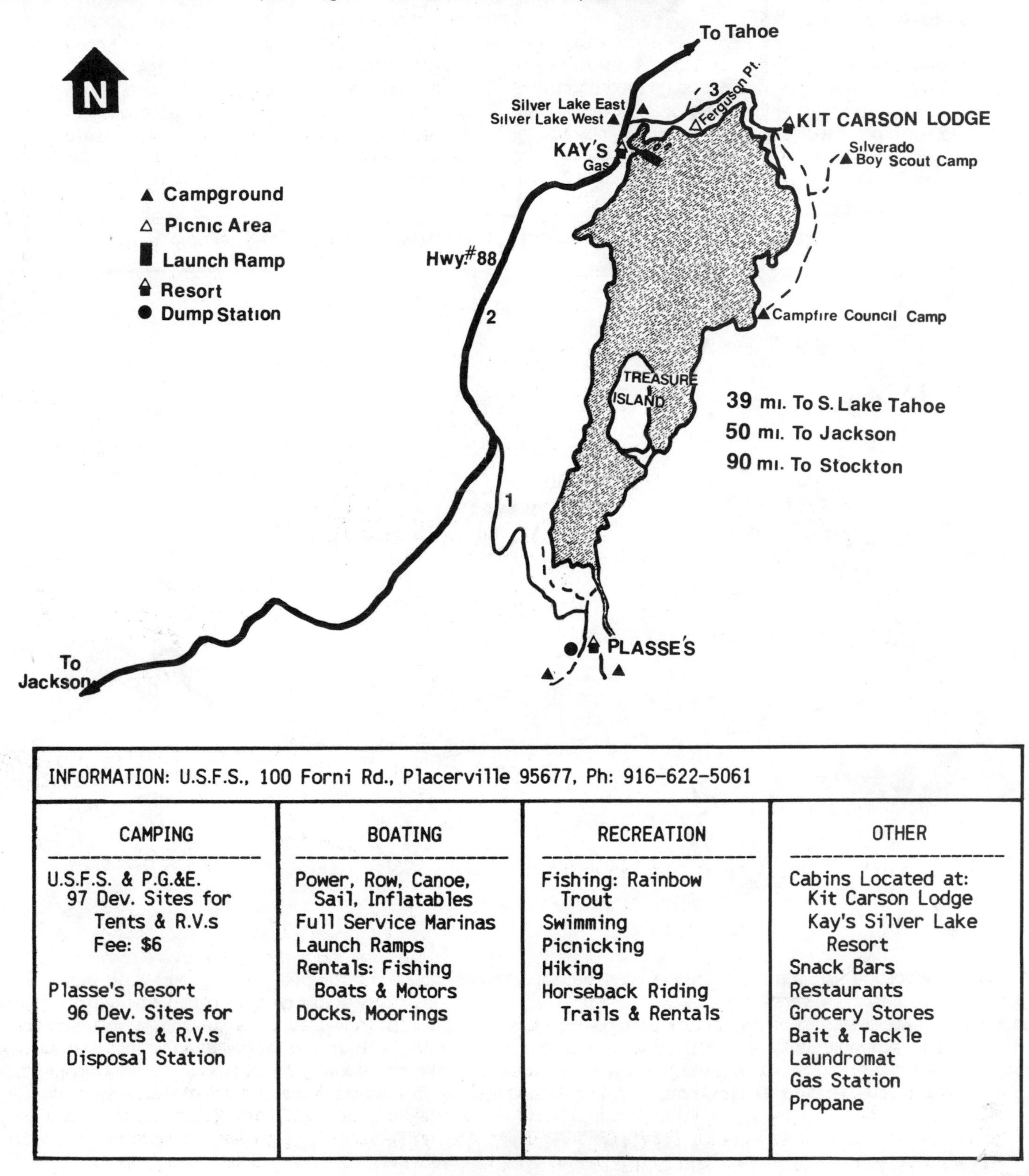

INFORMATION: U.S.F.S., 100 Forni Rd., Placerville 95677, Ph: 916-622-5061

CAMPING	BOATING	RECREATION	OTHER
U.S.F.S. & P.G.&E. 97 Dev. Sites for Tents & R.V.s Fee: $6 Plasse's Resort 96 Dev. Sites for Tents & R.V.s Disposal Station	Power, Row, Canoe, Sail, Inflatables Full Service Marinas Launch Ramps Rentals: Fishing Boats & Motors Docks, Moorings	Fishing: Rainbow Trout Swimming Picnicking Hiking Horseback Riding Trails & Rentals	Cabins Located at: Kit Carson Lodge Kay's Silver Lake Resort Snack Bars Restaurants Grocery Stores Bait & Tackle Laundromat Gas Station Propane

CAPLES LAKE

KIRKWOOD LAKE

Caples Lake is at an elevation of 7,950 feet in the Eldorado National Forest near the summit of Carson Pass. The nights and mornings are cool, and the water is cold in this 600 surface acre Lake. Kirkwood Lake is 3 miles to the west of Caples Lake at an elevation of 7,600 feet, and the road is not suitable for larger R.V.s or trailers. Motor boats are not allowed on Kirkwood, but you may use a motor up to 10 MPH on Caples. Fishing is good for a variety of trout in these Lakes as well as other nearby lakes and streams. Trails lead into the Mokelumne Wilderness to entice the hiker or horseback rider. This entire area is a photographer's delight.

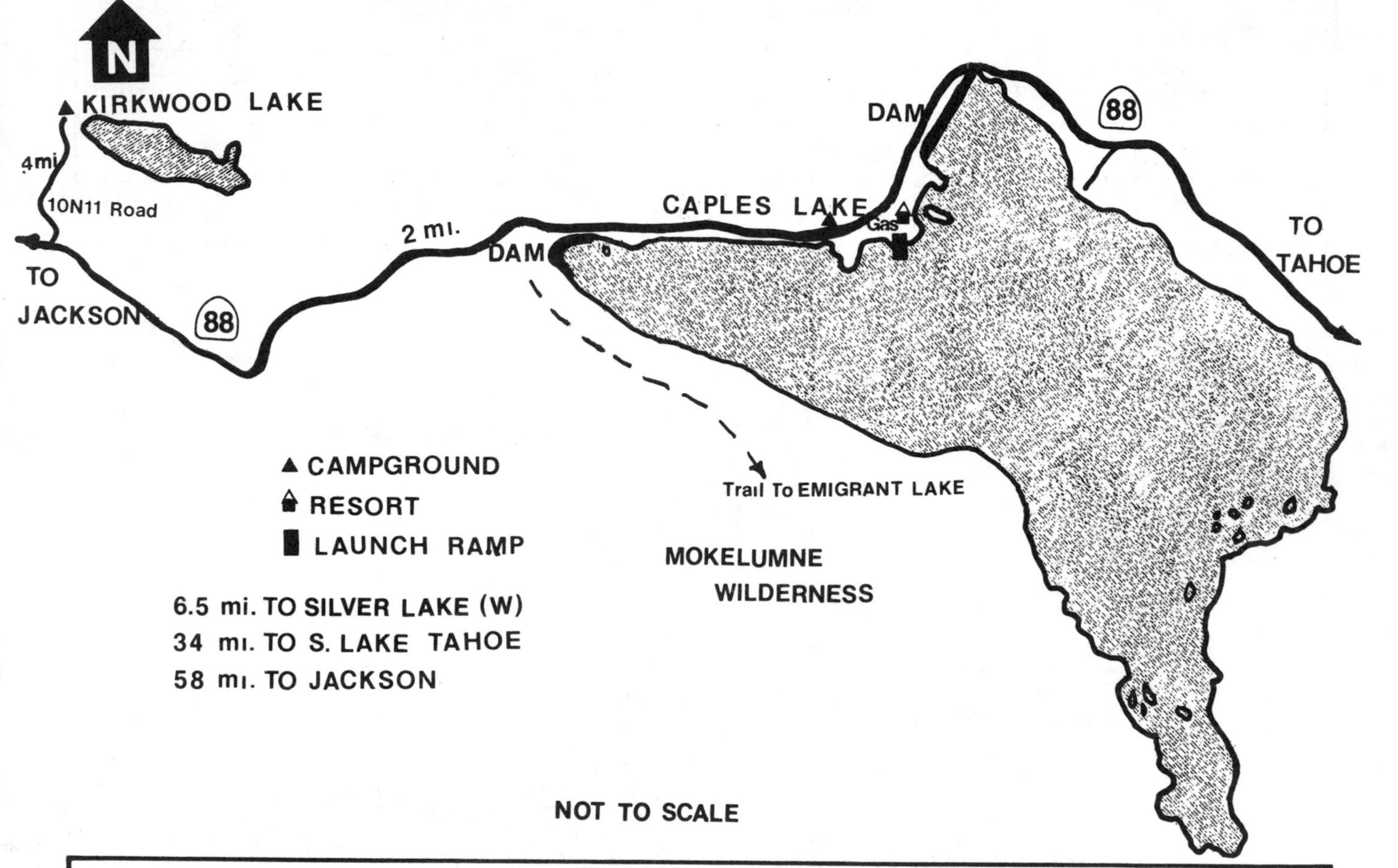

INFORMATION: Ranger Station, 26820 Silver Dr., Pioneer 95666, Ph: 209-295-4251

CAMPING	BOATING	RECREATION	OTHER
Caples Lake: 35 Dev. Site for Tents & R.V.s Fee: $6 Kirkwood Lake: 13 Dev. Sites for Tents & R.V.s Fee: $4	Power, Row, Canoe, Sail & Inflatables Speed Limit on Caples Lake - 10 MPH No Motors on Kirkwood Launch Ramp Rentals: Fishing Boats Water Taxi	Fishing: Rainbow, Brown, Brook & Cutthroat Trout Swimming Picnicking Hiking Backpacking Horseback Riding Trails Hunting: Deer	Caples Lake Resort P.O. Box 8 Kirkwood 95646 Ph: 209-258-8888 Lodge & Restaurant Housekeeping Cabins Grocery Store Bait & Tackle Gas Station

WOODS LAKE

Woods Lake is at an elevation of 8,200 feet southwest of the Carson Pass in the Eldorado National Forest. This lovely hidden retreat just 2 miles south of Highway 88 offers a variety of recreational opportunities. In addition to the campground, the Forest Service provides a nice picnic area at the water's edge with facilities for the handicapped. Fishing can be good from boat or along the bank as well as in the streams throughout the area. Motorboats are not permitted on the Lake. Trails lead to Winnemucca and Round Top Lakes and into the Mokelumne Wilderness. The Pacific Crest Trail runs to the east of Woods Lake. Most of Red Lake is private land with restricted access and limited facilities.

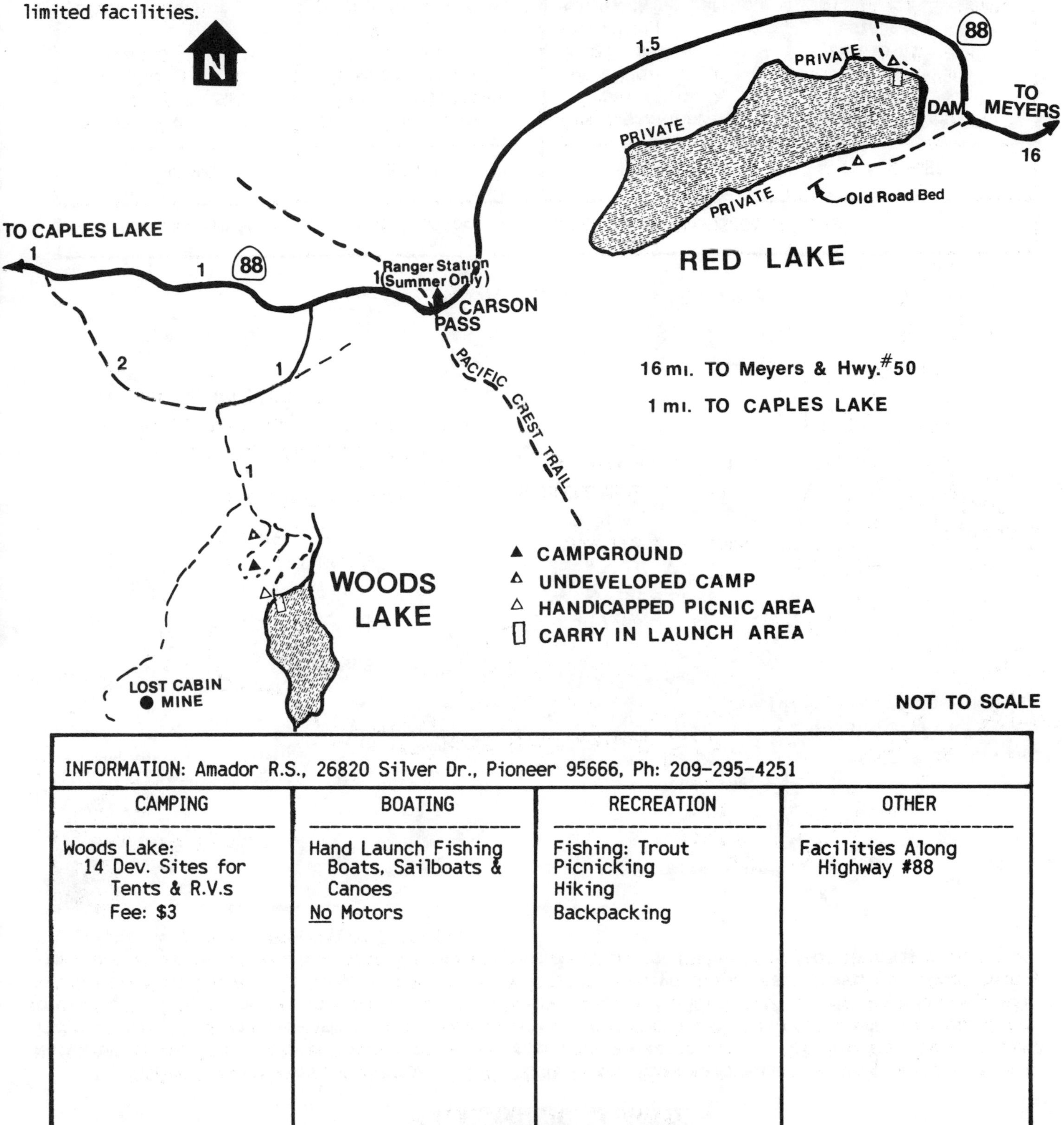

INFORMATION: Amador R.S., 26820 Silver Dr., Pioneer 95666, Ph: 209-295-4251

CAMPING	BOATING	RECREATION	OTHER
Woods Lake: 14 Dev. Sites for Tents & R.V.s Fee: $3	Hand Launch Fishing Boats, Sailboats & Canoes No Motors	Fishing: Trout Picnicking Hiking Backpacking	Facilities Along Highway #88

BLUE LAKES

ALPINE COUNTY

The Blue Lakes are at an elevation of 8,000 feet in this remote country of the Eldorado National Forest. The evenings and mornings are cool and the water is clear and cold. Boating is limited to small craft, and fishing can be good. There are numerous hiking trails, some leading into the Mokelumne Wilderness. The campgrounds are maintained by P.G.&E. except for Hope Valley which is operated by the U.S. Forest Service, Carson Ranger District, Toiyabe National Forest. Facilities are limited so come well prepared. Only the first seven miles of road are paved from Highway 88.

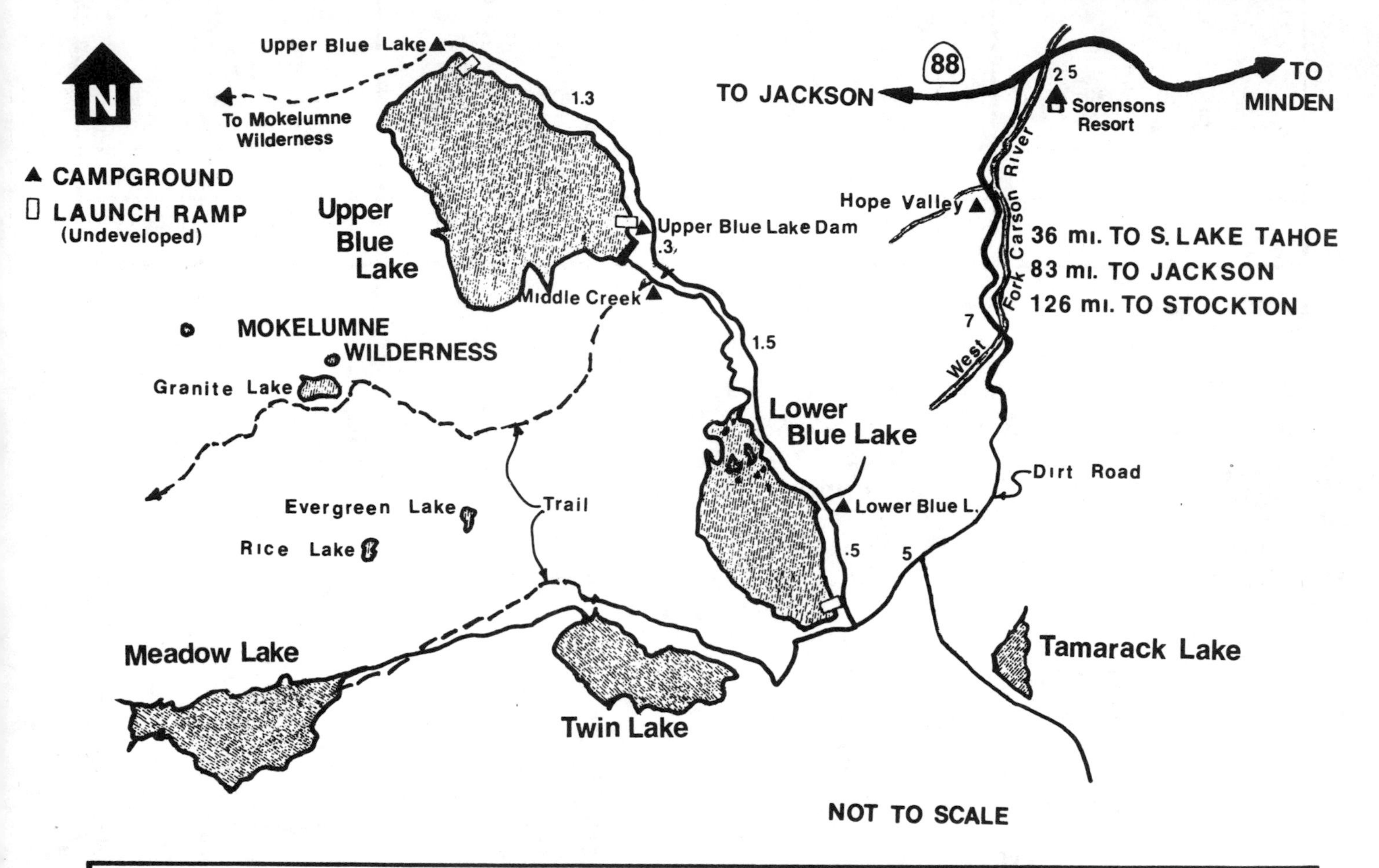

INFORMATION: P.G.&E. Div. Land Supervisor, P.O. Box 930, Stockton 95201

CAMPING	BOATING	RECREATION	OTHER
78 Dev. Sites for Tents & R.V.s P.G.&E. Fee: $5 26 Dev. Sites or Tents & R.V.s U.S.F.S. Fee: $4	Small Boats Only Undeveloped Launch Ramps	Fishing: Rainbow Trout Swimming Picnicking Hiking Backpacking-Parking	Sorensen's Resort Hope Valley 96120 Ph: 916-694-2203 20 Cabins Restaurant

INDIAN CREEK RESERVOIR AND HEENAN LAKE

Indian Creek Reservoir is at an elevation of 5,600 feet on the eastern slope of the Sierras. The Bureau of Land Management maintains more than 7,000 acres in this beautiful area of Jeffrey and Pinon Pines. This 160 acre Lake of recycled water offers good fishing and small craft boating. Nearby Heenan Lake, 129 acres, provides a good catch and release fishery. After 21 years of being off limits, this operating hatchery now provides for zero limit fishing by artificial lures and barbless hooks. Contact the California Department of Fish and Game at 916-355-7090 for specific regulations. A popular attraction in this area is Grover Hot Springs State Park where you can enjoy a hot mineral bath for $2.00. Camping reservations are advised.

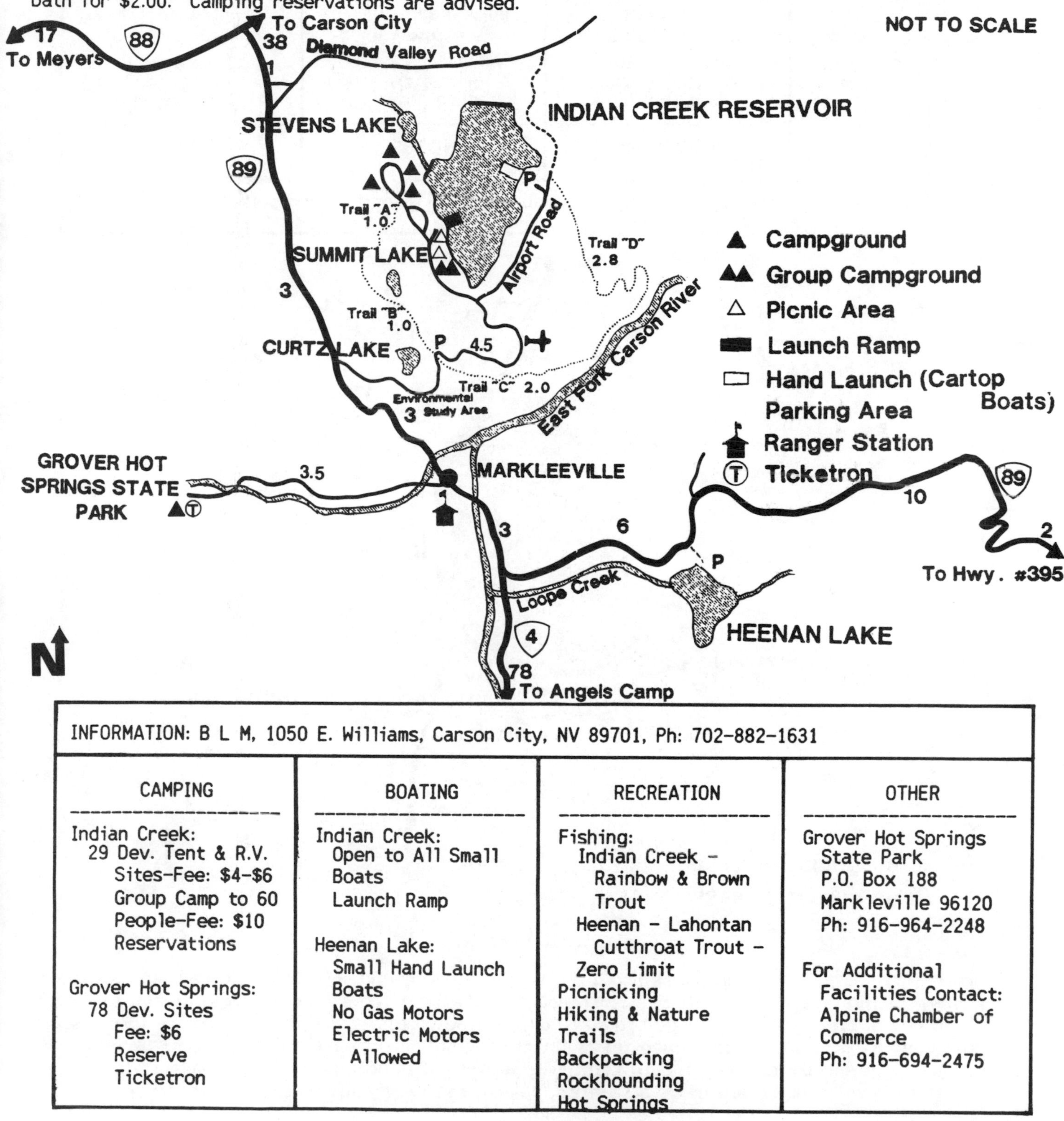

INFORMATION: B L M, 1050 E. Williams, Carson City, NV 89701, Ph: 702-882-1631

CAMPING	BOATING	RECREATION	OTHER
Indian Creek: 29 Dev. Tent & R.V. Sites-Fee: $4-$6 Group Camp to 60 People-Fee: $10 Reservations Grover Hot Springs: 78 Dev. Sites Fee: $6 Reserve Ticketron	Indian Creek: Open to All Small Boats Launch Ramp Heenan Lake: Small Hand Launch Boats No Gas Motors Electric Motors Allowed	Fishing: Indian Creek - Rainbow & Brown Trout Heenan - Lahontan Cutthroat Trout - Zero Limit Picnicking Hiking & Nature Trails Backpacking Rockhounding Hot Springs	Grover Hot Springs State Park P.O. Box 188 Markleville 96120 Ph: 916-964-2248 For Additional Facilities Contact: Alpine Chamber of Commerce Ph: 916-694-2475

TOPAZ LAKE

Topaz Lake rests on the California-Nevada State Line at an elevation of 5,000 feet. This 1,800 acre Reservoir is nestled amid sage covered mountains with a sandy shoreline of 25 miles. The Lake is open to all types of boating including overnight, but beware of potential heavy afternoon winds. Both California and Nevada stock the Lake which is closed to fishing for three months beginning October 1. As a result, trophy sized trout up to 8 pounds are no surprise. Since half of Topaz Lake is in Nevada, the nearby casinos offer games of chance for those so inclined.

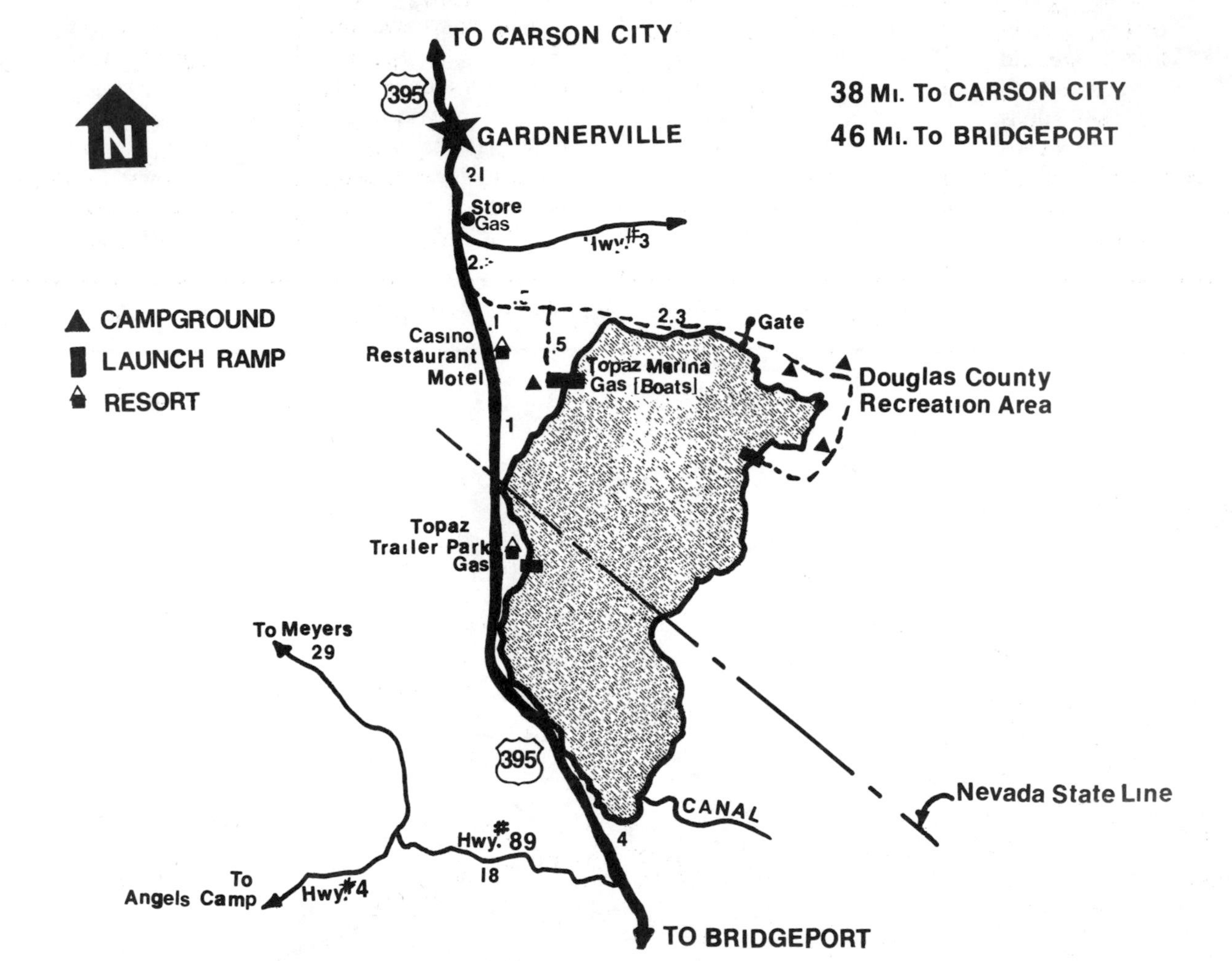

INFORMATION: Douglas Co., Rt.2,Box 176-A, Gardnerville, NV 89410, Ph: 702-266-3343

CAMPING	BOATING	RECREATION	OTHER
Douglas County: 125 Dev. Sites for Tents & R.V.s, Some Hookups - $4 Topaz Trailer Park 50 R.V. Sites - $12 Full Hookups Topaz Marina 28 Dev. Sites for Tents & R.V.s, Some Hookups Fee: $3 - $6	Power, Row, Canoe, Sail, Waterski, Jet Ski, Windsurf, & Inflatables Full Service Marina Launch Ramps - $2 Rentals: Fishing Boats Docks, Berths, Dry Storage, Moorings & Gas Overnight Boating	Fishing: Rainbow, Brown & Cutthroat Trout Swimming - Beaches Picnicking Hiking Playgrounds	Topaz Lake Trailer Park Phone: 916-495-2357 Topaz Marina Phone: 702-266-3236 Motel Restaurant & Lounge Casinos Bait & Tackle at Topaz Marina Disposal Station

LAKE ALPINE

Lake Alpine is at an elevation of 7,320 feet in the Stanislaus National Forest. The Lake has a surface area of 180 acres and is regularly stocked with Rainbow Trout. All boating is allowed within a 10 MPH speed limit, and the steady breezes make this a good sailing Lake. Trails leading to the new Carson-Iceberg Wilderness to the south of Lake Alpine and the Mokelumne Wilderness a few miles to the north, are accessible to the hiker, backpacker and horseman. The Forest Service maintains 4 campgrounds near the Lake plus a special area set aside for backpackers. The historic Lake Alpine Lodge overlooks this beautiful Lake in its heavily timbered mountain setting.

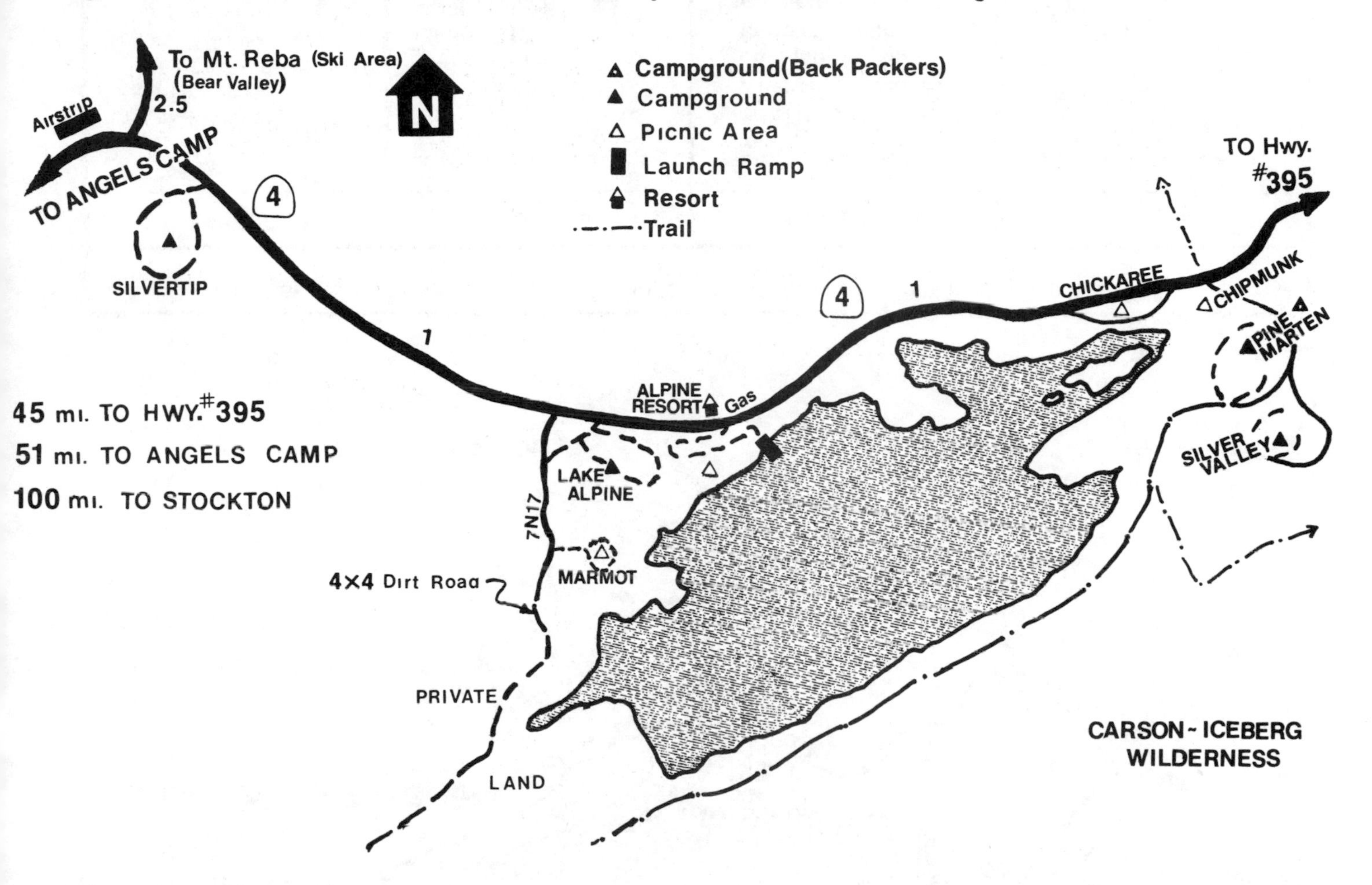

45 mi. TO HWY. #395

51 mi. TO ANGELS CAMP

100 mi. TO STOCKTON

INFORMATION: U.S.F.S., P.O. Box 500, Hathaway Pines 95233, Ph: 209-795-1381

CAMPING	BOATING	RECREATION	OTHER
110 Dev. Sites for Tents & R.V.s Fee: $6 Plus Overflow Area Nearby Marmot Picnic Area Handicap Facilities & Group Sites	Power, Row, Canoe, Sail, Inflatable & Sailboards Speed Limit - 10 MPH Launch Ramp Rentals: Fishing, Sail Boats & Sailboards	Fishing: Rainbow Trout Swimming Picnicking Hiking Backpacking-Parking Horseback Riding Trails & Rentals Hunting: Deer & Bear 4-Wheel Drive & Motorcycle Trails	Lake Alpine Lodge Cabins Snack Bar Restaurant Grocery Store Bait & Tackle Gas Station Airstrip at Bear Valley

LAKE SONOMA

Lake Sonoma is Northern California's newest recreation facility. Nestled amid the rolling hills of Sonoma County at an elevation of 495 feet, Lake Sonoma is under the jurisdiction of the U.S. Army Corps of Engineers. The Lake began filling behind Warm Springs Dam on November 1, 1984. When full, it will cover 3,600 surface acres with 73 miles of shoreline. Extensive recreation, marine and camping facilities are planned over the next few years. This is a good boating Lake, and the fishing is proving to be excellent. Since the facilities are in the process of development, subject to the demands of nature, contact the Corps of Engineers or the Sonoma Lake Resort for current status.

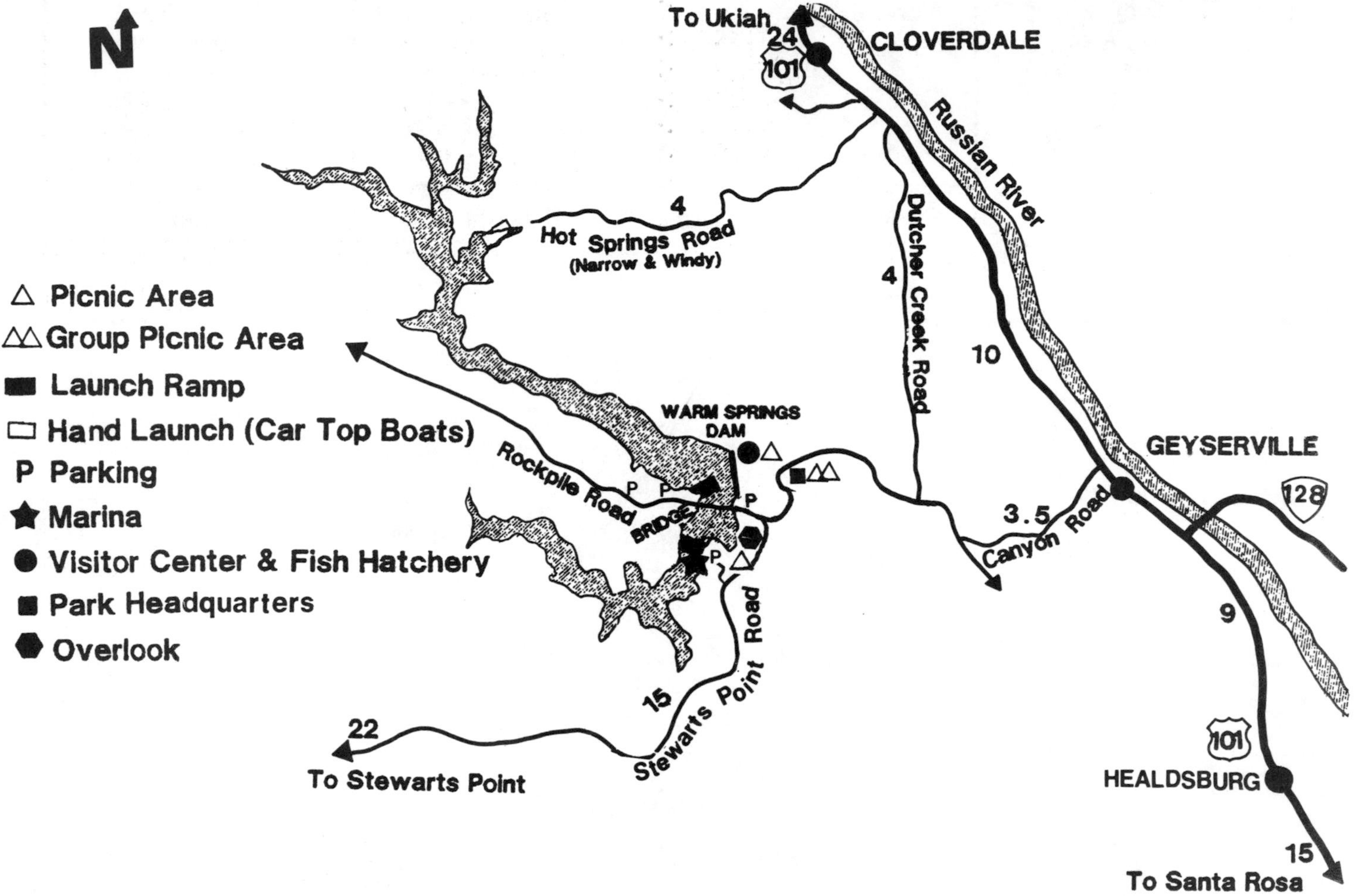

INFORMATION: Lake Sonoma, 3333 Skaggs Springs Rd., Geyserville 95441, Ph: 707-433-9483			
CAMPING	BOATING	RECREATION	OTHER
Contact Above for Current Information on Lake Sonoma Resort	Open to All Boating Jet Skis & Water-skiing Limited to Dry Creek Arm Launch Ramp - Fee: $10 Hand Launch - $4 Boat Rentals: Paddle, Canoe, Fishing, Sail, Ski and Windsurfers Hand Launch for Small Craft at Hot Springs Road	Fishing: Rainbow Trout, Large & Smallmouth Bass, Bluegill, Channel Catfish, Crappie, Redear Perch Picnicking Swimming Hiking & Nature Trail Horseback Riding	Lake Sonoma Resort P.O. Box 1345 Healdsburg 95448 Ph: 707-433-2200 Snack Bar Bait & Tackle Day Use - $2

SPRING LAKE AND LAKE RALPHINE

Spring Lake is under the jurisdiction of the Sonoma County Regional Parks Department. This nice 320 acre Park has picnic areas, a campground, swim lagoon and well maintained trails. This is a popular equestrian area. The 75 acre Lake is open to non-powered boating. Lake Ralphine is within the City of Santa Rosa's Howarth Park. This day use facility has an abundance of children's attractions. Lake Ralphine also allows non-powered boating with sailing being a special attraction. There is a warm water fishery in addition to planted trout at both Lakes. A bicycle path connects these Parks.

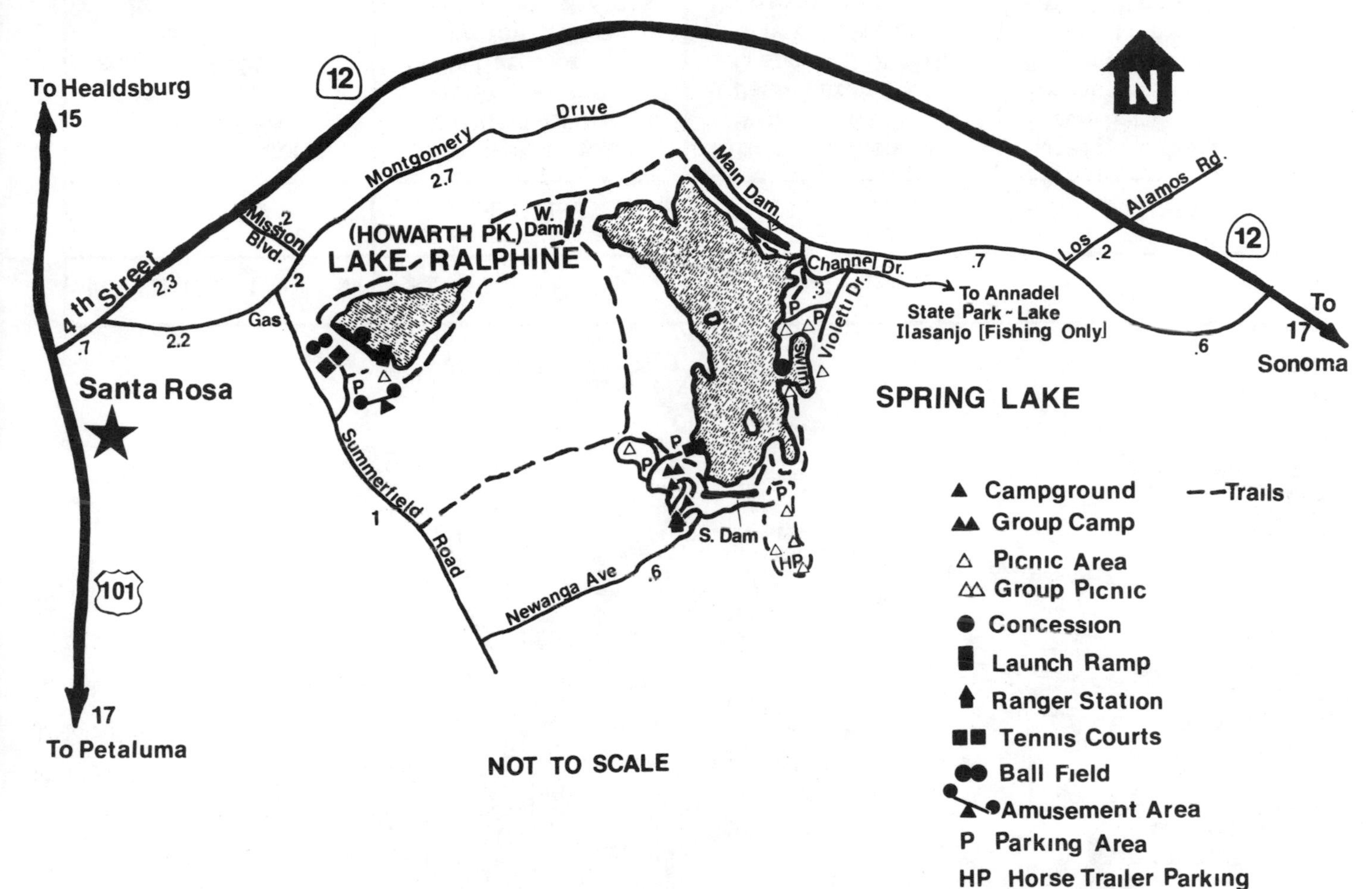

INFORMATION: Spring Lake, 5390 Montgomery Dr., Santa Rosa 95405, Ph: 707-539-8092

CAMPING	BOATING	RECREATION	OTHER
Spring Lake: 31 Dev. Sites for Tents & R.V.s No Hookups Hot Showers Fee: $6 Group Camp to 100 People - Reservations Required Disposal Station	Spring Lake: Row, Sail, Canoe & Inflatables (2 Chambers) Electric Motors Rentals: Row, Canoe & Sailboats (Summer Only) Lake Ralphine: Private Boats Under 20 ft. - No Motors Rentals: As Above	Fishing: Trout, Catfish, Redear Sunfish & Bass Swim Lagoon Picnic Areas: Group Reservations Available at Spring Lake Hiking, Riding & Bicycle Trails Tennis Courts	Howarth Park: Santa Rosa Rec. & Parks Dept. Ph: 707-528-5115 Miniature Steam Train, Merry-Go-Round, Roller Coaster, Pony Rides & Animal Farm, Frontier Village - For Info: Ph: 707-576-5169

LAKE BERRYESSA
LAKE SOLANO

Lake Berryessa and Lake Solano are in the beautiful wine country of the Napa Valley at an elevation of 440 feet.

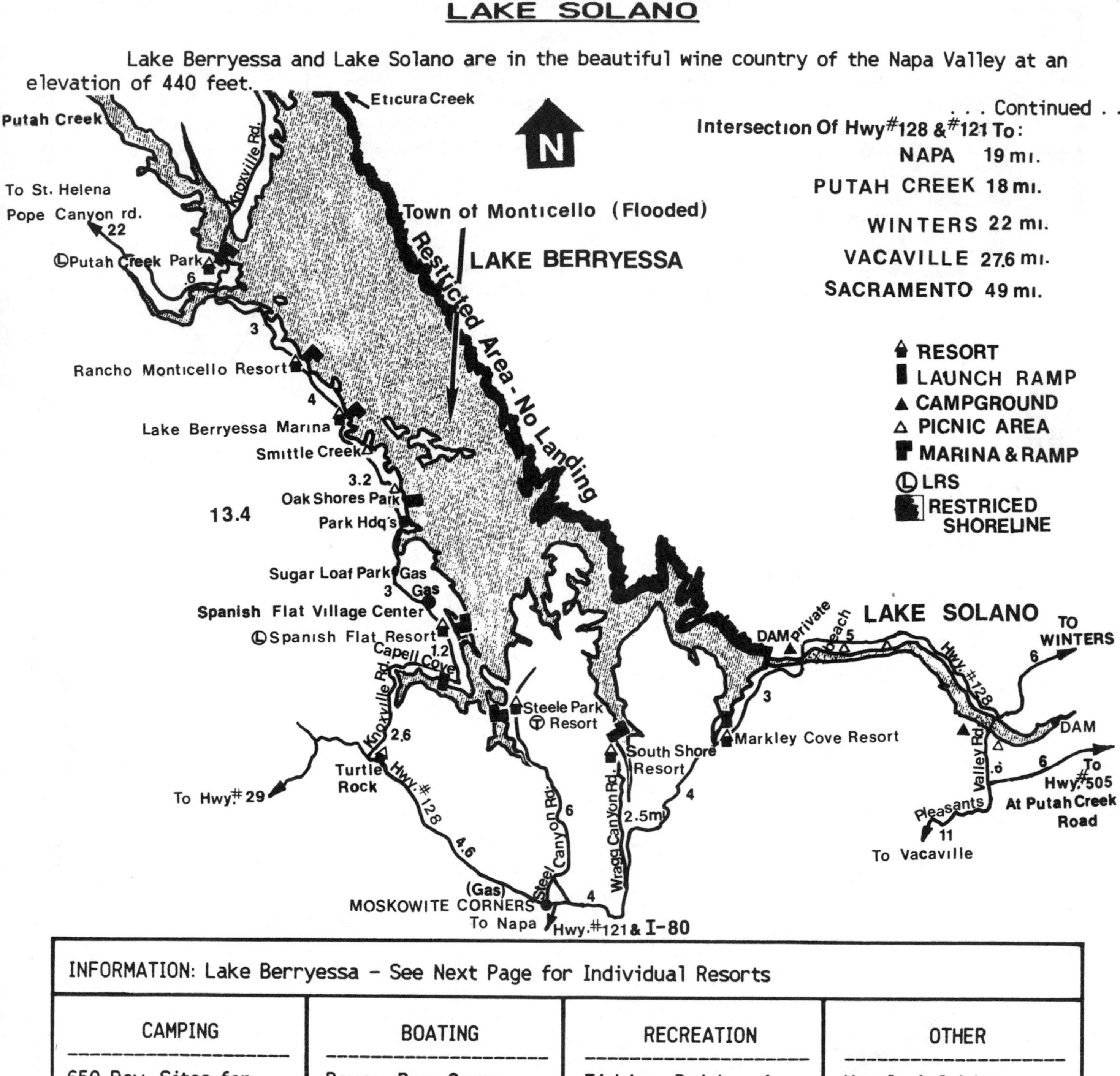

INFORMATION: Lake Berryessa - See Next Page for Individual Resorts

CAMPING	BOATING	RECREATION	OTHER
650 Dev. Sites for Tents & R.V.s at Resorts Fee: $6 - $8.50 Some Full Hookups	Power, Row, Canoe, Sail, Waterski, Jet Ski, Windsurf & Inflatables Restricted Areas Full Service Marinas Launch Ramps Rentals: Fishing, Waterski Boats, Jet Skis, Houseboats Docks, Berths, Gas No Power on Solano	Fishing: Rainbow & Brown Trout, Bass, Catfish, Crappie, Bluegill, Silver Salmon Swimming - Pools Picnicking Hiking Tennis Courts	Motels & Cabins Snack Bars Restaurants Grocery Stores Post Office Bait & Tackle Laundromat Disposal Stations Gas Stations Propane Beauty Shop Shirt Printing Shop

. . . Continued . . .

Lake Berryessa is one of the largest man-made lakes in California with a surface area of 13,000 acres. The often steep, hilly shoreline of 165 miles is covered by oak and manzanita. The 75 degree average summer water temperature makes for good swimming and waterskiing. Light and variable winds are a sailor's delight. The angler will find trophy trout and silver salmon in addition to the excellent bass and warm water fishery. Complete Resort, camping and marine facilities are available at the different Resorts. The Bureau of Reclamation maintains three-day use facilities including a launch ramp at Capell Cove and picnic sites at Smittle Creek and Oaks Shores which also has a cartop boat ramp.

PUTAH CREEK PARK - Ph: 707-966-2116 - 27 Unit Waterfront Motel, Camp, R.V. & Trailer Park with Electric Hookups, 50 with Full Hookups, Picnic Area, Launch Ramp, Docks, Boat Rentals, Storage, Full Service Marina, Tackle Shop, Grocery Store, Restaurant, Cocktail Lounge, Swim Beach, Snack Bar, Gas.

RANCHO MONTICELLO RESORT - Ph: 707-966-2188 - Camping, R.V.s & Trailers, Launch Ramp, Boat Rentals, Store, Swim Beach, Snack Bar, Storage, Gas.

LAKE BERRYESSA MARINA RESORT - Ph: 707-966-2161 - "Good Sam Park" - Camping, R.V.s & Trailers, Hookups, Launch Ramp, Berths, Storage, Fishing Boat, Waterski, Canoes and Patioboats, & Jet Ski Rentals, Marina Store, Restaurant, Snack Bar (in season), Swim Beach, Laundromat, Picnic Sites.

SPANISH FLAT RESORT - Ph: 707-966-2101 - Camping, R.V.s, Electric Hookups, Trailers, Launch Ramps, Berthing, Boat Rental: Fishing Boats, Waterski Boats, Jet Skis, Full Service Marina (Ph: 707-966-2338), Motor Repair, Store & Snack Bar (in season), Picnic Sites with Tables & Barbecues, Lake Swimming. LRS for Reservations - Ph: 800-822-CAMP.

SPANISH FLAT VILLAGE CENTER - Ph: 707-966-2101 - Country Store & Deli, Bait & Tackle, Shirt Printing Shop, Service Station, Laundromat, Restaurant & Bar (Spanish Flat Inn), Pizza, Mobile Home Park, Spanish Flat Woodlands, Post Office, Beauty Shop. LRS for Reservations - Ph: 800-822-CAMP.

STEELE PARK RESORT - Ph: 707-966-2123 - The largest Resort at Berryessa, Camping, R.V.s & Trailers, Motel, Housekeeping Cottages, Launch Ramp, Covered Berths, Boat Rentals, Full Service Marina, Store, Restaurant, Bar, Swim Beach, Pool, Tennis Courts, Dry Storage, Ski School.

SOUTH SHORE RESORT - Ph: 707-966-2172 - Camping, R.V.s & Trailers, Launch Ramp, Marina, Restaurant & Lounge, Boat Storage, Laundromat, Propane.

MARKLEY COVE RESORT - Ph: 707-966-2134 - Camping, Restaurant & Lounge, Store, Boat and Houseboat Rentals, Launch Ramp.

SUGAR LOAF PARK - Ph: 707-966-2347 - Fast Food Service, Grocery Store, Gas & Propane.

TURTLE ROCK - Ph: 707-966-2246 - Motel, Coffee Shop, Cocktail Lounge, Grocery Store, Off Sale Liquor, Bait & Minnows, Supplies.

FOR FURTHER INFORMATION CONTACT: Lake Berryessa Chamber of Commerce
P.O. Box 9164, Spanish Flat Station, Napa 94558

Lake Solano is a popular Lake in the summer with 110 surface acres and many lovely trees along 5 miles of shoreline. The County Park has 50 campsites for tents & R.V.s. No motors are allowed. There is a launch ramp and nice picnic sites along the shore. Rowboats and paddleboats can be rented, and trout season opens in March. There is a Snack Bar which also sells bait. Swimming is allowed in the lagoons.

FOR FURTHER INFORMATION CONTACT: County of Solano Parks Department, Ph: 707-447-0707
or Lake Solano Park: 916-795-2990.

LAKE AMADOR

Lake Amador is at an elevation of 485 feet in the Sierra Foothills, one mile east of historic Buena Vista. The surface area of the Lake is 425 acres. The shoreline of 13-1/2 miles is surrounded by black oak covered hills. The brush along the water's edge provides a thriving warm water fishery. A Northern California record limit of 80 pounds for Florida Bass was set in 1981, and in 1984 the individual Lake record was set for 15 pounds, 13-1/2 ounces. This is a nice boating Lake with good winds for sailing. The Lake is open to boating and fishing 24 hours a day. The visitor will find a 1 acre swim pond with sandy beaches and playgrounds for the children making Amador a good family recreation area.

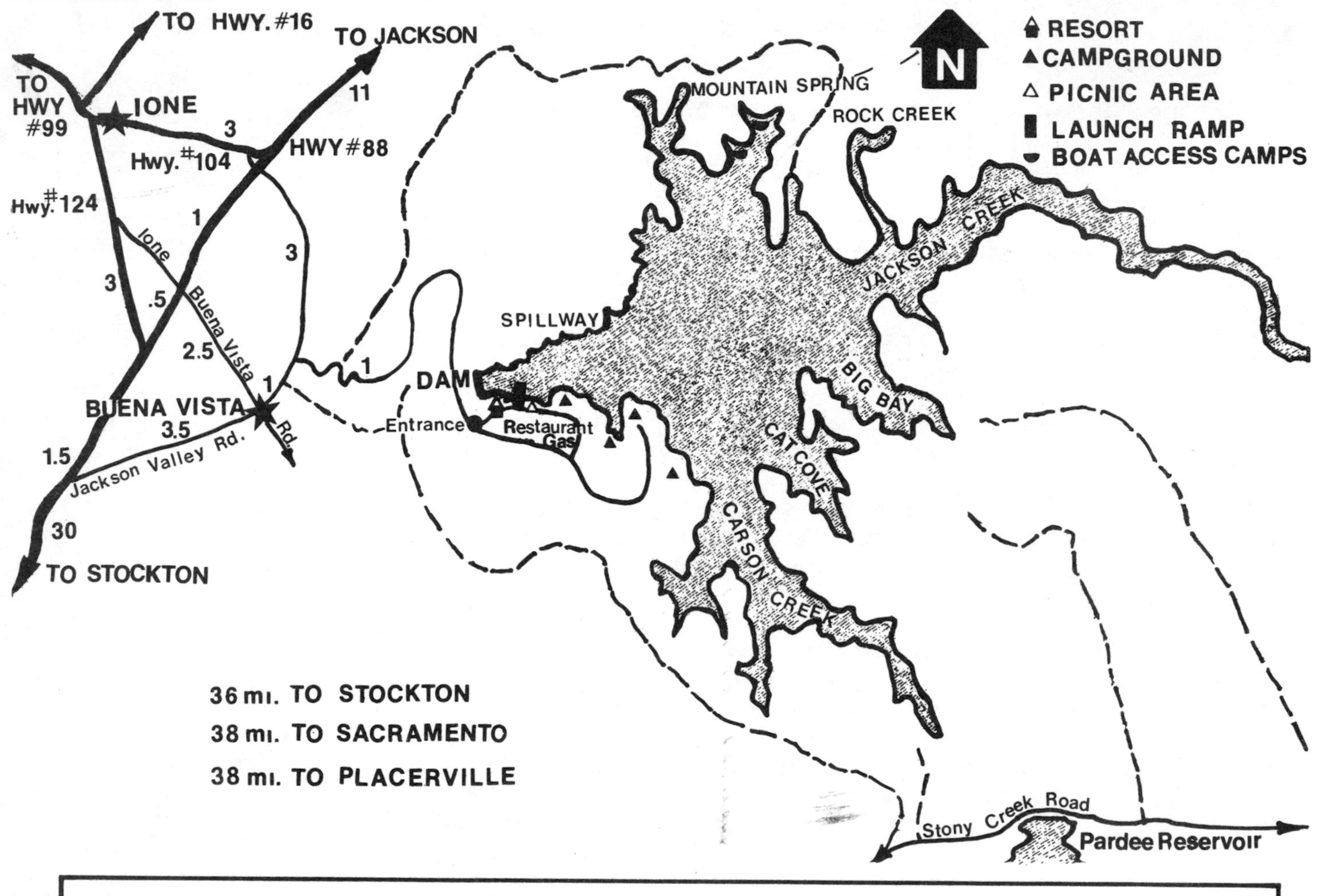

INFORMATION: Lake Amador Resort, 7500 Amador Dr., Ione 95640, Ph: 209-274-2625

CAMPING	BOATING	RECREATION	OTHER
150 Dev. sites for Tents & R.V.s Full Hookups Fee: $8.75 Plus 12 Boat-In or Walk-In Sites Group Camp to 50 Vehicles Reservations for All Sites Suggested	Power, Row, Canoe, Sail, Windsurf & Inflatables No Waterskiing or Jetskis Launch Ramp - $3.25 Rentals: Fishing Boats Docks, Storage Fishing Floats Around Shoreline	Fishing: Trout, Largemouth Bass, Catfish, Bluegill, Crappie & Perch Swimming - Pond Free Waterslides Picnicking Hiking Horseback Riding Trails	Snack Bar Restaurant Grocery Store Bait & Tackle Hot Showers Disposal Station Gas Station & Propane Club House & Recreation Room Children's Playground

PARDEE LAKE

Pardee Lake rests in the Mother Lode Country of the Sierra Foothills at an elevation of 568 feet. The surface area of the Lake is 2,200 acres with a shoreline of 43 miles of rolling woodland. Within easy distance of historic gold towns, Pardee is a complete family recreation area. The angler will find a good warm water fishery, trophy trout planted weekly in season, and a Tom Sawyer Island for the children. All boating is allowed except for waterskiing as no body contact with the water is permitted. There are modern, shaded camping facilities, picnic areas, playgrounds and a swimming pool. Law enforcement is strict so it is quite peaceful.

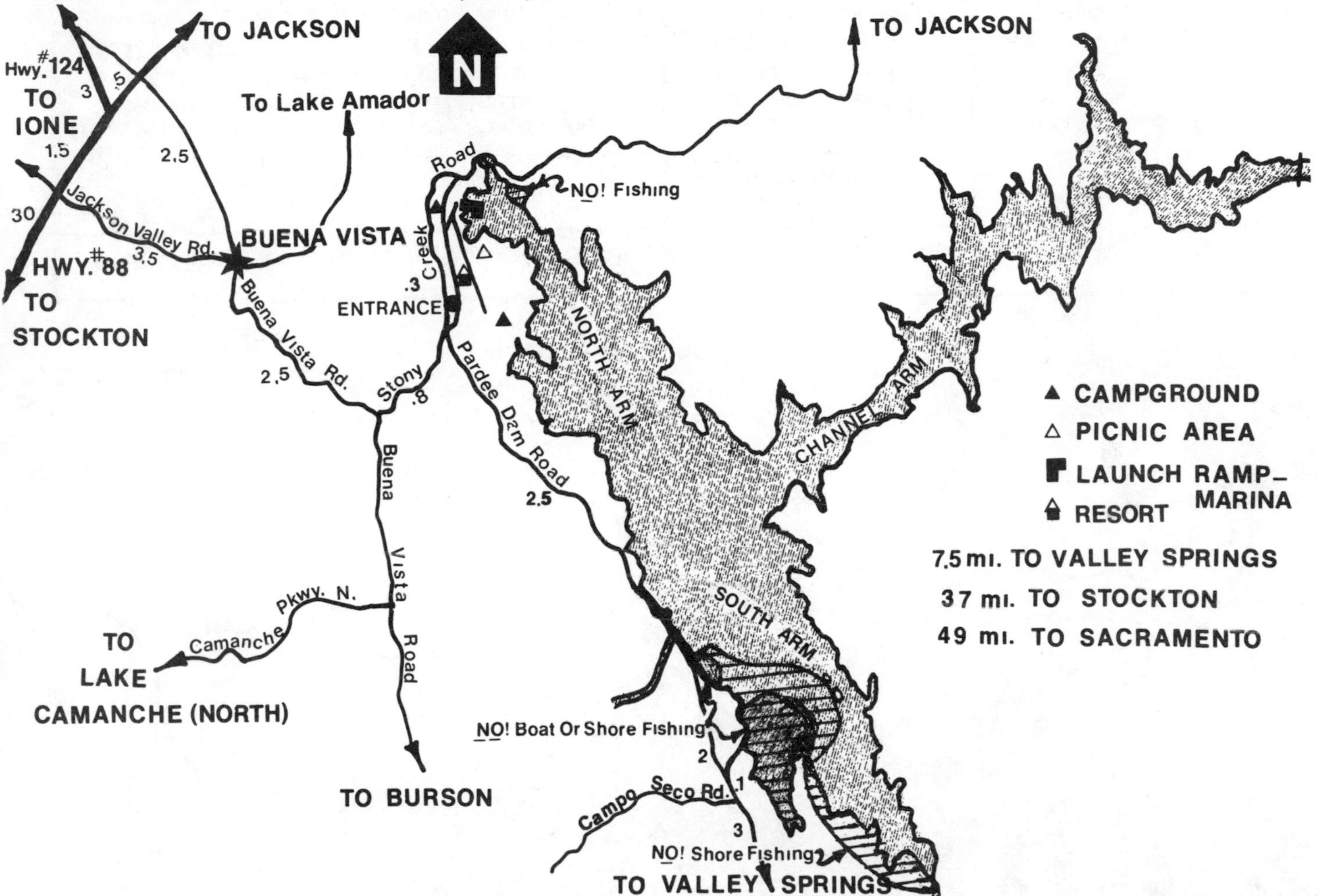

INFORMATION: Pardee Lake Resort, 4900 Stony Creek Rd., Ione 95640, Ph: 209-772-1472

CAMPING	BOATING	RECREATION	OTHER
100 Dev. Tent Sites Fee: $6 90 Dev. R.V. Sites With Full Hookups Fee: $10 Groups to 100 People Reservations Taken at R.V. Sites Only	Power, Row, Canoe, Sail & Inflatables No Body Contact With the Water Full Service Marina Launch Ramp Rentals: Fishing Boats & Pontoons Docks, Berths, Moorings, Gas Dry Storage	Fishing: Rainbow & Brown Trout, Kokanee Salmon, Catfish, Bluegill, Crappie & Bass Swimming in Pool Picnicking Bicycle Trails Playground Tom Sawyer Fishing Island	Snack Bar Restaurant Grocery Store Laundromat Disposal Station Gas & Propane

LAKE CAMANCHE

Lake Camanche is at an elevation of 235 feet in the foothills of the Sierra Nevada. This East Bay Municipal Utility District Reservoir has 7,700 surface acres and a shoreline of 53 miles. Located in the famous "Mother Lode" Country, panning for gold is still popular in the spring when streams are high. Indian grave sites are visible along the shoreline. The water is warm and clear making watersports a delight. Fishing for a variety of species can be excellent. The Resorts at Camanche Northshore and South Camanche Shore offer modern, complete camping, marine and recreation facilities. There are over 15,000 acres of park lands for the hiker and equestrian. Camanche is one of the most complete facility Lakes within easy distance of the San Francisco Bay Area.

. . . Continued . .

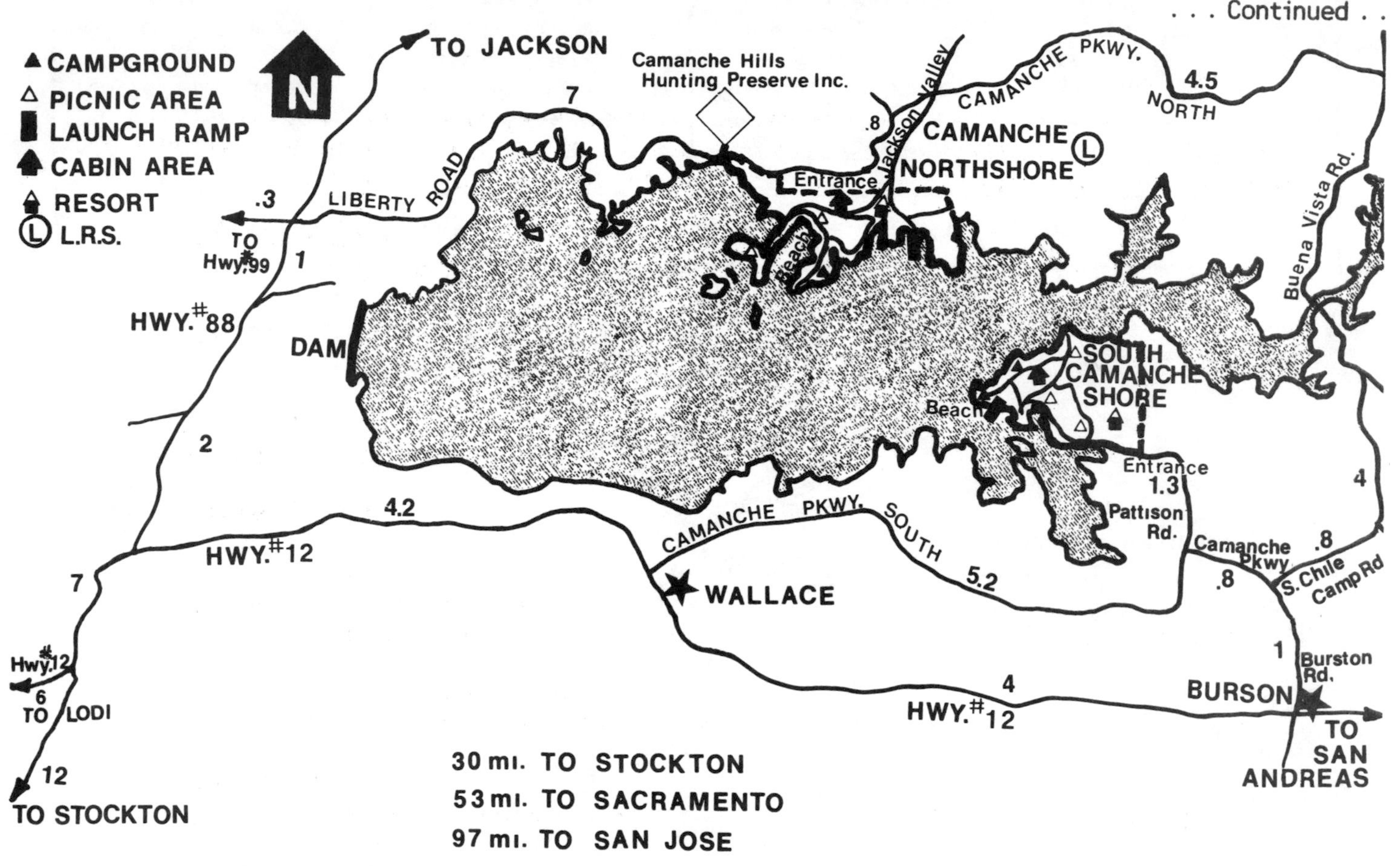

INFORMATION: Camanche North Shore and South Camanche Shore - See Next Page			
CAMPING	BOATING	RECREATION	OTHER
Over 1,100 Dev. Sites for Tents & R.V.s Full Hookups Available Disposal Stations Propane	Power, Row, Canoe, Sail, Waterski, Jet Ski, & Inflatables No Waterskiing in Upper Lake Full Service Marinas Launch Ramps Rentals: Fishing, Ski, Sail, Canoe, Patio Boats	Fishing: Trout, Catfish, Bluegill, Crappie, Bass & Kokanee Swimming, Waterslides Picnicking Hiking Horseback Riding Trails & Rentals Hunting: Ducks, Geese, Pheasant, Quail, Turkey	Extensive Vacation Facilities See Next Page For Details

CAMANCHE NORTHSHORE RESORT
2000 Jackson Valley - Camanche Road
Ione, California 95640
Ph: 209-763-5121

Reserve Campsites, Cottages & Motel Units Through Leisuretime Reservation System

500 Campsites for Tents & R.V.s - Water, Toilets, Showers, Disposal Station, Trailer Storage, Laundromat, Playgrounds, Store, Coffee Shop. Fees.

Full Service Marina - 10-lane Launch Ramp, Fee, Boat Rentals: Sail, Fishing, Canoes, Patio Boats, Storage, Berths, Moorings, Fishing & Waterskiing Equipment Rentals, Sailing School, Bike Rentals, Canoe River Trips, Patio Boat Tours, For Information Phone: 209-763-5511. General Store and Coffee Shop: Phone 209-763-5166

Riding Stables - Breakfast Rides, Cross Country, Sunset Rides, Barbecue Dinners and Campfires, Haywagon Rides, Pony Rides, Lessons, Training, Boarding. For Information Phone: 209-763-5295.

Cottages - Rentals of Deluxe Housekeeping Cottages for 2 to 12 People, Motel Rooms, Tennis Courts.

Conference and Seminar Facilities - Groups up to 100 People, Bird Hunting Preserve and Club, Golf Nearby, Special Events.

Other Facilities - Amphitheater with Movies and Entertainment. Pavilion for Dancing and Concerts. Two Mobile Home Parks with Sales Division, Restaurant and Cocktail Lounge.

SOUTH CAMANCHE SHORE
P.O Box 92
Wallace, California 95254
Ph: 209-763-5178

Over 678 Campsites for Tents & R.V.s - Water, Toilets, Showers, Full Hookups, Disposal Station, Laundromat, Store & Snack Bars. Fees.

Full Service Marina - 7-lane Launch Ramp, Boat Rentals: Fishing & Pontoon Boats, Storage, Berths, Moorings.

Other Facilities - Housekeeping Cottages, Horseback Riding, Tennis Courts, Waterslides, Fee. Amphitheater with Movies and Entertainment, Group Reservations for Camping or Picnicking, Mobile Home Park and Sales, Recreation Hall.

NEW HOGAN LAKE

New Hogan Lake is at an elevation of 713 feet in the foothills east of Stockton. The U. S. Army Corps of Engineers holds jurisdiction over the Lake and maintains the modern marine and camping facilities. The surface area of the Lake is 4,400 acres with 50 miles of shoreline covered with oak, digger pine and brushlands of chamise and manzanita. In spring a variety of wild flowers provide a colorful display. Wildlife is abundant with over 153 species of birds. New Hogan is ideal for water-oriented recreation. Waterskiing is allowed in the central Lake, but many coves and the swimming beaches are restricted.

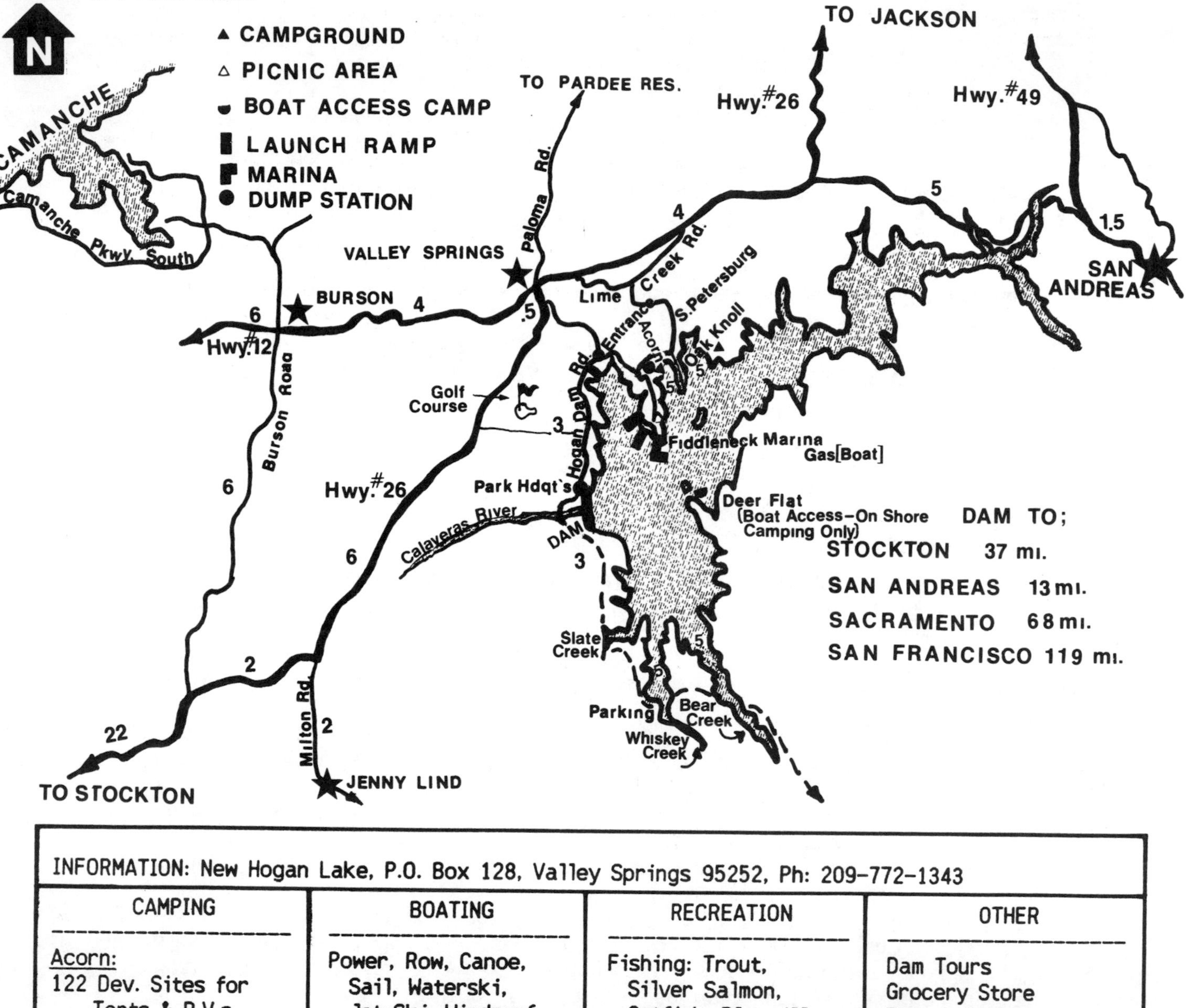

INFORMATION: New Hogan Lake, P.O. Box 128, Valley Springs 95252, Ph: 209-772-1343

CAMPING	BOATING	RECREATION	OTHER
Acorn: 122 Dev. Sites for Tents & R.V.s Fee: $6 Oak Knoll: 68 Undev. Sites - Free 30 Boat Access Camps - No Fee & No Water No Reservations	Power, Row, Canoe, Sail, Waterski, Jet Ski, Windsurf & Inflatable No Houseboats or Camping in Boats Full Service Marina Launch Ramps Rentals: Fishing Boats & Motors,	Fishing: Trout, Silver Salmon, Catfish, Bluegill, Crappie and Black & Striped Bass Swimming Picnicking Hiking, Nature & Equestrian Trails Campfire Program Bird Watching Hunting: Quail, Dove	Dam Tours Grocery Store Bait & Tackle Hot Showers Disposal Station Gas Station Docks, Moorings, Dry Storage La Contenta Golf Course Nearby Full Facilities-3 Mi. Valley Springs

LYONS LAKE

Lyons Lake is at an elevation of 4,200 feet on the western slope of the Sierras northeast of Sonora. This pretty Lake has 10 miles of tree-covered shoreline. There is a rocked launch ramp for small boats, and boating is limited to row, sail, canoe and electric motors. This is an excellent trolling Lake for Rainbow, Eastern Brook and German Brown Trout. Lyons Lake Resort provides a rustic campground with limited facilities. Large R.V.s and trailers are not advised due to road conditions. This is a quiet and peaceful area where you can relax and enjoy nature. Be sure to bring a camera.

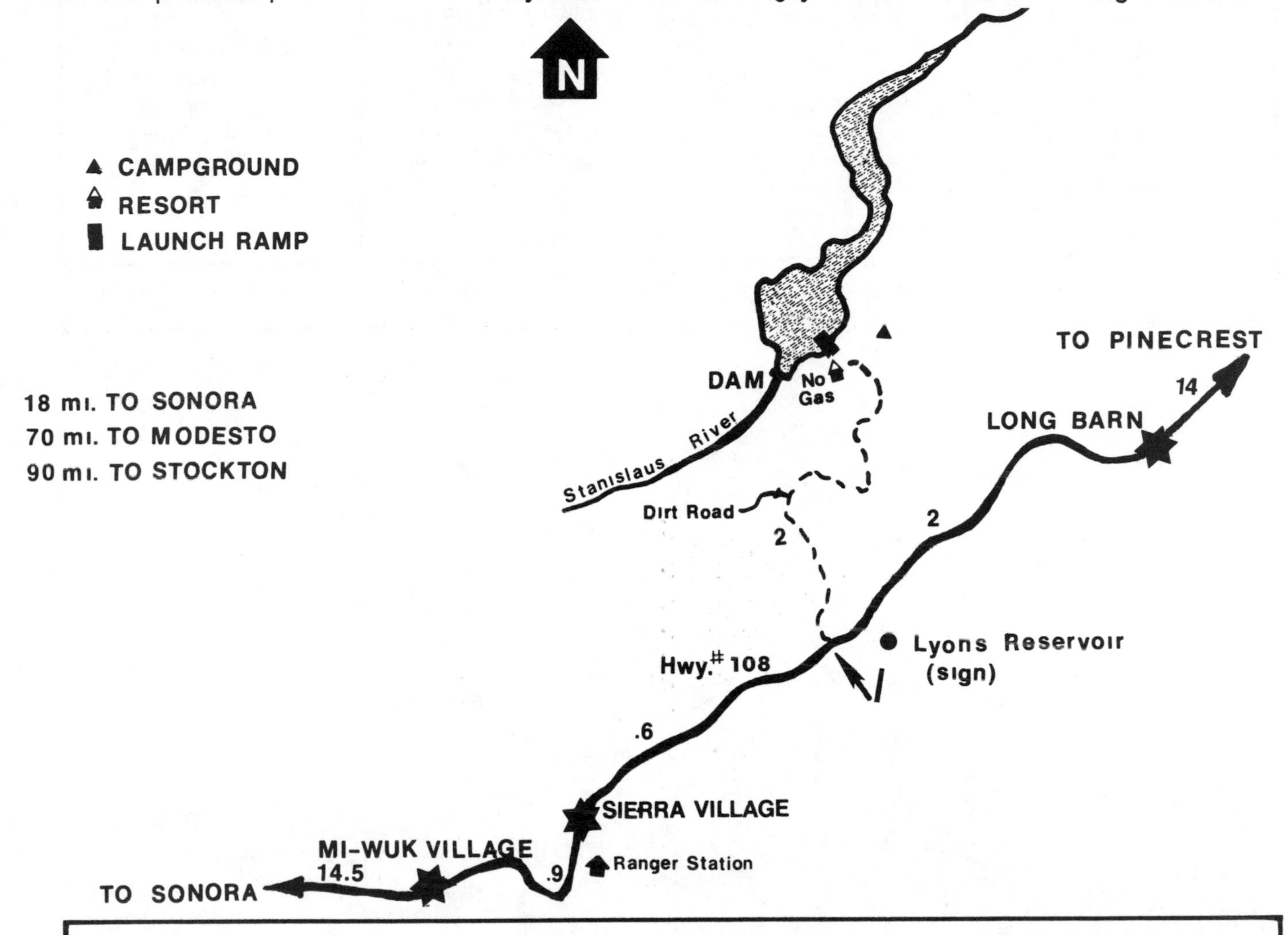

INFORMATION: Lyons Lake Resort, Star Rt., Box 1196, Sonora 95370, Ph: 209-586-3724

CAMPING	BOATING	RECREATION	OTHER
60 Dev. sites for Tents & Small R.V.s Fee: $5.50 Reservations Accepted	Electric Motors Only, Row, Canoe & Sail Unimproved Launch Ramp - $1.50 Rentals: Fishing Boats Dry Storage	Fishing: Rainbow, Eastern Brook & German Brown Trout, Black Bass & Channel Catfish Picnicking Hiking Backpacking-Parking Playgrounds No Swimming	Snack Bar Grocery Store Bait & Tackle Full Facilities - 16 Miles at Sonora

PINECREST LAKE

Pinecrest Lake is at an elevation of 5,600 feet in Stanislaus National Forest. At times called Strawberry Reservoir, Pinecrest has a surface area of 300 acres with 3.6 miles of mountainous, tree-covered shoreline. The Forest Service, under concession, maintains 300 campsites, a group camp, picnic sites next to the beach and a paved launch ramp. In addition, they provide nature trails and tours plus campfire programs. Pinecrest Lake Resort is a complete modern destination facility with extensive accommodations. Trout are planted weekly in season at Pinecrest Lake, and there are a number of other lakes and streams within easy walking distance to entice the angler. Boating is limited to 20 MPH, and waterskiing is not permitted. There is a large swim beach adjacent to the picnic area.

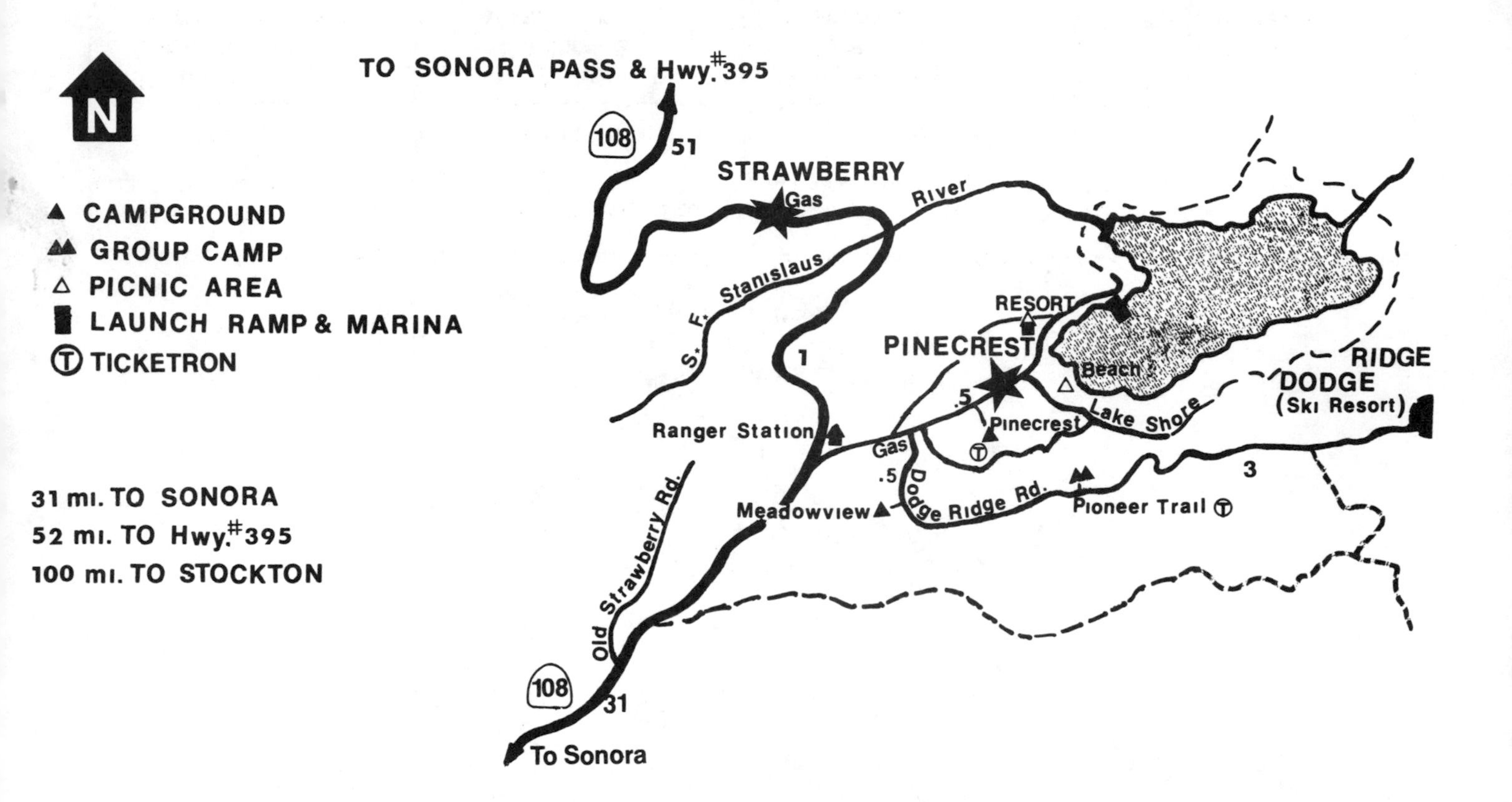

INFORMATION: Summit R.D., Star Rt. Box 1295, Sonora 95370, Ph: 209-965-3434

CAMPING	BOATING	RECREATION	OTHER
300 Dev. Sites for Tents Fee: $6 - $8 Ph: 209-965-3116 One Campground - Reservations One Campground - First Come Basis Group Camps - 3 Sites - 200 People Maximum No Trailers	Power, Row, Canoe, Sail, Windsurf & Inflatables Speed Limit - 20 MPH Full Service Marina Launch Ramp Rentals: Fishing, Sail, Paddle & Motor Boats, Windsurfers Docks, Berths, Gas	Fishing: Rainbow, Brown & Eastern Brook Trout Swimming - Beaches Picnicking Hiking & Nature Trails Backpacking-Parking Horseback Riding Rentals Nearby Campfire Programs - M-W Nights	Pinecrest Lake Resort P.O. Box 1216 Pinecrest 95364 Ph: 209-965-3411 Cabins & Condos Snack Bar Restaurant Grocery Store Bait & Tackle Gas Station Tennis & Movies Sports Store

MOSQUITO, HIGHLAND, DONNELLS, HARTLEY (BEARDSLEY) AND LEAVITT LAKES

Ascending the western slopes of the Sierra Nevadas to the Sonora and Ebbetts Passes, the Lakes along Highways 4 and 108 vary in elevation from west to east of 3,400 feet to 8,500 feet. Boating is limited to small hand-launched craft except for Hartley Lake which is open to all types of boating. There is good trout fishing in all of the Lakes, and there are numerous trails for the equestrian, hiker and backpacker. In addition to those campgrounds shown on the map, the Forest Service has campgrounds along both highways.

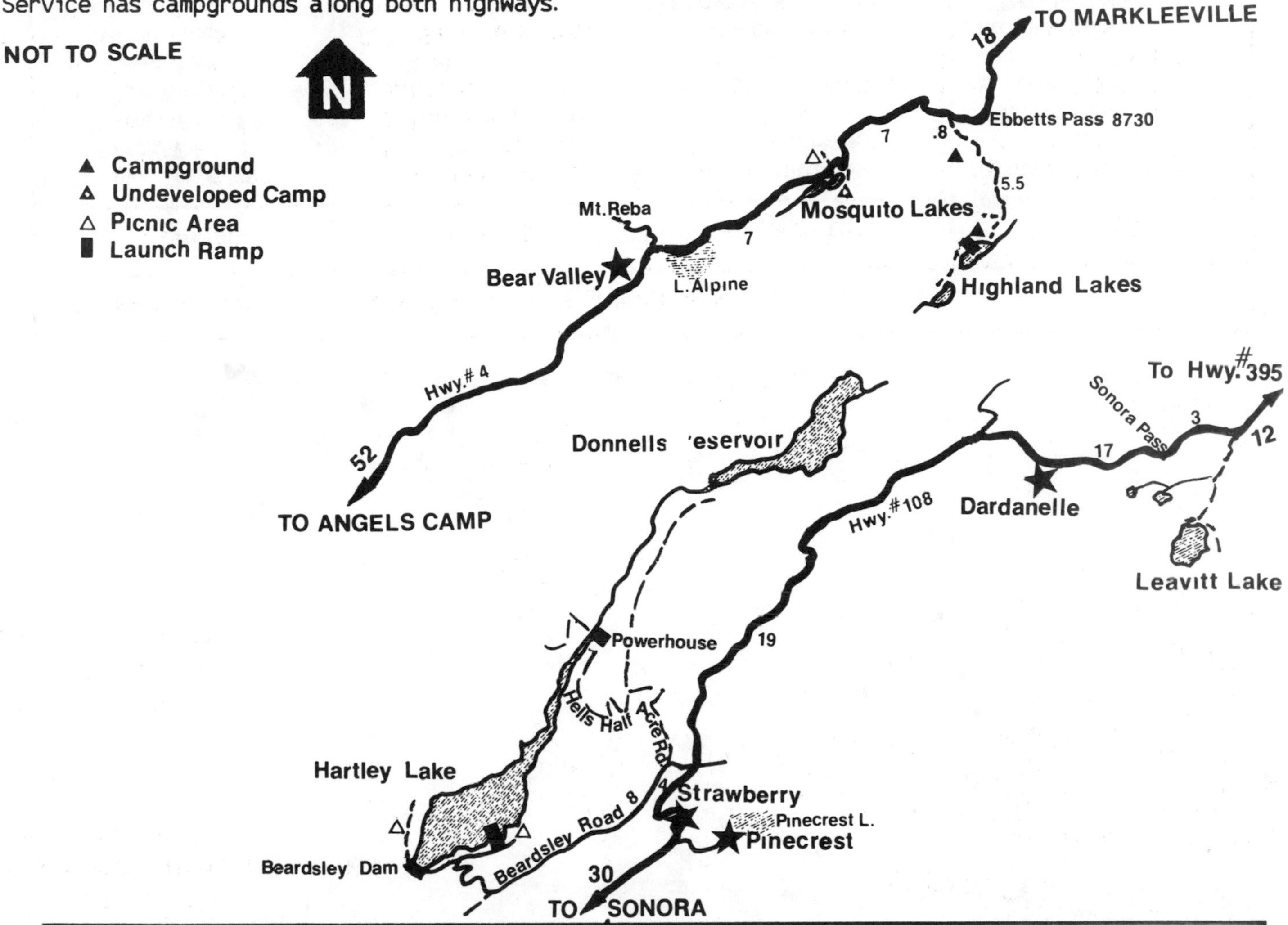

INFORMATION: Calaveras R.D., P.O.Box 500, Hathaway Pines 95233, Ph: 209-795-1381

CAMPING	BOATING	RECREATION	OTHER
Mosquito Lakes: 8 Undeveloped Sites - No Drinking Water Highland Lakes: 20 Sites	Hartley Lake - Open to All boats 2-Lane Paved Launch Ramp Highland Lakes - Open to All Boats Within a 15 MPH Speed Limit Mosquito & Leavitt - Small Hand-Launch Donnells - Not Advised	Fishing: Rainbow, German Brown & Brook Trout Picnicking Swimming Hiking & Riding Trails Backpacking Hunting: Deer	Highway 108: Numerous U.S.F.S. Campgrounds Along Highway: U.S.F.S. Summit R.D. Star Route Box 1295 Sonora Ph: 209-965-3434 Limited Facilities

CHERRY LAKE

Cherry Lake is at an elevation of 4,700 feet in the rugged back country of the Stanislaus National Forest. A 24-mile winding road from Highway 120 takes you into this Lake which has a surface area of 4 square miles. The surrounding mountains are heavily timbered with ponderosa pine, incense cedar, black oak and manzanita. The equestrian will find a Pack Station with horses and mules for day use or extended trips into the nearby Yosemite National Park and Emigrant Basin Primitive Area. The backpacker can enjoy fishing in the many other Lakes and streams throughout this vicinity.

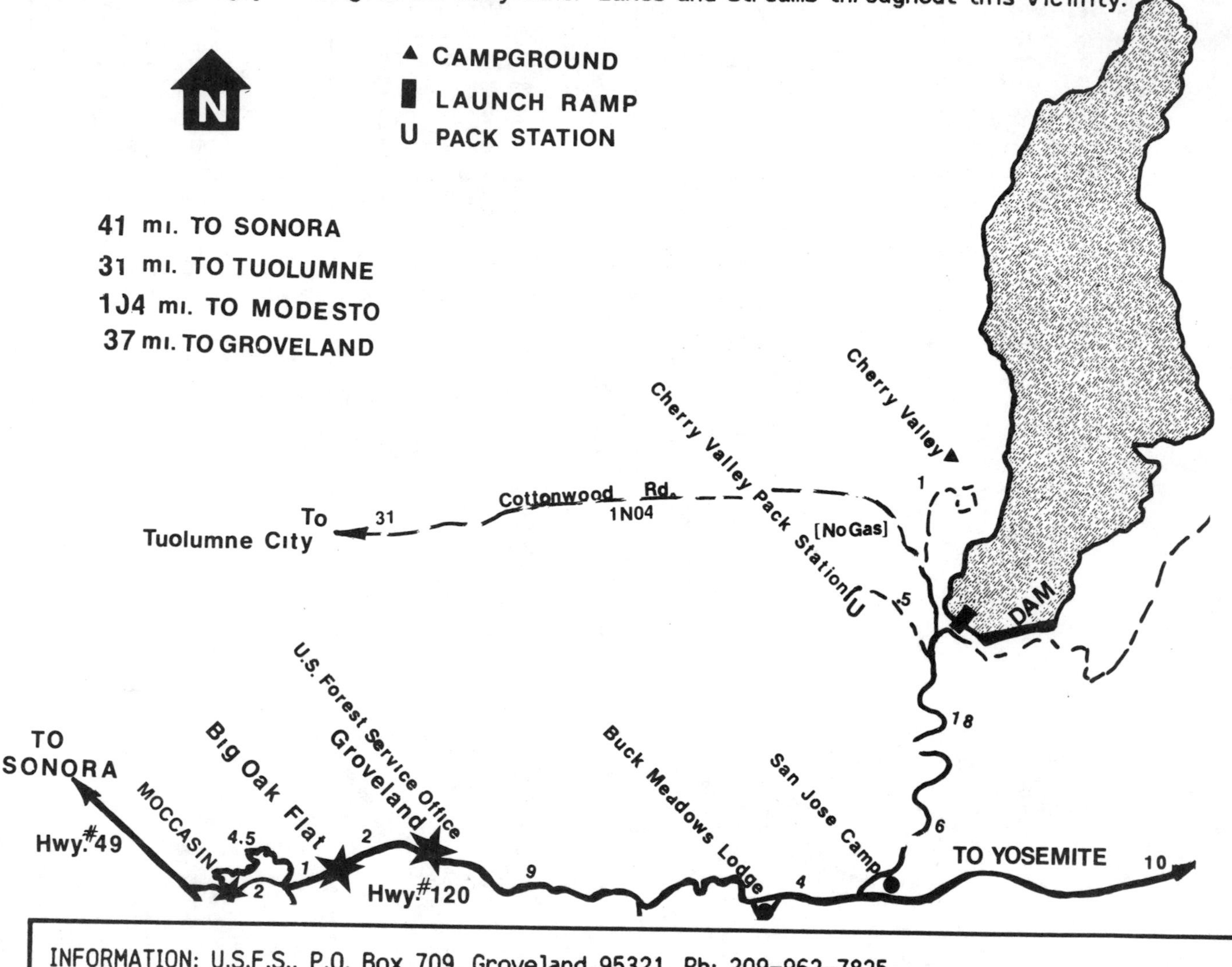

INFORMATION: U.S.F.S., P.O. Box 709, Groveland 95321, Ph: 209-962-7825			
CAMPING	BOATING	RECREATION	OTHER
46 Dev. Sites for Tents & R.V.s Fees: $4 - $8 Boat Camping Allowed on East Side of Lake	Power, Row, Canoe, Sail & Waterski Rocked Launch Ramp Varies with Water Level	Fishing: Rainbow, Brown & Brook Trout, Coho Salmon Swimming Backpacking Horseback Riding Trails & Rentals Pack Trips Hunting Nearby: Deer & Bear	Cherry Valley Pack Station P.O. Box 5500 Sonora 95370 No Services Available at Cherry Lake Full Facilities - 31 Miles at Tuolumne City

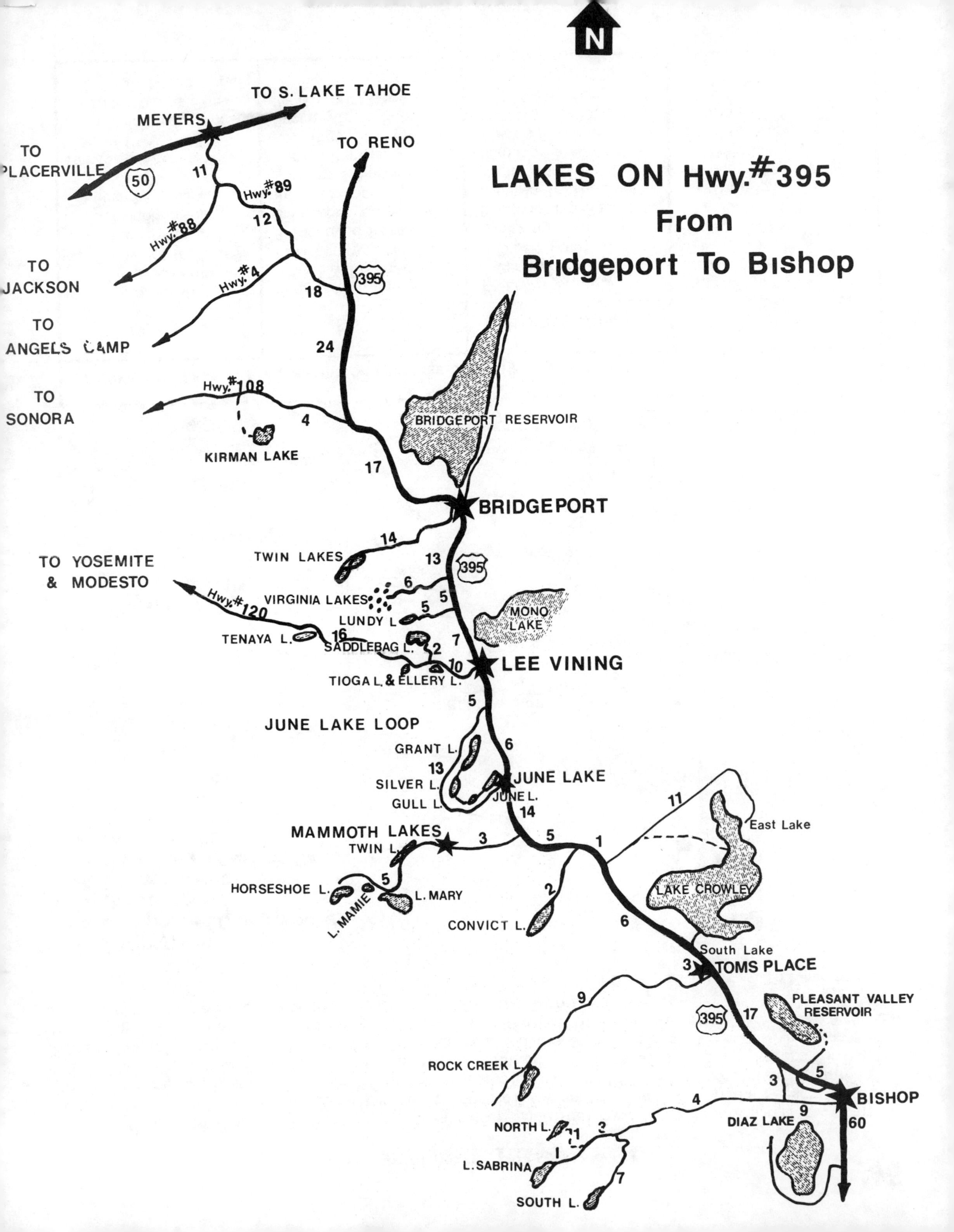
N
LAKES ON Hwy.#395
From
Bridgeport To Bishop
TO S. LAKE TAHOE
MEYERS
TO PLACERVILLE
50
11
Hwy.#89
12
Hwy.#88
TO JACKSON
Hwy.#4
18
395
TO ANGELS CAMP
TO RENO
24
TO SONORA
Hwy.#108
4
KIRMAN LAKE
BRIDGEPORT RESERVOIR
17
BRIDGEPORT
14
TWIN LAKES
13
395
TO YOSEMITE & MODESTO
Hwy.#120
6
VIRGINIA LAKES
5
LUNDY L.
5
MONO LAKE
TENAYA L.
16
SADDLEBAG L.
2
7
10
LEE VINING
TIOGA L. & ELLERY L.
5
JUNE LAKE LOOP
GRANT L.
6
13
SILVER L.
JUNE LAKE
GULL L.
JUNE L.
14
MAMMOTH LAKES
TWIN L.
3
5
1
11
East Lake
HORSESHOE L.
5
L. MARY
L. MAMIE
2
CONVICT L.
6
LAKE CROWLEY
South Lake
3
TOMS PLACE
9
395
17
PLEASANT VALLEY RESERVOIR
ROCK CREEK L.
3
5
BISHOP
4
9
DIAZ LAKE
60
NORTH L.
1
L. SABRINA
7
SOUTH L.

BRIDGEPORT RESERVOIR

Bridgeport Reservoir rests at an elevation of 6,500 feet in a large mountain meadow. This 4,400 surface acre Lake is famous for big trout, especially when trolling early in the season. In addition to the excellent fishing at Bridgeport, the angler will find 35 Lakes and streams within 15 miles. The East Walker River, designated as a Wild Trout Stream, is considered prime waters for large German Browns. Artificial lures or flies are required, and there is a 14-inch minimum with a two fish limit. The Lake is open to all boating. In addition to the facilities shown on the map, the U. S. Forest Service operates many campgrounds in this area. (See the Twin Lakes Page.)

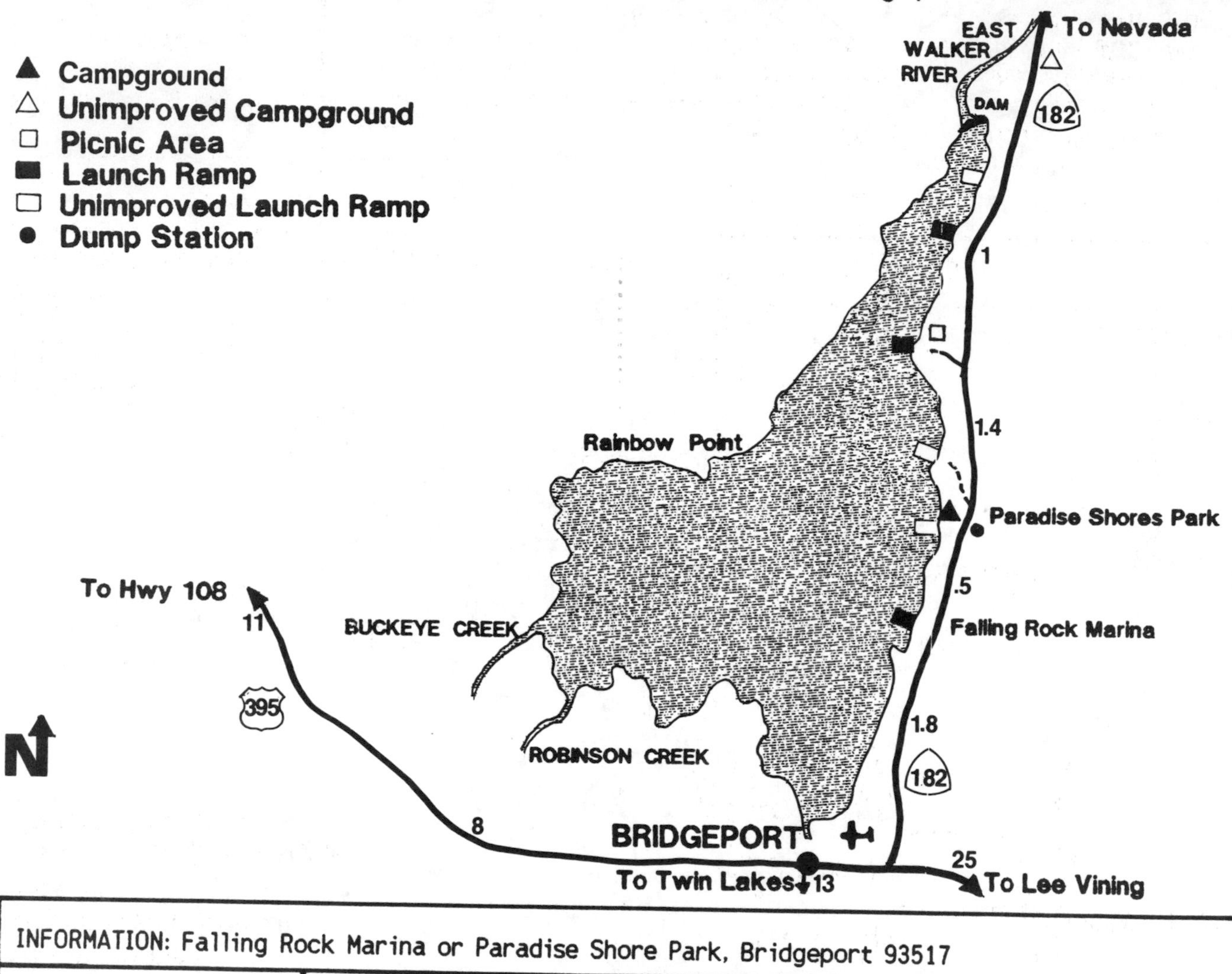

INFORMATION: Falling Rock Marina or Paradise Shore Park, Bridgeport 93517

CAMPING	BOATING	RECREATION	OTHER
Falling Rock Marina Ph: 619-932-7001 23 Dev. Tents Sites 19 R.V. Sites with Full Hookups Fees: $7 - $9 Paradise Shores Park Ph: 619-932-7735 35 R.V. Sites with Full Hookups Plus 10 with No Hookups	Power, Row, Canoe, Sail & Inflatables Full Service Marina 3 Improved Ramps 3 Unimproved Ramps Rentals: Fishing Boats & Motors Docks, Berths, Moorings, Storage Overnight in Boat Permitted Anywhere	Fishing: Rainbow, German Brown & Brook Trout Swimming Backpacking-Parking Bicycle Trails Rockhounding Hunting: Deer & Waterfowl	Snack Bar Restaurant Bait & Tackle Laundromat Trailer Rentals Gas Station Airport Full Facilities at Bridgeport

TWIN LAKES AND KIRMAN (CARMEN) LAKE

Twin Lakes are 12 miles southwest of Bridgeport in the Eastern Sierras at an elevation of 7,000 feet. The private campgrounds at the Lake are in a pine forest, and complete resort and marine facilities are available. There are 5 Forest Service Campgrounds along Robinson Creek. These Lakes provide excellent fishing for large rainbow and brown trout. Lower Twin Lake holds the State record for a German Brown at 26 pounds, 5 ounces. Doc and Al's Resort is a pleasant fisherman's retreat. The Hunewill Guest Ranch is a working cattle ranch offering excellent accommodations, food and excursions on horseback into this beautiful country. The nearby Hoover Wilderness invites the adventurous packer into its many scenic trails, lakes and streams. Kirman Lake is a designated Wild Trout Lake. There is a two trout limit at this hard-to-reach facility.

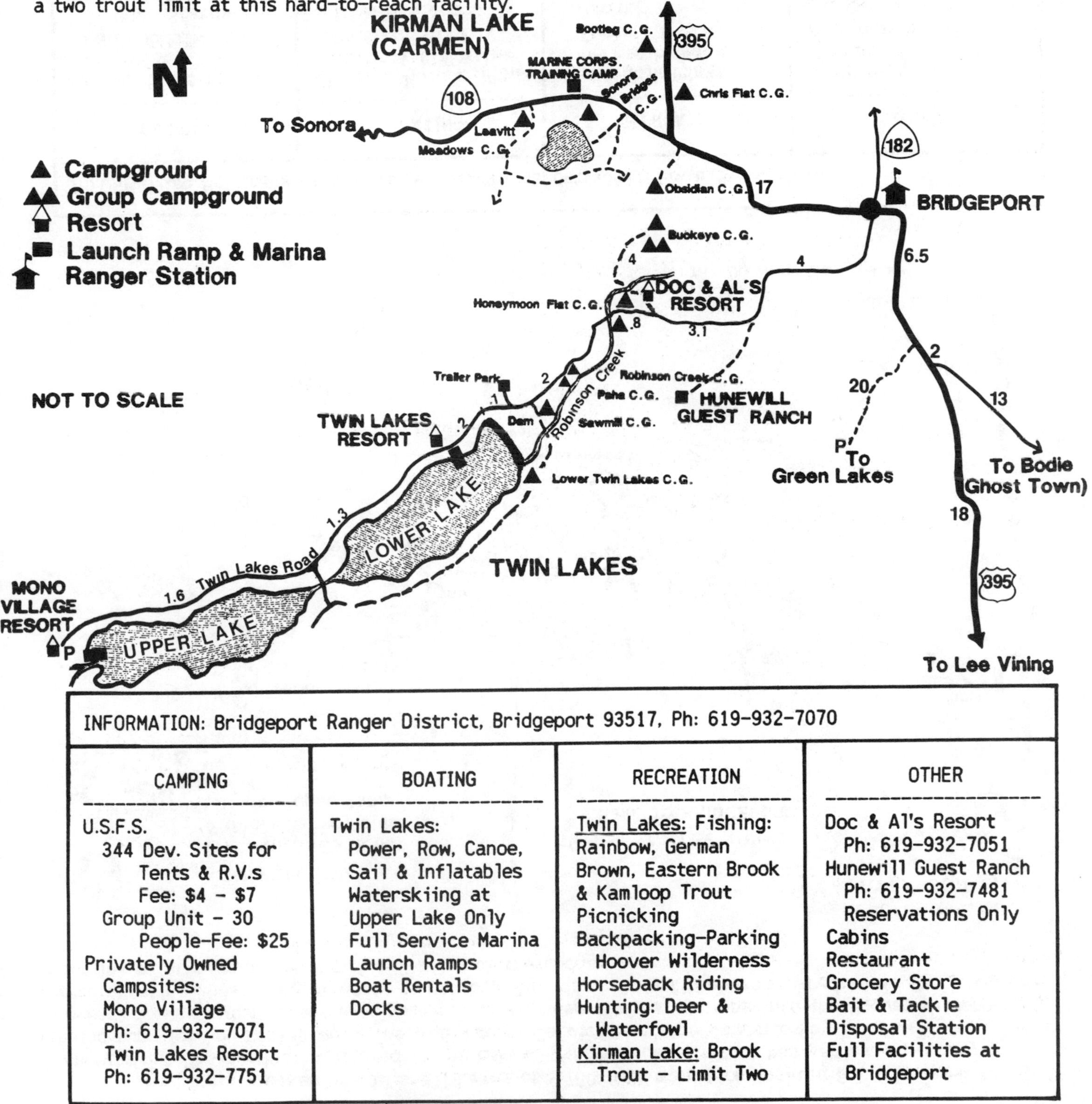

INFORMATION: Bridgeport Ranger District, Bridgeport 93517, Ph: 619-932-7070

CAMPING	BOATING	RECREATION	OTHER
U.S.F.S. 344 Dev. Sites for Tents & R.V.s Fee: $4 - $7 Group Unit - 30 People-Fee: $25 Privately Owned Campsites: Mono Village Ph: 619-932-7071 Twin Lakes Resort Ph: 619-932-7751	Twin Lakes: Power, Row, Canoe, Sail & Inflatables Waterskiing at Upper Lake Only Full Service Marina Launch Ramps Boat Rentals Docks	Twin Lakes: Fishing: Rainbow, German Brown, Eastern Brook & Kamloop Trout Picnicking Backpacking-Parking Hoover Wilderness Horseback Riding Hunting: Deer & Waterfowl Kirman Lake: Brook Trout - Limit Two	Doc & Al's Resort Ph: 619-932-7051 Hunewill Guest Ranch Ph: 619-932-7481 Reservations Only Cabins Restaurant Grocery Store Bait & Tackle Disposal Station Full Facilities at Bridgeport

VIRGINIA LAKES

The Virginia Lakes are 10 small Lakes at 9,700 feet elevation located 6.3 miles west of Highway 395. No swimming is allowed in the Lakes. Virginia Lake Resort has cabins, a grocery store, fishing supplies and restaurant. The U. S. Forest Service operates campsites by Trumbull Lake. There is a Pack Station with horses available for lovely scenic rides or trips into the Hoover Wilderness. The interesting Ghost Town of Bodie is nearby. This is truly a fisherman's paradise as the 10 Lakes and miles of streams are within 1-1/2 miles of the Lodge.

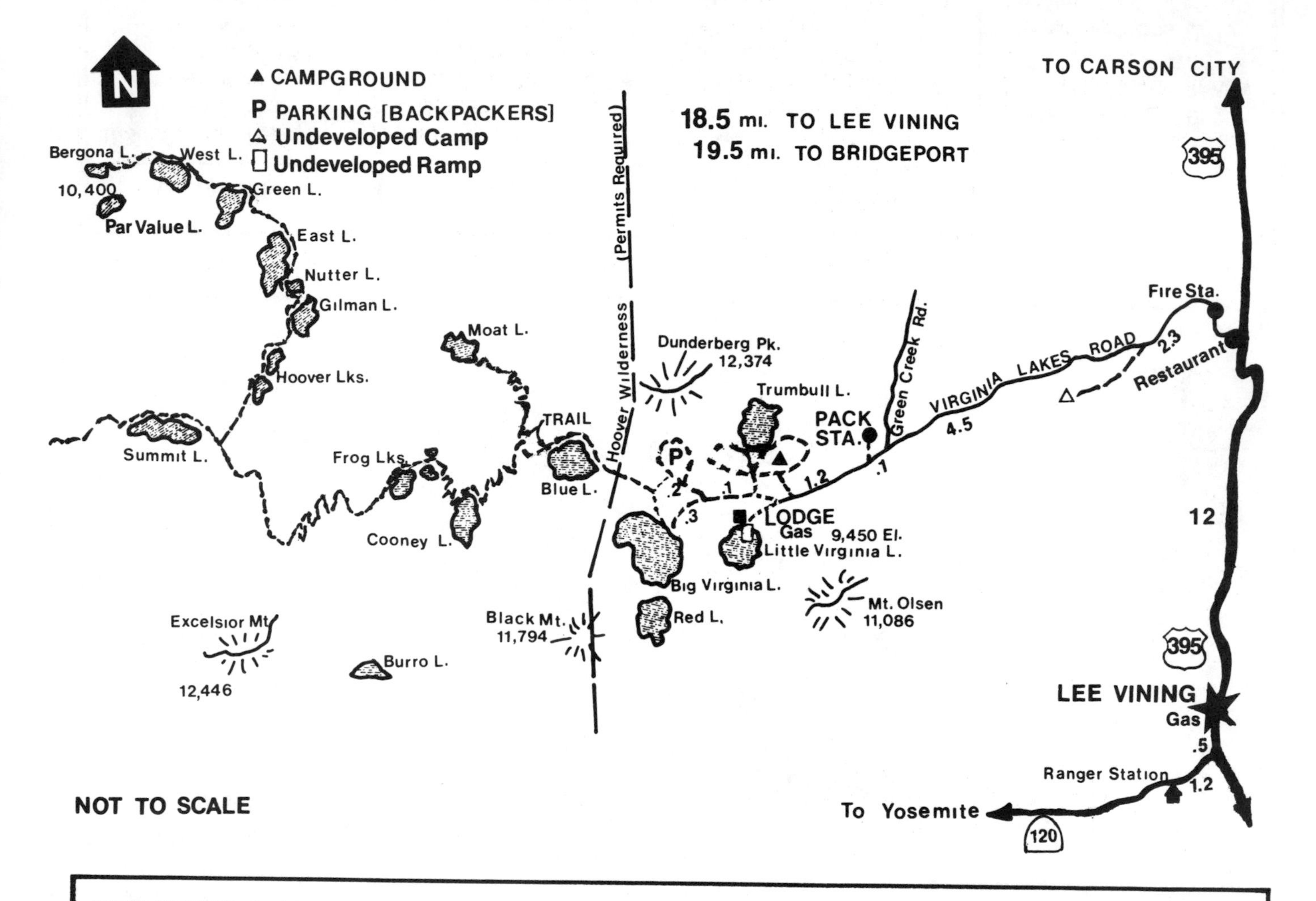

INFORMATION: Bridgeport Ranger District, Bridgeport 93517, Ph: 619-932-7070

CAMPING	BOATING	RECREATION	OTHER
45 Dev. Sites for Tents & R.V.s No Hookups or Dump Station Fee: $5 Group Camp to 30 People Maximum First-Come Basis Undeveloped Creekside Camping Fire Permit Required	Electric Motors, Row, Canoe & Inflatables No Gas Motors 10 MPH Speed Limit Unimproved Launch Ramp Rentals: Fishing Boats	Fishing: Rainbow, German Brown & Eastern Brook Trout Picnicking Hiking Backpacking Horseback Riding - Trails & Rentals Hunting: Deer	Virginia Lakes Resort Bridgeport 93517 Cabins Grocery Store Bait & Tackle Public Bath House Virginia Lakes Pack Outfit Star Route 1070 Bridgeport 93517

LUNDY LAKE

Nestled in a valley at an elevation of 7,800 feet, Lundy Lake is the Trailhead to the 20 Lakes Basin. High, majestic mountains and a rocky, Aspen and Pine covered shoreline provide for spectacular scenery. The Lake is 1 mile long and 1/2 mile wide, and the water is clear and cold. This is a popular fishing Lake where each year, fishermen stay for the summer at Mill Creek campground. Fishing is good at the Lake, in the streams and beaver ponds as well as many other Lakes above Lundy reached by trail. The atmosphere is relaxed and rustic with good facilities at the Resort. Mono Lake rests just off Highway 395. This huge, barren salt water Lake is the nesting site for 95 percent of California's Gulls.

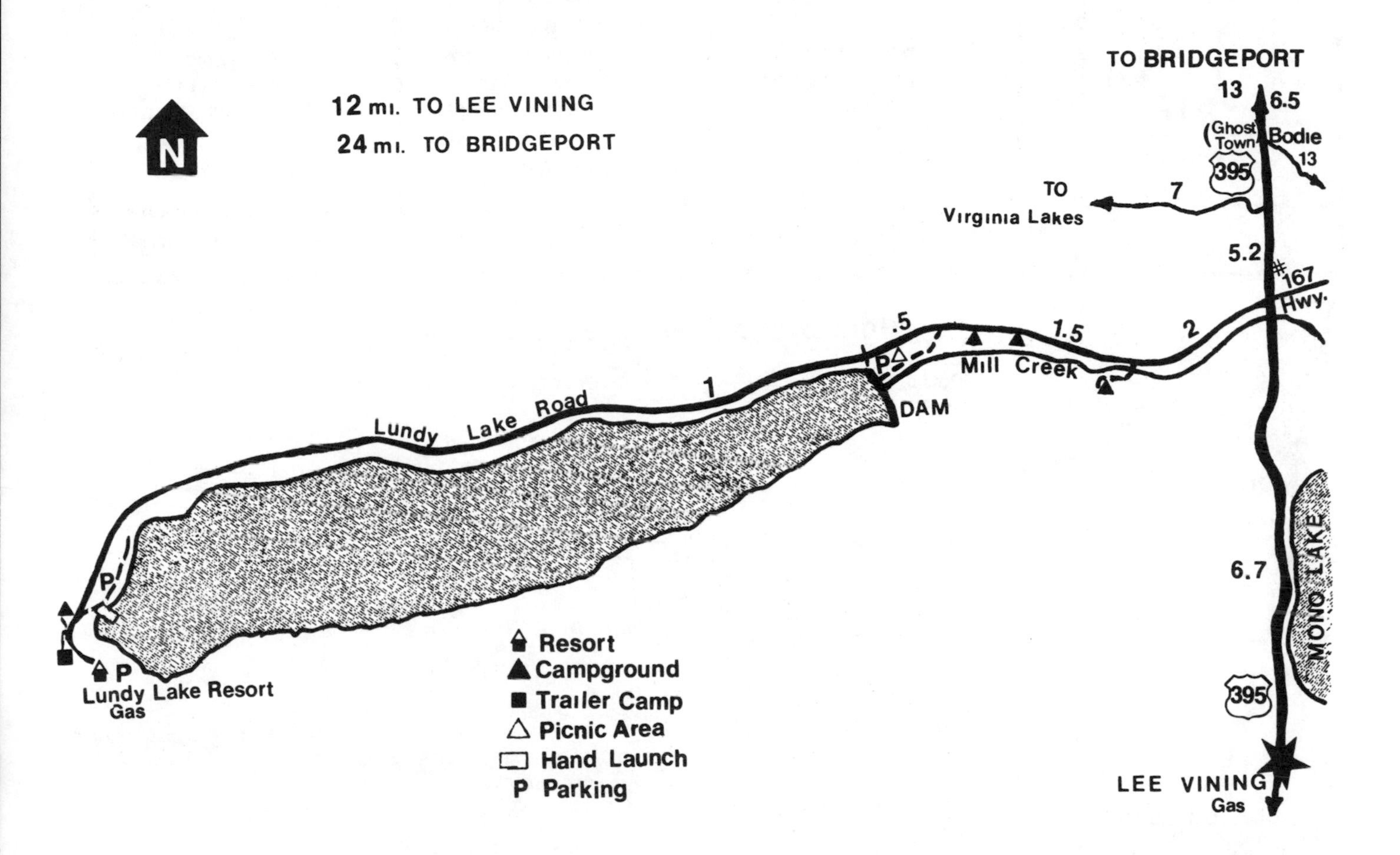

INFORMATION: Lundy Lake Resort, P.O. Box 265, Lee Vining 93541			
CAMPING	**BOATING**	**RECREATION**	**OTHER**
Lundy Lake Resort: 27 Tent Sites 3 Camp Huts 8 R.V. Sites with Full Hookups Mono County Parks P.O. Box 655 Bridgeport 93517 Ph: 619-932-7911 54 Sites at Mill Creek	Fishing Boats, Canoes & Inflatables Speed Limit-10 MPH Hand Launch Only Rentals: Fishing Boats & Motors	Fishing: Rainbow, German Brown & Eastern Brook Trout Picnicking Hiking Backpacking Bird Watching Hunting: Deer	Housekeeping Cabins Grocery Store Bait & Tackle Hot Showers Laundromat Camping Supplies Wilderness Permits

SADDLEBAG LAKE

Saddlebag Lake at an elevation of 10,087 feet is the highest Lake in California reached by public road. Just off Highway 120, 4 miles northeast of the Eastern Gate of Yosemite Park and near the South Entrance to Hoover Wilderness Area, Saddlebag Lake offers a beautiful rugged glacial environment. There are a series of 20 Lakes behind Saddlebag within an hour or less of easy hiking after a Water Taxi ride to the far end of the Lake. Fishing is excellent from boat, bank or stream. Mt. Conness Glacier is popular with experienced mountain climbers. The 2-1/2 mile road off Highway 120 to the Lake is steep, so large R.V.s or trailers over 22 feet are not advised.

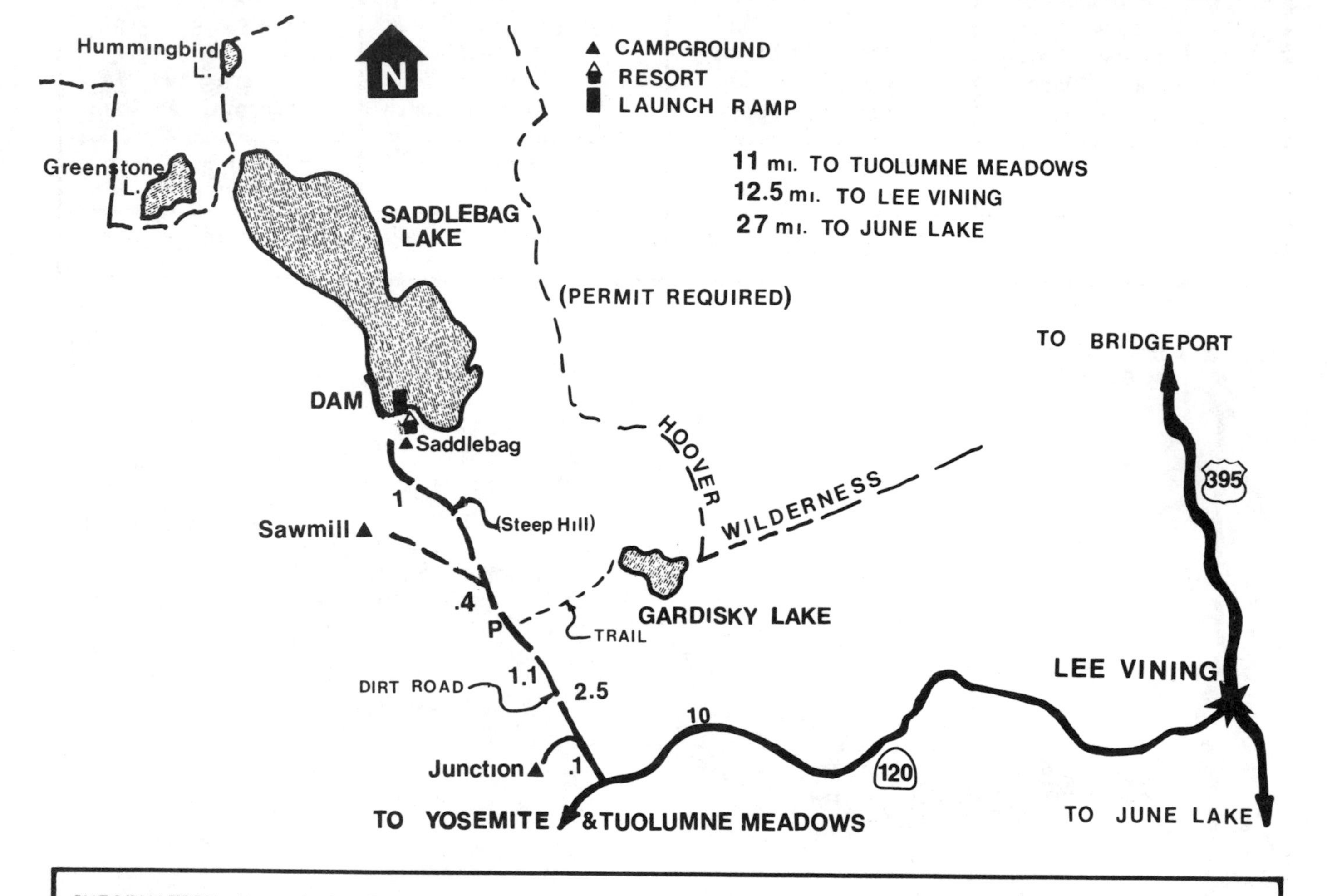

INFORMATION: Mono Lake Ranger Dist., Box 10, Lee Vining 93541, Ph: 619-647-6525

CAMPING	BOATING	RECREATION	OTHER
Saddlebag Campground 21 Sites for Tents & Small R.V.s Fee: $3 Sawmill Campground 5 Walk-In Sites No Fee	Fishing & Sail Boats, Canoes & Inflatables Unimproved Launch Ramp for Boats to 16 Feet - $2 Rentals: Fishing Boats & Motors Water Taxi	Fishing: Rainbow, Brook, Golden & Kamloop Trout Hiking Backpacking-Parking Mountain Climbing Nature Study	Saddlebag Lake Resort P.O. Box 36 Lee Vining 93541 (Winter Address: 389 O'Conner St. Palo Alto 94303) Snack Bar Grocery Store Bait & Tackle

ELLERY, TIOGA AND TENAYA

These lovely lakes are in the spectacular Eastern Sierras along Highway 120 west of Tioga Pass. Ellery and Tioga Lakes are 2 miles outside the eastern entrance to Yosemite National Park, and Tenaya is 15 miles inside the Park. An abundance of natural attractions are offered the outdoorsman. An interesting side trip into the Ghost Town of Bonnetville is a 20 minute hike from the Tioga Pass Resort. The water is clear and cold providing the fisherman with some excellent opportunities at all 3 Lakes along with numerous streams and other small Lakes in the area. While Highway 120 is often crowded, it is well worth a visit.

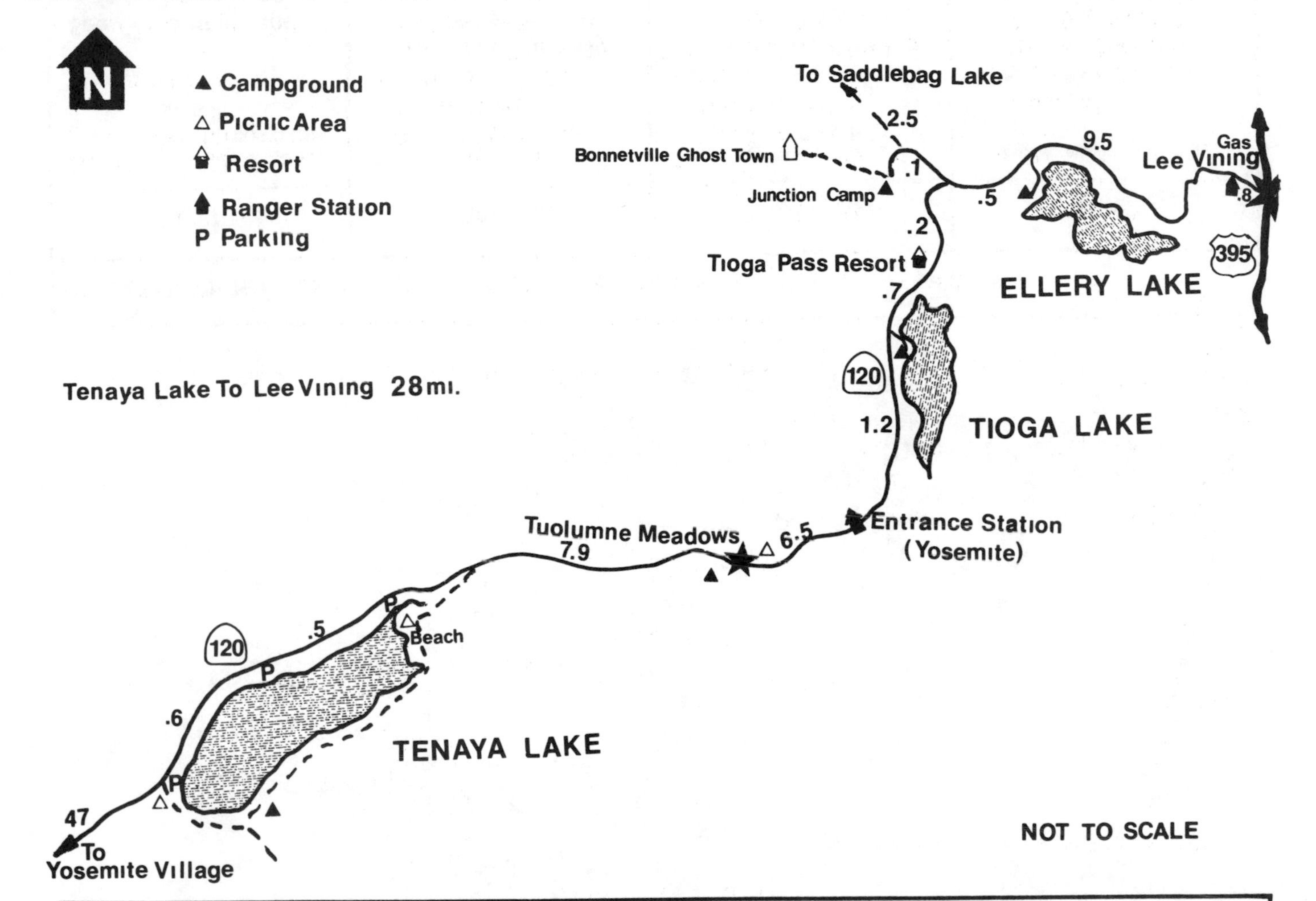

INFORMATION: Mono Lake Ranger District, Box 10, Lee Vining 93541, Ph: 619-647-6525

CAMPING	BOATING	RECREATION	OTHER
U.S.F.S. Ellery Lake: 12 Dev. Sites Tioga Lake: 13 Dev. Sites - Tents Junction Camp: 14 Dev. Sites Yosemite Nat. Park Tenaya Lake: 50 Walk-In Sites Tuolumne Meadows: 371 Dev. Sites	Ellery & Tioga Lakes: Motors Permitted Hand Launch at Ellery Small Trailered Boats At Tioga Tenaya Lake: No Motors Hand Launch Only	Fishing: Rainbow, Brook, Brown & Golden Trout Picnicking Hiking & Rock Climbing Nature Trails Campfire Programs Horseback Riding Hunting Outside Park Limits: Deer, Upland Game	Yosemite Nat. Park Box 577 Yosemite 95389 Ph: 209-372-4461 - - - - - - - - - - - Tioga Pass Resort Box 7 Lee Vining 93541 Cabins, Lodge Cafe - 7 am - 9 pm Groceries, Tackle & Sporting Goods

JUNE LAKE LOOP

June Lake Loop consists of 4 Lakes off Highway 395. Grant Lake is the largest with 1,100 surface acres. Silver Lake has 80 acres. Gull Lake, the smallest, has 64 acres, and June Lake has 160 acres, all interlocked by mountain streams. On the eastern slope of the High Sierras, the Lakes are at 7,600 feet elevation and the alpine scenery is quite spectacular. Full vacation facilities offer all types of accommodations and recreational opportunities as shown on the following page.

. . . Continued . . .

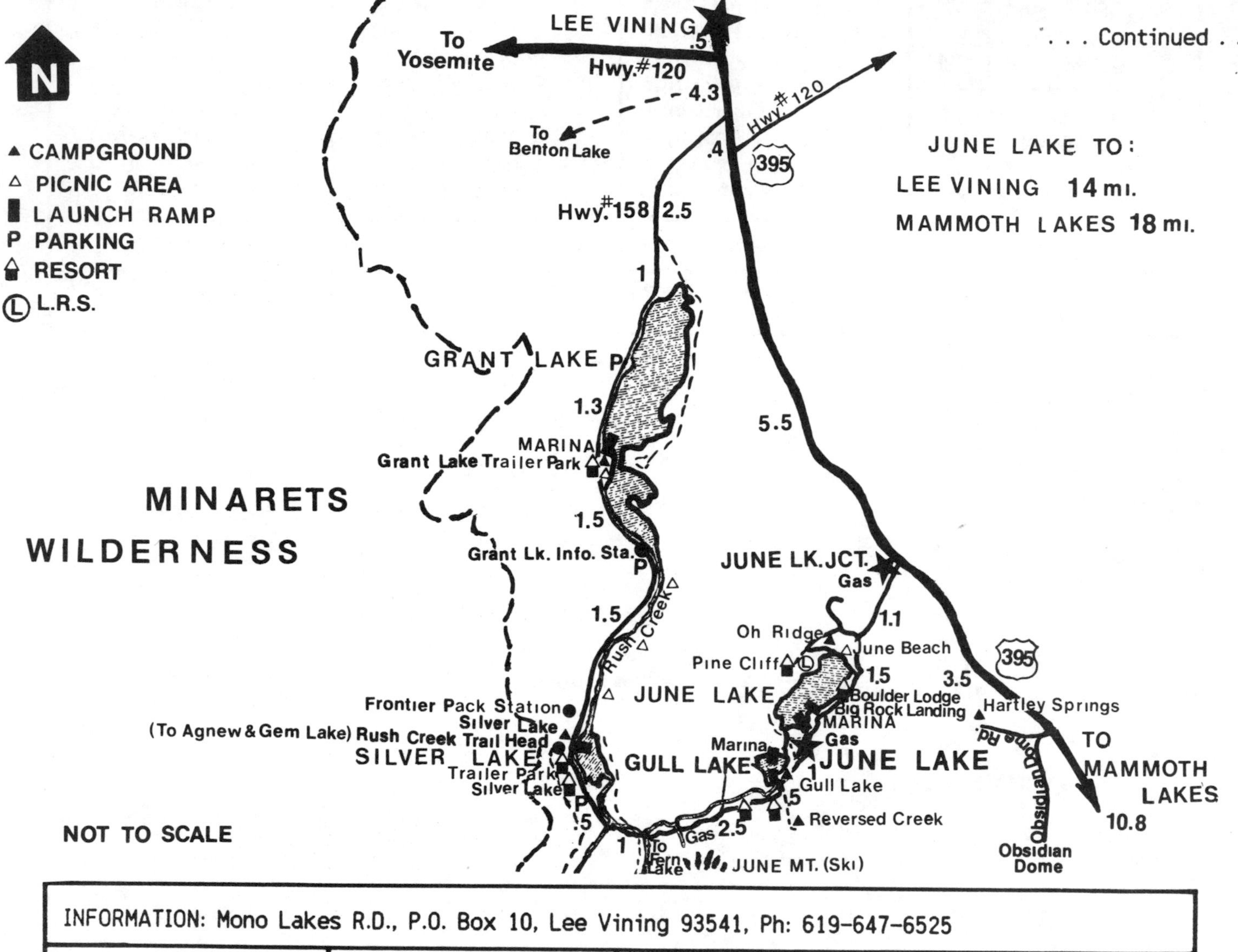

INFORMATION: Mono Lakes R.D., P.O. Box 10, Lee Vining 93541, Ph: 619-647-6525			
CAMPING	BOATING	RECREATION	OTHER
U.S. Forest Service 300 Plus Campsites for Tents & R.V.s Fee: $5 See Following Page for Details	Power, Row, Canoe, Sail, Windsurf & Inflatables Waterskiing At Grant Lake Only Other Lakes - Speed Limits Launch Ramps Rentals: Fishing Boats & Motors, Paddleboats Docks, Gas, Repairs	Fishing: Rainbow, Brown & Brook Trout Swimming - June Lake Backpacking-Parking Horseback Riding Trails & Pack Station Hunting: Deer, Dove Geese, Duck, Quail & Pheasant	Housekeeping Cabins Snack Bars Restaurants Grocery Stores Bait & Tackle Laundromats Further Info: June Lake Chamber of Commerce P.O. Box 2 June Lake 93529 Ph: 619-648-7584

GRANT LAKE

Grant Lake Marina, Star Route 3, Box 19, June Lake 93529, Ph: 619-648-7964

70 Developed Sites for Tents & R.V.s (Hookups). Fee: $9. Water, Toilets, Barbecues, Hot Showers, Disposal Station, Restaurant, Store, Bait & Tackle, Propane, Boat Rentals & Dock Rental, Trailer Rentals. Waterskiing Approximately April - October.

SILVER LAKE

U. S. Forest Service Campground

65 Developed Sites for Tents & R.V.s. Fee: $5. Water, Toilets & Barbecues.

Silver Lake Resort, P.O. Box 116, June Lake 93529, Ph: 619-648-7525

Full Housekeeping Cabins, Store, Bait & Tackle, Restaurant, Gas Station, Disposal Station, Launch Ramp, Rental Boats. 75-Unit Trailer Park with Full Hookups. 5 MPH Speed Limit on Lake.

Frontier Pack Train, Route 3, Box 18, June Lake 93529, Ph: 619-648-7701

Various Horseback and Pack Trips Into The Minaret Wilderness With Remote Lakes and Streams Nearly 2 Miles High.

GULL LAKE

U. S. Forest Service Campgrounds

Gull Lake Campground - 11 Sites. Fee: $5. Public Ramp.
Reversed Creek Campground - 17 R.V. Sites. Fee: $5. Ramp.

Gull Lake Boat Landing, P.O. Box 65, June Lake 93529, Ph: 619-648-7539

Full Service Marina, 30 Rental Boats & Motors, Paddleboats, Docks, Launch Ramps, Bait & Tackle, Beer & Wine, Ice.

JUNE LAKE

U. S. Forest Service Campgrounds

Oh Ridge - 148 Developed Sites for Tents & R.V.s. Fee: $5.
June Lake - 22 Developed Sites for Tents & R.V.s. Fee: $5.
Hartley Springs - South on Highway 395 - 20 Sites for Tents & R.V.s - No Fee.

June Lake Marina, P.O. Box 26, June Lake 93529, Ph: 619-648-7726

Full Service Marina, Boat Rentals, Docks, Bait & Tackle, Launch Ramp, Gas.

SOME RESORTS

Pine Cliff Trailer Park - 129 Trailer Sites, Full Hookups, Rentals. Ph: 619-648-7558. Reservations through LRS.
Golden Pines Trailer & Camper Park - Sites & Rentals. Ph: 619-648-7743.
Big Rock Resort - Housekeeping Cabins & Condos, Marina. Ph: 619-648-7717.
Fern Creek Lodge - Housekeeping Cabins. Ph: 619-648-7722.
Boulder Lodge - Housekeeping Cabins, Motel, Swimming Pool, Tennis. Ph: 619-648-7533.

MAMMOTH LAKES BASIN

The Mammoth Lakes Basin rests at the doorway to magnificent High Sierra scenery. These small glacial-formed Lakes range in elevation from 8,540 feet to 9,250 feet. They are easily accessible by road or pine-shaded trails. Fishing in Lake or stream is often excellent. This is an ideal area for the hiker, backpacker or horsepacker as trails lead into the John Muir and Ansel Adams Wilderness Areas. Numerous resorts are campgrounds are available, and complete facilities are located in the community of Mammoth Lakes. While Stocker Lake is outside the Lakes Basin, it shares a similar scenic and recreational abundance.

. . Continued . . .

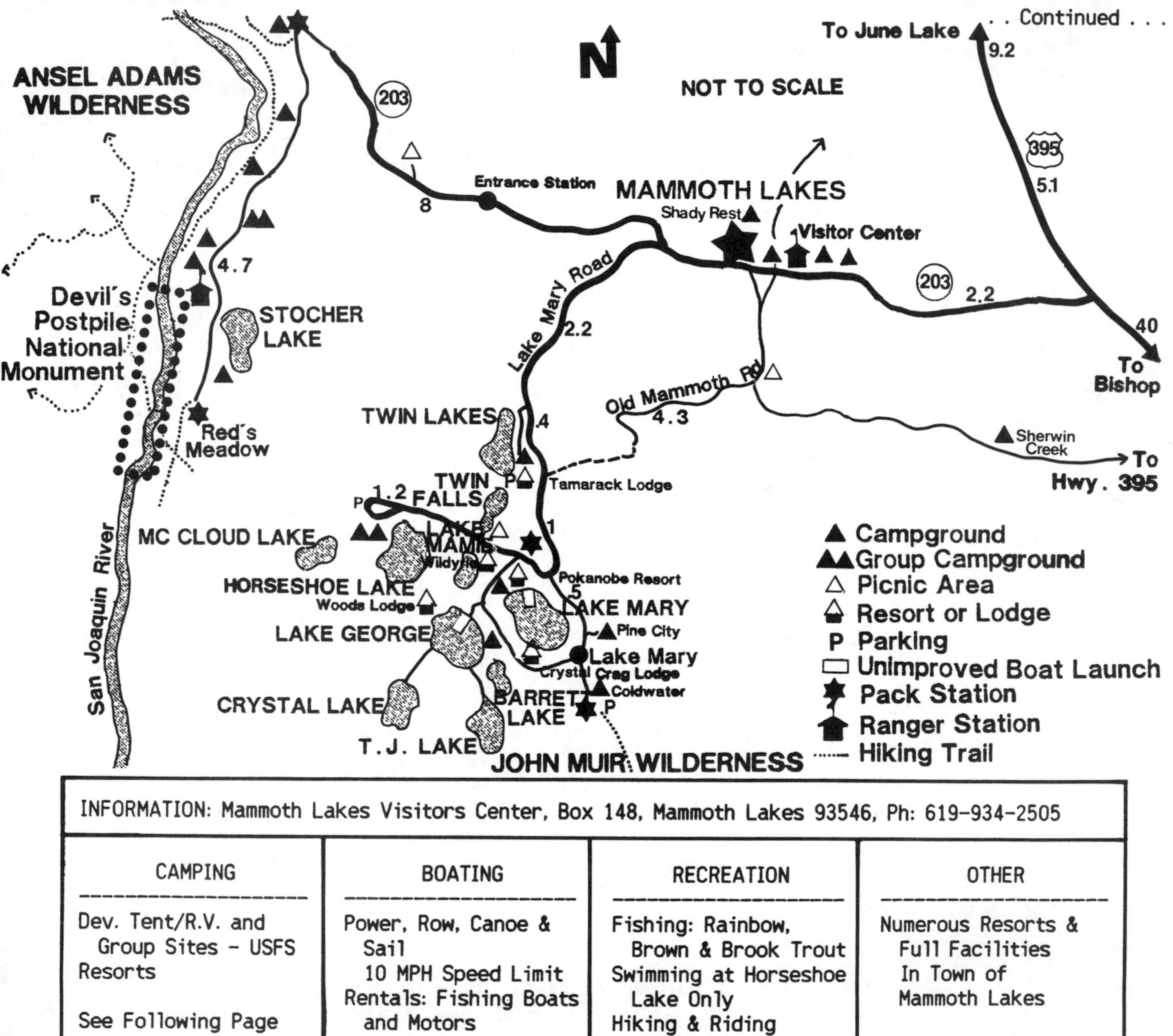

INFORMATION: Mammoth Lakes Visitors Center, Box 148, Mammoth Lakes 93546, Ph: 619-934-2505

CAMPING	BOATING	RECREATION	OTHER
Dev. Tent/R.V. and Group Sites - USFS Resorts See Following Page	Power, Row, Canoe & Sail 10 MPH Speed Limit Rentals: Fishing Boats and Motors Stocker Lake: Rowboats & Canoes Only	Fishing: Rainbow, Brown & Brook Trout Swimming at Horseshoe Lake Only Hiking & Riding Trails Nature Study Backpacking Picnicking Hunting: Deer Pack Stations & Horse Rentals	Numerous Resorts & Full Facilities In Town of Mammoth Lakes

TWIN LAKES: U.S. Forest Service Campground - 97 Developed Sites for Tents & R.V.s, Water, Toilets, Barbecues. Fee: $6 - 7 Day Limit.

Tamarack Lodge, P.O. Box 69, Mammoth Lakes 93546, Ph: 619-934-2442
Housekeeping Cabins, Restaurant, Grocery Store, Launch Ramp, Rental Boats.

LAKE MAMIE: ***Wildyrie Lodge***, P.O. Box 684, Mammoth Lakes 93546, Ph: 619-934-2444
Housekeeping Cabins, Grocery Store, Coffee Shop, Boat & Bicycle Rentals
Open - May 25 to October 1.

HORSESHOE LAKE: U.S. Forest Service Group Campground - 8 Group Sites - 320 People Maximum Tents & R.V.s, Water, Toilets, Barbecues - $15 Minimum a Day. Reserve through Ranger Station at Visitor Center.

LAKE GEORGE: U.S. Forest Service Campground - 10 Developed Sites for Tents & R.V.s. Fee: $6 - 7 Day Limit. Grocery Store, Boat Rentals, Boat Launch Ramp.

Woods Lodge, P.O. Box 105, Mammoth Lakes 93546, Ph: Summer - 619-934-2261
Winter - 619-934-2342. Housekeeping Cabins, Bait & Tackle, Unimproved Launch Ramp, Dock, Rental Boats & Motors.

LAKE MARY: U.S. Forest Service Campground - 50 Developed Sites for Tents, Water, Toilets, Barbecues. Fee: $6 - 14 Day Limit.

Crystal Crag Lodge, P.O. Box 88, Mammoth Lakes 93546, Ph: 619-934-2436
Housekeeping Cabins, Grocery Store, Boat & Motor Rentals, Open May 25 to Oct. 1.

Pokonobe Resort, P.O. Box 72, Mammoth Lakes 93546, Ph: 619-934-2437
Camp Sites, Boat Rentals, Grocery Store, Launch Ramp & Docks.

OTHER NEARBY U.S. FOREST SERVICE CAMPGROUNDS

PINE CITY CAMPGROUND - 36 Developed Sites for Tents Only. Fee: $6 - 14 Day Limit.

COLDWATER CAMPGROUND - Trailhead Into John Muir Wilderness - 79 Sites for Tents & R.V.s. Fee: $6 - 14 Day Limit.

SHERWIN CREEK CAMPGROUND - 86 Developed Sites for Tents & R.V.s. Fee: $6 - 21 Day Limit.

NEW SHADY REST - 96 Sites for Tents & R.V.s, Disposal Station, Fee: $6 - 14 Day Limit

OLD SHADY REST - 49 Sites for Tents & R.V.s Fee: $6 - 14 Day Limit.

PINE GLEN - Handicap Facilities - 18 Sites for Single Families & 3 Sites for Multiple Families for Tents & R.V.s. Fee: $15 - $40. Reserve through Ranger Station at Visitor Center.

SOTCHER LAKE: ***Red Meadows*** - U.S. Forest Service Campground - 55 Developed Sites for Tents and R.V.s, Water, Toilets, Barbecues. Fee: $6 - 14 Day Limit.

CONVICT LAKE

Crystal clear water surrounded by rugged peaks make Convict Lake one of the most beautiful places in the Eastern Sierra. At an elevation of 7,583 feet, the Lake is 1 mile long and 1/2 mile wide providing 3 miles of pine-covered shoreline. The fishing at the Lake can be good. The energetic hiker, backpacker or horseman will find a trail leading through a rock-walled canyon to 8 other Lakes and many streams offering superb fishing and scenery. The Resort Dinner House is excellent. In season, reservations are suggested.

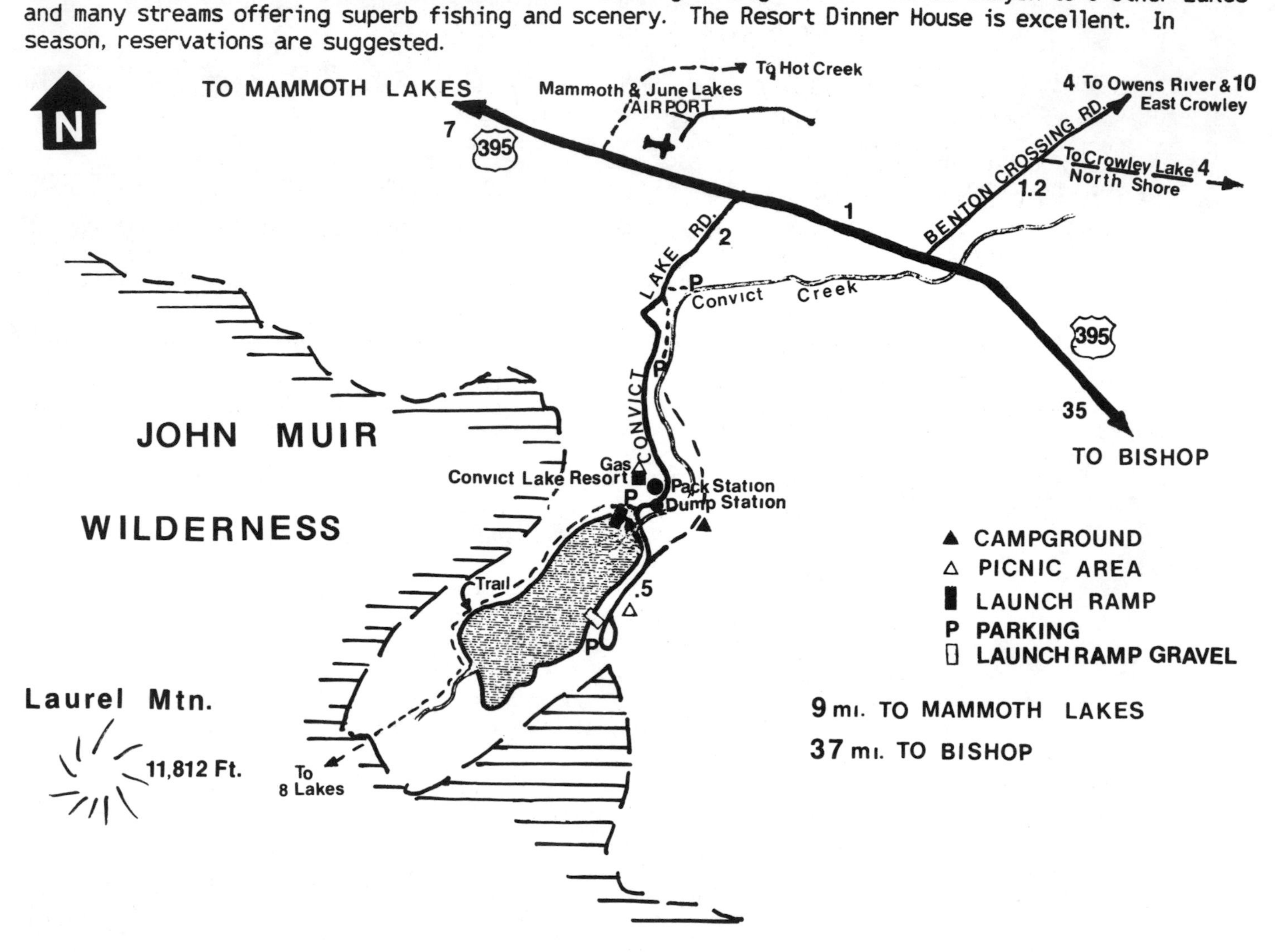

INFORMATION: Convict Lake Resort, Box 204, Mammoth Lakes 93546, Ph: 619-935-4213

CAMPING	BOATING	RECREATION	OTHER
U.S. Forest Service 96 Dev. Sites for Tents & R.V.s Fee: $6	Power, Row, Canoe, Sail & Inflatables Speed Limit-10 MPH Rentals: Fishing Boats Docks, Gas Dry Storage	Fishing: Rainbow & German Brown Trout Picnicking Hiking Backpacking-Parking Horseback Riding- Trails & Rentals Pack Station-Pack Trips Hunting: Deer, Rabbit	Housekeeping Cabins Restaurant Cocktail Lounge Grocery Store Bait & Tackle Disposal Station Gas Station Airport with Auto Rentals - 3 Miles

CROWLEY LAKE

At an elevation of 6,720 feet, Crowley is one of the top Eastern High Sierra Lakes. This 650 acre Lake is famous for its good fishing. It held the State Record of 25 pounds, 11 ounces for German Brown Trout until 1983, and currently holds the State Record for Sacramento Perch of 3 pounds, 10 ounces. There is a special trout season from August 1 to October 31 where single hook artificial lures are required. The minimum size trout is 18 inches, and there is a two fish limit. Float tubes are not allowed. In addition to the fishing season listed below, there is a single hook lure Perch season from August 1 to September 5. This is a good Lake for sailing with a strong program supported by the City of Los Angeles, and waterskiing is also popular. Heavy winds can be a hazard. There are numerous resorts and recreational opportunities in this area.

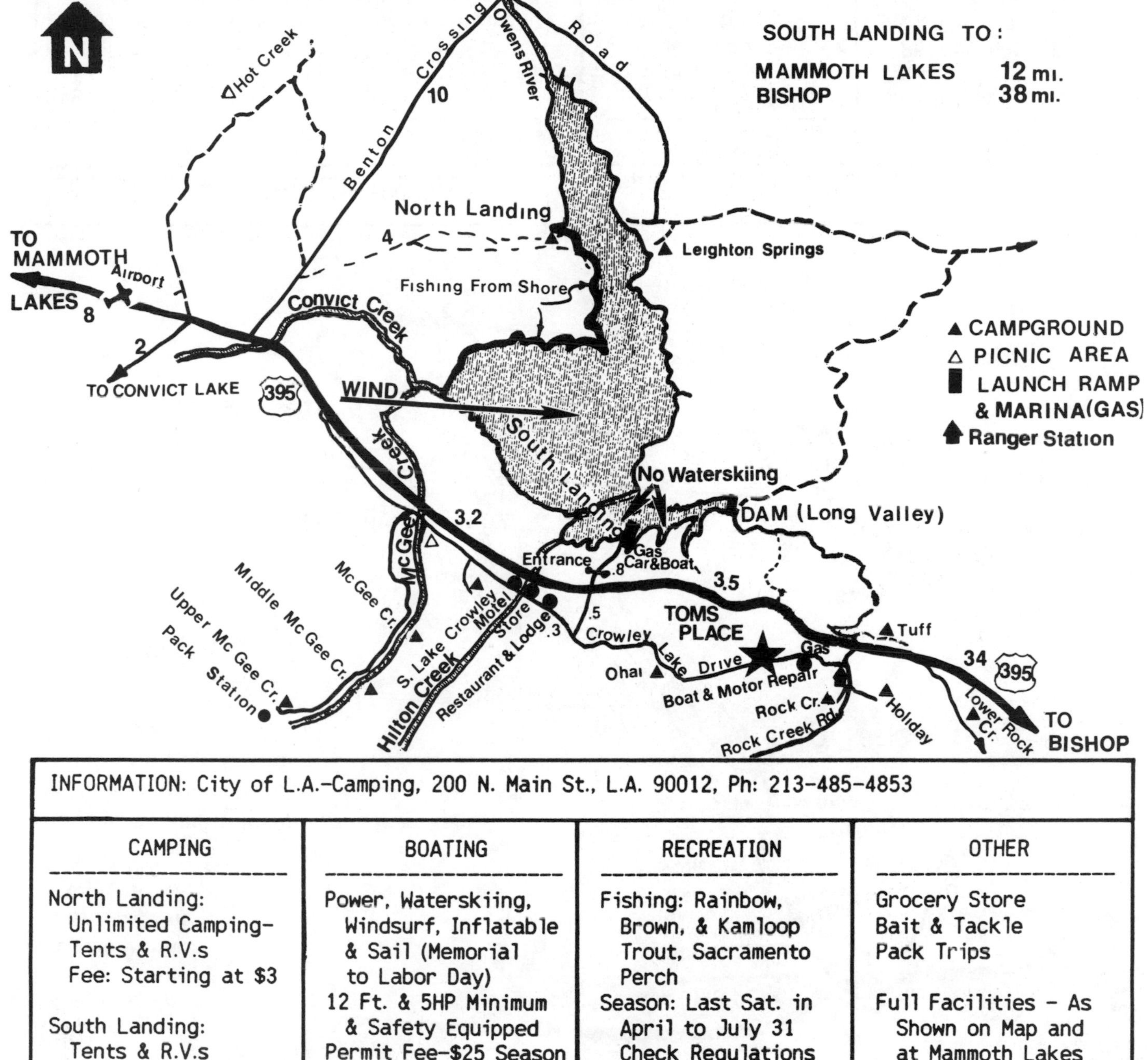

INFORMATION: City of L.A.-Camping, 200 N. Main St., L.A. 90012, Ph: 213-485-4853

CAMPING	BOATING	RECREATION	OTHER
North Landing: Unlimited Camping-Tents & R.V.s Fee: Starting at $3 South Landing: Tents & R.V.s Opening Weekend Only Other Campgrounds - See Map	Power, Waterskiing, Windsurf, Inflatable & Sail (Memorial to Labor Day) 12 Ft. & 5HP Minimum & Safety Equipped Permit Fee-$25 Season All Craft Must Register Launch Ramps Full Service Marina Rentals: Boat & Motor	Fishing: Rainbow, Brown, & Kamloop Trout, Sacramento Perch Season: Last Sat. in April to July 31 Check Regulations Waterskiing: Season: July 4 to Labor Day Picnicking Hiking & Backpacking	Grocery Store Bait & Tackle Pack Trips Full Facilities - As Shown on Map and at Mammoth Lakes

ROCK CREEK LAKE

Rock Creek Lake, at an elevation of 9,682 feet, is in the Rock Creek Canyon of Inyo National Forest on the Eastern Slope of the Sierras. Snow-fed streams flow into this natural Lake of 63 surface acres. Rainbow and German Brown Trout are planted throughout the season, and the more adventuresome will find native populations of Eastern Brook and Golden Trout in this area of more than 60 Lakes and streams. There are Pack Stations and an abundance of facilities for the camper, fisherman, backpacker or nature lover.

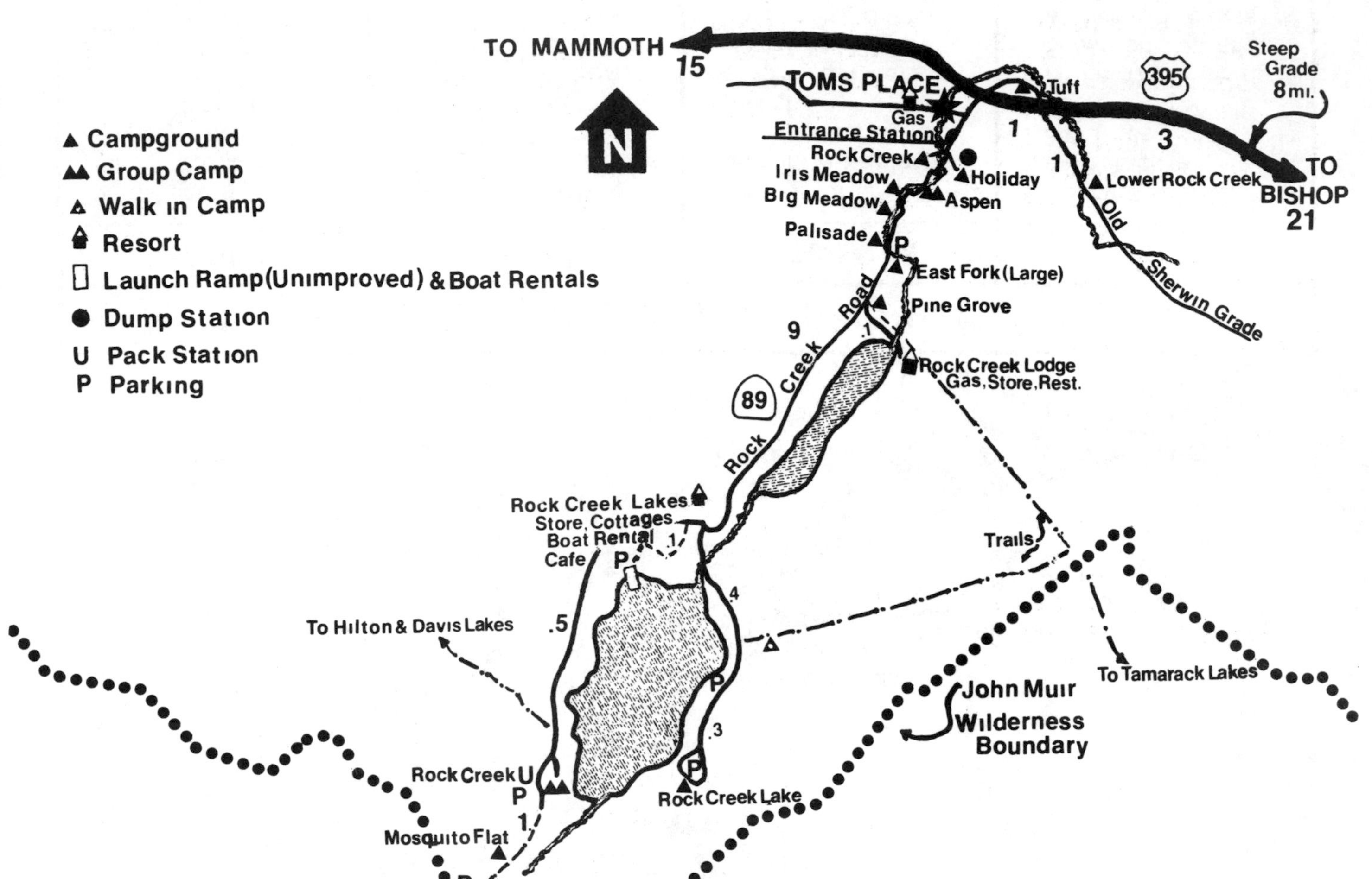

INFORMATION: White Mountain R.D., 798 N. Main St., Bishop 93514, Ph: 619-873-4207

CAMPING	BOATING	RECREATION	OTHER
U.S.F.S. in Area 63 Dev. Sites for Tents 174 Dev. Sites for R.V.s 10 Walk-In Sites Group Camps Fees: $4 - $25	Power, Row, Canoe, Sail & Inflatables Speed Limit - 5 MPH Unimproved Launch Ramp Rentals at Rock Creek Lakes Resort: Fishing Boats & Motors	Fishing: Rainbow, Eastern Brook & Golden Trout - Lake & Streams Picnicking Hiking Backpacking - John Muir Wilderness - Permit Required Horseback Riding - Rentals & Trails Hunting: Deer	Rock Creek Lakes Resort Ph: 619-935-4311 Rock Creek Lodge Ph: 619-935-4452 Tom's Place Resort Ph: 619-935-4239 Rock Creek Pack Station Ph: 619-935-4493

NORTH LAKE, LAKE SABRINA, SOUTH LAKE

BISHOP CREEK CANYON

Bishop Creek Canyon is on the Eastern slope of the Sierra Nevadas at elevations ranging from 7,500 feet to 9,500 feet. This area is popular with backpackers by both foot and horseback into the nearby John Muir Wilderness. Lake Sabrina has a surface area of 150 acres. South Lake has 180 acres, and North Lake is much smaller. These Lakes, along with Bishop Creek, are planted weekly with trout during the summer. The U.S. Forest Service offers numerous campsites in addition to private Resorts with full vacation facilities.

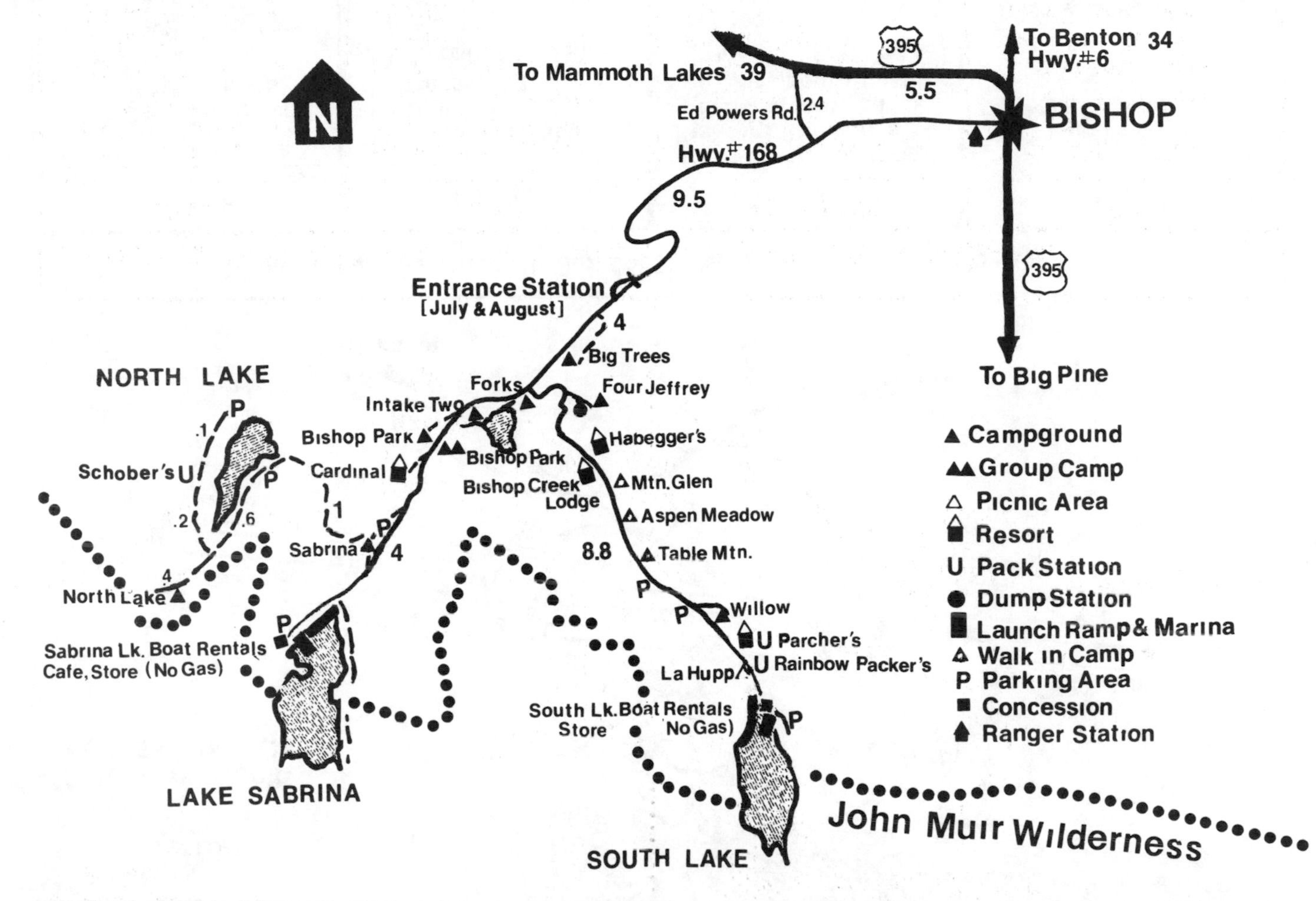

INFORMATION: U.S.F.S., 798 N. Main St., Bishop 93514, Ph: 619-873-4207			
CAMPING	**BOATING**	**RECREATION**	**OTHER**
146 Dev. Sites for Tents 187 Dev. Sites for R.V.s 15 Walk-In Sites Group Camps Fees: None to $25 Disposal Station	Power, Row, Canoe, Sail & Inflatables 5 MPH Speed Limit Unimproved Launch Ramps at South Lake and Sabrina Rentals: Fishing and Motorboats	Fishing: Rainbow & German Brown Trout Picnicking & Hiking Backpacking - Permit Required Horseback Riding Trails & Rentals Rainbow Packers: Ph: 619-873-8877	Resorts: Bishop Creek Lodge Cardinal Lodge Habegger's Resort Parcher's Rainbow Village Cabins Restaurants Grocery Stores Gas Stations Campfire Programs

NEW MELONES LAKE

New Melones rests at an elevation of 1,085 feet in the "Mother Lode Gold Country of Central California. Its Dam, completed in 1979, is the second largest earth and rock filled Dam in the United States. This damming of the Stanislaus River has created New Melones Lake which has 12,500 surface acres with over 100 miles of tree-covered shoreline. This is one of California's prime recreation Lakes. Extensive recreation facilities have been recently developed under the management of the U. S. Department of Reclamation. There are now two large campgrounds at Glory Hole and Tuttletown, as well as several day use areas. The boater will find launch areas and a full service marina under development. The fishing is considered good in the Lake and the nearby Stanislaus River.

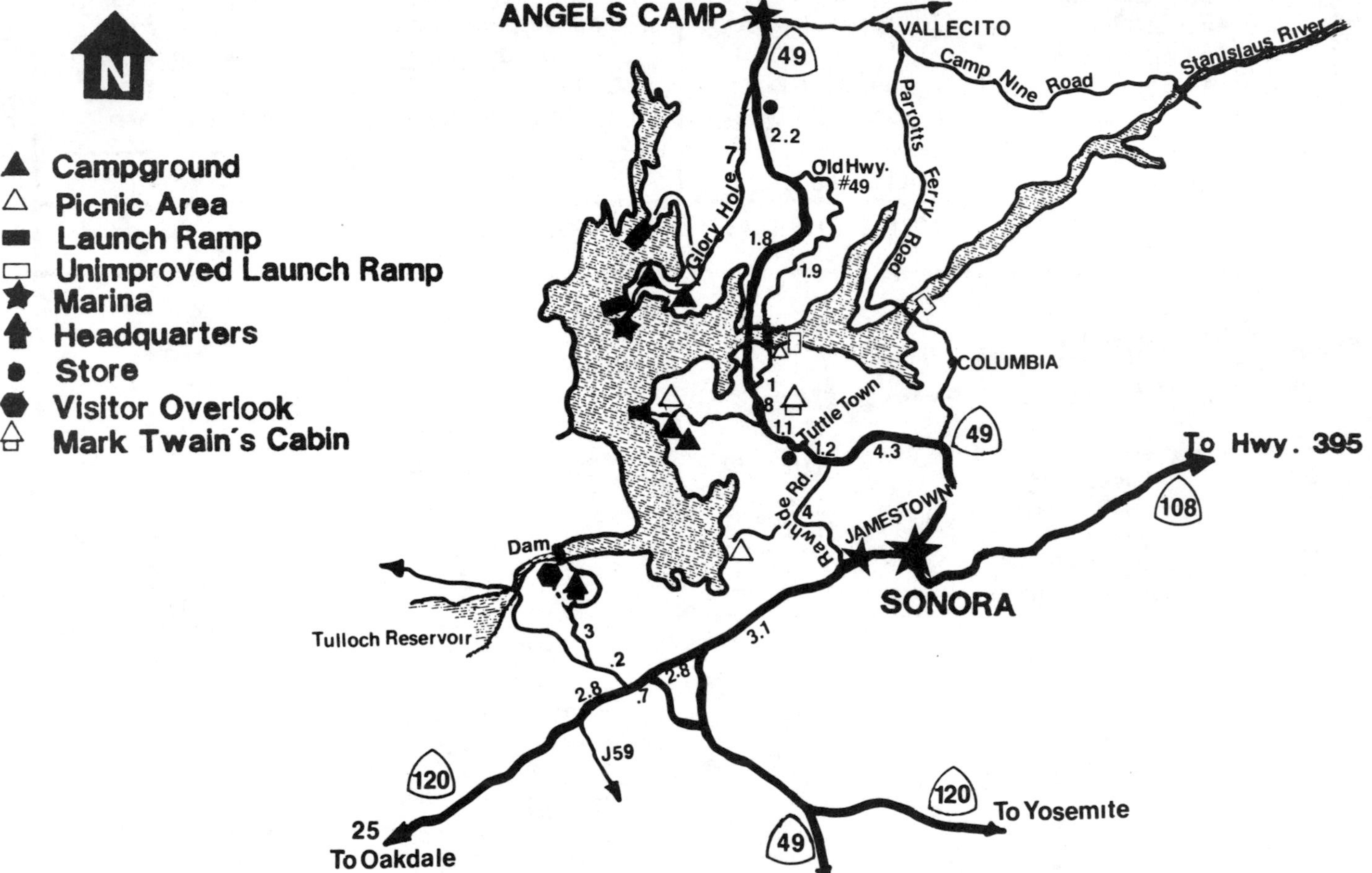

INFORMATION: Resource Manager, Star Rt. Box 155C, Jamestown 95327, Ph: 209-984-5248			
CAMPING	BOATING	RECREATION	OTHER
Glory Hole: 144 Dev. Sites for Tents & R.V.s Tuttletown: 89 Dev. Sites for Tents & R.V.s Fee: $5 2 Cars, 8 People Maximum Camping Only at Designated Sites	Open to All Boating, Sailing & Waterskiing 2 Unimproved Launch Areas 3 Improved Launch Ramps with 3 Floats Full Service Marina Being Developed at Glory Hole	Fishing: Rainbow & Brown Trout, Large & Smallmouth Bass, Bluegill, Catfish & Crappie Picnicking Hiking Gold Panning No ORV's Mark Twain's Cabin	Full Facilities in Nearby Towns

LAKE TULLOCH

Located in the Gold Country at an elevation of 510 feet, Lake Tulloch occupies two submerged valleys with 55 miles of shoreline. It is nestled between two high plateaus which are open to westerly winds making it a good Lake for sailing. Boating is very popular as the water is warm and clean. There is good trout and warm water fishing. Tulloch is one of the best smallmouth bass Lakes in California. Going towards Sonora on Highway 120, South Shore is the first exit. There are 64 developed campsites, by reservation, and 40 acres of undeveloped sites for self-contained units. Lake Tulloch Marina provides a launch ramp, snack bar, grocery store and gas. North Shore, 5 miles from Highway 120, has two facilities, Poker Flat and Copper Cove. Poker Flat has a luxury motel on the water with boat docks, gas, launch ramp, swimming pool, restaurant and bar. There is a private sandy beach in front of the motel. Copper Cove has a bar and restaurant on the water along with a launch ramp, moorings and a gas dock.

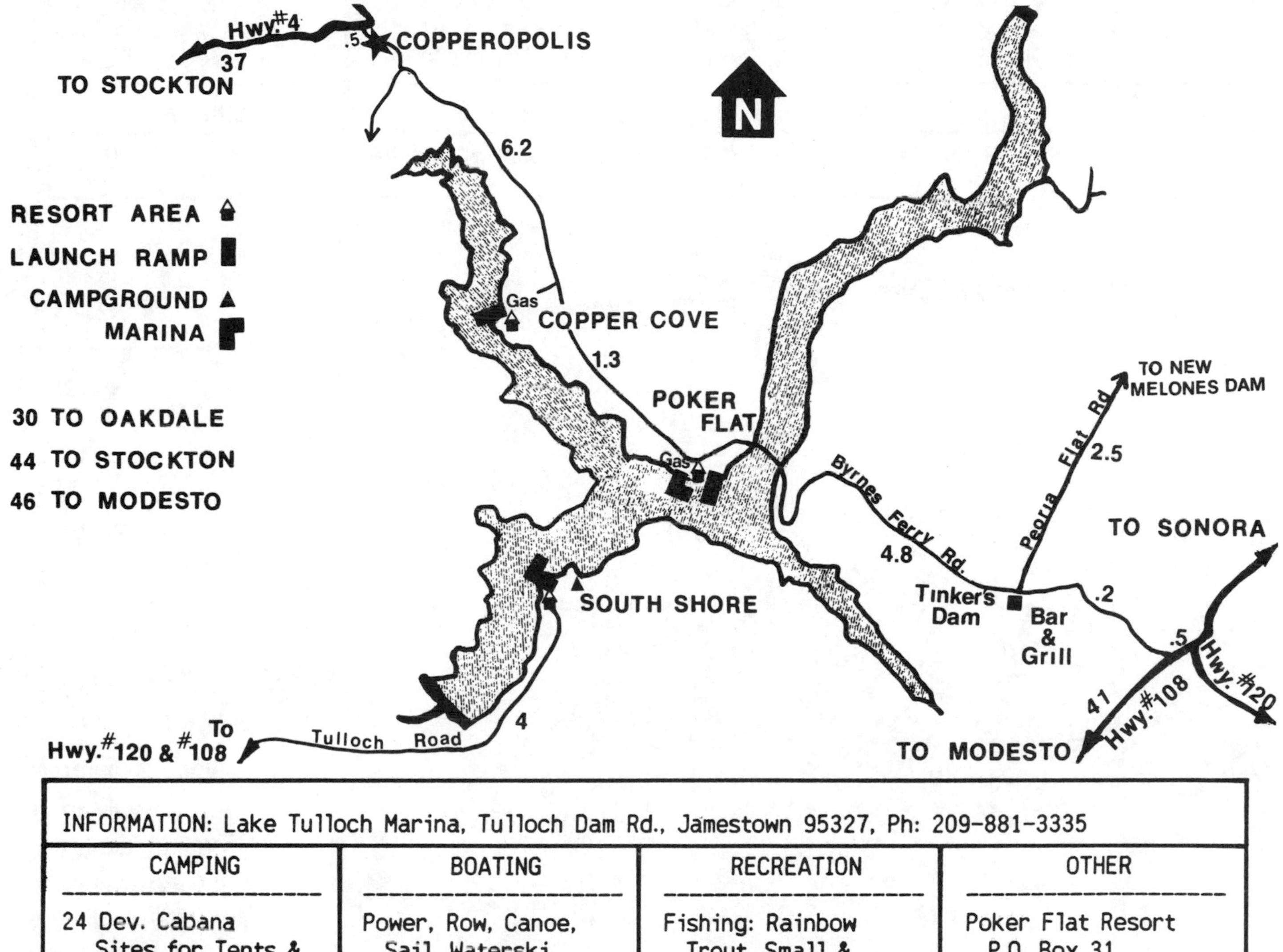

INFORMATION: Lake Tulloch Marina, Tulloch Dam Rd., Jamestown 95327, Ph: 209-881-3335

CAMPING	BOATING	RECREATION	OTHER
24 Dev. Cabana Sites for Tents & R.V.s on Lake 40 Dev. Sites for Tents & R.V.s - No Hookups Fee: $6 Plus Undeveloped sites for Self-Contained Units	Power, Row, Canoe, Sail, Waterski, Jet Ski, Windsurf & Inflatables Full Service Marina Launch Ramps Rentals: Fishing & Waterski Boats Overnight Boating Allowed Lake-shore Camping At Campground	Fishing: Rainbow Trout, Small & Largemouth Bass, Bluegill, Catfish, Crappie & Salmon Picnicking Swimming Hiking; Riding Trails Gold Panning Hunting: Quail, Dove, Pheasant, Waterfowl & Deer	Poker Flat Resort P.O. Box 31 Copperopolis 95228 Ph: 209-785-2286 Motel Restaurant & Bar Banquet Room Snack Bars Grocery Store Gas Station

Woodward Reservoir is at an elevation of 210 feet in the low, rolling, grassy foothills 6 miles north of Oakdale. The Lake has a shoreline of 23 miles and a surface area of 2,900 acres. The shallow shoreline has many coves and inlets, and the Lake is divided into areas to allow for waterskiing, sailing and fishing by speed limit restrictions which makes it very enjoyable for all boaters. Stanislaus County operates pretty tree-covered campgrounds on the edge of the Lake. This is a nice facility for a family outing.

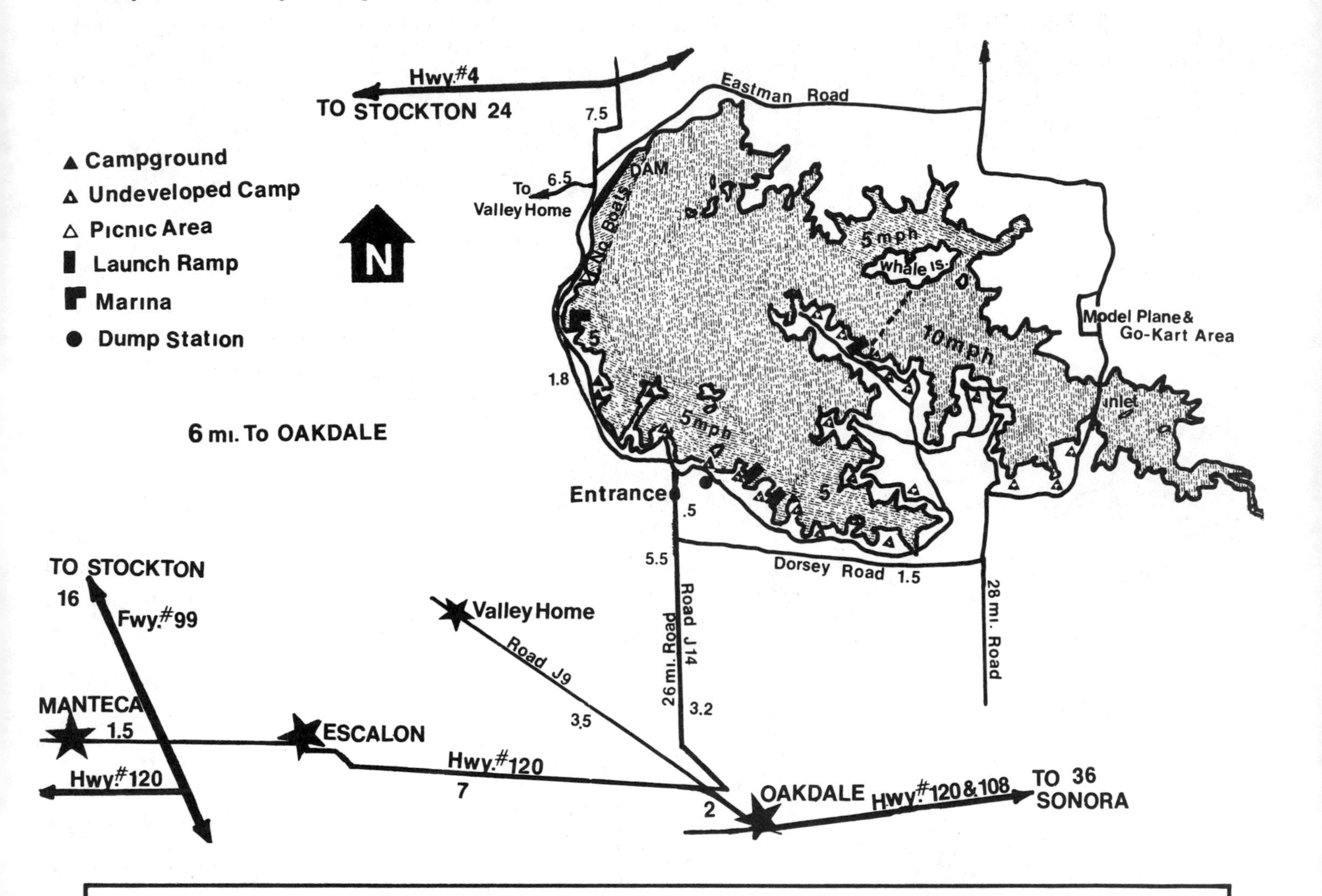

INFORMATION: Woodward Reservoir, 14528-26 Mile Rd., Oakdale 95361, Ph: 209-847-3304

CAMPING	BOATING	RECREATION	OTHER
78 Dev. Sites for Tents & R.V.s Fee: $7 1,200 Acres for Primitive Camping Fee: $5	Power, Row, Canoe, Sail, Waterski, Jet Ski, Windsurf, Inflatables Restricted Speed Limit Areas Launch Ramps - $2 Full Service Marina Rentals: Fishing, Sail & Canoe	Fishing: Catfish, Perch, Bluegill, Crappie, Large-mouth Bass Swimming Picnicking: Large Shelter to Reserve Hunting: Waterfowl With Permit Volleyball Court Horseshoe Pits	Snack Bar Grocery Store Bait & Tackle Disposal Station Hot Showers Full Facilities - 6 Miles at Oakdale

DON PEDRO LAKE

Don Pedro Lake rests at an elevation of 800 feet in the Sierra foothills of the Southern Mother Lode. This huge Lake has a surface area of 12,960 acres with a pine and oak dotted shoreline of 160 miles. There is an abundance of camping, marine and recreation facilities under the jurisdiction of the Don Pedro Recreation Agency. The vast size and irregular shoreline provides a multitude of boating opportunities from boat-in camping to waterskiing. The angler, from the novice to those on the Pro Bass Tour, will find the varied fishery satisfying. Emerging rocks and islands due to the fluctuating Lake levels can be a problem late in the season.

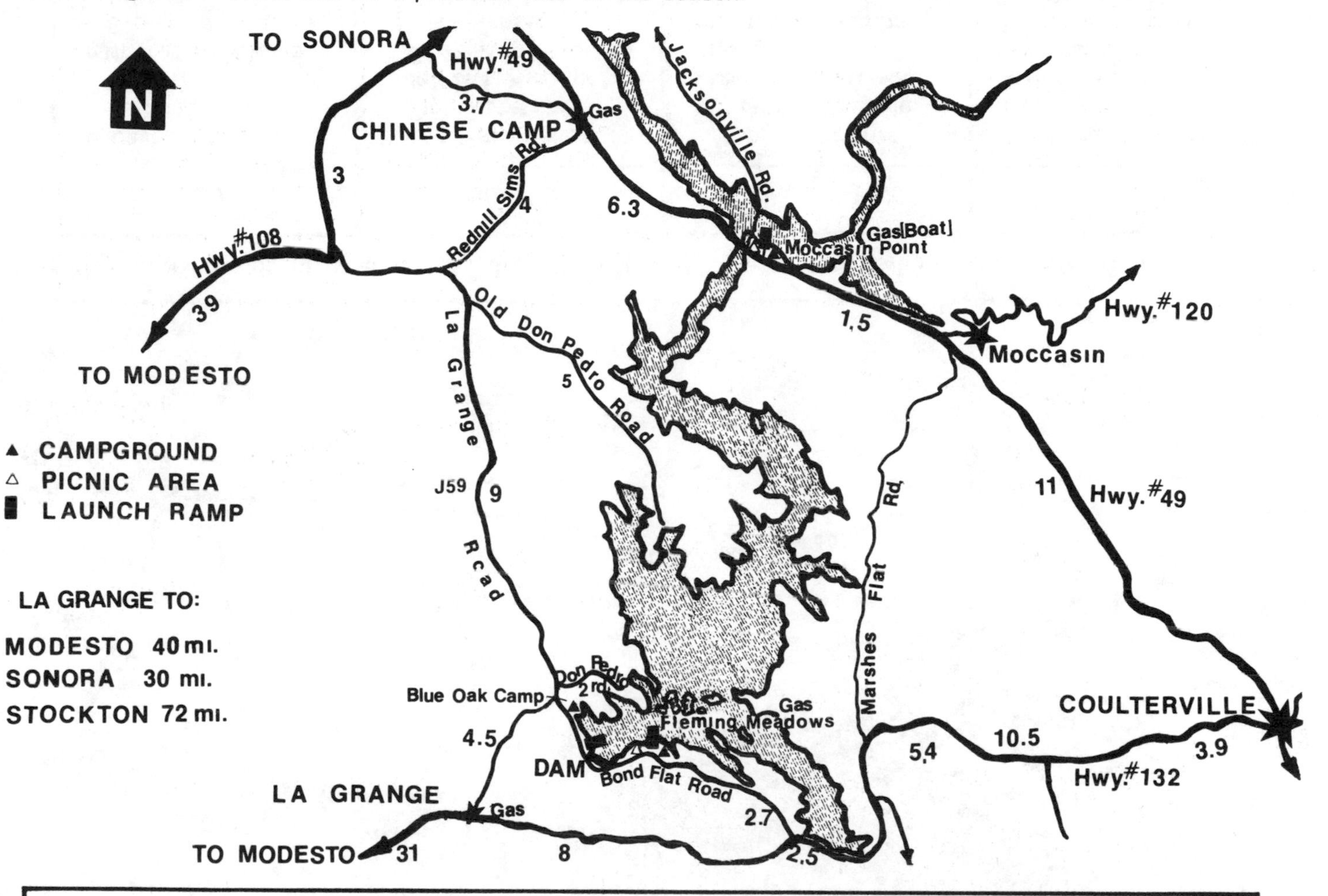

INFORMATION: Don Pedro Rec. Agency, Box 160, La Grange 95329, Ph: 209-852-2396

CAMPING	BOATING	RECREATION	OTHER
540 Dev. Sites for Tents & R.V.s Fee: $8 - Tents $12 - Full Hookup Group Camp - 200 People Maximum Boat-In & Walk-In Sites Reservations Accepted Overnight on Boat In Designated Areas	Power, Row, Canoe, Sail, Waterski, Jet Ski, Windsurf & Inflatable Full Service Marinas Launch Ramps - $4 Rentals: Fishing, Houseboats & Pontoons Docks, Berths, Moorings, Dry Storage & Gas	Fishing: Trout, Catfish, Bluegill, Crappie, Perch, Silver Salmon, Florida Black Bass Swimming Lagoon - Handicap Access Picnicking Hiking Private Houseboats Subject to Permit	Snack Bars Restaurant Grocery Store Bait & Tackle Hot Showers Laundromat Disposal Station Gas Station Propane Sailing Slalom Course

MODESTO RESERVOIR

Modesto Reservoir is at an elevation of 21 feet in the low hills, orchards and pastureland northeast of Modesto. The Lake has a surface area of 2,700 acres with 31 miles of shoreline. This is a good boating Lake with many pretty coves for unlimited boat camping, westerly breezes for sailing, and vast open water for the skier. Submerged trees along with the many coves provide a good warm water fishery. The facilities are under the jurisdiction of the Stanislaus County Parks Department.

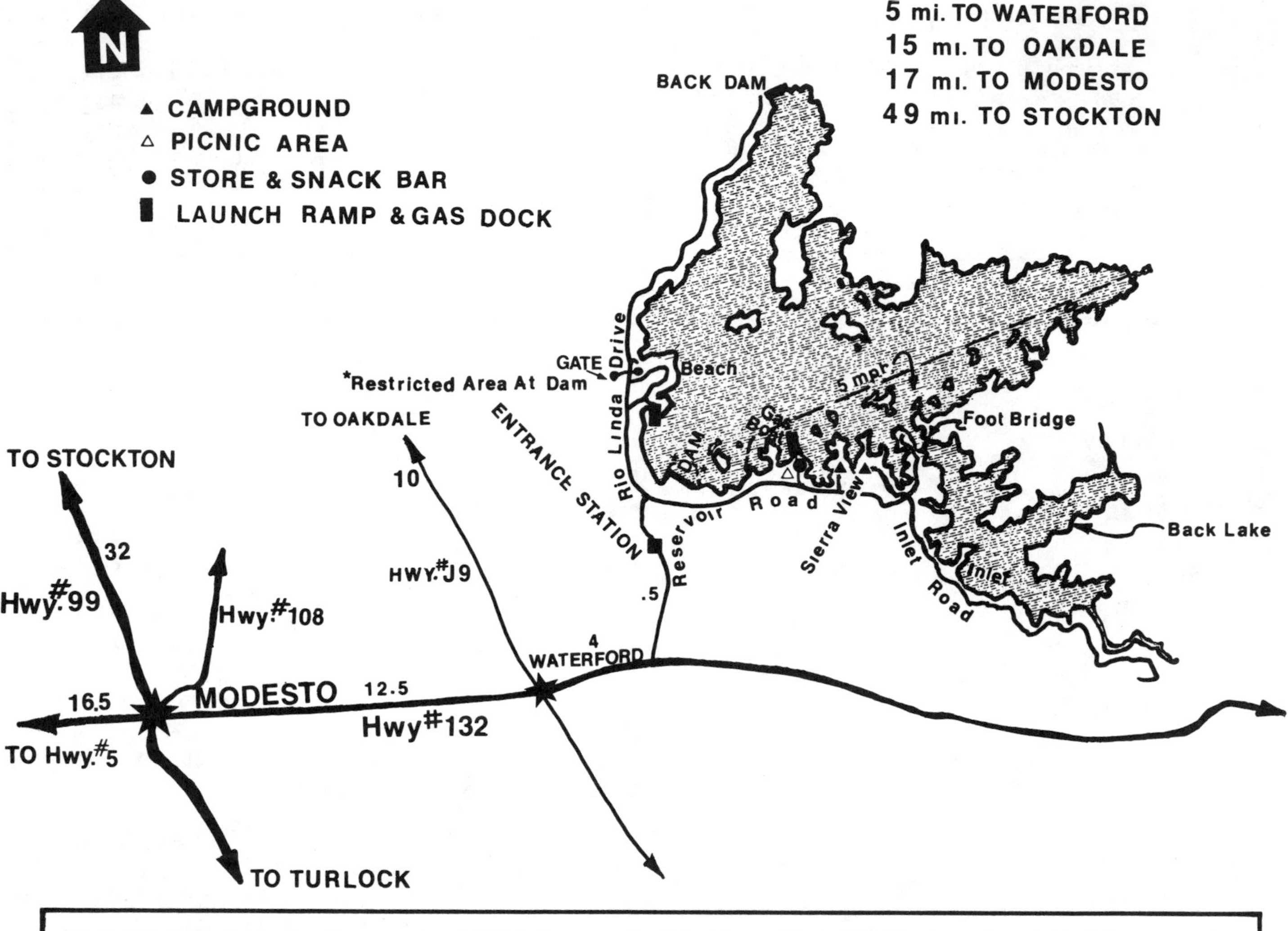

INFORMATION: Modesto Reservoir, 18139 Reservoir Rd., Waterford 95386, Ph: 209-874-9540

CAMPING	BOATING	RECREATION	OTHER
60 Dev. sites for Tents & R.V.s Fee: $7 Unlimited Primitive Sites Fee: $5 Entrance Fees Cars: $2 Boats: $2 Overnight in Boat Permitted Anywhere	Power, Row, Canoe, Sail, Waterski, Jet Ski, Windsurf & Inflatable Launch Ramps Full Service Marina Rentals: Paddleboats Docks, Moorings, Gas	Fishing: Catfish, Bluegill, Crappie, Large & Smallmouth Bass Swimming - Beaches Picnicking Hiking Backpacking-Parking Duck Hunting By Permit Only	Snack Bar Grocery Store Bait & Tackle Hot Showers Disposal Station Gas Station Full Facilities at Modesto

OAKWOOD LAKE

Bordering the San Joaquin River, Oakwood Lake is a unique camping and recreational experience. Boasting the "world's longest waterslide", there are 10 waterslides with 2 free for children. Arcades, roller skating, paddle boats and hot tubs are among the facilities to satisfy every member of the family. Boating is allowed on the Lake, no motors allowed. There are 400 campsites with full hookups located on shady lawns. If activities are part of vacation plans, this is the perfect Resort.

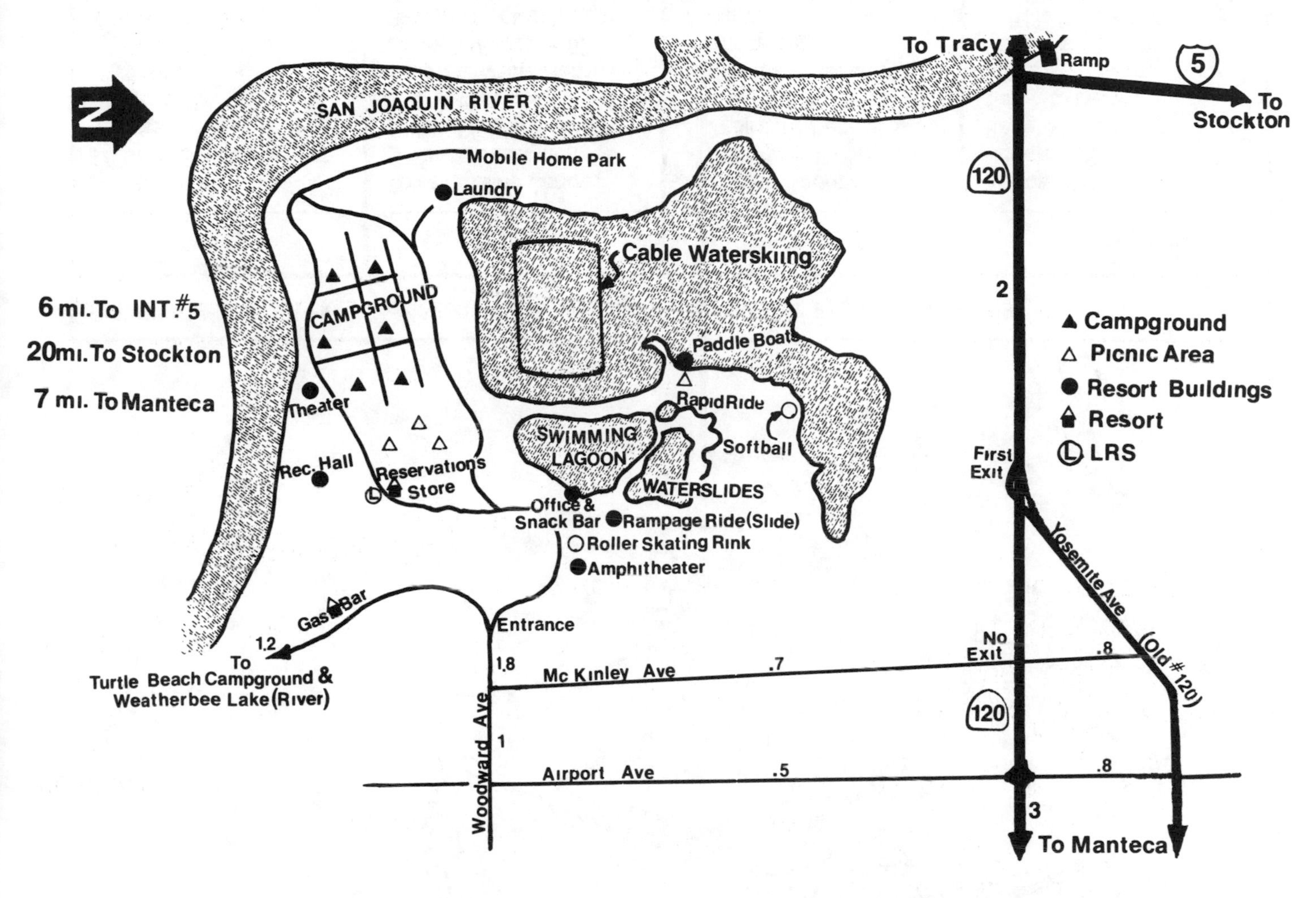

INFORMATION: Oakwood Lake, 874 E. Woodward, Manteca 95336, Ph: 209-239-2500

CAMPING	BOATING	RECREATION	OTHER
400 Dev. Sites for R.V.s with Full Hookups Tent Camping Fees Start @ $12 Group Sites Discount Rates for R.V. Clubs and Groups Reservations Only: Ph: 209-239-9566	Row, Sail, Canoe & Inflatables No Motors on Park Lake Hand Launch Only Rentals: Canoes, Paddle Boats San Joaquin River: Power Boats and Waterskiing-Launch Ramp off Hwy. 120	Fishing: Catfish & Bass - Guests Only Swimming Lagoon Picnicking 2 Large Day-Use Areas Waterslides Roller Skating Rink Rapids Ride Softball Complex Movies & Bingo Group Rates	Snack Bar Grocery Store Bait & Tackle Hot Showers Laundromat Playground Arcades R.V. Storage LP Gas Disposal Station

TURLOCK LAKE

Turlock Lake is at an elevation of 250 feet in the rolling hills of the Central Valley east of Modesto. The Lake has a surface area of 3,500 acres with 26 miles of shoreline. The Turlock Lake State Recreation Area is bordered on the north by the Tuolumne River. The Park is open year around, and this is a good warm water fishery. Trout are planted on a regular basis by the State Department of Fish and Game. The Marina is open from April though September. Reservations are advised for the campsites in season since this is a popular water recreation facility.

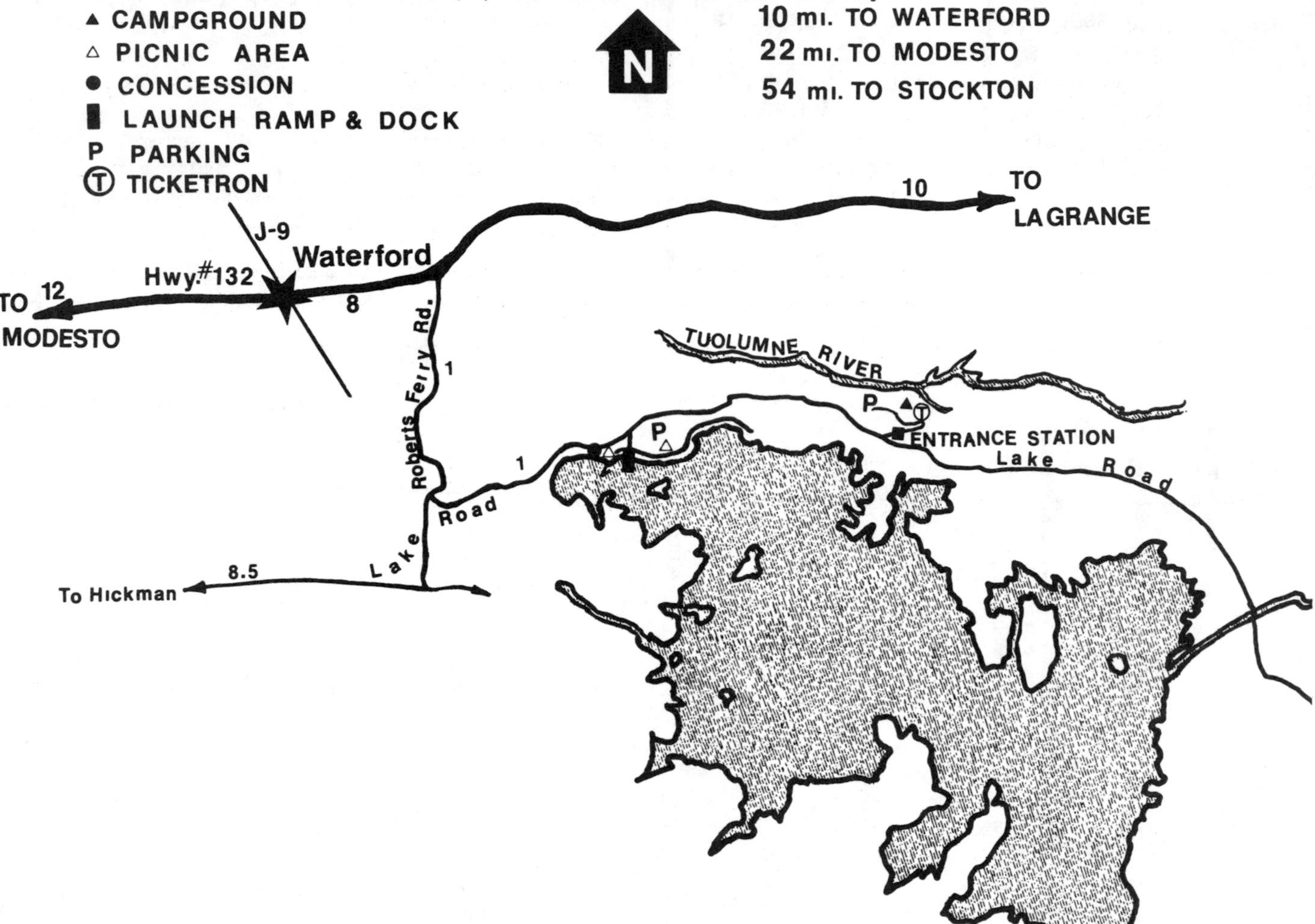

INFORMATION: Turlock Lake, 22600 Lake Rd., La Grange 95329, Ph: 209-874-2008			
CAMPING	BOATING	RECREATION	OTHER
State Park 67 Dev. Sites for Tents & R.V.s Fee: $6	Power, Row, Canoe, Sail, Waterski, Jet Ski, Windsurf & Inflatable Full Service Marina Launch Ramp - $2 Gas at Docks Rentals: Canoe, Rowboat & Paddleboats Low Water Late in Season	Fishing: Trout, Catfish, Bluegill, Crappie, Large & Smallmouth Bass Swimming - Beaches Picnicking Hiking Campfire & Junior Ranger Program Day Use Only: $2	Snack Bar Grocery Store Bait & Tackle Gas Station Full Facilities - 10 Miles at Waterford

LAKE MC CLURE AND LAKE MC SWAIN

At an elevation of 867 feet, these Lakes are in the Mother Lode Country of the Sierra Foothills. Lake McClure has a surface area of 7,100 acres with 82 miles of pine and oak covered shoreline. The fine recreation areas around the Lake have modern campgrounds, marinas and recreation facilities. Many coves are popular for houseboats, and the waterskier will find 26 miles of open water. Lake McSwain is actually the Forebay of Lake McClure. The cold flowing water from McClure has created a good fishery. Boating is popular, but waterskiing and houseboats are not allowed at McSwain.

. . . Continued . . .

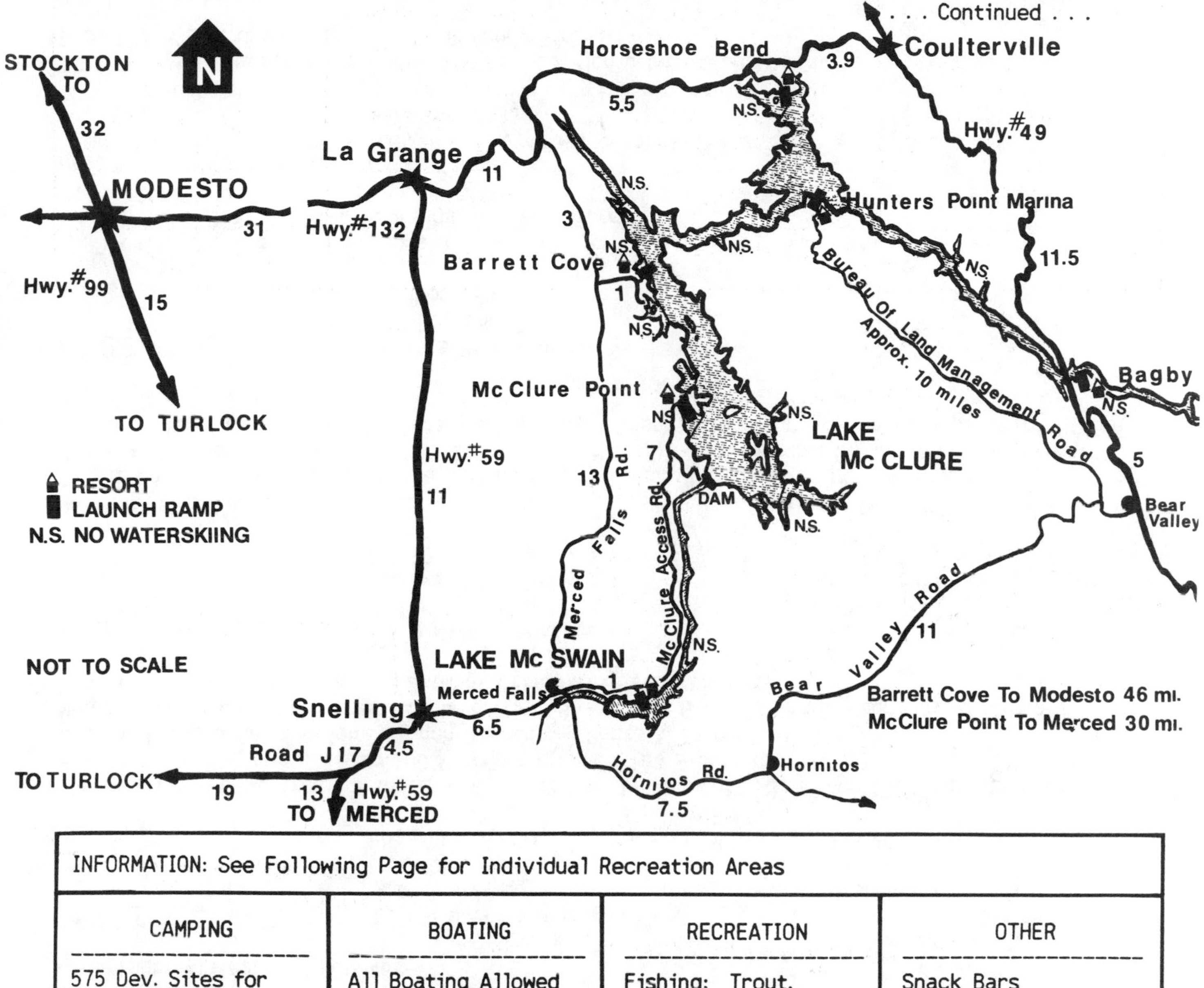

INFORMATION: See Following Page for Individual Recreation Areas

CAMPING	BOATING	RECREATION	OTHER
575 Dev. Sites for Tents & R.V.s Fee: $7 164 Electric & Water Hookups Fee: $8 15 Electric & Water & Sewer Hookups Fee: $9	All Boating Allowed at Lake McClure No Skiing/Houseboats at Lake McSwain Full Service Marinas Launch Ramps Rentals: Fishing, Houseboats, Pontoons & Jet Skis Docks, Berths, Moorings, Gas, Storage	Fishing: Trout, Catfish, Bluegill, Crappie, Perch & Bass Swim Lagoons Picnicking Hiking Sightseeing - Gold Rush Towns Playgrounds	Snack Bars Grocery Stores Bait & Tackle Hot Showers Laundromats Disposal Stations Gas Stations Propane

LAKE MC CLURE AND LAKE MC SWAIN

. . . Continued . . .

MC CLURE POINT	M I D Parks Department 9014 Village Drive Snelling 95369 Ph: 209-378-2521	McClure Point Marina 9561 Boat Club Road Snelling 95369 Ph: 209-378-2491

100 Developed Campsites for Tents & R.V.s, 41 Water & Electric Hookups. Fees: $7 - $8. Group Camp to 30 People Maximum. 64 Picnic Units. Full Service Marina with Gas for Boats & Cars, 5-Lane Launch Ramp, Boat Rentals: Fishing, Houseboats, Pontoons, Docks, Berths, Moorings, Storage. Swim Lagoon, Snack Bar Grocery Store, Laundromat, Showers. Reservations through Parks Department Office at 1-800-468-8889.

BARRETT COVE:	M I D Parks Department Star Route La Grange 95329 Ph: 209-378-2711	Barrett Cove Marina Star Route La Grange 95329 Ph: 209-378-2441

275 Developed Campsites for Tents & R.V.s, 33 Full Hookups, 35 Water and Electric Hookups. Fees: $7 - $9. Group Camp to 100 People Maximum. 100 Picnic Units. Full Service Marina with Gas for Boats & Cars, 4-lane Launch Ramp, Boat Rentals: Fishing, Houseboats, Pontoons, Jet Skis, Moorings, Storage. Swim Lagoon, Playground, Snack Bar, Grocery Store, Laundromat, Showers. Reservations through Parks Department Office at 1-800-468-8889.

HORSESHOE BEND:	M I D Parks Department 4244 Highway 132 Coulterville 95311 Ph: 209-878-3452	Horseshoe Bend Marina 4240 Highway 132 Coulterville 95311 Ph: 209-878-3119

90 Developed Campsites for Tents & R.V.s, 15 Water & Electric Hookups. Fees: $7 - $8. 32 Picnic Units. Full Service Marina, 2-lane Launch Ramp, Boat Rentals: Houseboats, Moorings, Storage, Gas for Boats & Cars, R.V. & Boat Repair Shop, Docks, Berths, Swim Lagoon, Snack Bar, Grocery Store, Laundromat, Showers, Barber Shop. Reservations through Parks Department Office at 1-800-468-8889.

HUNTERS POINT:	Hunters Point Marina P.O. Box 568 Mariposa 95338

15 Developed Campsites for Tents & R.V.s. 12 Picnic Units. Full Service Marina, Gas for Boats, Launch Ramp, Boat Rentals, Moorings, Grocery Store.

BAGBY:	A.M.S. Marina 8324 Highway 49 North Mariposa 95338

25 Developed Campsites for Tents & R.V.s. 25 Picnic Units. Full Service Marina, Launch Ramp, Boat Rentals, Moorings, Snack Bar, Grocery Store.

LAKE MC SWAIN:	M I D Parks Department 9014 Village Drive Snelling 95369 Ph: 209-378-2521	Lake McSwain Marina 8044 Lake McClure Road Snelling 95369 Ph: 209-378-2534

80 Developed Campsites for Tents & R.V., 30 Water & Electric Hookups. Fees: $7 - $8. Group Camp to 60 People Maximum. Picnic Area. Full Service Marina with Gas for Boats & Cars, 2-lane Launch Ramp, Rentals: Fishing Boats, Moorings. Snack Bar, Grocery Store, Laundromat, Showers, Playground Area. Reservations through Parks Department Office at 1-800-468-8889.

LAKE YOSEMITE

Lake Yosemite is nestled in the rolling foothills of the Sierra Nevadas, east of Merced. This 387 surface acre Lake is under the jurisdiction of the County of Merced. The County maintains a nice day use Park with shaded picnic areas for families and groups to 200 people. Group reservations are required. There are swimming beaches and excellent marine facilities. All types of boating are allowed with designated areas for waterskiing, sailing and rowing. Fishing can be productive at this pleasant Park in the San Joaquin Valley.

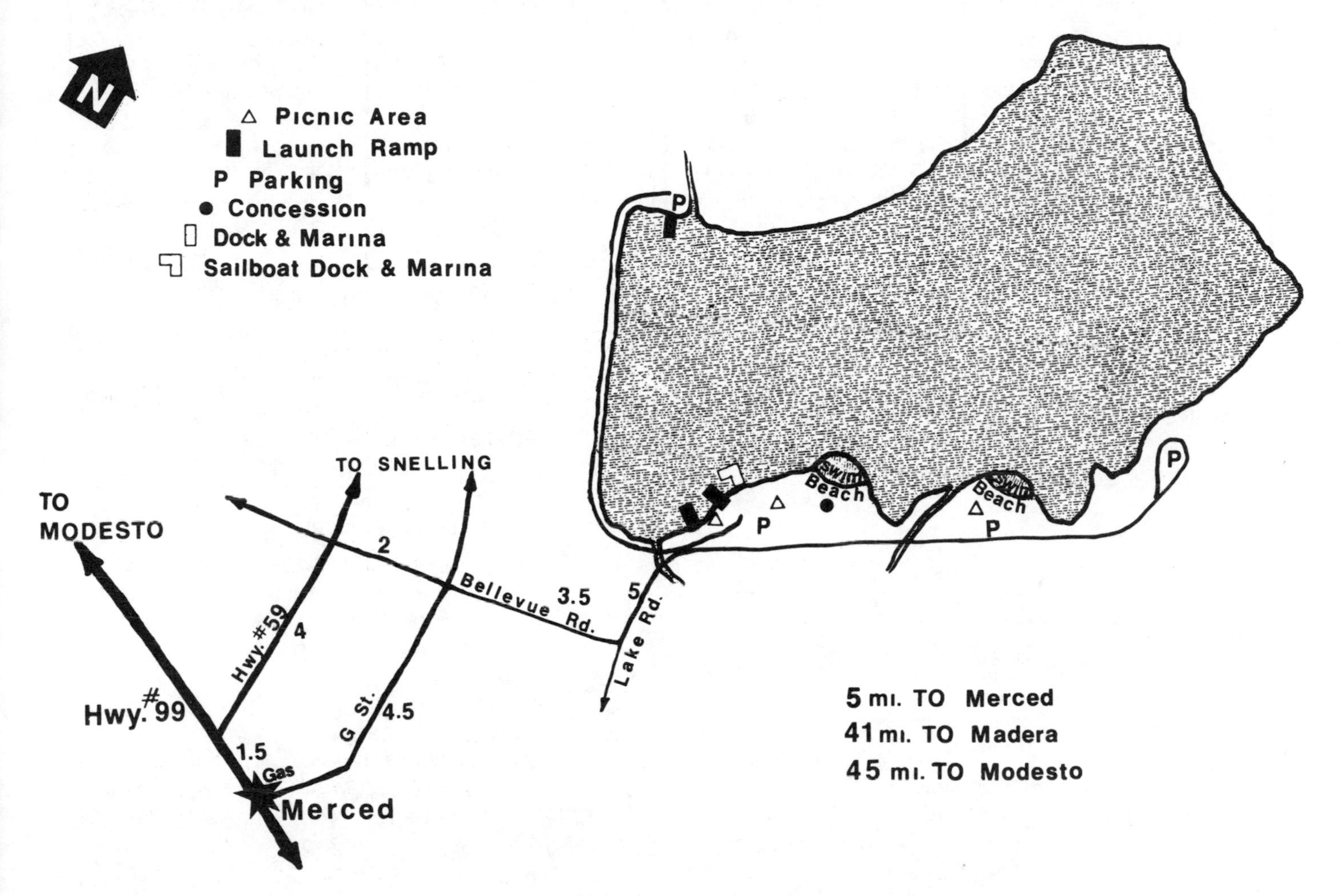

INFORMATION: Parks & Recreation, Merced County Courthouse, Merced 95340			
CAMPING	BOATING	RECREATION	OTHER
Youth Groups Only For Group Reservations Ph: 209-385-7426	All Boating Allowed with Designated Areas for Sailboats, Waterskiing, Rowboats & Powerboats Launch Ramp Docks and Marina Boat Rentals	Fishing: Trout, Largemouth Bass, Bluegill & Catfish Swimming - Beach Picnicking Group Picnic Facility	Snack Bar Park Fee: $1 Per Vehicle

SOULAJULE, STAFFORD, NICASIO, PHOENIX, LAGUNITAS, BON TEMPE, ALPINE AND KENT LAKES

Nestled on the slopes of Mt. Tamalpais, these pretty Lakes are under the jurisdiction of the Marin Municipal Water District. Picnic facilities are near each Lake, and beautiful redwood-shaded hiking and equestrian trails abound. While boating, swimming and wading are not allowed, fishing can be good for planted trout at all of the Lakes when water levels permit. The angler will also find a warm water fishery at Nicasio Reservoir. An interesting 19-mile bicycle loop from Samuel Taylor State Park around Nicasio Reservoir, and back to the Park, as shown on map, invites the skilled rider.

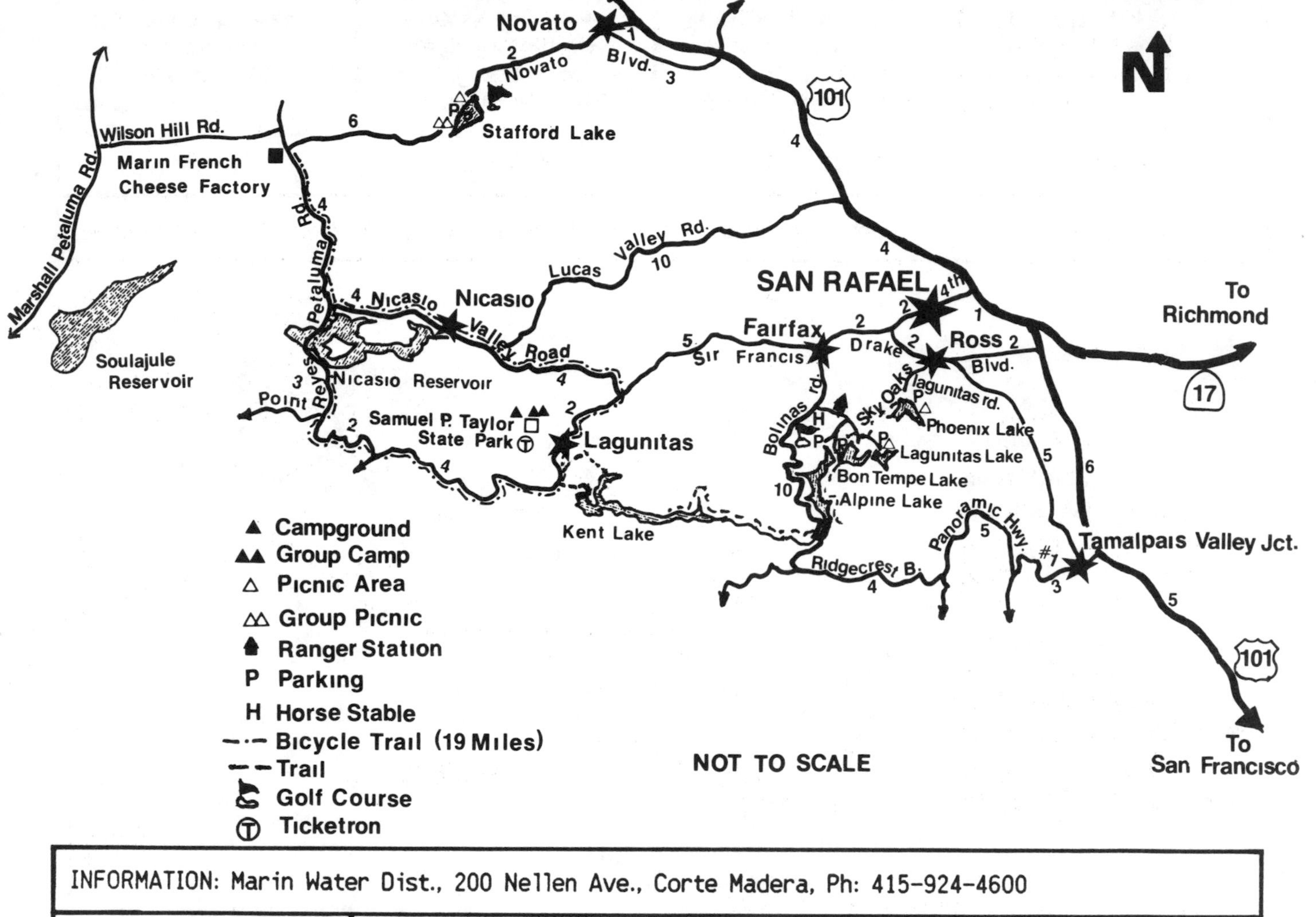

INFORMATION: Marin Water Dist., 200 Nellen Ave., Corte Madera, Ph: 415-924-4600

CAMPING	BOATING	RECREATION	OTHER
Samuel P. Taylor Park P.O. Box 251 Lagunitas 94938 Ph: 415-488-9897 65 Developed Sites Reserve Ticketron Lakes: Day Use Only Vehicle Fees: $3 Open: 8:00 a.m. to Sunset	No Boating	Fishing: Trout, Bass, Bluegill, Catfish & Crappie Hiking & Equestrian Trails Bicycle Loop Nature Study Picnicking No Swimming or Wading	Stafford Lake: North Marin Water District P.O. Box 146 Novato 94948 Ph: 415-897-4133 Cheese Factory: 4 Miles North of Nicasio Reservoir Full Facilities Nearby

ANZA, BERKELEY AQUATIC PARK, MERRITT AND TEMESCAL

Lake Anza is a small Lake within the beautiful Charles Lee Tilden Regional Park. While Lake Anza offers minimal water recreation, Tilden Park is one of the most extensively developed day use facilities in the Bay Area. Temescal is a small 13 acre Lake within the 48 acre Temescal Recreation Area. The City of Oakland administers the 160 acre saltwater Lake Merritt. The surrounding Lakeside Park provides expansive shaded lawns, picnic areas, children's playground and North America's oldest bird sanctuary. The Berkeley Aquatic Park is a popular rowing, sailing and windsurfing salt water Lake. While there are private facilities for waterskiing, it is not open to the public for power boating.

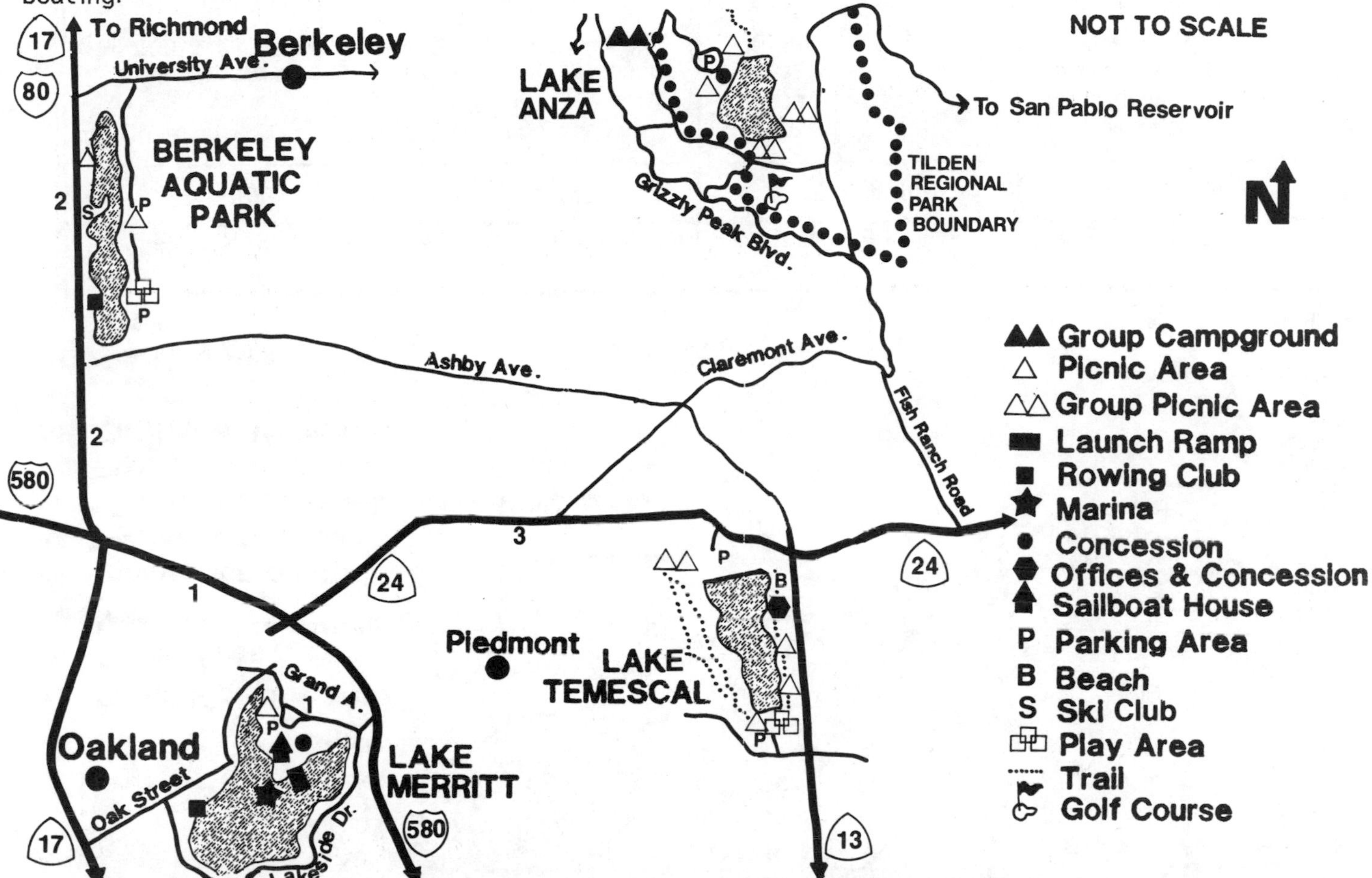

INFORMATION: East Bay Reg. Park, 11500 Skyline Blvd., Oakland 94619, Ph: 415-531-9300

CAMPING	BOATING	RECREATION	OTHER
No Camping Except for Youth Groups at Tilden Regional Park 14 Day Advance Reservations Ph: 415-531-9043	Lake Anza: No Boating Berkeley Aquatic: Sail, Windsurf & Row Private Facilities for Waterskiing Rental Sailboats Lake Merritt: Sail, Windsurf & Manually Powered Launch Ramp & Hoist Rental: Sail, Row Temescal: No Boating	Fishing: Trout, Bass, Catfish, Crappie & Perch Picnicking Hiking, Jogging & Riding Trails Playground Nature Study Bird Sanctuary Boat Tours Swimming: Anza & Temescal Only	Lake Merritt: 1520 Lakeside Dr. Oakland 94612 Ph: 415-444-3807 Berkeley Aquatic Park City of Berkeley 2180 Milvia Street Berkeley 94704 Ph: 415-644-6530

SAN PABLO RESERVOIR

San Pablo Reservoir rests at an elevation of 313 feet in the Berkeley hills. This 860 acre Lake is under the jurisdiction of the East Bay Municipal Utility District. The winds make for good sailing. Although windsurfing, waterskiing and speed boating are prohibited, this is a popular boating Lake with good marine facilities. Extensive fisheries habitat along with a tremendous planting schedule (300,000 trout planted in 1985) make this one of the most productive Lakes in the State. There are 142 picnic sites with barbecues overlooking the water in addition to a large children's play area. In addition, there are two large group picnic areas. Hiking and riding trails lead to Briones and Tilden Regional Park.

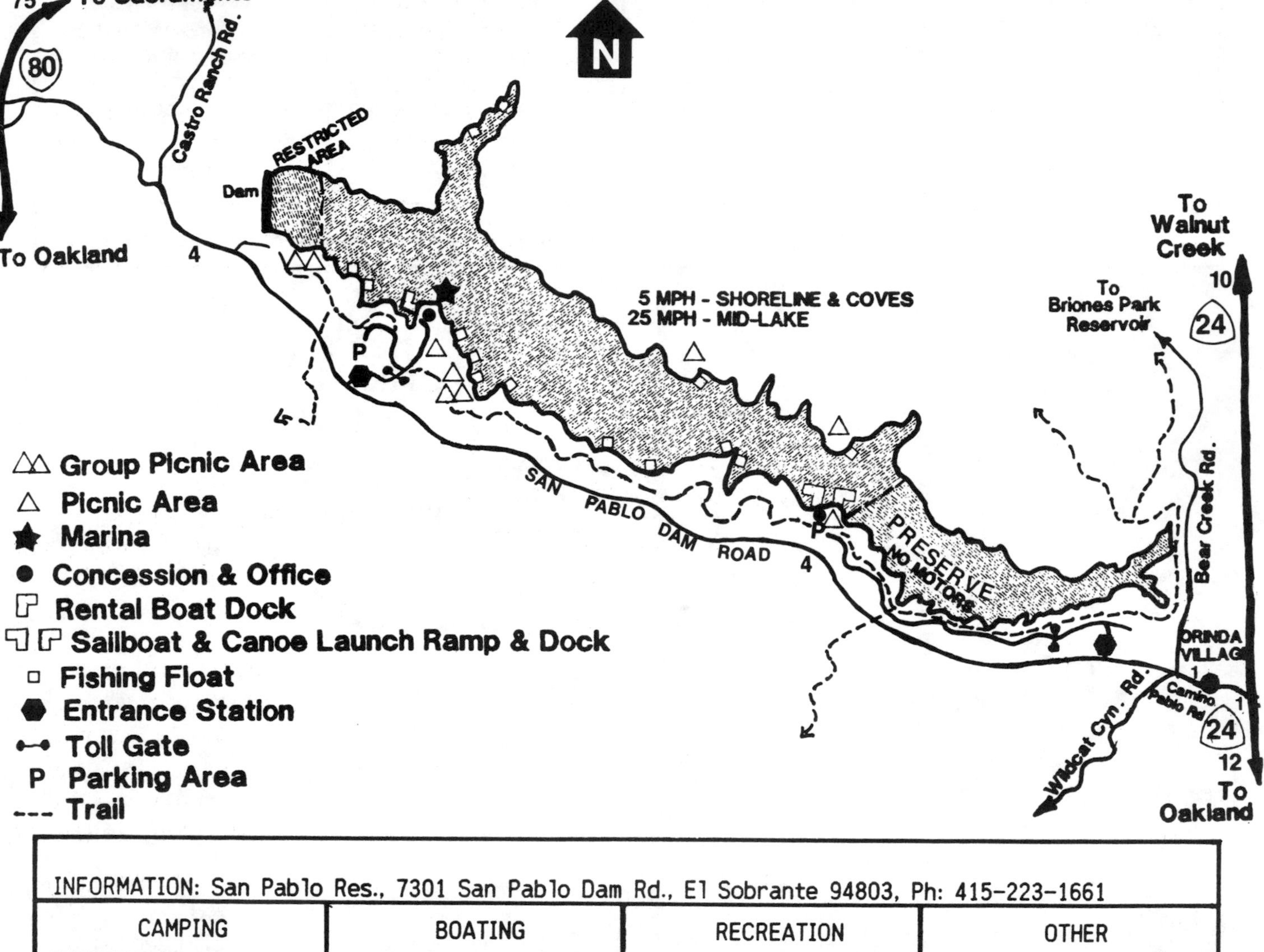

INFORMATION: San Pablo Res., 7301 San Pablo Dam Rd., El Sobrante 94803, Ph: 415-223-1661

CAMPING	BOATING	RECREATION	OTHER
Day Use Only 2 Group Picnic Areas for 100 & 250 People By Reservation	All Boating Subject to Permit Waterskiing, Windsurf & Racing Boats Not Allowed Full Service Marina 4-Lane Launch Ramp Docks Rentals: Fishing - 7-1/2 HP Motors, Row & Canoes	Fishing: Trophy Trout, Large, Smallmouth & Florida Bass, Catfish, Crappie & Perch Fishing Docks Picnic Areas Hiking, Bicycle & Riding Trails Children's Play Area No Swimming or Wading	Coffee Shop Restaurant Bait & Tackle

LAFAYETTE RESERVOIR

Lafayette Reservoir provides a natural retreat from the urban demands that surround it. Nestled amid the rolling oak-covered hills of Contra Costa County, this 115 acre Lake is popular among sailors, canoers and non-powered boaters. Electric motors are permitted. Although you must hand launch your boat, there is a boat house and sailing dock for the small boat owner. There are also rental boats. In addition to planted trout, the angler will find a warm water fishery. Most of the picnic sites surrounding the Lake have barbecues. There is a reserved group picnic area. A paved bicycle and walking trail surround the Lake, and in the hills above, there is a hiking trail. The facilities are under the jurisdiction of the East Bay Municipal Utility District.

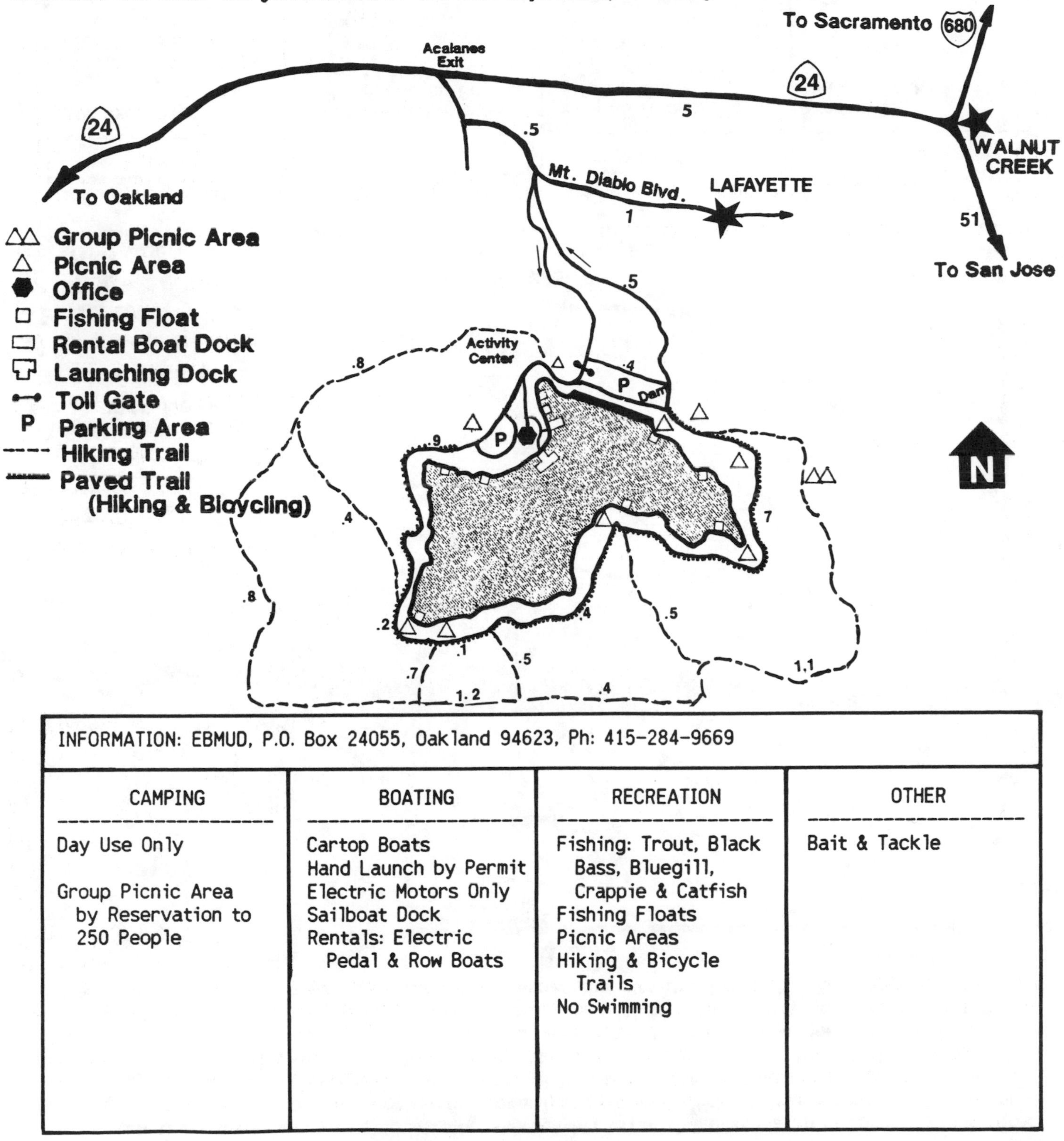

INFORMATION: EBMUD, P.O. Box 24055, Oakland 94623, Ph: 415-284-9669

CAMPING	BOATING	RECREATION	OTHER
Day Use Only Group Picnic Area by Reservation to 250 People	Cartop Boats Hand Launch by Permit Electric Motors Only Sailboat Dock Rentals: Electric Pedal & Row Boats	Fishing: Trout, Black Bass, Bluegill, Crappie & Catfish Fishing Floats Picnic Areas Hiking & Bicycle Trails No Swimming	Bait & Tackle

CONTRA LOMA RESERVOIR

Contra Loma Reservoir is located in the rolling hills of eastern Contra Costa County. This 71 acre Reservoir is within the 772 acre Contra Loma Regional Park. Hiking and riding trails run through the open grasslands of the Park into the adjoining Black Diamond Mines Regional Preserve. The concentration of greenery and facilities are near the water. Large shaded, turfed picnic areas and playgrounds await the visitor. There is a sandy swimming beach with a solar powered bathhouse. Wind, oar and electric powered boating is popular. The angler will find in addition to a warm water fishery, planted trout and striped bass. This facility is under the jurisdiction of the East Bay Regional Park District.

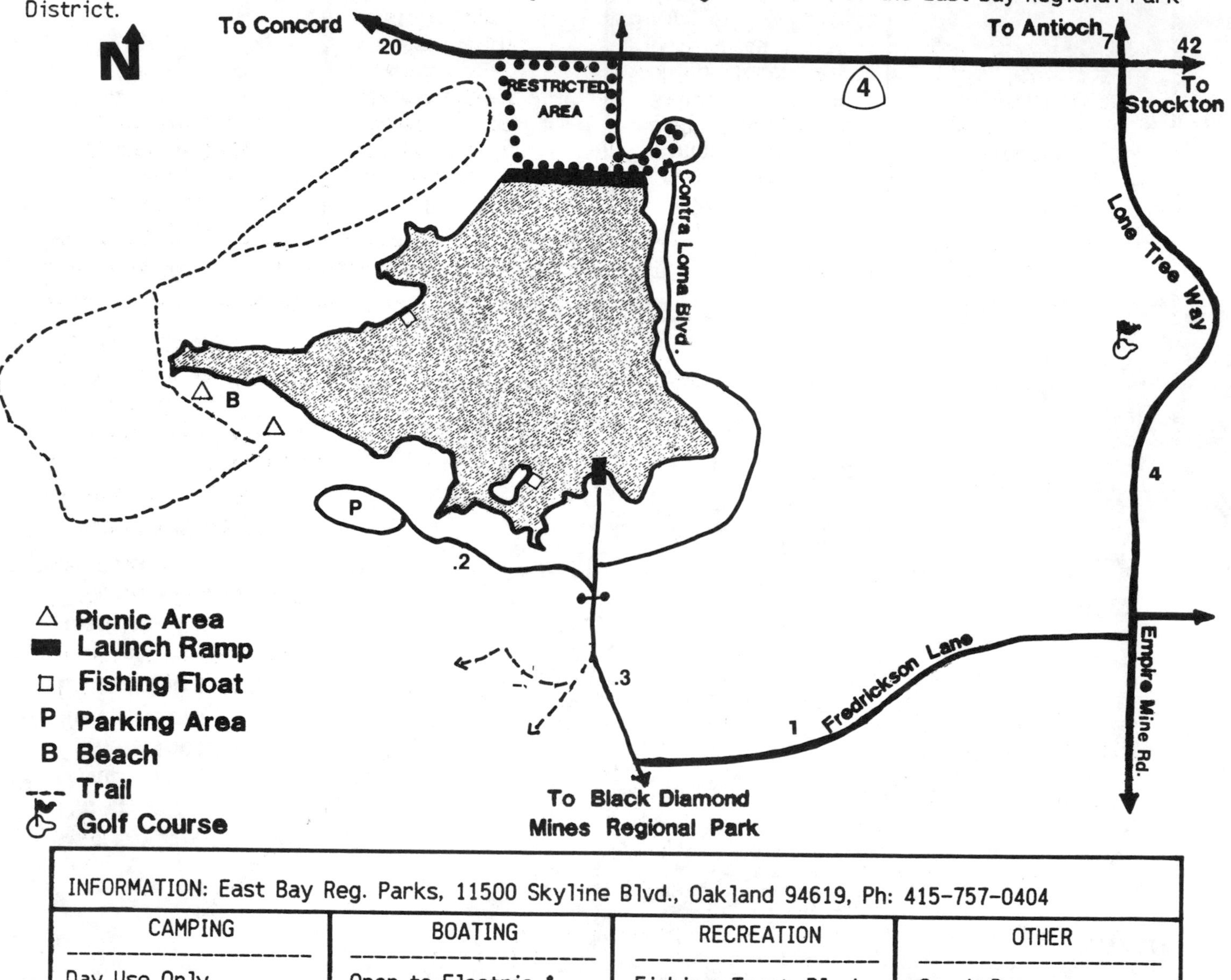

INFORMATION: East Bay Reg. Parks, 11500 Skyline Blvd., Oakland 94619, Ph: 415-757-0404

CAMPING	BOATING	RECREATION	OTHER
Day Use Only	Open to Electric & Non-Powered Boats to 17 feet By Permit Launch Ramp Rentals Windsurfing Lessons	Fishing: Trout, Black Bass, Bluegill, Catfish, Crappie, Perch & Striped Bass Fishing Docks Picnic Area Hiking & Riding Trails Swimming Children's Play Area Golf Course Nearby	Snack Bar Bait & Tackle

CHABOT, CULL CANYON, DON CASTRO AND JORDAN POND

These four small Lakes are within the East Bay Regional Park District. The angler will find a warm water fishery at all of these facilities and trout at Lake Chabot and Don Castro. Boating is limited to rentals at Lake Chabot. Each of these Regional Parks provide an abundance of natural attractions along with picnic facilities, hiking and riding trails. There are swimming lagoons at Cull Canyon and Don Castro. The 4,935 acre Anthony Chabot Regional Park provides an abundance of recreation facilities including an equestrian center, marksmanship range and motorcycle hill. Cull Canyon has won the Governor's Design Award for Recreation Development. Jordan Pond is within the 2,212 acre Garin and Dry Creek Pioneer Regional Park. This scenic Park offers an interpretive center and programs conducted by park naturalists.

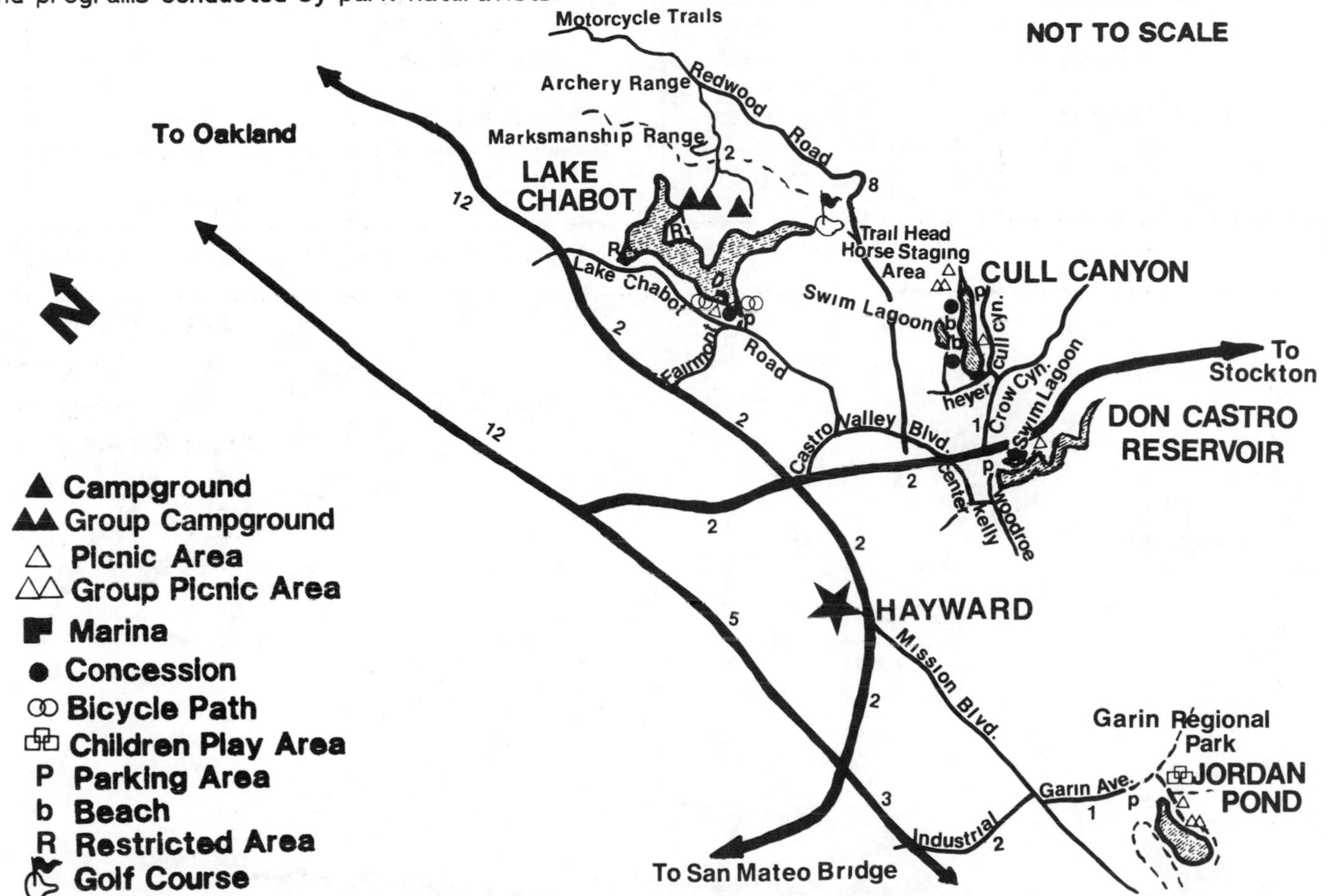

INFORMATION: East Bay Reg. Parks, 11500 Skyline Blvd., Oakland 94619, Ph: 415-531-9300

CAMPING	BOATING	RECREATION	OTHER
Lake Chabot: 73 Family Sites Youth Group Sites	Lake Chabot: No Private Boats Rentals: Electric, Row, Paddle & Canoe "Chabot Queen" Boat Tour No Boating at Other Lakes	Fishing: Trout, Black Bass, Bluegill, Catfish, Crappie & Perch Hiking, Jogging & Equestrian Trails Swimming: Don Castro & Cull Canyon Only Nature Study & Interpretive Center Playgrounds	Lake Chabot: Golf Course Motorcycle Hill Equestrian Center Horse Rentals Marksmanship Range

BETHANY RESERVOIR, SHADOW CLIFFS RESERVOIR, LAKE ISABEL, LAKE ELIZABETH

Within the greater Bay Area, these Lakes provide an abundance of recreational opportunities. The bicycler will find a 70 mile challenge at Bethany Reservoir on the California Aqueduct Bikeway or a leisurely ride on the 2 mile bikeway around Lake Elizabeth. Boating, fishing or a day at the Park can be found at these popular facilities.

. . . Continued. . .

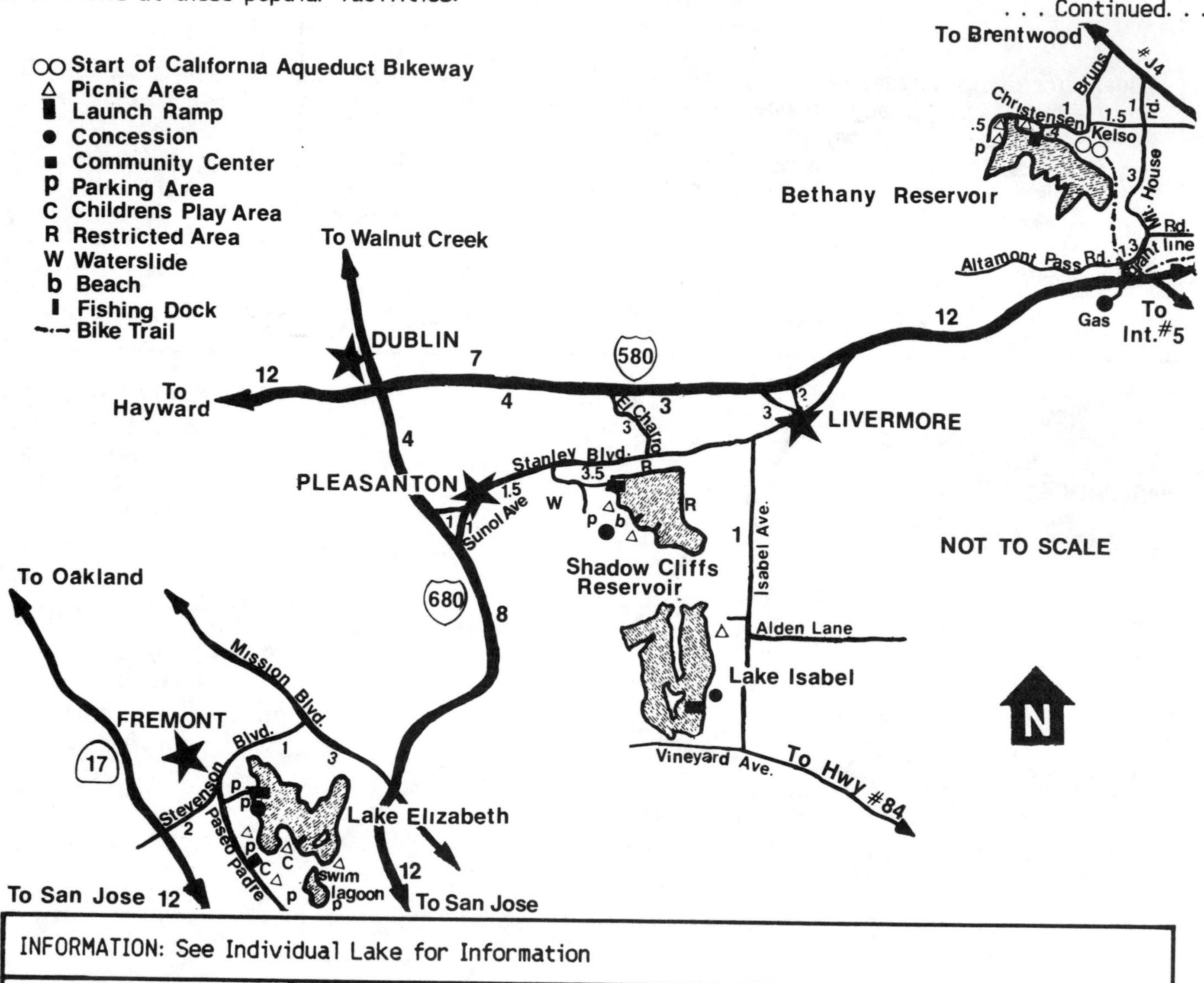

INFORMATION: See Individual Lake for Information			
CAMPING	**BOATING**	**RECREATION**	**OTHER**
Day Use Facilities Only	Varies at Each Lake - See Following Page	Fishing: Trout, Largemouth & Striped Bass, Catfish, Bluegill & Crappie Picnicking Nature, Hiking & Jogging Trails Bicycle Trails Swimming Beaches & Lagoons	Children's Play area Athletic Fields Waterslide Concessions at Shadow Cliffs, Isabel & Elizabeth Full Facilities Near Each Lake

. . . Continued . . .

BETHANY RESERVOIR, Department of Parks and Recreation, Diablo Area, 4180 Treat Blvd., Suite D, Concord 94521, Ph: 415-687-1800. Day Use Fee.

Bethany Reservoir State Recreation Area rests in gently rolling, grass-covered hills overlooking the vast Delta of the Sacramento and San Joaquin Rivers. This 162 acre Reservoir is open to all types of boating, but there is a 25 MPH maximum speed limit on the Reservoir, a 5 MPH speed limit within 200 feet of shore, and waterskiing is not allowed. Strong winds can be a hazard. This is a popular warm water fishery for striped bass and catfish. There is a parking lot for 120 cars, a 2-lane launch ramp and 4 picnic ramadas. Future plans call for campgrounds and a swimming beach. Bethany is the northern terminus for the California Aqueduct Bikeway.

SHADOW CLIFFS RESERVOIR, East Bay Regional Park District, 11500 Skyline Blvd., Oakland 94619, Ph: 415-531-9300. Parking Fee.

This Reservoir has been transformed from a bleak sand and gravel quarry to a complete 249 acre Park. The 74 surface acre Lake is open to all non-powered boating, and you may rent a fishing boat, canoe or paddle boat. Trout, largemouth bass, and channel and white catfish and bluegill await the angler. There is a sandy beach, swimming and waterslides in a separate area of the Park. The Park has picnic areas, turfed areas, hiking and equestrian trails and a food concession. Handicap facilities are available.

LAKE ISABEL, 1421 Isabel Avenue, Livermore 94550, Ph: 415-462-1281. Day Use. Fees: $8.50 Adults, $4.00 Children.

This 35 acre private Lake was opened to the public in the Fall of 1982. There are no facilities for private boats, but you may rent a fishing boat with electric motor. Rainbow trout range from 3/4 pounds to 10 pounds and are planted weekly in season. When the water is too warm for trout, channel catfish up to 10 pounds will be planted. There are plenty of bluegill, crappie and largemouth bass. The concession has tackle, bait, food and beer. Picnic areas and handicap facilities are available.

LAKE ELIZABETH, The Boathouse, P.O. Box 5006, Fremont 94538, Ph: 415-791-4340. Day Use.

This 63 acre Lake is within the beautiful Fremont Central Park. There are complete facilities for non-powered boating including ramps, docks, storage and rentals. This is a good sailing Lake with westerly winds which can become strong in the afternoons. Trout are planted except for the summer months when the water is too warm. There are also black bass, bluegill and catfish. The well maintained Park has an abundance of recreational facilities with open turfed areas, picnic areas, tennis courts, athletic fields, and a swim lagoon. The 2 mile Pedway around the Lake accommodates joggers, hikers and bikers at this complete City facility.

482 8044

DEL VALLE RESERVOIR

Del Valle Reservoir is at an elevation of 700 feet in oak-covered rolling hills near Livermore. The Lake has a surface area of 750 acres with 16 miles of shoreline. The 4,249 acre Del Valle Park is under the jurisdiction of the East Bay Regional Park District. In addition to the large tree shaded campgrounds, there are group campgrounds, picnic areas and marina facilities. Ten miles of scenic trails await the hiker or equestrian. Boating is limited to 10 MPH, and swimming is restricted to beach areas where lifeguards are on duty. This is a very popular sailing and windsurfing Lake.

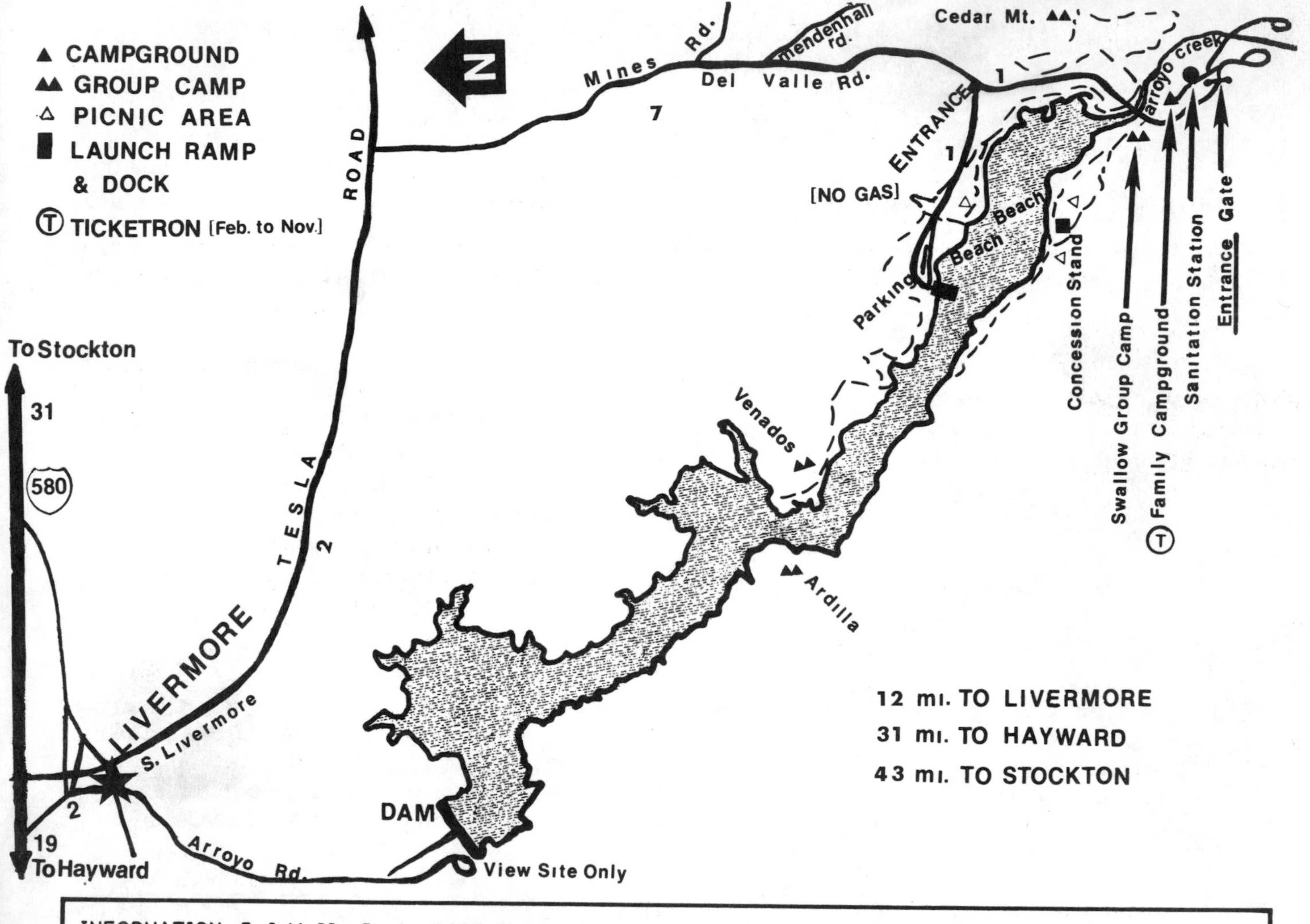

INFORMATION: Del Valle Park, 7000 Del Valle Rd., Livermore 94550, Ph: 415-443-4110

CAMPING	BOATING	RECREATION	OTHER
100 Dev. Sites for Tents & R.V.s Some Hookups Fee: $6 - $9 For Group Camp Reservations: Ph: 415-531-9043	Power, Row, Canoe, Sail, Windsurf & Inflatables Speed Limit - 10 MPH Launch Ramp Rentals: Fishing Boats & Canoes	Fishing: Trout, Catfish, Bluegill & Bass Swimming - In Season Picnicking - Groups Hiking Bicycle & Horseback Riding Trails Campfire Program	Snack Bar Bait & Tackle Disposal Station Full Facilities in Livermore

LAKE MERCED, SHORELINE PARK AND STEVENS CREEK RESERVOIR

These three urban Lakes provide a welcome variety of recreation opportunities. Lake Merced has a surface area of 396 acres. This is a popular sailing Lake. One of the better fishing Lakes in the State, rainbow and some brook trout grow to lunker size while feeding on fresh water shrimp. The relatively new Shoreline Lake provides the sailboarder and sailer with 50 acres of saltwater excitement. Shoreline Park is primarily open space with protected wildlife areas reached by paved trails. The prevailing north westerly winds make this a popular windsurfing Lake. Stevens Creek Reservoir, 765 acres, provides the angler with a warm water fishery and small craft boating. There are nice oak-shaded trails for the hiker and equestrian. Family and group picnic sites are available.

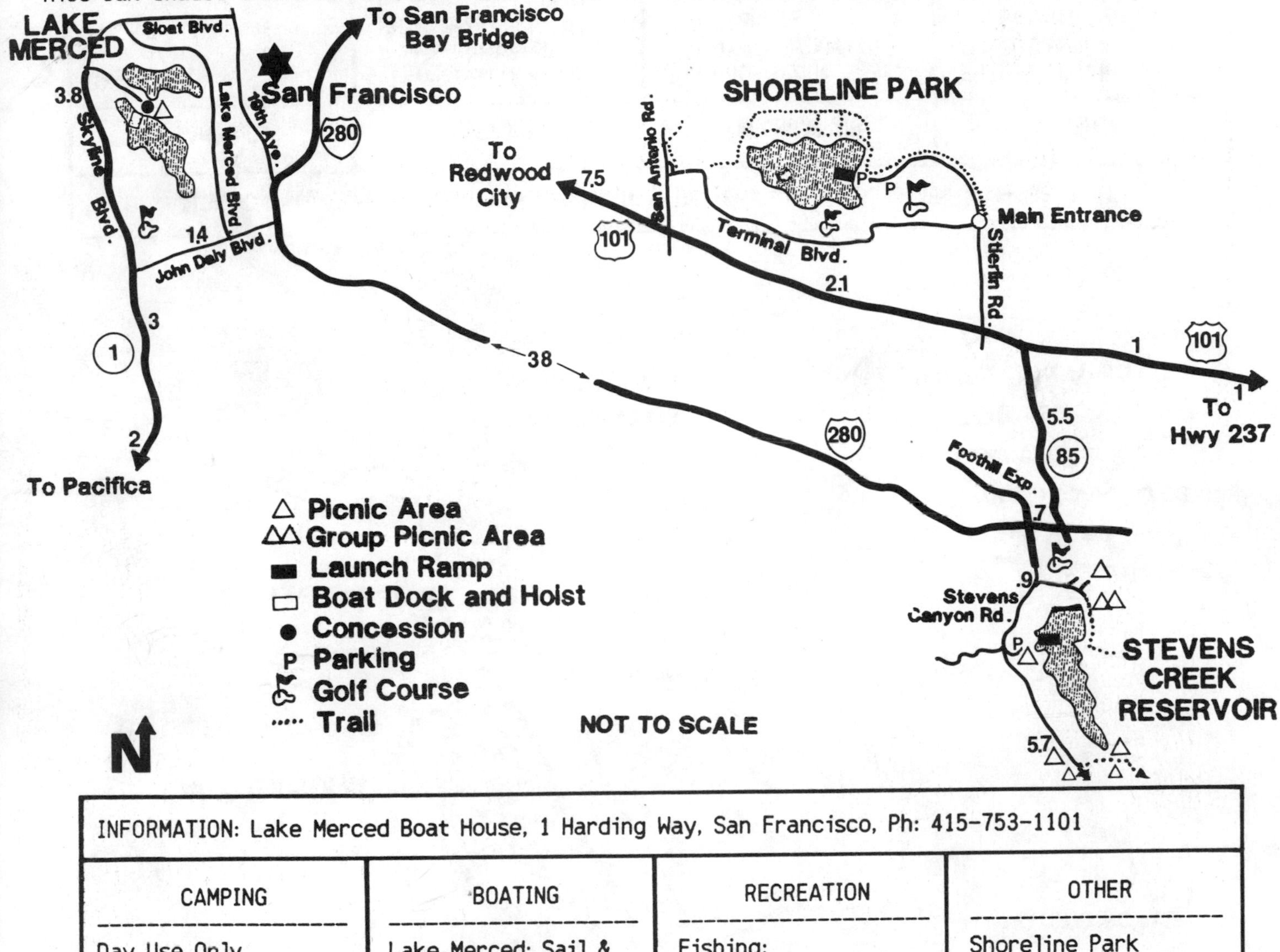

INFORMATION: Lake Merced Boat House, 1 Harding Way, San Francisco, Ph: 415-753-1101

CAMPING	BOATING	RECREATION	OTHER
Day Use Only No Camping	Lake Merced: Sail & Row to 18 Feet Hoist & Floats Rentals: Fishing Boats, Electric Motors Shoreline Park: Row, Sail & Windsurf to 14' Launch Ramp & Docks Stevens Creek: Sail & Row Boats No Power Boats 2-Lane Launch Ramp	Fishing: Rainbow & Brook Trout, Bass, Bluegill, Catfish & Crappie Picnicking Hiking, Bicycle & Riding Trails Nature Study Birdwatching	Shoreline Park Mountain View Ph: 415-965-7474 Stevens Creek Res. Santa Clara County Parks Dept. 298 Garden Hill Dr. Los Gatos 95030 Ph: 408-358-3741

VASONA, LEXINGTON AND LOS GATOS CREEK PARK

These three Lakes are located off Highway 17 in the Southwest corner of Santa Clara County. They are under the jurisdiction of the County's Parks and Recreation Department. Lexington is the largest of the three with 450 surface acres. While facilities are limited, rowers, windsurfers, waterskiiers and anglers find its waters attractive. Vasona is a pretty 57 acre Lake surrounded by 94 acres of turfed activity areas, picnic sites and paved paths. This popular family park offers good sailing and support facilities. Los Gatos Creek Park is commonly known as the "Campbell Perculation Ponds." Although boating is not allowed, seldom can you drive by on Highway 17 and not see the colorful sails of windsurfers. Fishing is popular and there are picnic facilities available.

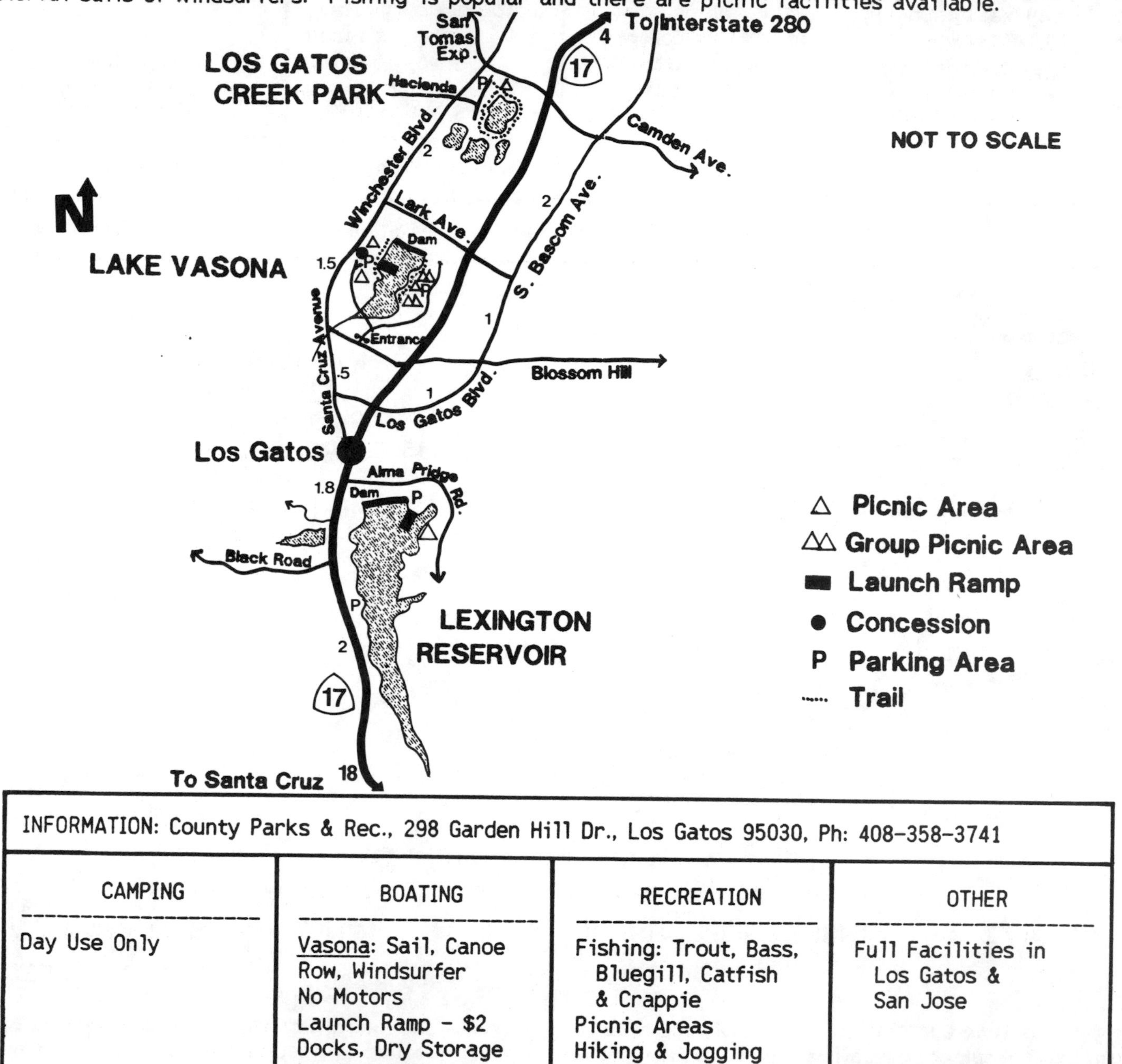

INFORMATION: County Parks & Rec., 298 Garden Hill Dr., Los Gatos 95030, Ph: 408-358-3741			
CAMPING	BOATING	RECREATION	OTHER
Day Use Only	Vasona: Sail, Canoe Row, Windsurfer No Motors Launch Ramp - $2 Docks, Dry Storage Lexington: Open to All Boating - Power & Waterskiing: Even-numbered Days Sail & Under 10 HP Odd-numbered Days Launch Ramp - $2	Fishing: Trout, Bass, Bluegill, Catfish & Crappie Picnic Areas Hiking & Jogging Trails Playground at Oak Meadow Next to Vasona and Bill Jones Railroad	Full Facilities in Los Gatos & San Jose Water Level is Often Low in Late Summer and Fall

ALMADEN LAKE, GUADALUPE, ALMADEN, CALERO, CHESBRO AND UVAS RESERVOIRS

Almaden Lake Regional Park is administered by the City of San Jose. There is a small 36 acre sailing and fishing Lake, a swim beach and lagoon and picnic sites within this 36 acre Park. The following Lakes are under the jurisdiction of Santa Clara County: Guadalupe and Almaden Reservoirs, approximately 60 acres each, are open to non-powered boating and fishing. They are adjacent to Almaden Quicksilver Park which is a popular hiking and equestrian facility. Chesbro and Uvas are primarily small fishing Lakes with picnic sites. Calero Reservoir, 349 surface acres, is a popular power boating and waterskiing Lake with a sandy beach and picnic facilities. At low water levels, from approximately October through January, the ramp can be closed.

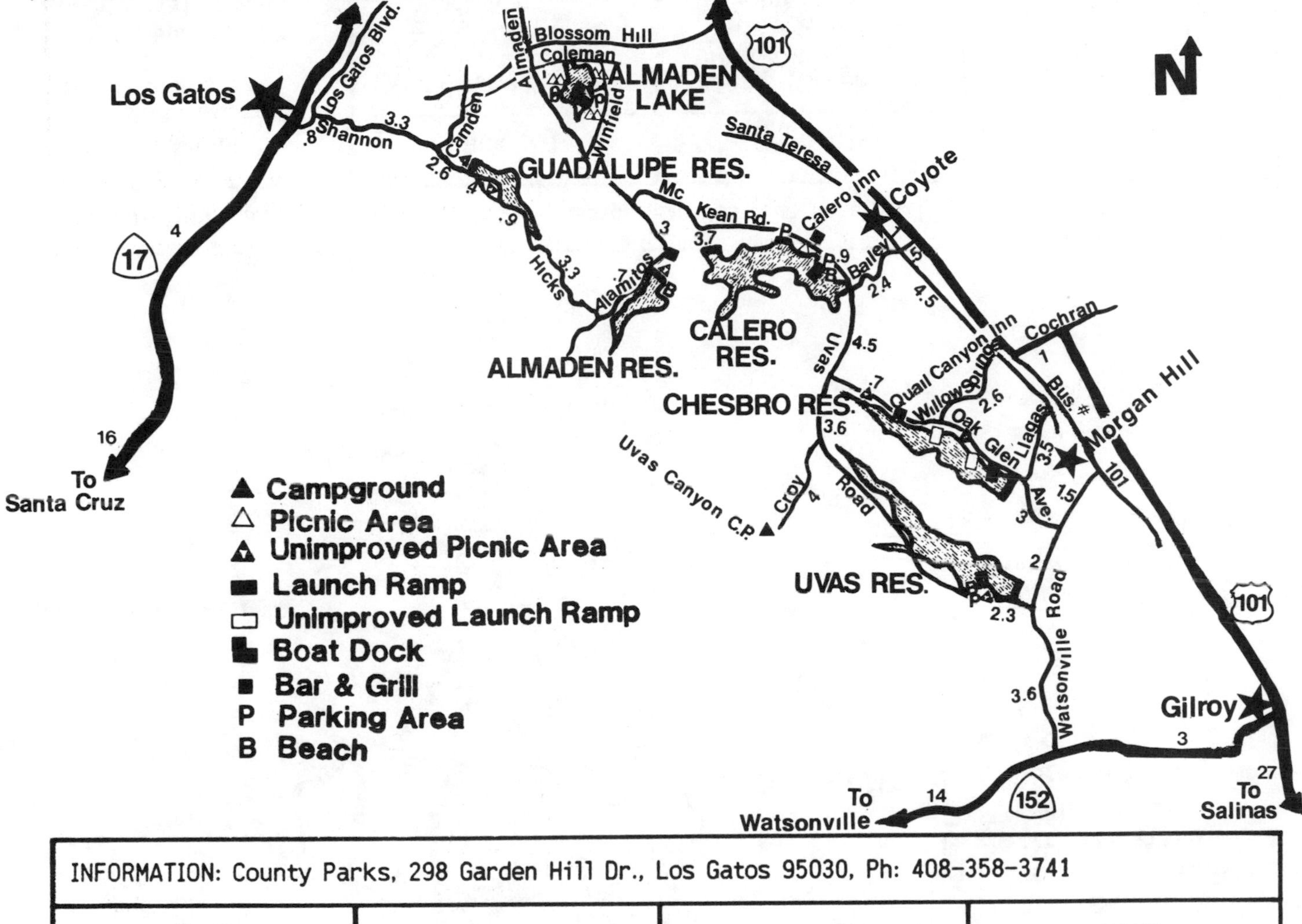

INFORMATION: County Parks, 298 Garden Hill Dr., Los Gatos 95030, Ph: 408-358-3741			
CAMPING	**BOATING**	**RECREATION**	**OTHER**
Uvas Canyon Park: 30 Dev. Sites for Tents & R.V.s Fee: $6 For Information: Ph: 408-779-9232	Almaden Lake: Sail & Non-Power Boating Launch Ramp Windsurf Rentals Guadalupe & Almaden Rs: Non-Power Boating Chesbro & Uvas: Sail, Row & Electric Motors - Launch Ramp Calero: Power, Waterskiing, Jet Boat Races, Ramp	Fishing: Bass, Catfish, Bluegill & Crappie Swimming: Almaden Lake & Calero Picnicking Hiking Riding Trails Almaden Lake: Parking: $2 Walk-In: 50 cents	Almaden Lake: c/o City of San Jose, Rm. 203 151 W. Mission St. San Jose 95110 Ph: 408-277-4661 Almaden Quicksilver Park: 3,598 Acres of Hiking & Equestrian Trails Ph: 408-268-3883

LAKE CUNNINGHAM, ED. R. LEVIN, J. D. GRANT AND COYOTE-HELLYER PARKS

Lake Cunningham Regional Park is under the jurisdiction of the City of San Jose. This 200 acre Park provides the visitor with numerous turfed picnic sites, walking and jogging paths and a 50 acre boating and fishing Lake. Its Raging Waters concession provides a variety of waterslides, pools, beach and a myriad of activities. The County of Santa Clara operates Ed R. Levin Park, Coyote-Hellyer Park and the mountainous J. D. Grant Park. Hellyer provides a Velodrome and an 8-foot wide, 5.9 mile long bicycle trail. The rugged 9,422 acres of Grant Park offers the adventuresome hiker, angler and equestrian a more remote experience. There are horse rentals at Grant Stables, Phone 408-274-9258.

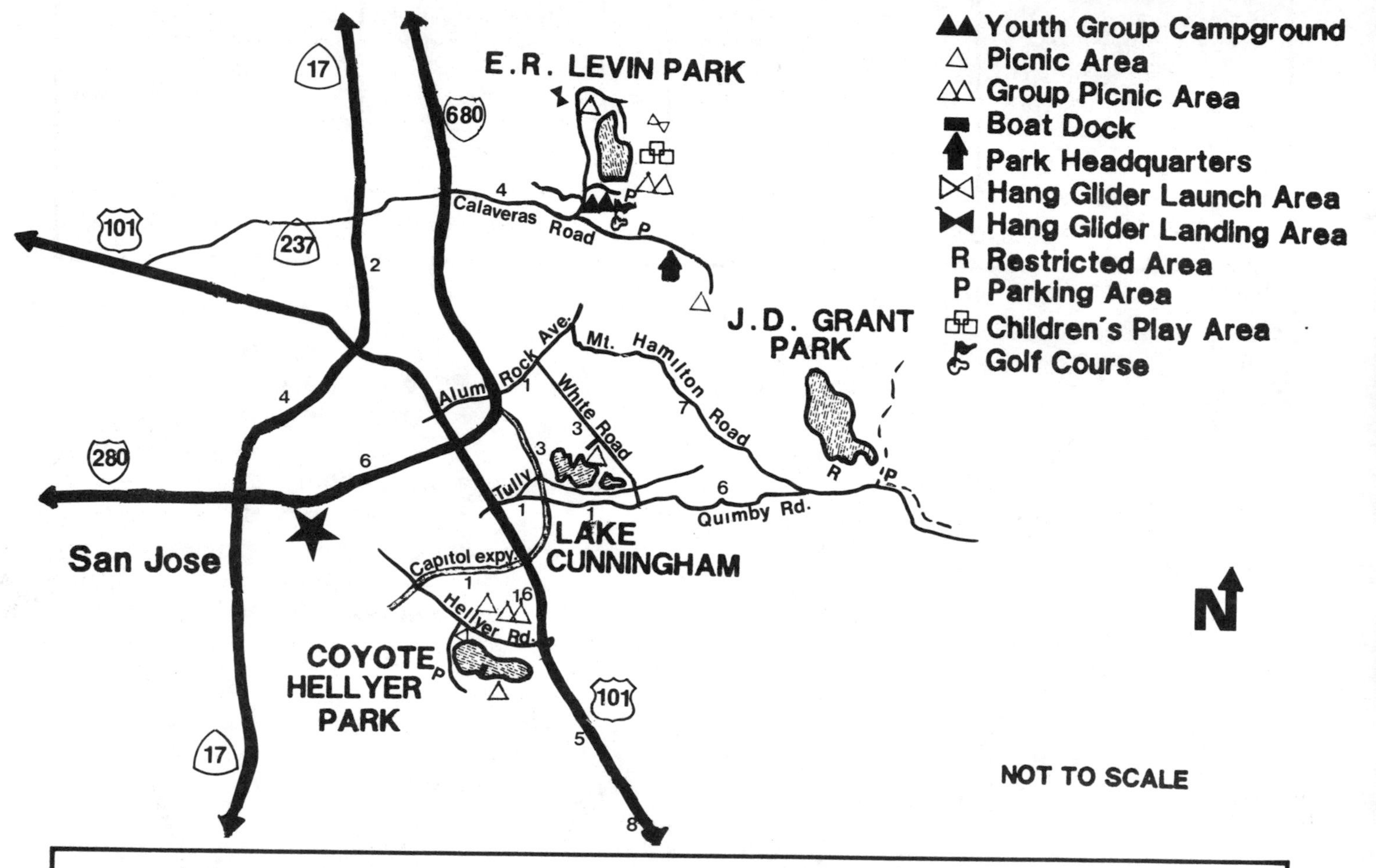

INFORMATION: Lake Cunningham - 151 W. Mission, Rm. 203, San Jose 95110, Ph: 408-277-4661			
CAMPING	BOATING	RECREATION	OTHER
Day Use Only Lake Cunningham Regional Park Parking Fee: $1 J. D. Grant Youth Group Camping & Picnicking Ph: 408-274-6121	Lake Cunningham: Non-Power Boats, Sail & Windsurf Launch Ramp Rentals Coyote-Hellyer & Ed R. Levin Small Sail, Row & Electric Motor Boats Launch Ramp at Coyote-Hellyer	Fishing: Largemouth Bass, Bluegill, Crappie & Catfish Coyote-Hellyer: Trout Picnicking Walking & Jogging Hiking & Riding Trails Horse Rentals Bicycling, Golf Hang Gliding	Levin, Grant & Hellyer Parks: Santa Clara Co. 298 Garden Hill Dr. Lost Gatos 95030 PH: 408-358-3741 Raging Waters: 2333 S. White Rd. San Jose 95148 Ph: 408-238-9900 Fees: $9.95 Group Rates

ANDERSON AND PARKWAY LAKES

Anderson Lake is the largest body of fresh water in Santa Clara County. It is 7 miles long with a surface area of 1,244 acres. This is a popular boating and waterskiing Lake. Afternoon winds make for good sailing and windsurfing. There are two privately operated marine facilities with launch ramps. The angler will find planted trout and a warm water fishery. The County of Santa Clara has picnic sites near the dam as well as a boat-in picnic area on the northwestern shore. Parkway is a 35-acre privately operated fishing Lake. Planted year around with large trout, channel catfish and Florida strain largemouth bass, the Lake usually rewards the angler with a good catch.

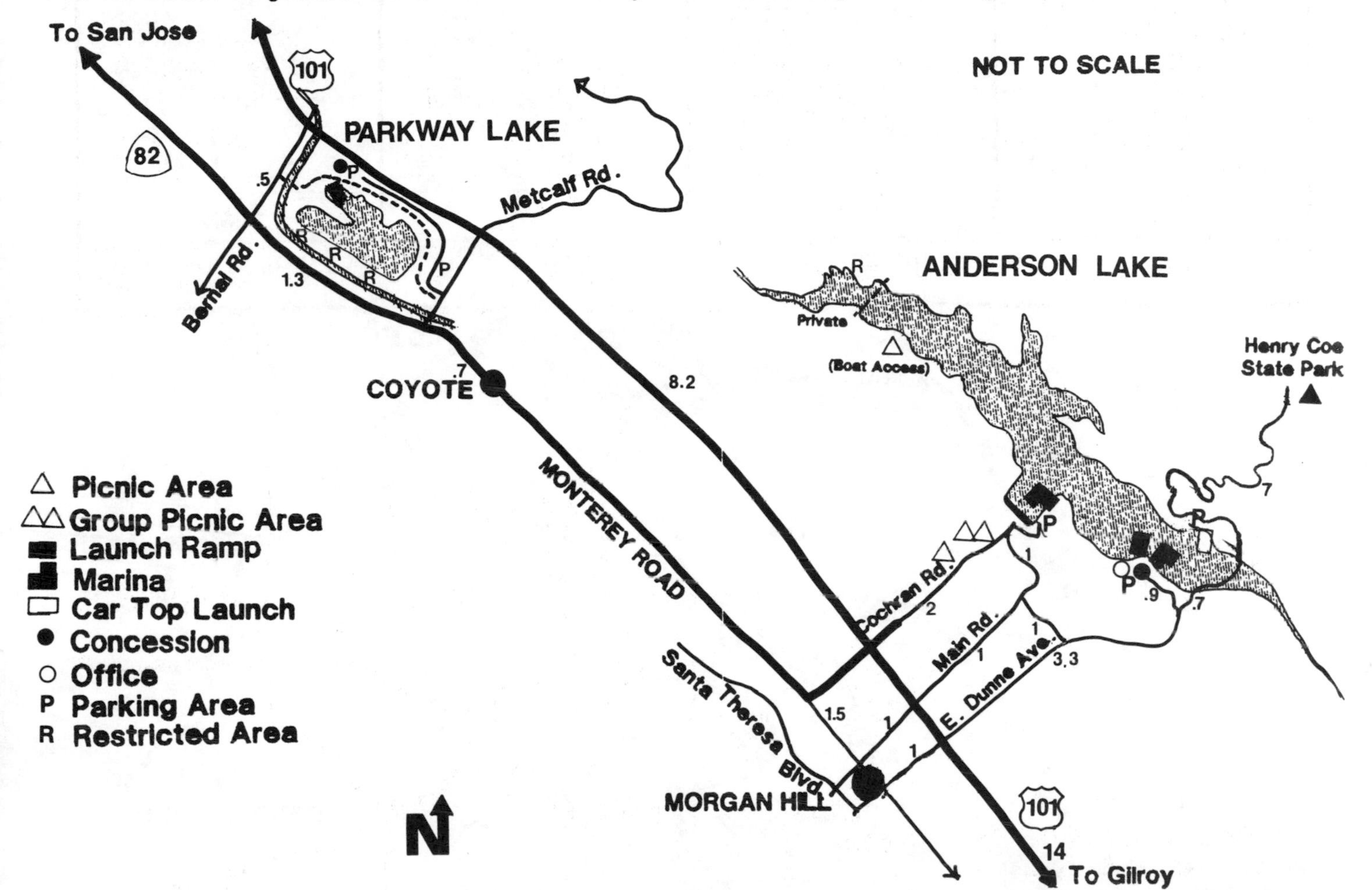

INFORMATION: Anderson Lake County Parks, 298 Garden Hill Dr., Los Gatos 95030, Ph: 408-358-3741

CAMPING	BOATING	RECREATION	OTHER
Day Use Only Henry Coe State Park 20 Tent & R.V. Primitive Sites P.O. Box 846 Morgan Hill Ph: 408-779-2728	Anderson: Open to All Boating; Launch Ramps & Docks Full Service Marinas Rentals: Fishing, Pontoon, Ski, Sail & Windsurfers, Wet Bikes Parkway: No Private Boats; Fishing Boat Rentals: $15	Fishing: Rainbow Trout, Largemouth Bass, Catfish, Crappie & Bluegill Picnicking Hiking Riding Trails Parkway: Fishing Fee: $8.50 - Adults $4.50 - Children	Parkway Lake: Metcalf Road Coyote 95013 Ph: 408-463-0383 Concession: Bait & Tackle Snacks

LOCH LOMOND

Loch Lomond rests at an elevation of 577 feet in the Santa Cruz Mountains. This scenic 3-1/2 mile long Reservoir is under the jurisdiction of the City of Santa Cruz. The Lake is open to quiet non-powered boating. Although there is a launch ramp, water level fluctuation can limit its use, so call for current status. Fishing is a prime attraction and often productive. There are over 100 picnic sites around the shoreline. Several hiking trails are along the shore and into the coniferous forest of oak, madrone, pine and redwood trees. In addition to naturalist programs, there is a self-guided Big Trees Nature Trail.

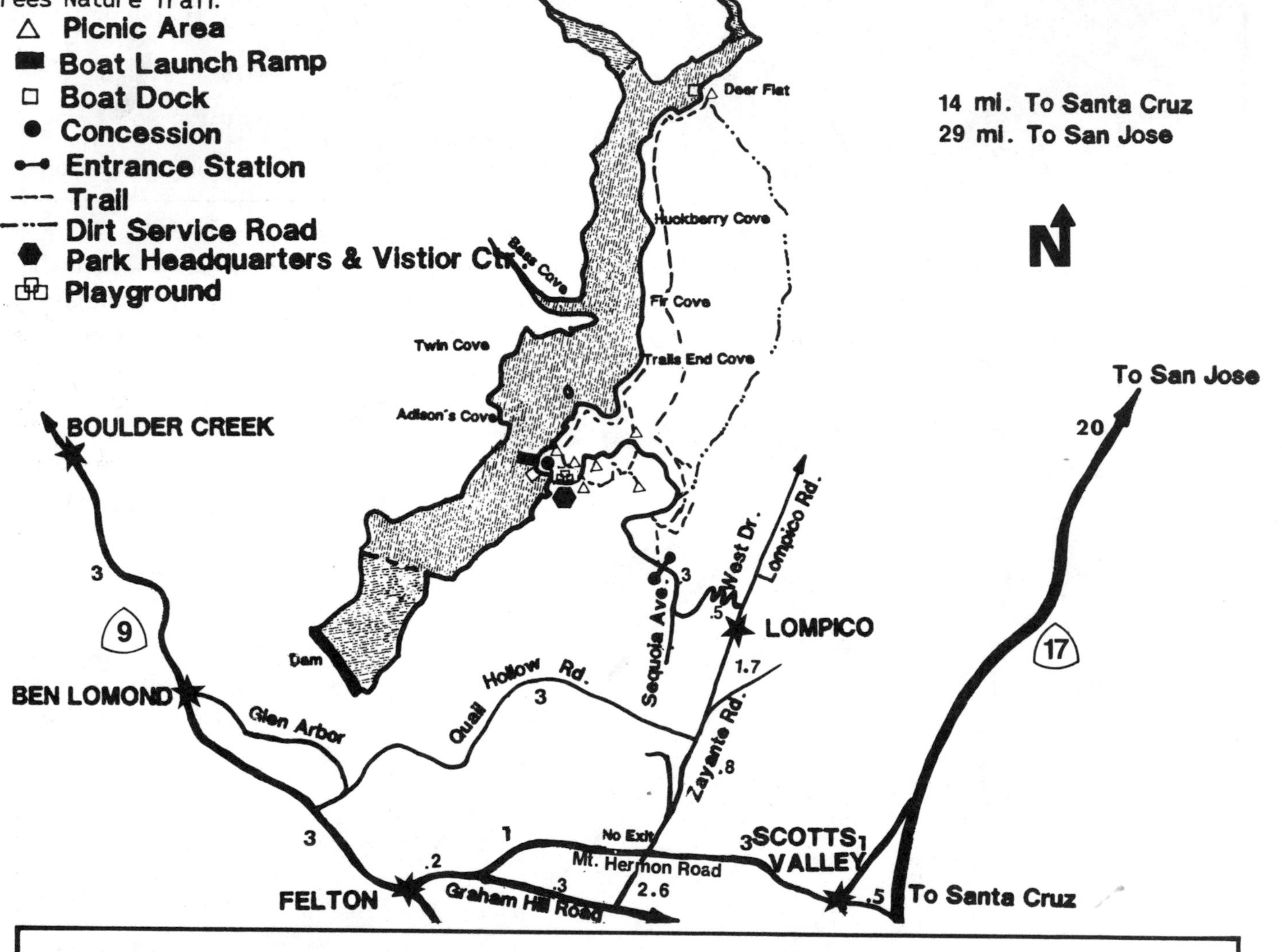

INFORMATION: Loch Lomond Rec. Area, P.O. Box 682, Santa Cruz 95060, Ph: 408-335-7424

CAMPING	BOATING	RECREATION	OTHER
Day Use Only Fee: $2.50 Open March Through September 15 6:00 a.m. to Sunset	Oar & Electric Motors Only Rentals: Row & Electric Launch Ramp Fee: $2 Water Level Limits	Fishing: Rainbow Trout, Largemouth Bass, Channel Catfish & Bluegill Picnicking Hiking & Nature Trails No Swimming	Bait & Tackle Refreshments

PINTO LAKE

Pinto Lake is under the jurisdiction of the City of Watsonville. This nice facility provides the visitor with a picnic area, a group picnic site, large turfed areas and a baseball field. This 92 acre Lake is popular with sailors and windsurfers who enjoy incoming Pacific breezes. There is a warm water fishery along with planted trout. Marmo's is a privately owned campground on the south westerly shore of the Lake offering campsites, a launch ramp, boat rentals and cafe. Santa Cruz County maintains a 180 acre wildlife refuge and park on the north end of the Lake with over 130 species of birds, nature trails and group picnic facilities. For reservations, Phone 408-425-2394.

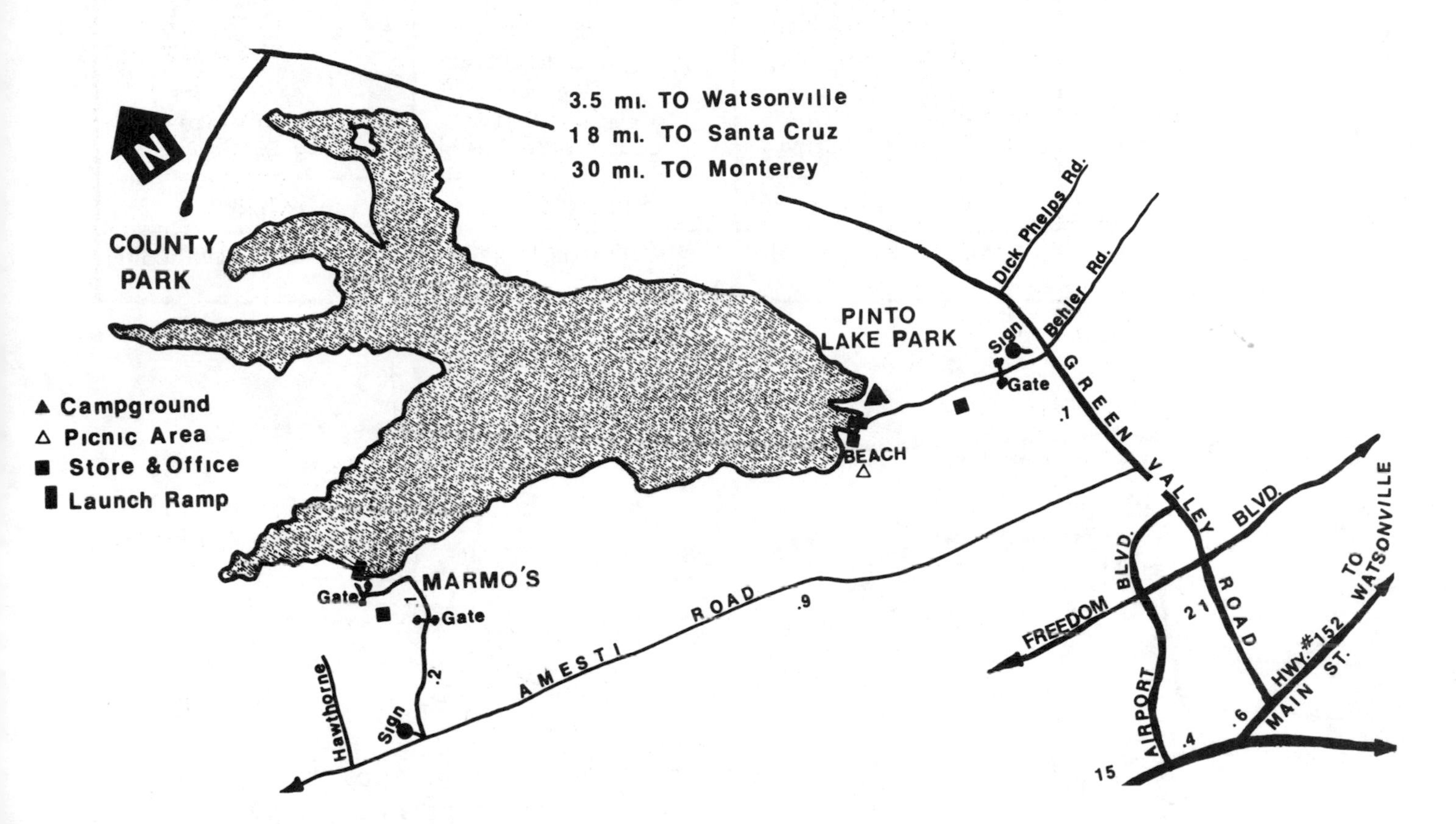

INFORMATION: Pinto Lake, 451 Green Valley Rd., Watsonville 95076, Ph: 408-722-8129			
CAMPING	**BOATING**	**RECREATION**	**OTHER**
Pinto Lake Park: 28 R.V. Sites Full Hookups Fee: $10 Marmo's Pinto Lake: 50 Tent & R.V. Sites Water & Electric Hookups Fee: $15	Power, Row, Canoe, Sail, Windsurf Speed Limit: 5 MPH Rentals: Fishing, Paddle, Canoe & Windsurfer Windsurfing Lessons	Fishing: Rainbow Trout, Largemouth Bass, Bluegill, Crappie & Catfish Picnicking Group Picnicking - Reservations Swimming - Designated Areas Hiking & Nature Trails Bird Watching	Snack Bar Bait & Tackle Marmo's Pinto Lake 324 Amesti Road Watsonville 95076 Ph: 408-722-4533

COYOTE RESERVOIR

Coyote Reservoir is at an elevation of 777 feet in the scenic, oak-covered hills near Gilroy. Santa Clara County provides facilities for lakeside camping, picnicking, hiking, fishing and all types of boating. This pretty Lake is open at the northwest end, so the breezes come down the length of the Lake which makes for good sailing and windsurfing. The Reservoir is open year around from 8:00 a.m. to sunset for day users. Campers may fish from shore during the night, but there is no night boating permitted.

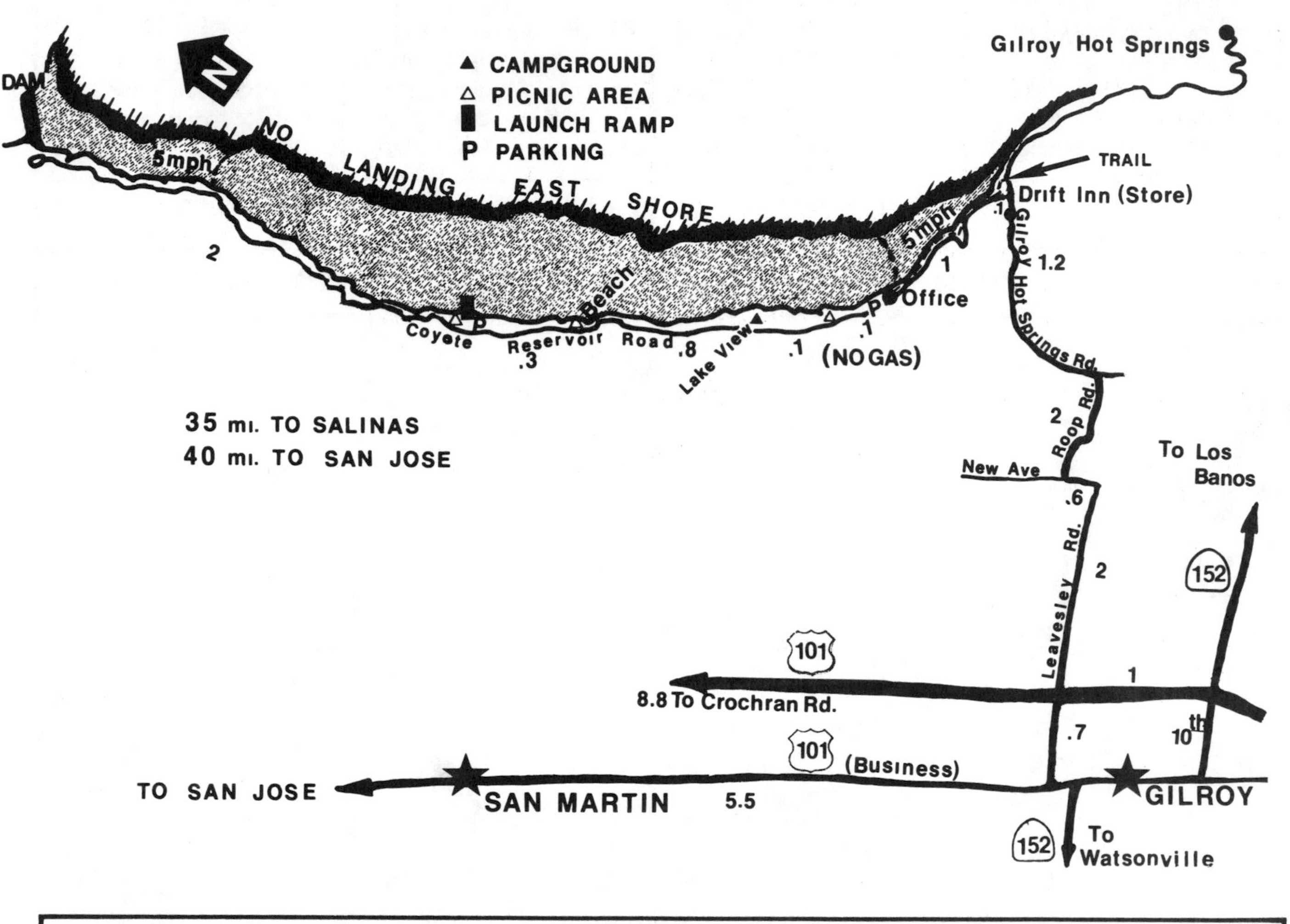

INFORMATION: Coyote Lake Park, 10840 Coyote Lake Rd., Gilroy 95020, Ph: 408-842-7800

CAMPING	BOATING	RECREATION	OTHER
75 Dev. sites for Tents & R.V.s Fee: $5 Pets: $1 - Allowed in Sites #31 - #42 Only	Power, Row, Canoe, Sail, Waterski & Jet Skis Speed Limit - 35 MPH Launch Ramp	Fishing: Trout, Catfish, Bluegill, Crappie & Bass Picnicking Hiking Day Use Fee: $2 Per Vehicle on Weekends and Holidays Only	Full Facilities - 8 Miles at Gilroy

EL ESTERO, LAGUNA SECA, LOWER AND UPPER ABBOTT LAKES

These three Recreation Parks in Monterey County range from a nice day use City Park in Monterey to a Forest Service Campground at Arroyo Seco. The Laguna Seca Recreational Area is one of the most complete Parks in the State with a modern campground and a small 10 acre Lake. El Estero is a pretty Lake in downtown Monterey with a children's play area, picnic facilities, athletic fields and a parcourse. The Abbott or Twin Lakes are in the Los Padres National Forest and offer family and group campgrounds and a warm water fishery. Trout fishing and swimming are popular in the Arroyo Seco River.

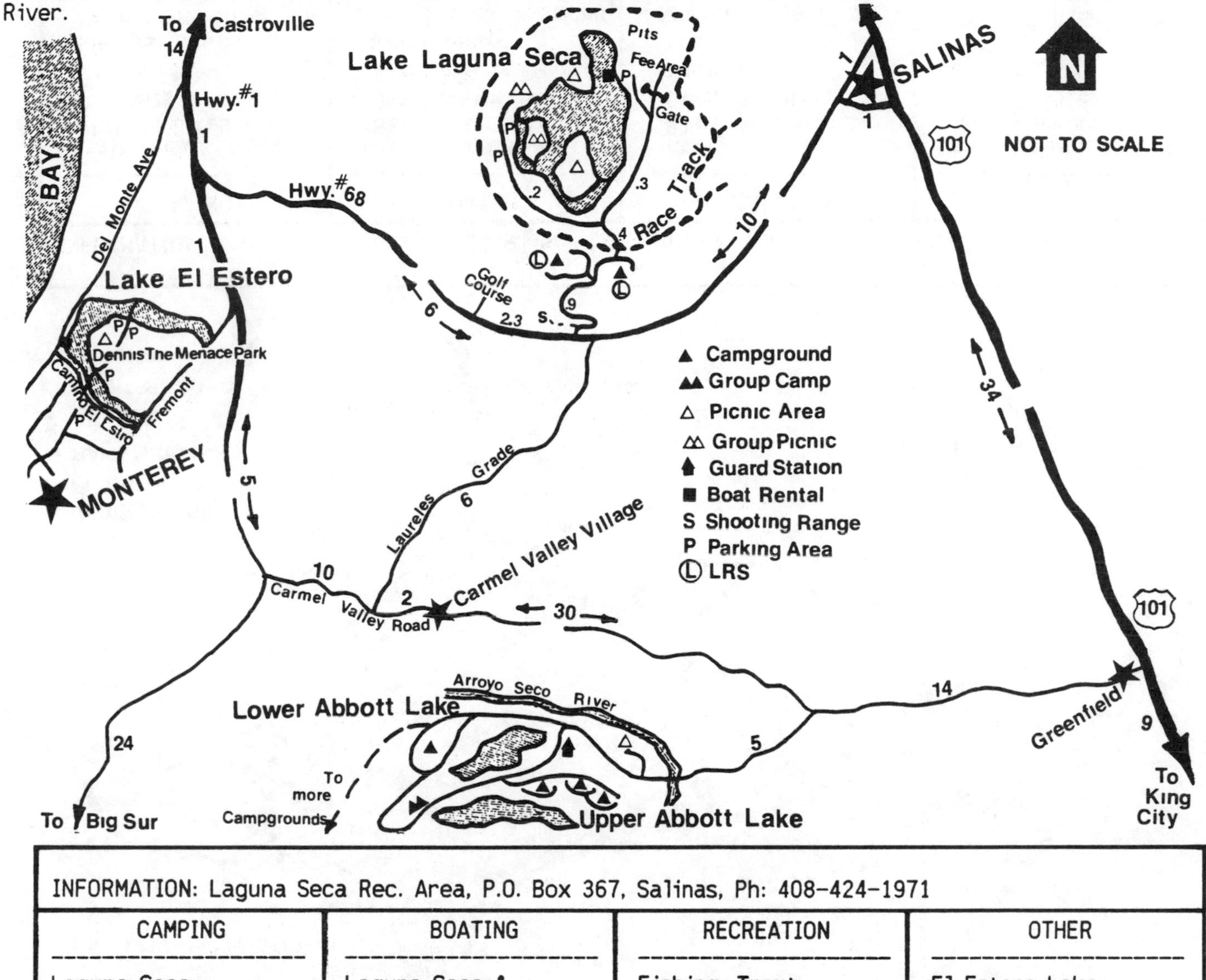

CAMPING	BOATING	RECREATION	OTHER
Laguna Seca: 93 Tents Sites 87 R.V. Sites with Electric & Water Ph: 800-822-CAMP U.S.F.S. Arroyo Seco - Abbott Lakes King City Ranger Station Ph: 408-385-5434 46 Sites & Group Site	Laguna Seca & El Estero: Paddle Boat Rental Abbott Lakes: Canoeing	Fishing: Trout, Bass & Catfish Picnicking Hiking Playgrounds Laguna Seca: Rifle & Pistol Range Motorcross Track Festivals Concerts Auto Races	El Estero Lake: City of Monterey Parks & Recreation Department 546 Dutra St. Monterey 93940 Ph: 408-646-3866 Full Facilities & Golf Courses in Monterey Salinas Rodeo Monterey Jazz Festival

INFORMATION: Laguna Seca Rec. Area, P.O. Box 367, Salinas, Ph: 408-424-1971

San Luis Reservoir is at an elevation of 544 feet at high pool in the eastern foothills of the Diablo Mountain Range west of Los Banos. This huge Reservoir has a surface area of 13,800 acres and 65 miles of grassy, oak-dotted shoreline. Although fish have never been planted, most species found in the Sacramento Delta are found at San Luis and the Forebay. In addition to good fishing, San Luis is popular for boating, swimming and waterskiing, but sudden strong winds can be a hazard. Warning lights are located at the Romero Overlook and on Quien Sabe Point on the Reservoir and at San Luis Creek Area on the Forebay. The O'Neill Forebay below San Luis Reservoir has a surface area of 2,000 acres with 14 miles of shoreline. The 67 mile San Joaquin Section of the California Aqueduct Bikeway ends at the Forebay. Boating and fishing are popular. Waterfowl hunting is allowed on the Lakes when in season.

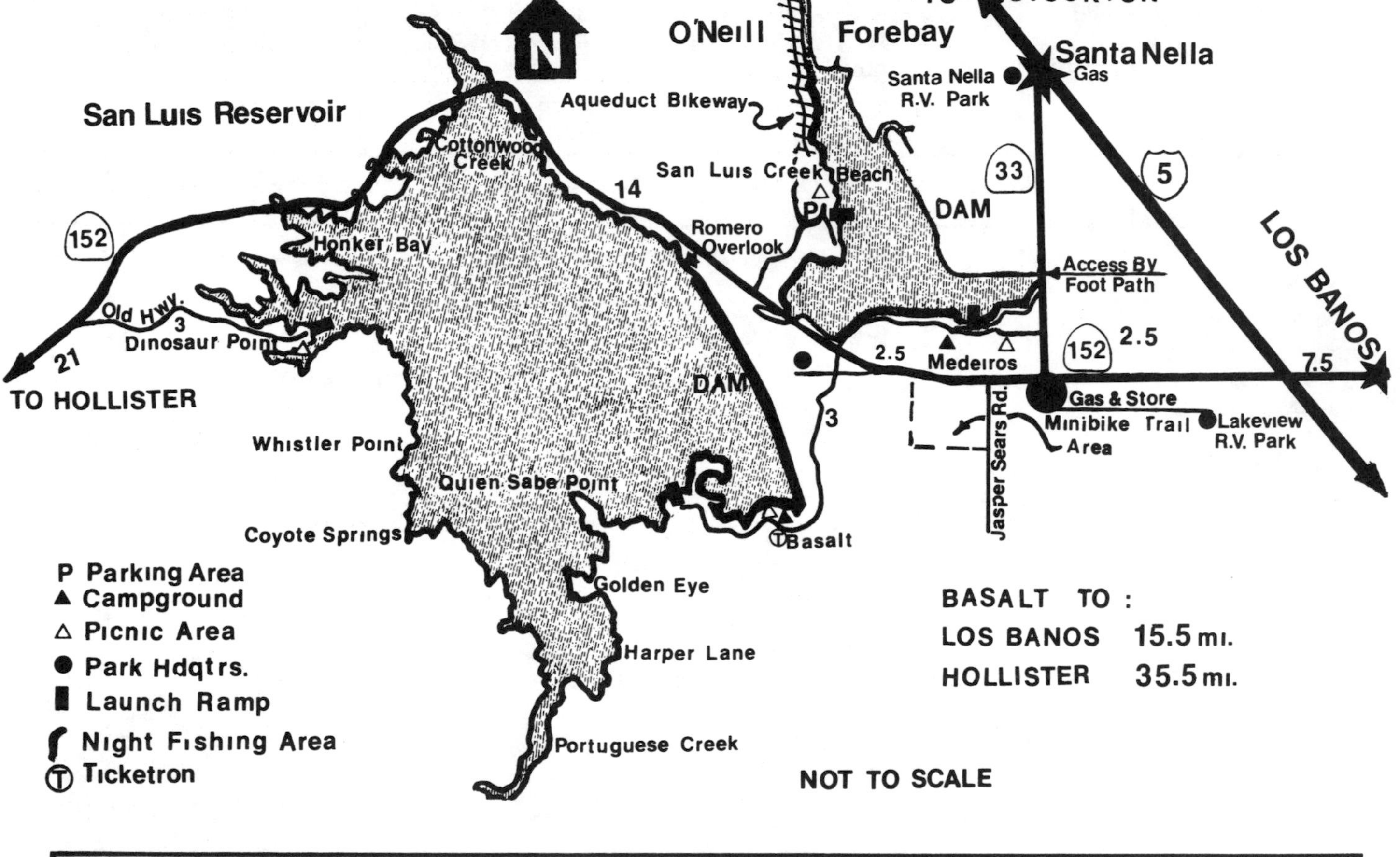

INFORMATION: Four Rivers Area, 31426 W. Hwy. 152, Santa Nella 95322, Ph: 209-826-1196

CAMPING	BOATING	RECREATION	OTHER
Basalt Area: 79 Dev. Sites for Tents & R.V.s Fee: $6 Medeiros: Undev. Sites for Tents & R.V.s Water & Porta Potties Available Fee: $3 Plus Area for 400 R.V.s	Power, Row, Canoe, Sail, Waterski, Jet Ski, Windsurf & Inflatable Launch Ramps - $2 Life Jackets Required for Everyone Except Windsurfers Beware of Sudden Strong Winds	Fishing: Catfish, Bluegill, Crappie, Striped & Black Bass, Sturgeon, Shad Swimming - Beaches Picnicking Hunting: Waterfowl 157 Acre Minibike Trail Area - 250cc Engine Only	Santa Nella R.V. Park Full Hookups Ph: 209-826-3105 Lakeview R.V. Park Full Hookups Ph: 209-826-1196 Full Facilities in Los Banos and Santa Nella California Aqueduct Bikeway

LOS BANOS RESERVOIR

Los Banos Reservoir is at an elevation of 328 feet in the hilly grasslands east of Los Banos. The surface area of this small Lake is 410 acres with 12 miles of shoreline. There are several planted trees around the campgrounds along with shade ramadas. Los Banos is under the jurisdiction of the Four Rivers District of the California Parks and Recreation Department. There is a small campground and a paved launch ramp. This facility is primarily used as a warm water fishery, and swimming is also popular. There are usually good winds for sailing and windsurfing.

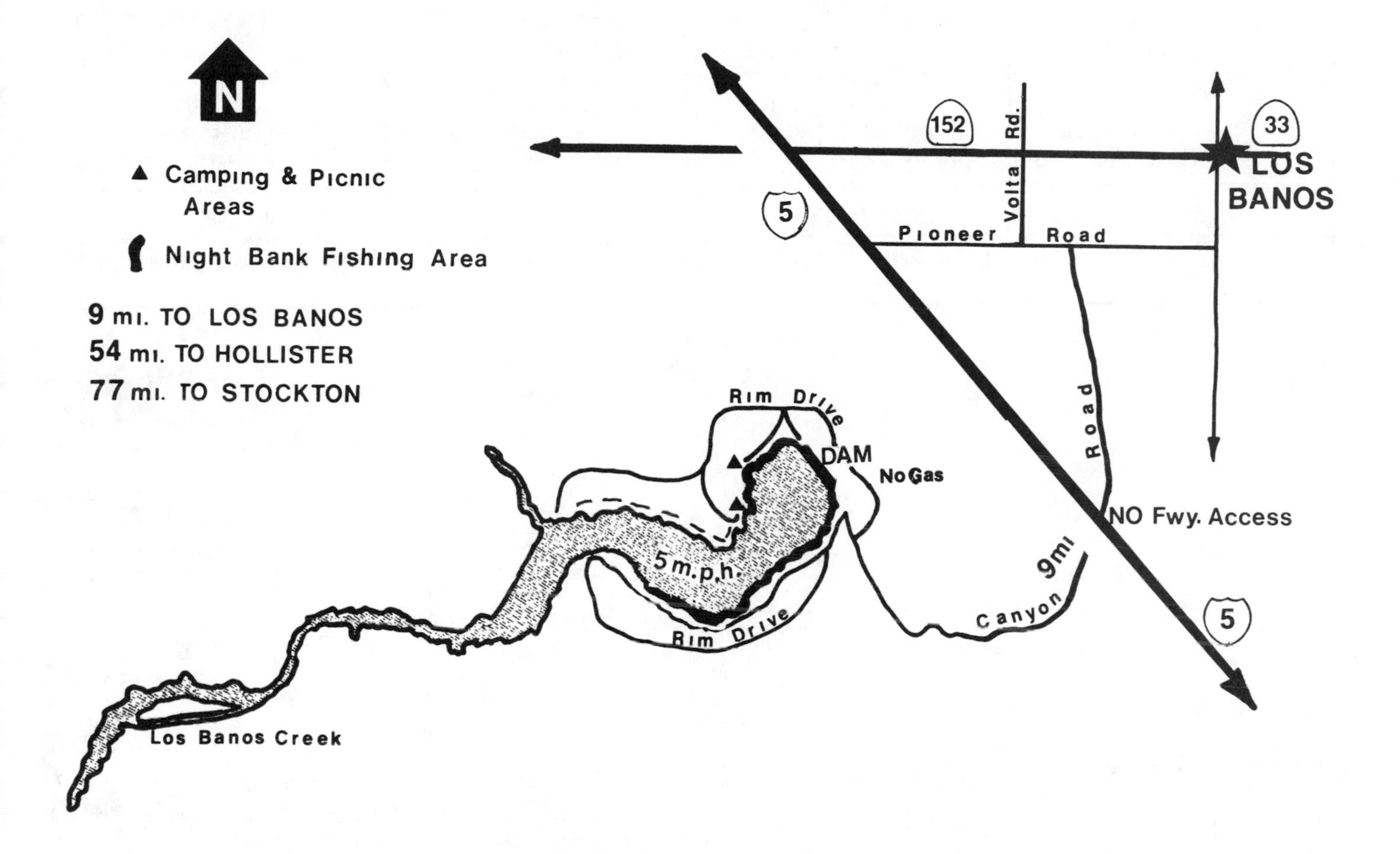

INFORMATION: Four Rivers Area, 31426 W. Hwy. 152, Santa Nella 95322, Ph: 209-826-1196			
CAMPING	BOATING	RECREATION	OTHER
20 Primitive Sites for Tents & R.V.s Fee: $3 (Hauled In Water)	Power, Row, Canoe, Sail, Windsurf & Inflatables Speed Limit - 5 MPH Up To 10 HP Motors Only Paved Launch Ramp	Fishing: Trout, Catfish, Bluegill, Large & Smallmouth Bass Swimming Picnicking Hiking Horseback Riding Trails Hunting: Waterfowl in Season	Full Facilities at Los Banos

HENSLEY LAKE

Hensley Lake lies at an elevation of 540 feet in the gently rolling foothills northeast of Madera. The surrounding hills are covered with majestic oaks and granite outcroppings. The Lake has a surface area of 1,570 acres with 24 miles of shoreline. The U. S. Army Corps of Engineers provides a campground, picnic areas and boating facilities. A large expanse of open water and many secluded quiet coves invites all types of boating. The fishing is good with an abundant warm water fishery. There are two swimming beaches. Hiking trails lead into the Wildlife Area where many birds, animals and native wildflowers may be observed.

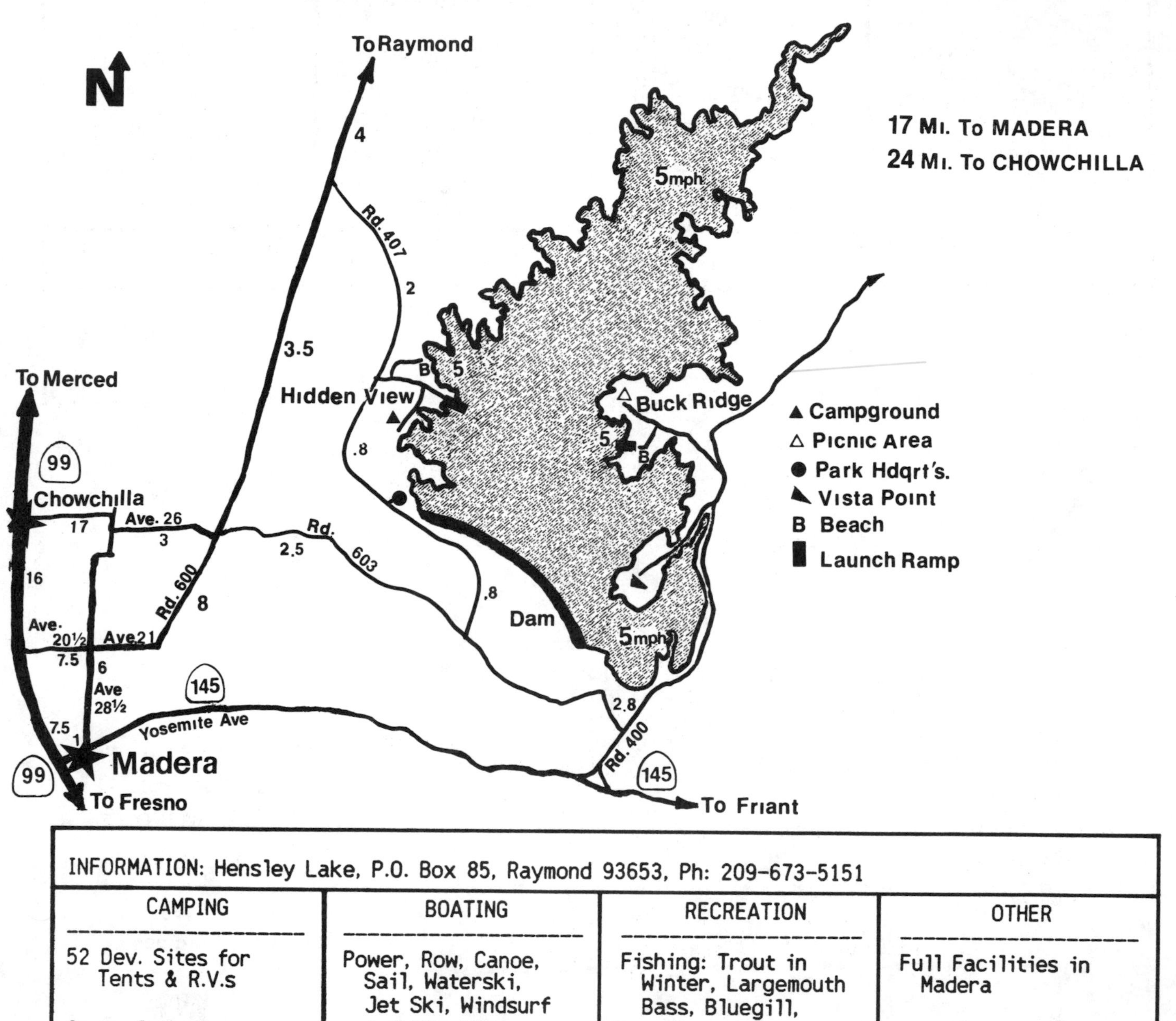

INFORMATION: Hensley Lake, P.O. Box 85, Raymond 93653, Ph: 209-673-5151

CAMPING	BOATING	RECREATION	OTHER
52 Dev. Sites for Tents & R.V.s Group Camp Area Disposal Station	Power, Row, Canoe, Sail, Waterski, Jet Ski, Windsurf & Inflatable 2 Paved Launch Ramps Submerged Hazards During Low Water	Fishing: Trout in Winter, Largemouth Bass, Bluegill, Catfish & Crappie Night Fishing Swimming - Beaches Picnicking: Family & Group Sites Hiking & Nature Trails	Full Facilities in Madera

EASTMAN LAKE

The U. S. Army Corps of Engineers completed Buchanan Dam in 1975, and the recreational facilities of Eastman Lake were opened to the public in 1978. Located in the oak-covered foothills 25 miles northeast of Chowchilla, this 1,780 acre Lake provides modern facilities for the outdoorsman. During construction, brush shelters were built for wildlife, and underwater fish shelters were also added. This is a good fishing Lake for warm water species. Boating and sailing are popular, and the well-maintained facilities are open year around. Berenda Reservoir to the west is a small day-use Lake with boating and fishing from shore.

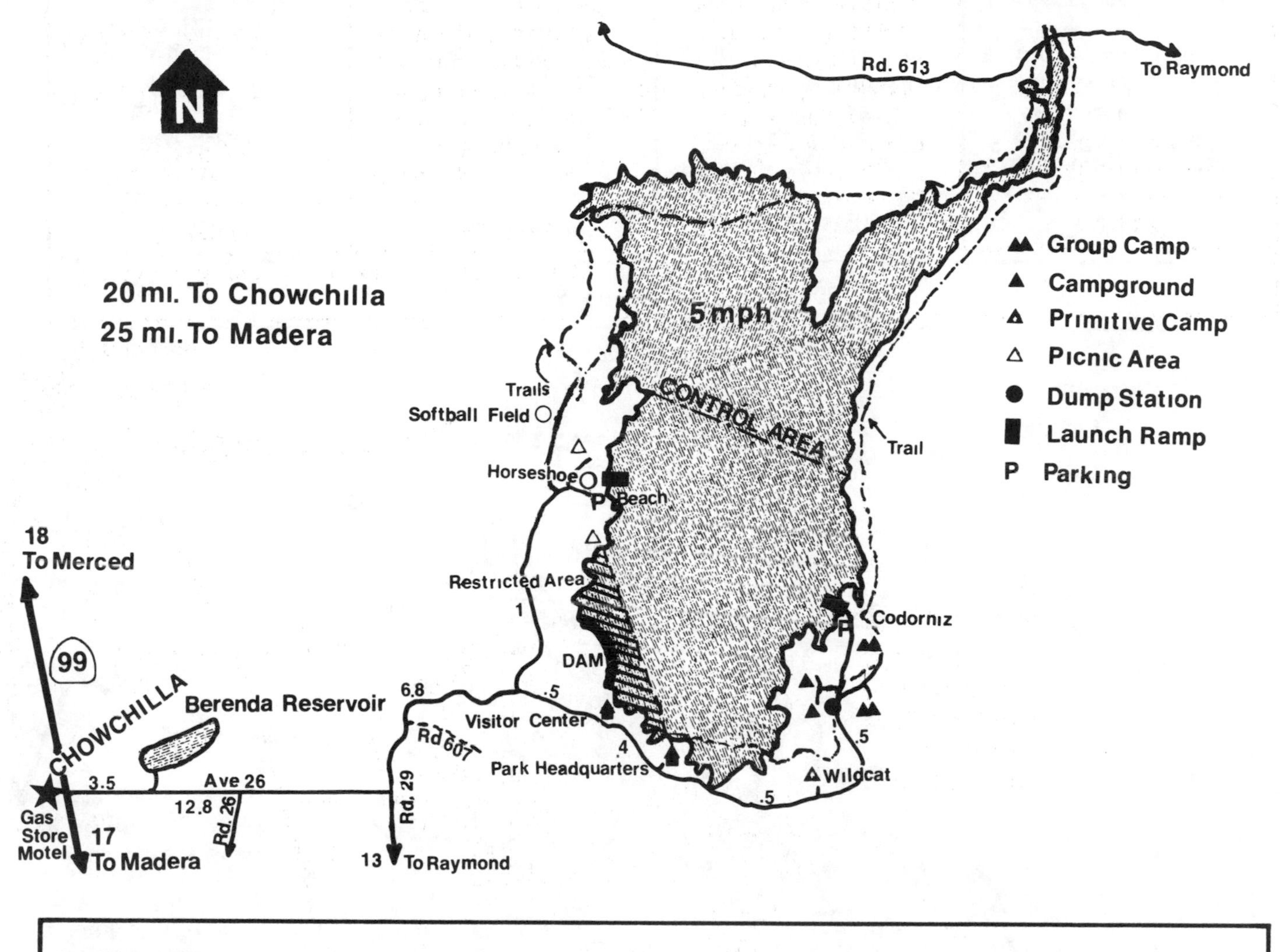

INFORMATION: Park Manager, Eastman Lake, Box 67, Raymond 93653, Ph: 209-689-3255

CAMPING	BOATING	RECREATION	OTHER
62 Dev. Sites for Tents & R.V.s Fee: $6 Mar. 1 Sep. 30 No Hookups 19 Primitive Sites Group Area to 100 People Max. Fee: $25	Power, Row, Canoe, Sail, Windsurf & Inflatables Launch Ramps Berenda Reservoir: Drag Boat Racing	Fishing: Trout, Catfish, Bluegill, Crappie & Black Bass Swimming Picnicking Hiking Horseback Riding Trails Nature Study Horseshoes Softball	Disposal Station Full Facilities in Chowchilla or Madera

MILLERTON LAKE AND LOST LAKE PARK

The Millerton State Recreation Area provides an abundance of modern picnic, camping and marine facilities. This extremely popular 5,000 surface acre Lake offers excellent sailing and boating, and the angler will find a good warm water fishery. Hundreds of picnic areas are scattered around the Lake, and there are nice sandy swimming areas. The Lost Lake Recreation area is a pretty 305 acre Park on the San Joaquin River just below Millerton. Lost Lake is a small 35 surface acre Lake which is open to non-powered boating and fishing. There are picnic areas, a campground and ball fields.

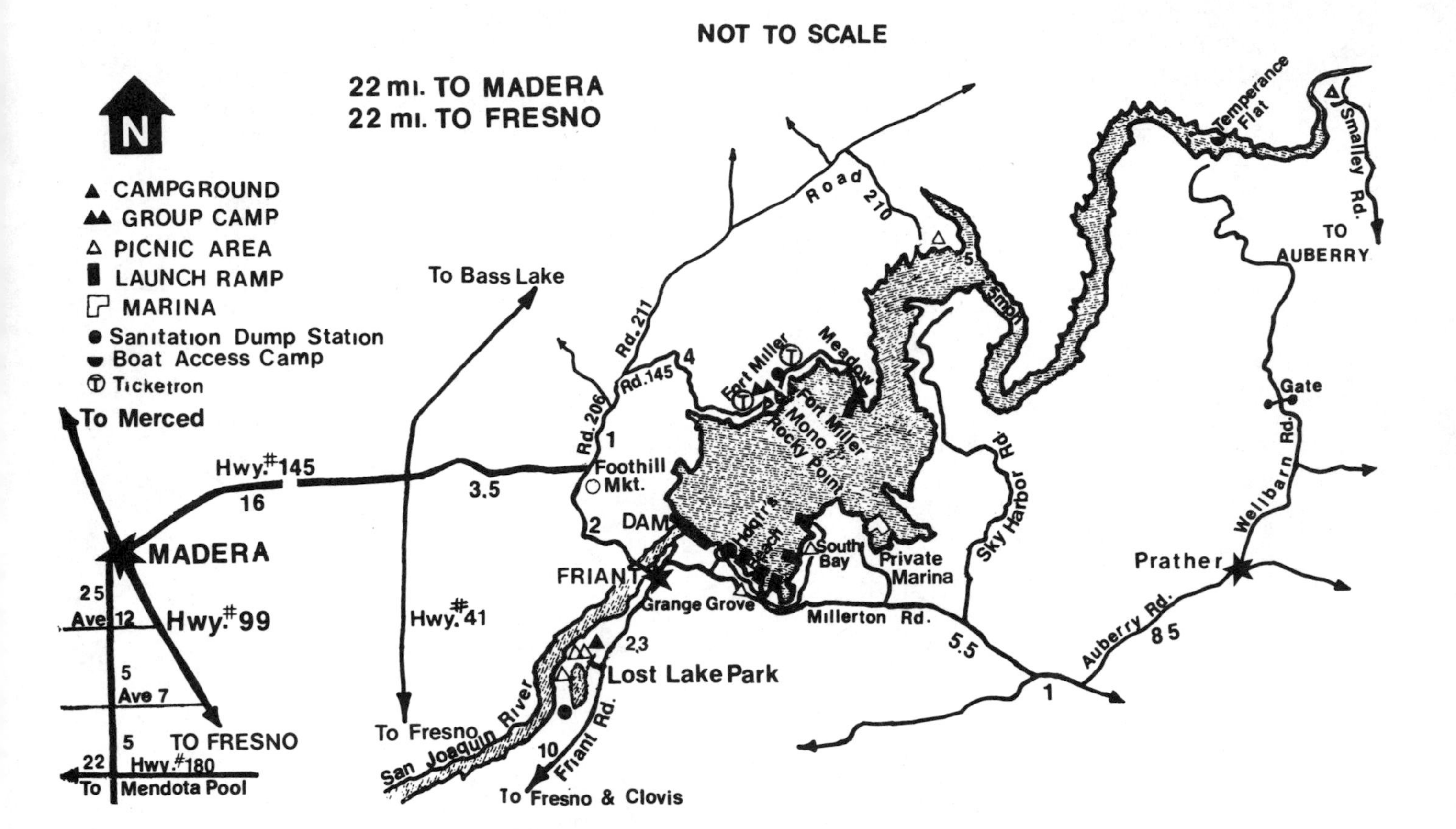

INFORMATION: Millerton Lake, P.O. Box 205, Friant 93626, Ph: 209-822-2332			
CAMPING	BOATING	RECREATION	OTHER
Millerton: 133 Dev. Sites for Tents & R.V.s Fee: $6 Group Sites for 75 and 125 People 15 Boat Access Sites Day Use Fee: $2 Lost Lake: 42 R.V. Sites Fee: $4	Millerton: Open to All Boats Full Service Marina Launch Ramps: $2 Rentals: Fishing Boats & Motors Lost Lake: No Gas-Powered Motors Hand Launch Only	Fishing: Alabama Spotted, Large & Smallmouth Bass, Catfish & Panfish Swimming - Millerton Only Picnicking Hiking & Horseback Riding Trails Birdwatching Nature Study Area Wildlife Refuge	Lost Lake Rec. Area Fresno County Parks 2220 Tulare St. Fresno 93721 Ph: 209-488-3004 - - - - - - - - - - Concessions, Bait & Tackle, Market, Disposal Stations

BASS LAKE

Bass Lake, at an elevation of 3,400 feet, is within the Sierra National Forest. This beautiful forested recreation area provides an abundance of recreational opportunities. Boating and sailing on this 1,165 surface acre Lake is extremely popular. Water levels are generally maintained through Labor Day. There are thirteen different species of fish to challenge the angler. Facilities on the South Shore are administered by the U. S. Forest Service and managed by California Land Management. Resorts, cabins and R.V. parks are available at privately owned areas around the Lake. For full information, contact the Bass Lake Chamber of Commerce.

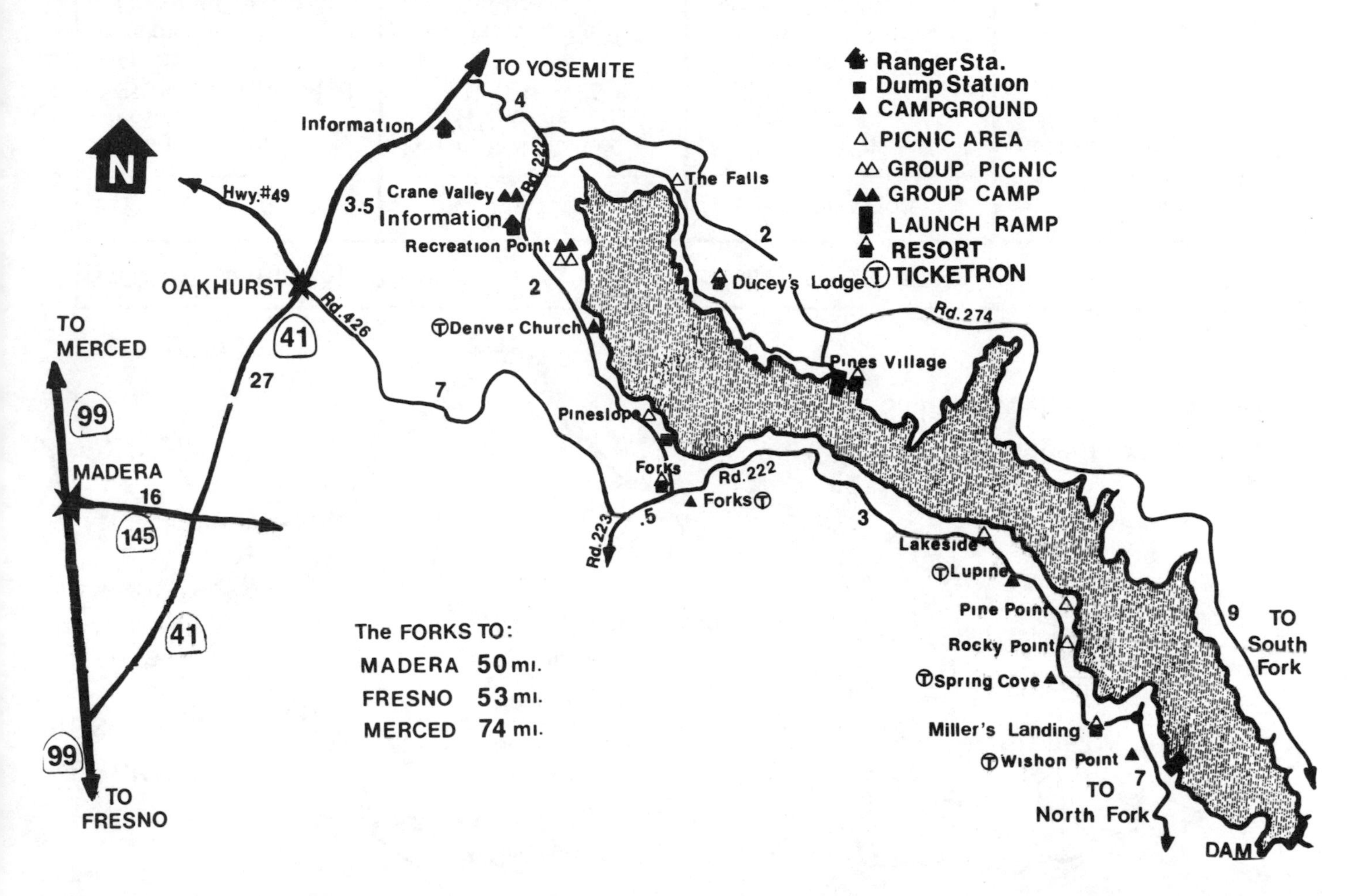

INFORMATION: U.S. Forest Service, 39900 Road 222, Bass Lake 93604, Ph: 209-642-3212			
CAMPING	**BOATING**	**RECREATION**	**OTHER**
237 Dev. Sites for Tents & R.V.s Fees: $6 - $8 Group Areas - Reserve through Calif. Land Mgmt. Bass Lake Chamber of Commerce P.O. Box 126 Bass Lake 93604 Ph: 209-642-3676	Power, Row, Canoe, Sail, Waterski, Jet Ski, Windsurf & Inflatables Full Service Marinas Launch Ramps Rentals: Fishing, Canoes & Waterski Boats Moorings, Gas	Fishing: Rainbow & Brown Trout, Catfish, Bluegill, Perch, Crappie, Black Bass & Kokanee Salmon Swimming - Beaches Hiking & Riding Trails Visitor Programs Nature Study	Cabins Snack Bars Restaurants Grocery Stores Bait & Tackle Disposal Station Gas Station Movie Theater Arcade

REDINGER LAKE & KERCKHOFF RESERVOIR

Redinger Lake is at an elevation of 1,400 feet in a narrow valley with surrounding mountains rising 1,000 feet above the Lake's surface. The Lake is three miles long and a quarter of a mile wide. The surrounding area of digger pine and chaparral is intermingled with live and valley oak, and there is a variety of wildlife that can be observed. Redinger is primarily a boating Lake as fishing is very limited. Kerckhoff Reservoir is located 6 miles to the west. Fishing for striped bass is the dominant activity, and boating is limited to carry-in boats. Camping is available at both Lakes, but the sites are not developed. Redinger has numerous sandy beaches and is a pretty Lake although remote.

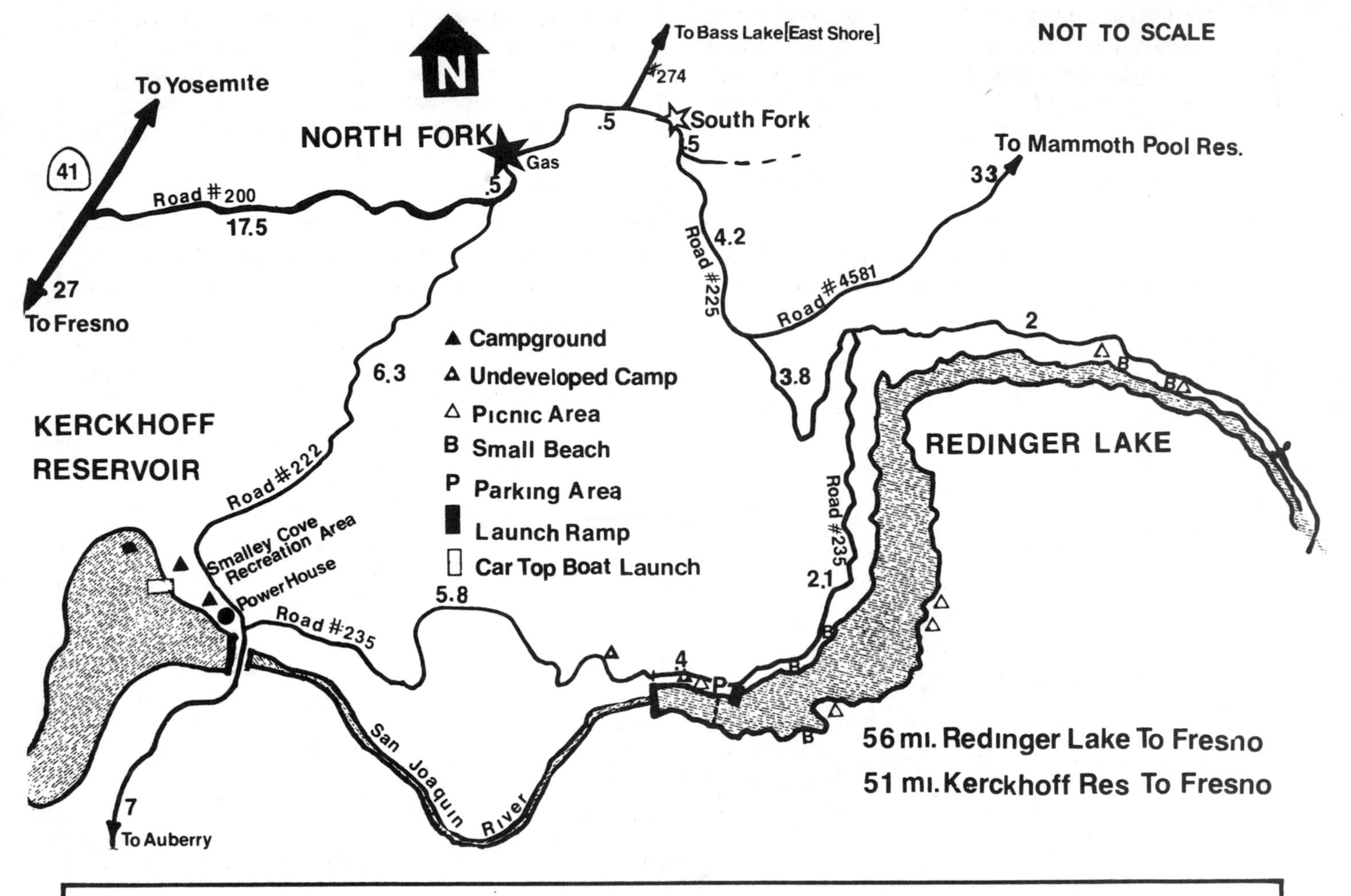

INFORMATION: Minarets Ranger District, North Fork 93643, Ph: 209-877-2218

CAMPING	BOATING	RECREATION	OTHER
Redinger Lake: Primitive Camp Sites in Designated Areas Only Kerckhoff: Smalley Cove Rec. Area 5 Campsites (1 for Handicap) 5 Picnic Sites Extreme Fire Danger No Campfires	Power, Row, Canoe, Sail & Inflatables Speed Limit - 35 MPH Launch Ramp at Redinger Lake Only Car Top Boats Only at Kerckhoff	Fishing: Striped Bass Swimming Picnicking Hiking Nature Study Hunting: Valley Quail, Rabbit & Deer	Nearest Facilities at North Fork

MAMMOTH POOL RESERVOIR

Mammoth Pool Reservoir is located on the San Joaquin River at an elevation of 3,330 feet. The Dam was completed in 1957 by Southern California Edison Company to produce hydroelectric power. The Lake is nestled in a narrow valley of Ponderosa Pine, Incense Cedar, Black and Live Oak with mountains rising 2,000 feet above its shoreline. The surface area of Mammoth Pool is 1,107 acres when full although the water level drops 90 feet in the Fall closing the improved launch ramp. The access road climbs to 5,300 feet rendering it impassable when winter snow arrives. Mile High Vista Point offers a 180 degree view of magnificent mountains including Mount Ritter and Mammoth Mountain.

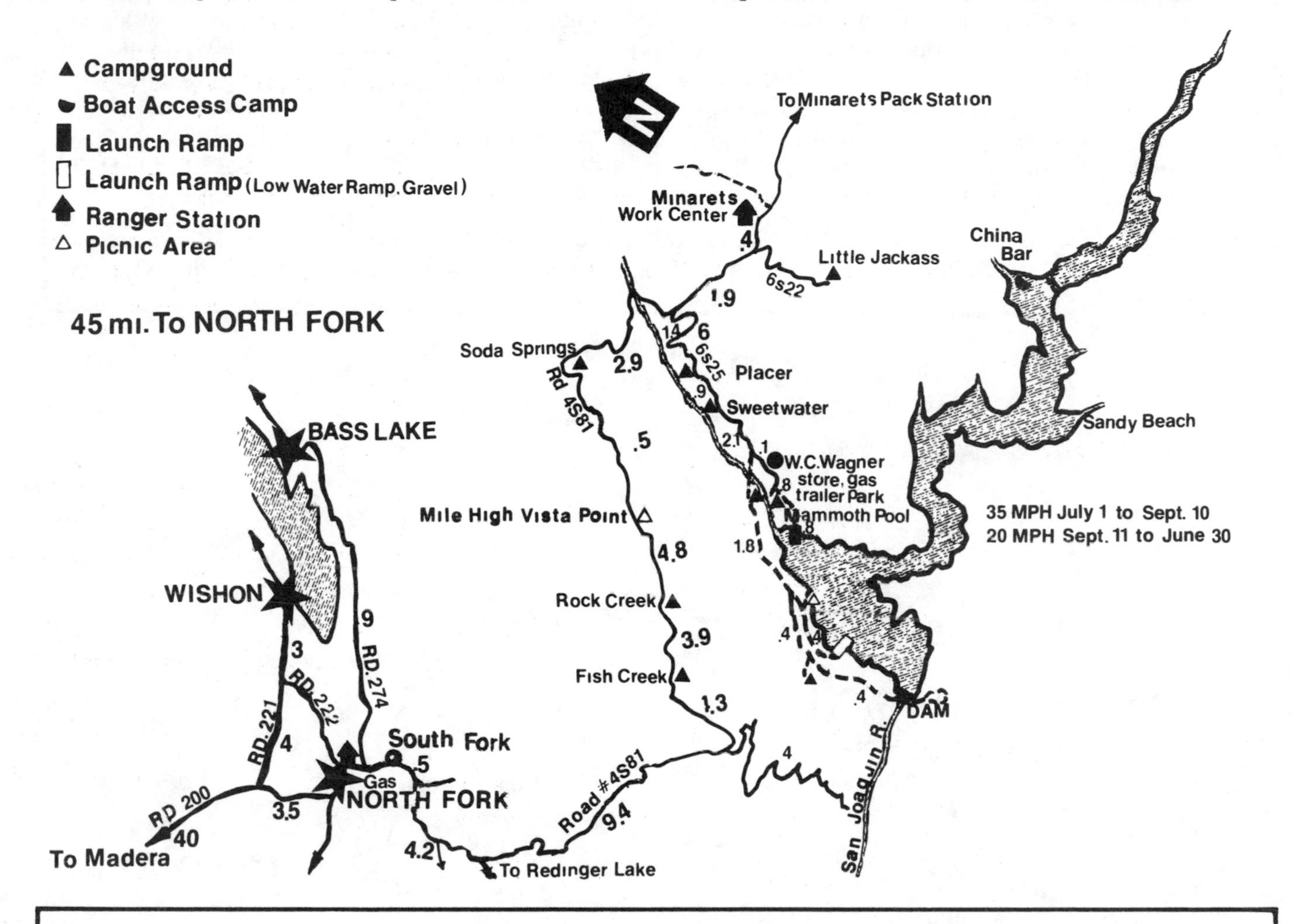

INFORMATION: Minarets Ranger District, North Fork 93643, Ph: 209-877-2218			
CAMPING	**BOATING**	**RECREATION**	**OTHER**
30 Dev. Sites for Tents 34 Dev. Sites for Tents & R.V.s Fee: Mammoth Pool Campground - $5 Fee: Placer Campground - $3 No Fee at Other Forest Service Campgrounds 6 Boat-In Sites	Power, Sail, Row, Canoe, Windsurf & Inflatables Waterskiing Subject to 35 MPH Speed Limit 7/1 to 9/10 Only Improved Launch Ramp & Gravel Launch Ramp	Fishing: Rainbow, Eastern Brook & German Brown Trout Lake Closed to Fishing & Boating May 1 to June 16 Swimming Picnicking Hiking-Nature Trail Pack Station Hunting: Deer	Wagner's Resort 21101 Rte. 209 Madera 93637 Ph: 209-822-2357 35 Dev. Sites for Tents & R.V.s Cabins Grocery Store Bait & Tackle Gas Station Open: Memorial Day to End Deer Season

These Lakes range in elevation from 8,200 feet at Courtright, 6,500 feet at Wishon to 4,200 feet at Black Rock. They are a part of the Kings River Drainage System. Located in the beautiful Sierra National Forest, these Lakes offer good fishing for native trout. In addition, the angler will find numerous Lakes and streams and the newly completed Upper King's River angler's access site. Wishon Village offers complete resort facilities in this relatively remote area. The Forest Service operates numerous campgrounds as shown on the map. Those seeking a wilderness adventure will find trailheads leading into the John Muir and Dinkey Lakes Wilderness Areas. The Helms Creek Hydroelectric Project affects water levels at Wishon and Courtright.

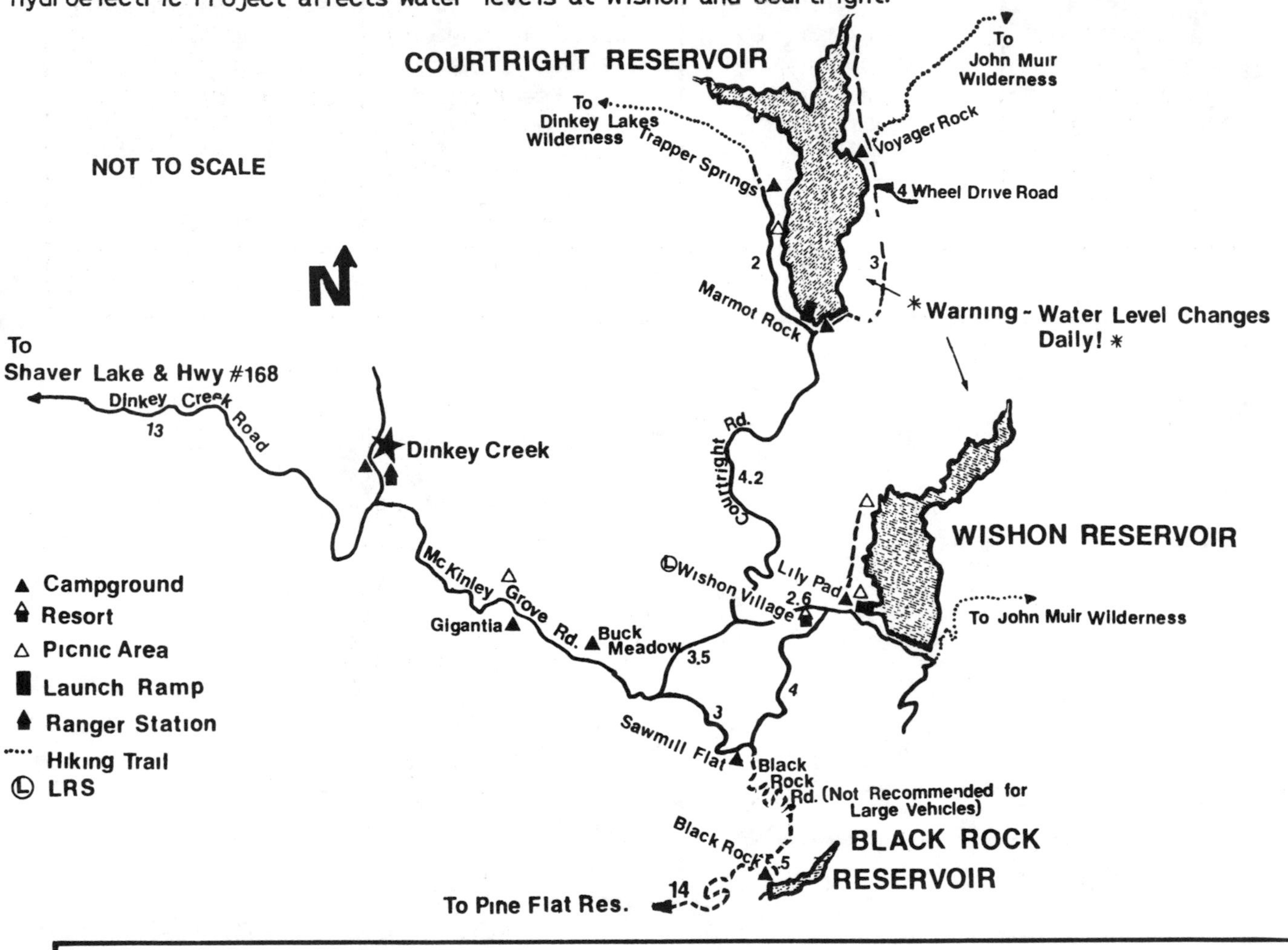

INFORMATION: U.S. Forest Service, P.O. Box 300, Shaver Lake 93664, Ph: 209-841-3311

CAMPING	BOATING	RECREATION	OTHER
Numerous U.S.F.S. Campgrounds in Area Dinkey Creek R.S. Ph: 209-841-3404 Wishon Village Dinkey Creek 93617 24 Tent Sites & 24 R.V. Sites Full Hookups Reserve LRS	Open to All Boating Except Waterskiing & Jet Skiing 15 MPH Speed Limit Rentals: Fishing Boats at Wishon	Fishing: Rainbow, Brown & Brook Trout Swimming Picnicking Hiking & Backpacking Horse Rentals & Pack Services Hunting: Deer ORV Roads	Wishon Village: Store Restaurant Gas Station Laundromat Propane Bait & Tackle Full Facilities at Shaver Lake

SHAVER LAKE

Shaver Lake is at an elevation of 5,370 feet in the Sierra National Forest. The Lake has a surface area of 2,000 acres with a shoreline of 13 miles. Tall pine trees blend with granite boulders to the water's edge. This is a popular boating Lake with good marine facilities. In addition to excellent fishing at Shaver, there are numerous trout streams nearby awaiting the expectant angler. The nearby John Muir and Dinkey Creek Wilderness Areas lure the hiker and backpacker. Both the U. S. Forest Service and Southern California Edison offer well-maintained campgrounds in this beautiful setting.

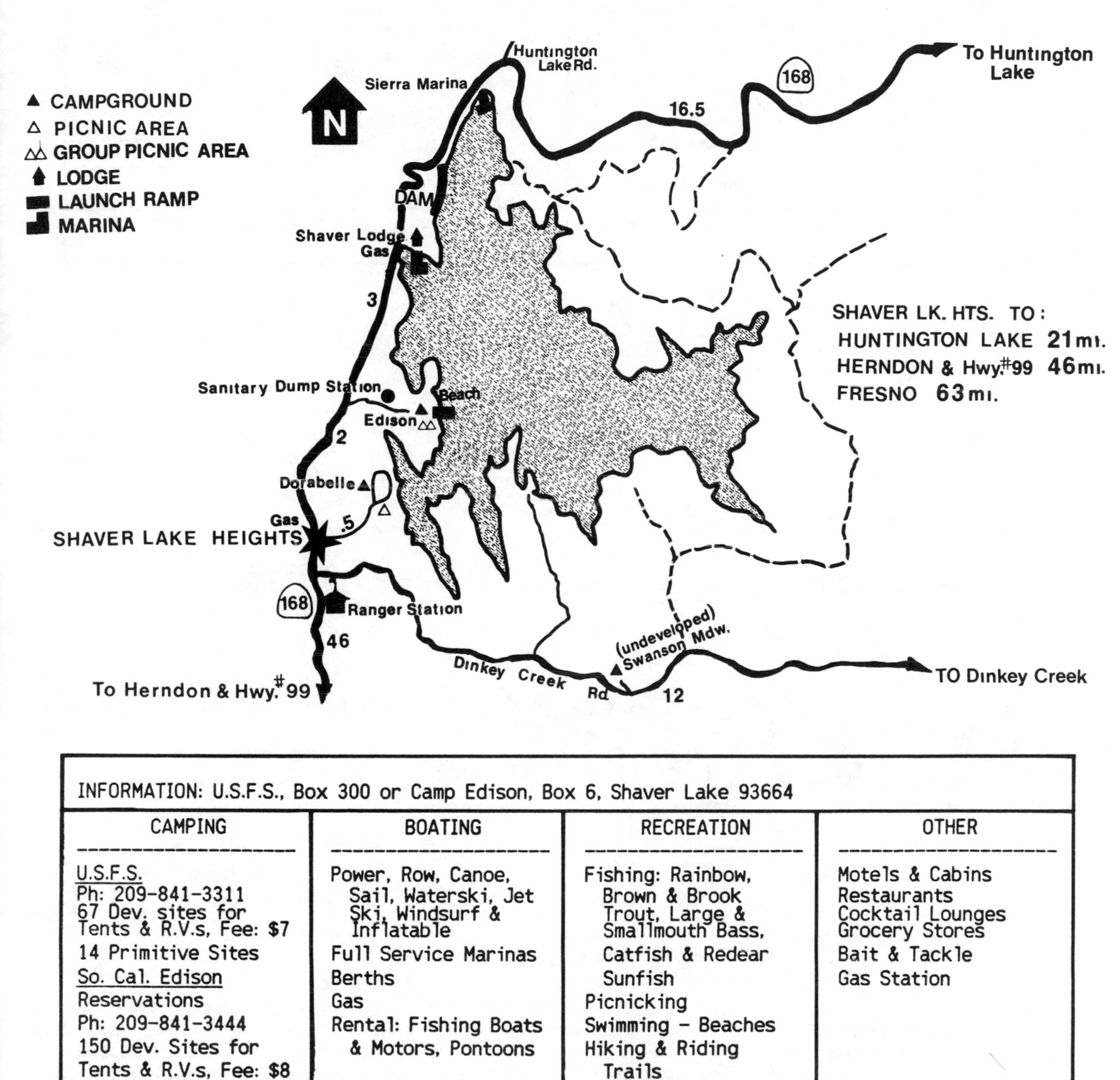

INFORMATION: U.S.F.S., Box 300 or Camp Edison, Box 6, Shaver Lake 93664

CAMPING	BOATING	RECREATION	OTHER
U.S.F.S. Ph: 209-841-3311 67 Dev. sites for Tents & R.V.s, Fee: $7 14 Primitive Sites So. Cal. Edison Reservations Ph: 209-841-3444 150 Dev. Sites for Tents & R.V.s, Fee: $8 Electric Hookups Disposal Station	Power, Row, Canoe, Sail, Waterski, Jet Ski, Windsurf & Inflatable Full Service Marinas Berths Gas Rental: Fishing Boats & Motors, Pontoons	Fishing: Rainbow, Brown & Brook Trout, Large & Smallmouth Bass, Catfish & Redear Sunfish Picnicking Swimming - Beaches Hiking & Riding Trails Horse Rentals Packstation	Motels & Cabins Restaurants Cocktail Lounges Grocery Stores Bait & Tackle Gas Station

HUNTINGTON LAKE

Huntington Lake is at an elevation of 7,000 feet in the Sierra National Forest. Resting in a forested natural basin, this man made Lake is 6 miles long and 1/2 mile wide with 14 miles of shoreline. The Forest Service maintains campsites around the Lake. There are many private Resorts under Special Use Permits. This is a good Lake for sailing, and regattas are held in the summer to take advantage of the westerly winds. Hiking and horseback riding trails surround Huntington. The backpacker will find the nearby Kaiser Wilderness with its 22,750 timbered acres an exciting adventure. Permits are required. Fishing from shore or boat is usually productive and nearby Lakes and streams offer a variety of opportunities.

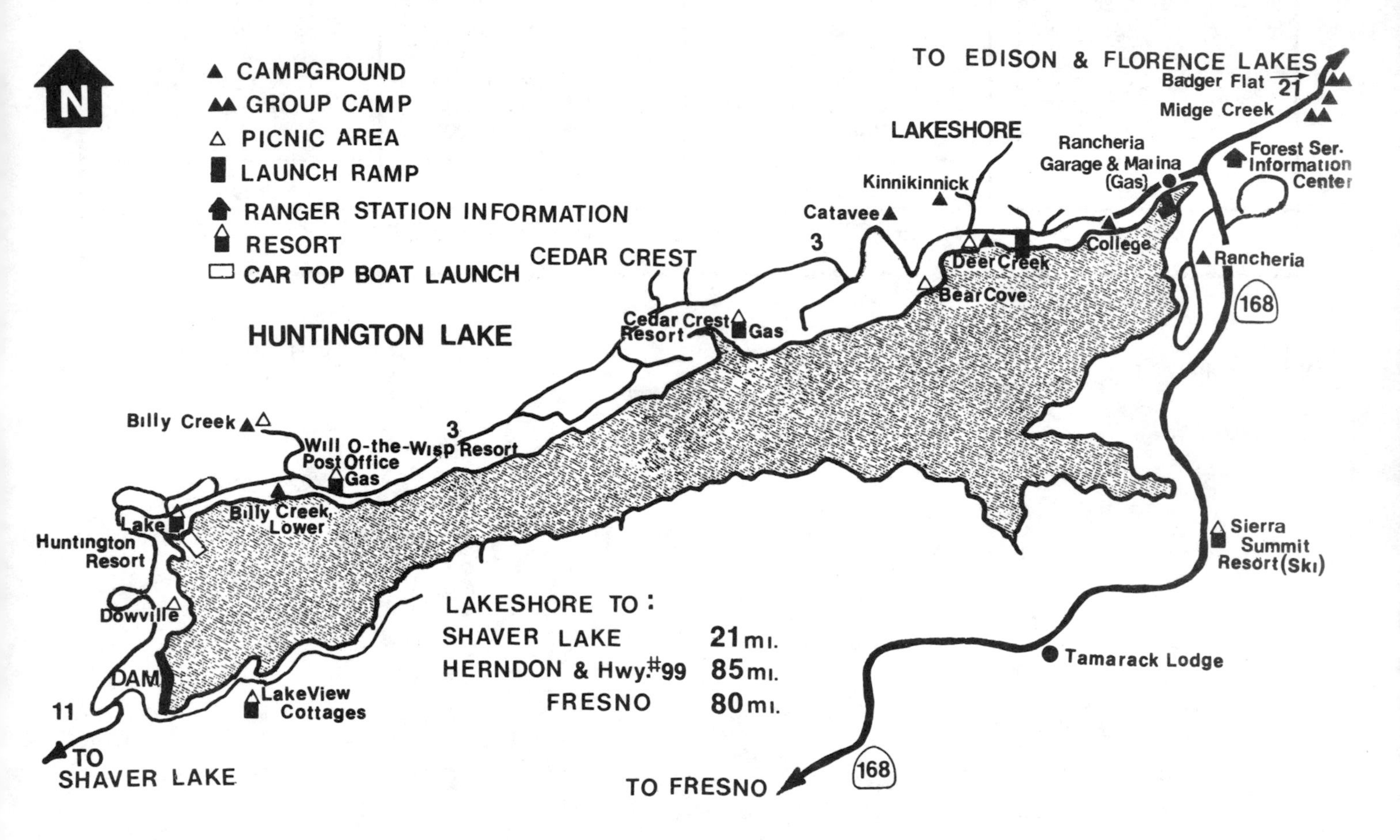

INFORMATION: Pineridge Ranger District, P.O. Box 300, Shaver Lake 93664, Ph: 209-841-3311

CAMPING	BOATING	RECREATION	OTHER
311 Dev. Sites for Tents & R.V.s Fee: $6 Double Sites: $12 Group Campgrounds Reservations Accepted After March 1 for Midge Creek & Badger Flat Group Campgrounds	Power, Row, Canoe, Sail, Waterski, Windsurf & Inflatable Full Service Marinas Launch Ramp Rentals: Fishing & Sailboats, Canoes, Paddleboats	Fishing: Rainbow, Brown & Brook Tout, Kokanee Swimming Picnicking Hiking Backpacking-Parking Horseback Riding Trails & Rentals Nature Study	Motels & Cabins Restaurants Grocery Stores Bait & Tackle Gas Station Summer Ranger Station

EDISON LAKE AND FLORENCE LAKE

Edison Lake is at 7,700 feet and Florence Lake is at 7,400 feet elevation in the beautiful high Sierras bordering the John Muir and Ansel Adams Wilderness Areas. Granite boulders and sandy beaches around the timbered shorelines make a lovely setting. In addition to the Forest Service Campgrounds, Vermillion Valley Resort at Edison Lake offers cabins, restaurant, grocery store, boat rentals and launch facilities. Florence Lake has a small store with limited supplies. A Resort with store, cabins, restaurant and hot mineral baths is located at Mono Hot Springs. A ferry service for backpackers into the Wilderness areas is available at both Lakes. Fishing in both Lakes and streams is excellent in this truly delightful high mountain retreat.

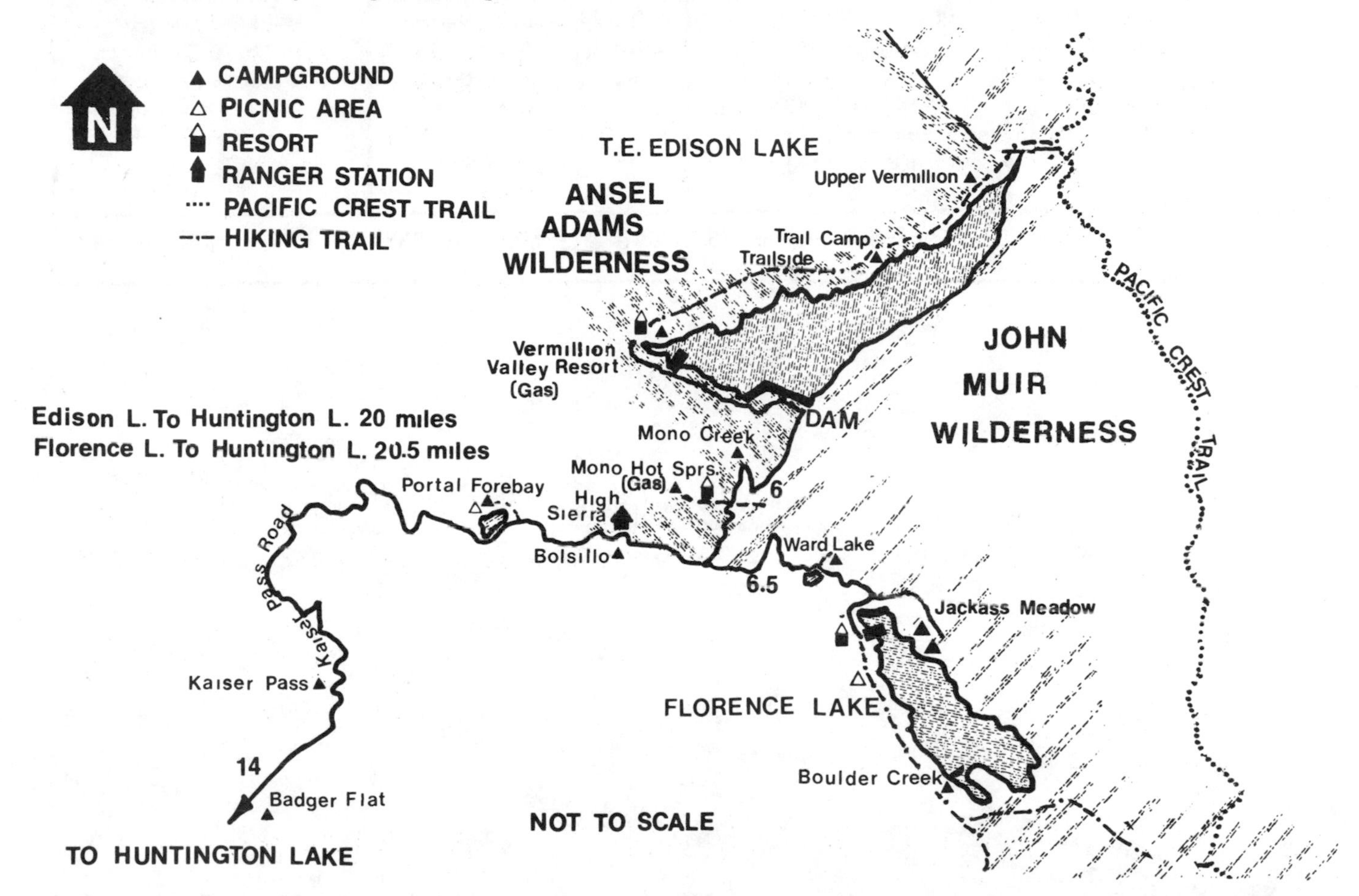

INFORMATION: U.S.F.S., P.O. Box 300, Shaver Lake 93664, Ph: 209-841-3311

CAMPING	BOATING	RECREATION	OTHER
120 Sites for Tents In This Area R.V.s and Trailers Use Caution Due To Narrow One-Lane Winding Rds. Primitive Camping Allowed Anywhere With Campfire Permit	Power, Row, Canoe & Inflatable Speed Limit - 15 MPH Launch Ramps Rentals: Fishing Boats & Canoes	Fishing: Rainbow, Brown & Brook Trout Picnicking Hiking Horseback Riding & Pack Trips Ferry Service for Backpackers Entry Point to John Muir & Ansel Adams Wilderness Permit Required	Cabins Restaurants Grocery Stores Bait & Tackle Gas Station High Sierra Ranger Station (Seasonal) Ph: 209-841-3203

PINE FLAT LAKE AND AVOCADO LAKE PARK

Pine Flat Lake is at an elevation of 961 feet in the Sierra Foothills east of Fresno. This 21 mile long Lake has 67 miles of generally open shoreline. There is a moderate growth of pine, oak and willow trees throughout the area. The U. S. Army Corps of Engineers has jurisdiction over the Lake. In addition to the public campgrounds around the Lake, there are private developments along Trimmer Springs Road which offer overnight lodging and R.V. accommodations. Good marine facilities and warm water are attractive to waterskiers, boaters and swimmers. A variety of fish await the angler at this popular Lake. Avocado Lake Park is on the Kings River below Pine Flat Dam. This small 83 surface acre Lake offers non-powered boating and a warm water fishery. There is no camping permitted, but there are nice picnic areas and a pleasant swimming beach.

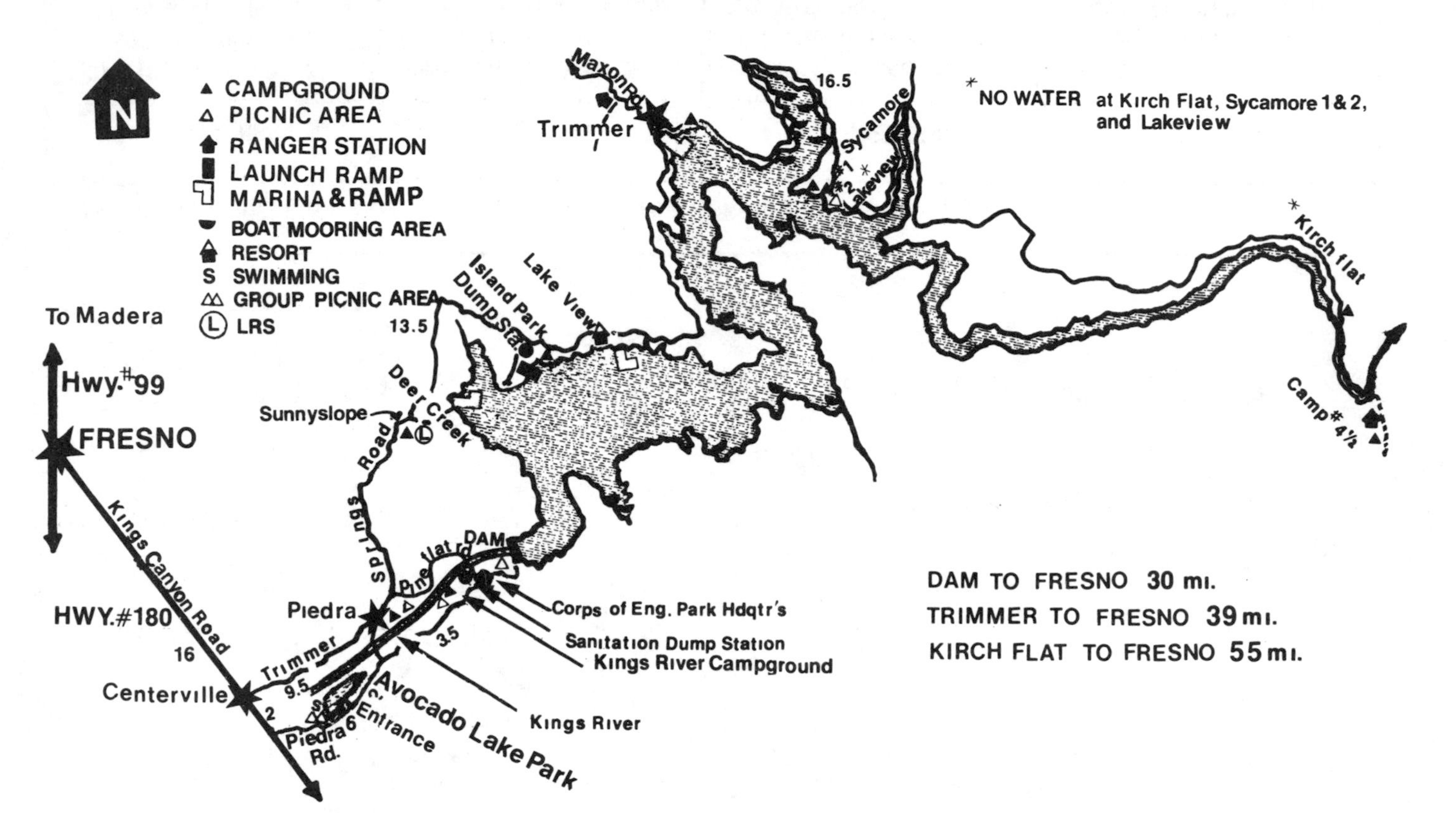

INFORMATION: Pine Flat Lake, P.O. Box 117, Piedra 93649, Ph: 209-787-2589

CAMPING	BOATING	RECREATION	OTHER
Island Park: 75 Dev. Sites for Tents & R.V.s Plus Overflow Fees: 0 - $6 Handicap Sites Sunnyslope Camp: P.O. Box 146 Piedra 93649 Ph: 209-787-2730 95 R.V. Sites Hookups - $10	Pine Flat: Open to All Boats Full Service Marina Overnight Mooring - No Shoreline Camping Rentals: Fishing, Pontoon & Jet Skis Avocado Lake Park: No Gas-Powered Boats-Hand Launch	Fishing: Rainbow Trout, Large & Smallmouth Bass, Catfish & Panfish Swimming Picnicking Campfire Program River Raft Trips Hunting: Deer, Quail, Dove, Pigeon & Squirrel-Designated Areas	Motel & Cabins Restaurants-Lounges Snack Bars - Stores Bait, Tackle & Gas Avocado Lake Fresno Co. Parks 2220 Tulare St. Fresno 93721 Ph: 209-488-3004

HUME AND SEQUOIA LAKES

Hume Lake, at 5,200 feet, and Sequoia, at 5,300 feet, are in the beautiful Sequoia National Forest. Hume Lake has 85 surface acres and Sequoia has 77 acres. The angler will find trout, and the boater is restricted to small non-powered crafts; electric motors are allowed at Hume. Sequoia Lake is operated by the YMCA and early reservations are advised at this popular camp. Since Sequoia is a private family camp, there is no day use. Be sure to bring your camera to this beautiful country of the Giant Sequoia Trees (survivors of the Ice Age), and the majestic Kings Canyon National Park.

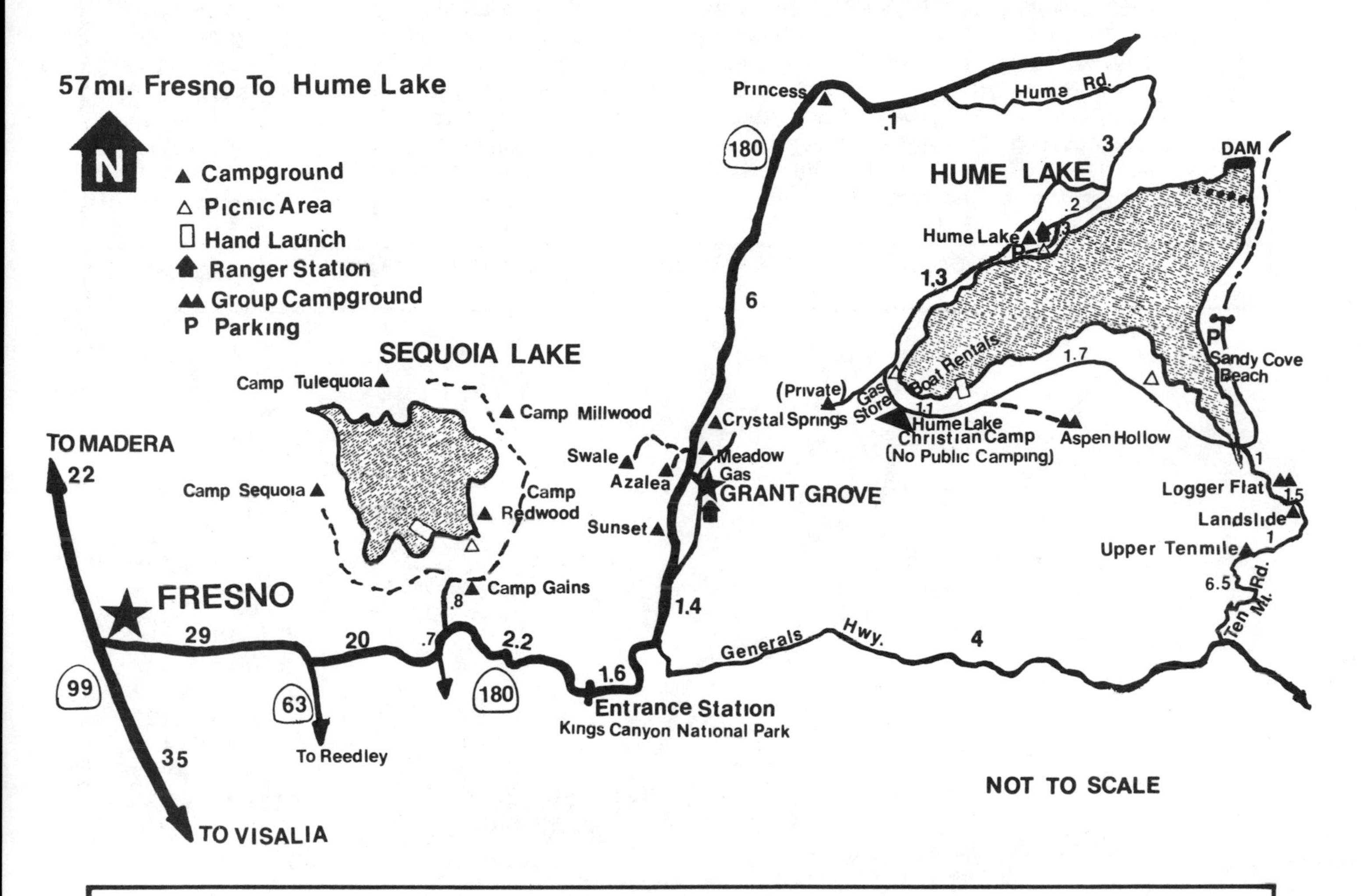

INFORMATION: USFS, 36273 E. Kings Canyon Rd., Dunlap 93621, Ph: 209-338-2251			
CAMPING	**BOATING**	**RECREATION**	**OTHER**
Hume Lake: 75 Dev. Sites for Tents & R.V.s, Fee: $5 2 Group Camps by Reservation Nearby Campgrounds 180 Plus Sites Sequoia Family Camp Central Valley YMCA P.O. Box 5618 Fresno 93755	Hume Lake: Open to All Non-Powered Boats, Electric Motors O.K. 5 MPH Speed Limit Hand Launch Boat Rentals at Christian Camp Sequoia: Sail&Canoes Furnished. Non-Powered Boats O.K. No Motors	Fishing: Rainbow & German Brown Trout Picnicking Swimming Hiking & Backpacking Horseback Riding & Rentals at Hume Lake Christian Camp Hunting: Deer Nature Study Photography	Hume Lake Christian Camp - Gas, Store Restaurant Ph: 209-335-2881 Sequoia Family Camp Meals, Store, Craft Materials, Laundry Before July 1 - Ph: 209-226-2267 After July 1 - Ph: 209-335-2886

DIAZ LAKE AND PLEASANT VALLEY RESERVOIR

Diaz Lake rests at an elevation of 3,700 feet on the eastern slope of the Sierras, 15 miles from the Mt. Whitney Trailhead. This 86 surface acre Lake offers varied boating and is popular with waterskiers during the season. There is a good warm water fishery plus brown and rainbow trout. Pleasant Valley Reservoir, at 4,200 feet, also offers trout fishing, but boating is not permitted. There is a 15 minute hike to the Lake from the campground. Inyo County operates the campgrounds at these Lakes.

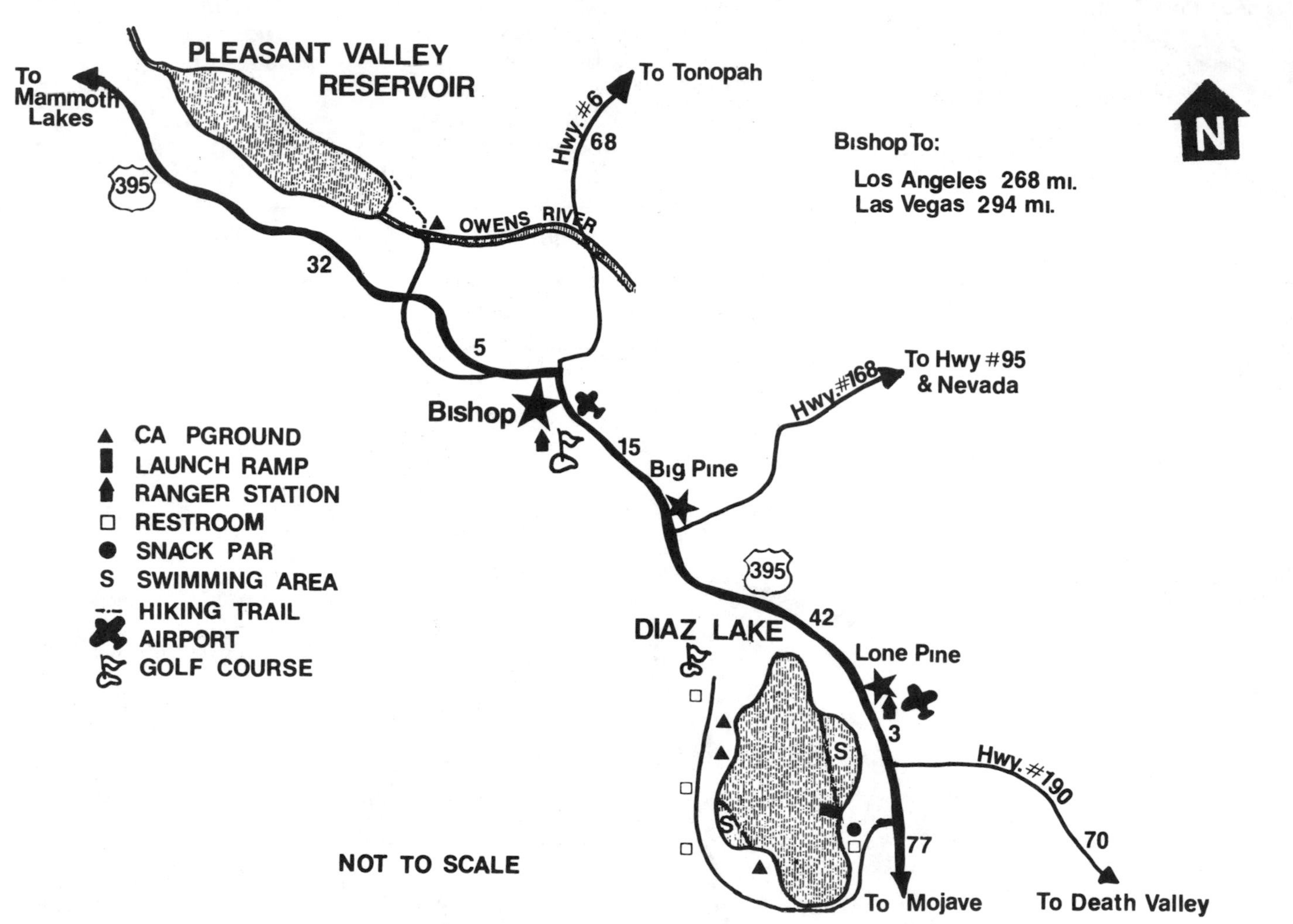

INFORMATION: Inyo County Parks, P.O. Box 237, Independence 93526, Ph: 619-878-2411

CAMPING	BOATING	RECREATION	OTHER
Pleasant Valley: 200 Tent & R.V. Sites No Hookups-Fee: $4 Diaz Lake: 300 Tent & R.V. Sites No Hookups-Fee: $5 Group Camping 2 Week Advance Reservations Required	Diaz Lake: Power, Row, Canoe, Sail, Waterski & Inflatables Launch Ramp - $5 Speed Limit - 35 MPH May through Oct. Speed Limit - 15 MPH Nov. through Apr. Noise Level Laws are Strictly Enforced Maximum Boat Size-22'	Fishing: Rainbow & Brown Trout, Small-mouth Bass, Bluegill & Catfish Swimming - Beaches Picnicking Hiking &Backpacking Horse & Plane Trips into Back Country Hang Gliding Hunting: Waterfowl No ORV's Allowed	Full Facilities in Bishop & Lone Pine Diaz Lake: P.O. Box 503 Lone Pine 93545 Ph: 619-876-5656

SOUTH SECTION

LAKES 148 - 194

NUMBERS REPRESENT LAKES IN NUMERICAL ORDER IN BOOK

LAKE KAWEAH

Lake Kaweah is at an elevation of 694 feet in the rolling foothills 17 miles east of Visalia. The Lake has a surface area of 1,945 acres, but there is a severe drop of over 100 feet in the fall each year. The Lake is 6 miles long with 22 miles of steep oak-covered shoreline. The U. S. Army Corps of Engineers maintains Terminus Dam along with camping, picnic and marina facilities. This is a good boating Lake with houseboating being very popular in the many coves and inlets. Boaters should beware of submerged rocks during low water. The angler will find trout in addition to a wide variety of warm water fish.

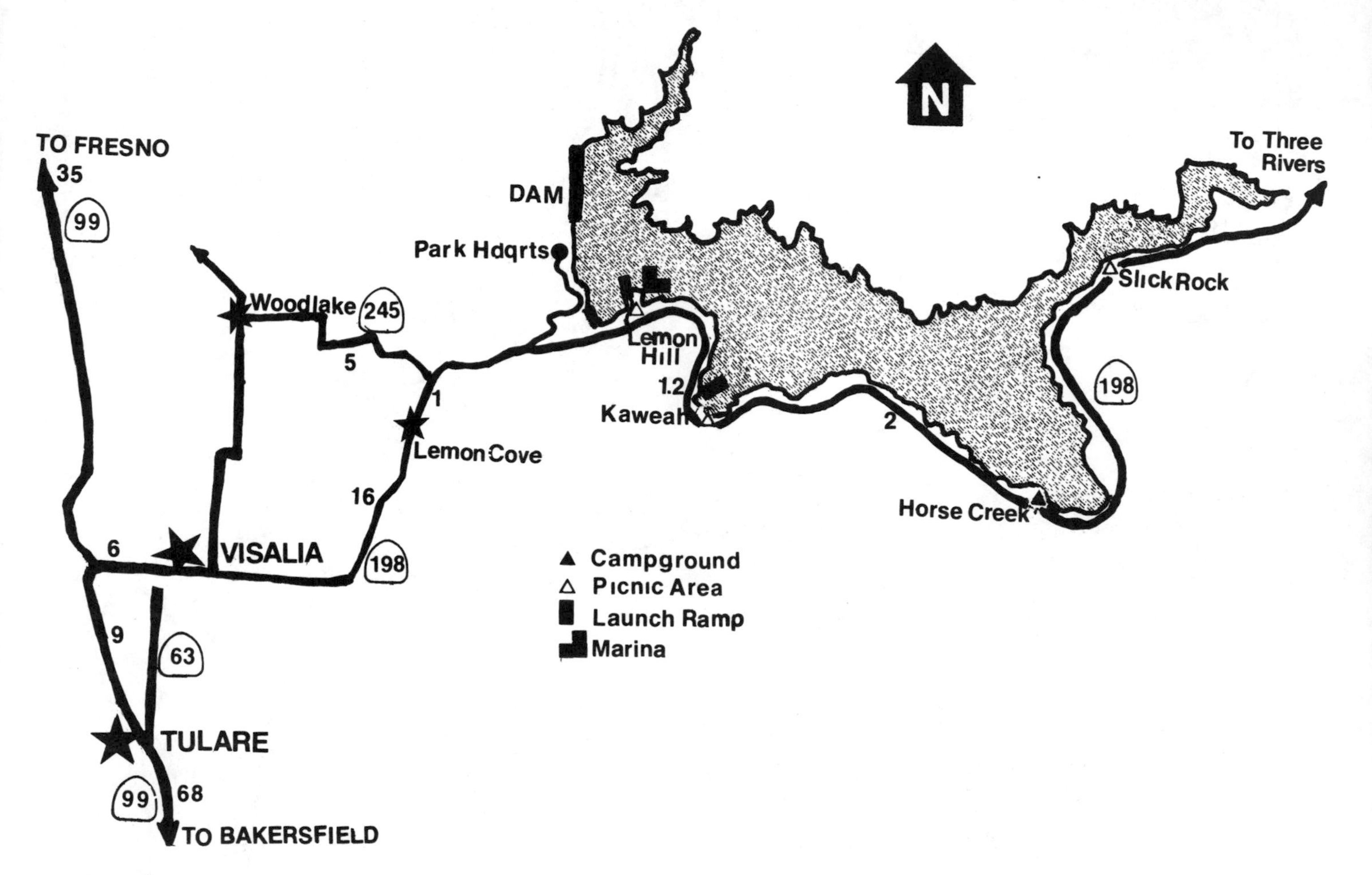

INFORMATION: Corps of Eng., P.O. Box 346, Lemon Cove 93244, Ph: 209-597-2301

CAMPING	BOATING	RECREATION	OTHER
80 Dev. Sites for Tents & R.V.s (Handicap Site by Reservation) Overnight On Boat Permitted Anywhere Away From Shore	Power, Row, Canoe, Sail, Waterski, Jet Ski Full Service Marina Launch Ramps Rentals: Fishing Boats, Houseboats & Pontoons Docks, Berths, Moorings, Gas	Fishing: Rainbow Trout, Catfish, Bluegill, Crappie, Large & Smallmouth Bass, Redear Perch Swimming Picnicking Campfire Program	Snack Bar Bait & Tackle Disposal Station Full Facilities at Woodlake and Three Rivers

SUCCESS LAKE

Success Lake rests at an elevation of 640 feet in the southern Sierra Foothills. The Lake has a surface area of 2,450 acres with 30 miles of shoreline. The U. S. Army Corps of Engineers has jurisdiction over the abundant and well-maintained camping, marine and recreation facilities. There is a Wildlife Area open for public use with hunting allowed, shotguns only, during appropriate seasons. The bird watcher may find several rare or endangered species, such as the Bald Eagle and California Condor. There is good fishing year around, and all types of boating are permitted from houseboats to waterskiing at this complete facility.

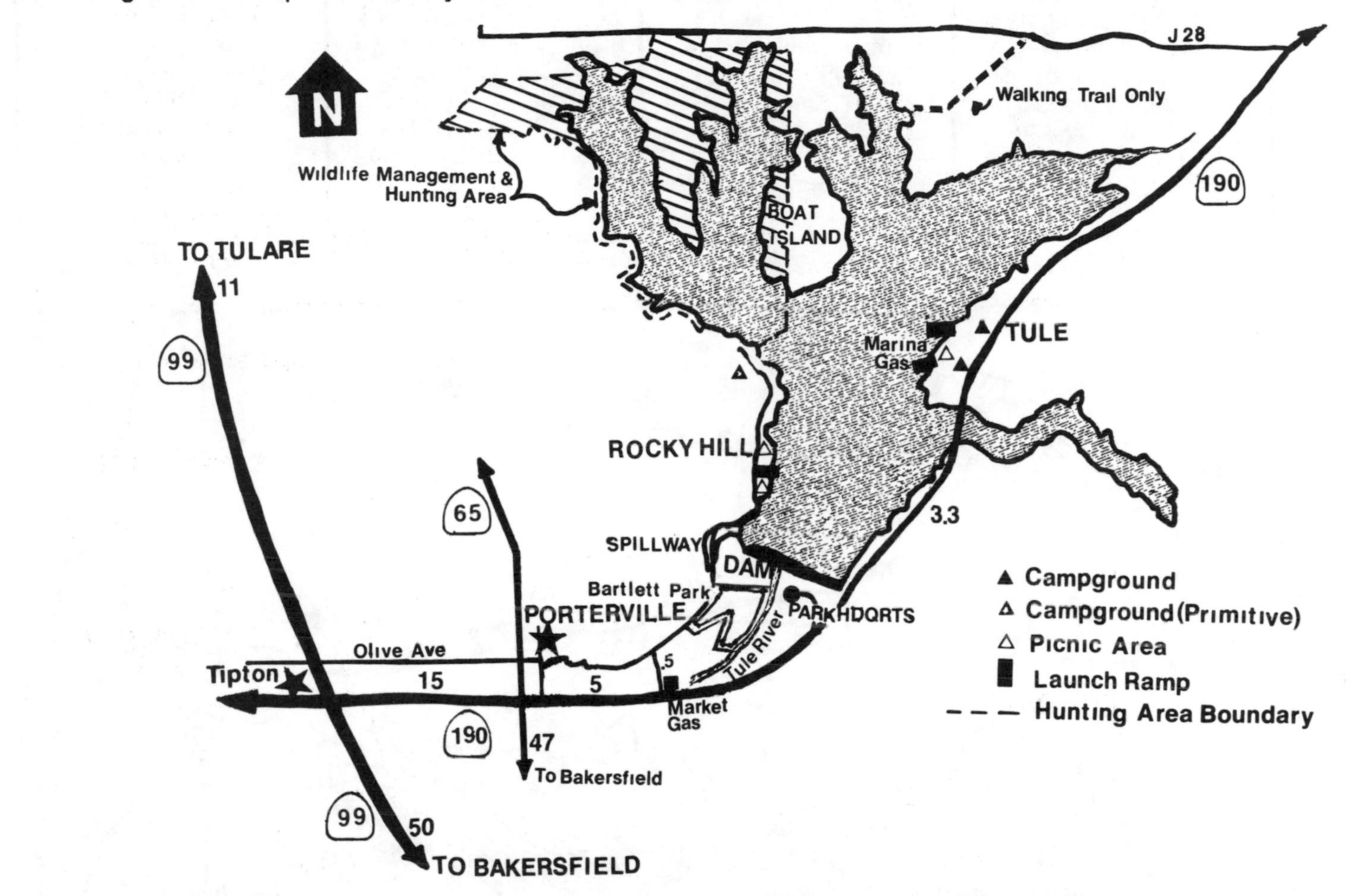

INFORMATION: Park Manager, P.O. Box 1072, Porterville 93258, Ph: 209-784-0215			
CAMPING	**BOATING**	**RECREATION**	**OTHER**
104 Dev. Sites for Tents & R.V.s Fee: $6 (Extra Vehicle: $3) - April-October No Fee Other Times 110 Primitive Sites No Fee Overnight in Boat Permitted Anywhere	Power, Row, Canoe, Sail, Waterski, Jet Ski, Windsurf & Inflatable Full Service Marina Launch Ramps Rentals: Fishing, Houseboats & Pontoons Berths (Maximum Boat Length - 30 ft.) Docks, Moorings, Gas	Fishing: Trout in Winter, Catfish, Bluegill, Crappie, Striped&Black Bass Swimming Hiking Bird Watching Hunting: Pheasant, Dove & Rabbit Horseback Riding & Dog Trails in Wildlife Area	Grocery Store Bait & Tackle Hot Showers Disposal Station Full Facilities - 5 Miles at Porterville

WOOLLOMES, HART AND MING LAKES AND BRITE VALLEY RECREATION AREA

The nice facilities at Hart, Woollomes and Ming Lakes are under the jurisdiction of Kern County. Lake Woollomes, 300 surface acres, and Hart Lake, 18 surface acres, offer non-powered boating and fishing. Ming Lake, 107 surface acres, is primarily a waterskiing, power boating and drag racing Lake, but sailing and fishing as scheduled below are newly added attractions. Brite Valley is under the jurisdiction of the Tehachapi Valley Recreation and Parks Department. This 90 surface acre Lake rests at an elevation of 4,000 feet. It is open during the warmer months for non-powered boating and fishing, but closed from November through April.

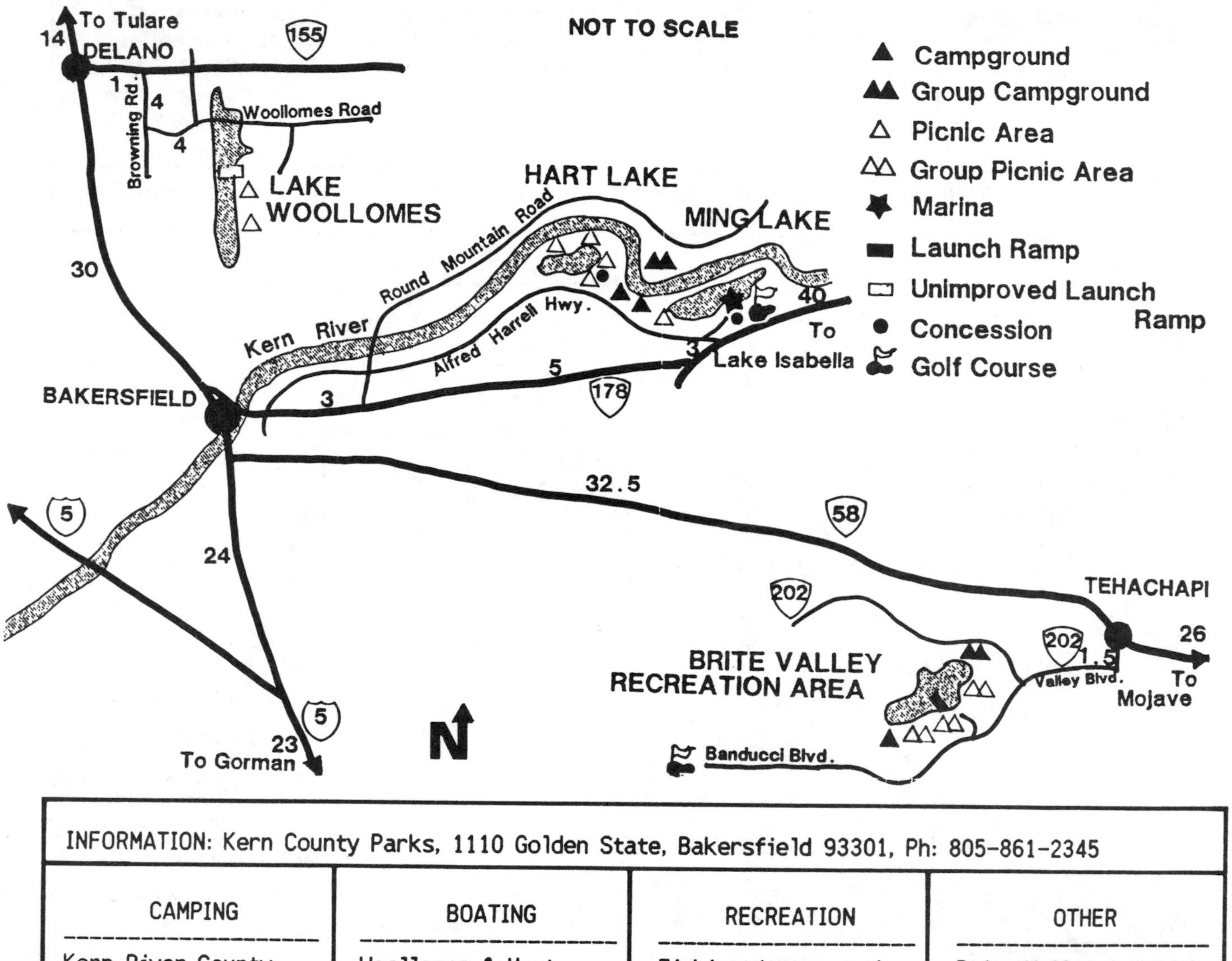

INFORMATION: Kern County Parks, 1110 Golden State, Bakersfield 93301, Ph: 805-861-2345

CAMPING	BOATING	RECREATION	OTHER
Kern River County Park: 50 Dev. Sites for Tents & R.V.s No Hookups Fee: $8 Brite Valley: Unlimited Open Camping No Hookups Fee: $4	Woollomes & Hart: Sail, Canoe, Row & Pedal Boats Only Ming: Power Boating & Drag Races, Sailing Allowed on Tuesdays & Thursdays and the 2nd weekend of month Brite Valley: No Power Except Electric Motors	Fishing: Largemouth Bass, Bluegill, Crappie & Catfish Hart & Ming: Trout in Winter Family & Group Picnicking Hiking Swimming at Woollomes Only Golf Course	Brite Valley Aquatic Recreation Area: Information - Tehachapi Valley Recreation & Parks 490 West "D" Tehachapi 93561 Ph: 805-822-3228

ISABELLA LAKE

Isabella Lake lies at an elevation of 2,605.5 feet in the foothills east of Bakersfield. The surface area of the Lake is 11,400 acres with a shoreline of 38 miles. The U. S. Army Corps of Engineers maintains the excellent and ample facilities at this complete recreation Lake. The main attractions at Isabella are boating, fishing and waterskiing. Activities range from white water rafting to bird watching. A trap range is available and hunting is allowed in designated areas. Winds can be a hazard so warning lights are located at 5 points around the Lake. Lake Patrol and Rescue Service, also Boat Permits, are handled by the Kern County Parks Department.

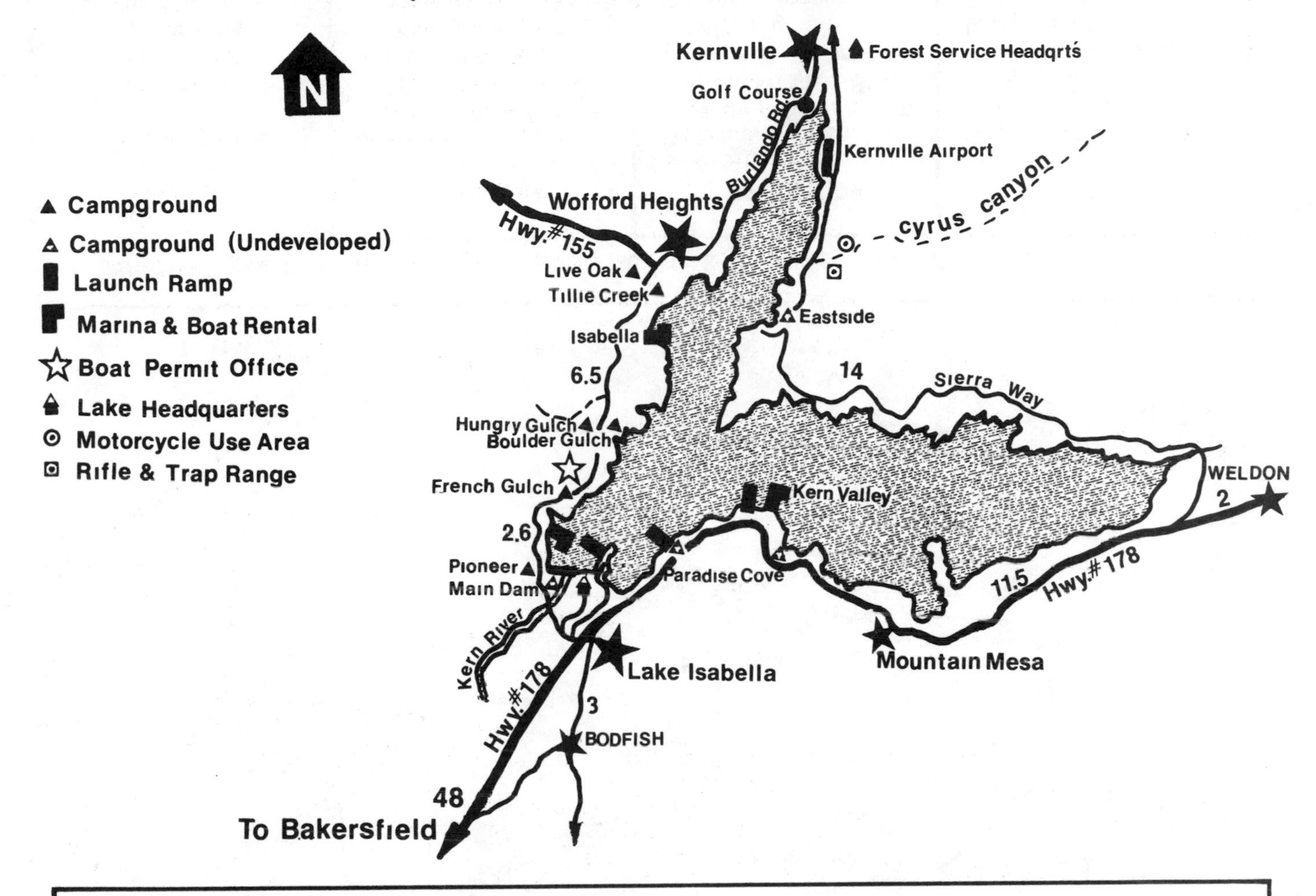

INFORMATION: Corps of Eng., P.O. Box 997, Lake Isabella 93240, Ph: 619-379-2742

CAMPING	BOATING	RECREATION	OTHER
623 Dev. Sites for Tents & R.V.s Water with "Y" Fee: $6 Group Camp - 25 to 200 People Per Area Call for Fee Info. Plus 1200 Undev. Campsites Disposal Station	Power, Row, Canoe, Sail, Waterski, Jet Ski, Windsurf & Inflatables With Restrictions Full Service Marinas Launch Ramps Rentals: Fishing & Waterski Boats Docks, Berths, Moorings, Gas	Fishing: Trout, Catfish, Bluegill, Crappie & Bass Swimming Picnicking Hiking Horseback Riding & Rentals White Water Rafting Bird Watching Hunting: Quail & Waterfowl	Full Facilities at Towns Near Lake Airport-Auto Rentals Golf - Movies Playgrounds Campfire Programs Nature Study Trailer Rentals & Storage ORV Use Area Rifle & Trap Range

SAN ANTONIO LAKE

San Antonio Lake is at an elevation of 900 feet in the oak-covered rolling hills of Southern Monterey County. The Lake has a surface area of 5,500 acres with 60 shoreline miles. There is an abundance of modern campsites, many with full hookups. This is an ideal Lake for waterskiing with its mild water temperature, its length of 16 miles, and calm waters protected by the surrounding hills. An excellent warm water fishery makes San Antonio a good year round angler's Lake. The facilities are open all year with complete services for vacation activities.

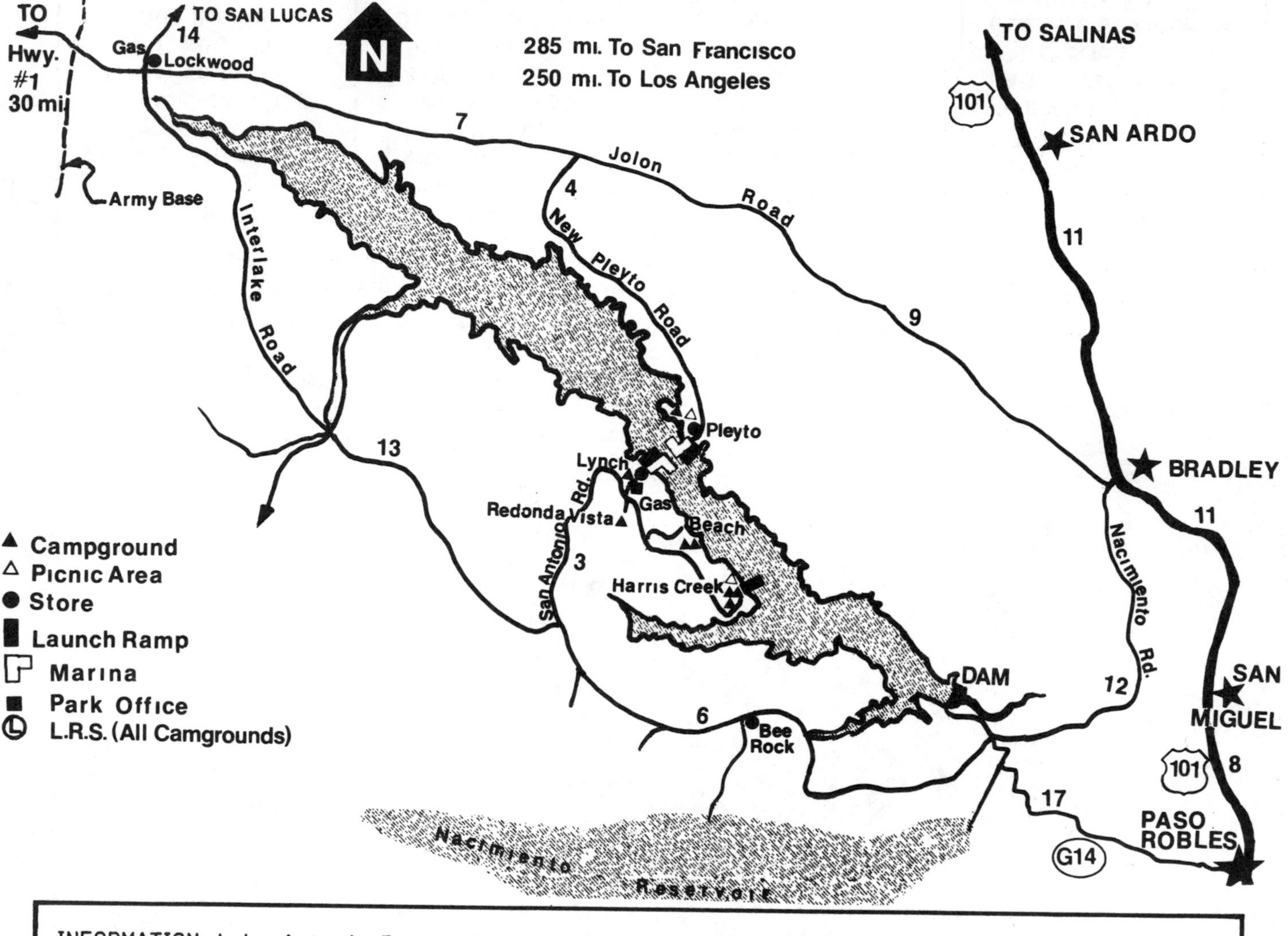

INFORMATION: Lake Antonio Resort, Bradley 93426, Ph: 805-472-2311 or 2313

CAMPING	BOATING	RECREATION	OTHER
650 Dev. Sites for Tents & R.V.s Some With Full Hookups Fees: Winter - $7 to $10 Summer - $8 to $11.50 Youth Campground to 60 People Disposal Station	Power, Row, Canoe, Sail, Waterski, Jet Ski, Windsurf & Inflatable Full Service Marina Launch Ramps - $3.50 Rentals: Fishing, Pontoons, Surf Jets & Jet Skis Docks, Mooring, Gas, Dry Storage	Fishing: Catfish, Large & Smallmouth Bass, Striped Bass Swimming - Beaches Picnicking Hiking & Horseback Riding Trails Campfire Program Nature Study Exercise Course	Snack Bar Restaurant Grocery Store Bait & Tackle Laundromat Gas Station Game Room Movies Dances Mobile Home Rentals: Reservations - Ph: 800-822-2267

LAKE NACIMIENTO

Lake Nacimiento is nestled in a valley of pine and oak trees at an elevation of 800 feet. The surface area is 5,370 acres with 165 miles of shoreline with many delightful coves. Fishing from shore or boat will usually produce bass, either large or smallmouth or the voracious white bass. Crappie, bluegill and catfish are also plentiful. Waterskiing is excellent on the 16-mile long Lake with water temperature about 68 degrees. The Resort offers an abundance of modern campsites, complete marina facilities and vacation activities, making it an excellent family recreation area.

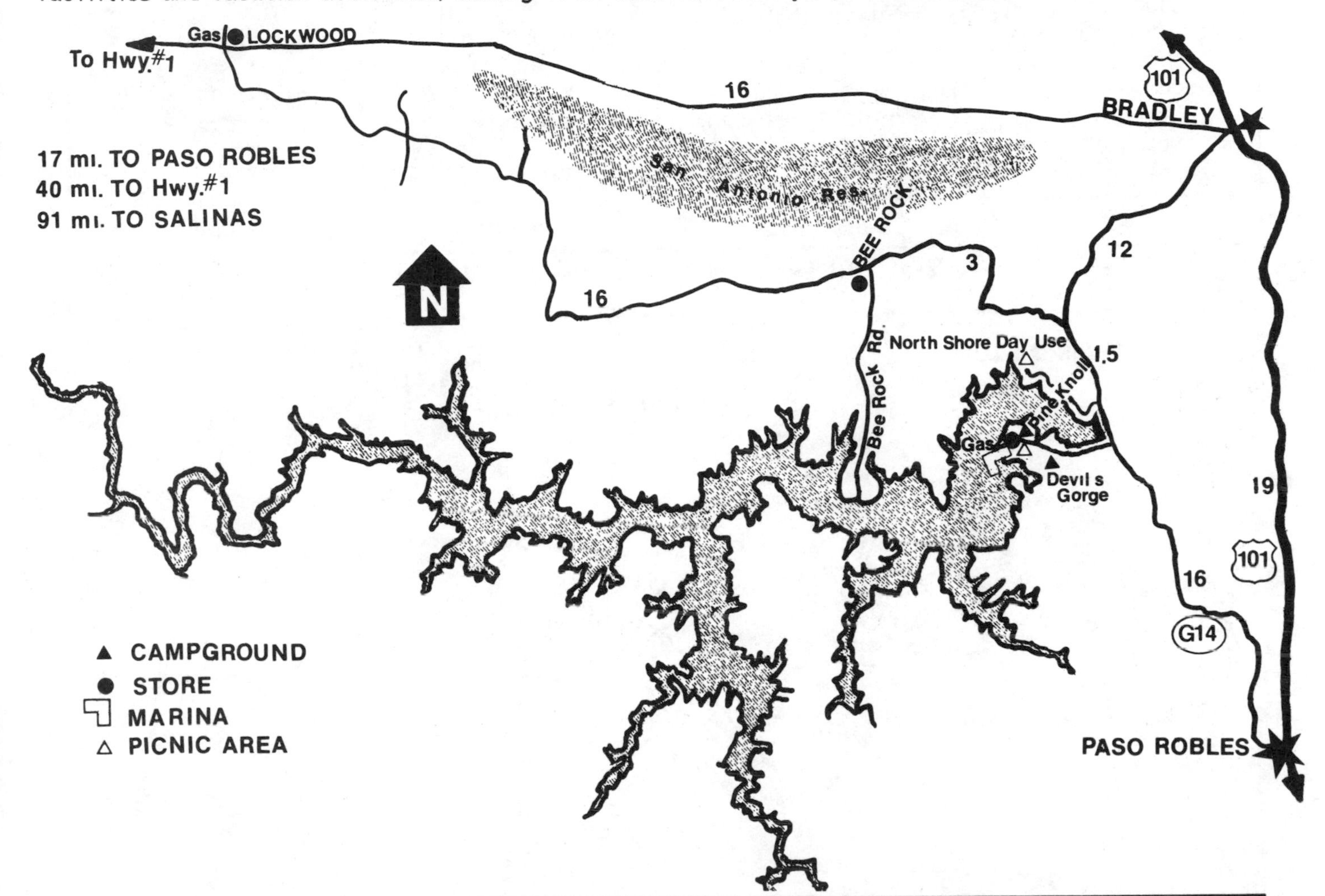

INFORMATION: Lake Nacimiento Resort, Star Rte., Bradley 93426, Ph: 805-238-3256

CAMPING	BOATING	RECREATION	OTHER
350 Dev. Sites for Tents & R.V.s Fees: $10/Night $60/Week 40 R.V. Sites With Full Hookups Fees: $14/Night $84/Week Group sites to 600 People Winter Rates in Effect 10-1 to 4-1	Power, Row, Canoe, Sail, Waterski, Jet Ski, Windsurf & Inflatable Min. Length - 8 ft. Full Service Marina 3 Launch Ramps Rentals: Fishing & Bass Boats, Pontoons County Water Fee: $3.50 a Day	Fishing: Catfish, Bluegill, Crappie, White, Large & Smallmouth Bass Swimming Picnicking Hiking No Motorcycles of Any type Day Use Fee: $5 - South Shore $3 - North Shore	Snack Bar Restaurant Grocery Store Bait & Tackle Hot Showers Disposal Station Gas & Propane Camp Trailer Rental Playgrounds Swimming Pool & Hot Tubs During Summer Only

ATASCADERO LAKE

Nestled amid Central California's coastal Range, these Lakes vary in recreational opportunities. Santa Margarita, the largest of the three with 1,070 surface acres, is a warm water fisherman's Lake with nearby camping facilities. Although waterskiing and windsurfing are not permitted, it is a good boating Lake. Atascadero is a small City Lake with picnic facilities, a concession and rental boats. Power boating is not allowed. You may fish for trout and bass. The City of San Luis Obispo does not allow boating or any water contact at Whale Rock Reservoir. There is three trout limit per day.

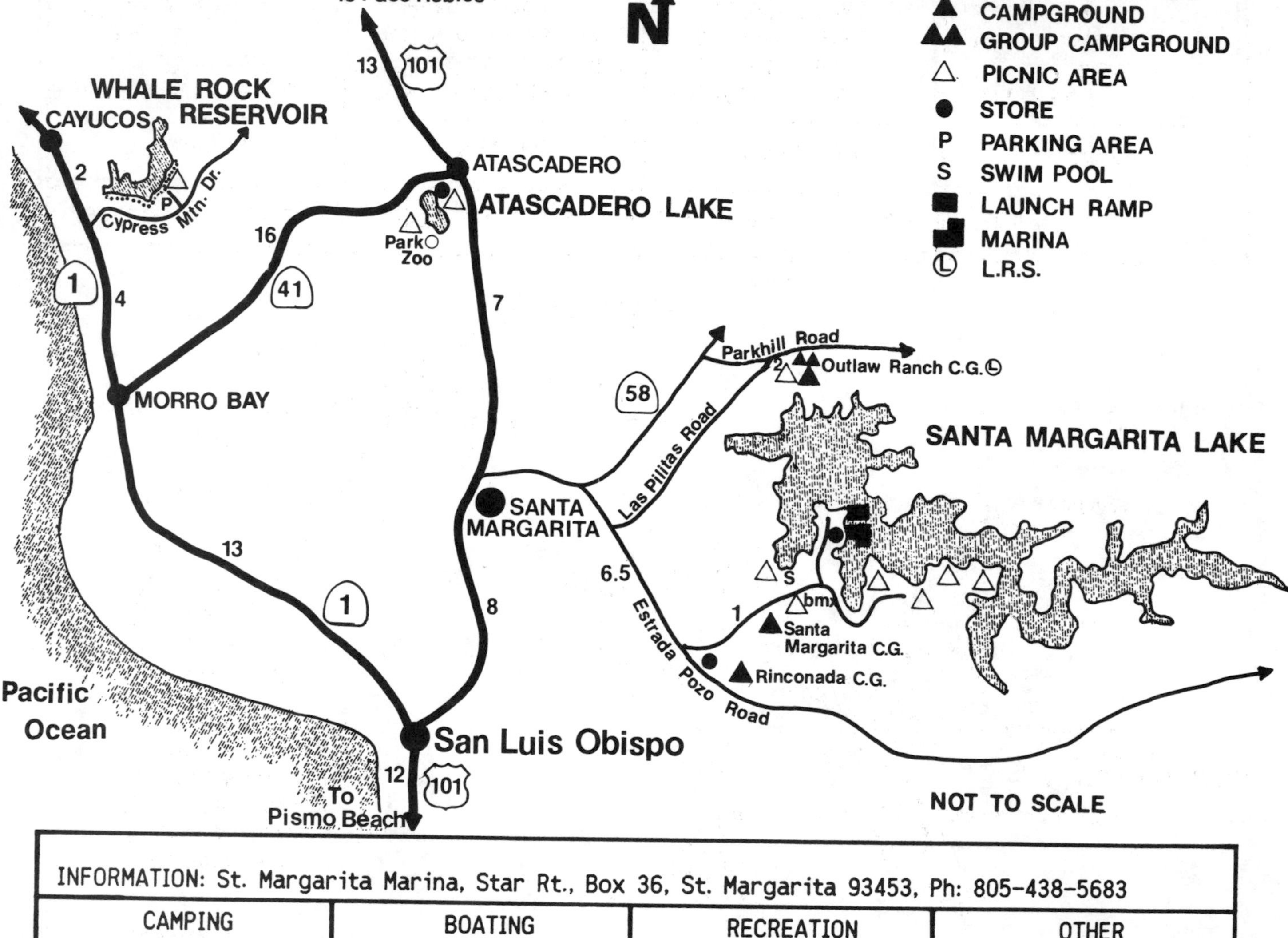

INFORMATION: St. Margarita Marina, Star Rt., Box 36, St. Margarita 93453, Ph: 805-438-5683

CAMPING	BOATING	RECREATION	OTHER
Santa Margarita: Star Rt., Box 34C Santa Margarita Ph: 805-438-5618 Rinconada Camp Star Rt., Box 36D Santa Margarita Ph: 805-438-5479 Outlaw Ranch Star Rt. 318 Santa Margarita Ph: 805-438-5605	Santa Margarita: All Boats Over 10 Feet Allowed - No Waterskiing or Windsurfing - Approved Inflatable Full Service Marina Rentals: Fishing Boats & Motors, Pontoons Whale Rock: No Boating	Fishing: Rainbow Trout, Bluegill, Catfish, Crappie, Striped & Large-mouth Bass Swimming: St. Margarita-Pool Atascadero-Kiddie Pool Only Whale Rock-None Picnicking Hiking&Riding Trails	Santa Margarita: Snacks & Drinks Bait & Tackle Cafe - Weekends Atascadero: Boating: Restricted No Power Boats 5 MPH Speed Limit No Waterskiing or Windsurfing Hand Launch Only

LOPEZ LAKE

Lopez Lake was opened in 1969 and is administered by the San Luis Obispo County Parks and Recreation Department. Its 950 surface acres are favored by westerly breezes coming off the Pacific which make it a popular Lake for sailing and windsurfing. There are good marine support facilities, and special areas are set aside for sailing, windsurfing, jet skis and waterskiing. The angler will find a variety of game fish. In addition to the well-maintained oak-shaded campsites listed below, there are overflow sites for a fee of $7 plus $3 for each additional vehicle. This is a complete recreation facility offering a good naturalist program which can be enjoyed on trails, by boat or at the campfire. The two 600-foot waterslides are a popular attraction.

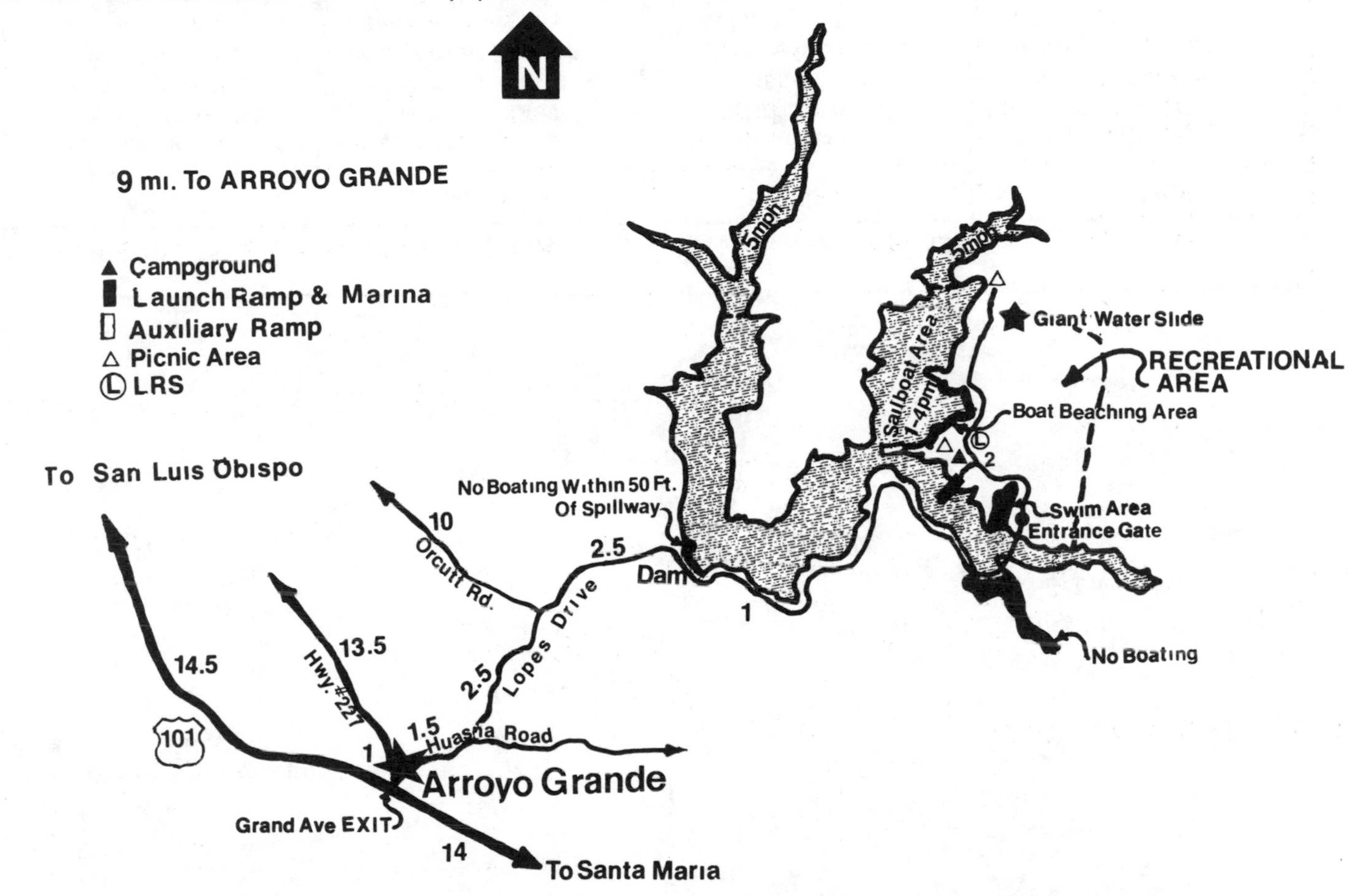

INFORMATION: Lopez Lake, 6800 Lopez Dr., Arroyo Grande 93420, Ph: 805-489-2095

CAMPING	BOATING	RECREATION	OTHER
148 Primitive Sites for Tents & R.V.s Fee: $7 67 Sites with Electric Hookups Fee: $8 135 Sites with Full Hookups Fee: $10 Pets: $1 a Day - Must Have Proof of Current Rabies Vaccination	Open to All Boating Speed Limit: 40 MPH Full Service Marina Paved Launch Fees: $3.50 per Day $25 per Year Boat & Trailer Storage Rentals: Fishing, Ski, Patio, Canoe, Sail & Sailboard	Fishing: Trout, Catfish, Bluegill, Crappie, Redear Sunfish & Black Bass Swimming: In Designated Areas Picnicking Hiking & Nature Trails Boat Tours Campfire Programs	Snack Bar General Store Bait & Tackle Laundromat Gas Station Game Room Waterslide Hot Spas

ZACA LAKE

Zaca Lake is Southern California's only natural private Lake and is operated by the Human Potential Foundation. It is at an elevation of 2,400 feet, 40 miles north of Santa Barbara and is surrounded by the Los Padres National Forest. This small Lake of 25 acres is in a semi-wilderness area, yet offers complete Resort facilities. The fisherman and boater who enjoy the quiet atmosphere of a Lake with no power boating, will find Zaca a pleasant retreat. Nature has blessed this environment with an abundance of wildlife and a variety of plants and trees. Hunting is not permitted. Some of California's most gorgeous trails await the hiker and equestrian. The atmosphere is rustic and relaxed while providing complete vacation activities.

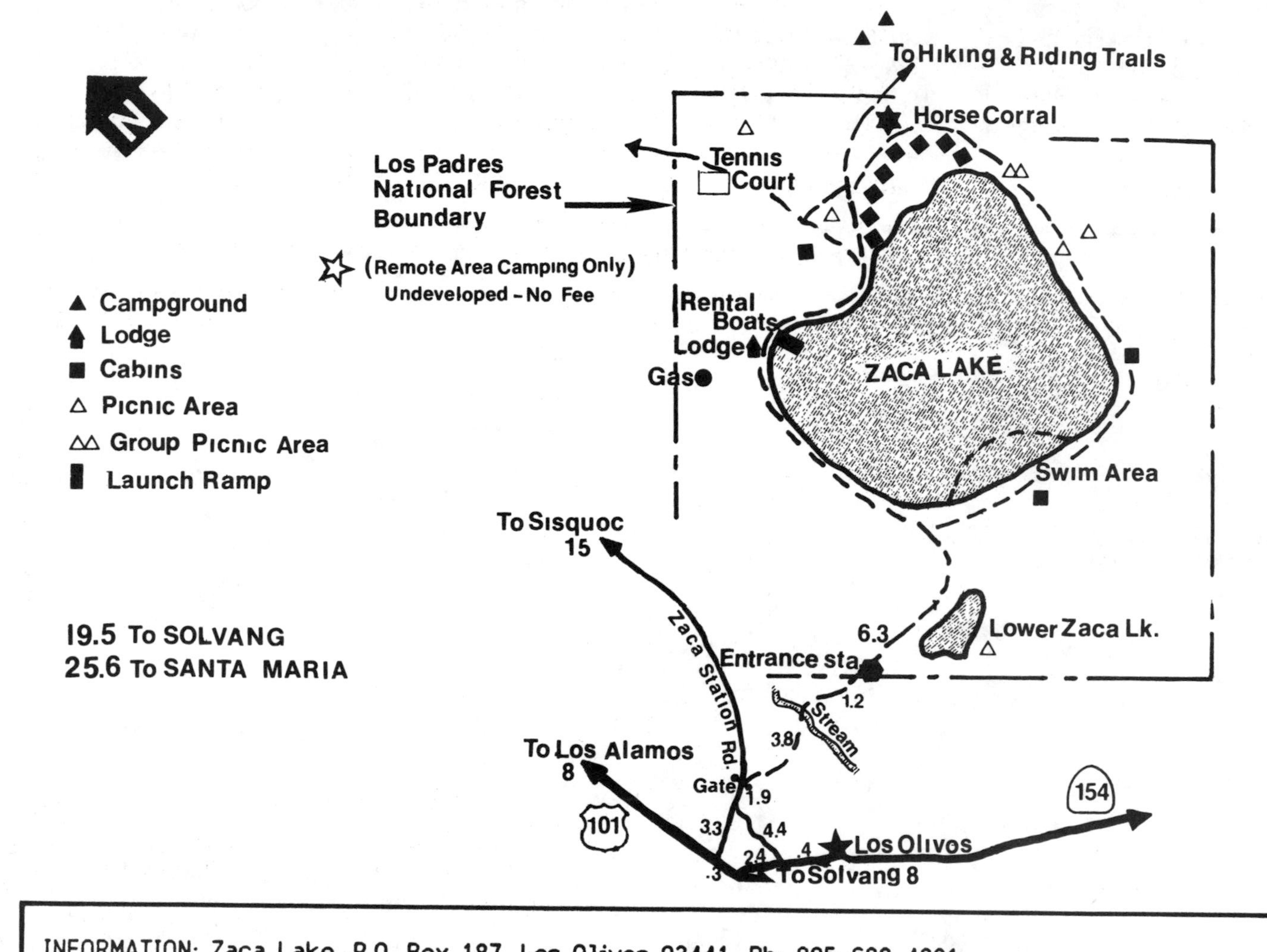

INFORMATION: Zaca Lake, P.O. Box 187, Los Olivos 93441, Ph: 805-688-4891

CAMPING	BOATING	RECREATION	OTHER
Lodge, Cabins, Housekeeping Houses Camping: $10 Los Padres National Forest Remote Camping 100 Sites No Open Fires	Row, Pedal, Canoe, Sail & Sailboards No Motors Unimproved Launch Fee: $4 Boat Rentals	Fishing: Catfish, Bluegill, Bass & Sunfish Hiking & Riding Trails Backpacking Horse Rentals Swimming Picnicking Tennis Mineral Baths Massages	Restaurant Snack Bar Cocktail Lounge Game Room Gas

LAKE CACHUMA

Lake Cachuma is nestled at an elevation of 650 feet amid the oak-shaded hills of the Santa Ynez Valley. This is one of the most complete recreation Parks in the State providing an abundance of modern camping, marine, recreation and other support facilities. In addition to the campgrounds at the Lake, the Cachuma Recreation Area includes the San Marcos Camp which will accommodate large groups to 4,000 people with complete facilities. This 3,200 acre Lake is open to most boating. Waterskiing, kayaks, rafts and canoes are not allowed. Fishing can be excellent. There are hiking, nature and riding trails. Park naturalists conduct a variety of programs. Gibraltar Reservoir is open for trout fishing on a limited permit basis through the City of Santa Barbara.

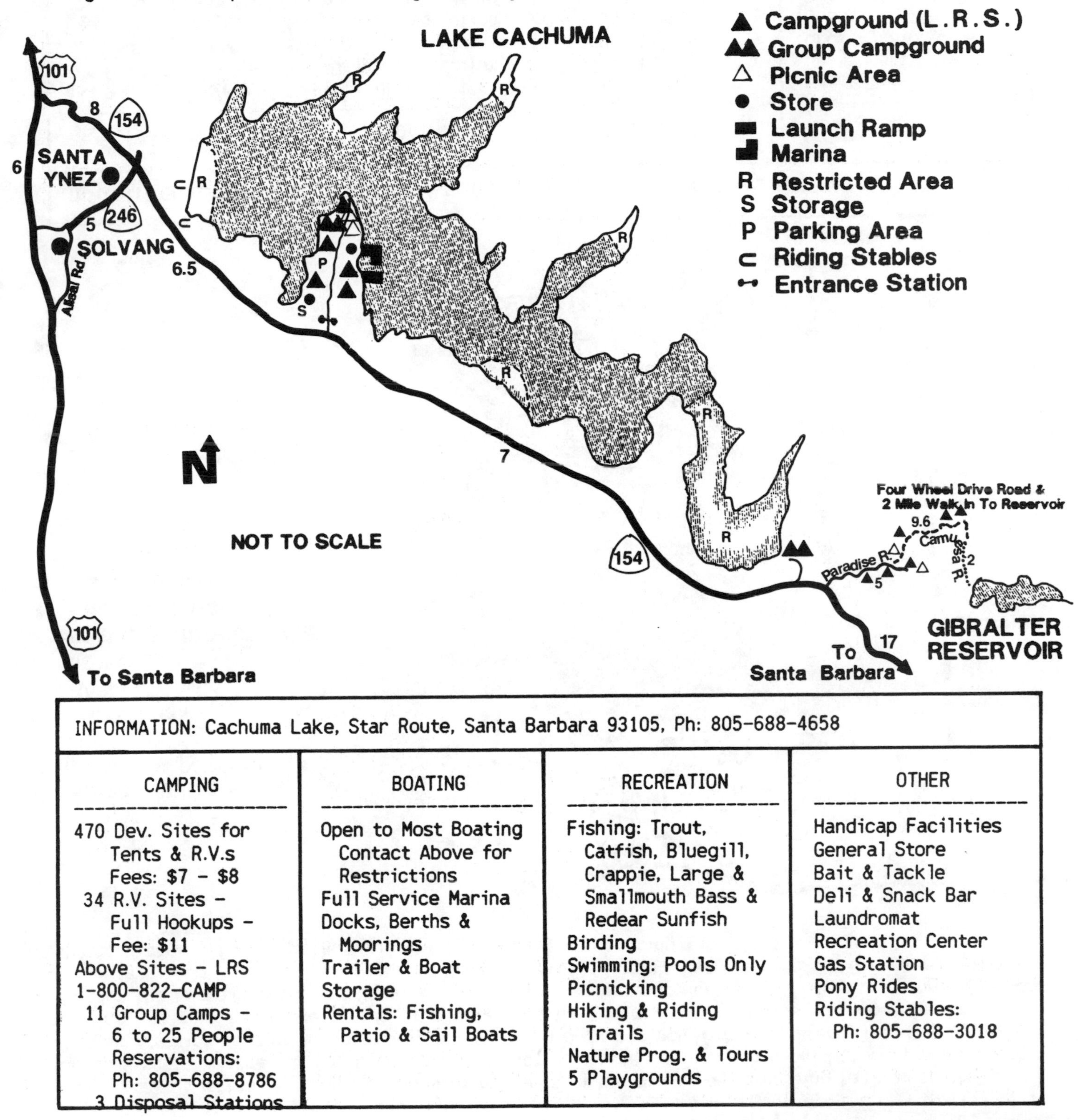

INFORMATION: Cachuma Lake, Star Route, Santa Barbara 93105, Ph: 805-688-4658

CAMPING	BOATING	RECREATION	OTHER
470 Dev. Sites for Tents & R.V.s Fees: $7 - $8 34 R.V. Sites - Full Hookups - Fee: $11 Above Sites - LRS 1-800-822-CAMP 11 Group Camps - 6 to 25 People Reservations: Ph: 805-688-8786 3 Disposal Stations	Open to Most Boating Contact Above for Restrictions Full Service Marina Docks, Berths & Moorings Trailer & Boat Storage Rentals: Fishing, Patio & Sail Boats	Fishing: Trout, Catfish, Bluegill, Crappie, Large & Smallmouth Bass & Redear Sunfish Birding Swimming: Pools Only Picnicking Hiking & Riding Trails Nature Prog. & Tours 5 Playgrounds	Handicap Facilities General Store Bait & Tackle Deli & Snack Bar Laundromat Recreation Center Gas Station Pony Rides Riding Stables: Ph: 805-688-3018

LAKE CASITAS

Lake Casitas is at an elevation of 600 feet in the oak-covered rolling hills west of Ojai. This 2,700 surface acre Lake is under the jurisdiction of the Casitas Municipal Water District which maintains a strict boating and swimming policy of no body contact with the water. The 32 miles of shoreline has many restricted areas, so please note them on the map. Casitas is famous for big fish and holds the State Records for Bass at 21 pounds, 3 ounces, and Redear Sunfish at 3 pounds, 7 ounces. You can fish from boat, bank or pier and perhaps catch a World's Record. The 6,200 acre tree-shaded recreation area offers excellent picnicking, camping and boating facilities.

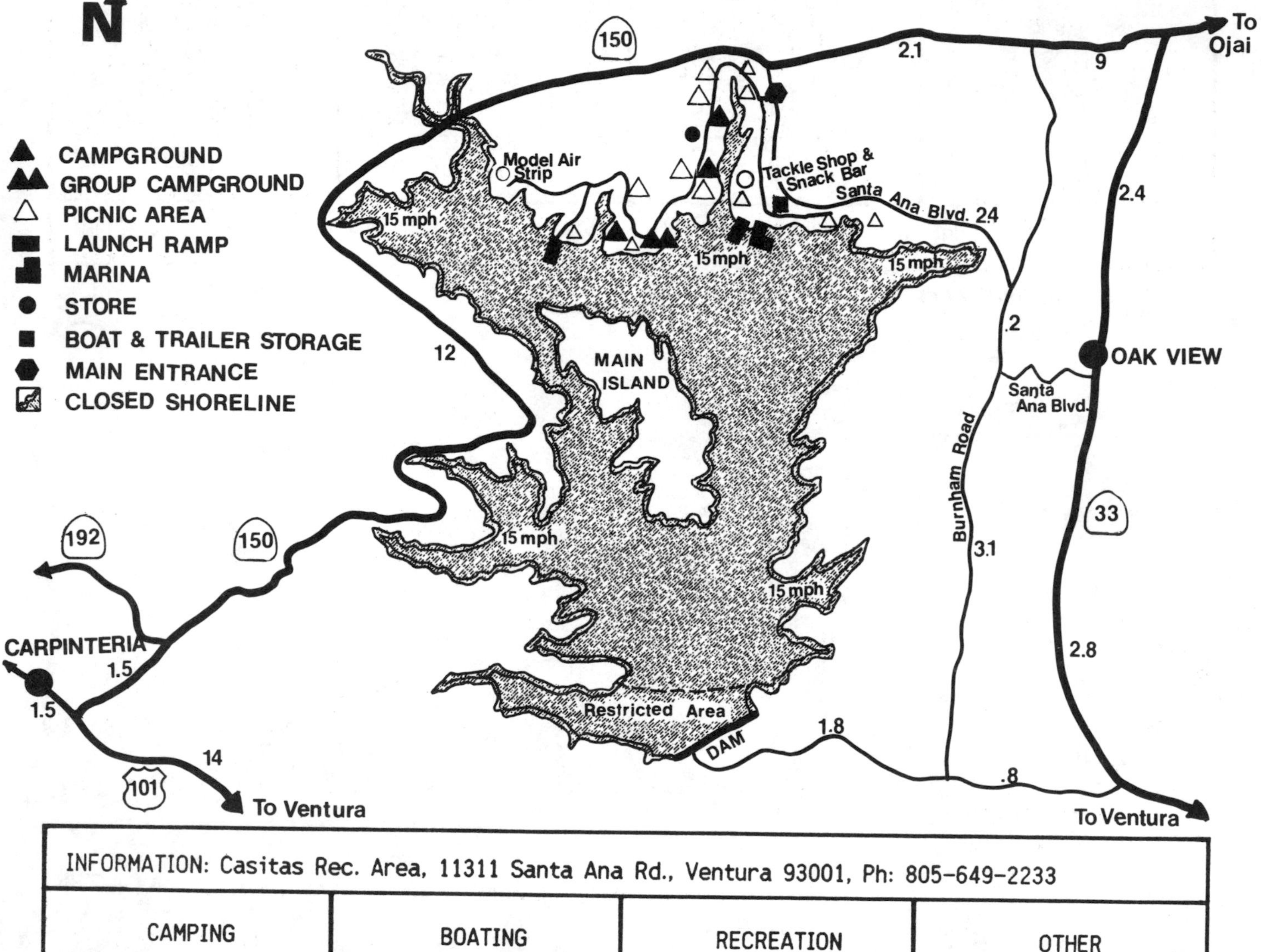

INFORMATION: Casitas Rec. Area, 11311 Santa Ana Rd., Ventura 93001, Ph: 805-649-2233

CAMPING	BOATING	RECREATION	OTHER
454 Plus Dev. Sites - Tents & R.V.s Plus Overflow Fees: $7 per Night $7 per Night for Extra Vehicle; $1 per Day for Pet Disposal Stations Reservations: Groups Only Handicap Facilities	Power, Row, Sail Only - 11 ft. Min. to 24 ft. Max. - Strict Regulations Speed Limit - 40 MPH Boat Permit: $3 a Day Full Service Marina Launch Ramps Rentals: Fishing & Row Boats, Pontoons Docks, Moorings, Berths, Gas	Fishing: Trout, Bluegill, Largemouth & Florida Bass, Redear Sunfish, Perch & Crappie No Swimming Picnicking Hiking Playgrounds Model Airplane Strip	Snack Bar Restaurant Grocery Store Showers - 25 cents Bait & Tackle Ph: 805-649-2043 Trailer Rentals: Ph: 805-649-1202 Trailer & Boat Storage

LAKE EVANS AND LAKE WEBB

BUENA VISTA AQUATIC RECREATION AREA

Buena Vista Recreation Area is at an elevation of 293.5 feet in the semi-arid south San Joaquin Valley. This is Kern County's newest recreation area consisting of 1,586 acres and two Lakes with complete modern facilities for camping, picnicking, swimming and boating. Lake Evans has a surface area of 86 acres and Lake Webb has 873 acres. Both Lakes are stocked with warm water fish continually and trophy trout in the winter months at Lake Evans. All boating is allowed in both Lakes, but Lake Evans is restricted to 5 MPH speed limit. Waterskiing is permitted at Lake Webb in a counterclockwise pattern. There is a no-ski area for sailboats and power boats without skiers.

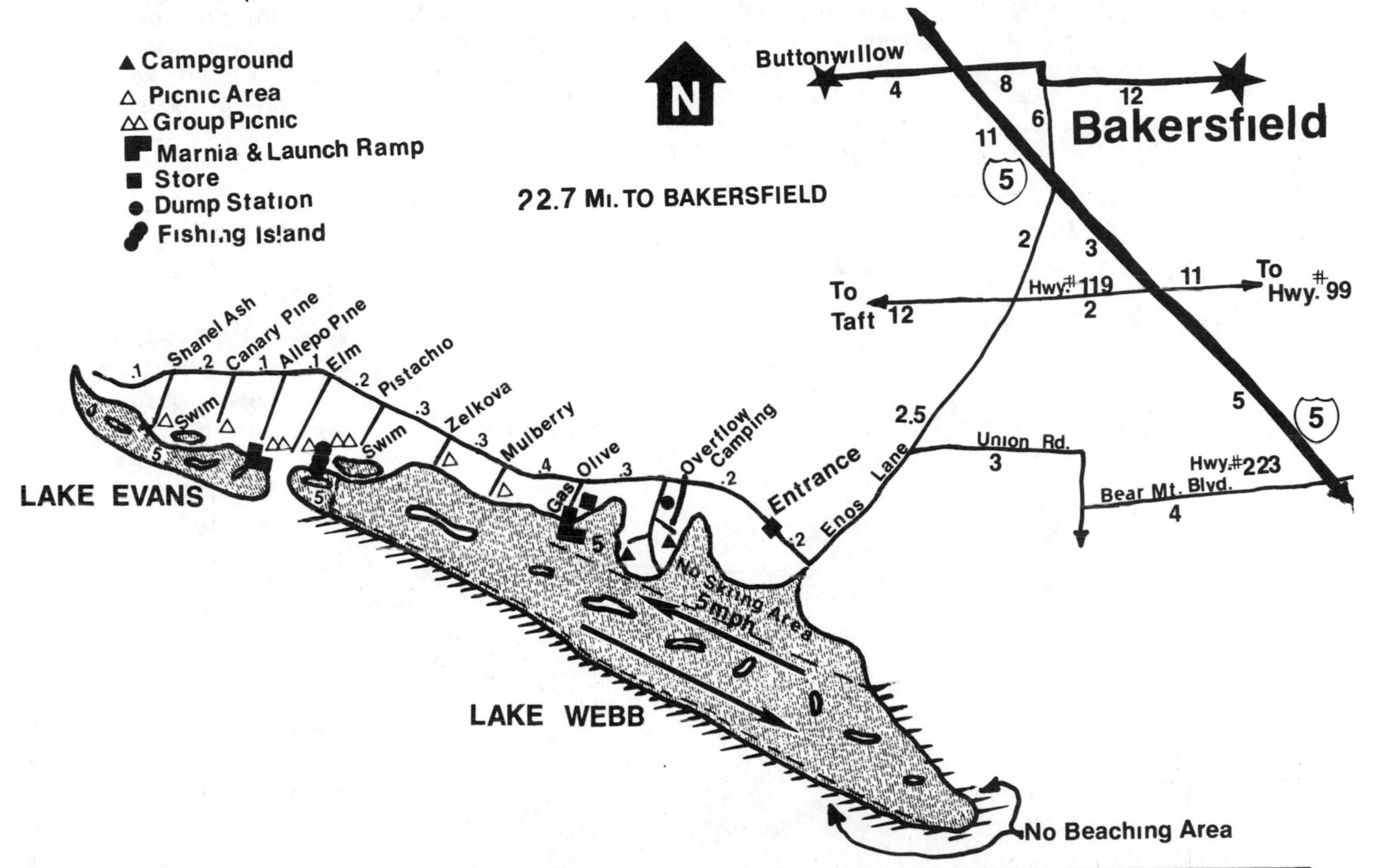

INFORMATION: Kern Co. Parks, 1110 Golden State, Bakersfield 93301, Ph: 805-861-2345			
CAMPING	BOATING	RECREATION	OTHER
112 Dev. Sites for Tents & R.V.s Fees: $10 No Hookup $12 Full Hook-up Plus Overflow Area Fee: $6 Pets - $2 a Day No Reservations Buena Vista Recreation Area Ph: 805-763-1526	Power, Row, Canoe, Sail, Windsurf, Jet Ski & Inflatable Meet Requirements Speed Limits: 5 MPH-Lake Evans 45 MPH-Lake Webb Launch Ramps Waterski Beaches Rentals: Fishing & Paddle Boats Docks, Moorings, Gas	Fishing: Trout in Winter, Catfish, Bluegill, Crappie, Largemouth & Striped Bass Swimming: Lagoons Only Picnicking Deep Pit Barbecues Playgrounds	Snack Bar Grocery Store Beer & Wine Bait & Tackle Laundromat Gas Station Propane Waterski & Equipment Rental Full Facilities - 14 Miles at Taft

PYRAMID LAKE

Pyramid Lake is at an elevation of 2,606 feet in the Angeles National Forest in Northwestern Los Angeles County. This popular Lake has a surface area of 1,297 acres. Most of its 21 miles of rugged shoreline is accessible only by boat. There are boat-in picnic sites and restrooms scattered around the Lake. Chumash Island is a favorite spot with its picnic site and swim beach. While there is a good trout and warm water fishery, Pyramid is known as one of Southern California's prime striped bass waters. There are good marine and campground facilities under concession from the U. S. Forest Service. Quail Lake, the beginning of the Southern portion of the California Aqueduct Bikeway, offers no facilities. The angler, however, may fish for stripers from the bank.

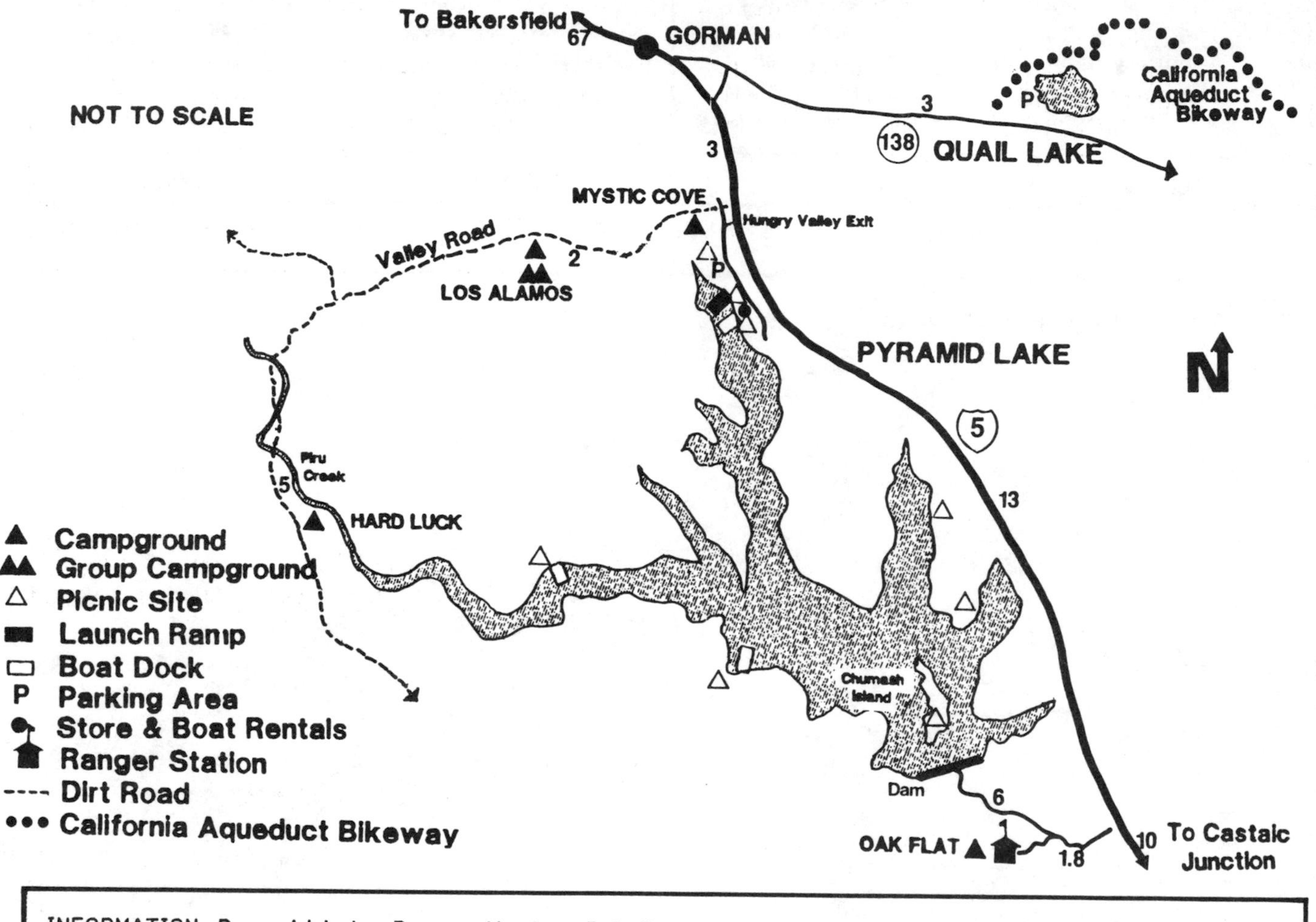

INFORMATION: Pyramid Lake Resort Marina, P.O. Box 102, Gorman 93243, Ph: 805-257-3330

CAMPING	BOATING	RECREATION	OTHER
Los Alamos: 93 Dev. Sites Tents & R.V.s Fee: $8 - $10 Group Sites for 6 to 75 People Fee: $50 - $130 Hard Luck: 26 Dev. Sites Tents & R.V.s Fee: $6 - $8 Reservations: Ph: 805-257-3532	Open to All Boating, Waterskiing & Windsurfing Speed Limit 35 MPH Full Service Marina Docks & Gas Launch Ramp Boat Rentals: Fishing, Ski & Recreational Boats	Fishing: Rainbow Trout, Channel Catfish, Striped & Largemouth Bass, Bluegill, Crappie & Sunfish Swimming Beaches Picnicking Boat-In Picnic Sites	Snack Bar Bait & Tackle Mystic Cove Trailer Park 38 R.V. Sites Full Hookups Hot Showers Ph: 805-248-6394

CASTAIC LAKE

Castaic Lake and the Afterbay Lagoon, at an elevation of 1,500 feet, are a part of the California State Water Project and is operated by Los Angeles County. The Castaic Lake facility is Los Angeles County's largest recreation area with 9,000 acres. There are two separate Lakes. The Main Reservoir has a surface area of 2,500 acres and the Afterbay Lagoon has 180 surface acres. The Main Reservoir's east arm is open to slower boating, 20 MPH speed limit, while the west arm is for waterskiing and fast boating. The Lagoon is open to non-power boating and swimming daily from mid-June through September and weekends and holidays from October through May. Boat-in camping areas are being developed. Future plans will include rustic as well as R. V. camping. Fishing at the Main Reservoir is from sunrise to sunset, but the Lagoon offers 24-hour fishing on the shoreline of the east side of the Lake.

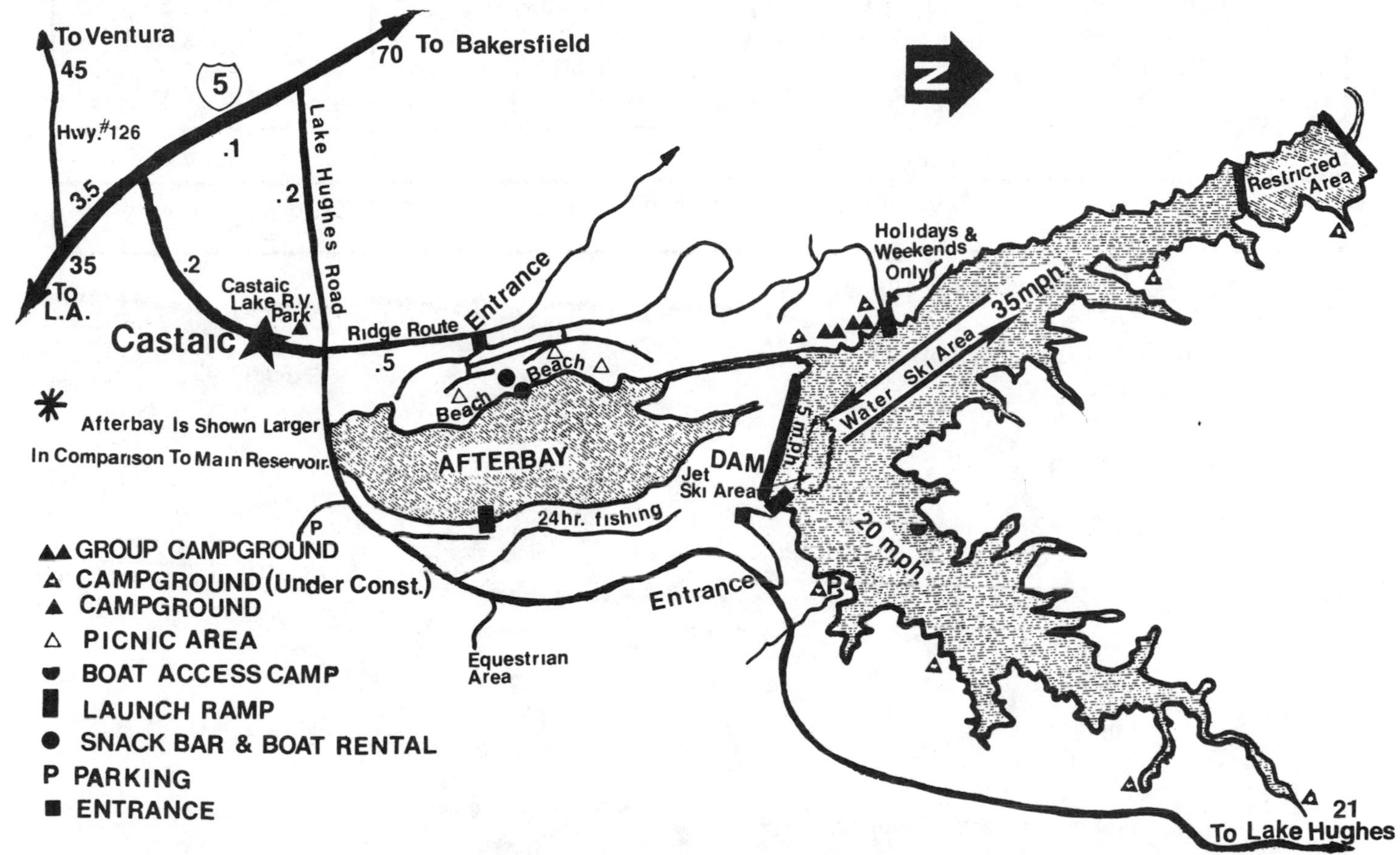

INFORMATION: Castaic Lake, P.O. Box 397, Castaic 91310, Ph: 805-257-4050

CAMPING	BOATING	RECREATION	OTHER
Main Reservoir In Development Stages Castaic Lake R.V. Park Ph: 805-257-3340 Group Camping - Organized Groups Only to 200 Plus People - 3 Nights Maximum $12.50 - $100	Main Reservoir: All Boating Allowed 35 MPH Speed Limit Launch Ramps, Docks Rentals: Fishing Boats & Windsurfers Afterbay: Non-Power Boats Launch Ramp: $2 Rentals: Sail & Row	Fishing: Trout, Catfish, Bluegill, Large & Smallmouth Bass Swimming Beaches at Afterbay Only Picnicking Backpacking	Snack Bar Bait & Tackle Full Facilities at Castaic Boaters Should Arrive Early as Launch is Closed After 100 Boats

LAKE PIRU

Lake Piru is at an elevation of 1,055 feet in the Los Padres National Forest near Metropolitan Los Angeles. It is owned and operated by the United Water Conservation District. The surface area of the Lake ranges from a maximum of 1,200 acres to a minimum of 750 acres. The water is deep and clear. This is a proven fishing Lake with warm water species growing to large sizes. Trout are planted bi-weekly in season. A popular boating attraction is the Competition Slalom Ski Course for members only, but membership is open to the public. The campgrounds are located amid oak and olive trees above the launch ramp. The Forest Service has also opened the Blue Point Campgrounds 6 miles north of Olive Tree.

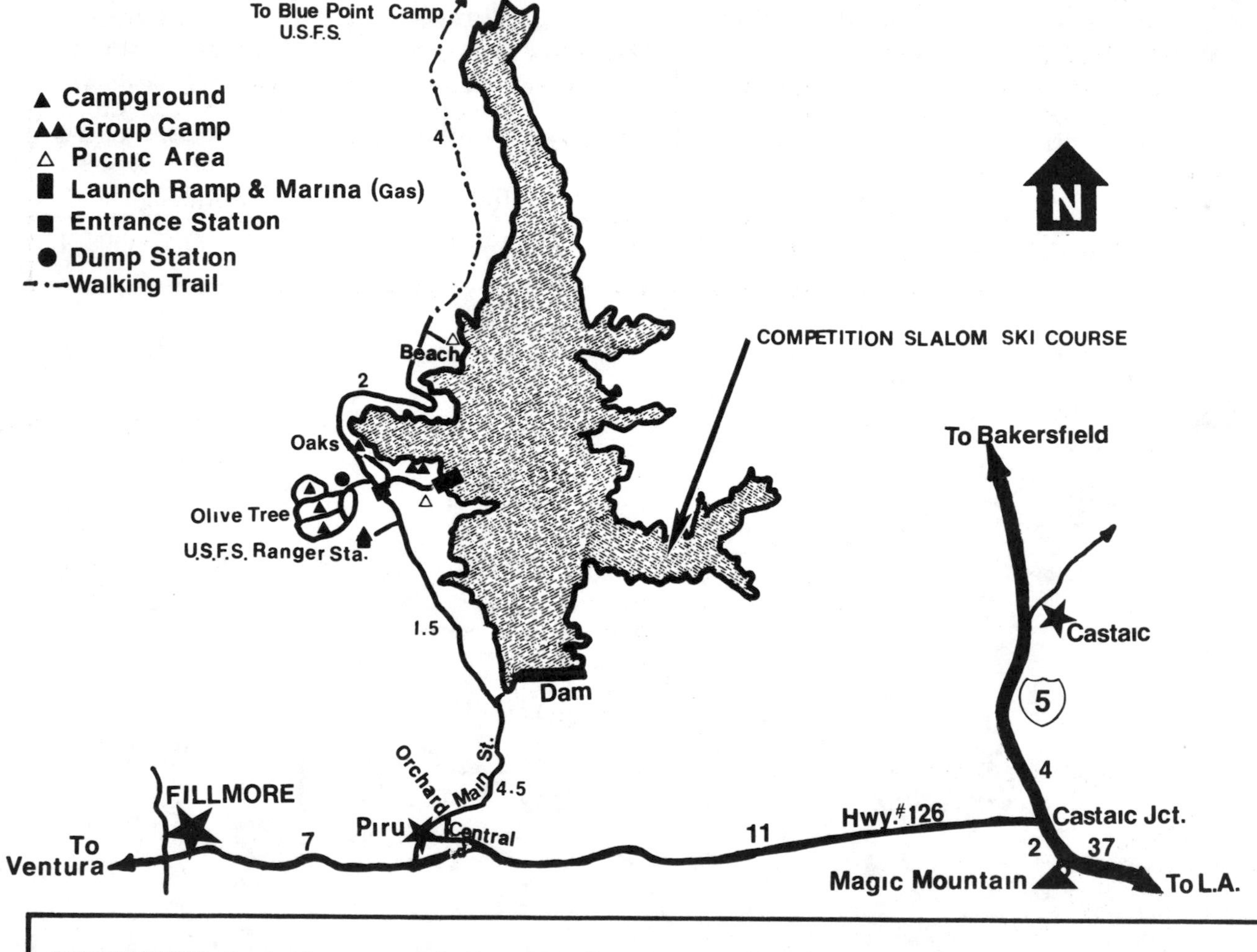

INFORMATION: Park Manager, P.O. Box 202, Piru 93040, Ph: 805-521-1500

CAMPING	BOATING	RECREATION	OTHER
187 Tent Sites Fee: $7 60 R.V. Sites Electric Hookups Fee: $10 Group Camp: 4 to 12 Sites Day Use Fee: $2.50 U.S.F.S.: 36 Dev. Sites & 6 Walk-In Sites	Power, Waterskiing, Sail & Inflatables (Must by 12' long with 3 Separate Compartments & 3 HP Minimum) No Windsurfing, Jet Skis, Canoes or Rowboats Full Service Marina 5-Lane Launch Ramp Rentals	Fishing: Rainbow & Brown Trout, Bass, Catfish, Crappie, Bluegill & Perch Swim Beach Picnicking Hiking & Riding Trails in Los Padres Nat'l. Forest Backpacking Playgrounds	Snack Bar Bait & Tackle Disposal Station Marine Supplies Dock, Fuel & Dry Storage Store & Gas in Piru Full Facilities at Castaic

LAKE HUGHES AND ELIZABETH LAKE

Elizabeth Lake and Lake Hughes are at an elevation of 3,300 feet in the Angeles National Forest north of Los Angeles. These small Lakes are within 5 miles of each other and are separated by an even smaller private membership Lake. Lake Hughes has a surface area of 35 acres. Access is through a resort which is open to the public year around and offers camping, fishing and all boating. The western half of Elizabeth Lake is owned and operated by the U. S. Forest Service which maintains picnic sites and allows swimming at your own risk in the Lake. There are warm water fisheries at both Lakes and trout in Elizabeth Lake.

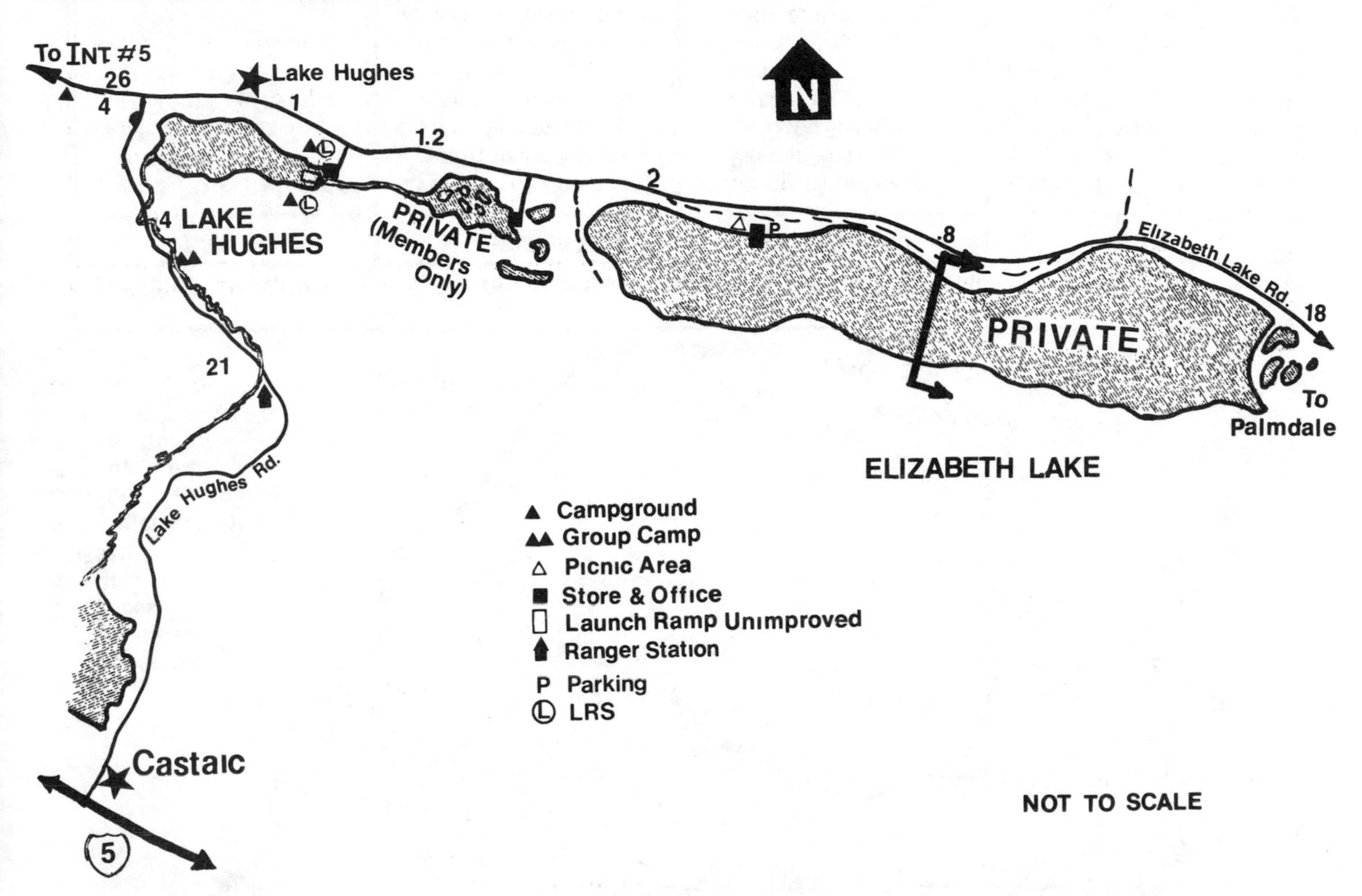

INFORMATION: Saugus R.D., 30800 Bouquet Canyon Rd., Saugus 91350, Ph: 805-252-9710

CAMPING	BOATING	RECREATION	OTHER
Hughes Lakeshore Park Ph: 805-724-1845 Water & Electric Hookups Hot Showers Fee: $10 Weekly & Monthly Rates	Open to Sail & Power Boating 5 MPH Speed Limit 10 HP Motors Max. Launch Ramps Rentals: Row & Paddle Boats at Lake Hughes	Fishing: Catfish, Bass, Bluegill & Crappie Trout at Lake Elizabeth-Winter Picnicking Hiking Hunting: Deer & Upland Game	Snack Bar Arcade Pool Tables Horseshoes General Store Restaurant Playground

APOLLO PARK, FRAZIER PARK AND LITTLE ROCK RESERVOIR

Little Rock Reservoir, at 3,400 feet elevation, is in the Angeles National Forest. This 150 surface acre Lake is usually very low by September. Fishing is often good for rainbow and brown trout, and it is stocked every other week in season. Apollo County Park is a part of the Los Angeles County Regional Park System. There are three Lakes, named after the three astronauts of the Apollo flight, providing a recycled water trout fishery. Frazier Lake is a very small fishing Lake for trout, bass and catfish.

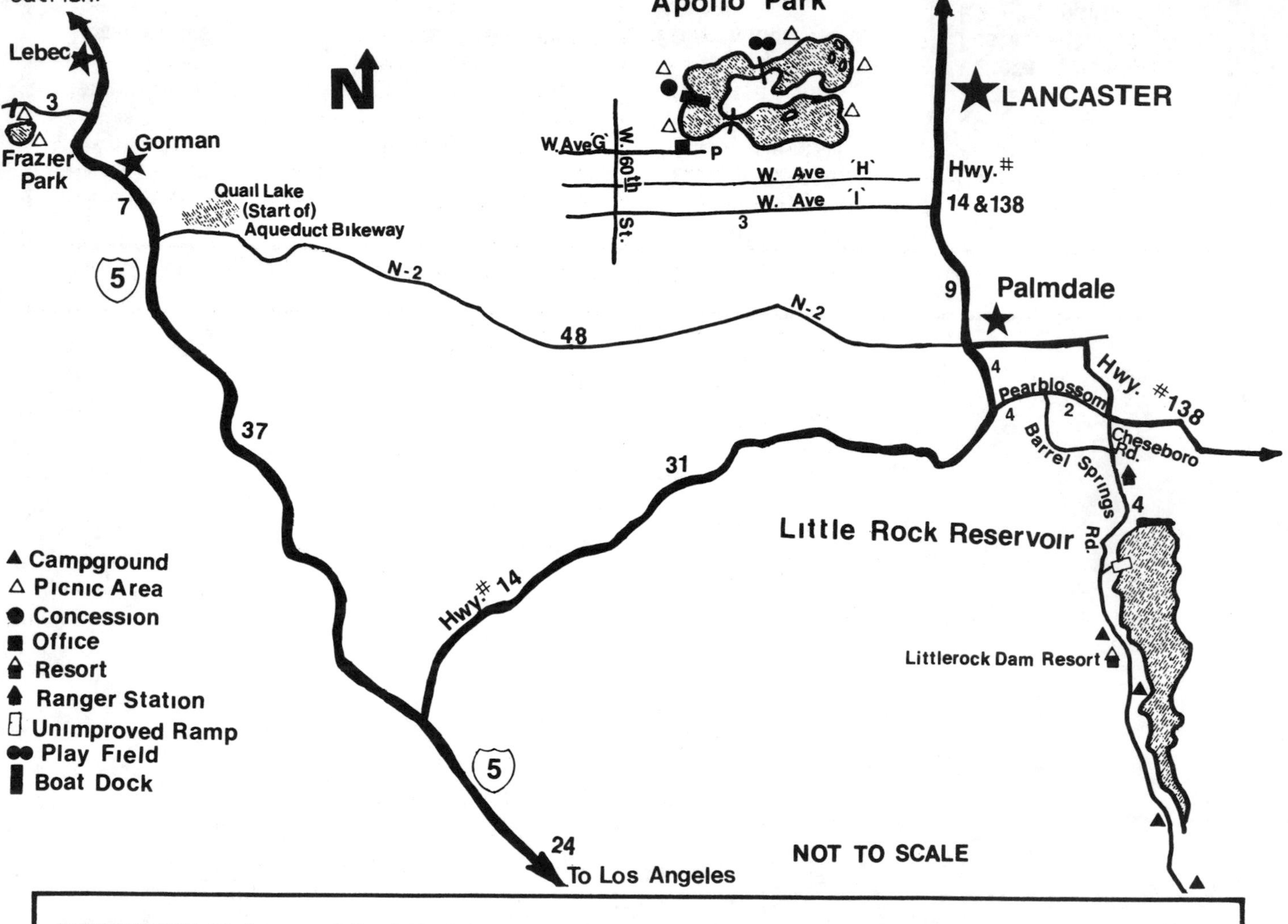

INFORMATION: Valyermo R.D., 34146 Longview Rd., Pearblossom 93553, Ph: 805-944-2187

CAMPING	BOATING	RECREATION	OTHER
Little Rock Reservoir U.S.F.S. 37 Dev. Sites for Tents & R.V.s Fee: $3	Little Rock Reservoir Fishing Boats Only Speed Limit: 5 MPH Launch Area - No Ramp Rentals at Resort: Rowboats & Motors Apollo Park: No Boating Frazier Park: No Boating	Fishing: Rainbow, German Brown, Kamloop Trout, Catfish Picnicking Hiking Rockhounding Hunting: Deer Children's Play Area Apollo Capsule	Little Rock Dam Resort 32700 Cheseboro Rd. Palmdale 93550 Ph: 805-944-1923 Grocery Store Cafe, Bait & Tackle Apollo County Park West Ave. G Lancaster 93534 Ph: 805-945-8290

MOJAVE NARROWS PARK, JACKSON LAKE AND GLEN HELEN PARK

Mojave Narrows Regional Park is at an elevation of 2,700 feet in the high desert. Jackson Lake, at an elevation of 6,500 feet, is in the Big Pines Recreation Area. Glen Helen Regional Park is at 1,000 feet elevation just 15 minutes from downtown San Bernardino. These Lakes offer a wealth of recreational opportunities. Boating is limited, but the angler will find winter trout, bass and channel catfish at Glen Helen and Mojave Narrows. Spring, summer and fall trout will be found at Jackson Lake. Excellent campgrounds, picnic areas, hiking, nature and riding trails await the visitor.

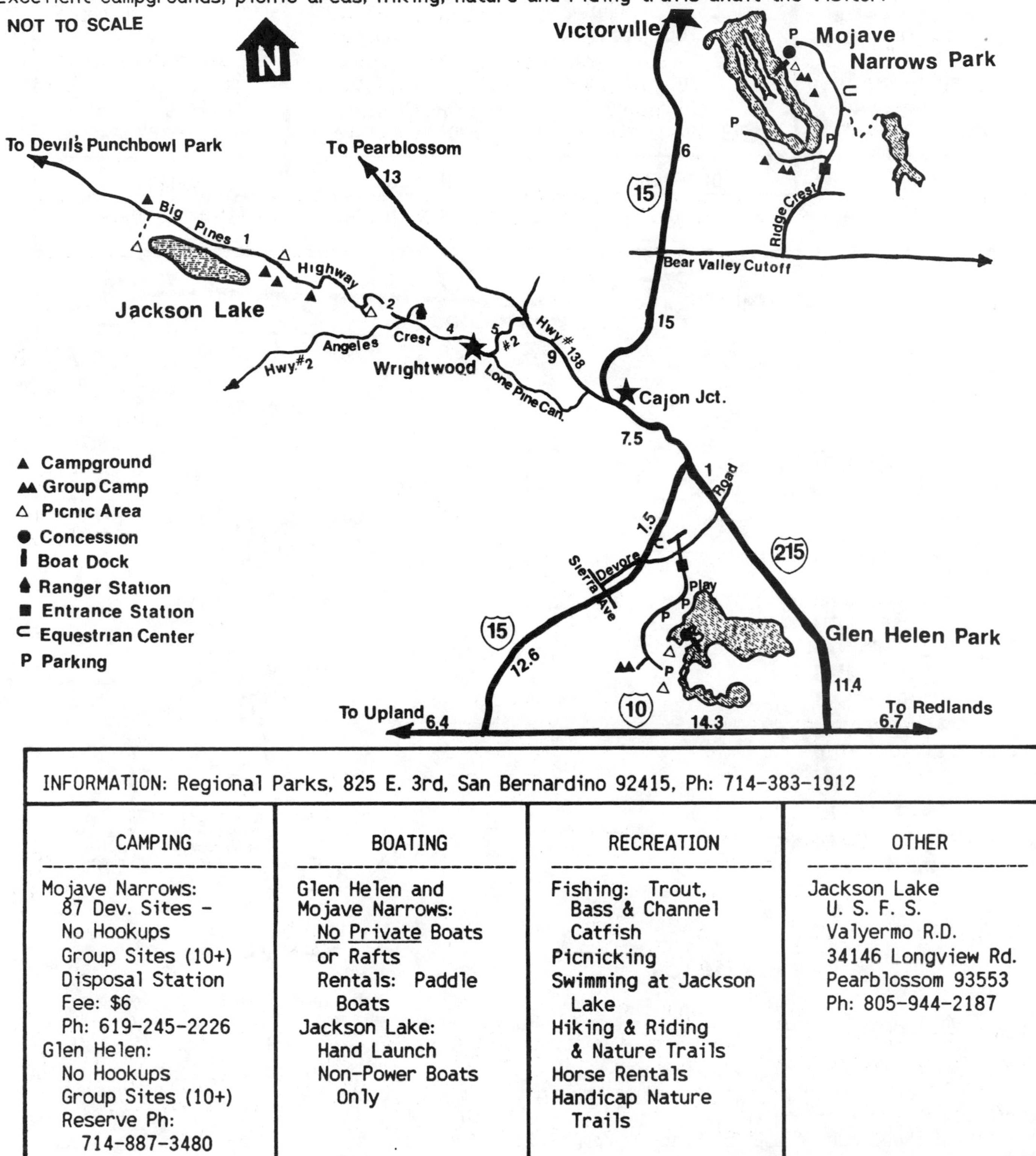

INFORMATION: Regional Parks, 825 E. 3rd, San Bernardino 92415, Ph: 714-383-1912

CAMPING	BOATING	RECREATION	OTHER
Mojave Narrows: 87 Dev. Sites - No Hookups Group Sites (10+) Disposal Station Fee: $6 Ph: 619-245-2226 Glen Helen: No Hookups Group Sites (10+) Reserve Ph: 714-887-3480	Glen Helen and Mojave Narrows: No Private Boats or Rafts Rentals: Paddle Boats Jackson Lake: Hand Launch Non-Power Boats Only	Fishing: Trout, Bass & Channel Catfish Picnicking Swimming at Jackson Lake Hiking & Riding & Nature Trails Horse Rentals Handicap Nature Trails	Jackson Lake U. S. F. S. Valyermo R.D. 34146 Longview Rd. Pearblossom 93553 Ph: 805-944-2187

Crystal Lake is at an elevation of 5,700 feet in the Angeles National Forest. Located in the Canyon near the San Gabriel Wilderness Area, this popular facility provides an abundance of recreational facilities and opportunities. This small 7 acre Lake (Map is Not to Scale), offers good fishing and limited small craft boating. Numerous trails invite the hiker and backpacker. The San Gabriel River's North, East and West Forks lures the dedicated angler. While hunting is popular in the San Gabriel Canyon, there are shooting restricted areas so check with the Ranger Station before scheduling your hunt. The San Dimas and San Gabriel Reservoirs are open to bank fishing only, but there are no facilities or boating.

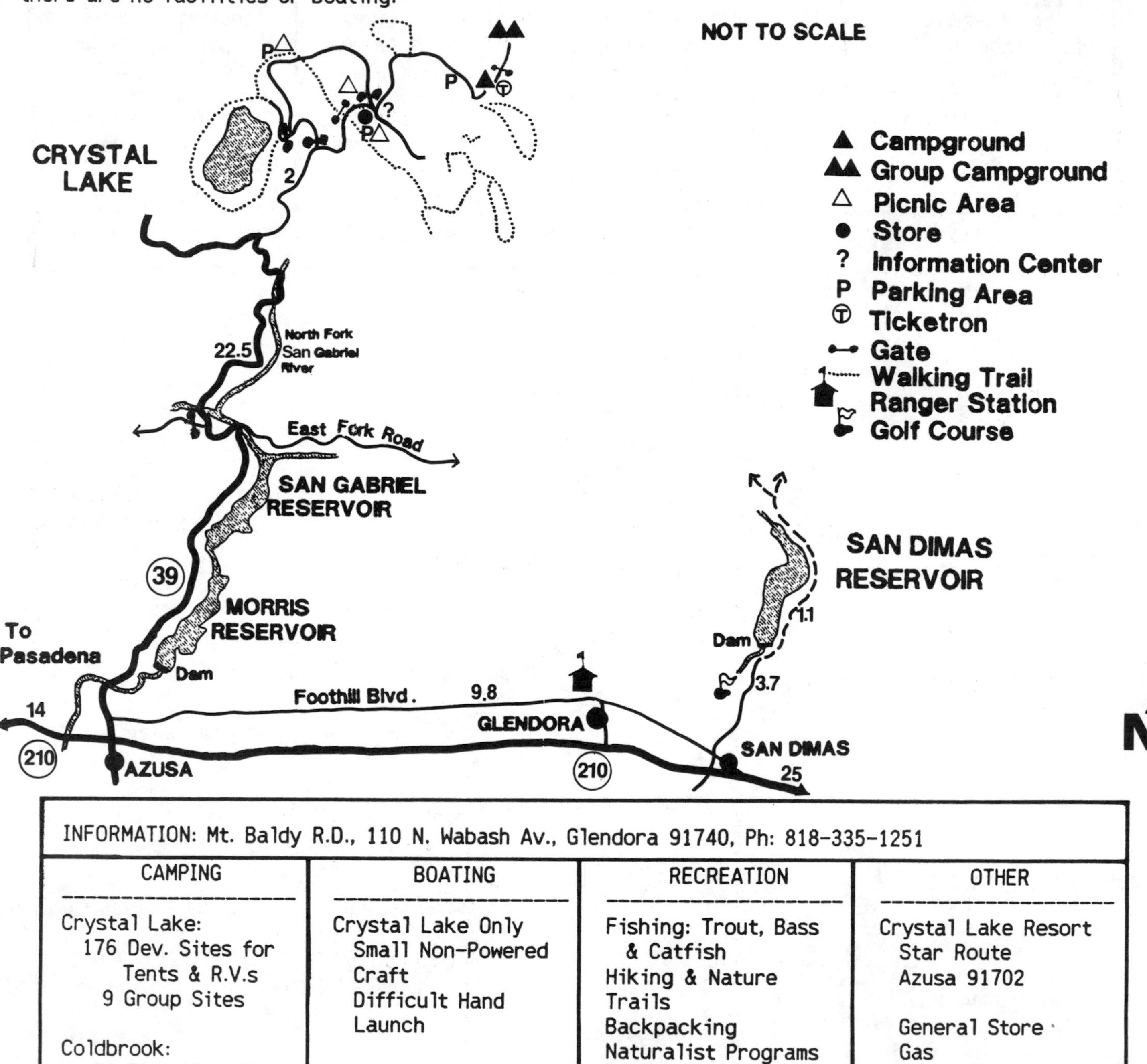

INFORMATION: Mt. Baldy R.D., 110 N. Wabash Av., Glendora 91740, Ph: 818-335-1251

CAMPING	BOATING	RECREATION	OTHER
Crystal Lake: 176 Dev. Sites for Tents & R.V.s 9 Group Sites Coldbrook: 24 Dev. sites for Tents & R.V.s Ph: 818-910-1161	Crystal Lake Only Small Non-Powered Craft Difficult Hand Launch	Fishing: Trout, Bass & Catfish Hiking & Nature Trails Backpacking Naturalist Programs No Swimming Hunting: Quail, Bear & Deer Restricted Areas	Crystal Lake Resort Star Route Azusa 91702 General Store Gas Snack Bar

ALONDRA PARK AND HARBOR LAKE

Alondra Park is under the jurisdiction of Los Angeles County. Within this 84 acre urban Park is a small 8 acre fishing Lake. Boating is not allowed. There are picnic sites, a swimming area, community gardens, paddle tennis courts and a children's play area. There are also group camping areas. Harbor Lake Park is under the jurisdiction of the City of Los Angeles. There is no private boating at this small Lake, but there are canoe and sailing lessons. The angler will find largemouth bass, bluegill, perch and catfish. There are youth group campgrounds, picnic areas and a playground. Harbor Lake Park is a wildlife sanctuary where a variety of plants, birds and animals may be observed in their natural habitats.

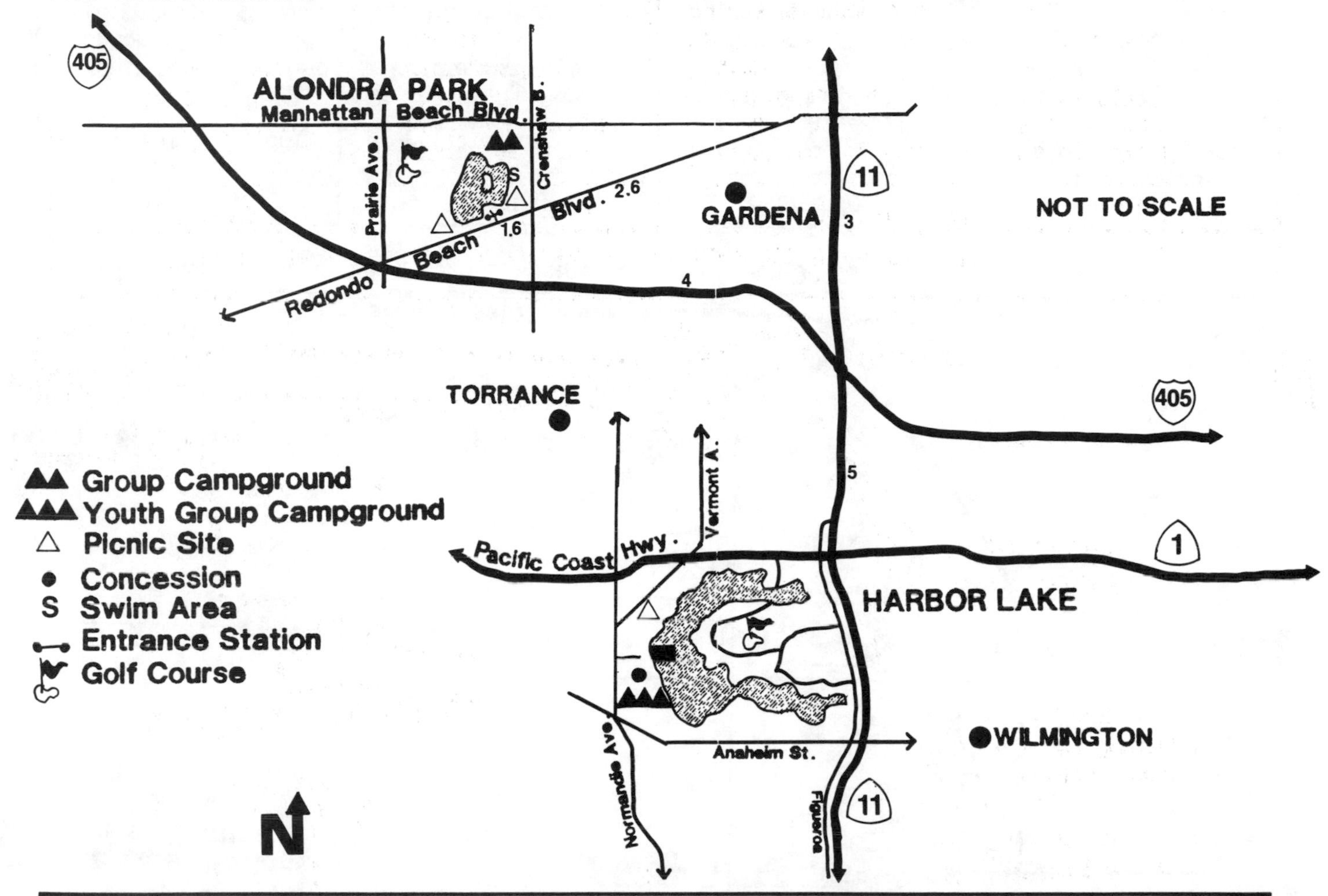

INFORMATION: Harbor Lake Park, 25820 S. Vermont, Harbor City 90710, Ph: 213-485-2844			
CAMPING	BOATING	RECREATION	OTHER
Alondra County Park 3850 W. Manhattan Beach Blvd. Lawndale 90260 Ph: 213-323-8125 Group Campsites Harbor Lake: Youth Group Camping	Alondra Park: No Boating Harbor Lake: No Private Boats Only Open to Group Boating by Request Non-Powered Boats Canoe & Sail Lessons	Fishing: Largemouth Bass, Bluegill, Catfish & Perch Picnic Areas Playgrounds Athletic Fields Birding & Nature Study Golf Course Swimming Area: Alondra Only	Full Facilities Nearby

EL DORADO EAST REGIONAL PARK

El Dorado East is a 450 acre urban Park under the administration of the City of Long Beach. Nestled amid the rolling green hills of the Park are 4 small Lakes of approximately 40 acres. Boating is limited to rentals since private boats are not allowed. Fishing from the shore for trout and warm water species is often rewarding. There are nice family group and company picnic areas. A network of paved trails awaits the bicycler and roller skater. There is a vita course along with a number of running courses for the casual jogger or serious runner. An 85 acre nature center with 2 miles of self-guided nature trails awaits the stroller or hiker. The Olympic Archery Range is the finest in Southern California. Facilities abound at this complete recreation Park.

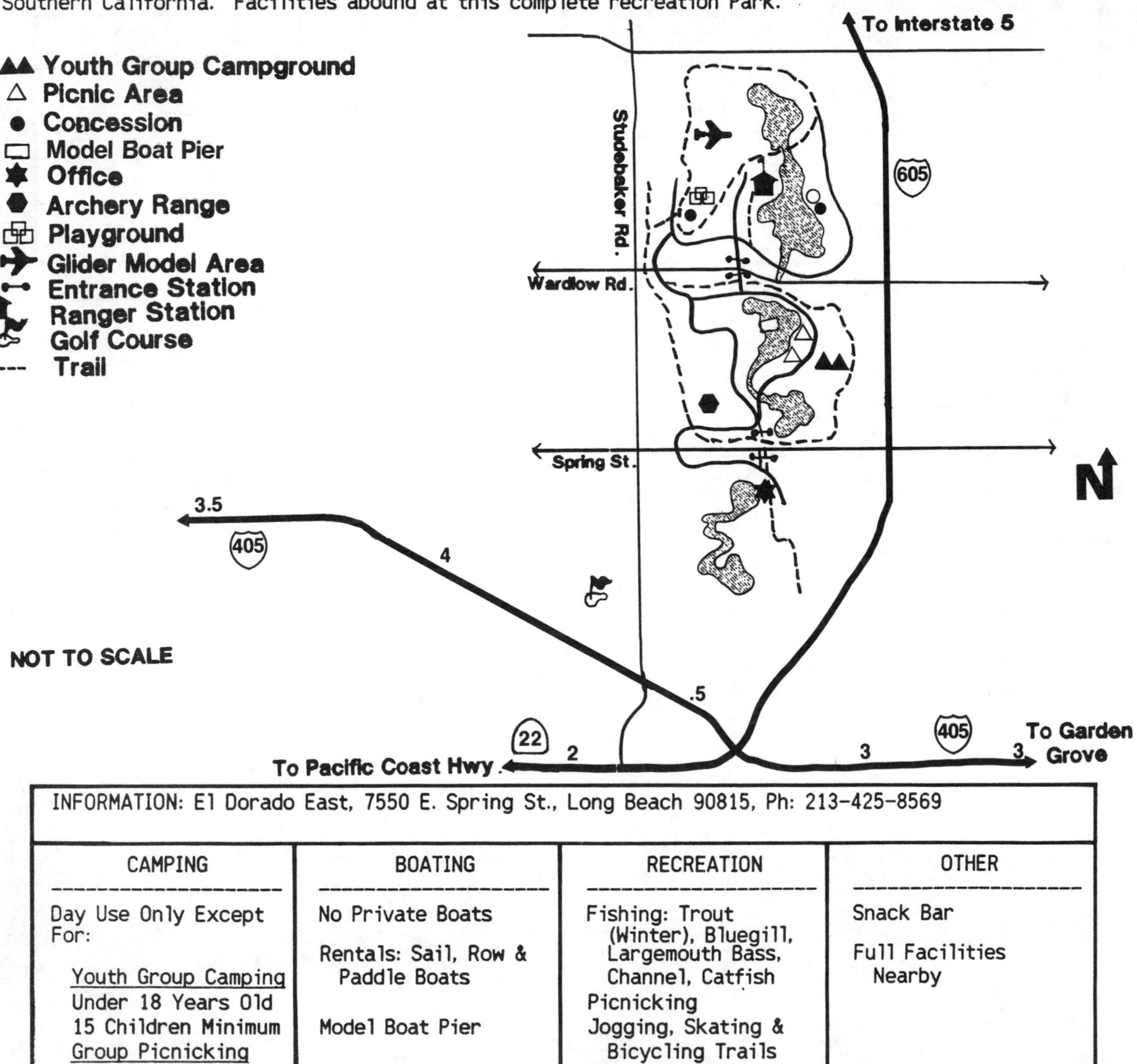

INFORMATION: El Dorado East, 7550 E. Spring St., Long Beach 90815, Ph: 213-425-8569

CAMPING	BOATING	RECREATION	OTHER
Day Use Only Except For: Youth Group Camping Under 18 Years Old 15 Children Minimum Group Picnicking to 400 - Permit Required for 25 or more Ph: 213-432-5931 Ext. 271 or 272	No Private Boats Rentals: Sail, Row & Paddle Boats Model Boat Pier	Fishing: Trout (Winter), Bluegill, Largemouth Bass, Channel, Catfish Picnicking Jogging, Skating & Bicycling Trails Vita Course, Olympic Archery Range Nature Center & Trails No Swimming	Snack Bar Full Facilities Nearby

PECK ROAD, SANTA FE AND LEGG LAKE

These three Los Angeles County Parks provide picnic areas, hiking and bicycle trails and Lakes for fishing. The 80 acre Lake at Peck Road Water Conservation Park is closed to boating and swimming. This natural area is open from Wednesday through Sunday. Santa Fe Dam Park has a 70 acre Lake open to non-powered boating. There are also swim beaches, horse rentals, a nature center and preserve. Group picnic areas may be rented. Legg Lake, actually three small Lakes totaling 76.5 acres, is within the Whittier Narrows Recreation Area. This 1,092 acre multi-purpose Park has a sporting dog area, a skeet and trap shooting range, archery range, model hobby areas, athletic field, horseback riding, golf course and lighted tennis courts. There is no private boating or swimming, but you may rent a rowboat. Group camping is available at Whittier Narrows.

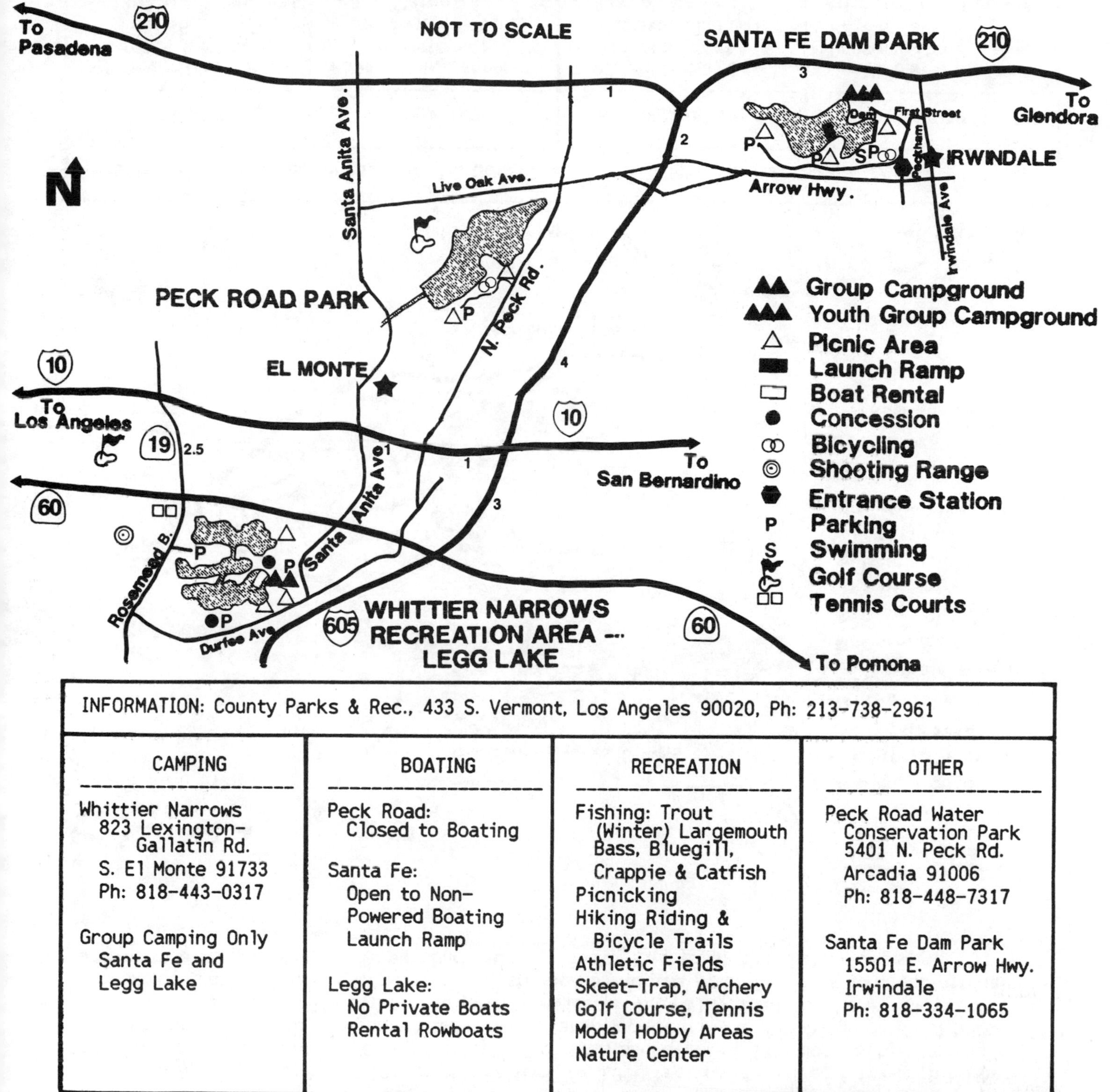

INFORMATION: County Parks & Rec., 433 S. Vermont, Los Angeles 90020, Ph: 213-738-2961

CAMPING	BOATING	RECREATION	OTHER
Whittier Narrows 823 Lexington-Gallatin Rd. S. El Monte 91733 Ph: 818-443-0317 Group Camping Only Santa Fe and Legg Lake	Peck Road: Closed to Boating Santa Fe: Open to Non-Powered Boating Launch Ramp Legg Lake: No Private Boats Rental Rowboats	Fishing: Trout (Winter) Largemouth Bass, Bluegill, Crappie & Catfish Picnicking Hiking Riding & Bicycle Trails Athletic Fields Skeet-Trap, Archery Golf Course, Tennis Model Hobby Areas Nature Center	Peck Road Water Conservation Park 5401 N. Peck Rd. Arcadia 91006 Ph: 818-448-7317 Santa Fe Dam Park 15501 E. Arrow Hwy. Irwindale Ph: 818-334-1065

SILVERWOOD LAKE

Silverwood Lake is located at an elevation of 3,350 feet on the edge of the high Mojave Desert. The Lake has a surface area of 1,000 acres and a shoreline of 13 miles. Silverwood is a complete boating Lake with designated areas for waterskiing, boating and fishing. Several brushy areas were left uncleared when filling the Lake which provides a natural habitat for fish. There are 12 miles of paved trails for the hiker and bicyclist. Nearby Mojave River Forks is an added attraction to the area with a modern 90-unit campground with full hookups in 25 of the units.

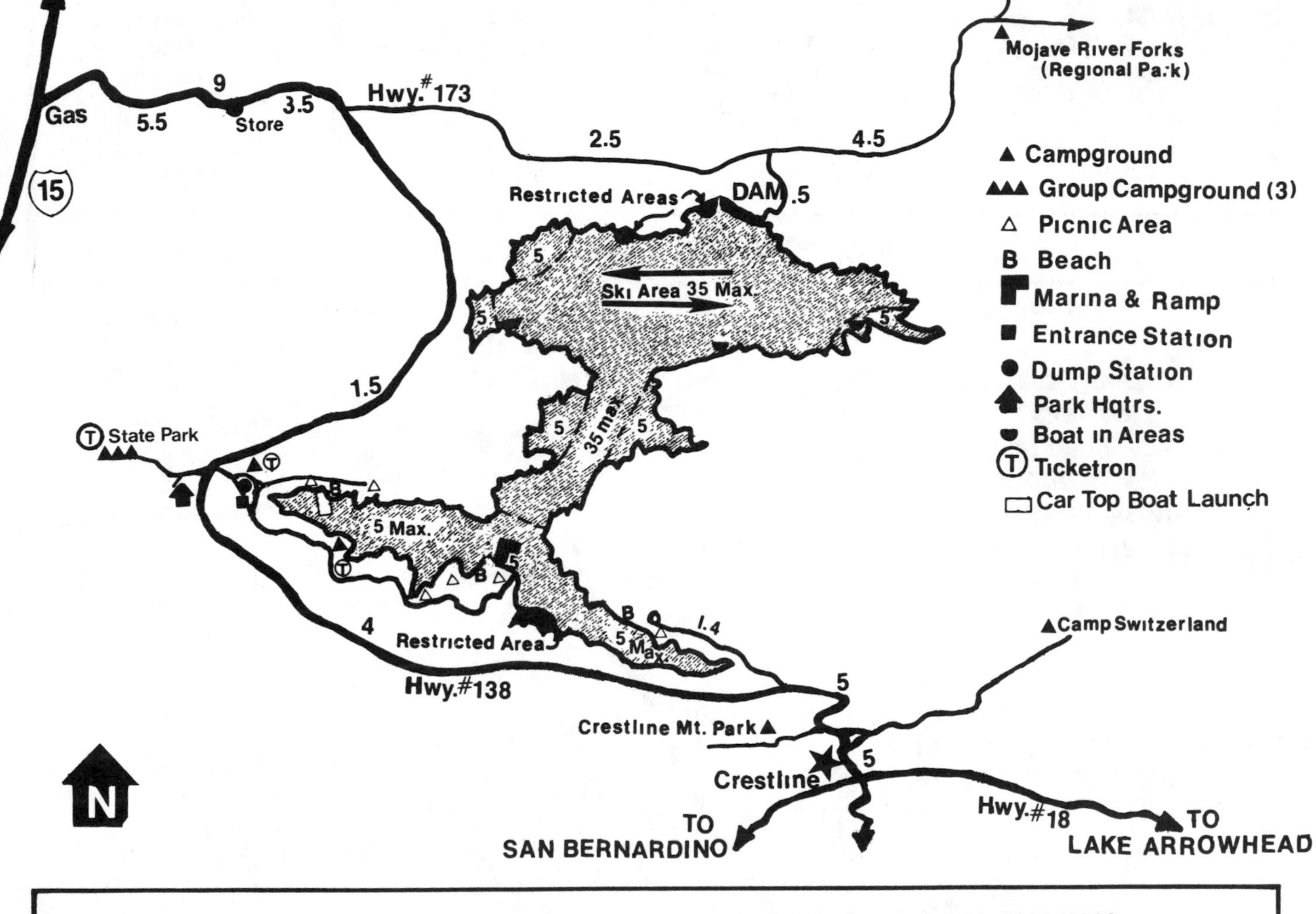

INFORMATION: State Rec. Area, Star Rt., Box 7A, Hesperia 92345, Ph: 619-389-2281/2303

CAMPING	BOATING	RECREATION	OTHER
135 Dev. Sites for Tents & R.V.s Fee: $6 3 Group Sites - 120 People Each 7 Bike-In or Hike-In Sites - Fee: 50 cents Paved Sites With Ramp for the Handicapped	Power, Row, Canoe, Sail, Waterski, Jet Ski, Windsurf & Inflatables Speed Limit - 35 MPH Launch Ramp Rentals: Fishing Boats & Pontoons Docks, Berths, Gas Hazards: High, Unpredictable Winds	Fishing: Brown & Rainbow Trout, Catfish, Bluegill, Perch, Striped & Largemouth Bass, & Silver Salmon Swimming Picnicking Hiking Campfire Program	Snack Bar Grocery Store Bait & Tackle Disposal Station Mojave River Forks P.O. Box 1005 Hesperia 92345 Ph: 619-389-2322

GREGORY, ARROWHEAD, GREEN VALLEY, ARROWBEAR AND JENKS LAKES

In the scenic San Bernardino National Forest, these Lakes are at elevations ranging from 4,520 feet at Lake Gregory to 7,000 feet at Green Valley Lake. While trout is the primary game fish in these Lakes, the angler will find catfish and other warm water species. There are many trails for hiking and riding. The San Gorgonio Wilderness is near Jenks Lake for the equestrian and backpacker. Permits are required. Lake Arrowhead is a private facility and public access is limited.

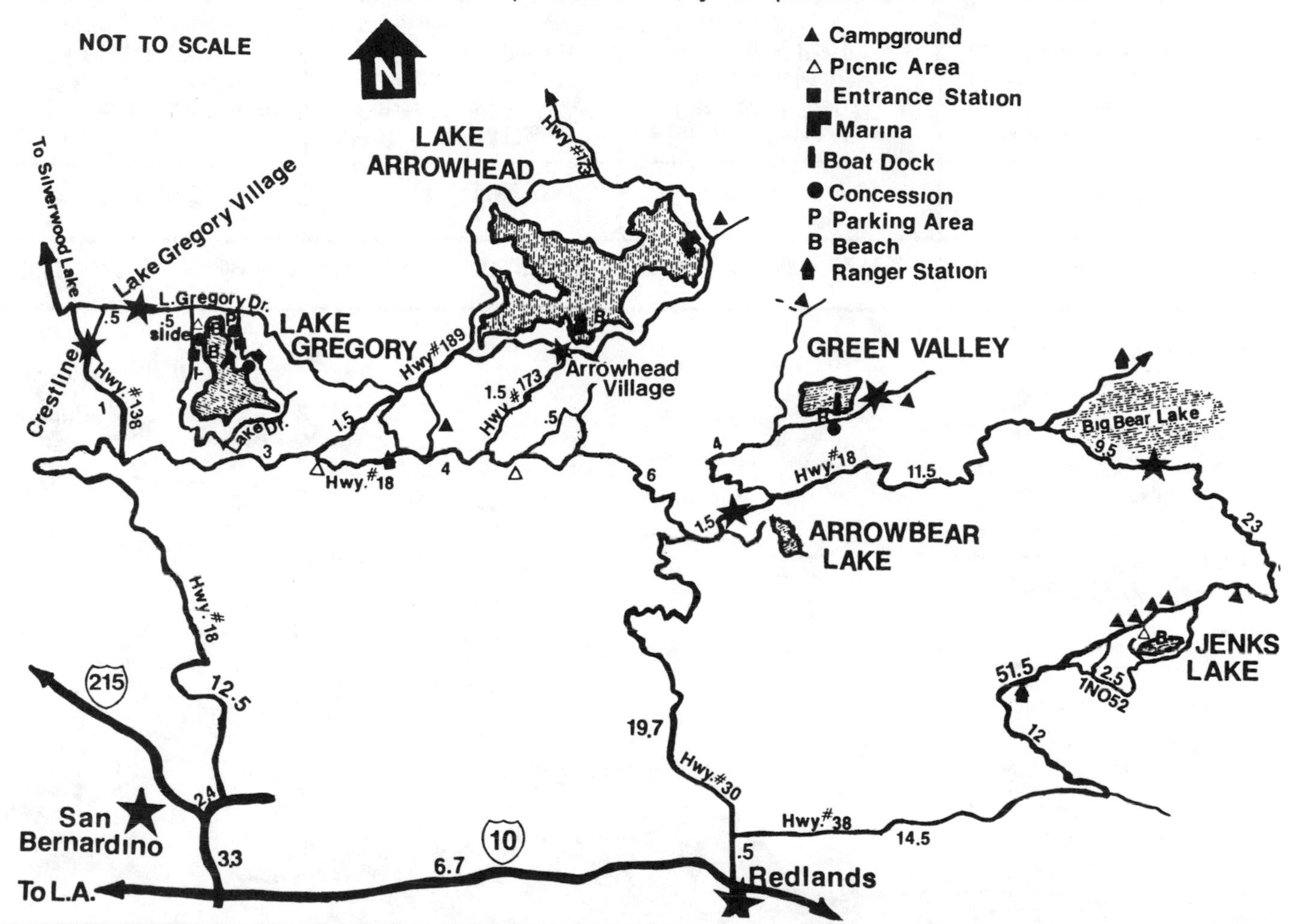

INFORMATION: Arrowhead Ranger District, Rimforest 92378, Ph: 714-337-2444			
CAMPING	**BOATING**	**RECREATION**	**OTHER**
U.S.F.S. Near Jenks Lake: San Gorgonio R.D. Rt. 1, Box 264 Mentone 92359 Ph: 714-794-1123 Lake Arrowhead & Green Valley: Arrowhead R.D. P.O. Box 7 Rimforest 92378 Ph: 714-337-2444	Gregory: Rental Fishing Boats Only Arrowhead: Rental Ski Boats, Canoes, Sail & Fishing Boats Only No Private Boats Green Valley: Non-Power Rentals Only Arrowbear: No Boats Jenks: Non-Power, No Rentals	Fishing: Trout, Bass, Bluegill, Catfish & Kokanee Salmon Picnicking Backpacking Hiking & Equestrian Trails - Horse Rentals in Area Swimming Beaches	Lake Gregory Regional Park P.O. Box 656 Crestline 92325 Ph: 714-338-2233 Resorts & Facilities at Nearby Cities as Shown on Map

BIG BEAR LAKE

Big Bear Lake is in the San Bernardino National Forest at an elevation of 6,750 feet. Originally dammed in 1884, improved by another dam in 1911, the Lake now has a surface area of over 3,000 acres and 22 miles of shoreline. This beautiful mountain Lake is owned and administered by the Big Bear Municipal Water District. Although all boating is allowed, there are size restrictions, and all boats must have a valid Lake permit. There are many campsites operated by the Forest Service as well as extensive private facilities. This is one of Southern California's most popular Lakes and mountain resorts with unlimited recreational opportunities.

. . . Continued . . .

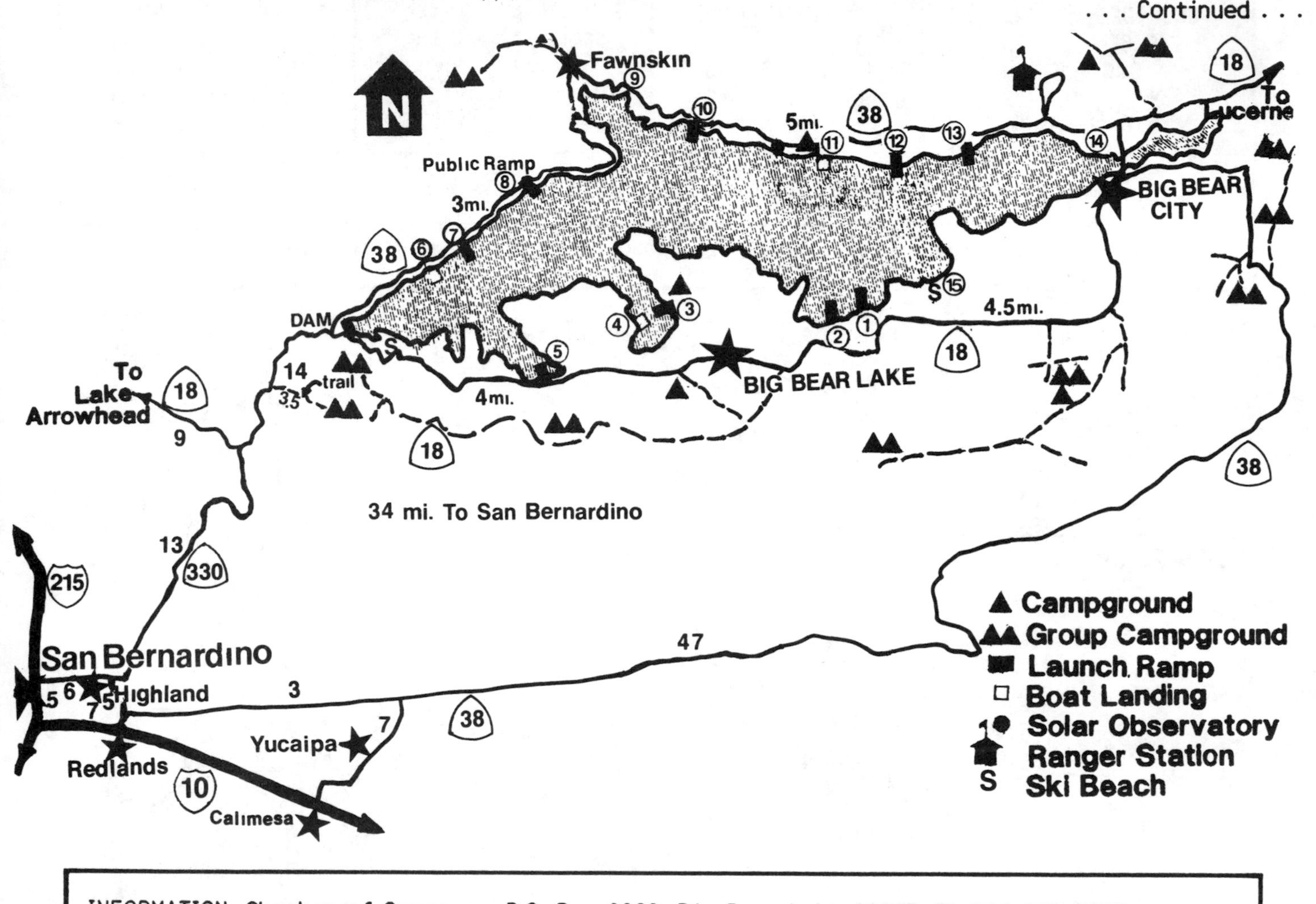

INFORMATION: Chamber of Commerce, P.O. Box 2860, Big Bear Lake 92315, Ph 714-866-5652

CAMPING	BOATING	RECREATION	OTHER
U.S.F.S. 7 Campgrounds With 254 Dev. Sites for Tents & R.V.s Fee: $5 Remote Area Also at No Charge Group Sites - $15 No Reservations Privately Operated Facilities	All Boating Allowed Power & Sail: 6-26' Rowboat: 12-26' Valid Lake Permit Required 35 MPH Speed Limit Full Service Marinas Launch Ramps Rentals: Power, Sail, Fishing, Sailboard, Jet Ski & Surfjet Berths-Docks-Storage	Fishing: Trout, Bass, Catfish, Bluegill, Silver Salmon Swimming - Pools Beaches Hiking & Backpacking Horseback Riding: Trails & Rentals Golf & Tennis Picnicking	Motels & Cabins Restaurants Grocery Stores Complete Resort Facilities See Following Page for Information

GENERAL INFORMATION: Big Bear Chamber of Commerce, 41647 Big Bear Blvd., Big Bear Lake 92315, Ph: 714-866-5652
LAKE INFORMATION: Big Bear Municipal Water District, P.O. Box 2863, 42169-D Big Bear Blvd., Big Bear Lake 92315, Ph: 714-866-5796
CAMPING/HIKING INFORMATION: Big Bear Ranger District, Box 290, Fawnskin 92333 Ph: 714-866-3437
LODGING INFORMATION: Central Reservation Service, Ph: 714-866-5877

MARINE FACILITIES - See Map for Number Location

1. PINE KNOT LANDING & MARINE - Ph: 714-866-2628 - Boat Permit Sales, Rentals, Docks, Moorings, Launch Ramp, Gas, Storage, Bait & Tackle, Marine Store, Lake Tours.

2. BIG BEAR MARINA - Ph: 714-866-3218 - Boat Permit Sales, Rentals, Docks, Moorings, Launch Ramp, Gas, Storage, Bait & Tackle, Marine Store, Lake Tours.

3. HOLLOWAY'S MARINA - Ph: 714-866-5706 - Boat Permit Sales, Rentals, Docks, Moorings, Launch Ramp, Gas, Bait & Tackle, Grocery Store, R.V. Facilities.

4. PLEASURE POINT LANDING - Ph: 714-866-2455 - Boat Permit Sales, Rentals, Docks, Moorings, Launch Ramp, Gas, Bait & Tackle.

5. BOULDER BAY MARINA & LANDING - Ph: 714-866-7557 - Boat Permit Sales, Rentals, Docks, Moorings, Gas, Bait & Tackle, Cabins.

6. GRAY'S LANDING - Ph: 714-866-2443 - Boat Rentals, Bait & Tackle, Fishing Pier.

7. NORTH SHORE LANDING - Ph: 714-866-3123 - Boat Rentals, Small Grocery Store.

8. DUANE BOYER PUBLIC LAUNCH RAMP - Ph: 714-866-2917 - Boat Permit Sales, Launch Ramp, Boat-Trailer Parking, Day Use Area.

9. FAWNSKIN LANDING - Ph: 714-866-3088 - Boat Rentals, Docks, Moorings, Bait & Tackle.

10. CLUSTER PINES - Ph: 714-866-2246 - Camping & Docking Facilities, Launch Ramp, Small Grocery Store.

11. LIGHTHOUSE LANDING - Ph: 714-866-7855 - Boat Rentals, Docks, Moorings, R.V. Facilities, Small Store.

12. BIG BEAR NORTH - Ph: 714-866-8217 - Camping & R.V. Facilities, Small Store.

13. JUNIPER MARINA - Ph: 714-866-4151 - Boat Rentals, Docks, Mooring, Launch Ramp, Day Use.

14. EAST LAUNCH RAMP, NORTH SHORE DRIVE, WEST OF STANFIELD CUTOFF - In process of Development, Boat Permit Sales, Launch Ramp, Boat-Trailer Parking, Day Use Area.

15. MEADOW PARK SWIM BEACH, PARK AVENUE NEAR KNIGHT AVE. - In Process of Development, Public Swimming Area, Sandy Beach, Snack Bar.

U.S.F.S. CAMPGROUNDS

There are 17 Campgrounds in Area: 254 Developed Sites for Tents and Some R.V.s, No Hookups, No Showers Plus 10 Group Sites for 15 to 40 People. Fees: $6 - $15.

PUDDINGSTONE LAKE

Puddingstone Lake is at an elevation of 941 feet within the 2,000 acre Frank G. Bonelli Regional Park. This complete recreation facility is administered by the Department of Parks and Recreation of Los Angeles County. The 250 surface acre Lake has good marina facilities and is open to all boating. The angler will find trout and a warm water fishery. This well landscaped Park has turfed picnic areas, sandy swim beaches, multi-purpose trails and a full facility R.V. Park and Campground. The Equestrian Center complements the riding trails throughout the Park. Raging Waters is the largest water theme park west of the Rockies. There is a Park Entrance Fee of $2 for vehicle towing a boat.

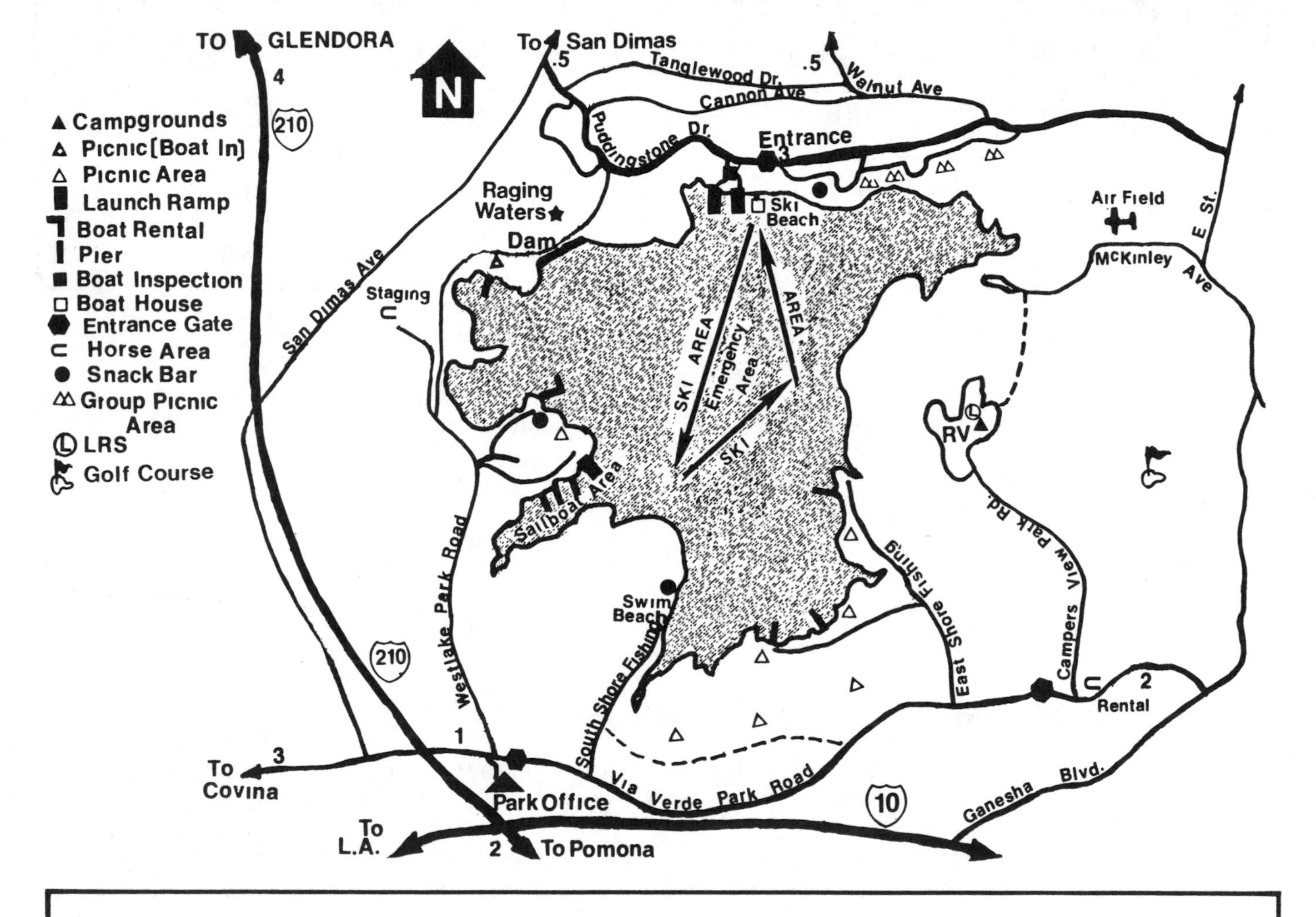

INFORMATION: Bonelli Park, 120 E. Via Verde, San Dimas 91773, Ph: 714-599-8411

CAMPING	BOATING	RECREATION	OTHER
56 Dev. Sites for Tents 389 Dev. Sites for R.V.s - Full Hookups Group Sites, Swim Pool, Spa, Rec. Rm. Volleyball Courts & General Store Disposal Station Fees: $9.50-$15.50 Ph: 714-599-8355	Open to All Boating All Boats Must be Min. 8 ft., Max. 26 ft. Power Boats Must be 12 ft. Jet Skis Allowed Check at Entrance for All Regulations Boat Rentals Paved Launch Ramps Fee: $2	Fishing: Trout, Bass, Bluegill, Crappie & Perch Swimming at Designated Areas Picnicking Group Picnic Areas by Reservation Hiking & Equestrian Trails - Horse Rentals Tram & Raging Waters	Equestrian Center: Horse Boarding, Rentals & Roping Arena Ph: 714-599-8830 Raging Waters: Water Slides, Wave Pool, Rapids, & Children's Pool, Ph: 714-599-1251 Restaurants, Snack Bars, Bait & Tackle

LAKE PERRIS

The Lake Perris State Recreation Area is the southern terminus of the California State Water Project. The Lake's 2,200 surface acres are surrounded by rocky mountains towering to more than a thousand feet above the water's surface. Alessandro Island provides a popular boat-in picnic area. This Island rises 230 feet creating an interesting view of the surrounding area. The complete Recreation Park provides an abundance of activities and support facilities. The fishing is good from boat or shore. Lake Perris holds the world record for Alabama Spotted Bass at 9.06 pounds. This is a popular Lake for waterskiing, sailboarding, sailing and boating. There are specific areas for waterfowl and upland game hunters. The hiker, bicycler and horseback rider will find extensive trails, and there is even a rock climbing area.

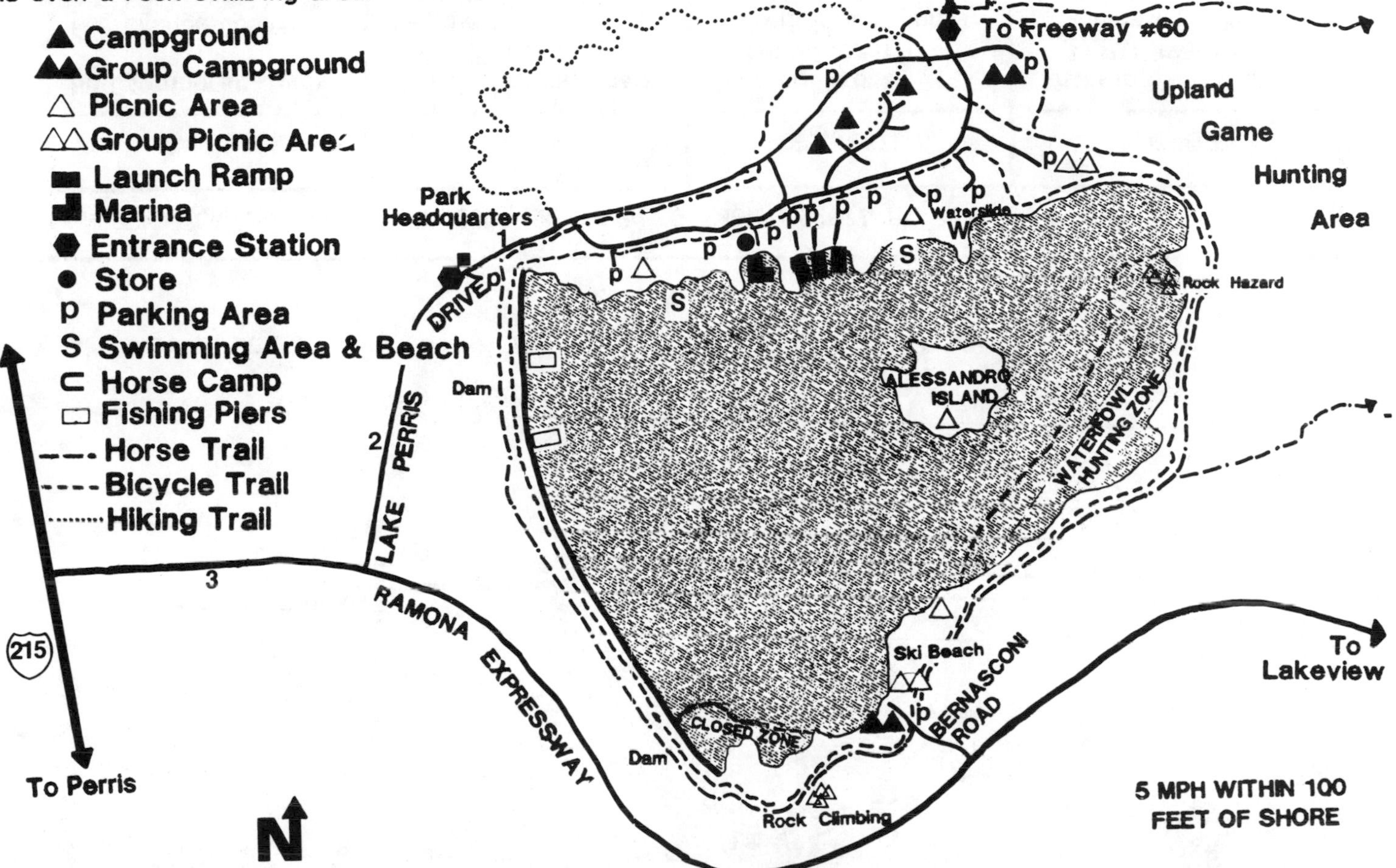

INFORMATION: State Rec. Area, 17801 Lake Perris Dr., Perris 92370, Ph: 714-657-0676			
CAMPING	BOATING	RECREATION	OTHER
167 Dev. Tent Sites Fee: $6 254 R.V. Sites - Hookups-Fee: $12 2 Group Campgrounds 25-100 People & 25-80 People Disposal Station Boat Camping in Slips Only	Open to All Boating 35 MPH Speed Limit 5 MPH Zoned Areas Full Service Marina Launch Ramps-Fee: $2 Boat Storage, Gas Dock Rentals: Fishing Boats Hobie Cats. Jet Skis, Sailboards & Paddle Boats	Fishing: Trout, Alabama Spotted & Largemouth Bass, Bluegill, Channel Catfish, Sunfish Picnicking & Swimming Beaches & Waterslide Hiking, Bicycle & Riding Trails Rock Climbing Area Hunting: Waterfowl & Upland Game	Regional Indian Museum Horse Camp: Corrals, Water Troughs, Picnic Tables to 50 People Coffee Shop, Snack Bar Restaurant & Motel Bait & Tackle Marina Supplies Boat Repairs

ANAHEIM, SANTA ANA RIVER, IRVINE & LAGUNA NIGUEL LAKES

Anaheim, Santa Ana River, and Irvine Lakes are all private facilities geared to the fisherman. Trout and a good warm fishery await the angler. Laguna Niguel Regional Park also offers good fishing in addition to a nice 154 acre park. Laguna Niguel and Irvine Regional Park (near Irvine Lake), are a part of Orange County's Recreational Facilities which provide an abundance of Regional Parks, Camping Parks, and Harbors throughout the County.

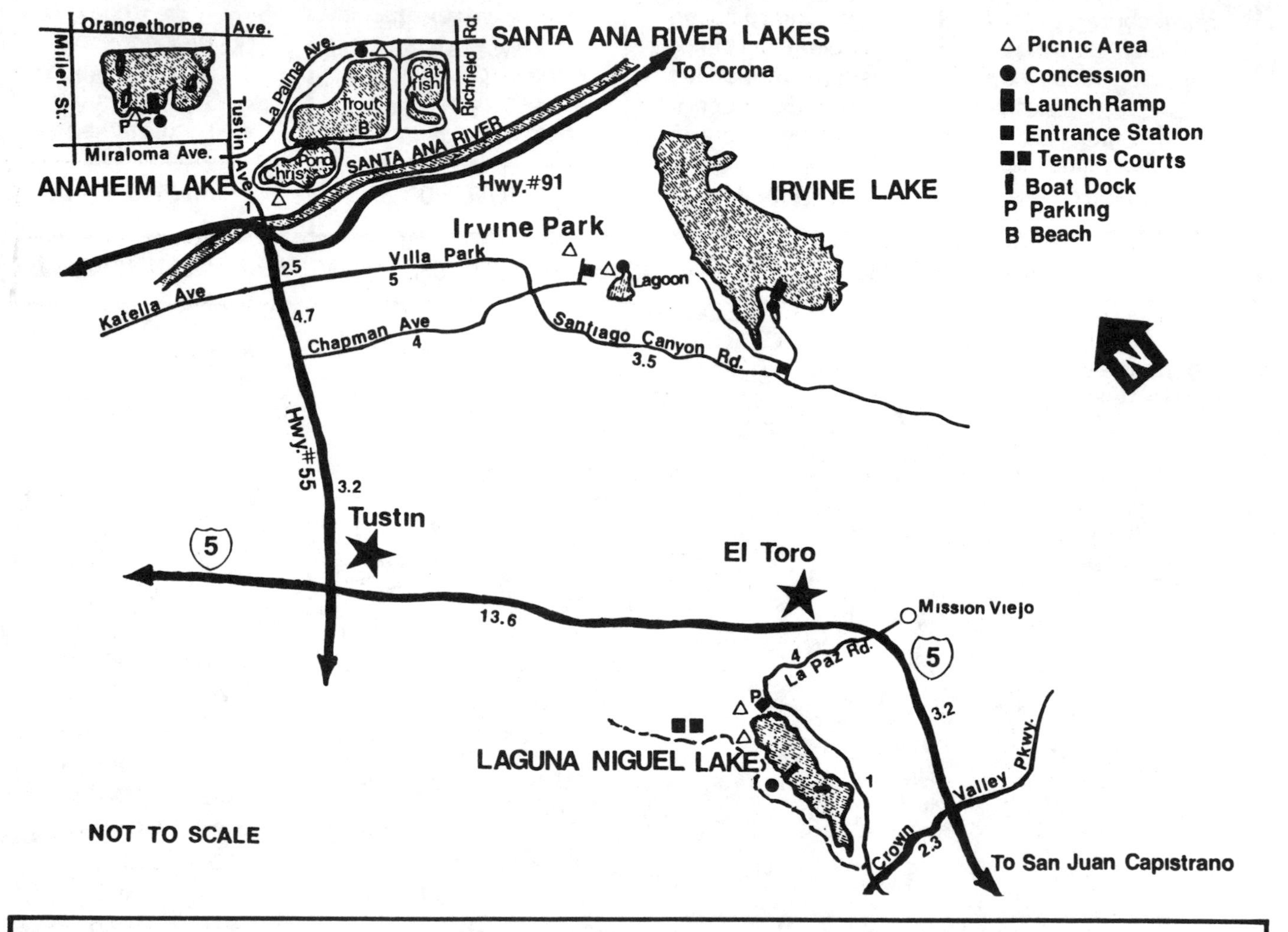

INFORMATION: Laguna Niguel, 28241 La Paz Rd., S. Laguna 92677, Ph: 714-831-2790

CAMPING	BOATING	RECREATION	OTHER
No Camping at Lakes For Orange County Campgrounds: County of Orange Recreational Facilities 10852 Douglas Road Anaheim 92806 Ph: 714-634-7034	Rental Fishing Boats at All Lakes Laguna Niguel: No Private Boats Other Lakes Allow Private Boats Phone for Specific Rules	Fishing: Trout, Bass, Bluegill, Crappie & Channel Catfish No Swimming Picnic Areas Hiking, Jogging & Bicycle Trails Athletic Fields Tennis Courts Playgrounds	Anaheim Lake 3451 Miraloma Anaheim 92806 Ph: 714-524-7100 Irvine Lake Star Route 38 Orange 92667 Ph: 714-649-2560 Santa Ana River Lakes 4060 E. La Palma Anaheim 92807 Ph: 714-632-7830

CUCAMONGA–GUASTI, YUCAIPA PARK, PRADO PARK AND FAIRMONT PARK

These relatively small Lakes offer limited boating, but the surrounding Parks offer an abundance of recreational opportunities. Cucamonga-Guasti, Yucaipa Park and Prado Park are a part of the San Bernardino County Regional Park System. Fairmont Park is administered by the City of Riverside. Fishing is popular the year around for bass and channel catfish, and during the winter months, the angler will find planted trout. In addition to modern campgrounds, Yucaipa and Prado offers the horseback rider trails and equestrian centers. There is a variety of recreational opportunities unique to each Park from trap shooting to waterslides.

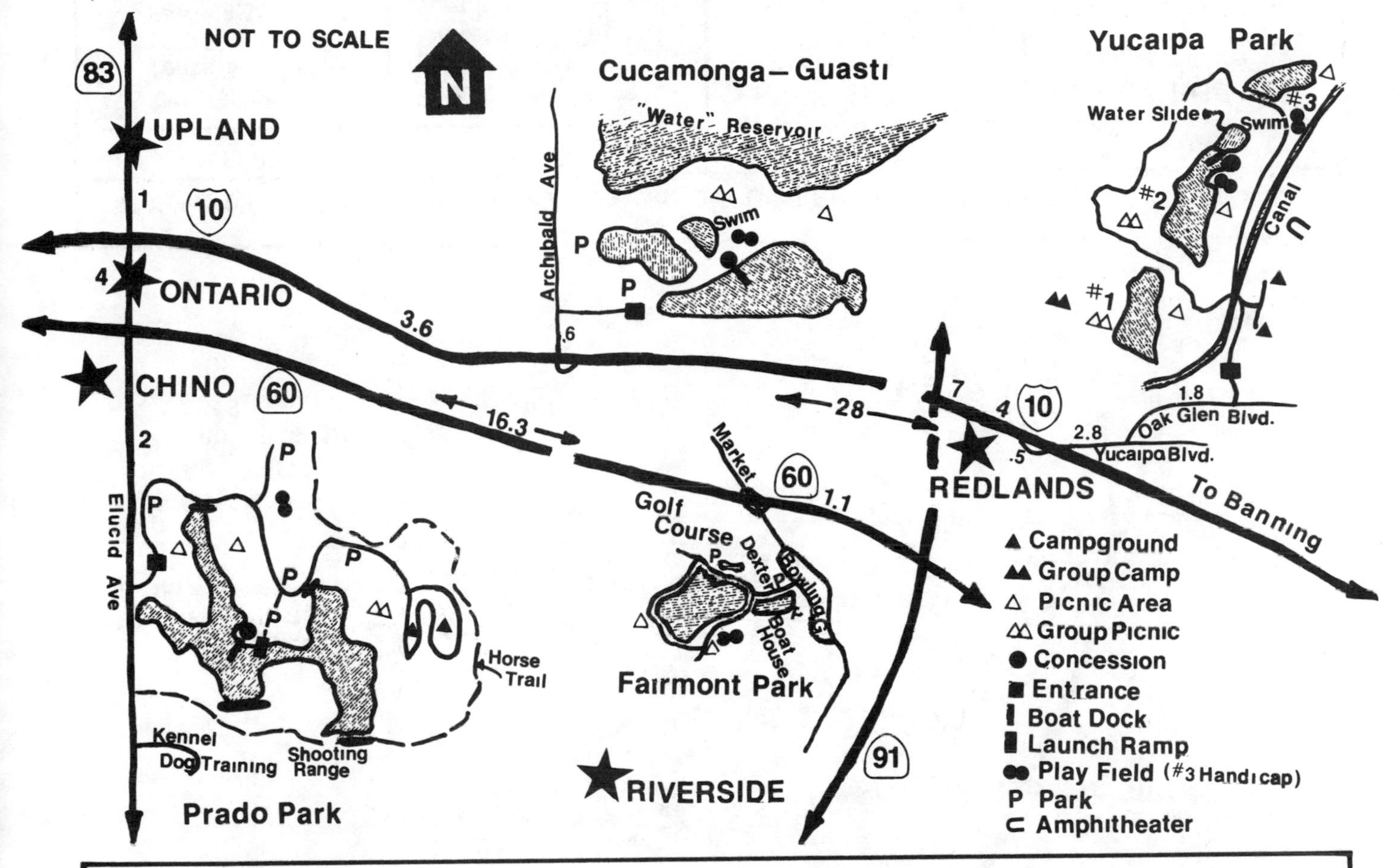

INFORMATION: Regional Parks, 825 3rd St., San Bernardino 92415, Ph: 714-383-1912

CAMPING	BOATING	RECREATION	OTHER
Yucaipa Park: Ph: 714-790-1818 26 R.V. Sites to 60 Rigs Overflow Tent Sites 13 Group sites to 35 Rigs No Hookups Prado Park: Ph: 714-597-4260 50 R.V. Sites with Full Hookups	Prado: Non-Power Boats Launch Ramp Rentals: Rowboats & Paddle Boats Yucaipa & Cucamonga-Guasti Paddle Boat Rentals Only	Fishing: Trout (Winter), Bass & Channel Catfish Swimming Lagoons Waterslides Picnic Areas Hiking & Riding Trails Equestrian Center & Horse Rentals Athletic Fields	Trap & Skeet Range Golf Course - - - - - - - - - - - Cucamonga-Guasti Ph: 714-988-1061 Fairmont Park: City of Riverside Parks & Rec. 3900 Main St. Riverside 92522 Ph: 714-683-9449

LAKE ELSINORE

Lake Elsinore, at an elevation of 1,273 feet, has been described as "one of the most unruly and unpredictable bodies of water in California." In spite of its fickle nature, Lake Elsinore provides an abundance of water sports. This large fluctuating Lake offers sailing, boating and waterskiing. It is known as one of the best bass fishing Lakes in the West. The State Recreation Area is under concession to the Lake Elsinore Recreation Area, Inc., a private corporation. There are many walnut shaded lawns awaiting the camper at this well maintained facility. There are a number of private campgrounds, resorts and marinas around the Lake. Elsinore, long famed for its mineral springs, offers the visitor three spas.

. . . Continued . . .

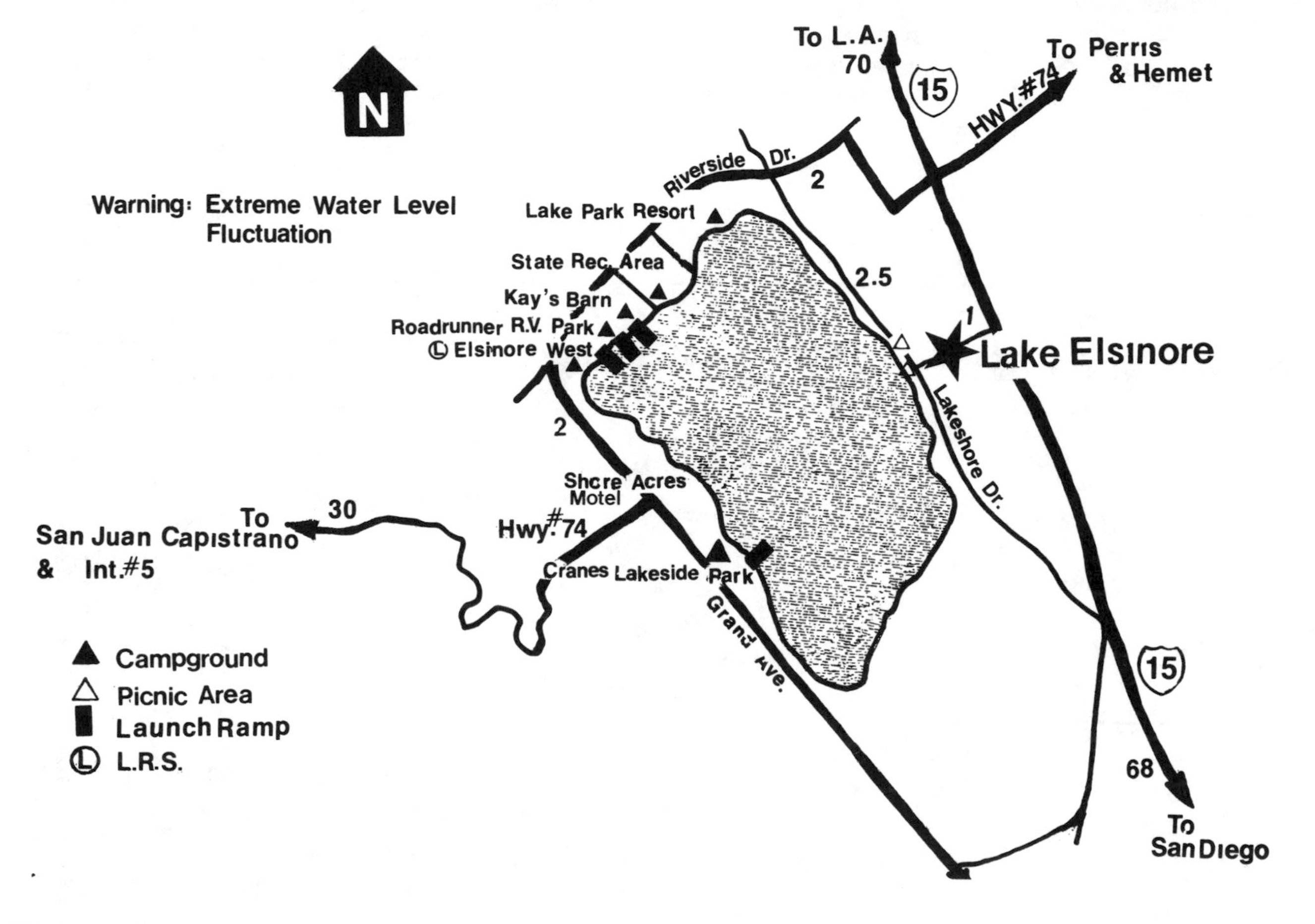

INFORMATION: State Rec. Area, 32040 Riverside Dr., Lake Elsinore 92330, Ph: 714-674-3177

CAMPING	BOATING	RECREATION	OTHER
176 Dev. Sites for Tents & R.V.s 132 Elec. Hookups Fee: $8.50 for 2 & $1 each add'l. Elec. Hookup: $3 Pets: $2 Disposal Station Group Site to 800 People Day Use Only Fee: $3	Power, Row, Canoe, Sail, Windsurf, Waterski & Jet Ski Boating Fee: $5 Day Annual Permits: $25-$65 Launch Ramps, Marinas Slips, Docks, Gas 35 MPH Speed Limit Rentals: Fishing Boats Kayaks, Paddle Boats Noise Level Restrict.	Fishing: Small & Largemouth Bass, Carp, Crappie, Bluegill & Catfish Swimming: In Pools & Designated Areas Picnicking Hiking, Riding & Bicycle Trails Hang Gliding & Ultra Lite Planes Mineral Baths	Full Facilities in Lake Elsinore See Following Page

LAKE PARK RESORT

32000 Riverside Dr., Lake Elsinore 92330, Ph: 714-674-7911
Beach Tent & R.V. Camp Area, Fee: $8, 121 R.V. Sites, Full Hookups, Fee: $11, Cable T.V., Hot Showers, Flush Toilets, Disposal Station, Laundry, Swim Beach & Olympic Size Pool, Recreation Center, Picnic Area, Hand Launch & Dock, Rentals: Fishing Boats & Jet Skis.

ROAD RUNNER R.V. PARK

32500 Riverside Dr., Lake Elsinore 92330, Ph: 714-674-4900
145 R. V. Sites, 100 Full Hookups, Hot Showers, Flush Toilets, Disposal Station, Laundry, Launch Ramp.

ELSINORE WEST MARINA

32700 Riverside Dr., Lake Elsinore 92330, Ph: 714-678-1300
Open Tent & R.V. Camp Area, 170 R.V. Sites, Full Hookups, Hot Showers, Flush Toilets, Cable T.V., Picnic Area, Launch Ramp, Docks.

SHORE ACRES MOTEL RESORT

15712 Grand Ave., Lake Elsinore 92330, Ph: 714-678-2052
R.V. Parking, Motel, Kitchenettes, Swimming Beach & Pool, Picnic Area, Barbecue, Boat Dock, No Pets.

CRANE LAKESIDE PARK

15980 Grand Ave., Lake Elsinore 92330, Ph: 714-678-2112
21 R.V. Sites, Water & Electric Hookups, Hot Showers, Flush Toilets, Snack Bar, Swim Area, Recreation Center, Laundry, Launch Ramp & Boat Slips.

FOR OTHER FACILITIES AND ACCOMMODATIONS CONTACT:

Lake Elsinore Chamber of Commerce
132 W. Grand Avenue
Lake Elsinore 92330
Ph: 714-674-2577

LAKE SKINNER

Located at an elevation of 1,500 feet in the transitional area between coast and desert, Lake Skinner rests amid semi-arid vegetation, rolling hills of wild flowers and oak trees. The Lake has a surface area of 1,200 acres, and the 14 miles of irregular shoreline is surrounded by the 6,000 acre Lake Skinner Park. This new and developing facility is operated by Riverside County Parks Department. In addition to the campsites, there is a half-acre swimming pool, beaches, ecology ponds, marine facilities, camp store and fishing areas. Equestrian facilities are in the planning stages. This is a good sailing Lake with moderate winds. Power boating is restricted to 10 MPH with low wake conditions. It is well stocked with trout and warm water fish. The facilities are nicely maintained with grassy areas and sandy beaches.

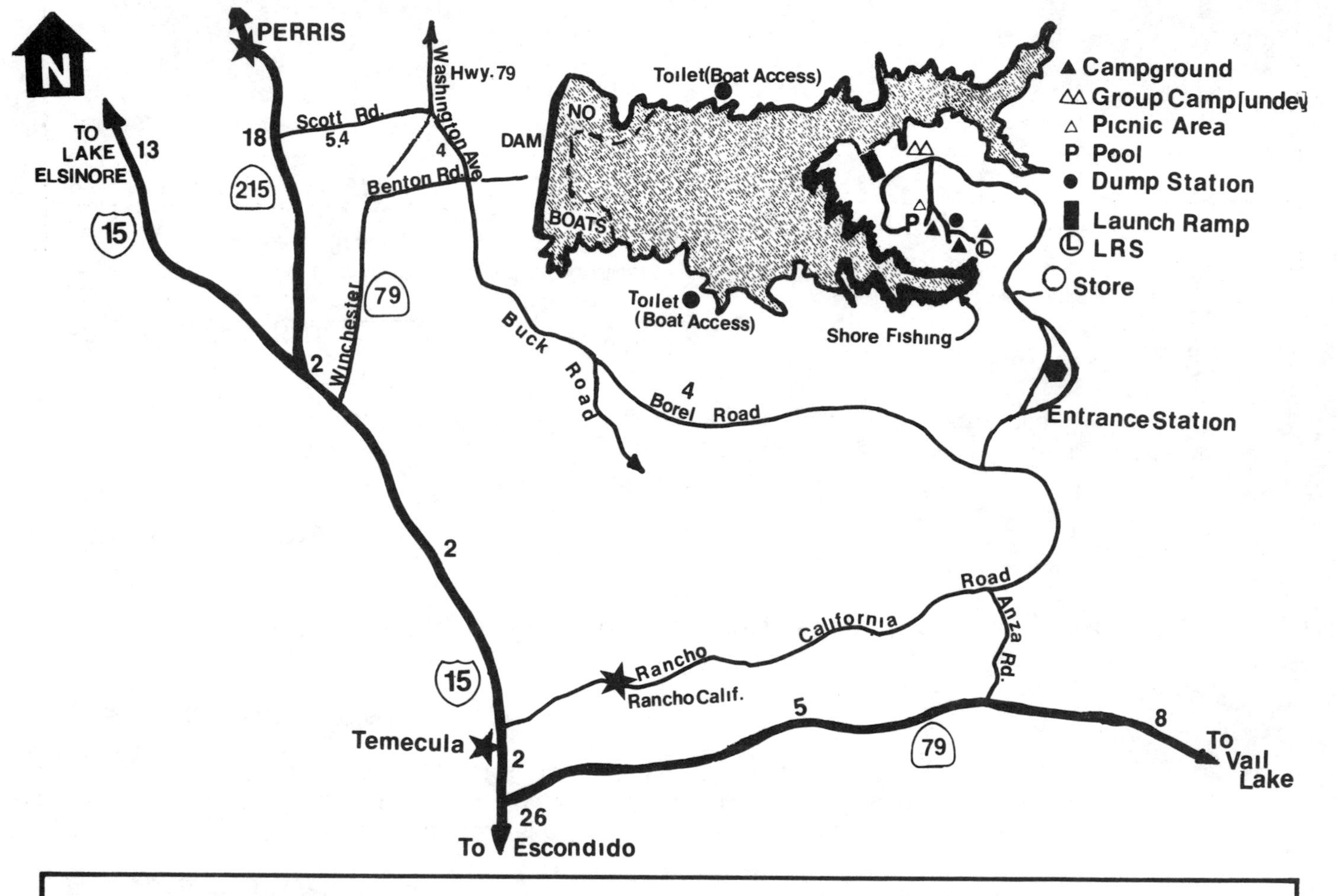

INFORMATION: Parks Department, P.O. Box 3507, Rubidoux 92519, Ph: 619-787-2553			
CAMPING	**BOATING**	**RECREATION**	**OTHER**
43 Dev. Sites for Tents - Fee: $6 Dev. Sites for R.V.s 18 Partial Hookups Fee: $8 209 Full Hookups Fee: $9 Primitive Sites for Overflow Fee: $4 Group Camp to 125 People - Reserve	All Boats Must Be 42" Wide, Sailboats Must Be 12' Long & 12" of Freeboard No Canoes, Kayaks or Multihulled Boats Without Solid and Fixed Decking Speed Limit - 10 MPH Launch Ramp Rentals: Row & Motor Boats	Fishing: Trout, Catfish, Bluegill, Crappie, Perch, Bass, Carp Swimming in Pool Only Picnicking Hiking Horseback Riding Trails Nature Study	Snack Bar Grocery Store Bait & Tackle Complete Facilities - 9 Miles at Rancho California

LAKE FULMOR, REFLECTION LAKE AND ANGLER'S LAKE

Lake Fulmor is at an elevation of 5,300 feet near the beautiful mountain resort community of Idyllwild. Although facilities are limited at this small trout Lake, the visitor is sure to enjoy the relaxed atmosphere in this area of the San Bernardino National Forest. Angler's and Reflection, at 1,600 feet elevation, are small private fishing Lakes. Angler's Lake provides open camping and no limit fishing. Reflection Lake offers a developed campground with full hookups. Boating is limited to canoes, inflatables and rowboats. Electric motors are allowed. Trout and Channel Catfish are planted weekly in season at both Angler's and Reflection Lakes, and State fishing licenses are not required at these private facilities.

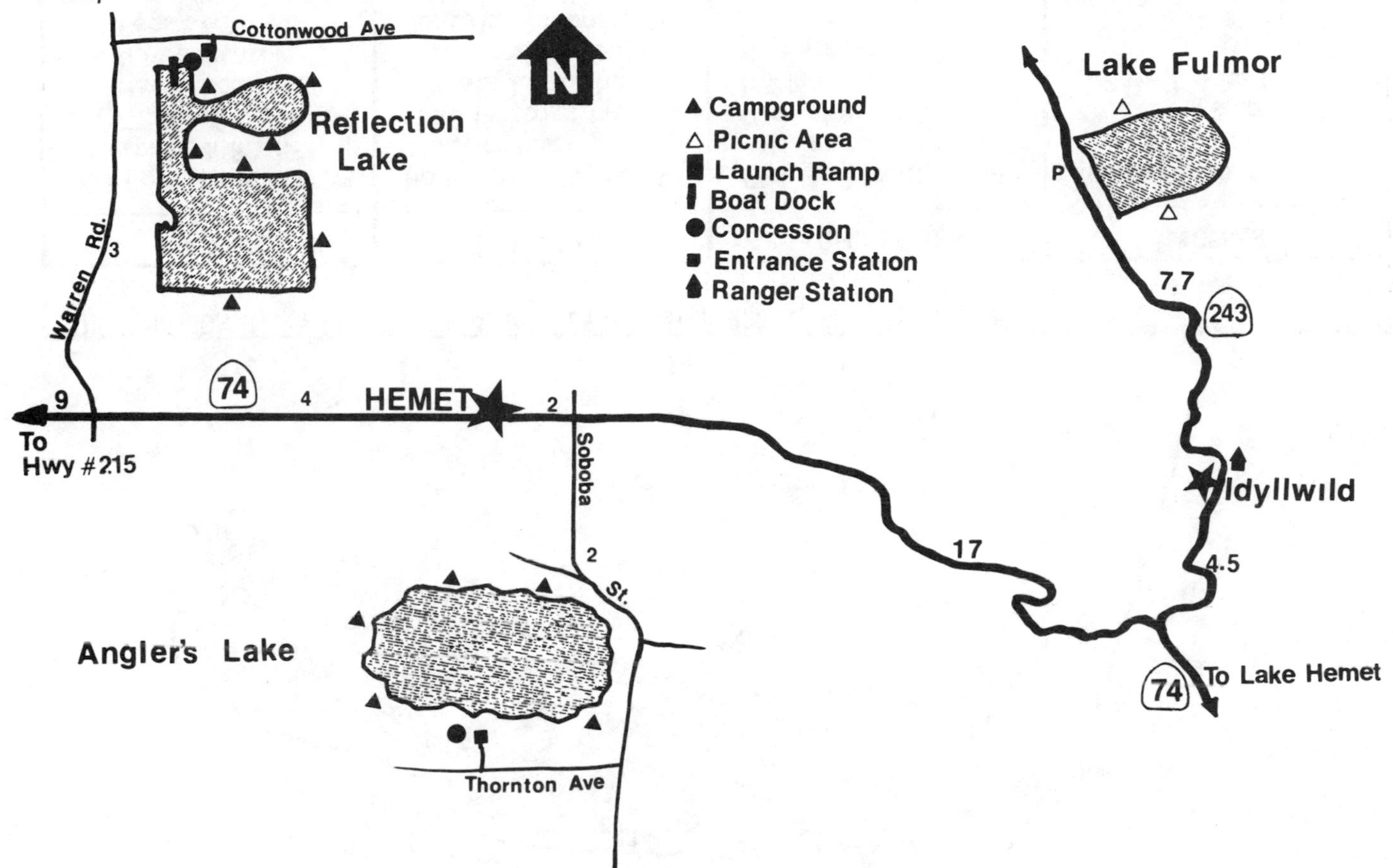

NOT TO SCALE

INFORMATION: Reflection Lake, 36151 Cottonwood Rd., San Jacinto 92383, Ph: 714-654-7906

CAMPING	BOATING	RECREATION	OTHER
Reflection Lake: 121 Sites - Water and Electric Hookups Disposal Station Fee: $11.25 Angler's Lake: Open Campsites to 300 People Fee: $7	Reflection Lake: Row, Canoe & Inflatables, Electric Motors Only Rentals: Rowboats Angler's & Fulmor: No Boating	Fishing: Trout, Bass, Bluegill & Catfish Picnicking Hiking No Swimming	Angler's Lake 42660 Thornton Ave. Hemet 92343 Ph: 714-927-2614 Lake Fulmor: Idyllwild R.S. P.O. Box 518 Idyllwild 92349 Ph: 714-659-2117

LAKE HEMET

Lake Hemet rests at an elevation of 4,400 feet in a pleasant mountain meadow of the San Bernardino National Forest. Surrounded by chaparral covered hills, this 420 acre Lake is under the jurisdiction of the Lake Hemet Municipal Water District. Boating is limited to fishing boats. This is primarily a fishing Lake. Large trout are caught throughout the year. In addition, the angler will find a good bass and catfish fishery. There is a large developed campground at the Lake, and nearby Herkey Creek has a 300-site campground operated by Riverside County. Although swimming is not allowed in Lake Hemet, swimming is permitted at Herkey Creek.

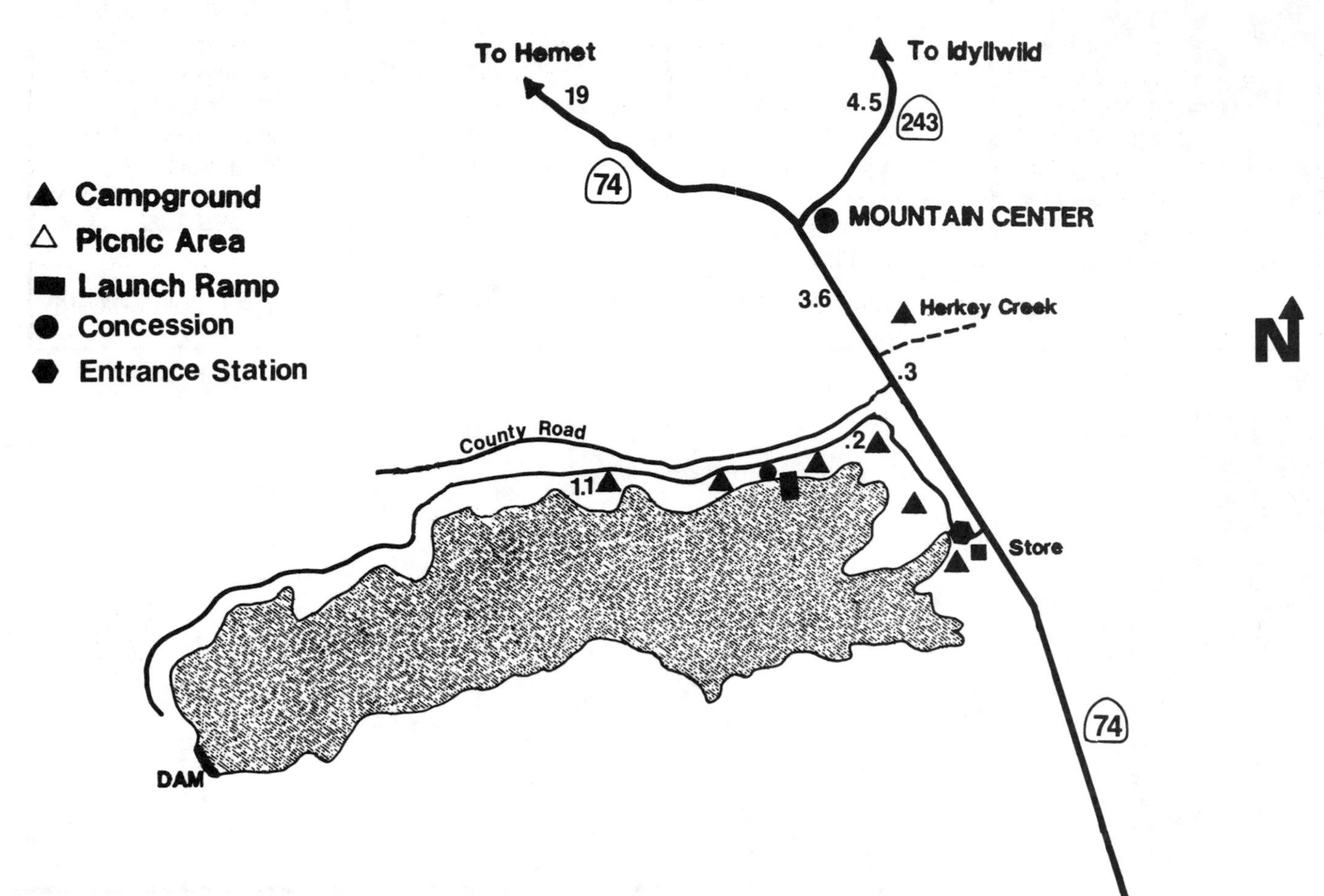

INFORMATION: Lake Hemet, Box 4, Mountain Center 92361, Ph: 714-659-2680

CAMPING	BOATING	RECREATION	OTHER
900 Dev. Sites for Tents & R.V.s Electric & Water Hookups No Generators Fee: $7.25 Herkey Creek: 310 Sites for Tents & R.V.s; No Hookups Group Sites; Fee: $6 Reserve Ticketron	No Canoes, Kayaks, Sailboats, Inflatables or Boats Less Than 10 Feet in Length Rentals: Rowboats & Motors 10 MPH Speed Limit Unpaved Launch Ramp	Fishing: Trout, Bass & Catfish Picnicking Hiking No Swimming	General Store: Food Camping Supplies Bait & Tackle

LAKE CAHUILLA

Lake Cahuilla is at an elevation of 44 feet, 6 miles southwest of Indio. This 135-surface acre Lake is owned by the Coachella Valley Water District, and the palm-shaded Park is operated by Riverside County. Located in the desert with temperatures up to 100 degrees, Cahuilla offers a pleasant retreat. There is a 10-acre beach for swimming and an adjacent water play area for the children. This oasis offers an abundance of well-maintained campsites along with a secluded group campground and a shady picnic area. The winter months can be delightful with temperatures of 75 degrees luring the camper and fisherman to this nice facility.

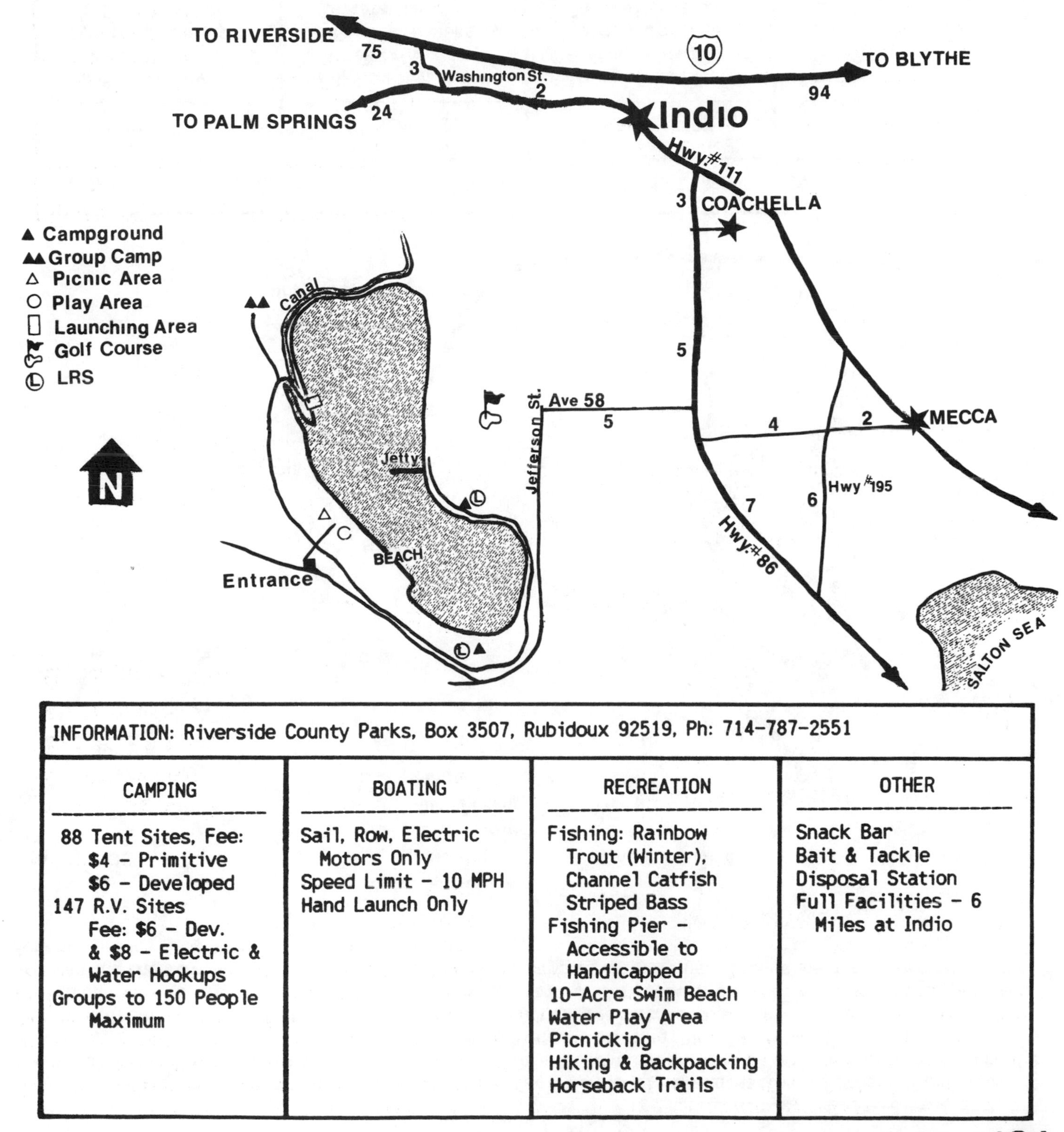

INFORMATION: Riverside County Parks, Box 3507, Rubidoux 92519, Ph: 714-787-2551

CAMPING	BOATING	RECREATION	OTHER
88 Tent Sites, Fee: $4 - Primitive $6 - Developed 147 R.V. Sites Fee: $6 - Dev. & $8 - Electric & Water Hookups Groups to 150 People Maximum	Sail, Row, Electric Motors Only Speed Limit - 10 MPH Hand Launch Only	Fishing: Rainbow Trout (Winter), Channel Catfish Striped Bass Fishing Pier - Accessible to Handicapped 10-Acre Swim Beach Water Play Area Picnicking Hiking & Backpacking Horseback Trails	Snack Bar Bait & Tackle Disposal Station Full Facilities - 6 Miles at Indio

VAIL LAKE

Vail Lake rests at an elevation of 1,426 feet in the Cleveland National Forest. Giant oak trees dot the mountainous shoreline of 15 miles. This 1,000 acre private Lake provides the angler with a quiet environment to wet his line. Although small craft boating is allowed, boating is secondary to fishing. Trout are planted from November through April, and Channel Catfish are planted monthly. In addition, there is a good fishery for the Florida strain of largemouth bass, bluegill and crappie. There are snacks and bait and tackle at the Lake, but no camping facilities. The nearest campground is the Forest Service Campground at Dripping Springs.

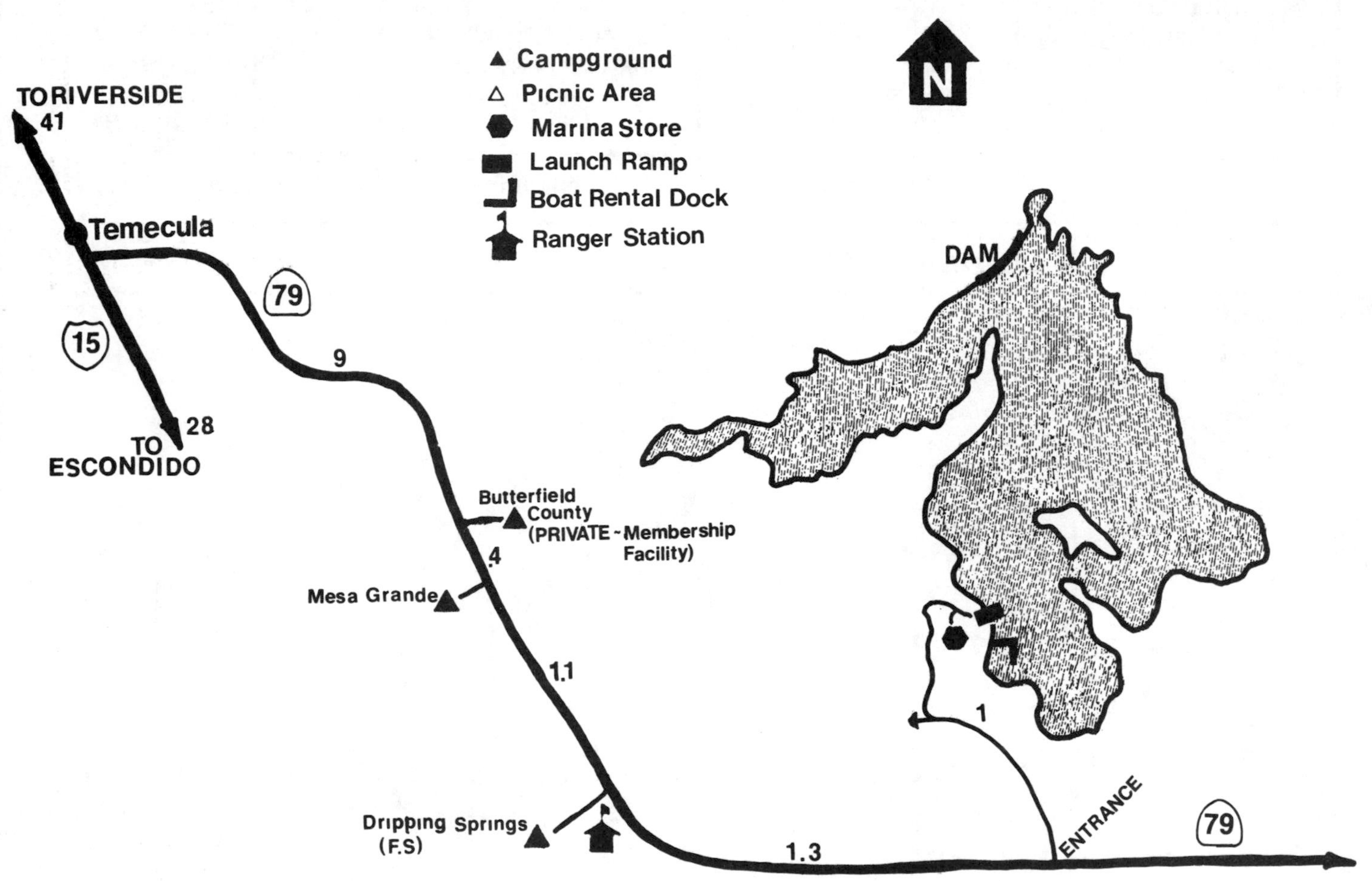

INFORMATION: Vail Lake, 44500 Vail Lake Rd., Aguana 92302, Ph: 714-676-5280			
CAMPING	BOATING	RECREATION	OTHER
U.S.F.S. - Palomar Ranger District Dripping Springs: 26 Dev. Sites for Tents & R.V.s Fee: $5	Sail, Row & Motor Boats Only No Canoes, Kayaks or Inflatables 10 MPH Speed Limit Launch Ramp: Free for Fishing Boats $10 for Sailboats Rentals: Fishing Boats & Motors Docks, Gas, Moorings	Fishing: Trout in Winter, Bluegill, Largemouth Bass, Channel Catfish & Crappie Picnicking No Swimming	Snack Bar Bait & Tackle Facilities in Temecula

SALTON SEA

The Salton Sea is located in a desert valley 228 feet below sea level surrounded by mountains reaching to 10,000 feet. It is one of the world's largest inland bodies of salt water with a surface area of 360 square miles. Although summer temperatures range well over 100 degrees, fall, winter and spring temperatures are in the 70's. This warm, shallow Sea provides an abundance of food for its game fish. Orangemouth Corvina, Croaker (Bairdiella) and Sargo were introduced from the Gulf of California, and the Tilapia was imported from Africa. These fish have flourished and the angler is rewarded with California's richest inland fishery. Numerous marinas, campgrounds and resorts support the recreational abundance of this desert oasis.

. . . Continued . . .

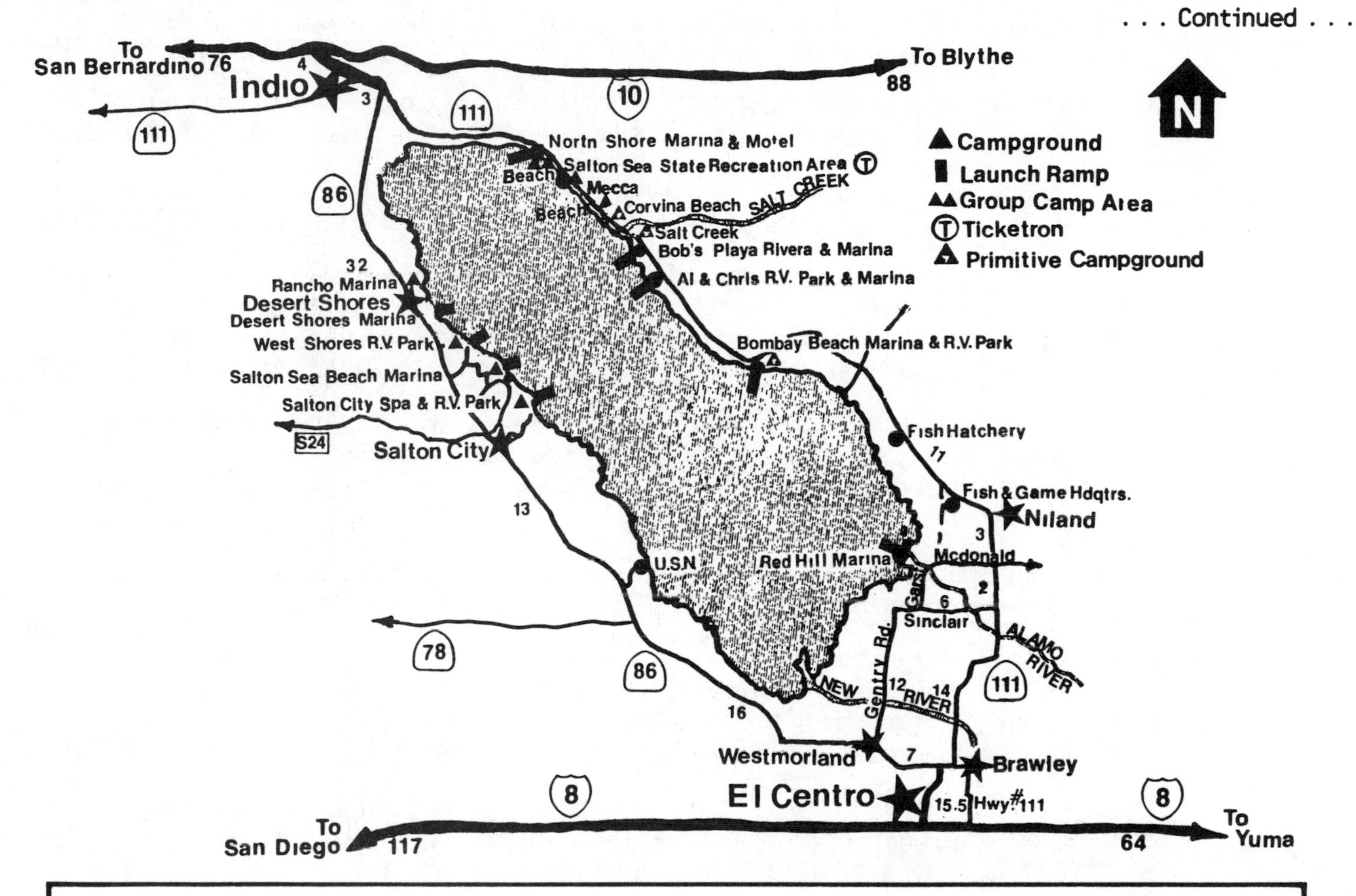

INFORMATION: See Following Page			
CAMPING	**BOATING**	**RECREATION**	**OTHER**
See Following Page for Campgrounds	Open to All Boating Full Service Marinas Launch Ramps Gas, Docks Dry Storage Caution: Sudden Strong Winds Many Unmarked Underwater Hazards Especially at North & South Ends	Fishing: Corvina, Sargo, Gulf Croaker, Tilapia Frogging Swimming Beaches Picnicking - Shade Ramadas Nature Trails Birdwatching Hunting: Waterfowl, Pheasant, Dove & Rabbit	Full Facilities Around the Lake Mineral Spas For Additional Information Contact Westshores Chamber of Commerce P.O. Box 5185 Salton City 92275 Ph: 619-394-4112

SALTON SEA - A PARTIAL LIST OF FACILITIES: . . . Continued . . .

SALTON SEA STATE RECREATION AREA - P.O. Box 3166, North Shore 92254, Ph: 619-393-3052

Headquarters Campground: 53 Tent/R.V. Sites, Wheelchair Accessible, 15 Full Hookups, Disposal Station, Flush Toilets, Solar Showers, Shade Ramadas, Shaded Picnic Area, Campfire Programs, Nature Trail to Mecca Beach. Fee: $6 - $12. Reservations: October - May - Ticketron

Mecca Beach Campground: 110 Tent/R.V. Sites, Wheelchair Accessible, Flush Toilets, Solar Showers, Shaded Picnic Area. Fee: $6

Covina Beach, Salt Creek & Bombay Beach Campgrounds: 800 Primitive Sites on Water's Edge, Chemical Toilets Beach Launch. Fee: $3

RED HILL MARINA - Imperial County Resident Ranger, P.O. Box 1419, Niland 92257
Ph: 619-348-2310
240 Acre Primitive Tent/R.V. Dry Camp, 80 R.V. Sites, Electric & Water Hookups, Showers, Shade Ramadas, Disposal Station, Picnic Tables, Launch, Docks, Dry Storage, Boatwash Rack, Snack Bar, Bait & Tackle, Beer, Ice.

NORTH SHORE MARINA - P.O. Box 5003, North Shore 92254, Ph: 619-393-3952
Motel, Campground, Swimming Pool, Full Service Marina, Boat Storage, 2 Ton Hoist, Launch Ramp, Fishing & Marina Supplies, Restaurant, Cocktail Lounge.

BOB'S PLAYA RIVIERA, North Shore 92254, Ph: 619-348-1835.
67 Tent/R.V. Sites, 40 Full Hookups, 7 Electric & Water Hookups, Hot Showers, Flush Toilets, Boat & Trailer Storage, Full Service Marina, Launch Ramp, Bait, Gas, Groceries, Laundry, Row Boat Rentals.

AL 'N' CHRIS R.V. PARK - P.O. Box 3106, North Shore 92254, Ph: 619-348-1272
80 Full Hookups. Season Lease Sites, Flush Toilets, Hot Showers, Full Service Marina, Launch Ramp, Laundry, No Tents.

BOMBAY MARINA - Star Route 1, Box 61, Niland 92257, Ph: 619-348-1694
Tent/R.V. Sites, 16 Full Hookups, Trailer Rentals, 18 Shaded Sites, Open Tent Camping, Hot Showers, Flush Toilets, Snacks, Bait & Tackle, Ice, Drinks, Boat Slips, Launch Ramp, Rental Boats.

DESERT SHORES MARINA - Desert Shores 92274, Ph: 619-395-5700
Launch Ramp, Tie Ups, Charters, Snacks, Drinks.

RANCHO MARINA - 301 N. Palm Dr., Desert Shores 92274, Ph: 619-395-5410
76 Tent/R.V. Sites, 47 Full Hookups, Flush Toilets, Hot Showers.

SALTON SEA BEACH MARINA - Route 3, Box 512, Thermal 92274, Ph: 619-395-5212
144 R.V. Full Hookups, Overflow Site for Tents & R.V.s, Water & Electric Hookups, Gas Groceries, Bait & Tackle.

SALTON CITY SPA & R.V. PARK - P.O. Box 5375, Salton City 92275, Ph: 619-394-4333
315 Tent/R.V. Sites, Full Hookups, Cable T.V., Flush Toilets, Hot Showers, Sauna, Hot Mineral Spa, Tennis Courts, Swimming Pool, Pool Tables, 2 Launch Ramps, Docks, Dry Storage, Mini Market.

WEST SHORES R.V. PARK - P.O. Box 5312, Salton City 92275, Ph: 619-394-4755
108 Tent/R.V. Sites, Full Hookups, Hot Showers, Flush Toilets, Disposal Station, Launch Ramp, Dock, Bait & Tackle, Restaurant & Bar.

WISTER UNIT, FINNEY, RAMER AND WIEST LAKES

Finney-Ramer Lakes and Wister Pond are a part of the Imperial Wildlife Area. This wildlife habitat is the home of a rich variety of birds, amphibians and mammals. Nature lovers, hunters, anglers, bird watchers, photographers and campers are drawn to this area of natural abundance. Located below sea level, hot July, August and September temperatures are a deterrent, but the visitor will find a more temperate 70 degrees in the fall, winter and spring. Wiest Lake offers a complete recreation facility with a modern campground, all types of boating and a good warm water fishery in this 50 acre Lake.

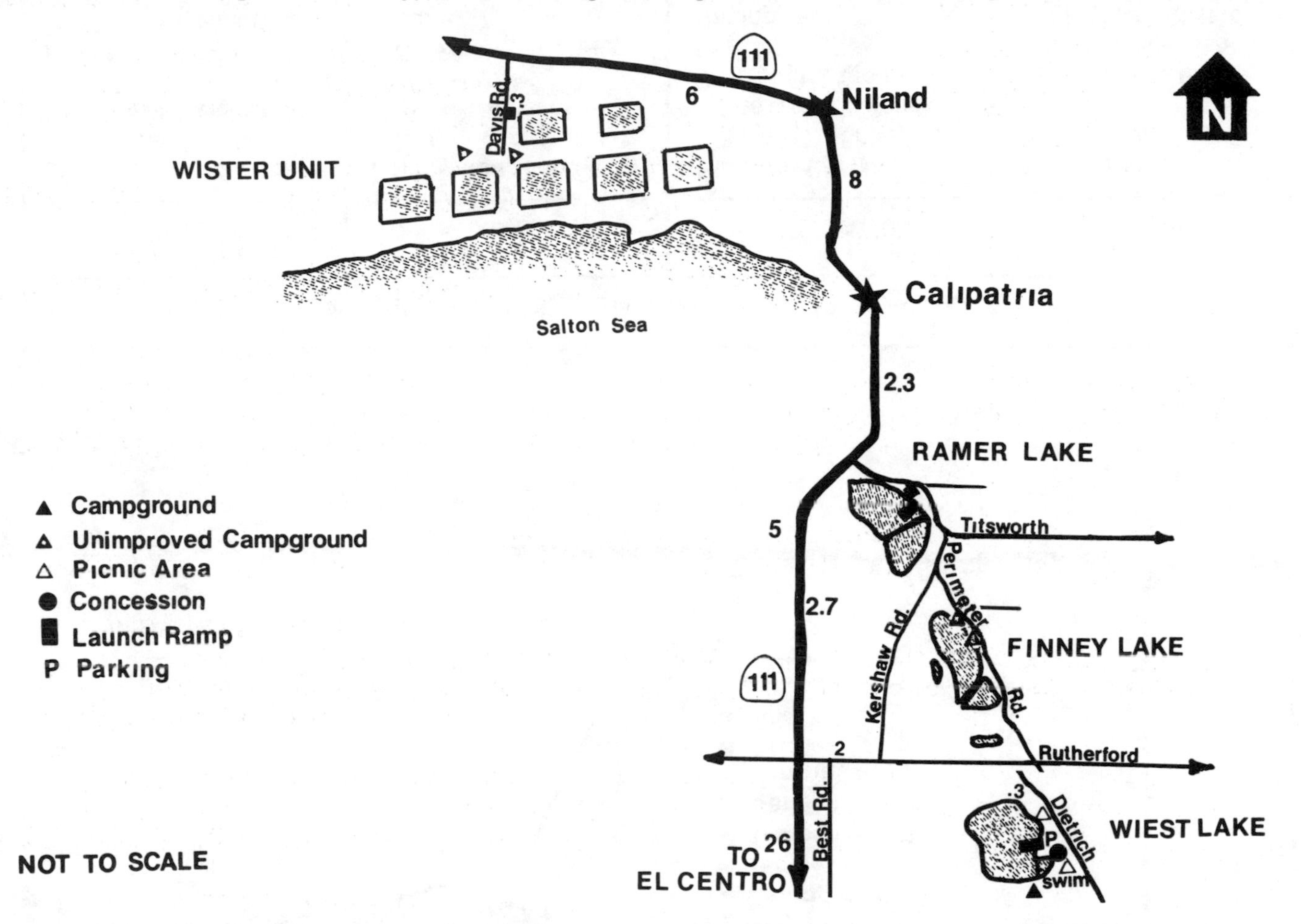

INFORMATION: Imperial Wildlife Area, Rt. 1, Box 6, Niland 92257, Ph: 619-348-0577

CAMPING	BOATING	RECREATION	OTHER
Wister & Finney-Ramer: Primitive Open Camping	Finney-Ramer: No Power Boats Electric Motors Only Wister Ponds: No Boating Wiest Lake: Open to All Boats Paved Launch Ramp	Fishing: Largemouth Bass, Bluegill, Crappie, Catfish & Carp Picnicking Hiking Nature Study Swimming-Wiest Lake Hunting: Duck, Geese, Dove, Rabbit	Wiest Lake 5351 Dietrich Rd. Brawley 92227 Ph: 619-344-3712 30 Tent Sites 20 R.V. Sites Water & Electric Hookups Handicap Facilities

SUNBEAM LAKE

Sunbeam Lake is actually two small Lakes totaling 14 surface acres with a large camping facility. Owned and operated by Imperial County, the Park offers a variety of recreational opportunities. Although boating is allowed in both Lakes, power boating is limited to only one of the Lakes. There is a spring fed swimming lagoon, and the fisherman will find a variety of warm water fish. These Lakes are 43 feet below sea level where summer temperatures average over 100 degrees. Fall, winter and spring are in the 70's. Surrounded by palm trees, Sunbeam Lake is a pleasant oasis.

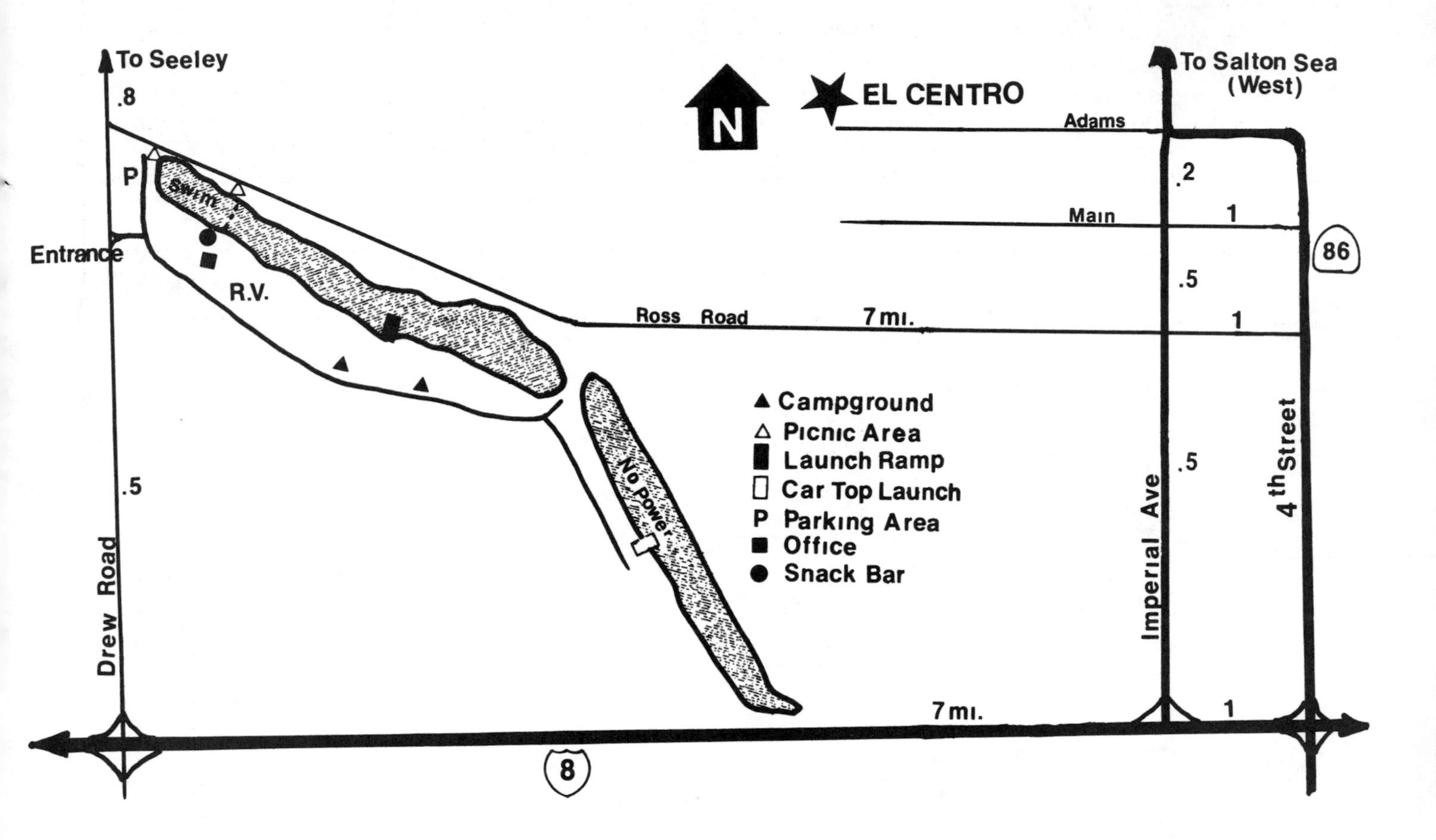

INFORMATION: Park Ranger, P.O. Box 806, Seeley 92273, Ph: 619-352-3308

CAMPING	BOATING	RECREATION	OTHER
256 Dev. Sites for Tents 44 Dev. Sites for R.V.s Fee: $3 - Site Plus $2 Electric Hookup Storage - $15	Power, Row, Canoe, Sail, Waterski, Jet Skis, Windsurf, Inflatables No Power in Lower Lake Docks Dry Storage	Fishing: Catfish, Bluegill, Crappie, Smallmouth Bass Swimming Lagoon Picnicking Hiking Frogging Hunting Nearby: Quail, Dove, Waterfowl & Rabbit	Snack Bar Bait & Tackle Restaurant, Grocery Store, Gas Station, Disposal Station - 1 Mile No Alcoholic Beverages in Park

DIXON LAKE

The Dixon Lake Recreation Area is operated by the City of Escondido Community Services Department. Nestled in chaparral and avocado-covered foothills, Dixon Lake is at an elevation of 1,045 feet. It has a surface area of 70 acres with 2 miles of shoreline within this 527 acre Park. The facilities are excellent for camping, fishing and picnicking. Originally stocked with fish in 1971, the Lake was not open until 1977, and as a result, many large bass and catfish await the angler. Trout are stocked from November through May.

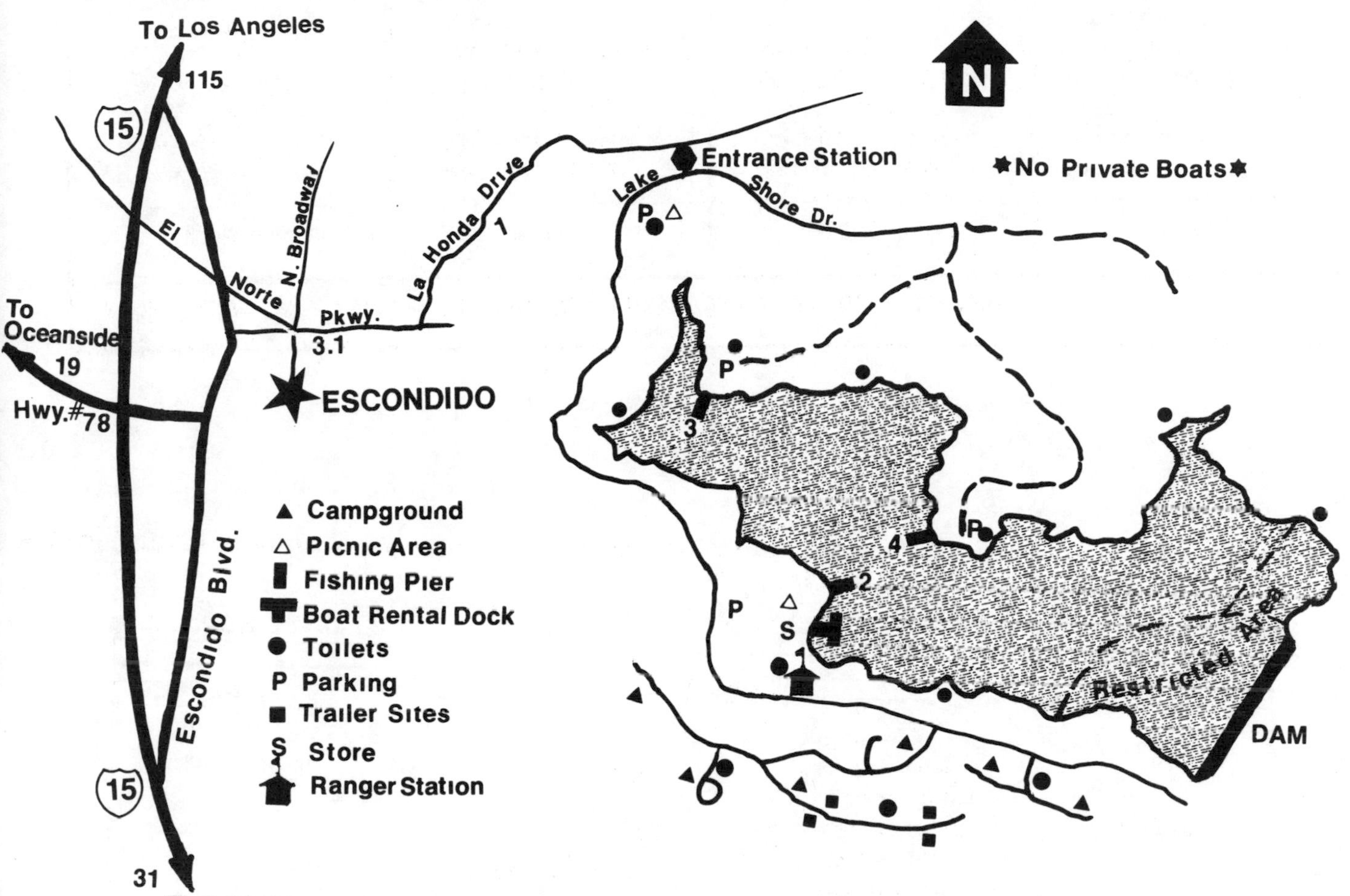

INFORMATION: Community Services, 100 Valley Blvd., Escondido 92025			
CAMPING	**BOATING**	**RECREATION**	**OTHER**
35 Dev. Sites for Tents & R.V.s Fee: $6 10 Dev. Sites for R.V.s - Full Hookups Fee: $9 Reservations Accepted Fee: $5 Ph: 619-741-3328 9 am - 2 pm	No Private Boats Rentals: Rowboats with Electric Motors	Fishing: Trout, Catfish, Bluegill, Crappie, Redear Sunfish, Florida Bass No Swimming or Wading Picnicking: Reservations Ph: 619-741-3328 8 am - 5 pm	Hiking - Nature Trails Campfire Programs Snack Bar Bait & Tackle Disposal Station Fishing Pier with Handicapped Facilities Full Facilities in Escondido

LAKE HENSHAW

Lake Henshaw is at an elevation of 2,740 feet in a valley on the south slopes of Palomar Mountain. The water level varies with the demands of man and nature. In 1942, the Lake reached its highest mark of nearly 25 miles of shoreline. The present shoreline is approximately 5 miles with a surface area of 1,137 acres. The large oak trees around the Resort area create a pleasant contrast to the surrounding semi-arid mountains. Long known for its fishing, Henshaw is stocked yearly with trout and channel catfish to supplement the native population of bass, crappie and bluegill.

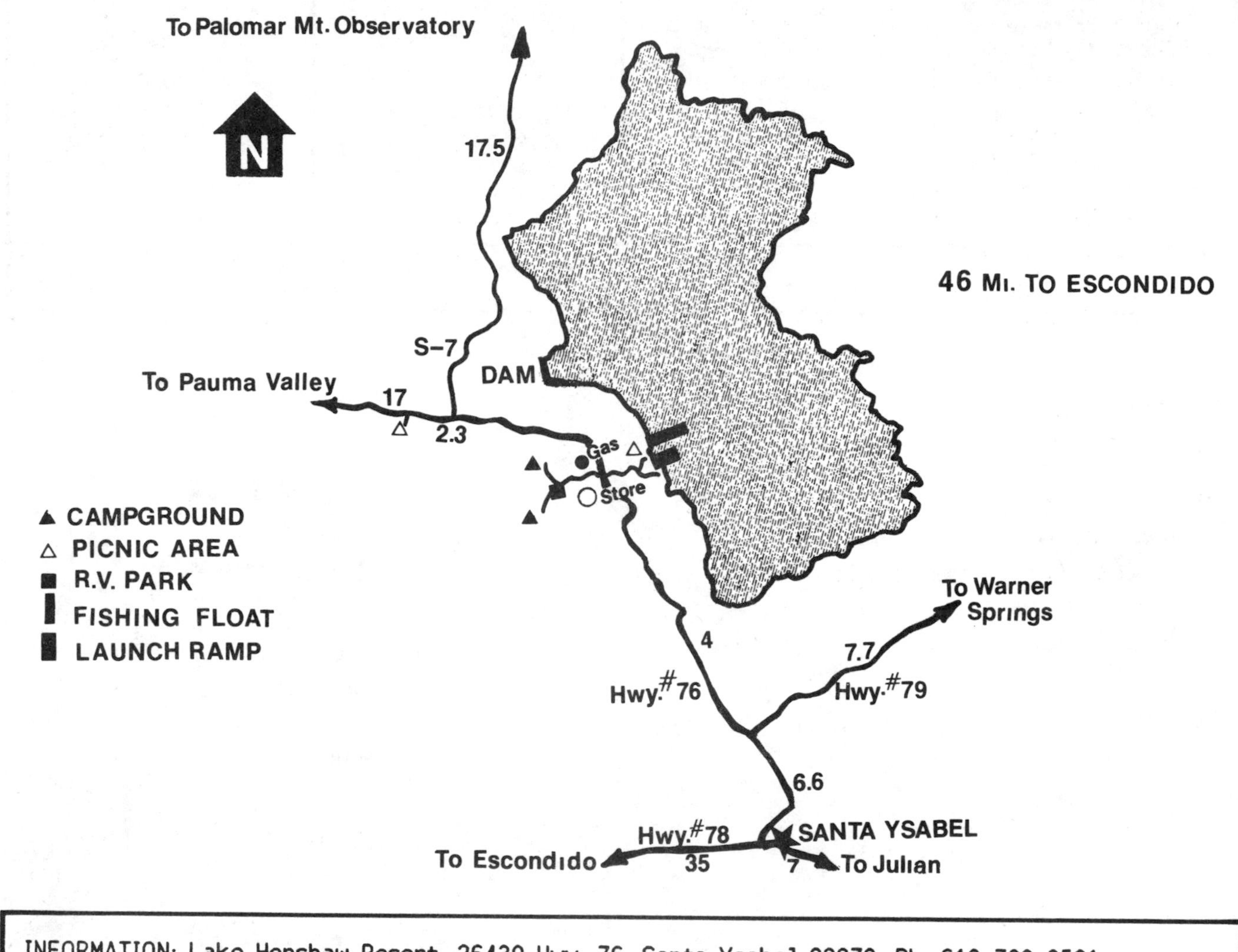

INFORMATION: Lake Henshaw Resort, 26439 Hwy. 76, Santa Ysabel 92070, Ph: 619-782-3501

CAMPING	BOATING	RECREATION	OTHER
400 Dev. Sites for Tents Fee: $7.50 100 Dev. Sites for R.V.s Full Hookups Fee: $9.50 Disposal Station	Power & Row 10 Feet Minimum Length 10 MPH Speed Limit Launch Ramp Rentals: Fishing Boats	Fishing: Trout, Catfish, Bluegill, Crappie & Bass Swimming - Pool Only Picnicking Hiking Playgrounds Club House	Cabins Snack Bar Restaurant Grocery Store Bait & Tackle Hot Showers Laundromat Propane Gas Station Trailer Storage Therapy Pool

AGUA HEDIONDA LAGOON, LAKE WOHLFORD, PALOMAR PARK (DOANE POND)

From a saltwater lagoon to a coniferous mountain meadow pond at 5,500 feet, the Lakes on this page offer a striking contrast. Doane Pond is in the Palomar State Park with hiking and nature trails, picnic sites and a campground. The Palomar Observatory is also nearby. Trout are caught seasonally; November through June are the best months. Wohlford, at 1,500 feet, is a good fishing Lake with trout (in season), Florida bass, channel catfish and pan fish. Sailboats, canoes, kayaks, rafts and collapsible boats are not permitted. Agua Hedionda Lagoon is a large saltwater lagoon off Interstate Highway 5 which offers all types of boating. This is a popular waterskiing and jet ski facility. There are also waterski and jet ski schools, a 3-lane paved launch ramp, dry storage and a concession.

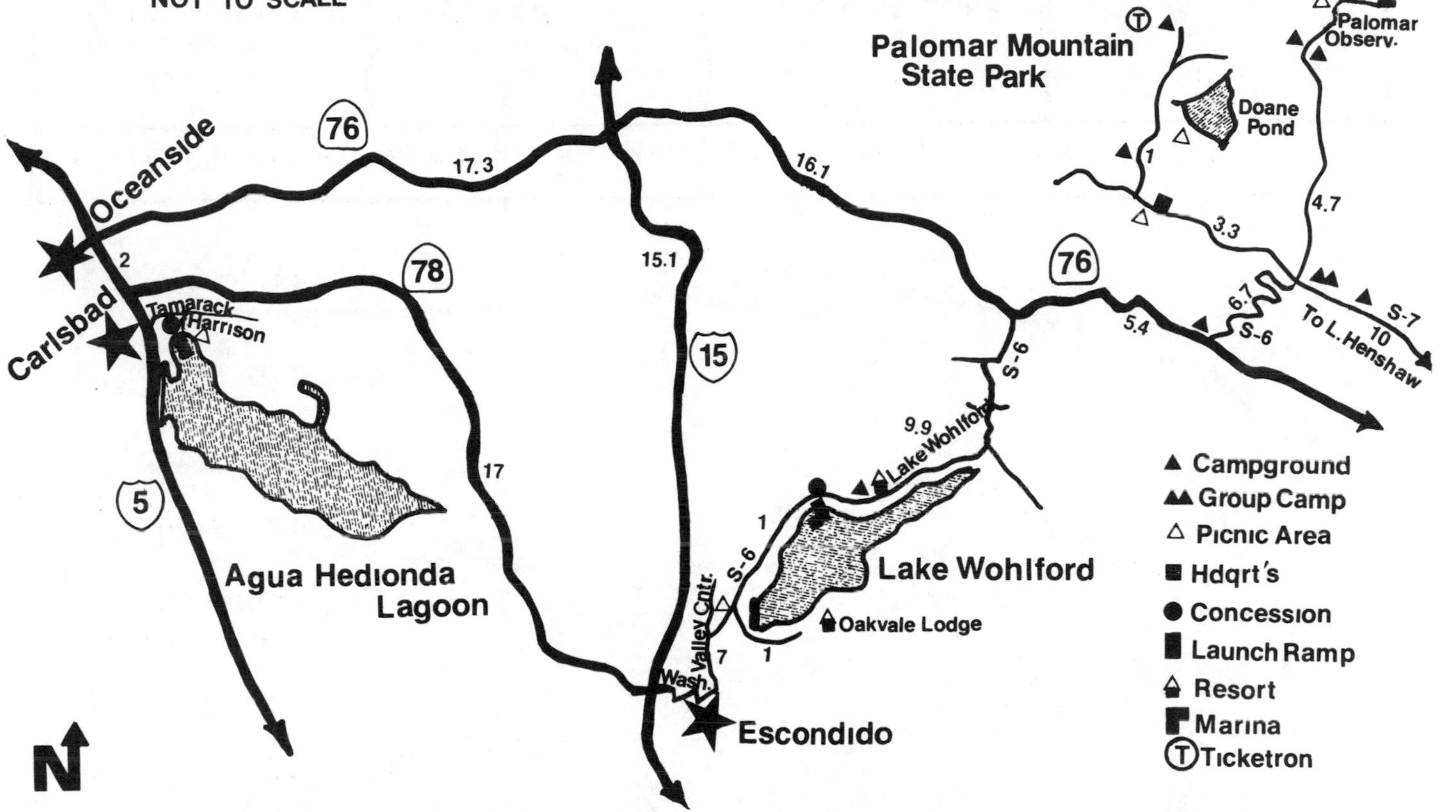

INFORMATION: Palomar Mountain State Park (Only), Palomar 92060, Ph: 619-742-3462

CAMPING	BOATING	RECREATION	OTHER
Doane Valley Campground: 30 Dev. Sites Reservations Advised Ph: 619-765-0755 Agua Hedionda Lagoon (No Camping) 4145 Harrison St. Carlsbad 92008 Ph: 619-434-3089	Agua Hedionda: Open to All Boats, Windsurfing and Parachutes - Not Allowed Speed Limit: 45 MPH Jet Ski Rentals Water Ski School Lake Wohlford: 18 Feet Max. Length Speed Limit: 5 MPH Rental Fishing Boats	Doane Pond: No Boating No Swimming Fishing: Trout, Florida Bass Catfish, Crappie & Bluegill Picnicking Hiking Nature Study	Lake Wohlford: Resort Rt. 1 - Box 204 Escondido 92025 Ph: 619-749-2755 100 Campsites 7 Full Hookups Hot Showers Cabins Concessions

These three Lakes in the San Diego area provide a popular warm water fishery. In addition, the angler will find trout planted during the winter months at Poway and Santee. The Lake Poway Recreation Area provides a primitive camping area, picnic sites, nature and equestrian trails. The 60 acre Lake is open to row and electrical boating, and night fishing is allowed. The Santee Lakes Recreational Area offers a large number of modern campsites with a swimming pool, picnic facilities, playgrounds, volleyball courts and horseshoe pits. The seven small Lakes are closed to private boating, but rentals are available. Hollins Lake is a private membership facility geared to Senior Citizens, but it is open to the public on a fee basis.

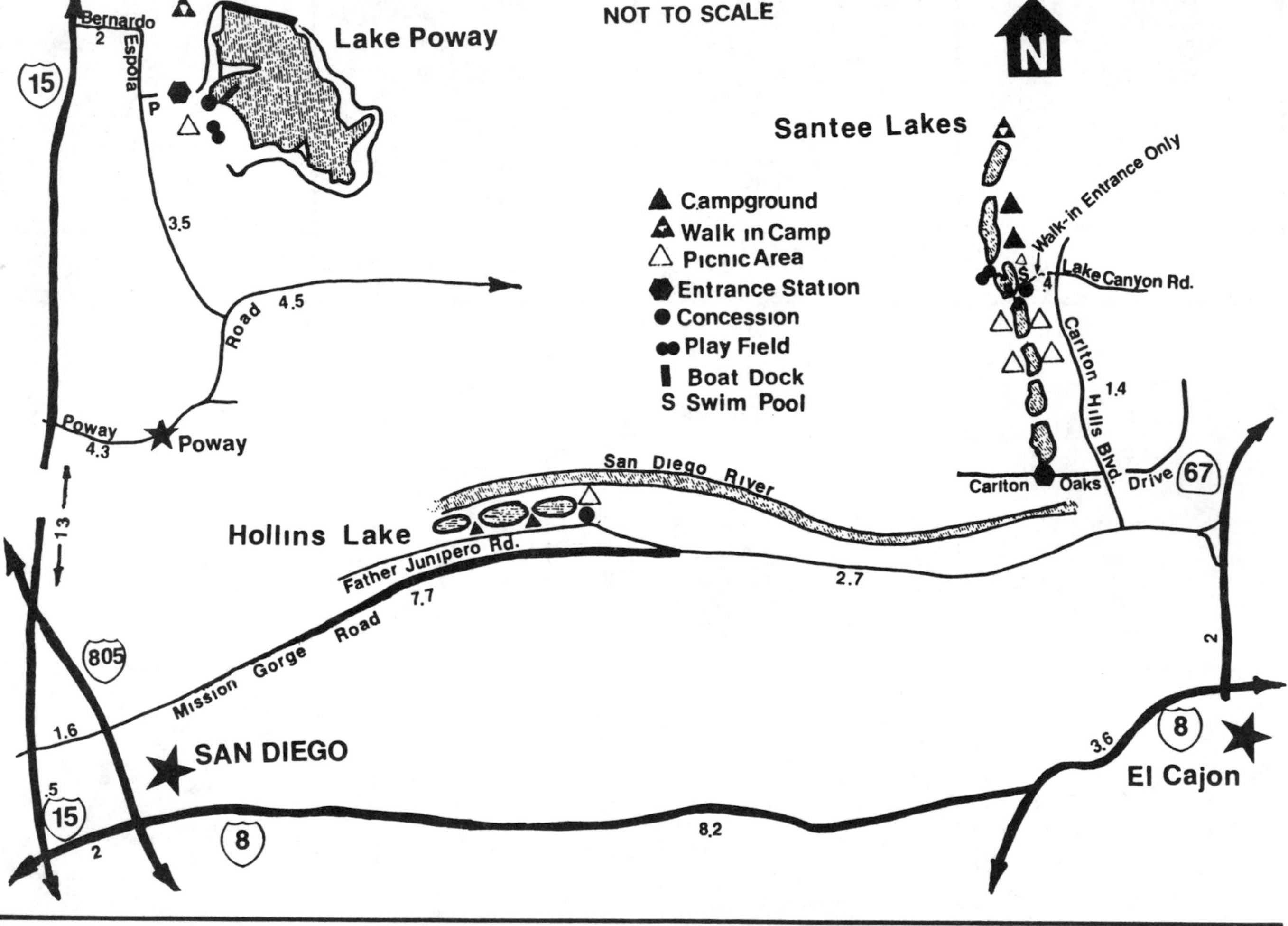

INFORMATION: Santee Lakes, P.O. Box 70, Santee 92071, Ph: 619-448-2482

CAMPING	BOATING	RECREATION	OTHER
Santee Lakes: 152 R.V. Sites - Full, Partial Hookups 62 Overflow Sites Disposal Station Laundry & Groceries Hollins Lake: P.O. Box 924 Santee 92701 Ph: 619-448-5859 50 Sites for Self-Contained Units	Lake Poway: Row & Electric Motors Only Rental Row Boats Santee Lakes: No Private Boats Rentals: Row, Paddle & Canoe Hollins Lake: No Boating	Fishing Trout (Winter at Poway & Santee), Florida Bass, Bluegill & Channel Catfish Family & Group Picnic Hiking, Riding & Nature Trails-Poway Playgrounds Volleyball Courts Horseshoe Pits	Lake Poway P.O. Box 785 Poway 92071 Ph: 619-748-2224 Snack Bar Bait & Tackle Full Facilities Nearby

LAKE CUYAMACA

Lake Cuyamaca is at an elevation of 4,650 feet in a mountain setting of oak, pine and cedar forests. The Dam was originally built in 1887. Thanks to a dedicated group of residents and sportsmen, the minimum pool is 110 surface acres. Normally the only Lake in San Diego County that stocks trout all year, Cuyamaca offers excellent fishing for warm water fish as well. Cuyamaca Rancho State Park has over 100 miles of scenic horseback riding and hiking trails. Los Caballos Campground offers 16 developed sites including corrals for families with horses. In addition, Los Vaqueros Campground is for equestrian groups with facilities for 80 people and 50 horses.

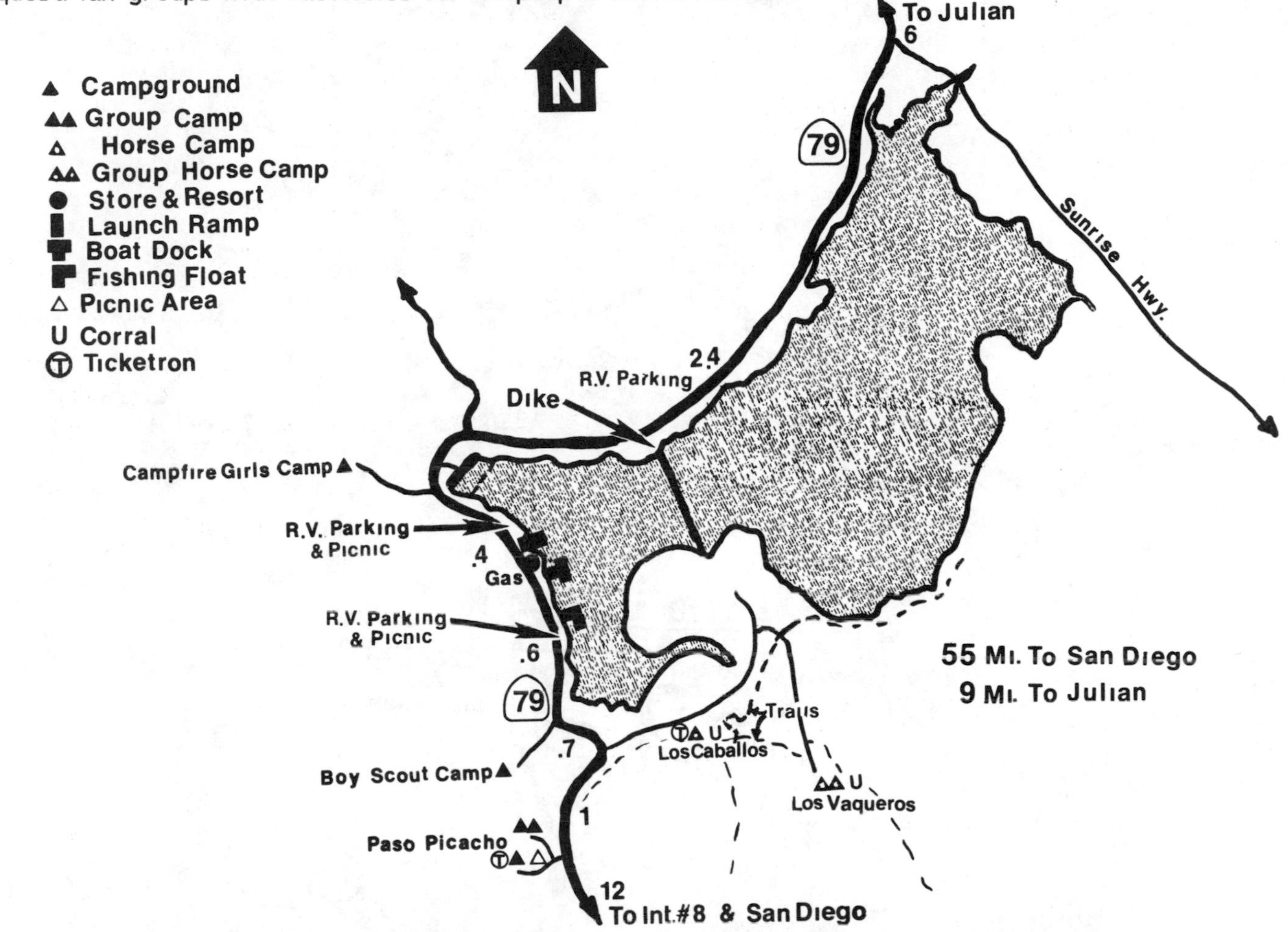

INFORMATION: Park Ranger, Star Rt., Box 2300, Julian 92036, Ph: 619:765-0515

CAMPING	BOATING	RECREATION	OTHER
At Lake: 50 Sites for Self-Contained Units Only - Fee $6 Cuyamaca Rancho State Park Paso Picacho: 85 Dev. Sites for Tents & R.V.s Group Camp - 160 People Maximum	Power & Row Boats Between 10 ft. & 18 Ft. Only Inflatables Must Have Discernible Bow & Stern, 9-18 ft., Wood Bottom or Multiple Inflatable Compartments Speed Limit - 10 MPH Launch Ramp Rentals: Boat & Motor	Fishing: Trout, Perch, Catfish, Bluegill & Bass No Swimming or Body Contact with Water Hiking Backpacking-Parking Hunting: Duck - Wed. & Sun. A.M. in Season	Snack Bar Restaurant Grocery Store Bait & Tackle Disposal Station Gas Station State Park - To Reserve Individual Sites: Ticketron Group Camps: Ph: 619-765-0755

SAN DIEGO CITY LAKES
HODGES, SUTHERLAND, MIRAMAR, SAN VICENTE, EL CAPITAN, LOWER OTAY

These popular Lakes provide some of the best bass fishing in America. They are operated by the City of San Diego. The Lakes are open from sunrise to sunset, but the days each Lake is open varies and is subject to change, so it is advisable to call for current schedules. The Water Utilities Department provides a daily Hot Line with fishing and hunting information. Phone 619-465-3474.

. . . Continued . . .

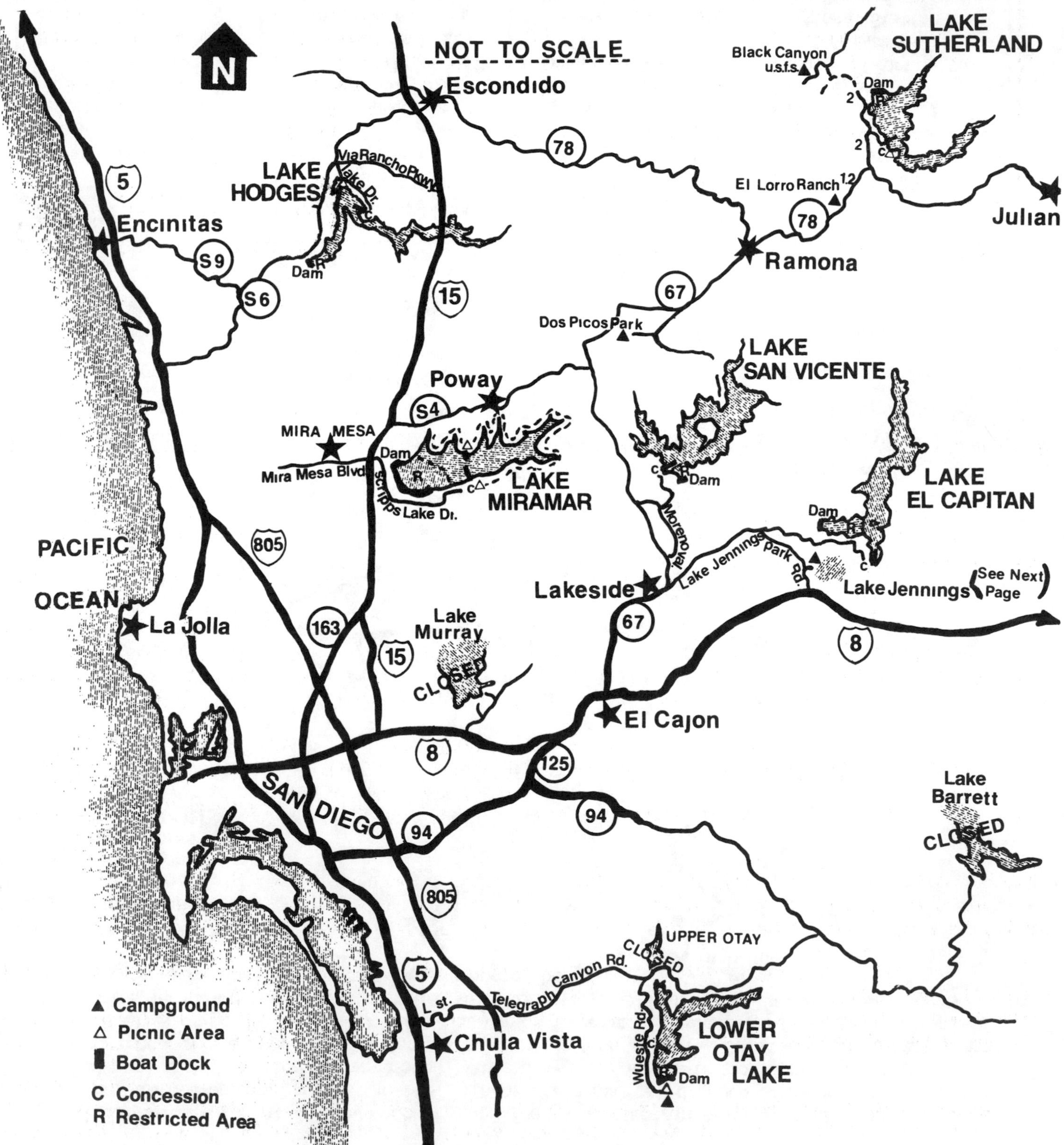

LAKE HODGES is at elevation of 330 feet with a surface area of 1,234 acres and 12 miles of chaparral covered shoreline. Bass, bluegill, channel catfish, crappie and bullhead are in the Lake. The nearest facilities are in Escondido.

LAKE SUTHERLAND is at an elevation of 2,074 feet with a surface area of 557 acres and 11 miles of oak and chaparral covered shoreline. The closest campgrounds are Dos Picos Park and Ramona and William Heise Park in Julian, both operated by the County of San Diego. Florida Bass, bluegill and channel catfish are in the Lake. There is also waterfowl hunting in season. (Oct.-Jan. Duck Hunting)

LAKE MIRAMAR is at an elevation of 714 feet in the rolling hills below Poway. The Lake has a surface area of 162 acres with 4 miles of shoreline. Florida Bass, bluegill, channel catfish and redear sunfish can be caught in the Lake. Trout season is from November through May. The nearest facilities are at Mira Mesa.

LAKE SAN VICENTE is at elevation of 659 feet in the low mountains east of El Cajon. The Lake has a surface area of 1,069 acres with 14 miles of shoreline. The County operates Dos Picos Park Campground to the north as well as the Campground at Lake Jennings. Florida Bass along with channel catfish, crappie and bluegill are in the Lake. Trout season is from November to May.

LAKE EL CAPITAN is at elevation of 750 feet in the foothills east of Lakeside. The Lake has a surface area of 1,574 acres with 20 miles of shoreline. The only publicly operated campground is at Lake Jennings County Park (Ph: 619-565-3600). Other facilities are in Lakeside and El Cajon. Florida Bass, bluegill, bullhead, channel and blue catfish and crappie are in the Lake.

LAKE LOWER OTAY is in the rolling chaparral covered hills at an elevation of 492 feet east of Chula Vista. The surface area of the Lake is 1,266 acres with 13 miles of shoreline. The County of San Diego maintains a campground with 44 sites including 26 with full hookups for R.V.s (Ph: 619-565-3600). There are full facilities in Chula Vista. Florida Bass, channel and white catfish, bullhead, crappie and bluegill are in the Lake.

LAKE BARRETT is closed to fishing, but open for waterfowl hunting on Thursdays and Sundays in season.

INFORMATION: Water Utilities Dept./Lakes, 5520 Kiowa Dr., La Mesa 92041			
CAMPING	BOATING	RECREATION	OTHER
See Above for Camping Information - - - - - - - - - - - Boat Reservations: Lake Miramar - Ph: 619-571-0690 Lake San Vicente - Ph: 619-562-1042 All Other Lakes - Ph: 619-562-9365	Power, Row, Inflatables & Sail (12' or Longer, 12" Freeboard & Fixed Deck) Subject to Inspection Fee: $3.25 Launch Ramps Rentals: Fishing Boats & Motors	Fishing: See Above for Types of Fish Fishing Permit Fees: Trout-$4.00 - Adult $2.50 - Junior - 8-15 Years Old Other Fish $3.50 - Adult $2.00 - Junior Picnicking & Hiking Hunting as Shown Above	No Swimming or Body Contact With Water Privately Operated Concessions at Each Lake: Fishing Licenses Food & Beverages Bait & Tackle

LAKE JENNINGS

Lake Jennings is east of El Cajon at an elevation of 690 feet. It is owned by the Helix Water District which administers strict sanitation standards for this domestic water supply Reservoir of 145 surface acres. The 4 miles of fairly steep shoreline is semi-arid dotted with sumac trees and a few pine trees. The primary recreation is fishing. Although campers may fish from the shore of the campground every day year around, the season for all other fishing is October through May on Fridays, Saturdays and Sundays only. This is the Lake for big Channel or Blue Catfish. A 41-pound Blue Catfish was caught recently.

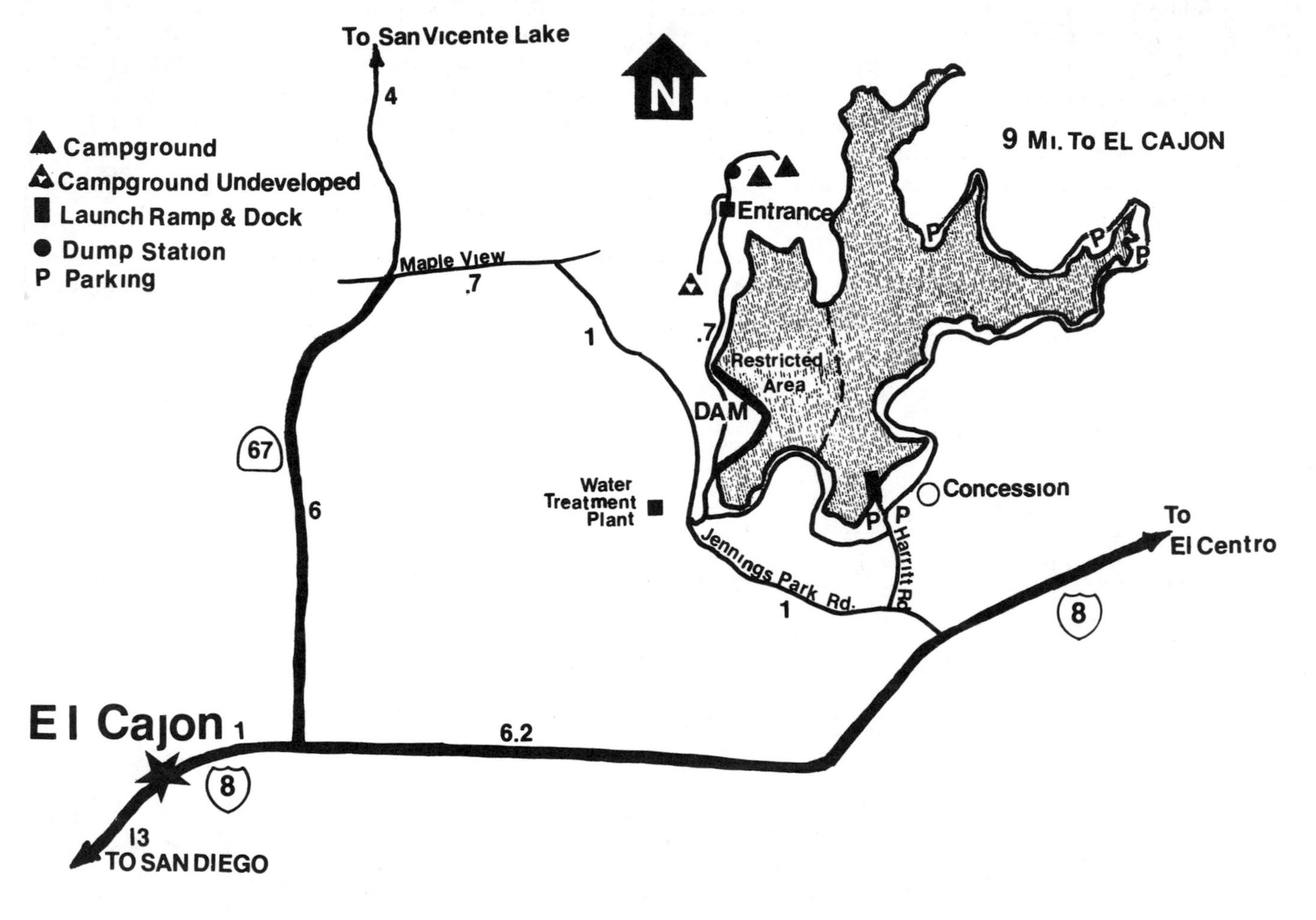

INFORMATION: County Parks, 5201 Ruffin Rd., "P", San Diego 92123, Ph: 619-565-3600

CAMPING	BOATING	RECREATION	OTHER
26 Dev. Sites-Tents Fee: $7 29 Dev. Sites-R.V.s Electric & Water Hookups, Fee: $9 34 Dev. Sites-R.V.s Full Hookups Fee: $9 Pets - $1 Per Night 15 Primitive Sites for Tents Only Fee: $5	Fishing Boats Only Speed Limit - 10 MPH Launch Ramp - $4 Rentals: Fishing Boats & Motors	Fishing: Trout, Catfish, Bluegill, Bass Fridays, Saturdays & Sundays - Oct. - May Permit Required No Swimming	Snack Bar - Open In Season Bait & Tackle Full Facilities in El Cajon Campers Only Can Fish From Shore In Campgrounds Year Around

LAKE MORENA

Lake Morena is at an elevation of 3,000 feet in the Cleveland National Forest east of San Diego. San Diego County maintains a nice Lake front Park in a setting of live oak trees among rocky foothills. In addition to the developed campground, there is an undeveloped open camping area on the north end of the Lake. This 80 year old Lake has a surface area of over 1,000 acres. Morena has an abundant population of warm water fish including the Florida strain of bass. Fishing is the primary activity. Boating is limited to 10 MPH, and inflatables are subject to rigid standards. The nearby Pacific Crest Trail invites the hiker, backpacker and equestrian.

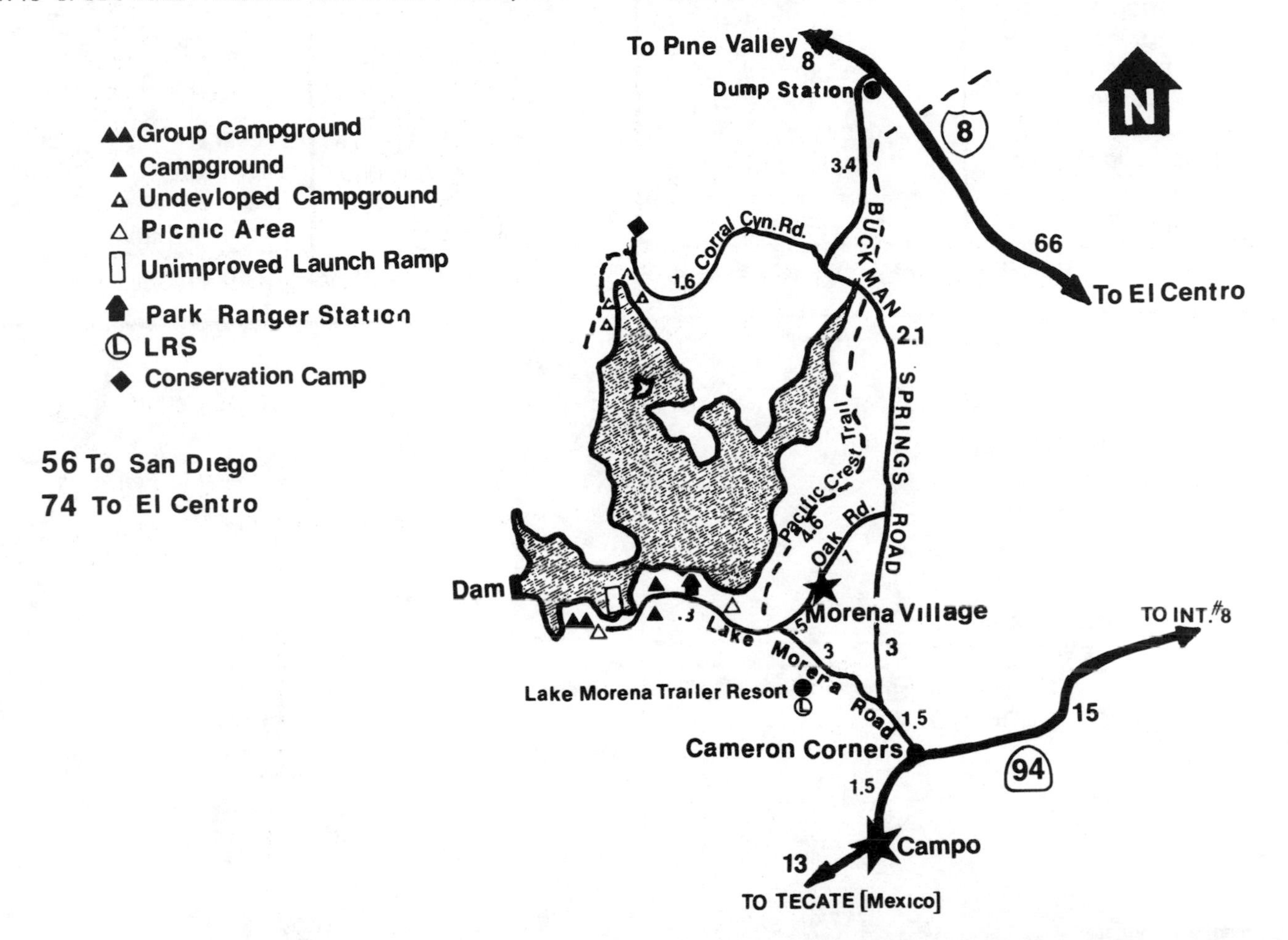

INFORMATION: County Parks, 5201 Ruffin Rd., San Diego 92123, Ph: 619-565-3600

CAMPING	BOATING	RECREATION	OTHER
90 Dev. Sites for Tents & R.V.s Fee: $7 Undeveloped Open Camping Fee: $5 2 Group Camps to 35 People Maximum Reservations Accepted	Power, Row, Sail & Inflatables (Strict Regulations) 10 MPH Speed Limit Unimproved Launch Ramp Rentals: Fishing & Row Boats	Fishing: Florida Bass, Bluegill, Catfish & Crappie Picnicking Hiking Backpacking Riding Trails Nature Study	Lake Morena Trailer Resort Rt. 1, Box 137 Campo 92006 Ph: 619-478-5677 42 R.V. Sites, Full Hookups Fee: $10 Disposal Station LP Gas Morena Village: Gas, Restaurant & Store

Lake Havasu is at an elevation of 482 feet in the desert between Arizona and California. Flowing out of Topock Gorge, the Colorado River becomes Lake Havasu. This 19,300 acre Lake of secluded coves, quiet inlets and open water backs up 45 miles behind Parker Dam. Famed for its outstanding fishery and excellent boating, Lake Havasu attracts thousands of visitors. Major fishing, powerboating and waterskiing tournaments are held yearly. Numerous campgrounds, resorts and marinas are located around the Lake. The hub of the area is Lake Havasu City and Pittsburg Point which offer complete facilities. The boat camper and houseboater will find the 13,000 acres of Lake Havasu State Park a pleasant retreat.

. . . Continued . . .

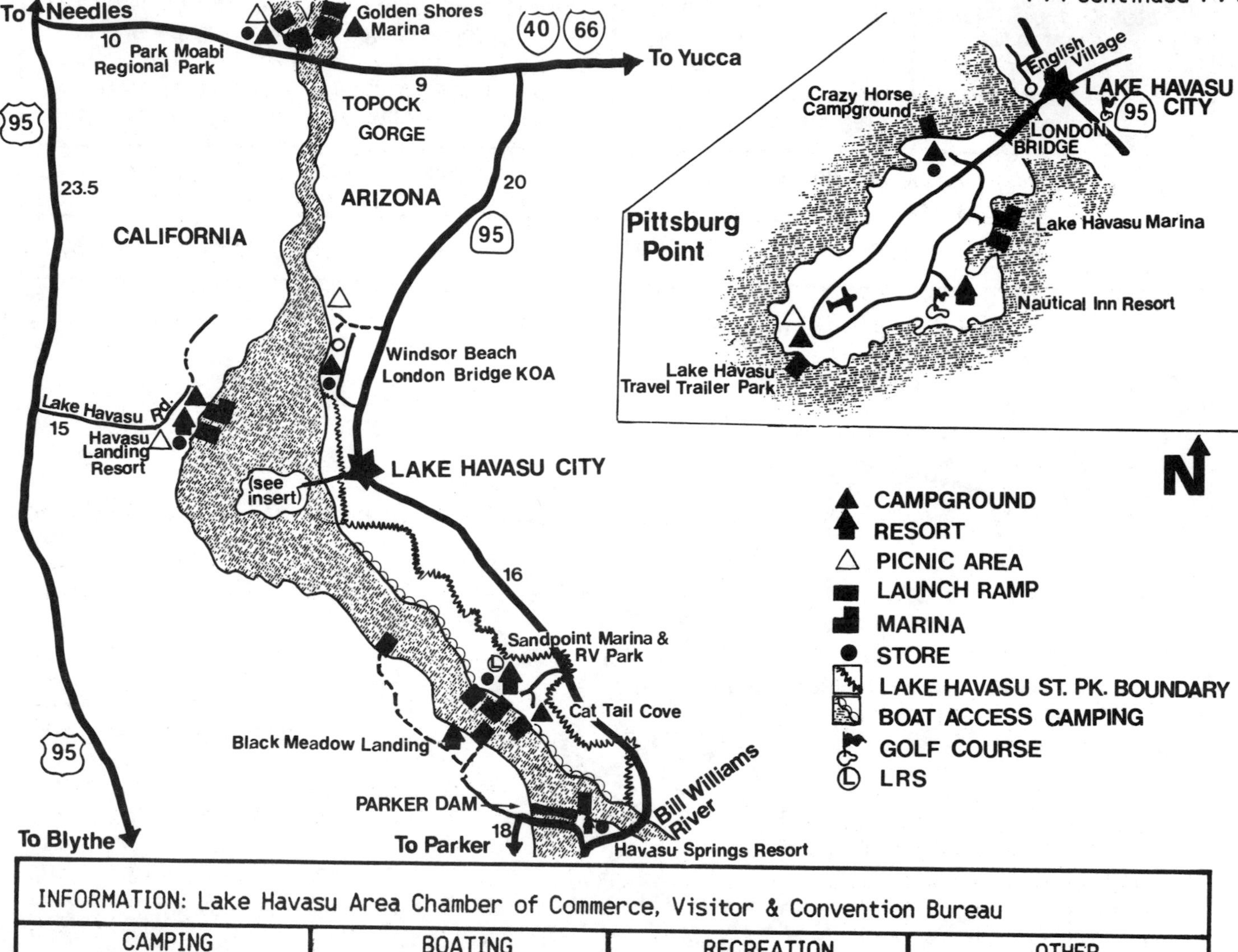

INFORMATION: Lake Havasu Area Chamber of Commerce, Visitor & Convention Bureau			
CAMPING	BOATING	RECREATION	OTHER
Chamber of Commerce 65 N. Lake Havasu Avenue Suite 2-B Lake Havasu City AZ 86403 Ph: 602-855-4115 or 602-453-3444 Numerous Campgrounds Around Lake - See Following Pages	Power, Row, Canoe, Sail, Waterski, Jet Ski, Windsurf & Inflatable Full Service Marinas Rentals: Fishing, Power, Pontoons & Houseboats High Winds Can be A Hazard in Fall & Spring Each Year	Fishing: Catfish, Bluegill, Crappie, Largemouth & Striped Bass Swimming Picnicking Hiking Backpacking Nature Study Hunting: Waterfowl, Quail & Dove	Full Resort Facilities Airport Golf Courses Tennis Courts Boat Excursions Casino Trips Home of the London Bridge See RECREATION ON THE COLORADO RIVER for Full Details

. . . Continued . . .

CAMPGROUNDS & RESORTS AS SHOWN ON MAP - NUMEROUS OTHER FACILITIES - CONTACT THE CHAMBER OF COMMERCE FOR FURTHER DETAILS.

PARK MOABI REGIONAL PARK, Park Moabi Rd., Needles 92363, Ph: 619-326-3831. 648 T/R.V. Sites, Full & Partial Hookups - Fee: $6-$10 - Hot Showers, Laundromat, Flush Toilets, Picnic Sites with Tables & Barbecues, Disposal Station, Swim Beach, 5-Lane Launch Ramp, Waterfront Cabanas, Fishing Area, Dry Storage, Recreation Hall & Arcade, General Store, Ice, Full Service Marina, Gas Docks, Rentals: Houseboats and Fishing Boats, Courtesy Dock, 37 Boat Slips, Bait & Tackle.

GOLDEN SHORES MARINA, HC-12, Box 502, Topock, AZ 86436, Ph: 602-768-2325. R.V. sites, Full Hookups - Fee: $10, Store, Restaurant, Gas, Fuel Dock, Slips & Launch Ramp.

HAVASU LANDING RESORT, P.O. Box 1975, Chemehuevi Valley 92363, Ph: 619-858-4593. Owned by the Chemehuevi Tribe. 1,500 Tent Sites, 175 R.V. & Trailer Sites, Full Hookups. Fees: $10 a Day in Season, $8 a Day Off Season. Plus Unlimited Boat Access, Camping Along the Shoreline of the Reservation. Complete Destination Campground with Hot Showers, Flush Toilets, Laundromat, Snack Bars, Grocery Store, Restaurant & Lounge. Full Service Marina - Two Launch Ramps, 202 Slips, Courtesy Dock & Houseboat Rentals. 5 Star Mobile Home Park - 500 Spaces.

BLACK MEADOW LANDING, P.O. Box 98, Parker Dam 92267, Ph: 619-663-3811. 150 sites for Tents - Fee: $5 for 2 Adults. 31 Sites for R.V.s - Full Hookups, Disposal Station. Hot Showers, Flush Toilets, Laundromat. Ice, Restaurant, Boat Ramp. Boat Rentals: Fishing Boats & Pontoons. Grocery Store, Tackle Shop, Motel with 32 Rooms and 20 Kitchen Cabins.

LONDON BRIDGE KOA, 3405 London Bridge Drive, Lake Havasu, AZ 86403. 84 R.V. Sites, Full & Partial Hookups, Tents allowed - Fee: $13, Hot Showers, Swim Pool, Store, & Cafe.

HAVASU SPRINGS RESORT, Route 2, Box 624, Parker AZ 85344, Ph: 602-667-3361. Fee: $5, 100 R.V. Sites with Full Hookups, Cable TV - Fee: $11.50 Plus $1 for Electricity. Hot Showers, Flush Toilets, Laundromat. Restaurant & Lounge, Motel, Grocery Store, Swimming Pool & Beach, Boat Ramp, 250 Slips, Boat Rentals: Fishing, Waterski, Patio, Jet Ski, Camp-a-Float, Houseboats, Dry Storage, Gas, Ski Beach, Video Game Room.

CAT TAIL COVE, Lake Havasu State Park, 1350 W. McCulloch Blvd., Lake Havasu City, AZ 86403, Ph: 602-855-1223. 40 Sites for Tents & R.V.s, Fee: $7 for Residents, $8 for Non-Residents. Electrical & Water Hookups, Disposal Station, Hot Showers, Flush Toilets. Boat Ramp. 15 Miles South of Lake Havasu City.

> The Lake Havasu State Park has provided miles of shoreline for boat access camping and picnicking. 160 Boat Access Only Sites are scattered along the Arizona Shore South of Lake Havasu City. The campgrounds are all named and range from "Solitude" with 1 site to "Hi Isle" with 14 sites. Most have a table, trash barrel, firepit and vault-type toilets nearby. Fees: $4 for Residents, $5 for Non-Resident per Night. Day Use Only: $2 for Residents, $3 for Non-Residents.

SANDPOINT MARINA AND R.V. PARK, P.O. Box 1469, Lake Havasu City, AZ 86403, Ph: 602-855-0549. 170 Sites for Tents & R.V.s - Full Hookups, Disposal Station. Hot Showers, Flush Toilets, 2 Laundromats, 24-Hour Ice Service, Snack Bar, Game Room, Grocery Store & Tackle Shop, Gas Pumps Available on Land and Water. Playground, Swim Beach, Launch Ramp, Boat Slips with Electrical Hookups, Cable T.V., Rentals: Fishing Boats, Houseboats, Pontoons, Pedal Boats, Travel Trailer, Ski Boats and Addictor Boats. For Reservations: Ph: 800-822-CAMP (LRS).

. . . Continued . . .

PITTSBURG POINT

CRAZY HORSE CAMPGROUND, 1534 Beachcomber Dr., Lake Havasu City, AZ 86403, Ph: 602-855-2127. At State Park: 742 Sites for Tents & R.V.s with Full Hookups. Fees: $8 for Water & Electric Hookup, $8.50 for Water, Electric & Sewer Hookup. Disposal Station, Hot Showers, Flush Toilets, Laundromat. Grocery Store, Ice. Boat Ramp, Docks, Swim Beach, Arcade, 3 Waterslides.

LAKE HAVASU MARINA, 1100 McCulloch Blvd., Lake Havasu City, AZ 86403, Ph: 602-855-2159. 6-Lane Launch Ramp, Permanent Docks, Temporary Slips, Pumpouts for R.V. Boat-A-Floats. Boat Rentals: Fishing, Waterski & Pontoons, OMC & Mercury Repairs, Boat Cleaning, Fiberglass Repairs. Grocery Store, Beer & Wine, Ice, Bait & Tackle, Waterski Equipment, Dry Storage.

NAUTICAL INN RESORT, P.O. Box 1885, Lake Havasu City, AZ 86403, Ph: 602-855-2141. Lake Havasu's Only Lake Front Resort, 120 Rooms & Suites Overlooking the Lake, Private Beach & Dock, Swimming Pool, Lighted Tennis Courts, 18-Hole Executive Golf Course, Conference Center, Restaurants & Cocktail Lounges, Rental Boats: Catamarans, Windsurfers, Sail Lessons, Para Sailing. Gift Shops, Beauty Salon, Convenience Store.

LAKE HAVASU TRAVEL TRAILER PARK, P.O. Box 100, Lake Havasu City, AZ 86403, Ph: 602-855-2322. 167 R.V. & Trailer Sites with Full Hookups. Fee: Winter--$12.96 (Summer--$15.67) per Night for 2 People, Monthly Rates. Parking Area for Self-Contained Units. Hot Showers, Flush Toilets, Laundromat, Ice. Launch Ramp. Swimming Pool, Therapy Pool, Recreation Hall, Docks (Free to Guests).

FOR ADDITIONAL ACCOMMODATIONS AND FACILITIES CONTACT:

Lake Havasu Area Chamber of Commerce
VCB Division
65 N. Lake Havasu City, AZ 86403
Ph: 602-855-4115 or 602-453-3444

For a complete guide to the Colorado River, order "Recreation on the Colorado River." Order form on back page of this book.

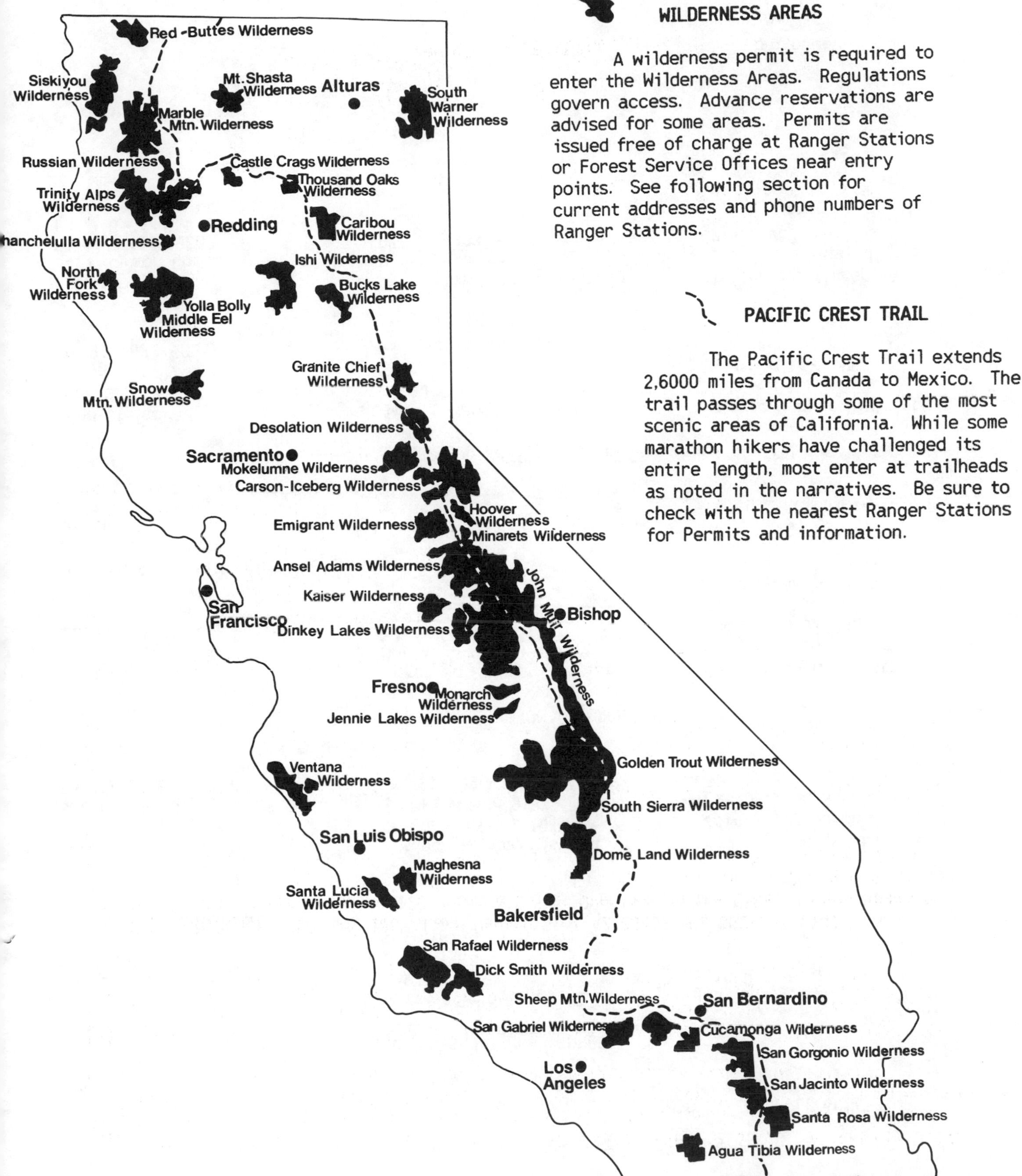

WILDERNESS AREAS

A wilderness permit is required to enter the Wilderness Areas. Regulations govern access. Advance reservations are advised for some areas. Permits are issued free of charge at Ranger Stations or Forest Service Offices near entry points. See following section for current addresses and phone numbers of Ranger Stations.

PACIFIC CREST TRAIL

The Pacific Crest Trail extends 2,6000 miles from Canada to Mexico. The trail passes through some of the most scenic areas of California. While some marathon hikers have challenged its entire length, most enter at trailheads as noted in the narratives. Be sure to check with the nearest Ranger Stations for Permits and information.

RANGER STATIONS AND FOREST SERVICE OFFICES

CALIFORNIA REGION OF THE U.S. FOREST SERVICE

GENERAL INFORMATION, MAPS AND WILDERNESS PERMITS MAY BE OBTAINED AT THE FOLLOWING LOCATIONS:

ANGELES NATIONAL FOREST

Head Office
150 So. Los Robles Ave.
Room 300
Pasadena 91101
Ph: 818-577-0050 or
213-684-0350

Arroyo-Seco Ranger District
Oak Grove Park
Flintridge 911011
Ph: 818-790-1151

Mt. Baldy Ranger District
110 N. Wabash Ave.
Glendora 91740
Ph: 818-335-1251

Saugus Ranger District
27757 Bouquet Canyon Rd.
Saugus 91350
Ph: 805-252-9710

Tujunga Ranger District
12371 N. Little Tujanga Cny.
San Fernando 91342
Ph: 818-899-1900/(1447)

Valyermo Ranger District
34146 Longview Rd.
Pearblossom 93553
Ph: 805:944-2187

CLEVELAND NATIONAL FOREST

Head Office
880 Front St., Rm.
San Diego 92188
Ph: 619-293-5050

Descanso Ranger District
Descanso Ranger District
Alpine 92001
Ph: 619-445-6235

Palomar Ranger District
Palomar Ranger District
Escondido 92025
Ph: 619-745-2421 or
169-566-0130

Trabuco Ranger District
1147 E. Sixth Street
Corona 91720
Ph: 714-736-1811

EL DORADO NATIONAL FOREST

Head Office
100 Forni Rd.
Placerville 95667
Ph: 916-622-5061

Amador Ranger District
26820 Silver Dr. & Hwy. 88
Star Route 3
Pioneer 95666
Ph: 209-295-4251

Pacific Ranger District
Pollock Pines 95726
Ph: 916-644-2348

Placerville
3491 Carson Court
Placerville 95667
Ph: 916-644-2324

Georgetown Ranger District
Georgetown 95634
Ph: 916-333-4313

Placerville Nursery
2375 Fruitridge Rd.
Camino 95709
Ph: 916-622-9600 or 01

. . . Continued. . .

. . . Continued. . .

INYO NATIONAL FOREST

Head Office
873 No. Main St.
Bishop 93514
Ph: 619-873-5841

Mammoth Ranger District
P.O. Box 148
Mammoth Lakes 93546
Ph: 619-934-2505

Mono Lake Ranger District
P.O. Box 10
Lee Vining 93541
Ph: 619-647-6525

Mt. Whitney Ranger District
P.O. Box 8
Lone Pine 93545
Ph: 619-876-5542

White Mountain Ranger District
798 NO. Main Street
Bishop
Ph: 619-873-4207

KLAMATH NATIONAL FOREST

Head Office
1312 Fairlane Road
Yreka 96097
Ph: 916-842-6131

Goosenest Ranter District
37805 Hwy. 97
Macdoel 96058
Ph: 916-398-4391

Happy Camp Ranger District
P.O. Box 377
Happy Camp 96039
Ph: 916-493-2243

Oak Knoll Ranger District
2254 Hwy. 96
Klamath River 96050
Ph: 916-465-2241

Salmon River Ranger District
Sawyers Bar 96027
Ph: Ft. Jones Operator and ask for Sawyers Bar 4600 or
P.O. Box 280
Etna 96027
Ph: 916-467-5757

Scott River Ranger District
11263 S. Hwy. 3
Fort Jones 96032
Ph: 916-468-5351

Ukonom Ranger District
P.O. Box 410
Orleans 95556
Ph: 916-627-3291

LAKE TAHOE BASIN MANAGEMENT UNIT

THIS UNIT COVERS PARTS OF EL DORADO, TAHOE AND TOIYABE NATIONAL FORESTS.

Head Office
P.O. Box 8465
870 Emerald Bay Rd.
South Lake Tahoe 95731
Ph: 916-544-6420

Tahoe Visitor Center
1/2 Mi. from Camp Richardson
Ph: 916-541-0209
Open Summers Only

William Kent Info. Station
William Kent Campground
West Shore
Ph: 916-583-3642
Open Summers Only

LASSEN NATIONAL FOREST

Head Office
55 South Sacramento St.
Susanville 96130
Ph: 916-257-2151

Almanor Ranger District
P.O. Box 767
Chester 96020
Ph: 916-258-2141

Eagle Lake Ranger District
472-013 Johnstonville Rd.
Susanville 96130
Ph: 916-257-2595 or 2161

Hat Creek Ranger District
P.O. Box 220
Fall River Mills 96028
Ph: 916-336-5521

Engineering Department
1800 Main St.
Susanville 96130
Ph: 916-257-5507

. . . Continued . . .

. . . Continued . . .

LOS PADRES NATIONAL FOREST

Head Office
6144 Calle Real
Goleta 93117
Ph: 805-683-6711

Monterey Ranger District
406 S. Mildred
King City 93930
Ph: 408-385-5434

Mt. Pinos Ranger District
Star Route, Box 400
Frazier Park 93225
Ph: 805-245-3731 or 3462

Ojai Ranger District
1190 E. Ojai Ave.
Ojai 93023
Ph: 805-646-4348

Santa Lucia Ranger District
1616 N. Carlotti Dr.
Santa Maria 93454
Ph: 805-925-9538 or 39

Santa Barbara Ranger Dist.
Star Route, Los Prietos
Santa Barbara 93105
Ph: 805-967-3481 or 82

MENDOCINO NATIONAL FOREST

Head Office
420 E. Laurel St.
Willows 95988
PH: 916-934-3316

Corning Ranger District
22000 Corning Rd.
Corning 96021
Ph: 916-824-5196

Covelo Ranger District
Route 1, Box 62-C
Covelo 95428
Ph: 707-983-6118

Stonyford Ranger District
Stites Ladoga Road
Stonyford 95979
Ph: 916-963-3128

Upper Lake Ranger District
Middlecreek Rd.
P.O. Box 96
Upper Lake 95485
Ph: 707-275--2361

Chico Tree Improvement
Center
2741 Cramer Lane
Chico 95926
Ph: 916-895-1176 or 77

MODOC NATIONAL FOREST

Head Office
441 N. Main St.
Alturas 96101
Ph: 916-233-5811

Big Valley Ranger District
P.O. Box 885
Adin 96006
Ph: 916-299-3215, 16, 17

Devil's Garden Ranger Dist.
P.O. Box 5
Canby 96015
Ph: 916-233-4611, 12, 13, 14

Doublehead Ranger District
P.O. Box 818
Tulelake 96134

Warner Mountain Ranger District
P.O. Box 220
Cedarville 96104

PLUMAS NATIONAL FOREST

Head Office
P.O. Box 1500, 159 Lawrence
Quincy 95971
Ph: 916-283-2050

Beckwourth Ranger District
Mohawk Ranger Station
P.O. Box 7
Blairsden 96013
Ph: 916-836-2575

Greenville Ranger District
P.O. Box 329
Greenville 95947
Ph: 916-284-7126

La Porte Ranger District
Challenge Ranger Station
P.O. Drawer F
Challenge 95925
Ph: 916-675-2462

Milford Ranger District
Laufman Ranger Station
Milford 96121
Ph: 916-253-2223

Oroville Ranger District
875 Mitchell Ave.
Oroville 95965
Ph: 916-534-6500

Quincy Ranger District
1400 E. Main, Box 69
Quincy 95971
Ph: 916-283-0555

. . . Continued . . .

SAN BERNARDINO NATIONAL FOREST

. . . Continued . . .

Head Office
144 N. Mt. View Ave.
San Bernardino 92408
Ph: 714-383-5588

Arrowhead Ranger District
Rimforest 92378
Ph: 714-337-2444

Big Bear Ranger District
P.O. Box 290
Fawnskin 92333
Ph: 714-866-3437

Cajon Ranger District
Lytle Creek Ranger Station
Star Route
Fontana 92335
Ph: 714-887-2576

San Gorgonio Ranger District
Mill Creek Station
Route 1, P.O. Box 264
Mentone 92359
Ph: 714-794-1123

San Jacinto Ranger District
Idyllwild Ranger Station
P.O. Box 518
Idyllwild 92349
Ph: 714-659-2117

SEQUOIA NATIONAL FOREST

Head Office
900 W. Grand Ave.
Porterville 93257
Ph: 209-784-1500

Cannell Meadow Ranger District
P.O. Box 6
Kernville 93238
Ph: 619-376-3781

Greenhorn Ranger District
Federal Bldg., Rm. 322
800 Truxtun Ave.
Bakersfield 93301
Ph: 805-861-4212

Hot Springs Ranger District
Route 4, Box 548
Ca. Hot Springs 93207
Ph: 805-548-6503

Hume Lake Ranger District
36273 E. Kings Canyon Rd.
Dunlap 93621
Ph: 209-338-2251

Tule Ranger District
32588 Highway 190
Porterville 93257
PH: 209-539-2607

SHASTA-TRINITY NATIONAL FOREST

Head Office
2400 Washington Ave.
Redding 96001
Ph: 916-246-5222

Big Bar Ranger District
Star Route 1, Box 10
Big Bar 96010
Ph: 916-623-6106

Hayfork Ranger District
P.O. Box 159
Hayfork 96041
Ph: 916-628-5227

McCloud Ranger District
District
Drawer 1
McCloud 96057
Ph: 916-964-2184, 85

Mt. Shasta Ranger District

204 West Alma
Mt. Shasta 96067
Ph: 916-926-4511

Shasta Lake Ranger

6543 Holiday Drive
Redding 96003
Ph: 916-275-1587

Weaverville Ranger District
P.O. Box T
Weaverville 96093
Ph: 916-623-2131 or 21

Yolla Bolla Ranger District
Platina 96076
Ph: 916-352-4211

NCSC
6106 Airport Road
Redding 96002
Ph: 916-246-5285

SIERRA NATIONAL FOREST

Head Office
Federal Building
1130 "O" St.
Fresno 93721
Ph: 209-487-5155

Bass Lake Ranger District
41969 Highway 41
Oakhurst 93644
Ph: 209-683-4665

Kings River Ranger District
Trimmer Route
Sanger 93657
Ph: 209-855-8321 or 22

Mariposa Ranger District
P.O. Box 747
Mariposa 95338
Ph: 209-966-3638

Minarets Ranger District
North Fork 93643
Ph: 209-877-2218 or 19

Pineridge Ranger District
P.O. Box 300
Shaver Lake 93664
Ph: 209-841-3311

Kings River Ranger District
Dinkey Ranger Station, Dinkey Route
Shaver Lake 93664
PH: 209-841-3404 (Summer Only)

. . . Continued . . .

. . . Continued . . .

SIX RIVERS NATIONAL FOREST

Head Office
507 "F" Street
Eureka 95501
Ph: 707-442-1721

Gasquet Ranger District
P.O. Box 228
Gasquet 95543
Ph: 707-457-3131

Lower Trinity Ranger Dist.
P.O. Box 668
Willow Creek 95573
Ph: 916-629-2118

Mad River Ranger District
Star Route, Box 300
Bridgeville 95526
Ph: 707-574-6233

Orleans Ranger District
Drawer B
Orleans 95556
Ph: 916-627-3291

Salyer Fire Station
(No Mail Service)
Lower Tr. Rd.
Salyer 95563
Ph: 916-629-2114

Zenia Fire Station
General Delivery
Zenia 95495
Ph: Zenia Toll Station
#6069 - through Operator

Big Flat Station on:
Gasquet Ranger District
(Summer Station Only)
No Phone or Mail Service

Humboldt Nursery
4886 Cottage Grove
McKinleyville 95521
Ph: 707-839-3256

STANISLAUS NATIONAL FOREST

Head Office
19777 Greenley Rd.
Sonora 95370
Ph: 209-532-3671

Calaveras Ranger District
Highway 4
P.O. Box 500
Hathaway Pines 95233
Ph: 209-795-1381

Groveland Ranger District
Highway 120
P.O. Box 709
Groveland 95321
Ph: 209-962-7825

Mi-Wuk Ranger District
Highway 108 E
P.O. Box 100
Mi-Wuk Village 95346
Ph: 109-586-3234

Summit Ranger District
Highway 108 E at Pinecrest
Star Route, Box 1295
Sonora 95370
Ph: 209-965-3434

TAHOE NATIONAL FOREST

Head Office
Highway 49 & Coyote St.
Nevada City 95959
Ph: 916-265-4531

Downieville Ranger District
N. Yuba Ranger Station
Star Route, Box 1
Camptonville 95922
Ph: 916-288-3231

Foresthill Ranger District
22830 Auburn-Foresthill Rd.
Foresthill 95631
Ph: 916-367-2224

Nevada City Ranger District
12012 Sutton Way
Grass Valley 95945
Ph: 916-273-1371

Sierraville Ranger District
P.O. Box 95, Hwy. 89
Sierraville 96126
Ph: 916-994-3401

Truckee Ranger District
P.O. Box 399
Truckee 95734
Ph: 916-587-3558

NATIONAL PARKS

Lassen Volcanic National
Park
Mineral 96063
Ph: 916-595-4444

Sequoia-Kings Canyon
National Park
Three Rivers 93271
Ph: 209-565-3341

Yosemite National Park
P.O. Box 577
Yosemite National Park
95389
Ph: 209-372-4461

CALIFORNIA STATE PARKS SYSTEM
1416 Ninth Street
Sacramento, CA 95814
Ph: 916-445-6477

DEPARTMENT OF FISH & GAME OFFICES

CENTRAL OFFICE:

1416 Ninth Street
Sacramento, CA 95814
Ph: 916-445-3531

REGIONAL OFFICES:

Region 1
601 Locust Street
Redding, CA 96001
Ph: 916-225-2300

Region 2
1701 Nimbus Road
Rancho Cordova 95670
Ph: 916-355-0978

Region 3, (Yountville)
7329 Silverado Trail
Napa, CA 94558
Ph: 707-944-2011

Region 4
1234 E. Shaw Avenue
Fresno, CA 93710
Ph: 209-222-3761

Region 5
245 W. Broadway
Long Beach, CA 90802
Ph: 213-590-5132

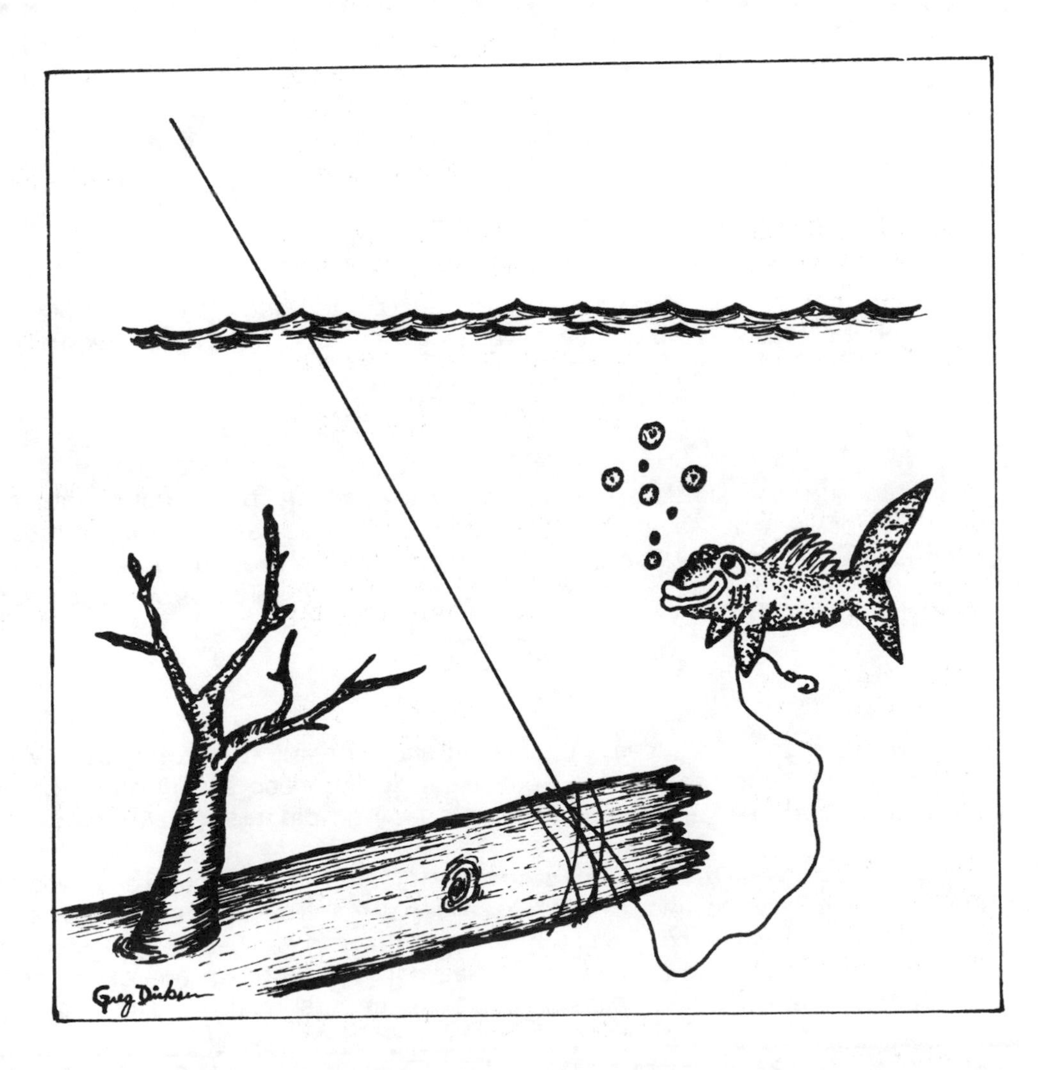

DO NOT DRINK UNTREATED NATURAL WATER

Is the water safe? Giardiasis, an intestinal disorder, is a serious problem. This disease can cause extreme discomfort which has to be treated by a physician. Giardiasis is caused by a microscopic organism, Giardia lamblia, which is found in many mountain lakes and streams. Where drinking water is not available, bring your own or boil the water for at least one minute at sea level and for at least five minutes at higher elevations.

Giardia is easily transmitted between humans and animals. All feces, human and animal, should be buried eight inches deep and at least one hundred feet away from natural waters. Protect those who follow you by keeping our Lakes and streams free of contamination.

PETS

Pets are normally welcome at most facilities. Often a nominal fee is charged, and there are some general rules to follow. Proof of a current rabies vaccination, a current license, and a leash no longer than ten feet are usually required. Pets are not allowed to contaminate water, nor are they allowed into Wilderness Areas, on trails or on swimming beaches.

BOATING

For State Boating Regulations, see the Department of Motor Vehicle's booklet, "ABC's of California Boating Law." This booklet may be obtained at your local DMV office.

THE CALIFORNIA AQUEDUCT

The California Aqueduct provides the angler with 343 miles of open canals and 18 developed fishing access sites with parking and toilets. Striped bass, largemouth bass, catfish, crappie, green sunfish, bluegill and starry flounder are found in the San Joaquin Valley section. Striped bass, bluegill, and catfish are found south of the Tehachapis where the Aqueduct splits into west and east branches.

In addition to fishing, the California Aqueduct Bikeway provides the adventurous cyclist with an interesting challenge. While parking and rest stops are provided every ten miles, careful planning is advised since water, food and spare parts are not always available.

Caution is advised. There are often strong currents. Although safety ladders are provided every 500 feet along the steep, slippery concrete sides of the Aqueduct, stay out of the water. It is dangerous. The 17 pumping stations are closed for 400 yards at each location.

FOR INFORMATION CONTACT:

The Department of Water Resources
P.O. Box 388
Sacramento, CA 95802
Ph: 800-952-5530

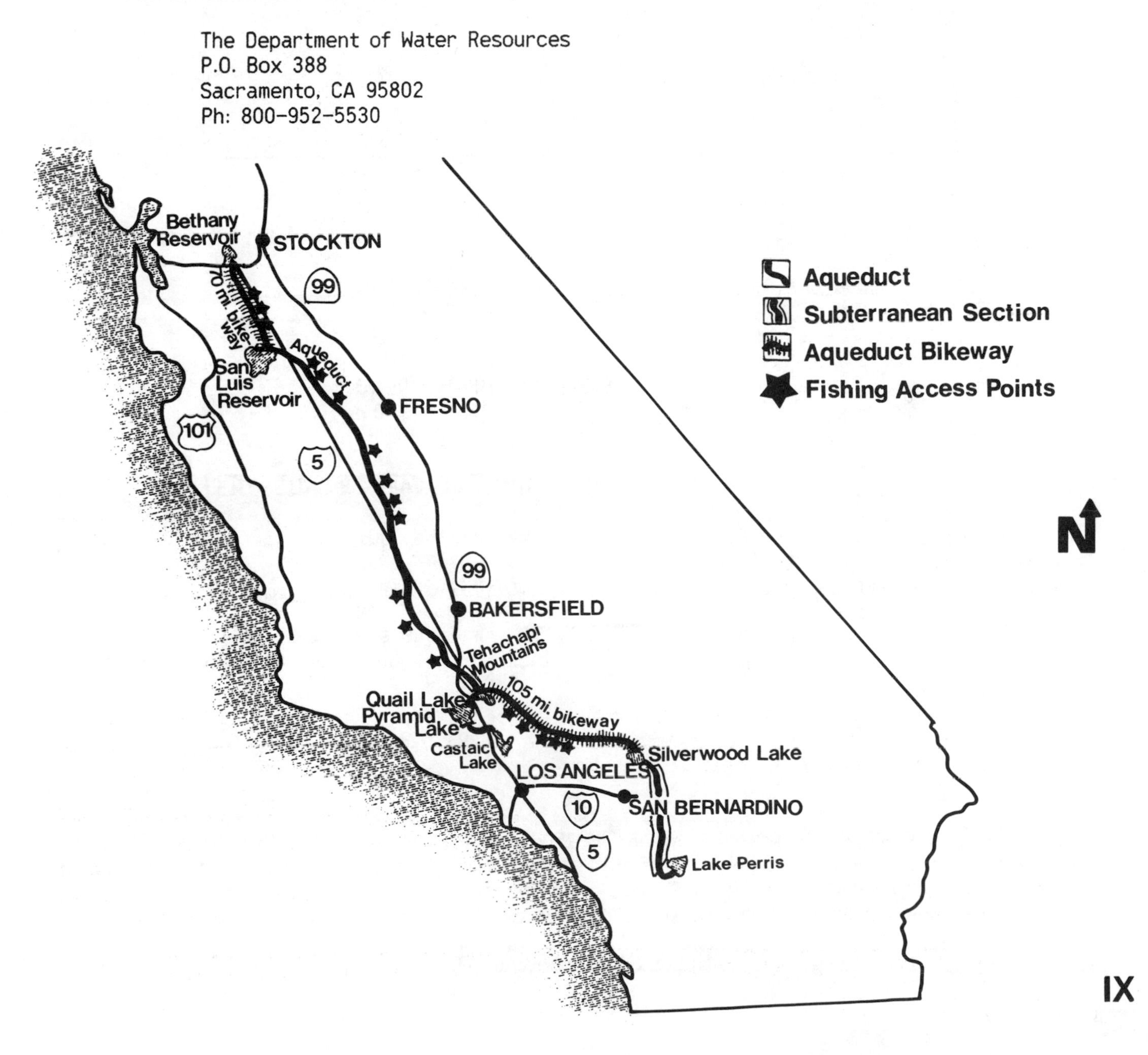

RESERVATION INFORMATION

While reservations are not taken nor required at many campgrounds, they are often advised. Group reservations are normally required. We have noted an address and phone number at each lake where information may be obtained. Where reservations are accepted by Ticketron (as noted by the Ⓣ) and Leisuretime Reservations Systems (noted by the symbol Ⓛ), they are placed next to the facility on the map.

TICKETRON: P.O. Box 26430
San Francisco, CA 94126

Or Call:		
	General Information	800-952-5580
	Los Angeles Area	213-216-6666
	San Diego Area	619-565-9949
	San Francisco Area	415-393-6914
	Sacramento Area	916-445-8828
	TDD (for the Deaf)	916-324-1891

LEISURETIME RESERVATION SYSTEMS, INC:

LRS
P.O. Box 1010
Citrus Heights, CA 95611-1010 or call

California	800/822-CAMP
Outside California	800/824-CAMP
Information Only	916-722-5602

ALL FEES ARE SUBJECT TO CHANGE

INDEX — ALPHABETICAL ORDER

ORDER FORM

SEND TO: Sail Sales Publishing
P.O. Box 1028
Aptos, CA 95001

☐ "Recreation Lakes of California" - Seventh Edition

$ 10.95	Book
.71	Tax
1.84	Postage & Handling
$ 13.50	CHECK ENCLOSED

☐ "Recreation on the Colorado River" - First Edition

$ 9.95	Book
.65	Tax
1.25	Postage & Handling
$ 11.85	CHECK ENCLOSED

Both Publications (Free Postage & Handling)

$ 19.90	Books
1.29	Tax
$ 22.26	CHECK ENCLOSED

NAME: ______________________________

ADDRESS: ______________________________

____

zzzZZ